A HISTORY OF
MODERN CRITICISM
1750–1950

2. *The Romantic Age*

OTHER BOOKS BY RENÉ WELLEK

Immanuel Kant in England

The Rise of English Literary History

Theory of Literature (with Austin Warren)

Concepts of Criticism

Essays on Czech Literature

Confrontations

A HISTORY OF MODERN CRITICISM 1750–1950

BY

RENÉ WELLEK

2. The Romantic Age

CAMBRIDGE UNIVERSITY PRESS

CAMBRIDGE

LONDON   NEW YORK   NEW ROCHELLE

MELBOURNE   SYDNEY

Published by the Press Syndicate of the University of Cambridge
The Pitt Building, Trumpington Street, Cambridge CB2 1RP
296 Beaconsfield Parade, Middle Park, Melbourne 3206, Australia

First published in Great Britain by Jonathan Cape Ltd 1955
This paperback edition first published by the
Cambridge University Press 1981

Printed in Great Britain at the
University Press, Cambridge

British Library Cataloguing in Publication Data
Wellek, René
A history of modern criticism 1750-1950.
Vol. 2: The romantic age
1. Literature – History and criticism
I. Title   II. Series
801'.95'0903   PN86
ISBN 0 521 28296 9

CONTENTS

INTRODUCTION

By the turn of the 19th century the romantic movements, at least in Germany and England, had definitely got under way. In Germany the review written largely by the Schlegels, *Das Athenaeum* (1798–1800), is the crucial document; in England it is *Lyrical Ballads* (1798), by Wordsworth and Coleridge, to which Wordsworth added his theoretical *Preface* in 1800. France seems to lag behind, since the French romantic movement is usually dated from the triumph of *Hernani* (1830) or the appearance of Hugo's preface to *Cromwell*, three years earlier. Yet in 1813 Madame de Staël had expounded the classical-romantic distinction in *De l'Allemagne*, drawing on August Wilhelm Schlegel. In Italy the classical-romantic debate started in 1816 under the influence of an article by Madame de Staël. But these recognized landmarks are somewhat deceptive: we shall see that even the Schlegels were not conscious of forming or founding a romantic school. The designation of contemporary German literature as romantic was due only to the enemies of the Heidelberg group (Arnim, Brentano, Görres), which today is usually called the Younger or Second Romantic School. Jens Baggesen, a Danish poet residing in Germany, published a parodistic *Klingelklingelalmanach* (1808) with the subtitle *Ein Taschenbuch für vollendete Romantiker und angehende Mystiker*. Arnim and Brentano took up with eagerness a term which was meant to be mere mockery. As far as I know, the first extended account of the new literary party of the so-called "Romantiker" can be found in the eleventh volume (1819) of Friedrich Bouterwek's monumental *Geschichte der Poesie und Beredsamkeit*. In England none of the romantic poets recognized himself as a romanticist or recognized the relevance of the Continental debate to his own time and country. In Italy and France one can speak of definitely "romantic" groups: in Milan after 1816, in Paris after 1824.

But if we ignore the question of self-awareness and conscious

1

advocacy of a romantic creed, I think we must recognize that we can speak of a general European romantic movement only if we take a wide over-all view and consider simply the general rejection of the neoclassical creed as a common denominator. In a history of criticism the rise of an emotional concept of poetry, the establishment of the historical point of view, and the implied rejection of the imitation theory, of the rules and genres are the decisive signs of change, and these must be ascribed to the 18th rather than to the early 19th century. Diderot and Herder are the key figures. There is no profound change in doctrinal positions and concepts of poetry between them and such "romantic" (in a more narrow sense) figures as Wordsworth or Hazlitt, Madame de Staël or Foscolo. In a European perspective, in a history of critical thought, the technical romantic movements mean no radical change. Whatever their importance in literary politics, they did not, in themselves, make for a break in critical ideas. These had been formulated long before.

But within this very large movement there arose in Germany a new concept of poetry, symbolistic, dialectical, and historical, which must be ascribed largely to Kant, Goethe, and Schiller. The Schlegels, while hostile to Schiller, codified this view and gave it a turn which proved of great contemporary relevance. Germany, which in the early 18th century had passively received the main doctrines of French neoclassicism, became the center of radiation for critical thought. Especially did August Wilhelm Schlegel play a large role as its most effective propagandist.

The situation in England was, however, totally different: there Jeffrey and Wordsworth, though enemies, developed further the empirical, psychological view of poetry inherited from the 18th century, and only in Coleridge can we speak of a dialectical and symbolistic view of poetry. This seems to have been imported from Germany, though Coleridge nourished it by reading in the Platonic tradition, which lies back of the Germans. Coleridge, however, remained isolated in his time and country, though he influenced Wordsworth and Hazlitt and later Carlyle. But both Wordsworth and Hazlitt remained in the empirical psychological British tradition, and after Coleridge English criticism resumed its course in the empirical tradition, almost unaffected by Coleridge's ideas.

In France Madame de Staël was the importer of the romantic-classical distinction, but otherwise she and her opponent Chateaubriand can be described as adherents of the emotionalistic concept. With Hugo there emerges in France for the first time a concept of poetry which can be defined as symbolistic and dialectical.

In Italy romanticism was largely a slogan recommending truth and contemporaneity in literature. The Italian romanticists anticipated what was later proclaimed by the *Junge Deutschland* and the early French realists. Foscolo, though no romanticist in his formal creed, must be described as close to Madame de Staël in his emotionalistic concept and his grasp of the historical point of view. Leopardi stands apart, with a profoundly personal, completely "lyrical" concept of poetry. But there is, I believe, no trace of the dialectical symbolistic view in Italy before De Sanctis.

Thus one can speak of a romantic movement in criticism in two very different senses: in a wider sense it was a revolt against neoclassicism, which meant a rejection of the Latin tradition and the adoption of a view of poetry centered on the expression and communication of emotion. It arose in the 18th century and forms a wide stream flooding all countries of the West.

In a more narrow sense we can speak of romantic criticism as the establishment of a dialectical and symbolistic view of poetry. It grows out of the organic analogy, developed by Herder and Goethe, but proceeds beyond it to a view of poetry as a union of opposites, a system of symbols. In Germany this view was in constant danger of becoming mystical and thus of losing its grip on the aesthetic fact itself, but in the Schlegels and a few critics around them a satisfying theory of poetry was developed which guarded its fences against emotionalism, naturalism, and mysticism and successfully combined symbolism with a profound grasp of literary history. This view seems to me valuable and substantially true even today. We find it at that time, outside of Germany, only in two prominent critics: Coleridge and Hugo.

For a modern theory of literature this view needs to be described in all its implications and wealth of suggestions. We shall therefore start with the Schlegels, whom we shall discuss not according to their seniority but according to priority in ideas: first the younger Friedrich Schlegel, and then August Wilhelm. They deserve to be treated separately because they are distinct individualities with different points of view. We shall then take up the other prominent German romantics: the philosopher Schelling, the mystical poet Novalis, the friends Wackenroder and Tieck, and finally Jean Paul, who seems to stand somewhat apart. They provide a body of thought and a definition of taste which can be considered as the background for Coleridge. But before discussing him, we have to turn to the minor English critics of the time from Jeffrey to Shelley, and to analyze Wordsworth's frequently misjudged position. After this, Lamb, Hazlitt, and Keats form a distinct group held together by identical doctrines and a new method of metaphorical criticism which proved to be highly influential throughout the 19th century. In France we must couple Madame de Staël and Chateaubriand in spite of their apparent antagonism, and in the following chapter we shall confront Stendhal and Hugo, who both seem champions of the same romantic cause but hold completely opposite views concerning the nature of poetry. The Italians, stimulated as they were by both Madame de Staël and August Wilhelm Schlegel, follow naturally. We shall return to Germany to describe the new developments there, which were not, however, effective outside of Germany at the time under consideration: the mythic, collectivist concept of poetry in Jakob Grimm, the view of poetry as irony in Solger, an expressionist theory of art in Schleiermacher, the new concept of tragedy in Schopenhauer, and the final synthesis of German aesthetic speculation in the grandiose system of Hegel. In the Conclusion we shall look briefly at the other minor countries and open a vista into the future.

1 : FRIEDRICH SCHLEGEL

FRIEDRICH SCHLEGEL (1772–1829)—five years younger than his brother August Wilhelm (1767–1845)—was the more original and seminal mind of the two. His critical activity and effect precedes, to a large degree, that of August Wilhelm. It is admittedly difficult to decide questions of priority with exactness in the case of two intimate brothers and friends, but there seems little doubt that the initiative was almost always Friedrich's. However, August Wilhelm developed distinct critical theories of his own and cannot be described as a mere echo of his brother, even though he served as codifier and popularizer of Friedrich's doctrines. One can hardly deny the greater effectiveness of August Wilhelm's expositions, especially outside of Germany. His Vienna *Lectures on Dramatic Art and Literature,* which were delivered 1808–09 and published 1809–11, affected the course of critical thought very widely, especially after they had been translated into French (1814), English (1815), and Italian (1817). It is also true that Friedrich Schlegel was far less influential outside of Germany, since his conversion to Roman Catholicism in 1808 prevented him from republishing most of his early writings and on the whole limited the appeal of his later work to the definitely conservative and Catholic world of the Restoration period. *The Lectures on Ancient and Modern Literature,* translated into English by J. G. Lockhart in 1815, was the only book of Friedrich's which attracted international attention.

The early writings of Friedrich Schlegel, however, are of the greatest significance both for the history of romanticism and a general history of criticism. In close proximity to Schiller (whom he came to hate) Friedrich renewed the debate on ancients and moderns and developed from it the theory of the romantic which in his brother's version spread, literally, around the world. But Friedrich was not merely the propagandist of a catchword, the

writer of literary manifestoes which would give him purely historical importance; he was also the author of a critical theory which
anticipates many of the most urgent interests of our own time. In
Friedrich's theory of the romantic there were contained and implied theories of irony and myth in literature and the novel which
are pertinent even today. Moreover, Friedrich Schlegel reflected
on the theories of criticism, interpretation, and literary history so
fruitfully that he can be claimed as the originator of hermeneutics,
the theory of "understanding" which was later formulated by
Schleiermacher and Boeckh and thus influenced the whole long
line of German theoreticians of methodology. These are solid
claims to fame, to which we must add Friedrich's pioneering work
in Indic philology and philosophy and his wide-ranging historical and practical criticism of Goethe and Lessing, Homer, Camoēs, Boccaccio, and many other writers of almost all ages and nations.

Friedrich Schlegel started out as a classical philologist. His ambition was to become the "Winckelmann of Greek poetry," and
all his early publications, which include two books,* are devoted
to this plan. But Friedrich Schlegel's studies of Greek poetry were
not, of course, antiquarian contributions to literary history
(though they display an astonishing learning for so young a man).
As such they would necessarily be obsolete today and merit only
mention in a history of classical scholarship. Rather, he conceived
of literary history as so closely integrated with criticism that the
history of Greek literature appeared to him both the nourishing
soil and the proving ground of an aesthetic. Greek literature, in
these early writings, was considered uniquely suitable to such a
purpose, for Friedrich Schlegel not only saw the Greek works as
eternal models of perfection, as archetypes of poetry, but also
thought of Greek literary history as natural, spontaneous, undisturbed by outside interference, and complete in itself. Greek
culture is called "throughout original and national, a whole complete in itself, which merely by internal evolution reached its
highest summit and, in a complete cycle, then sank back into it-

---

* *Griechen und Römer* (1797), which contains a long paper, "Über
das Studium der griechischen Poesie," written in 1794–95, and some
smaller pieces; and *Geschichte der Poesie der Griechen und Römer*
(1798), which, however, breaks off before treating Greek tragedy.

self." [1] Greek poetry thus contains a complete collection of examples of all the different genres and contains them in a natural order of evolution. It serves both as a theory of genres and as a picture of the whole cycle of the organic evolution of an art, as a kind of laboratory for theory, as "the eternal natural history of taste and art." [2] This evolution is conceived on the analogy of biological evolution, in terms of growth, proliferation, blossoming, maturing, hardening, and final dissolution,[3] an analogy which during the 19th century received a great deal of impetus from Darwinian evolutionism and led to such curiosities of literary history as Brunetière's evolutionary histories or John Addington Symonds' *Shakspere's Predecessors in the Drama.* Though this Greek evolution must be thought of as somehow necessary and fated and the table of genres as complete, Friedrich Schlegel did not succumb to the relativistic implications of his theory. When he said over and over again that the "best theory of art is its history" [4] he did not mean the usual 19th-century historical relativism which is still crippling our present-day literary scholarship. He did not give up the task of evaluation or hide behind neutral history. In these early writings Friedrich Schlegel found his standard in the prescriptive nature, the ideal model of the great Greek classics; and late in his life he came to impose more and more religious criteria derived from his Christian philosophy. But in his middle stage, which clearly is the most interesting today, he recognized that the Greeks cannot command the unique position he had claimed for them and that his theory of the relation between history and criticism must be extended to the whole of literature without idolatry of any one nation or age. He saw that the whole history of the arts and sciences forms an order, one whole, or as he came to call it, an "organism" or an "encyclopedia," and that this order is the "source of objective laws for all positive criticism." [5] For Schlegel literature thus forms "a great completely coherent and evenly organized whole comprehending in its unity many worlds of art and itself forming a peculiar work of art." [6] T. S. Eliot in "Tradition and the Individual Talent" has said substantially the same. But Schlegel—differing from the unhistorical Eliot—can say that he is "disgusted with every theory which is not historical" [7] and that the "completion of every science is often nothing but the philosophical result of its history." [8] Schlegel thus rejects both unhistorical theorizing and historical relativism. He recognizes that the result of Herder's universal tolerance is the denial of any general standard of evaluation, in effect the abdication of criticism. The method of Herder to "contemplate every flower of art, without evaluation, only according to place, time, and kind, would finally lead to the result that everything must be as it is and was." [9] Also, in later years Friedrich Schlegel rejected Adam Müller's similar concept of "mediating" (*vermittelnd*) criticism, since it abolishes the difference between the good and the bad and amounts to saying, "Providence orders everything for the best, and everything had to come about as it did according to the philosophy, so dear to our contemporaries, of King Gorboduc: 'All that is, is.' " But the critical view cannot be simply absorbed by the historical because books are not "original creatures." [10] These protests against historical relativism are timely even today and were timely especially in Germany, where in the later 19th century historical relativism destroyed criticism more thoroughly than in any other country.

Beyond formulating convincingly the relation between history and criticism and stressing the aim of criticism as the "ascertaining of the value and nonvalue of poetic works of art," [11] Schlegel made many fruitful suggestions concerning the nature of critical procedure and interpretation. It is obvious that he derives from the tradition of philology. [12] He always stresses the share of philology in critical practice: "one cannot read out of pure philosophy or poetry without philology." [13] Philology means to him the love of words, the detailed attention to the text, "reading," interpretation. A critic, he can say wittily, "is a reader who chews his cud. He should have more than one stomach." [14] Reading or interpretation is always understood to be the right combination of micrology and attention to the whole. "One should exercise the art of reading both very slowly in a constant analysis of the detail and more quickly, in one swoop, for a survey of the whole." [15] One should not merely be sensitive to beautiful passages but be able to seize the impression of the whole, since "the first condition of all understanding, and hence also of the understanding of a work of art, is an intuition of the whole." [16]

Schlegel wants the critic to "spy on what he wanted to hide from our sight or at least did not want to show himself at first: on the author's secret intentions, which he pursues in silence and of which we can never assume too many in a genius." [17] We should uncover the deeply hidden, the unfathomable, and understand an author even better than he understood himself.[18] These are dangerous and paradoxical theories, with a measure of truth which has been exploited by much modern criticism far beyond Friedrich Schlegel's dreams. Mostly, though, Schlegel suggests sound and sober principles of interpretation. He repeats the commonplaces of the historical spirit, the necessity of sympathetic entry into remote times and countries, and he always stresses that one must know all the writings of an author in order to grasp their common spirit. In "art history," he understands, "one mass explains and illuminates the other. It is impossible to understand a part by itself." [19] The construction and knowledge of the whole (of art and poetry) is the one and essential condition of all criticism.[20] History and criticism are one. Every artist illuminates every other artist: together they form an order.

Schlegel attempts to describe what is needed in good criticism: "(1) a kind of geography of a world of art; (2) a spiritual and aesthetic architectonics of the work, its nature, its tone; and finally (3) its psychological genesis, its motivation by laws and conditions of human nature." [21] He speaks constantly of the whole: the spirit, the tone, the general impression. Mostly he thinks of criticism as a "reconstructive" process. The critic must "reconstruct, perceive, and characterize the more subtle peculiarities of a whole. . . . One can say that one has understood a work and a mind only if one can reconstruct its course and structure. This profound understanding, if expressed in definite words, is called characterization and is the actual business and inner essence of criticism." [22] Yet Schlegel has no use for the psychology of the reader, and he is strongest in his condemnation of the British psychological critics like Kames.[23] He makes the sensible distinction between "fantastics" (i.e. the theory of creation, of imagination) and "pathetics" (a theory of the psychology of the reader, of the effects of poetry), but comes then to the conclusion that "not much is gained for criticism so long as one wants only to explain the aesthetic sense in general, instead of thoroughly exercising, applying, and forming it." [24] He therefore rightly remarks that "almost all judgments on art are either too general or too specific. The critics should look for the golden mean here in their own productions, not in the works of the poets." [25]

Schlegel recognizes also the dangers of what we might call exclamatory criticism. "If many mystical lovers of art who consider all criticism dissection and every dissection a destruction of enjoyment were to think consistently, 'I'll be damned!' would be the best judgment on the greatest work. There are critics who do not say more, though at much greater length." [26] In general he describes the aim of criticism as "to give us a reflection of the work, to communicate its peculiar spirit, to present the pure impression in such a way that the presentation itself verifies the artistic citizenship of its author: not merely a poem about a poem, in order to dazzle for a moment; not merely the impression which a work has made yesterday or makes today on this or that person; but the impression which it should always make on all educated people." [27] This recognizes the universal appeal any critical judgment makes, a claim which Schlegel apparently found excessive at times: he would say merely that the "finished view of a work is always a critical fact" and that it can make no other claims than its "invitation to everybody to seize his own impression just as purely and to define it just as strictly" [28] as the critic himself. At times, however, he can embrace the fallacy of "creative" criticism. "Poetry can only be criticized by poetry. A judgment on art which is not itself a work of art, either in its matter, as presentation of a necessary impression in its genesis, or in its beautiful form and a liberal tone in the spirit of old Roman satire, has no citizens' rights in the realm of art." [29] But possibly the subclauses limit the demand of the main clause: actually a work of criticism is artistic to Schlegel if it is a precise reproduction of an impression or if it simply has the satirical polemical tone, the verve he loved and admired in himself and others.

"Polemics" is one of Friedrich Schlegel's favorite words and concepts. One of the functions of criticism is negative, the removal of the false, the making of room for the better, and this is polemics as practiced by writers like Lessing. "Polemics" is only the obverse side of "productive" criticism, by which Schlegel means something much more practical and useful than "creative" criticism. He means criticism which we might possibly better call "incitory" or "anticipatory," criticism which is not the "commentary on an existing, completed, even exhausted literature" but the *organon* of a literature which is just beginning to form itself. It is thus a criticism which is not merely explanatory and conservative but productive—at least indirectly so, by guidance, command, or instigation.[30] His own criticism was surely "productive" in his great years, when he stimulated a whole emerging literature and helped to give it direction. Instigating, directing, "producing" a new literature will always be one of the tasks of criticism which cannot be reduced—as is fashionable today—to the preservation and winnowing of tradition. But "creative" criticism, the production of another work of art, is an aberration, a needless duplication of a work of art, a blurring of necessary distinctions.

Schlegel's actual standards of evaluation and conception of poetry changed at least twice in his career: about 1796, when he abandoned his "Graecomania"—apparently under the impact largely of Schiller's treatise on *Naive and Sentimental Poetry*—and, more slowly and gradually, after 1801, when he moved toward a purely religious conception which finally led him to his conversion in 1808. But long before, poetry had become subordinated in his mind to philosophy and religion. In the early writings on Greek poetry, especially "Über das Studium der griechischen Poesie," which, we must remember, was finished before Schlegel could have read Schiller's treatise, Schlegel expounds a view of the contrast between the ancients and the moderns which in many ways is very similar to Schiller's. It derives, of course, from Winckelmann, from Schiller's *Letters on Aesthetic Education,* and from Goethe, yet it is elaborated with sharp distinctiveness and dogmatic assertiveness. The ideal of poetry is Greek poetry which is objective, "disinterested" (in the Kantian sense), perfect in form, impersonal, pure in its genres, and free from merely didactic and moralistic considerations. But more important than this rehearsal of the familiar traits of Winckelmannian "classicity" is Schlegel's negative characterization of the moderns.

Modern poetry is artificial, "interesting" (i.e. not disinterested, involved in the author's personal ends), "characteristic," "mannered" (in Goethe's sense, which contrasts subjective manner with objective style), impure in its mixing and confusion of genres, impure in its admixture of the didactic and philosophical, impure in its inclusion of even the ugly and the monstrous, and anarchic in its rejection of laws. Modern literature has "the terrible and yet fruitless desire to spread itself into the infinite, the eager thirst to penetrate the individual." [31] Against the closed cycle of antiquity there stands the moderns' system of infinite progression, their unsatisfied "yearning" (*Sehnsucht*), a word which later became one of the shibboleths of romanticism.[32] Even Shakespeare, though he is called the "summit of modern poetry," [33] is never totally beautiful. He is mannered throughout, even though his manner is the greatest. Goethe alone affords hope for a return to objective art, to classical beauty, though Schlegel recognizes that he is still in between the interesting and the beautiful, the mannered and the objective.[34] Schlegel, of course, conceives of the hoped-for German classicism not as actual imitation of the ancients but as a rebirth of an objective philosophy of art. No individual Greek writer, nor even less, of course, Greek theory and criticism, can become the model and authority. Schlegel always had a low opinion of Aristotle's *Poetics*.[35]

"Über das Studium der griechischen Poesie," then, contains the germ of the theory of the romantic. What was needed was only to change the minus signs into plus signs in front of the characterization of the moderns. Schlegel even in that treatise admits the necessity of the modern situation and praises many modern authors. He must have recognized that his dream and ideal, the harmony and objectivity of Greek poetry, is completely contrary to the actual bent of his own mind and the trend of the times. His reading of Schiller's treatise on *Naive and Sentimental Poetry* strengthened (as Schlegel acknowledged) this recognition and speeded up his change of heart or possibly, rather, his change of front. Fortified by Schiller's defense of the "sentimental," Schlegel, in the preface to *Die Griechen und Römer* (1797), which included the hitherto unprinted "Über das Studium," takes an intermediate position admitting the provisional aesthetic value of the "interesting." The conversion to the modern is complete when in the same year (1797) Schlegel surprisingly calls his essay, "Über das Studium," "a mannered prose hymn on the objective in poetry." [36] A year later comes the famous "fragment" (No. 116) of the *Athenaeum* which defines romantic poetry as "progressive universal poetry." This fragment has been quoted over and over again and has been made the key for the interpretation of the whole of romanticism. But one should recognize that it is only one of his deliberately mystifying pronouncements and that in it Schlegel uses the term "romantic" in a highly idiosyncratic way which he himself very soon abandoned. The use of the term in this fragment had actually no influence on its establishment as a contrast to classical. Schlegel adopted the term in preference to "modern" or "interesting" because it had no pejorative or strictly chronological connotations and because at this time he was apparently playing with its etymological affinity with the *Roman,* the novel.[37] The fragment in the *Athenaeum* wavers bewilderingly between a characterization of a poetry of the future and a novel of the future. The mission of romantic poetry is not only to "reunite the separate genres of poetry, to put poetry in touch with philosophy and rhetoric . . . it should combine poetry and prose, genius and criticism, the poetry of art and the poetry of nature. . . . Romantic poetry is still becoming: indeed its real essence is that it is always only becoming and never completed. . . . Romantic poetry is the only kind which is more than a kind; it is, so to speak, poetry itself: in a certain sense all poetry is or should be romantic." This is a program, a claim, a "vista toward a limitless growing classicity," [38] as he says paradoxically; something so all-inclusive, all-embracing, and vague that the whole fragment assumes concrete meaning only if we think of his aspiration for the romantic novel to embrace all genres and of his earlier speculations which contrasted the cyclical course of Greek poetry with the unlimited perfectibility of the moderns.

In the *Gespräch über die Poesie* (1800) Schlegel returns to the old meaning of the term romantic. In his sketch of the "Epochs of Poetry" which is part of the *Gespräch*, Shakespeare is characterized as laying the "romantic foundations of modern drama." [39] In the speech on mythology, another part of the piece, Cervantes and Shakespeare are referred to as belonging to "romantic poetry." Thus "romantic" is not simply identical with Schiller's "sentimental," since Shakespeare is romantic in Schlegel and naive in Schiller. Schiller considers the immediate relation to reality, the imitation of nature, as naive, while Schlegel sees a romantic trait in the avidity for the fullness of life. The terms clearly overlap on many points; Schlegel, however, draws a further contrast between the romantic and the modern. They differ, according to him, as a painting by Raphael or Correggio differs from a fashionable copper engraving. Lessing's *Emilia Gallotti* is called "unutterably modern" and "not in the least romantic," while Shakespeare is the "real center and core of romantic imagination." The romantic thus can be found rather in the Renaissance and the Middle Ages, "in that age of knights, of love and fairy tales, whence the thing and the word are derived." [40] But then the romantic is said to be not a genre but an element of poetry, which may dominate or recede more or less yet must never be totally absent. All poetry, Schlegel concludes illogically, must be romantic. These passages contain the essential distinctions of the romantic from the classical and the modern (i.e. pseudo-classical). But Friedrich Schlegel does not consider his own age romantic: he singles out the novels of Jean Paul as the "only romantic products of an unromantic age." [41] Nor does he expressly contrast the classical and the romantic (though he alludes to their possible union).[42] The most influential formulations of the great dichotomy belong only to his brother, August Wilhelm, even though all its elements are in Friedrich Schlegel.

Schlegel's poetic ideal takes on much more concrete meaning if we examine his demands for irony, myth, and the mysterious, his conception of the novel, in fact his whole new hierarchy of genres. He does not call irony "romantic irony." All the early passages using the term comment on the irony of Socrates, on his "sublime urbanity," without any particular modern application.[43] Only the review of *Wilhelm Meister* (1798) and the *Gespräch über die Poesie* (1800) give it a meaning in the context of modern literature. Irony is, in part, associated with Schiller's play-concept of art, the Kantian view of art as free activity. We demand irony, "we demand that the events, the people, in brief the whole play of life, should really be conceived and represented as play." [44] Irony is associated with paradox. It is "a form of paradox. Paradox is what is at the same time good and great." [45] Irony is his recognition of the fact that the world in its essence is paradoxical and that an ambivalent attitude alone can grasp its contradictory totality. For Schlegel irony is the struggle between the absolute and the relative, the simultaneous consciousness of the impossibility and the necessity of a complete account of reality.[46] The writer must thus feel ambivalent toward his work: he stands above and apart from it and manipulates it almost playfully. "In order to be able to describe an object well," Schlegel can say, "one must have ceased to be interested in it . . . as long as the artist invents and is inspired he remains at least for communication in an illiberal frame of mind." [47] Thus art demands the "liberal frame of mind," the power of the artist to raise himself above his own "highest." [48] "Irony is a clear consciousness of the infinitely full chaos," [49] of the dark and inexplicable world, but it is also highly self-conscious, for irony is self-parody, "transcendental buffoonery" which "rises above one's art, virtue, and genius." [50] Irony is thus associated with "transcendental poetry," with the "poetry of poetry" which Schlegel finds in Pindar, Dante, and Goethe. Irony to Schlegel is objectivity, complete superiority, detachment, manipulation of the subject matter. Schlegel praises *Wilhelm Meister* for the irony with which the hero is portrayed by Goethe, who seems to "smile down from the heights of his spirit upon his masterwork"; [51] and he looks for similar attitudes in Aristophanes, Cervantes, Shakespeare, Swift, Sterne, and Jean Paul.

There is no evidence that Schlegel found irony in the constant interference of the author in his work, in the deliberate breaking of the illusion. Only in one fragment (No. 42 of the *Lyceum*) is there an allusion to the Italian *buffo* which might be so interpreted.[52] But Schlegel speaks there of poetry in general, not of the drama, and the reference to the buffo means only that the ironic author always smiles at his imperfect medium just as the buffo laughs at his comic role. There is no recommendation of very old devices of art: the playwright on the stage, the play within the play, the author appearing in his own novel, which became such particular favorites of Tieck and Brentano, E. T. A. Hoffmann and Heine, and came to be known as "romantic irony." At the time that Schlegel formulated his ideas on irony he did not know Tieck's comedies and he never considered them realizations of his ideals. Goethe, Shakespeare, and Cervantes were his ironists, not his fellow romanticists.*

* Schlegel's interpretation of irony has been argued over rather heatedly, e.g. by Käthe Friedemann, "Die romantische Ironie," *Zeitschrift für Aesthetik, 13* (1919), 270–82; Carl Enders, "Fichte und die Lehre von der romantischen Ironie," *op. cit., 14* (1920), 279–84; Alfred Lussky, *Tieck's Romantic Irony*, Chapel Hill, 1932; and Oskar Walzel, *Romantisches* (Bonn, 1934), pp. 73–93. I am convinced by Raymond Immerwahr, "The Subjectivity or Objectivity of Friedrich Schlegel's Poetic Irony," *Germanic Review, 26* (1951), 173–91.

Still, Schlegel's theory easily lent itself to a subjectivist interpretation; in his own novel *Lucinde* he certainly exemplified extreme subjectivism, playing with illusion, moral and artistic irresponsibility. There is no contradiction between these two attitudes, and in dialectical thinking one extreme easily passes into the other.

Friedrich Schlegel introduced the term irony into modern literary discussion. Before, there are only adumbrations in Hamann. Schlegel's use of the term differs from the earlier purely rhetorical meaning and from the view of tragic irony in Sophocles which was developed early in the 19th century by Connop Thirlwall. Schlegel's concept was taken up by Solger, in whom it first assumed a central position for critical theory and for whom all art becomes irony. Hegel and later Kierkegaard criticized Schlegel's concept, utterly mistaking it as a consequence of his adherence to the Fichtean philosophy of ego, as sheer opportunism, artistic and moral frivolity.* But in the actual texts there is no justification for such disparagement. One must realize, moreover, that irony for Schlegel is only one element of modern self-consciousness and is combined with very different requirements.

Among these, Friedrich Schlegel's demand for a new myth, an ironical, self-consciously elaborated, philosophical myth, is the most striking. In the speech on mythology, which also forms a part of the *Gespräch über die Poesie* (1800), Schlegel develops the thesis —familiar today and still relevant—that modern literature lacks the support, the mother-soil, of myth. Classical and Christian mythology had been used throughout the course of modern literature, and Germans preceding Schlegel, especially Herder and Klopstock, had loudly called for the revival of Teutonic mythology, a return to the sources of folk imagination. But Schlegel suggests a new and different mythology which would derive a new system of relationships, a "hieroglyphical expression of surrounding nature," [53] from the new idealistic philosophy (Fichte) and the new physics (Schelling's *Naturphilosophie*). The exact nature of the new mythology is left vague in this manifesto. Schlegel suggests as further sources

---

* Connop Thirlwall, "On the Irony of Sophocles," reprinted in *Remains Literary and Theological* (London, 1878), *3*, 1–57. On Solger and Hegel see below, p. 299 f, 324. Sören Kierkegaard, *Der Begriff der Ironie* (1841); two Ger. trans., Munich, 1929.

the pantheism of Spinoza and the Orient, especially India, a hint which he later pursued systematically in his own Indic studies. But Schlegel apparently does not mean by myth merely a new cosmology or an exploitation of philosophical concepts; he thinks of it, rather, as a system of correspondences and symbols. Myth is an analogue of the "wit of romantic poetry," as it is exemplified in the works of Cervantes and Shakespeare, which are full of "artfully arranged confusion, charming symmetry of contrasts, marvelous eternal alteration of enthusiasm and irony." Myth is something he calls "an indirect mythology," [54] a new world view which abolishes the course of logical reason and returns us to the "beautiful confusion of imagination, the original chaos of human nature, for which I do not as yet know any more beautiful symbol than the colorful milling throng of the ancient Gods." [55] However obscurely this is phrased, the sense becomes clear if we see the passage in the light of the other pronouncements on irony and the romantic. "Idealism" (i.e. Fichtean philosophy) means free play; life as play and all art as symbolic. Schlegel does not yet use the distinction between allegory and symbol drawn by Goethe and Schelling. He thus can say, "All beauty is allegory" and "Because it is inexpressible, one can express the highest only allegorically." [56] Art, therefore, is myth, symbolism, even "divine magic." [57]

More light is thrown on Schlegel's conception of poetry by several recently published fragments on beauty. Schlegel distinguishes there between multiplicity, unity, and totality in beauty. The triad is derived from Kant's table of the categories of quantity,[58] which he interprets as plenty, richness, and life in a work of art; harmony, organization; and perfection or divinity. The first two criteria are the well-known requirements of unity and variety, local texture and general structure, or whatever we may call them today. The third category is clearly the same as the mythic or the infinite of other passages. At times, Schlegel has in mind simply the cosmic quality of art which was familiar to Schiller and Kant. The "infinite" is the morally sublime, the assertion of man's moral freedom, his resistance to suffering in tragedy; [59] but mostly, with increasing emphasis and frequency, poetry becomes a part of divine creation, a smaller parallel to the work of art which is nature. "All holy plays of art are only distant imitations of the infinite play of the world, of the eternally self-creating work of art" [60]—so runs an early passage formulated in a pantheistic terminology. But soon we get phrases like "Art is a visible appearance of God's Kingdom on earth," [61] and "Only that can be beautiful which has a relation to the infinite and divine," [62] or poetry "is nothing else than a pure expression of the inner eternal word of God." [63] Poetry becomes more and more identified with philosophy and religion. Philosophy and poetry are proclaimed different forms of religion and the union of philosophy and poetry is envisaged as an ultimate aim.[64] In effect, poetry is pronounced, at first, to be "only another expression of the same transcendental view of things, differing only in its form" from idealistic philosophy.[65] After Schlegel's conversion, poetry for him forms, along with history, mythology, language, science, and art, only one of the rays of the single light of higher knowledge, revelation.[66] Poetry thus loses more and more of its specific meaning and becomes confused and amalgamated with religion, philosophy, and the whole universe itself. Even before this, the *Gespräch über die Poesie* (1800) had spoken of the "formless and unconscious poetry which stirs in plants, shines in light, smiles in a child, glistens in the flower of youth, glows in the loving breast of women." [67] But then one of the interlocutors could still ask mockingly: "Is then everything poetry?" [68] But later if someone had asked Schlegel whether everything good and beautiful is religion, he would have received a roundly affirmative answer. One must recognize how influential this cosmic extension of the meaning of poetry (with its antecedents and parallels in Plato and Shelley) became during the 19th century. It was a development detrimental to the establishment of a genuine theory of literature.

Schlegel's many speculations about particular genres proved more fruitful than his mystical generalities on the significance of poetry. In his early writings on Greek literature he is most interested in the theory of genres because the development of Greek literature presented him with a survey of the main genres. He did not get to the discussion of tragedy in detail but in connection with Homer devoted long arguments to the epic. He violently rejected Aristotle's approximation of the epic and tragedy and argued, using Wolf's theories about the gradual composition of the Homeric poems, for a theory of the epic in which each larger or smaller member has, like the whole, its own life and internal unity.[69] An epic thus has a different structure from that of a drama: it not only

begins *in medias res* but also ends in it. It is always both a con-
tinuation and the beginning of something else.[70] The events in the
epic are not free actions or necessary decisions of fate but contingent, chance events, for everything marvelous is contingent.[71] The
affinity to some of the contemporary discussions between Schiller
and Goethe is clear, but Schlegel's contrast between the almost
atomistic epic and the unified drama, the epic as a series of chance
events and the tragedy of fate and inexorable necessity, seems
exaggerated and scholastic in its rigidity.

The novel is later discussed by Schlegel with much greater originality and suggestiveness, in close relation with his theories of the
romantic, myth, and irony and with actual contemporary practice.
His "Letter on the Novel" (which is also a part of the *Gespräch
über die Poesie*) presents a program, a history, and an implied defense of his own attempt at a novel, the unlucky *Lucinde* (1799).
Schlegel has no patience with realistic art, though he is full of avid
lust for life in its variety and fullness. He condemns the realistic
novel of the English, including even Fielding.[72] He admires Swift,
Sterne, and Diderot. *Jacques le Fataliste* is superior to Sterne, as
it is free from sentimental admixtures. Jean Paul also excels Sterne
in that his "imagination is much more diseased, and hence much
odder and much more fantastic." [73] But all these recent novelists
seem to him only preparatory to an understanding of the "divine
wit," the imagination of an Ariosto, a Cervantes, and a Shakespeare. The novel is thus not grouped with the epic at all, for the
epic (he still thinks mostly of Homer) is impersonal, objective, and
heroic, while the novel in his sense expresses a subjective mood
and allows indulgence in an author's humor which would be quite
out of place in an epic. By a novel, a *Roman,* Schlegel means the
"ironic, fantastic, romantic" art of Cervantes, Sterne, Diderot, Jean
Paul, and his own *Lucinde.* The realistic novel, he would admit,
tells us (as does Fanny Burney's *Cecilia*) how people get bored in
London or (as Fielding) how a country squire curses. But in novels
he loves the "arabesque" (a term derived from Goethe), the play of
imagination, the irony, and the subjective. Thus, Rousseau's *Confessions* are called a better novel than *La Nouvelle Héloïse.*[74] His
own *Lucinde* consisted of such arabesques, or what the century
called "rhapsodies," and of highly personal erotic confessions. Novalis' *Heinrich von Ofterdingen* combines the novel and the myth.

In the "Letter on the Novel" Goethe's *Wilhelm Meister* has lost its earlier central position and is praised only for attempting the impossible ideal of uniting classical and romantic.[75]

The romantic, irony, and myth are all combined in this all-embracing genre, the *Roman,* which contains narration, song, and other forms. The old hierarchy of genres is overthrown. Drama and epic are dethroned, the novel exalted. But it is a very peculiar novel: Thomas Mann's ironic myths, Joyce, or Kafka would come nearer to a fulfillment of his prophecy than the realistic novel of the 19th century. Schlegel even saw the consequences of writing novels "out of psychology": "It seems very inconsistent and pusillanimous to want to shy away even from the slowest and most detailed analysis of unnatural lusts, most gruesome tortures, revolting infamy, and disgusting sensual and spiritual impotence."[76] But he could hardly have endorsed his mock proposal, as nothing was further from his taste than plodding, "lifelike" art.

In the early writings on Greek poetry, tragedy is considered the summit of Greek and presumably of all literature. Sophocles, especially, is so completely identified with the highest beauty, the harmony of the whole, that praise could hardly go higher.[77] Greek tragedy is interpreted as a necessary strife between mankind and fate, but that strife is resolved in harmony and mankind is victorious even though physically defeated. Hercules, in the *Trachiniae,* though dying, "wings upward at last, free."[78] Shakespeare, on the other hand, the example of modern, "interesting," or "philosophical" tragedy, centers his art around character rather than fate. The total impression of *Hamlet* is a maximum of despair. Its end result is the "eternal colossal dissonance which divides mankind and fate forever."[79] During the fruitful middle years Schlegel's interest in tragedy receded in favor of the novel. It re-emerges in the *History of Ancient and Modern Literature* (1812), where, in the context of the discussion of Calderón, a new three-type or three-stage theory of tragedy is expounded. A purely picturesque art of depiction is the lowest stage. The second is the characterization of the whole, "where the world and life in its full variety, in its contradictions and odd complications, where man and his existence, this involved riddle, is depicted as such a riddle." Shakespeare is the greatest master of this stage. But beyond it there arises a third stage, in which the dramatist not only expounds but solves the riddle of existence and shows how "the Eternal arises from the earthly catastrophe." [80] This threefold distinction is explained by a further and different classification of three kinds of catastrophes in tragedy, which are compared to the *Inferno, Purgatorio,* and *Paradiso.* The hero may perish completely, like Macbeth or Wallenstein or Faust (in the German legend, for Schlegel could not yet know Goethe's happy ending). The second kind of solution is that of reconciliation, as at the end of the *Oresteia* or in *Oedipus at Colonus.* The third and highest stage is that of spiritual transfiguration of the hero, for which the Christian endings of Calderón's plays are Schlegel's example and the justification of the exalted position which he now ascribes to Calderón.

On the whole, Schlegel obviously holds to the doctrine of the distinction and even purity of genres. In his early writings he severely condemned the mixing of genres as a modern disease,[81] and even later he praised Lessing for showing that each work "should be only excellent in its genus and species, as otherwise it would become an unsubstantial thing in general." [82] He condemns pedantic classifications but obviously agrees with the interlocutors in his *Gespräch über die Poesie* who argue that the "imagination of the poet must not pour itself into a chaotic poetry in general, but every work must have its completely distinct character according to form and genre." A theory of genres would be a specific theory of poetry. This point of view is somewhat modified, in the later revised version, when another interlocutor admits that the "essential form of poetry lies in its distinct genres and their theory," but not the "essence of poetry itself, which is alone ceaselessly inventive and creative, eternal imagination." [83] When Schlegel recommended the romantic novel he rather formulated the principles of a new inclusive genre than advocated the mingling of the old ones.

Moreover, in discussing Lessing's *Laokoon* Schlegel does not favor an actual union of the arts. He sensibly criticizes Lessing for ignoring the differences between sculpture and painting and argues that each art should try to overcome the limitations of its material. Just because sculpture uses so heavy and dead a material as stone, it should try to make it alive and living. Just because music is so fluid and flowing, it must attempt to express the permanent, to "build a proud temple out of the eternal relations of harmony" and leave "the whole firm as a monument in the soul of the listener." The poet also uses sound which occurs successively in time, but at the end of a poem the "whole must stand clearly like a picture in one presentation before the eyes of the listener or even reader." Poetry is the universal art, and thus there can be poems which are written wholly in the spirit of painting and others which are musical, or even both simultaneously. Several works of Cervantes and Tieck are referred to without specification, and some poems of the ancients and Goethe are given as examples of poems that draw something from sculpture. Descriptive poetry in the 18th-century sense is, however, condemned, not because it tried to achieve the effects of painting in poetry but because it was atomistic, concerned only with particulars. "This is the death of all feeling for art, which first of all and primarily is based on a view of the whole." [84] The way is open here for the picture poems of the romanticists, the musical songs in words, the sculpturesque poetry of Keats, Landor, and Gautier. But no union of the arts, no absorption of one art by another, is advocated, and poetry keeps its central position as the most universal of the arts.

The creative act is thought of by Schlegel as a combination of the conscious and subconscious, of "instinct" and "intention." However, in the *Gespräch* there are passages which speculate on the possibility of schools of poetry. Even the hope is expressed that poetry which had been a "tale of heroes, and then a game of the knights, and finally the handicraft of burghers would become a thorough science of true scholars and the honest art of inventive poets." [85] Though this might sound like a recommendation for sheer academicism, for art as a craft (and has been interpreted as such),[86] it surely cannot be taken literally in the light of all of Schlegel's other writings. His concept of poetry is far too closely related to that of Schelling and Novalis, who actually use the term "unconscious." The idea of a "school" is merely a paradoxical formula for Schlegel's desire for collective art, the social art of the future, for the whole romantic ideal of "symphilosophizing." His school is a *côterie*, a *cénacle*, not a *Singschule* in the style of the *Meistersänger*. Also in his allusions to the role of the artist in society Schlegel is only apparently contradictory. He can call him an "isolated egoist" and suggest that "even in its outward customs the manner of life of artists should be thoroughly distinct from that of other people. They are Brahmins, a higher caste, ennobled not by birth but by free self-dedication."[87] This attitude best suited his own manner of life, his pride, his hatred of the German *Philister* and the cultural representatives of the Berlin Enlightenment, and his ever present desire to *épater le bourgeois,* so prominent in his paradoxes and witty formulas. But Schlegel opposed the purely individual isolated artist, what he called the "Stubenluft,"[88] of earlier German literature. At a period when his liberalism was at his height, in a defense of the German revolutionary Georg Forster, Schlegel praised him as a "social" writer who lived up to his ideal of the total man.[89] In describing Lessing's position in German literature he dwelt on the loneliness, the single-handedness of his struggle more than on anything else.[90] Schlegel's whole conception of polemical criticism, of an "encyclopedia," presupposes teamwork, some kind of association, a group of friends, or possibly a class of clerics, an élite. When the flood of enthusiasm for folk poetry was at its highest in Germany, Schlegel did not share it, though he admired ancient mythic poetry. He even wrote a satirical review of a collection of German folk songs in which he parodied Goethe's review of *Des Knaben Wunderhorn,*[91] and in the *History of Ancient and Modern Literature* he considered folk poetry as valuable only as a survival of ancient heroic poetry. He even calls it a proof of the dissolution of real national poetry.[92] "It is not always the right condition that poetry, which should inspire, keep alive and further develop the spirit of a whole nation, be left to the people alone."[93] The emphasis is now laid on poetry as an expression of a nation and its peculiar character: national literature should be based on its legends, its history, its myth, and should appeal to the whole nation. But when Schlegel praises Spanish literature as the "most national" of all, he pulls himself up and declares that he is far from "considering the national point of view as the only one from which the value, in world history, of a literature should be judged."[94] The overriding value is now religion, revelation.

Schlegel never shared the latecomer's prophecy of the extinction of poetry, precisely because he never conceived of it as an isolated skill. Poetry, he believed with Herder, is the mother-tongue of the human race, a natural function of man. He rejected the view that poetry is only "the symbolic child's language of mankind in its youth." [95] It is to him an activity of the human mind which cannot disappear, rather to be perfected in the future than perfect in the past. Man, he feels, is gaining rather than losing in the strength and sensitivity of his feeling, in true aesthetic vital force.[96] Schlegel has no patience with the worship of a golden age of poetry, and the golden ages of the French and English seem to him not golden or poetic at all.[97] He rejects, at least for modern times, the idea of a cycle, of growth and decay, quoting the example of Calderón as that of a sudden rebirth in an age of apparent total decadence, of a phoenix rising out of its own ashes.[98] He believed, even in his Catholic years, in perfectibility, in the open structure of modern literature, in its great civilizing role. He could not otherwise have been a leader of a group, the herald of an "aesthetic revolution" in Germany. After all, romantic poetry, modern poetry, was for him "progressive universal poetry." [99]

We shall glance only briefly at Friedrich Schlegel's achievements as a literary historian, scholar, and practical critic. Literary history was his earliest ambition, fulfilled by his fragmentary history of Greek poetry. A brief sketch, the "Epochs of Poetry," takes a central position in the *Gespräch*, and later in life he considered the *History of Ancient and Modern Literature* (delivered in 1812, published in 1815) the culmination of his literary career. Heine, in his malicious account of the Schlegels, suggested that "Friedrich Schlegel there surveyed the whole of literature from an elevated point of view, but that elevation is always the bell tower of a Catholic church." [100] But this is grossly exaggerated. The book, one must admit, is in many ways disappointing with respect to literary criticism. It attempts, rather, a general survey of the intellectual, religious, philosophical, and literary history of mankind on a scale which is small for the tremendous scope of its ambition. It includes a philosophy of history which predicts the ultimate victory of Roman Catholicism over the forces of the Enlightenment and all other forms of secularism. Literary history and criticism is thus crowded out by unctuous exhortations, philosophical and religious reflections, and speculations on the history of language which today are totally obsolete. But in spite of these long stretches of irrelevancy the book contains much literary criticism and history in the strict sense, and most of it, based in large part on his earlier researches and reflections, represents his most considered and systematic view of many authors and problems.

We have sufficiently discussed Schlegel's early views of the history of Greek poetry, its cyclical rise and fall, its explication of the sequence of genres, and the theory of the epic and tragedy he elicits from Homer and Sophocles. In spite of his glorification of Greek classical beauty, even his early conception of the Greeks had some original features which were later developed by him in much greater fullness. He apparently was one of the first to sense the dark background or underground of Greek life, the element which Nietzsche exalted seventy years later as "Dionysian." Schlegel emphasizes that we should consider the "Greek orgies and mysteries not as foreign stains and chance aberrations but as an essential part of ancient culture, as a necessary step in the gradual development of the Greek spirit." [101] With the appreciation of the Orphic in Greek poetry and in the mysteries goes Schlegel's exaltation of Aristophanes, which was then a comparative novelty. A very early paper is devoted to the "Aesthetic Value of Greek Comedy," [102] which is seen in its joy, sublime freedom, and unlimited autonomy. The social purpose and the realistic detail of the old comedy are ignored completely. Aristophanes seems to anticipate romantic irony. Even in Sophocles Schlegel finds fused the "divine drunkenness of Dionysus, the deep inventiveness of Athene, the quiet serenity of Apollo." [103] But with Schlegel's turn toward the romantic and Christian his sight was sharpened for the nonclassical elements in the Greeks. He sees the ancient Greeks now as less unique in the context of the ancient Orient. He stresses in Aeschylus the "struggle between the old chaos and the idea of law and harmonious order," [104] and he condemns Greek naturalism and materialism much more strongly and sees it now everywhere. In this he goes along with the development of German classical studies of his time: he shares, though moderately, in the attacks on the glorification of the Greeks by the medieval enthusiasts among his contemporaries and by those who saw the limitations of Greek civilization from the point of view of Christianity. He sympathizes with the new interest in Greek myth and its symbolist interpretation introduced by Creuzer. He also looks for anticipations of the Christian spirit among the Greeks and finds them in Sophocles, who has an "intuition of the divine," [105] whose tragedies end in reconciliation and a hint of transfiguration.

With his shift to the romantic Schlegel's concrete interest in the Middle Ages grew considerably. Here the stimulation of his brother was probably decisive. He devoted some research in the Paris libraries to manuscripts of Provençal poetry in preparation for an edition which never materialized and laboriously read through the scarce minor works of Boccaccio. The piece which he devoted to a characterization of Boccaccio (1801) [106] has pioneering value and some critical interest, for Schlegel suggests there an aesthetic of the *novella* in which he sees the presentation of a subjective mood and view in an indirect and symbolic manner.[107] Schlegel belongs also to the early German admirers of Dante (following his brother). He sees in him a proof of the artificial character of the oldest modern poetry,[108] as Dante's poem is contrived in its structure according to scholastic concepts and thus contrasts with Homer's naturally growing work. Without knowing it Schlegel here contradicts Vico, who had seen in Dante the Italian Homer, the representative of a heroic age. Also in the *History* Schlegel admits that in Dante poetry and Christianity are not in complete harmony and that the *Divine Comedy* is, at least in places, only a theological didactic poem.[109]

The revival of Nordic and Old Germanic studies in Germany, in which his brother and his friend Tieck took a prominent part, turned Schlegel's attention also to the Nordic Middle Ages. He wrote elaborately on Ossian (expressing grave doubts of its authenticity and speculating on its date), on the *Edda,* and more sketchily on the *Nibelungenlied* and Wolfram von Eschenbach.[110] In the *History* Schlegel characterizes the German *Minnesang,* trying to differentiate it from the Provençal courtly lyric.[111] Later he more and more stressed the value for modern poetry of national history, legends, and memories, and these memories were, for the Nordic nations, mostly medieval. He also argues against the term "Dark Ages" [112] and gives a favorable account of medieval civilization, stressing the survival of antiquity, the beginnings of the Renaissance as early as the times of Charlemagne, the advantages of chivalry, courtly love, the beauties of Gothic architecture, and so forth. But one cannot say that his medievalism is extreme or exclusive like that of many of his contemporaries. One has also the definite impression that his acquaintance with the actual literature was limited and that he did not overrate its artistic value. Strangely enough he rated Chaucer below Hans Sachs [113] and shows little concrete knowledge of Old French literature, though he had encouraged and supervised his wife's German version of the Old French Merlin romance.

The Renaissance (not yet called so) is much more fully in his mind. It is to him *the* romantic age. His admiration for Shakespeare, Cervantes, and Camoẽs is almost unbounded. French literature of the Renaissance, however, is almost completely ignored (with the exception of meager remarks on Montaigne and Rabelais) and Italian literature is rated curiously low. Schlegel considers Tasso a subjective sentimentalist, unsuccessful in the heroic epic, and he definitely prefers Camoẽs to Ariosto. Machiavelli, though treated with respect, is singled out as a strange un-Christian anomaly. Surprising and even odd is the praise for Guarini's *Pastor Fido* as "permeated with the spirit of antiquity, great and noble, even in its form, like the drama of the Greeks." [114] Shakespeare attracted Schlegel very early, especially *Hamlet*, which at that time he saw as a philosophical tragedy (a contradiction according to his theory), a tragedy of despair, of the disproportion between thinking and acting powers.[115] Schlegel's Hamlet clearly is a development of Goethe's in the direction of Coleridge's philosophical prince. With his brother, Friedrich was one of the first critics to stress that Shakespeare was a "most purposeful artist" (1797),[116] but his concrete discussions of Shakespeare seem quite divided in purpose and conception. He shows the then prevalent German interest in Shakespeare's histories as a national myth and can express the preposterous opinion that *Henry V* is the "summit of Shakespeare's power." [117] He also shares Tieck's and his brother's uncritical predilection for the apocrypha. *Locrine* especially is considered by him as important for an understanding of Shakespeare, apparently in contrast to the sonnets and poems, which for Schlegel are a proof of the sweetness of Shakespeare's personality and hence, in reverse, a proof of Shakespeare's own "immense remoteness from the stage." [118] It is strange that Schlegel, with all his interest in the fantastic and idyllic Shakespeare, the Italian Shakespeare one might say, could still come to the conclusion that Shakespeare is basically an "old Nordic and not a Christian poet," [119] and can even speak of his feeling as "generally Nordic and truly German." [120] German here means, of course, Germanic as it was used at that time, but Schlegel also claims that only the German critics have understood Shakespeare and that he is peculiarly theirs. Schlegel was caught in the general wave of German nationalism during the Napoleonic era and was enticed by the whole North and South contrast which, in the case of the English Shakespeare, was complicated by a violent antipathy for the commercial, utilitarian, and materialistic England of the 18th century which made Shakespeare appear a lonely survivor of an almost prehistoric Nordic age.

No literature elicited as much admiration and interest from Friedrich in his later years as Spanish literature. Cervantes especially is to him a romantic, poetic writer in spite of his satire against chivalry.[121] *Don Quixote* is the model of the novel, fantastic, poetic, humorous. The *Novelas, Galatea,* the play *Numancia,* and even *Persiles* are also highly admired. The Spanish medieval romances are the most beautiful he knows, and in later years Calderón rises in his estimation to the highest position among all dramatists, being "preeminently Christian and therefore the most romantic of all." * Schlegel, besides, took an intense interest in Camoës. The *Lusiads* is praised as the greatest heroic poem of modern times, right after Homer, by far exceeding Ariosto in color and fullness of imagination.[122] A special article elaborates this praise in a lyrical description of the contents,[123] coupled with a comparative disparagement of Virgil and Tasso.

French tragedy and literature in general was the pet aversion of the German romanticists and the main polemical butt of his brother. Friedrich's early writings are full of violent invectives. French tragedy is called a mere "empty formality without power, charm, and substance; even its form is an absurd barbaric mechanism, without internal vital principle and natural organization." [124] The French are considered a nation "without poetry," and the so-called classics of the French and English are dismissed

* *Sämtliche Werke, 2,* 87: "Unter allen andern dramatischen Dichtern vorzugsweise der christliche und eben darum auch der am meisten romantische." To what height the idolatry of Calderón could rise is shown by a letter addressed to August Wilhelm before the conversion (May 24, 1805): "Was ist schöner als die *Puente de Mantible* [by Calderón]? Die ist mehr wert als die ganze Französische und Englische Litteratur" (*Krisenjahre der Frühromantik, 1,* 198).

as not even worthy of mention in a history of art.[125] But this violence abated considerably with time, his stay in France, and his turn to Catholicism. In the *History*, though there is still no sympathy shown for neoclassical theory, Corneille's *Cid* and Racine's *Athalie* are praised very warmly.[126] Surprisingly, even Voltaire's *Alzire* finds favor in Schlegel's eyes,[127] though otherwise Voltaire is one of the villains of his *History*. Schlegel, moreover, does not endorse his brother's attack on Molière; the praise for Bossuet is very generous for obvious reasons, while Pascal is mainly characterized as a sophistical enemy of Schlegel's friends, the Jesuits.[128] Rousseau, though Schlegel considers him merely a negative force without positive creed, is exalted as the greatest French author of the 18th century.[129]

English literature outside Shakespeare interested Friedrich Schlegel (possibly for linguistic reasons) least. Praise and appreciation of Milton is very limited and the influence of his Latinized vocabulary is called unfortunate.[130] The Christian theme of *Paradise Lost* is considered to erect insuperable barriers to success. Richardson is mildly appreciated, as well as Sterne, but in general the English of the 18th century are attacked as the representatives of the modern spirit, "modern" meaning secular and commercial. Gibbon especially is singled out for frequent ridicule; the *Memoirs* is considered an "immensely comic book." Gibbon merely loved the material magnificence of the Romans and might as well have written on the Turks.* The English 18th-century critics are mercilessly dismissed: "there is not the most modest hint of a sense for poetry in Harris, Home [Lord Kames], and Johnson." [131]

There is comparatively little criticism of contemporary foreign literature in Friedrich Schlegel: the *History* shows Schlegel's sympathetic awareness of the French Catholic revival, De Bonald, Lammenais, and Joseph de Maistre. Schlegel wrote a warmly appreciative review (1820) of Lamartine,[132] especially of the first volume of the *Méditations*, which fitted into a scheme for contrasting Lamartine the poet of faith with Byron the poet of despair.

---

* Minor, 2, 375: "ein unendlich drolliges Buch." Cf. 2, 237. Schlegel's criticism is unjust. In writing *The Decline and Fall of the Roman Empire* Gibbon constantly has the British empire and its ideals in mind. Cf. Lewis P. Curtis, "Gibbon's Paradise," in *The Age of Johnson* (New Haven, 1949), pp. 73–90.

Still, Byron, though condemned as the poet of negation, is, as was usual on the Continent at that time, grossly overrated. Lucifer in *Cain* is, for instance, preferred to Goethe's Mephistopheles.[133] Among more recent English writers Schlegel praises only Burke for political reasons and gives a very critical account of Scott's poetry as a mere "mosaic of isolated fragments of romantic legend." [134]

One feature of the *History* should be singled out for particular praise. Schlegel tries to pay some attention to the minor nations of Northern and Eastern Europe. In a spirit of tolerant nationalism he insists that every nation has a right to its language and peculiar literature. He refers to the existence at least of Russian and medieval Czech literature and shows some awareness of the revival of Hungarian literature, even mentioning one author, Kisfaludy.[135]

Naturally, Schlegel's main efforts in practical criticism were devoted to German literature. Considering his general outlook, one must admire his generous appreciation of Luther, even in the *History*. The praise of Opitz is unusual for the time and setting, and Schlegel shares the extravagant admiration of his friends for Jakob Böhme.[136] Some of the most detailed criticism Schlegel wrote was devoted to Lessing, his great favorite among the older German authors. As Lessing is usually considered the representative author of the German Enlightenment and can hardly be divorced from the rationalistic Protestant tradition, this sympathy seems surprising at first. It cooled considerably after the conversion, yet in his most romantic years Schlegel wrote an enthusiastic article and edited a three-volume anthology with introductions, one of them on the "Character of Protestants." Part of Schlegel's sympathy must be explained by his desire to capture the great palladium of the Enlightenment for himself and his friends: to show that Lessing is by no means the ordinary rationalist, that especially the *Education of the Human Race* points toward a new religion. Schlegel quite frankly surrenders Lessing's claim to greatness as a poet and dramatist and is interested primarily in his character, his "great free style of life," his open-mindedness, and the strength of his unpopular opinions even more than in his prose style, his "mixture of literature, polemics, wit, and philosophy." [137] Lessing's fragmentary form, his "combinatory spirit," is for Schlegel the model and the justification of his own fragments, many of which he quoted as "iron filings" in the article on Lessing. His anthology is, in part, made up of snippets: the antiquarian or theological context is dropped in order to isolate the passages which Schlegel felt to be of contemporary import and to reveal Lessing's spirit rather than his opinions. One must recognize that posterity has, on the whole, endorsed Schlegel's view: the position of Lessing the poet has decreased and that of the thinker has increased, just as Schlegel himself desired.

The relations of Friedrich Schlegel to Goethe and Schiller underwent such changes and were so complicated by personal clashes, literary politics, and even the background influence of women that a complete exposition hardly belongs in a history of criticism.[138] Still, Friedrich Schlegel was also a serious critic of Schiller and Goethe, and thus his opinions need attention in our context. At first, Schlegel admired Schiller, and undoubtedly his early aesthetic writings were profoundly influenced by Schiller's. "Über das Studium der griechischen Poesie" contains praise of Schiller's lyric poetry—which is compared to Pindar—the power of his feeling, the nobility of his mind, the dignity of his language, his "chest and voice" [139]—indeed, praise so extravagant that Schlegel has been suspected of irony or insincerity. The change was certainly marked very soon when Schlegel reviewed Schiller's *Musenalmanach,* and there slyly ridiculed Schiller's poem "Die Würde der Frauen," suggesting it should be read backwards stanza by stanza.[140] The feminist in Schlegel simply could not tolerate Schiller's middle-class ideal of women. In "Die Ideale" Schlegel sees the "convulsion of despair," an "almost sublime excess," and even suggests that "the health of the imagination once disrupted is incurable." [141] That Schlegel did not like Schiller's epigrams (*Xenien*), some of which were directed against him, is not surprising, but he made a tactical mistake when he pointed out that Schiller's periodical *Die Horen* published mostly translations.[142] Schiller then broke with August Wilhelm, who had supplied a majority of these translations and had been very glad to get paid for them. After this break the Schlegels adopted a policy of public silence toward Schiller, partly in order not to endanger their good relations with Goethe. But privately Schlegel voiced the most unfavorable opinions of everything that Schiller published and even his most personal notes show that he considered him merely a "rhetorical sentimentalist,"

a "poetical philosopher but not a philosophical poet." [143] Even the
aesthetic writings are roundly condemned. But with the years—
after the personal animosities faded and Schiller died—Schlegel
came to a much more favorable appreciation of Schiller's works.
The *History* recognizes that Schiller was the "real founder of the
German drama," that he was "through and through a dramatist,"
and that his "passionate rhetoric" [144] was essential to it. Even his
philosophical preparations for poetry are defended, and the possibility of the philosophical lyric is illustrated from Schiller's example. Schlegel seems to have recognized that he himself belonged
to Schiller's generation: he sees him passing from the modern to
the romantic and once groups him with Jean Paul, Tieck, Novalis,
and himself.[145]

The relation to Goethe developed differently and found much
fuller public expression in detailed discussions of Goethe's works.
It is difficult to realize today that Goethe, after the great success of
Werther, had fallen into comparative oblivion in the 80's and that
the Schlegels did very much to rebuild his fame on quite different
grounds. The initiative there belongs to August Wilhelm, but
Friedrich also played an important role. Friedrich Schlegel
printed, as a fragment of his forthcoming book "Über das Studium
der griechischen Poesie," a piece on Goethe (1796) in which he
hails him as the "dawn of true poetry and pure beauty." Goethe
opens a vista toward a new stage of aesthetic culture. His works are
the "irrefutable proof that the objective is possible and that the
hope of beauty is not a vain illusion of reason." [146] Friedrich even
claims that *Faust,* when finished, will probably far excel *Hamlet.*[147]
Very soon afterward, however, the ratio is strangely defined in
favor of *Hamlet* as something like 100:7.[148] But it would be hard
to think of higher praise than that Friedrich heaped on Goethe's
idyll "Alexis und Dora," [149] and he never wrote better and more
appreciative criticism than the essay on *Wilhelm Meister* (1798)
and the "Essay on the Different Styles of Goethe's Early and Late
Works," included in the *Gespräch* (1800). The review of *Wilhelm
Meister* is justly famous, as it succeeds in defining the attitude of
the author, the general impression and the particular character of
each part, and the main characters of the action. Schlegel also puts
his finger on the break in the book (which he did not know was
caused by Goethe's rewriting and incorporation of the *Theatrical*

Mission), though he prefers the later parts with their mysteries and philosophies to the earlier realistic sections that seem so much more alive today. The attempt to survey Goethe's whole artistic development is also highly successful in its somewhat schematic distinction of three stages, represented by *Goetz von Berlichingen, Tasso,* and *Hermann und Dorothea* respectively. Schlegel's sense of style is remarkable if one considers how clearly he arranges works whose dates of composition were unknown to him and how well he ranks Goethe's works according to their importance.

But apart from these public pronouncements Schlegel's private notes show increasing misgivings about Goethe and a slow but decided turning away from complete adoration. Very early Schlegel notes that "Goethe is without the word of God," and *Meister* is considered "imperfect, because it is not mystic enough." [150] Goethe's works are even called "much more similar to mechanical works of art than the ancients, Shakespeare, and the romantics. . . . Goethe's works have no unity, no totality: only here and there is there a faint beginning." [151] But nothing of this appeared in public, and as late as 1802 Goethe went far out of his way to produce Schlegel's play *Alarcos.* Friedrich's first public criticisms of Goethe were directed against the neoclassicism of his views on art propounded in the *Propyläen,* but the formal pronouncements continued to be very favorable and respectful. Among them the review of four volumes of Goethe's works (1808) is the most elaborate. It is most vocal in its praise of Goethe's lyrics and lyrical romances, with discriminating remarks on individual poems. Much that Goethe wrote in classical meters is especially admired and classed together as the outline of a great didactic cycle. *Wilhelm Meister* is again reviewed, with a difference. Schlegel now defends it against his friend Novalis' famous saying that *Meister* is a novel directed against poetry. He even recants his theory of the romantic novel. The novel is now called "no real genre . . . every novel . . . that is really poetic forms an individual in itself." [152] But there are reservations, blaming Goethe for the way he scattered his energies in mere sketches, outlines, fragments, and minor experimental works.[153] The treatment in the *History* is very perfunctory and hurried. *Meister* is now ranked below *Faust, Iphigenie, Tasso,* and *Egmont,* which (with the best lyrics) will preserve Goethe's fame; and Goethe is called the

Shakespeare of his age. But in conclusion it is suggested that to his way of thinking Goethe should be called rather a German Voltaire: [154] a malicious comparison if one considers the context of the times and Voltaire's reputation among the public Schlegel was addressing. The private notes show that this classification had been long in Schlegel's mind and that his resentment of Goethe's paganism and supposed enmity to Christianity went so far that he spoke in private letters of his "meanness." [155] Whatever one may think about the convolutions of Schlegel's opinions and their often very personal motivations, one must recognize that he suggested many important critical views of the works of both Goethe and Schiller. Considering his close analysis of *Wilhelm Meister* and many poems, Saintsbury's judgment that he "blenches at the book—still more at the passage and the phrase" (*3*, 402) seems strange, to say the least. It is probably suggested by a reading of the *History* which, in its very scope, demanded large generalizations, wide vistas, and sweeping opinions. But there is a place for such synthesis, of which Friedrich Schlegel, after all, was an early pioneer.* His brief history of recent German literature there included is remarkable, even if one considers only such a feature, in recent times hailed as a great discovery, as its division according to three generations: those who matured in the 50's and 60's of the 18th century, Klopstock, Lessing, Wieland, etc.; those who entered literature in the 70's, such as Goethe and Herder; and a third generation appearing late in the 80's and early 90's, with which he classed himself.

One cannot say that Schlegel was a systematic critic of his own friends and contemporaries, but he has written an excellent impressionistic characterization of Jean Paul, of his "piquant lack of taste," his "attractive clumsiness"; one of Tieck,[156] of whom, in spite of personal friendship, he was not uncritical; and has pronounced on many other of his German contemporaries. His high regard for the tawdry and hollow Zacharias Werner [157] must be

* There is, I believe, no comparable book which precedes Friedrich's. They are either long bibliographical and biographical *compendia* such as those by Andrés, Eichhorn, and Bouterwek or very thin general sketches such as Carlo Denina, *Discorso sopra le vicende di ogni letteratura* (Torino, 1760; also Glasgow, 1763) or what could be extracted from Herder's scattered writings.

classed as an aberration caused by his sympathy for a fellow convert.

One aspect of Schlegel's criticism deserves special emphasis: its
form. His early works were conventional treatises written in an
abstract expository style. In his late writings, such as the *History*,
Schlegel returned again to formal exposition and rotund periods.
But in his middle period he developed forms which were, at least
in Germany, new in criticism. The "Charakteristik" is the critical
essay on a single author or book in which Schlegel applies a vocabulary of criticism which mingles abstract definitions or approxima-
tions with impressionistic and even lyrical passages. Impressionism
became a doubtful blessing of criticism in the course of the 19th
century when it degenerated into the purple patches of Pater and
Oscar Wilde, but at the time, Schlegel's evocations must have
struck readers as something novel and welcome compared to the
formalism of the treatises on aesthetics or the cut-and-dried report
of the conventional book review. Besides the "Charakteristik,"
Schlegel discovered the "fragment," the aphorism, as a vehicle for
criticism. It was not, of course, a totally new discovery—Lichten-
berg and Chamfort are his masters—but he quite definitely and
consciously used the fragment in order to indulge in the mere unsupported pronouncement, the metaphorical surprising analogy,
the oracular and even mystifying statement, the witty paradox. At
its best he can open, with a glimpse, wide vistas; at its worst he can
note down pretentious witticisms and even trivialities. But one
must be literal-minded indeed not to recognize that Schlegel was
engaged in warfare, that he wanted and needed attention at the
price of paradox and offense, and that he loved the grandiose,
mysterious, and irrational too much to suppress it. The most con-
centrated masterpiece of Schlegel's criticism, *Gespräch über die
Poesie,* is a Platonic dialogue in a very free form, with interspersed
lectures and papers read aloud by the interlocutors. It seems the
right medium for Schlegel, neither too formal nor too informal,
too short to be merely mystifying nor too long to be misty and
nebulous, as he can become at his worst. But with all due reservations Friedrich Schlegel seems—if we think only of what he said
on criticism, myth, irony, the romantic, and the novel—one of the
greatest critics of history.

2 : AUGUST WILHELM SCHLEGEL

AUGUST WILHELM SCHLEGEL'S work could be viewed as mainly an application and exposition of the ideas of his younger brother. It would be possible to compile a long series of parallel passages in which August Wilhelm repeats and develops what has been said by his brother on the nature of poetry and criticism, the character of the main literary genres, the role of myth in literature, etc. In almost every case the priority seems to belong to Friedrich. We thus might be inclined to dismiss August Wilhelm as an unoriginal mind, a kind of middleman and even popularizer of the ideas of his brother. There is some truth in this view, though we would need to stress the enormous historical importance of August Wilhelm's mediating and popularizing role. To many Englishmen he became "our national critic," "the new Stagyrite," the one clear voice of criticism out of Germany. Precisely because he did not take part in Friedrich's turn toward Catholicism and because (in spite of all his professed enmity to the ideals of the Enlightenment) he kept away from the excesses of the mystical view of poetry, his effect without and within Germany was much greater and more lasting than Friedrich's.

But we must not succumb to the temptation of making August Wilhelm a mere reflex of his brother, to treat him as an undistinguishable twin. August Wilhelm has his own characteristic physiognomy, his own quite different development, and his own personal stresses and nuances, which make him a critic in his own right. Not only did August Wilhelm frequently write on topics his brother never touched and vice versa, not only are there psychological differences between the two, but there is also a distinct difference of doctrine which it will be our purpose to discern and define. Psychologically and temperamentally, the difference is very obvious and great: August Wilhelm, from the beginning of his career, had an air of judicious objectivity, the detachment of a learned man of the world, a tolerant historical spirit, which was mostly absent in the more volatile, more polemical and more incisive brother. At times August Wilhelm also indulged in polemics, satire, and jokes, but one cannot help feeling that he is awkward at a game which is essentially foreign to his nature. Still, the tone of restraint, the careful weighing of evidence, the clauses and limitations in the writings of August Wilhelm constitute at times (compared with his brother's pronouncements) the difference between truth and mere paradox, cautious hypothesis and hazardous assertion.

Like his brother, August Wilhelm was trained as a classical scholar: in Göttingen as a pupil of the famous Heyne he wrote a learned dissertation on Homeric geography in Latin. Unlike his brother he came early under the influence of the poet Bürger, whom he admired personally and to whose poems he devoted his first elaborate reviews. Very early he also developed his talents as a poetic translator, and his intense interest in poetic and metrical forms. In him there always remained a very strong vein of the technician, the metrist, the virtuoso who can look on meter and poetic diction with an eye almost exclusively trained on the detail. Goethe asked August Wilhelm to examine his hexameters and docilely corrected them in accordance with August Wilhelm's theories. Throughout his career August Wilhelm advocated strict rules for the writing of German verse modeled on classical metrics, and with equally pedantic ingenuity developed theories of the sonnet, ottava rima, terzina, and even the sestina and canzone. August Wilhelm's criticism of this kind ranges all the way from an application of rigid formulas to an extraordinarily subtle exploitation of his experiences as a translator. He can indulge in fanciful speculations about the geometrical analogies of squares and triangles to sonnet structure,[1] but he can also sensibly and sensitively criticize the details of many German poetic translations. August Wilhelm has the true philologist's devotion to the word, to close examination and close reading. One of his first reviews was devoted to Schiller's poem "Die Künstler," [2] whose consistency and coherence of metaphor and sentence structure he examined with minute care. This vein persisted throughout Schlegel's critical career: from his review of Voss's Homer [3] and Herder's translations from the German Latin poet Jakob Balde,[4] to Goethe's *Hermann und Dorothea* [5] and German translations of Propertius, Aeschylus, and Ariosto. The method of close comparison and minute investigation of motivation is also employed in the famous *Comparaison des deux Phèdres*,[6] where Euripides' *Hippolytus* is shown to be preferable, in every respect except diction, to Racine's *Phèdre*. Similarly, in the Berlin and Vienna lectures August Wilhelm elaborately compares the treatment of the Electra theme in Aeschylus, Sophocles, and Euripides in order to show the immense inferiority of Euripides to his two predecessors. On occasion the interest in technical metrical perfection blinded Schlegel's critical judgment. He made much of a now forgotten poem on mineral baths, W. V. Neubeck's *Gesundbrunnen*,[7] because it appealed to him by its correct handling of the German hexameter and its charming invention of details. The man who translated Spanish "trochees" with all their assonances and closely imitated the most elaborate verse-schemes of Italian canzoni and in his own poetry experimented with all kinds of meters could not help being a craftsman also in his criticism. There is hardly anything of this in his brother Friedrich.

The preoccupation with meter and diction of the young August Wilhelm was soon modified by his enthusiasm for the Herderian ideal of world literature, for literary cosmopolitanism, which subsequently runs like a leading motif through his lifework. When August Wilhelm introduced specimens of his metrical translations from Dante (1791), he formulated his ideal of "entering into the structure of a foreign being, to know it as it is, to listen to how it became." [8] The very first words of the *Dramatic Lectures* are an expression of a need for a "universality of the spirit," a "flexibility which enables us, by renouncing personal predilection and blind habit, to transfer ourselves into the peculiarities of other nations and ages, to feel them, as it were, from their own center." [9] Thus August Wilhelm can say, with a good conscience, that French criticism of his time lacks the "necessary knowledge of the universal history of poetry" [10] and can recommend to the Germans universality of education as the only possible return to nature,[11] for he felt this to be true of himself. In a late rather slight piece, "Abriss von den europäischen Verhältnissen der deutschen Litteratur" (1825), written for an English public, Schlegel extolls the Germans as the "cosmopolites of European civilization" [12] and historical criticism as their most characteristic recent achievement. Even if this were not true of the Germans in general, Schlegel could rightly point to himself and his brother as fulfilling this ideal.

August Wilhelm certainly had the scholar's avidity for the variety of world literature. He had an intense curiosity for the unexplored and unknown, which led him to the study of Old French, Italian, and Spanish literature, made him a pioneer in the study of Middle High German and the *Nibelungenlied,* and finally the initiator of Sanscrit studies in Germany. His late French dissertations on the language and literature of the Provençals [13] and on the origin of chivalrous romances [14] display a learning very unusual for its time, and his research on the *Nibelungenlied,* which included collation of manuscripts and elaborate speculations on the historical facts behind its theme, have to be mentioned honorably in any history of Old German scholarship.[15] But one must admit that in a rigorous sense none of August Wilhelm's great scholarly projects (with the exception of the late Sanscrit editions and translations) came to fruition. He was, in each case, outstripped by rivals and disciples: in France by Raynouard and Fauriel; at Bonn by Diez, his friend and younger colleague, on the Provençals; and by von der Hagen and Lachmann on the *Nibelungen*. His stimulation and critical praise proved more important than his actual technical contributions. August Wilhelm was one of the first to extoll the world of Arthurian romance, at least in Germany, and to praise adequately as figures Tristan and Parzival, which since then have entered European imagination. He was one of the first to take seriously the dictum of Johannes Müller that the *Nibelungenlied* was a German *Iliad:* he analyzed and praised the characterization of the heroes and the composition in a way that opened the poem for the first time to modern readers. But he also anticipated the extravagances of praise which have since been showered on the poetic value of the *Nibelungenlied,* and unfortunately he also was so deeply impressed by Wolf's theory of the origins of the Homeric epics that he suggested and initiated the long aberration of *Nibelungen* scholarship which was concerned with speculations about collective authorship and composition from individual "ballads" by a later "collector." Also, Schlegel's view of Provençal and Old French poetry, though sound in his rejection of the extravagances of Fauriel's claims for Provence, errs in emphasizing Teutonic influences. Schlegel argues that the Charlemagne romances owe their remote origin to Germanic epic traditions, a view which since has been thoroughly refuted by Joseph Bédier.

We might conclude from Schlegel's adherence to the Wolfian view of the origin of the Homeric poems that he hardly differs from Herder's outlook on universal natural poetry. Very early he was even interested in the speculative natural history of the origins of poetry, which engaged so many great men of the 18th century from Vico to Herder. Schlegel's "Briefe über Poesie, Silbenmass und Sprache" [16] are inspired by Rousseau and Herder. They argue for the original union of the arts, music, dance, and poetry, and hence deduce the absolute original necessity of meter: in the rhythms of heartbeat and breathing and in the rhythms of labor (rowing, threshing, mowing),[17] an idea which has found an elaborate modern development in Bücher's book *Arbeit und Rhythmus*. But meter, according to Schlegel, is the beginning of conscious art: the expression reacts back to the feeling. The passions, whose powerful outbursts are transformed by introducing the orderly measure of song and dance, are thus moderated.[18] The origins, and hence in Schlegel's view the nature, of poetry are connected closely with the origins of language, which itself is a kind of poetry,[19] since poetry is made from sounds and words.[20] Although he later disavowed the naturalism of his early essay,[21] Schlegel kept this ultimately Vichian view of poetry all his life. All poetry aims to restore the original "Bildlichkeit" of language; hence the indirect, transferred, tropical expression is the essentially poetic expression.[22] Poetry is thus a re-creation of original language on a higher level: [23] i.e. it consciously overcomes the arbitrariness of modern sign languages and returns to the symbolic use of language, in which the linguistic sign actually represents the object.

Thus metaphor, symbol, and myth hold the central position in Schlegel's theory of poetry. Metaphor is constantly defended as the basic procedure of poetry. August Wilhelm even defended the "baroque" (as we would say today) style of poetry which was then generally despised. In discussing the German "secentists" (as he calls them) Hofmannswaldau and Lohenstein he says that "poetry cannot be too fantastic; in a certain sense it can never exaggerate.

No comparison of the most remote, of the largest and the smallest, if it is only apt and meaningful, can be too bold." [24] Metaphor has its justification not only in this restoration of original vision (*Anschauung*) and immediacy of perception, but also in a total conception of the system of nature and the universe. "All things are related to all things; all things therefore signify all things; each part of the universe mirrors the whole." [25] The whole mutual concatenation of things is to be restored through constant symbolizing. Thus, metaphor suggests "the great truth that each is all and all is each." [26] "Imagination removes this disturbing medium [commonplace reality] and plunges us into the universe, while making it move within us like a magic realm of eternal metamorphoses, where nothing exists in isolation, but everything rises out of everything by a most marvelous creation." [27] Schlegel here propounds a theory of correspondences, of symbolism, which is practically identical with that of the much later French symbolist movement. It is quite genuinely a rhetoric of metamorphoses which follows from a conception of the universe. Poetry, to Schlegel, is "speculation by imagination." [28] There are no outworn metaphors. Even the oldest comparisons may have their place, for "really beautiful images are eternal and however frequently used will be rejuvenated in the hands of a genuine poet." [29]

Metaphor is, of course, only one poetic device; all devices which restore the original language are legitimate tools of poetry. Thus it seems to Schlegel utter nonsense to identify prose and poetry. Poetic diction should differ as far as possible from the speech of ordinary life. The listener should not skim over each detail.[30] Word play does on a small scale what poetry does with the form of language as a whole. Word play shows the poet's sensitivity to the most distant relationships. The whole of nature thus can become the mirror of a beloved object. Petrarch is defended for playing on the name of Laura (*l'aura,* breeze, *lauro,* laurel, *l'auro,* gold) and Shakespeare and Cervantes are celebrated as masters of puns.[31] Schlegel praises the dying John of Gaunt's moving quibble on his own name.

Schlegel clearly sees that a distinction must be drawn between the merely decorative and intellectual use of these devices of metaphor and symbolism and their legitimate poetic function. In a very early discussion of the *Divine Comedy* (1791) he defends

Dante's allegory as being more than a mere concept of the understanding. Allegory must be lost in the sensuous shape, and shine through it only as a soul shines through its body. In Dante imaginary beings have coherence, independently of their hidden meaning; there is more in them than can be resolved into concepts. "We everywhere tread solid ground, surrounded by a world of reality and individual existence." [32] Though we may doubt the complete justice of the praise, we must realize that the distinction here drawn is valid. August Wilhelm returned to it frequently; in discussing Aeschylus in the *Dramatic Lectures* he calls allegory "the personification of a concept, a fiction contrived only for this purpose; but [symbolism] is what the imagination has created for other reasons, or what possesses a reality independent of concept, what is at the same time spontaneously susceptible of a symbolic interpretation; indeed it even lends itself to it." [33]

Later, Schlegel came to prefer the German word "Sinnbild" to "symbol." All art must be "sinnbildlich," i.e. it must present meaningful images. Nature itself creates symbolically; it reveals the inner by the outer; each thing has its own physiognomy. The artist points up the physiognomy of things; he lends the reader his sense for the penetration of the inner core.[34] Art is thus a way of knowledge through signs, a thinking in images. Poetry is "bildlich anschauender Gedankenausdruck," according to the almost untranslatable formula of the 1798 lectures on aesthetics.[35] The Kantean and Fichtean term "Idea" is then introduced in the Vienna lectures. Poetry must present "Ideas," i.e. necessary and eternally true thoughts and feelings which soar above earthly existence, in images.[36] Here and elsewhere Schlegel is in acute danger of falling into the intellectualistic misunderstanding of art. The formula "thinking in images" made a great impression outside of Germany also: Belinsky must have derived it from some German source and Hegel's "sinnliches Scheinen der Idee" is substantially identical with it. Schlegel's critical practice usually keeps him firmly to his original view (derived from Herder) that poetry must be concrete, to which he adds only the necessity of a symbolic relationship to the whole universe: a microcosmic-macrocosmic parallelism which has its ultimate roots in neo-Platonism. A work of art has the "inexhaustibility of creative nature whose counterpart it is in miniature." [37] The great artist is himself a mirror of the universe, its representative. Schlegel quotes Moritz: "Every beautiful whole from the hands of the forming artist is an offprint in miniature of the highest beautiful in the great whole of nature." [38] The greatness of an artist must be judged by his success in constituting such a mirror himself: in clarity, energy, and all-embracing breadth. [39]

This symbolist view of poetry, an analogy of the totality of the universe and its relationships, is a precarious position, which has to be guarded carefully against two dangers: intellectualism and mysticism. Schlegel has not entirely escaped either of them. Intellectualism tempted him most in the discussion of the didactic philosophical poem and in the shape of the false ideal of a union of poetry and philosophy. He believed that they strive for the same end by different means and that poetry could be called "exoteric philosophy" and philosophy "esoteric poetry." [40] A fusion of philosophical and poetic enthusiasm seems to him the solution of the problem of a perfect philosophical poem. [41] But to excuse these formulas, of course, we must think of philosophy not as a technical subject but in the sense in which the romantics understood it: a poetic philosophy, a thinking in symbols as it was practiced by Schelling or Jakob Böhme.

But while Schlegel, on occasion, seems near to this perilous identification of poetry and philosophy, he is much oftener subject to the danger of mysticism. From Schelling he drew the phrase "beauty is the infinite represented finitely" and modified it to read "beauty is the symbolic representation of the infinite." [42] The infinite is meant to be not something completely beyond this world but rather the mystery behind appearances and the mystery in us: it is something cosmic, obscure, the "oracular verdict of the heart, these deep intuitions in which the dark riddle of our existence seems to solve itself." [43]

These passages often seem written under the influence of his environment: of his brother, Schelling, Creuzer, or many others of his contemporaries. Centrally, August Wilhelm held a view of poetry which is neither intellectualistic nor mystical. Poetry is metaphor, symbol, and myth but not mysticism. Myth is the concept which holds the view together: man poetizing is neither a philosopher nor a mystic but a myth-maker. Myth is the system of symbols on which the poet draws and which he restores to con-

sciousness.[44] Schlegel accepts the view that man went through a
state dominated by myth and that such a state is natural to him.
Hume's *History of Natural Religion,* which explains the origin
of religion in fear and priestcraft, is thus completely mistaken.
There is an indefinite and boundless shudder in man which cannot
be abolished by any degree of physical security. What is usually
called Enlightenment should thus rather be called Darkening, because it means the extinction of the inner light of man.[45] Myth is
not merely raw material of poetry. It is nature itself in a poetical
costume, it is poetry itself, it is a complete view of the world. Since
myth is a transformation of nature, it is itself capable of endless
poetic transformations.[46] Greek and Christian mythology are, historically, the main sources of poetic inspiration; nevertheless,
August Wilhelm recognizes that they are drying out today [47] and
that it is necessary to search for a new poetic myth. At times, he
backslides into an external view of the use of mythology when
he defends the use of Catholic symbols [48] without actually accept-
ing Catholicism. But we must remember that he had to defend
himself against the suspicion of sharing in the turn of his brother
toward Roman Catholicism and even of sharing in a secret Catholic conspiracy. Usually he understands that poetry is not identical
with myth and that myth is not merely an inert reservoir of images,
gods, and stories. He propounds the possibility of a new nature
myth, a union of "physics" and poetry, where "physics" means the
new Schellingian *Naturphilosophie.* He argues that myth can be
favorable to poetry only if it is a living myth, if it arose as an unconscious fiction of mankind, by which nature can be humanized,
and if it is a belief still existing among the people. It cannot be
the artificial invention of an individual.[49] Yet apparently he would
have argued that this is no objection to the new nature mythology
which incorporates the folk symbolism of the fairy tales, the magic
power of stones and plants, the significance of animals and even
chemical forces. In characterizing Dante, August Wilhelm states
that the "most essential forces of nature become for the poet symbols of spiritual existence, and thus out of the union of his physics
with his theology arises a scientific mythology. If one doubts that
poetry can become an organ of idealism, one can see it realized in
Dante." [50] Schlegel here appeals to a passage in Gravina's *Ragion
poetica* [51] to fortify his view of a union of physics and theology in

Dante, a passage which to him sounds like an anticipation of the endeavors of Novalis. Idealism, in Schlegel's and Novalis' view, is like a "magic wand that materializes spirit easily and spiritualizes matter, for poetry must keep hovering between the sensuous and the intellectual world." [52] Even descriptive poetry (condemned in its English form) can be saved by a symbolic view of nature. [53]

While the renewal of myth, the creation of a system of symbols and correspondences, is thus central to Schlegel's concept of poetry, we must stress that Schlegel did not identify modern poetry with folk poetry, unconscious "natural" poetry in Herder's sense. What has been expounded must not be mistaken for a variation of the similar passages in Vico, Herder, and Diderot. Schlegel has a very different view of the history of poetry and the role of "natural" poetry in it. He uses the term "natural" poetry and distinguishes three stages in it: (1) elementary poetry in the shape of original language, poetry in language; (2) rhythm; and (3) myth. The poetry actually preserved today is not natural poetry in this sense. Schlegel concedes that there is a sense in which one can speak of Greek poetry as the poetry of nature, a sense which is obviously close to Schiller's term "naive." There was then no division between unconscious instinct and self-conscious free activity. [54] But even Homer was not a popular poet in the sense that he would have addressed the lower classes. He sang first of all for princes and noblemen. Still, he was a poet of the people, in that he belonged to the whole nation and was comprehensible to all classes. His poems did not contain any inert learning which would close them to the uneducated. [55] Only in this all-national sense can Homer be described as the greatest of all popular poets. [56] Nor were the *Minnesänger*, Schlegel early recognized, in any way popular poets. [57] Shakespeare, of course, was no popular poet either, as Herder and the *Sturm und Drang* had thought. Schlegel repeated over and over again that Shakespeare was a "deep-thinking artist" and found in him "superb cultivation of mental powers, practiced art, and worthy and maturely considered intentions." [58] Thus folk poetry is really a term which should be limited to songs written expressly for the lower classes or written among them. [59] August Wilhelm, while not deficient in taste for Scottish ballads, German folk songs, and even 16th-century chapbooks, had a detached attitude toward them: he recognized them as often being dim and remote echoes of genuine antiquity and did not share the un-critical enthusiasm for every snatch of song or romance that was common among his Teutonizing contemporaries. In his famous essay on Bürger (1800), which professedly was to serve as a rebuttal to Schiller's harsh review, Schlegel actually throws up the case of "popular" poetry rather lightly.[60] Throughout his life, however, he held the Herderian view that poetry is a universal language of mankind and is thus possible among all sorts and conditions of men, in all ages and in all societies. But he sees no particular virtue in the merely popular, nor does he see any particular vice in the sophisticated and learned, addressed to a limited audience.

Schlegel could not commit the error of the nature worshipers, for he had a sound view of the relation between the conscious and the unconscious, inspiration and craft, imagination and reason, in the composition of poetry. He rejected both intellectualism and mystical inspiration, just as he had rejected (though less firmly) both extremes in his description of poetry. Schlegel constantly criticized the *Sturm und Drang* glorification of mere genius and was also very severely critical of Kant's discussion of genius in the *Critique of Judgment*. Kant, according to Schlegel, makes genius a mere blind tool of nature. It is true that there is something in art which cannot be learned, but purpose and all motives which can incite our free activity influence the exercise of art. Great works of art, such as the Greek tragedies, have come about as the result of competitions.[61] All creation is simultaneously judging, all expression of creative power is linked with constant introspection.[62] Genius is the intimate union of the unconscious and the self-conscious activity of the human spirit, of instinct and intention, freedom and necessity.[63] Genius embraces the whole inner man, all his powers: not only his fancy (*Einbildungskraft*) and understanding (*Verstand*), but also his imagination (*Fantasie*) and reason (*Vernunft*).[64] In passing, Schlegel here draws the distinction between *Einbildungskraft* and *Fantasie,* with the last clearly considered the higher power, associated with reason. "Creative imagination" is both unconditionally free and lawful: there cannot be any lawlessness in it. "One must merely know," Schlegel explains, "that imagination through which the world first originated for us and through which works of art are created, is the same power, only in diverse kinds of activity." [65] This is the distinction, drawn by

Schelling, between the primary and secondary imagination of which Coleridge made so much.

Schlegel does not seem to realize that there is a contradiction between this view of art—which identifies it if not with nature at least with the creative processes of nature, the *natura naturans*—and his usual stress on the consciousness, the reflectiveness of the artist. If he rejects the neoclassical and Aristotelian view of "imitation" and admits only that imitation may mean that art "should create living works like nature creating independently, organized and organizing," [66] there seems no room for the artist's self-reflection and self-criticism which he otherwise stresses as necessary, especially for the poet of his age. "Today's poet," he says, "must be clearer in his knowledge of the nature of art than great poets of former ages could be, whom we must therefore understand better than they understood themselves: a higher reflection must in its works submerge itself again in the Unconscious." [67] Presumably, in the Schellingian system here adopted the emergence of consciousness out of nature is conceived of as so continuous and gradual that no dualism of consciousness and the unconscious in a strict sense would be admitted: on the highest level, consciousness and the unconscious, freedom and necessity are one. It is one of the advantages of the dialectical method to have things both ways. And frequently, as in the argument about inspiration versus conscious purpose in the composition of poetry, the solution which affirms that both are necessary is the right one; it is verified by observation and introspection and a study of the historical evidence. But such solutions say little about the share and order of the two contradictory elements and while disposing of false extremes do little to advance the cause of knowledge.

The same is true of the solutions propounded for reconciling the opposition of form and content, unity and variety, by means of the magic words "whole" or "organism" so prominent in Germany since Herder, Goethe, and the Schlegels. August Wilhelm constantly appeals to the organism metaphor, pressing it sometimes very far. In discussing Wilhelm Meister's proposed adaptation of *Hamlet* Schlegel finds Goethe's own parallel between a work of art and a tree too weak. Branches can be lopped off a tree and others can be grafted on without disturbing the "free royal growth" or leaving visible traces of the shears. "But," he asks, "what if a

dramatic poem of this kind had more similarity with higher organizations, in which, sometimes, the inborn deformation of a
single limb could not be cured without endangering the life of the
whole?" [68] In criticizing Euripides' luxurious versification and his
use of the chorus as mere external ornaments, Schlegel again draws
the parallel between a work of art and a living being very closely.
"If works of art are to be looked at as organized wholes, then the
insurrection of individual parts against the unity of the whole is
exactly what in the organic world is putrefaction, which is usually
the more horrible and repulsive the nobler the organic shape it
destroys, and it thus must fill us with the greatest disgust in this
most eminent of literary kinds [tragedy]. However, most men are
less sensitive to the impression of spiritual than to the impression
of bodily putrefaction." [69]

These extreme formulas which identify a work of literature
with an animal have made less impression than Schlegel's contrast
between organic and mechanical form which he expounded at the
very beginning of the third volume of the *Dramatic Lectures:*
"The form is mechanical when through outside influence it is im-
parted to a material merely as an accidental addition, without
relation to its nature (as e.g. when we give an arbitrary shape to a
soft mass so that it may retain it after hardening). Organic form,
on the other hand, is innate; it unfolds itself from within and ac-
quires its definiteness simultaneously with the total development
of the germ." Such forms occur in nature, from the crystallization
of salts and minerals to plants and flowers and up to the human
race. "Also in the fine arts all genuine forms are organic, i.e. determined by the content of the work of art. In a word, form is nothing but a significant exterior, the speaking physiognomy of everything which, undistorted by any disturbing accidents, bears true
witness to its hidden nature." [70] Here the analogy is extended to
minerals and plants and the contrast to an external superimposed
mold is worked out very clearly. Coleridge was to quote these formulas literally.

Schlegel usually emphasizes the "unity and indivisibility" of a
work of art,[71] the "inner mutual determination of the whole and
the parts," [72] the fact that in a real work of art everything exists
relative to the whole.[73] A beautiful whole can never be pieced together from beautiful parts; the whole must first be posited abso-

lutely and then the particular evolved from it.[74] Schlegel speaks of
a work of art as ideal if "in it matter and form, letter and spirit
have interpenetrated so completely that we are unable to distinguish them." [75] In rejecting objections to the form of the sonnet
as a Procrustean bed for the poet, Schlegel rightly says that the
objection would apply to any metrical form and that it assumes
writing poetry is an exercise in which what is first drafted in formless prose is then forced into verse. But "such people have no conception that form is rather a tool, an organ for the poet, and that
from the first conception of a poem, content and form are, like
soul and body, indivisible." [76] Yet if this totality is conceived to
be so absolute that no element is distinguishable within it, criticism will be paralyzed, for we must draw distinctions in order to
speak at all, and the process of exposition in criticism is necessarily a slow consecutive one in which one part has to precede another.

In practice Schlegel often attends mainly to form or to "inner
form." In discussing Voss's famous translation of Homer he asks
whether Voss has actually hit upon "the form, the style, the tone,
the color of the Homeric poems, which is really the most important
matter, since it encompasses the whole and since all the content of
a poem is known only through the medium of form." [77] Such a wide
conception of form is also at the base of Schlegel's most practically
effective discussion of the three unities. They are discarded in
favor of a 'much deeper lying, more intimate, more mysterious
unity," [78] for which Schlegel accepts the term "unity of interest,"
drawn from De La Motte,[79] an early 18th-century French critic.
But Schlegel recognizes the difference between his use and that of
De La Motte, who thought of the psychology of the audience.
Schlegel's unity is rather "inner form," an idea, such as fate in
Greek tragedy.

At times Schlegel seems to admit that there is some contradiction
between form and matter even in good art. He praises the Spanish
drama for the way Spanish poets transformed the merely marvelous and adventurous, breathed into it a "musical soul," wholly
purified it of gross materiality, changed it to color and perfume.
Schlegel finds an irresistible charm in this very contrast between
matter and form,[80] a formula which seems to abandon the purely
organic theory of the whole. In discussing the didactic poem

Schlegel makes an even further concession to the distinction between form and matter. He does not, it is true, recognize didactic poems as the highest poetry, because their whole is not poetic but is held together merely by logic. Still, he does not deny the possibility of the genuineness of the individual poetic elements. Poetry, he says now, has its spirit and its letter; it should be allowed at times to cultivate the letter in isolation, without the spirit.[81] Here the virtuoso, the technician and experimenter, rebels against his own general theory.

It is remarkable how skillfully and consciously Schlegel can combine a "holistic," organic view of poetry with a recognition of a theory of genres. The concept of the completely self-sufficient unity of a work of art leads to the concept of its complete "uniqueness" and, in Croce and other moderns, to the logical consequence of rejecting the genre concept altogether. Not so with Schlegel, who holds firmly to the biological metaphor which would imply that every individual, however individual, also belongs to a species. "Genuine forms must be looked upon as species of organizations to which life is attached, but which still give much leeway to individuality." [82] "A certain law of form is the condition of free individuality in art just as in nature; for anything that does not belong to any species of organizations is monstrous." [83] Monstrosity, hybridization is thus the objection to an improper mixture of genres which Schlegel always points out as disadvantageous to art. Aristotle is repeatedly criticized for trying to judge the epic by the laws of tragedy,[84] and much of Schlegel's own criticism is straight genre criticism, which disapproves of any violation of the purity of genre and could thus be considered a survival of the neoclassical point of view. Nonetheless, in his actual conception of the genres Schlegel differs considerably from neoclassical doctrines.

The epic is most elaborately discussed, according to Friedrich's theory of Greek epic, in a review of Goethe's *Hermann und Dorothea* (1797). August Wilhelm shares Friedrich's view that chance may play a large part in the epic, that it can be easily divided and combined, and that its presentation must be objective and passionless. There must be no artificial intrigue, no accumulated difficulties, no sudden surprises, no tension tending toward one point. Throughout there should be superior calm and impartiality of representation.[85] Schlegel argues that the differences between epic and drama cannot be deduced from that between narration and dialogue. Dialogue both in the epic and in tragedy is not natural dialogue but is modified, in its most subtle details, by the character of the whole to which it belongs.[86] In criticizing Virgil—whom Schlegel ranks far below Homer—he uses these criteria effectively: the history of Dido is a tragic fragment of a sentimental character [87] rather than properly an episode in an epic. Virgil betrays or affects sympathy with his characters and even indulges in "mannered exclamations" about his heroes, or addresses them directly.[88] Schlegel compares the epic with a bas-relief; in both the figures are presented in profile. The bas-relief is endless by nature, while tragedy is like a group of statues. Virgil's heroes are like painted portraits whose eyes are always turned toward the viewer wherever he may stand. Virgil has made the epic rhetorical and subjective and has thus destroyed its "ideality." [89]

The novel, according to Schlegel, has little to do with the epic. It is subjective: its figures are mere tools in the hand of the author.[90] The novel aims at all-inclusiveness and thus can use almost all the other genres. It hints at those riddles of life which cannot actually be expressed and thus every detail in it becomes meaningful and symbolic.[91] The epic is *the* classical genre, the novel *the* romantic. Schlegel's idea of the novel is modeled on *Don Quixote*, *Wilhelm Meister*, and *Heinrich von Ofterdingen*, while the English realistic novel and its German imitations are dismissed as an inferior subgenre, since all naturalism is disparaged.[92] The novel is neither the end nor the aberration of modern poetry. It is its first genre, a species which can represent the whole genus of romantic literature, for *Roman* and *romantic* both come from *romance*.[93]

As opposed to Friedrich, August Wilhelm's main interest among the genres was the drama, and the *Lectures on Dramatic Art and Literature* were the most sustained and influential of his published works. Tragedy interested him more than comedy. Greek tragedy, on the one hand, and Shakespearean and Spanish drama, on the other—their differences and contrasts are the pivots around which Schlegel's speculations revolve. He has little use for Aristotle's *Poetics*, though he praised it for suggesting the organic analogy.[94] He not only rejects the three "Aristotelian" unities; he even decides that Aristotle did not understand the nature of tragedy at all.[95] Aristotle's view of poetry is purely logical and physical.[96] *Catharsis* conceals a purely moralistic theory.[97] The other usual explanations of tragic pleasure are equally unconvincing. We do not enjoy seeing misfortune because we are safe ourselves and we are not improved by seeing poetic justice done and the evil-doers punished.[98] Poetic justice, if it means a nice distribution of rewards and punishments, is not necessary to good tragedy. Tragedy can end with the defeat of the righteous man and the triumph of the wicked, provided our inner consciousness and a vista into the future restore the equilibrium.[99] At most, poetic justice in the genuine sense of the word is only a "revelation of the invisible blessing or curse which hangs over human sentiments and actions." [100] Tragedy thus must be explained differently. Clearly, Schlegel's theory derives from Kant's definition of the sublime. The tragic mood is man's recognition of his dependence on unknown powers, of the transience of pleasures, affections, and life itself. It is a feeling of inexpressible melancholy, for which there is no other defense than the consciousness of a vocation transcending the limits of earthly life. When this mood pervades the representation of violent revolutions in a man's fate, either subduing his will or calling forth his heroic fortitude, we can speak of tragic poetry.[101] If one had to formulate the purpose of tragedy as a doctrine, one would have to say that earthly existence must be considered as nothing, that all suffering must be endured and all difficulties overcome merely in order to affirm the claims of the mind to the divine.[102] In tragedy, thus, man's struggle with fate is resolved into harmony, but it need be only an ideal harmony.[103]

Similarly, comedy is deduced from the comic mood. It means forgetting all the gloomy considerations in the pleasant feeling of present happiness. We are then inclined to view everything in a playful light. The imperfections and irregularities of man must no longer be objects of dislike or pity but must entertain and amuse. A comic poet must refrain from letting his characters excite moral indignation or real sympathy.[104] In tragedy every emotion is channeled in one direction, in comedy there is an "apparent lack of purpose" and a breakdown of all limits in the use of our mental faculties. Comedy is the more perfect the more vivid is the illusion of our purposeless play and unlimited caprice.[105] In comedy

Schlegel approves the breaking of illusion, the address to the public, even the pointing at individual spectators in the audience.
Comedy "seeks the most colorful contrasts and continually crossing
opposites." [106] It is obvious that Schlegel can have little sympathy
for the comedy of manners and character: he specifically censures
French critics for considering character comedy superior to the
comedy of intrigue. With his usual, apparently unromantic preference for the pure genre, however romantic in itself the genre
may be, Schlegel prefers the comedy of fantasy and caprice to the
realistic comedy in which he sees an approach to seriousness and
hence an impure genre. Irony is one of the marks of comedy and
comic writing. It does not, however, occupy the central theoretical
position which it has in the writings of his brother. It extends beyond the limits of comedy but stops before genuine tragedy.[107] It
is a "recognition, more or less clearly stated, that the presentation
is one-sidedly exaggerated, that there is a high share of imagination
and feeling in it." [108] It shows the superiority of the artist over his
material, "his power to annihilate, if he so wanted, the beautiful,
irresistibly attractive illusion he has conjured." [109]

The lyric is hardly discussed in the published writings of August
Wilhelm except for a passage in the Vienna lectures which calls
it a "musical expression of emotion in language," an attempt to
fix or even to eternize an emotion which must have already been
softened by memory: "we want to be at home in a single moment
of our existence." [110] But these brief remarks are only the quintes-
sence of the theories much more fully developed in the 1798 lectures on aesthetics and in the Berlin lectures. The 1798 lectures
are, as usual in this series, the most technically speculative in their
formulations: at that time Schlegel stood nearest to Schelling and
for the academic audience he was addressing tried to give his
theories a verbal garb resembling that of the school jargon of his
colleagues. Stripped of its technical language, his theory is that the
lyric must be musical and must be the expression of a genuine
emotion which is individual and particular; hence the lyric can
use only objects which are linked with the emotion. Everything
discordant and contradictory is excluded from lyrical poetry: a
dissonant emotion can be included only if the resolution into complete harmony is fully prepared. Thus anything immoral, as well
as emotions such as anger, envy, or even genuine despair, are ex-

cluded. The unity of a lyrical poem is its dominant mood: its mechanical forms are the most varied of any genre, since they must correspond to these moods, and its diction can be the most divergent from prose; the boldest metaphors, the greatest "poetic licenses" are permitted.[111]

Fortunately, in the actual elaborate discussions of the historical variety of the lyric Schlegel forgets his narrowly defined ideal and undertakes sympathetic considerations of all the historical forms. His theories are always modified by his critical practice, by his genuine historical sympathy, and by the wide interests of a literary historian and lover of literature.

Schlegel holds a theory of criticism which is remarkably conscious of the cooperation and interpenetration of criticism and history, theory and practice. He argues that there cannot be history without theory, since history, if it is not to be a mere chronicle, requires a principle of selectivity. Each phenomenon of art can be assigned its true position only by relating it to the idea of art.[112] On the other hand, no theory of art can exist without the history of art, for obviously history, especially art history, has to teach by examples. Schlegel recognizes the central difficulty of art history, which since his time Croce has made the main argument against all of art history. Each genuine work of art is perfect by itself; but if history means progress, approximation to perfection, then art history must be made up of imperfect phenomena which actually should not have a place in the realm of genuine art. Schlegel solves the dilemma by appealing to an art spirit (*Kunstgeist*) that always appears modified by its environment, a nation, a specific age. This spirit organizes its own shape and thus has a history. "Each work of art must be considered from its own point of view: it need not achieve the absolutely highest; it is perfect, when it is the highest of its kind, in its sphere, its world; and thus we can explain that it can simultaneously be a member in an infinite series of progressions and still be satisfying and independent by itself." [113] Schlegel also disposes of the other common objection to art history or literary history: that art is created by geniuses and thus is a mere freak of nature, a series of chance events. He answers that phenomena are objectively necessary while subjectively accidental; the person of the artist is contingent, but the style of a time is essential and necessary. We can think of all individual geniuses as single parts and appearances of the *one* great genius of mankind which cannot perish and must rise again from its ashes. Art history thus must comprehend whole ages and great masses and ignore the learned and human detail. It must look on history as an organic whole.[114]

In that way Schlegel is able to formulate our aim as leading art criticism to "the historical point of view, i.e. even though each work of art ought to be closed within itself, we must consider it as belonging to a series according to the relations between its origin and existence and comprehend it from what has preceded and what follows or is still following from it." [115] Schlegel said much earlier (1795) that "by explaining how art became what it is, we show also in the most convincing manner what it should be." [116] This is not, in Schlegel's view, mere historical determinism: all genetic explanation, e.g. by biography, does not absolve us from forming an independent judgment. The laws of the beautiful are valid everywhere and at all times.[117] Thus biography is not decisive for criticism. A work of art "is as much detached from the person of its author as fruit which is being eaten is detached from its tree; and even if all the poems of a man represent his poetic biography and together form, as it were, an artistic personality in which the individuality of the real one is revealed more or less, directly or indirectly, we must still consider them as products of free will, even of caprice, and must leave it undecided whether a poet could not have mirrored his individuality in his works quite differently, if he had only willed to do so." [118]

Criticism, in relation to theory and history, is conceived of as the mediating middle link.[119] In discussing criticism Schlegel by no means underrates the role of intuition, of mere feeling. At times he concedes a final appeal to feeling. "In every criticism, be it ever so formal, there comes a point where motivation ends and where everything depends on whether the reader can or will agree with the judge." [120] But mostly Schlegel defines the aim of criticism in more intellectual terms. He can speak ambitiously in the terminology of idealist philosophy of "construing a work in its totality according to its structure and nature" [121] or he can, more moderately, define its function as "comprehending and interpreting the meaning of a work in a pure, complete, and sharply definite manner." The critic thus aims to raise less independent but susceptible

spectators to the insight of his own point of view.[122] The actual
process of grasping the meaning of a work of art is described
largely as the reproduction of a general or total impression. Parallel
to his conception of the wholeness of a work of art Schlegel thinks
of the critical act as a whole and contrasts the right criticism—
which is of an organic nature in which the individual exists only
through the whole—with atomistic criticism—which views the
work of art as a mosaic, a painstaking combination of mere par-
ticles.[123] Schlegel thus prefers like Chateaubriand the criticism of
beauties. It is much easier to "scold with reason than to praise with
spirit. One can do that and still not go beyond the surface, the
technical scaffolding of a work of the mind; but praise presupposes
that one has really penetrated to the inside and is, at the time,
master of expression in order to grasp the peculiarity of the aesthetic impression which eludes mere concept." [124]

Schlegel also faces the problem of the subjectivity of criticism.
He first argues that some kind of objectivity is achieved by distinguishing between a total impression and a mere mood. Ideally a
critic should be able to tune himself at will, i.e. be able at any
moment to evoke the purest and liveliest susceptibility for any
work of the mind.[125] Merely by being conscious of our transitory
mood we may raise ourselves above it or realize, at least approxi-
mately, how another mood would have affected us. Objectivity is
enhanced by historical study, by a knowledge of art history, since
the critic must know the most eminent works and they cannot be
found in any one time and place. Objectivity is also increased by
constant reference to theory. A judgment can be clarified and expressed only in concepts, and concepts assume distinctness only
in an assumed system. "Critical reflection is thus a constant experi-
mentation to discover theoretical statements." In the end we must,
however, recognize that something subjective will remain in every
critical judgment. One can do nothing else than be aware of one's
personality, "treat it liberally," express it by the manner of our
communication. Thus Schlegel opposes colorless "dignified" criticism which suppresses everything that is characteristic. If criticism
is to be individual in its matter it must be so in its form as well.

The fact that people disagree about works of art does not disturb
Schlegel; we disagree with ourselves at different times in our life,
but this does not justify general skepticism in matters of art. "Dif-

ferent people may very well have their eyes on the same center, but since each of them starts from a different point of the circumference, they inscribe also different radii." [126] Here is stated a conception which has since been called "perspectivism" and which happily mediates between mere historicism and the old dogmatism. It does not give up the ideal of one poetry and yet does not deny the variety of its historical forms.

These are, one can say without exaggeration, still wonderfully pertinent reflections on the nature and procedure of criticism and its relations to theory and history. They are best exemplified in Schlegel's most famous distinction: that between the classic and the romantic. It oscillates, as Schlegel wanted it to do, between theory and history. It mediates, as a truly critical idea, between them.

Schlegel did not invent the contrast but he formulated it in a manner which gained general acceptance and spread widely in Germany and beyond. His writings are by no means full of discussions of "romantic." Even the term is used comparatively rarely. In the 1798 lectures on aesthetics given at Jena the contrast is not yet drawn explicitly. It is merely implied in the lengthy discussion of modern genres, which include the romantic novel, culminating in the "perfect masterwork of higher romantic art," *Don Quixote;* the "romantic" drama of Shakespeare, Calderón, and Goethe; and the "romantic" poetry of the Spanish *romances* and Scottish ballads.[127] The sonnet is called a "romantic epigram." [128] In the review of Bürger (1800), where the term occurs several times in conventional uses, it is used once rather apologetically: Bürger's loose use of "romance" is defended, since genres in romantic poetry did not develop "immediately from pure laws of art" but accidentally under the influence of the historical circumstances which accompanied the rebirth of a new world in the Middle Ages.[129] Friedrich Schlegel's contrast between the history of Greek literature, which is somehow necessary and systematic, and modern literature, which is determined by historical chance, is here employed to defend a popular poet against the rigors of Schiller's genre criticism.

But the first Berlin lectures (1801–02) contain the full proclamation of the contrast, praised as a recent discovery, whose function is to allow an impartial recognition of both antinomies. "The his-

torian and theoretician should try to keep to the point of indifference between the two poles." [130] If actually carried out, the implications of this professed impartiality are those of extreme historicism and of the view that there are two ideals of poetry, both
equally valid but mutually incompatible. Toward the end of the
course of lectures the contrast is formulated as one between the
classical emphasis on purity of genre and the romantic mixture
of all poetic elements. Romantic poetry strives for the infinite not
only in an individual work of art but in the whole course of art.
Saying that "romantic art is limitless progressivity," August Wilhelm echoes Friedrich's famous "fragment." [131]

The second lecture course (1802–03) adds to the contrast the
idea that classical poetry is plastic and architectonic, while modern
poetry is picturesque.[132] Only the third lecture course (1803–04)
attempts a systematic survey of romantic literature. The theoretical
formulation is, however, surprisingly meager: it stresses that romantic poetry has its own necessary course of development and the
actual discussion concerns mainly the historical role of Christianity, chivalry, courtly love, etc. as explanation for the rise of modern
(i.e. medieval) literature. The emphasis is on the historical approach. In passing, Schlegel recognizes that "romantic poetry is
indisputably much nearer to our mind and heart than classical"; [133]
yet, on the whole, he tries to preserve a judicious balance and
even grants that the division is not absolute and that elements of
each can be found on both sides, though in different order.[134]

The Vienna *Lectures on Dramatic Art and Poetry* (1809–11)
contain the most systematic and influential discussion. There the
whole history of the drama is based on the contrast between classical and romantic. The contrast is seen as all-pervasive, affecting the
other arts as well. Schlegel appeals to Rousseau, who showed that
"rhythm and melody are the ruling principle of ancient, and harmony of modern, music." [135] Hemsterhuis is quoted as saying that
the ancient painters were too much sculptors, the modern sculptors
too much painters. The spirit of ancient art and poetry, Schlegel
concludes, is plastic, that of modern art picturesque. The contrast
between Gothic and classical architecture is then applied to literature in a famous comparison, used also by Coleridge. "The
Pantheon is no more different from Westminster Abbey or St. Stephen's Church in Vienna than the structure of a tragedy by Sopho-

cles is from that of a drama by Shakespeare." [136] Schlegel then repeats his account of the origin and spirit of romantic literature. The Greeks lived in the limits of the finite. Their religion was a deification of natural forms and earthly life. They thus invented the poetry of joy. But with the advent of Christianity everything changed. Poetry became the poetry of the infinite. The poetry of possession yielded to the poetry of desire (*Sehnsucht*). Harmony yielded to inner division. Chivalry, courtly love, and honor, determined by the spirit of Christianity, shaped the new literature. "In Greek art and poetry there is an original unconscious unity of form and matter; in the modern, so far as they have remained true to their peculiar spirit [i.e. did not become neoclassical], a more intimate penetration of both as two opposites is sought for. The Greeks solved their task to perfection; the moderns can satisfy their striving for the infinite only by approximation." [137] This exposition is then supplemented at the beginning of the third volume, which is devoted to the romantic drama. There all the stress is on the romantic mixture of genres. Romantic drama is neither tragedy nor comedy in the strict sense, but drama (*Schauspiel*). Romantic poetry differs from classical by its delight in insoluble mixtures of everything antithetical: nature and art, poetry and prose, earnest and jest, memory and intuition, spirituality and sensuality.[138] "Ancient poetry and art is a rhythmical *nomos*, a harmonious promulgation of the eternal legislation of a beautifully ordered world mirroring the eternal Ideas of things. Romantic poetry, on the other hand, is the expression of a secret longing for the chaos which is perpetually striving for new and marvelous births, which lies hidden in the very womb of orderly creation . . . [Greek art] is simpler, clearer, more like nature in the independent perfection of its separate works; [romantic art], in spite of its fragmentary appearance, is nearer to the mystery of the universe." [139] Greek drama is then compared with a group sculpture, modern drama with a large painting.

If we analyze these passages we can easily recognize the diverse elements drawn from Schiller and Friedrich Schlegel, but all the distinctions are brought together and worked out in a historical context. The antitheses, mechanical—organic, plastic—picturesque, finite—infinite, closed or perfect—progressive and unlimited, pure in the distinction of genres—indulging in mixtures,

simple—complex, or rather these reconciled contrasts and opposites, are memorably phrased and brought into relationship with
the historical contrasts between the Gothic and the classical style in
the fine arts and with the differences between pagan and Christian
religion and pagan and Christian morality. Schlegel himself tried
to preserve an impartial balance, at least in these theoretical pronouncements; his genuine admiration for antiquity is obvious
from his writings, but in the bulk of his critical practice the scales
are heavily weighted in favor of the romantic. To Schlegel's contemporaries in search of a loosely organized, complex, and Christian art, the terms "mechanical," "finite," "pagan," and "simple"
must have sounded as a condemnation of the classical. It seems
excessive, however, to charge Schlegel either with complete subordination of the classical to the romantic ideal or, from a different
point of view, with an extreme theory of the bifurcation of poetry,
a splitting up of its ideal into two equally valid concepts. Schlegel
does neither. It is clear that his own sympathies are largely with
the romantic, that his general conception of poetry, with its stress
on metaphor and symbol, leans in that direction. On the other
hand, he has so general a concept of poetry that he could find it exemplified in works belonging to the classical type. Fundamentally
he did not quite face the issues raised by the recognition of the
two types and was not entirely certain how to distinguish between
a historical category and an ever-recurring type. He also could not
quite separate the descriptive use from the normative and thus
never quite solved the actual difficulties raised by historical relativism.

Nonetheless, in this very lack of sharp decision there was some
critical virtue: unlike his successors in the 19th century Schlegel
never succumbed to completely amorphous, opinionless, and direc-
tionless relativism, to the total passive comprehension of everything ever written, which inevitably led later to mere factualism,
to the indiscriminate accumulation of information about everything at any time anywhere. In Schlegel the methods and assumptions of *Geistesgeschichte*—the view that all cultural activities are
closely parallel, that, for instance, ancient architecture, sculpture,
religion, philosophy, literature, etc. implicate each other—are anticipated, but again the method is not pressed to the fantastic extremes of the 20th century: it still illuminates and does not ob-

fuscate, as it does in Spengler and many other German parallel
hunters who conceive of history as a sequence of sharply defined
ages and types and talk very glibly of the Gothic or the baroque
man. The germ of this method is in Schlegel, but only the germ.
Schlegel still remained a critic who preserved a positive frame of
reference, who, in spite of all his theoretical and practical universality, kept the needs of his time and of creative art in mind, who
knew how to judge according to an ideal of poetry and literature.
It may have made him blind to many values and many authors, but
it preserved him at least from losing his grip on a set of principles
and norms. Without them a critic ceases to be a critic and becomes
a mere antiquary.

The vast range of Schlegel's pronouncements, the scope of his
literary histories, and the boldness and decisiveness of many of his
opinions, which were new or unusual especially in their time,
necessitate a brief survey of his critical opinions.

Greek literature was for August Wilhelm as for Friedrich the
basis of our tradition, and all his sympathies are with Greek literature in opposition to Latin. Almost every Greek poet is discussed
by Schlegel in one context or another: Homer is treated in terms
of the theory of the epic sketched previously in connection with
Hermann und Dorothea.[140] Schlegel quite radically rejects the view
of Homer as a primitive bard, a rude singer, yet he was apparently
too deeply impressed by Wolf's hypothesis to come to a clear decision about the nature of the Homeric epic. The very detailed exposition of the *Iliad* and the *Odyssey* [141] seems to me critically un-
fruitful and disappointing.

Far more original and influential were the discussions of Greek
drama in the Berlin Lectures,[142] the French *Comparaison des deux
Phèdres* (1807), and the Vienna series.[143] In those works the distinction between classical and modern drama as one of fate versus character was clearly formulated, the background of Greek tragedy in
religion was explained, and the technical conditions of Greek
drama were expounded. Among the three tragedians Schlegel ex-
tols Sophocles—though he has his reservations about *Oedipus* because of its complex intrigue and improbability [144]—and systematically disparages Euripides, who lost the idea of fate, was of doubtful piety, and was corrupted by rhetoric and naturalism.[145] Schlegel
shares his brother's fervid admiration for Aristophanes, whose

irony and complete freedom from restraint correspond to their ideal of art as free play and the artist's superiority to his materials.[146]

Latin literature was too closely associated with pseudoclassicism and the French to find much favor in Schlegel's eyes. He criticized Virgil very severely, especially the *Aeneid,* which seems to him an academic piece: subjective, pathetic, contrived, made out of brilliant passages like a mosaic, with a hero who is a mere "vehicle of Providence." [147] The *Georgics* find more favor in his eyes, as they seem to him to be more congenial to Virgil's gifts.[148] Lucretius, though praised, is praised with reluctance; the contrast between a materialistic system and poetry does not seem to Schlegel to be resolved and he does not acknowledge that Lucretius poeticized his matter throughout.[149] Among the elegiac poets Schlegel prefers Propertius, whom he calls "a poet of the first rank," [150] while he seems to have a positive aversion for Ovid: for his character, which he calls despicable, and his writings, which seem to him sentimental, mannered, and cold.[151] Also Horace, though praised as a character, is treated coolly as a derivative and artificial poet.[152] The whole Augustan age is disparaged. Schlegel's antinaturalistic views and his extolling of Aristophanes make him cool toward the new comedy and hence also toward Plautus and Terence.[153]

August Wilhelm had a much greater concrete knowledge of medieval literature than his brother. There are elaborate discussions in his writings of the Provençal lyric, the German *Minnesang,* the Spanish *romancero,* chivalric romances, etc. Most of it, however, is descriptively historical, hardly critical in the narrower sense. The *Nibelungenlied* is the one German work of the Middle Ages which elicited Schlegel's analytical praise, in special articles,[154] in the Berlin lectures, and on other occasions. It is always praised as a "work of colossal character, not only of unsurpassed sensuous energy but also of admirable sublimity of sentiment; it ends like the *Iliad,* only on a much larger scale, with the overwhelming impression of general destruction." [155]

Dante was one of Schlegel's first loves and remained so for him as translator and critic. The early characterization (1791) is mostly descriptive and historical: an attempt to explain the times, the world view, the general question of allegory. The preference shown for *Paradiso,* which is recognized as the most important part of the *Comedy*, seems for that time remarkable. The interest in the *Vita nuova* was also rare then, at least in Germany.[156] Critically more interesting is the later discussion in the 1803–04 course of the Berlin lectures, which very sharply denounces the view that the *Divine Comedy* is merely a series of fine passages, and tries to explain its over-all structure in terms of number symbolism, the trinity, and so on. In Dante Schlegel sees the successful reconciliation of philosophy and poetry, and he parallels him with Calderón, whose *autos* seem to him shorter "Christian allegorical representations of the universe" which came at the end of romantic poetry, while Dante stands at its beginning.[157] Petrarch's poetry, especially the form and technique of the sonnet and the *canzone,* also excited Schlegel's interest and elaborate study, which were almost wholly technical.[158] Though Schlegel translated from Boccaccio, there is no extended comment on him except in a general context of the discussion on the romantic novel.[159]

The Renaissance was, understandably, much more in Schlegel's mind than the still largely unexplored Middle Ages. But Schlegel disappoints us if we ask him for a detailed discussion of the Italians: he thought Ariosto overrated, not comparable to Homer, lacking in heart (*Gemüth*). Contrary to Schiller, who classed Ariosto with the sentimental poets, Schlegel sees him as a sensual realist.[160] The comments on Tasso are slight and far between. Schlegel seems hardly to have known French Renaissance literature, and Spanish *siglo de oro* literature outside of Cervantes seems to have been beyond his ken. Cervantes, of course, was one of his great favorites; he even planned a complete translation of his works and sponsored Tieck's *Don Quixote.* Nothing remains of his translation but a fragment of the *Numancia,* a play he admired inordinately.[161] Critically most important, however, was the discussion of *Don Quixote* in 1799 which gives for the first time, I believe, an out-and-out defense of all the inserted *novelle,* the whole "great contrast between the parodistic and the romantic masses, which is always inexpressibly charming and harmonious, but at times, as in the meeting of the mad Cardenio with the mad Don Quixote, passes into the sublime." [162] Schlegel also must have been one of the first critics who thought the second part equal to the first.

Shakespeare, of course, is the center of Schlegel's critical interest, the author to whom he devoted more effort and time than to any other. He translated seventeen plays; he wrote elaborately on Shakespeare, from the early comment on Falstaff in 1791 [163] (which rejected Morgann's view that he is no coward) to the full systematic survey of all the plays in the Vienna lectures. The leading motif of Schlegel's discussion, even very early, is Shakespeare's conscious artistry, the opposition to the view of Shakespeare as a mere force of nature, the praise of Shakespeare's works as miracles of harmony and composition. The first extended comment on *Hamlet,* occasioned by Goethe's discussion in *Wilhelm Meister* (1796), is still Herderian in its stress on Hamlet's obscurity as a character, which he shares with people in real life and with unfathomable nature. "Shakespeare knew more of his Hamlet than he was conscious of." [164] Still, the praise of Fortinbras' moving appearance on the battlefield, the praise of the sonnets, and the defense of Shakespeare's instinctively right changes from poetry to prose all show the familiarity of the critic with his subject and his courage to deviate from the beaten path. But Schlegel's view of Shakespeare is first developed in the remarkable paper on *Romeo and Juliet* (1797), which is all centered around the one idea that Shakespeare had "finer, more spiritual concepts of dramatic art than one usually tends to ascribe to him." [165] There is an inner unity in the play; it is a "harmonious miracle," "one great antithesis," [166] "at one and the same time enchantingly sweet and painful, pure and glowing, tender and fervent, full of elegiac softness and tragically overwhelming power." [167] Every detail is then defended as contributing to this final effect: Romeo appearing in love with Rosalind is justified because we must not see Romeo in an indifferent state of mind. "His first appearance is enhanced by seeing him walking on the sacred soil of imagination, separated from the environment of cold reality." [168] Our seeing his first inclination overcome in one moment by the new passion demonstrates so much the better its omnipotence. The tyrannical fury of Juliet's father and the meanness in the behavior of both parents seem objectionable, yet they save Juliet from the struggle between love and filial piety; and the faithlessness and cynicism of the nurse also contribute to Juliet's isolation and thus prepare us for her readiness to take the Friar's potion. The quibbles and the antithetic word play are similarly defended as representing the "great antithesis," the contrasts of love and hate, embraces and suicide. A good word is said even for the killing of Paris and the final speech of the Friar.

Shakespeare thus is a deep-thinking artist who might go "against our conventions but not against the conventions of his time and people." [169] Shakespeare is more correct than any modern poet in the sense that he deliberately developed even the smallest detail of his work according to the spirit of the whole. "He is more systematic than any other author: through those antitheses which contrast individuals, masses, and even worlds in picturesque groups; or through the musical symmetry of the same great scale, by gigantic repetitions and refrains; often through parody of the letter and irony at the spirit of the romantic drama." [170] Shakespeare, in short, is an "abyss of deliberateness, self-consciousness, and reflection." [171]

This conception also pervades the chapter in the Vienna lectures, which is Schlegel's most systematic pronouncement on Shakespeare. Much that is said there is still right and true and much was novel in its time. Other parts indulge in the romantic bardolatry from which Schlegel was not exempt or go far in the modernizing and psychologizing of Shakespeare. We need not rehearse Schlegel's defense of Shakespeare's neglect of the unities, by now a commonplace. We must expect Schlegel to say a great deal on Shakespeare's irony of characterization. He expressly states that "we would be ill-advised to take literally the utterances of Shakespeare's characters about themselves and others." [172] The view that one cannot add or remove or order anything differently in Shakespeare [173] will appear to us extravagant; still, the emphasis on a "central point" or on a "main idea" [174] in each play [175] (in opposition to the criticism of passages and details as practiced by Dr. Johnson and other commentators) was right and useful, though it soon led to the abuses of the "central idea" by the Hegelians and to the exaggerations of the "organic" point of view. Schlegel shows his historical imagination in defending Shakespeare's anachronisms (and presumably all anachronisms) as proof of the health and self-confidence of a society which believed that things had always been as they were then and would be so forever. [176]

The individual plays are, on the whole, well characterized, and much of the detailed praise seems judicious and possibly new:

e.g. the emphasis on *Measure for Measure*,[177] the defense of the sub-plot of *King Lear*,[178] or the psychological remarks on the triple dis-tribution and thus attenuation of Macbeth's guilt,[179] the ambiguity in the characterization of Cleopatra,[180] the symmetry of trickery in *Much Ado about Nothing*,[181] and the diversion of our interest to Iago's means rather than his ends.[182] The treatment of *Hamlet*[183] may surprise one if he thinks of Schlegel as the exponent of ro-mantic criticism. Hamlet as a character is treated with remarkable severity: he has a "natural inclination to go by crooked ways"; he is a hypocrite toward himself; he has a malicious joy in the destruc-tion of his enemies; he has no firm belief either in himself or in anything else. But on the whole Schlegel endorses Goethe's view of the weakness of Hamlet's character and agrees with the stress on the paralyzing influence on action of thought and intellect: "the native hue of resolution sicklied o'er with the pale cast of thought." It is Goethe's weak Hamlet but with some streaks of cruelty and crookedness added: an intellectual Hamlet without moral charm.

Whatever the limitations of this romantic character-study the distinction of the pages on Shakespeare is undeniable. It is only gratuitously spoiled when in an appendix[184] Schlegel defends the ascription of almost all apocrypha to Shakespeare and indulges in extravagant and uncritical praise of such plays as *Thomas Lord Cromwell, Sir John Oldcastle,* and *A Yorkshire Tragedy,* which, according to Schlegel, belong to "the most mature and most emi-nent of Shakespeare's works."[185] It seems significant, however, that Schlegel never said anything concrete on any figure or scene in these supposedly wonderful plays.

On the whole, Schlegel disappoints when he goes outside the main body of Shakespeare's great works, which he knew intimately. His discussion of Shakespeare's predecessors amounts to saying that Shakespeare owed almost nothing to them,[186] a view which can only be explained as an uncritical acceptance of Malone. But Schlegel *had* read Marlowe's *Edward the Second* and was not impressed. He cannot understand why Ben Jonson spoke of his "mighty line."[187] His treatment of Shakespeare's contemporaries and successors is also disappointing. He praises Heywood's *A Woman Killed with Kindness*[188] but is cool to Ben Jonson. Beaumont and Fletcher as well as Massinger are rated low. On the whole the successors of Shakespeare seem to him "mannered"[189] or as we would say, baroque. Schlegel, at times, seems to have no sympathy for such "decadent" art.

Generally speaking, the 17th century comes off badly in Schlegel's writings compared to the 16th. It is to him the century of transition from romantic to artificial poetry, and French neoclassicism is to him the type of art to which he felt most antagonistic. Schlegel is most favorably inclined to the early Corneille, as *Le Cid* is still near the Spanish drama; he expresses regret that the French theater was not allowed to become truly national and romantic.[190] Still, in the Vienna lectures the tone of the comments on Racine is moderate and defensible if one accepts the premise that the French had an "abstract concept of tragedy," desired tragic dignity and greatness, tragic situations, passions and pathos completely naked and pure, and thus lost out on life and particularity.[191] But the earlier *Comparaison des deux Phèdres* (1807) must be dismissed as beside the point, for Schlegel there willfully (and one cannot help thinking maliciously) disparaged Racine's play in comparison to Euripides' *Hippolytus,* ignoring his own historical theories and concealing from the French audience his own low opinion of Euripides. Euripides there appears as the naive and classical poet, though Schlegel understood very well that Euripides represents a late stage of the decadence of classical drama.* In the *Dramatic Lectures, Athalie* is singled out for special praise,[192] but *Phèdre* is still ranked low among Racine's plays.[193]

The discussion of Molière has caused most offense, and rightly so, for Schlegel even uses an appeal to social snobbery in disparaging Molière's background and standing, accepts and elaborates the charges of plagiarism and unoriginality, suspects Molière's morality of flunkeyism [194] and gross servility, and discusses the plays in a very carping spirit, going to the grotesque length of denying them universality,[195] minimizing their psychological insights, and exaggerating their improbabilities. Nonetheless, one should grant that Schlegel, from his point of view, which consistently disapproved of realism and domestic drama, was not merely malicious in suggesting that Molière was best in his coarser, broader farces and that his

* See Philarète Chasles, *Études sur l'antiquité* (Paris, 1847), pp. 245–53. Chasles' good refutation of Schlegel's comparison is vitiated by his ignorance of Schlegel's real opinion of Euripides, which was actually quite close to Chasles'.

edging toward the tragic, in plays like the *Misanthrope,* was a violation of the purity of the comic style. The offense against Molière becomes aggravated when one thinks that Schlegel could praise a fantastic farce, *Le Roi de Cocagne* by Legrand,[196] and find interest in the operas of Quinault.[197] Undoubtedly nationalism in the case of Molière exaggerated Schlegel's dislike of realism, didacticism, and plain common sense.

The English 17th century also found little favor with Schlegel. He clearly did not know the metaphysicals. He disliked Milton, dismissing the early poems and criticizing *Paradise Lost* most severely. It is an impossible enterprise for an individual to invent a mythology.[198] The poem is deficient in religious mysticism and in the symbolic view of nature. The fall of Lucifer has become an external and accidental event, the fall of man is soon brought to bare rationality and deprived of mystery by moralizing detail.[199] Paradoxically and willfully Schlegel praises the allegory of Sin and Death which had aroused most objections; this is the way the subject should have been handled throughout, as a mystery, dramatically and allegorically.[200] One can understand why Schlegel was repelled by the coarse *Hudibras* and thought the dramas of Dryden unbelievably bad. But it seems inexcusable that he did not recognize the merits of Dryden as a critic and that he speaks of his confused gabble about the drama, the unities, the French, and the English, etc.[201]

The one kind of 17th-century art Schlegel admired is the drama of Calderón. Lope, of whom he seems to have known only little, is treated quite coolly, but Calderón, who was Schlegel's discovery (suggested by Tieck), is praised extravagantly, yet in such general terms that one would hardly suspect that Schlegel himself translated five plays completely and fragments of several others. The praise consists in a rhetorical evocation of Calderón's view of the world: religion is his real love, his heart of hearts. He writes in his works a hymn of rejoicing at the wonders of the universe.[202] He is the end and culmination of romantic poetry. Strangely enough his art, which seems baroque today, is contrasted with the mannered taste which had spread all over Europe.[203]

Needless to say, the 18th century found least favor in Schlegel's eyes. After all, his main polemical butts were the Enlightenment and neoclassicism. Voltaire's *Henriade* gets short shrift [204] and his tragedies are judged unfavorably (though *Alzire* is praised).[205] Diderot is dismissed and called, for his naturalism, no critic at all.[206] Pope is consistently disparaged: *Eloisa to Abelard* is called "frigid," [207] the *Essay on Man* confused,[208] the *Dunciad* without salt and wit,[209] the translation of Homer "the summit of perversion." [210] Johnson's comments on Shakespeare are frequently singled out for their "thick-skinned insensibility," [211] Burke's *Reflections on the Sublime and Beautiful* is elaborately ridiculed for its physiological explanations of the origins of the feelings it deals with.[212] The references to other English 18th-century authors are also very cool. One is a little surprised that Schlegel took the trouble (surely mainly for financial reasons) to translate in his youth a rather large selection from Horace Walpole [213] and that he seriously reviewed books such as Lewis' *Monk*,[214] as well as many minor novels. Among the Italians, Gozzi and his fairy tales appealed to Schlegel's taste for his friend Tieck and for irony.[215]

Schlegel understandably devoted most attention to German 18th-century literature. The earlier figures are judged severely and are generally dismissed: Gottsched and Klopstock, even Lessing, who, though praised at times,[216] is surprisingly passed over in silence on many occasions; August Wilhelm seems never to have shared his brother's enthusiasm. Wieland was the special target of Schlegel's criticism; some of it was gratuitously malicious, such as the advertisement in the *Athenaeum* [217] asking the creditors to submit their claims to Wieland's works; other, more elaborate criticism, as in the Berlin lectures,[218] contains much truth. Wieland's Epicurean rococo was quite distant from Schlegel's own sympathies. Herder—though Schlegel must have owed him a great deal —is also treated with scant respect. His *Ideas Toward a Philosophy of the History of Humanity* are said to contain neither ideas nor philosophy nor history.[219] In contradistinction to his brother, August Wilhelm was also cool to Jean Paul, whose talent he considered sickly and spoiled.[220]

The famous review of Bürger, [221] supposedly a defense against Schiller's harsh verdict, is really a very detached appraisal which, in spite of a favorable conclusion and a warm tone of personal apology, stresses Bürger's debasement of English and Scottish ballads, his "coarse manner," and his failure to overcome the handicaps and sorrows of his own life in his poetry.

Schlegel's intellectual relations to Goethe and Schiller are the most interesting and critically most fruitful. In part, of course, they were colored by his personal relations, by the conflict of his brother with Schiller, the opinions of his wife Caroline who disliked Schiller, and by many considerations of literary "policy." A full chronological discussion is out of place.[222] It may suffice to say that Schlegel took a violent dislike to Schiller because of his review of Bürger; that he later suppressed it as well as he could and expressed admiration for Schiller's philosophical poems and writings; but that after Schiller's conflict with Friedrich, which cost August Wilhelm his position on the *Horen,* he indulged in bitter parodies and invectives against Schiller in private, while adopting an almost consistent policy of silence toward him in public. Occasionally he would disparage the distinction between naive and sentimental and point out how it differed from the distinction between classical and romantic.[223] And occasionally he would refer critically to Schiller's reviews of Bürger and Matthisson.[224] But there is no formal criticism of Schiller's dramas until the *Dramatic Lectures,* from which Schiller could not be omitted. By then Schiller was dead and much more famous. Schlegel, with a slightly sour mien, surveyed the dramas, praising *Mary Stuart* and especially *Wilhelm Tell.* He is surely right in condemning the violation of history in the *Maid of Orleans* and in expressing dissatisfaction with the neither mythological nor historical, neither ideal nor natural, setting and theme of the *Bride of Messina.*[225] If one can believe the report of an English student, Schlegel, in his late Bonn lectures on German literature, went so far as to call Schiller completely "confused in his ideas respecting the theory of the drama" and to speak of the ballads as "among the worst which we possess." [226]

Nothing so unpleasant can be reported about Schlegel's relation to Goethe. His admiration for Goethe was genuine, though it cooled off toward the end. The very earliest reviews, from a later perspective, seem cool: *Tasso* and the *Faust* fragment of 1790 are praised but hardly appreciated in their greatness.[227] Schlegel, however, is at his finest as a critic in his praise of the *Roman Elegies* [228] and *Hermann und Dorothea.*[229] The elegies are characterized as both antique and original, and *Hermann und Dorothea* is justified in terms of a theory of the Homeric epic congenial to Goethe; it is praised as a "perfect work of art in the grand style." [230] Schlegel's

enthusiasm thus goes to the classical Goethe, the Goethe of the late
80's and 90's, rather than the early or late Goethe. When he spoke
of him again at length in the *Dramatic Lectures,* his enthusiasm
had cooled off: he had attacked Goethe's classicism in the fine arts
because he, with his brother, had become a convert to the medieval, "Old German," Gothic style in painting.[231] He now, in his
history of the drama, suggests, hardly unjustly, that Goethe has
"enormous dramatic but hardly as much theatrical talent." [232]
Goetz and *Faust* are praised but *Iphigenie* seems to him pale and
elegiac and the end of *Egmont* sounds an "ideal music of the
soul." [233] When in the Bonn lectures Schlegel said that Goethe did
not "shine in a critical capacity," [234] it was, one must suppose, in
self-defense, for he must have heard of Goethe's increasingly low
opinion of his character. Otherwise, Schlegel was largely interested
in the periphery of Goethe's works: he especially praised e.g. the
Triumph der Empfindsamkeit [235] and was much intrigued and
puzzled by the *Märchen.*[236] But the actual significance of *Faust* remained beyond his ken and he paid no formal attention to the bulk
of Goethe's works.

Schlegel cannot be charged with neglecting contemporary literature. He was for years a regular reviewer; between 1796 and 1799
in the *Jenaische allgemeine Literaturzeitung* alone he published
some 300 reviews. But paradoxically one cannot say that he paid
much analytical critical attention to his exact contemporaries. This
is, in part, due to the fact that he stopped reviewing current books,
except learned publications, about 1801 and that much of his reviewing was devoted to very ephemeral stuff. But he did not refrain
from polemics and severely critical surveys of contemporary literature: his writings are full of satires and attacks on the minor German novelists of the time (Lafontaine, etc.), dramatists (Kotzebue,
Iffland), and lyrical poets (Voss, Matthisson, Schmidt). In the 1802
Berlin lectures he surveyed the state of German literature very
critically, deploring the low general taste, the low level of the
periodicals, the decay of the theaters, etc. At the same time he did
little formal criticism of the great men of his age (except those
older than he), possibly because those who interested him most
were his brother and close friends like Tieck and Novalis, whom
he could not in later years review with good grace. He did welcome
the early writings of Tieck very sympathetically and yet judi-

ciously, recommending to their author more discipline and clarity.[237] And he also reviewed Wackenroder's *Herzensergiessungen*
sympathetically,[238] though rather coolly. But in later years he quar-
reled with Tieck over the edition of Novalis and fell silent about
his writings.[239] From letters one could cull a great many opinions
and pronouncements (especially on Tieck and Werner) [240] which
show that Schlegel gradually lost sympathy with the group of which
he was supposed to be a leader. He retired early from any attempt
to influence the shaping of opinion on current German literature.*
One would look in vain in his writings for any more extended and
analytical pronouncements on his English and French contemporaries: Schlegel had most definitely become a scholar and historian.

Novalis, writing to Friedrich Schlegel, expressly asks that he
keep his judgment separate from that of his brother and then
formulates the contrast between the two Schlegels: "yours is always
individual—his historical and general." [241] In retrospect it may
seem that Novalis was right: the voice of Friedrich Schlegel is
certainly more individual, more striking, his sensibility subtler,
more precise. The voice of August Wilhelm is often that of the historian, the man of detachment, of tolerance, of universality. But
one could also turn Novalis' dictum around: Friedrich Schlegel is
the more speculative, more "general" thinker of the two, the critic
who less frequently enters into a close discussion of technique, who
rarely analyzes a work of art; while August Wilhelm can become
absorbed in concrete detail, in aesthetic surface, in the craft of
literature. Friedrich certainly is preoccupied with irony and paradox, while his brother is not. Friedrich's theory of criticism makes
much more of the polemical, the incitory, anticipatory, forward-
looking function of criticism. Friedrich was much more interested
in the new novel, the synthetic genre of the future, than his
brother. Friedrich's conception of poetry early acquired a religious
tinge and finally became fused with religion and philosophy, an
evolution which was not shared by August Wilhelm.

August Wilhelm, in his turn, elaborated much more clearly and
systematically than his brother a theory of metaphor and symbol-

* In 1822 he could write "Je me moque de la littérature." Letter to
Auguste de Staël, Feb. 19, 1822, in *Krisenjahre der Frühromantik*, 2,
394.

ism which led him to a theory of symbolic correspondences, of art as the restoration of man's original animizing intuition. August Wilhelm also was much more consistently preoccupied with a theory of "organic" structure in literature; while Friedrich accepts the view, he is not so interested as Wilhelm in the term. Wilhelm defends it not only for the individual work of art but also for the great genres and the whole evolution of literature. August Wilhelm remained much more a follower of Herder than Friedrich: his view of literature permitted biological analogies, though his symbolism divorced him from all naturalism. August Wilhelm thought about the problem of literary history and its relation to criticism more consistently and systematically. He was more interested in the drama than his brother. But these differences of emphasis and tone as well as personal development should not obscure their profound agreement in all essentials during the time of their most intimate collaboration. The unity of their view seems to me only less striking than the general sanity of their position. The Schlegels, it seems, best formulated a view of literature and criticism which was transmitted by Coleridge to the English-speaking world and is, on many essential points, accepted by recent English and American criticism.

KANT is usually considered the fountainhead of German aesthetics, but one could argue that the German romanticists never adopted Kant's main position; certainly they do not share his cautious temper and his conservative taste. When in 1796 F. W. J. Schelling (1775–1854) drew up his program of a new philosophy, he completely ignored Kant's distinction between epistemology, ethics, and aesthetics. He put forward the grandiose claim that the idea of beauty, taken in the higher Platonic sense, "unites all other ideas." "I am convinced," he says, "that the highest act of reason is the aesthetic act embracing all ideas and that truth and goodness are made kindred only in beauty. The philosopher must have as much aesthetic power as the poet. Poetry thus assumes a new dignity; it becomes what it was in the beginning—the teacher of mankind: for there is no philosophy or history any more; poetry alone will outlive all other sciences and arts." [1] "Poetry" is used here in the all-embracing sense of human creativity, derived from Plato's *Symposium.* This claim for poetry is then linked with the demand for a "new mythology which would be in the service of ideas, a mythology of Reason." Ideas must become aesthetic, i.e. mythological, in order to be acceptable to the people, to be effective in the civilizing mission of art which Schelling conceives in terms of Schiller's *Letters on Aesthetic Education.* This claim for the pre-eminence of art must not, of course, be confused with later 19th-century aestheticism: it is rather an attempt to abolish all distinctions between art, religion, philosophy, and myth. While Kant was at great pains to distinguish between the good, the true, and the beautiful, Schelling enthrones beauty as the highest value. But his beauty is actually truth and goodness in disguise.

This strange early scheme remained in manuscript until 1917; nevertheless, Schelling's published writings of the next decade expound the same claims for art in a number of crucial passages which impressed the age as the most ambitious formulas for the view of art as revelation, philosophy, religion, and myth. One can distinguish at least three stages in Schelling's views: the conclusion of the *System of Transcendental Idealism* (1800) differs from the passages in *Bruno* (1802); and there is further change (partly a return to the earlier views) in the 14th lecture of *Vorlesungen über die Methode des akademischen Studiums* (1803) and in a speech, *Über das Verhältnis der bildenden Künste zu der Natur* (1807). Meanwhile, however, Schelling had developed a concrete and very full system of aesthetics and poetics in the lectures he gave first at Jena in 1802–03 and repeated in Würzburg in 1804–05. Only a small fragment from them, *Über Dante in philosophischer Beziehung*, was printed in 1802.[2] They circulated widely in manuscript but were not published until 1859, after Schelling's death. They must be counted as the first speculative poetics, though we must realize that Schelling had access to the Berlin lectures of August Wilhelm Schlegel and drew much of his concrete information from them. For our purposes the MS lectures are clearly the most important document, but something must be said about Schelling's general aesthetics, since his published pronouncements were most influential not only in but even outside of Germany— directly for Coleridge and Cousin, indirectly for Emerson and others.

In principle, Schelling revives neo-Platonism; art is vision or intellectual intuition (a term derived from Giordano Bruno). Both the philosopher and the artist penetrate into the essence of the universe, the absolute. Art thus breaks down the barriers between the real and the ideal world.[3] It is the representation of the infinite in the finite,[4] a union of nature and freedom, for it is both a product of the conscious and the unconscious,[5] of the imagination which unconsciously creates our real world and consciously creates the ideal world of art.[6] Schelling's views on the exact relation between philosophy and art shift: at times philosophy and art and truth and beauty are completely identified;[7] at other times they are conceived of as related like archetype and image,[8] art being "real" and philosophy "ideal," despite the fact that art has just been defined as the complete fusion of the "ideal" and the "real."[9] Especially in the oration "Über das Verhältnis der bildenden

Künste zu der Natur" Schelling expounds his central conception of art as an analogue of nature and of nature's creative power. Art constitutes an active link between the soul and nature.[10] Art does not imitate nature but has to compete with the creative power of nature, "the spirit of nature which speaks to us only through symbols." A work of art expresses the essence of nature and is excellent in the degree to which it shows us "this original power of nature's creation and activity, as if in a silhouette." [11] On its lowest level art faithfully represents the "characteristic," the peculiar nature of the individual object, but it should rise beyond this to true grace and beauty, to the complete reconciliation of all mental powers, to the "certainty that all antithesis is only apparent, that love is the tie between all beings and pure goodness the foundation and content of the whole of creation." [12] In Nature itself Schelling can see a "poem that lies enclosed in a secret marvelous cipher," an "Odyssey of the Spirit." [13] The poet is, as it were, the liberator of nature and as Novalis said of man in general, the Messiah of Nature.

Only the MS lectures on *Philosophy of Art* make these conceptions more concrete and relate them to actual literature. In them the role of mythology in Schelling's conception becomes clear. Mythology is the subject matter of art. Just as ideas are the subject of philosophy, so gods are the necessary subject of art.[14] These gods are accessible not through reason but only through imagination.[15] Schelling, of course, thinks primarily of the Greek gods, yet he exalts mythology in general terms as the subject matter of all art. While all art must present the absolute, it can do so only symbolically: mythology is a system of symbols and is therefore art itself. Schelling distinguishes between schematism (the general signifying the particular, as in abstract thought), allegory (the particular signifying the general), and symbolism (the union of the general and the particular), which alone is truly art. This union is achieved in mythology,[16] because in it there is a complete "indifference" of the general and the particular. Venus *is* beauty; she does not merely signify it. Mythology is the product not of an individual but of the race. True mythology seems to be only Greek mythology, inasmuch as Schelling elaborately argues that Christian mythology is either allegorical or historical. Only Christ is a God, "the last of the ancient Gods," [17] yet Christ is not a good subject for art because pure suffering is not poetic.[18] Angels also are useless for poetry, for they are unreal, incorporeal, and unconcrete.[19] Only Lucifer is a concrete individuality and he alone comes near being a mythological figure.[20] But then, of course, his origins are pagan.

One would think that there is no hope for poetry in the modern world, but actually Schelling does not adhere to a complete exaltation of ancient mythology. The historical elements of the Christian myth are recognized as usable: the apostles, the saints' legends, even the mythology of chivalry. The summit of Christian poetry is in Calderón, whom Schelling ranks above Shakespeare.[21] Protestantism and modern rationalism are, of course, inimical to mythology and hence to poetry. Milton is condemned as abstract and Klopstock as empty.[22] Catholicism is recommended as a necessary element of modern poetry and mythology.[23] By giving a slight shift to the meaning of the term "myth" Schelling is able to grant that some poets have overcome the modern handicaps. Dante, in some cases, has made his historical figures (e.g. Ugolino) mythological.[24] Shakespeare has created his own world of myths, and Don Quixote and Sancho Panza are truly mythological persons.[25] In *Faust* (then unfinished), the Germans will have a genuine mythological poem. "Mythology" thus does not mean an actual assemblage of Gods: Sancho Panza and Falstaff are not gods, they are true "myths," for they are universal and concrete, characters meaningful in themselves while remaining eternal symbolic types.

Schelling has hopes for a new mythology: he thinks that the truly creative individual will be able to fashion his own mythology,[26] that a new Homer will arise. He will apparently draw on the new physics, i.e. Schelling's own speculative *Naturphilosophie,* as a source for the final great epic that will realize the identity of philosophy and poetry.[27] While Schelling's hopes for the future are distressingly vague, his conception of the close relationship between symbol and myth, his distinction between symbolism and allegory, and his recognition of the mythic in the great figures of modern imagination are insights of striking originality and enduring value.

The discussions of the forms of art which follow are much less valuable. The new distinction between poetry as internal vision and art as external creation is arbitrary and confusing, and the discussions of the corresponding distinctions between the sublime and the beautiful, between the naive and the sentimental, between style and manner are unilluminating because Schelling always decides in favor of the first member of the dichotomy and thus actually dissolves it into a distinction between art and non-art. Naive art is the only good art, the sentimental is pseudo-art, and so with the rest. Nor do we need to follow Schelling's discussions of sculpture, painting, and music, which contain such famous fanciful analogies as the view that "music is a form of sculpture" [28] and architecture is "frozen music." [29]

Schelling's ingenious genre theory, however, deserves attention. Poetry itself is not differentiated from the other arts except on the obvious ground of medium: language is "ideal," while the media of the plastic arts—stone, sounds, and colors—are "real." The genres of poetry, though they all share the general character of art, the union of the finite and the infinite, are distinguished according to their various leanings toward one or the other of these two extremes. Moreover, by an elaborate scheme of involution they correspond to the other arts: the lyric to music, the epic to painting, the drama to sculpture. In the lyric the finite—i.e. the subject, the ego of the poet—predominates. The lyric is the most subjective, individualized genre, the most particular, and in Schelling's classification the nearest to music,[30] which also expresses subjective feelings. Within the lyric, however, Schelling prefers the more objective, more formally precise art of the Greeks and the set, conventionalized forms developed by Dante and Petrarch. The epic rises beyond subjective consciousness to the next power of man, action. It is thus an image of history. A balance between the infinite and the finite is achieved; there is no struggle, no fate, in the epic.[31] It is timeless, or rather "constant" (*stätig*), indifferent to time. Its actions are chance events: it may have no beginning or end. The poet is detached from his ego, objectively cool toward his world. In short, Schelling succeeds in working into his scheme all the characteristics of the epic as he knew them from the theories of August Wilhelm Schlegel or Humboldt.

Then come the subgenres of the epic: the elegy, the idyll, didactic poetry, and satire. The high position given to didactic poetry is remarkable in that Schelling envisages a new Lucretius, a new summary of man's philosophy, as an ideal for the future.[32] Besides these traditional genres, Schelling recognizes chivalric romances as another subgenre. Ariosto is the great exemplar, though Schelling could hardly have known him well, to judge from a gross error he makes.[33] The novel joins the verse romance. Only *Don Quixote* and *Wilhelm Meister* are considered true examples, because they alone show objectivity, the use of irony, chance, etc., which Schelling demands from the genre. The English novel is treated with severity. *Tom Jones* is a mere picture of manners painted in crude colors.[34] *Clarissa*, though it shows an objective power of representation, is vitiated by pedantry and diffuseness.[35] The short story (*Novelle*) is then described as a short novel, written in a lyrical manner, grouped around one center.

Schelling, from his mythological point of view, is worried by the absence in modern history of a single "generally valid event" that would be capable of epic treatment. Such an event would have to be general, national, and popular, as was the Trojan war according to his conception. He grants some epic qualities to Goethe's *Hermann und Dorothea* but has only faint hopes that such individual epics, if grouped around a center, could by synthesis or expansion achieve some final collective totality.[36] The Wolfian theory of Homeric origins is used here, surprisingly, to propose a collective epic of the future.

As the last epic genre, Schelling discusses Dante's *Divine Comedy*. It is an epic *sui generis,* not a novel or a didactic poem or an epic in the ancient sense, or a comedy or a drama, but the most insoluble of mixtures, and the most perfect interpenetration of all of them. As a species it is the most universal representative of modern poetry; it is the poem of poems.[37] Dante's *Comedy*, besides being a synthesis of religion, science, and poetry, is completely individual; yet it is also universal, generic, timely (in the sense of being characteristically medieval), and eternal. Dante's figures, Schelling admits, are both allegorical and historical, but by virtue of the eternal place in which they are put they assume eternity. Thus not only events and figures which Dante drew from his time (such as the story of Ugolino) but also purely fictional events (such as the end of Ulysses and his companions) assume in the context of the poem mythological certainty. Schelling distinguishes the three realms sharply: the Inferno is dark, sculpturesque, material; the Purgatorio colorful, pictorial; the Paradiso musical, full of bright, white light. But Schelling emphasizes that the three realms collaborate toward a total effect: the work is not plastic, or pictorial, or musical, but all at the same time; not lyrical or epic, or dramatic, but a fusion of all three. It is thus prophetic of modern poetry, since modern poetry is also individual and generic, topical and universal.

Every age, according to Schelling, could and should write its new *Divine Comedy:* a recommendation which is probably just another version of the hope for a new universal philosophical epic. No wonder that with this conception of Dante, Schelling indignantly rejects [38] the view of Bouterwek (in his *Geschichte der Poesie und Beredsamkeit*) that Dante's *Comedy* is only a gallery of pictures, a series of beautiful or "tasteless" passages. Croce is one of the few critics who have defended Bouterwek,[39] since he also wants to distinguish between system and poetry, theological scaffolding and art. But "totality" is Schelling's and the German romantics' watchword, and in the context of earlier Dante criticism Schelling has great merit in dismissing the discussion of what genre the *Divine Comedy* belongs to and stressing the general structure and unity.

Drama, we can easily anticipate, is in Schelling's scheme a union of the lyric and the epic, a struggle between freedom and necessity in which both come out victorious and defeated.[40] Necessity triumphs without freedom perishing and freedom triumphs without necessity perishing. Actually this final synthesis of necessity and freedom explains only tragedy. The tragic hero must necessarily be guilty of a crime and at the end he must accept punishment freely. Genuine tragedy is not the punishment of a conscious, deliberate crime but rather the acceptance of punishment by the guiltless guilty; it is the sacrifice of the individual which both asserts moral freedom and restores the moral order. Schelling's theory of tragedy thus differs widely from Kant's, Schiller's, and the Schlegels', and prepares the way for Hegel's. Schelling, of course, has mostly *Oedipus Rex* in mind, just as, in discussing the Greek tragedians, he clearly prefers Sophocles to the other two. Euripides is severely, though somewhat inconsistently, rebuked for altering the Greek myths too freely.[41]

Comedy is seen then as a reversal of the scheme of tragedy: while in tragedy necessity is objective (i.e. in the order of the universe) and freedom subjective (in the moral revolt of the hero), comedy turns the relation around. Necessity is now the subject, freedom the object. If I understand this rightly, Schelling means merely that in comedy, character is fixed and fated, while the world and its order are treated with freedom and irony. Obviously, Aristophanes is Schelling's great example.

Modern dramatic poetry is viewed as a mixture of tragedy and comedy and thus something like a return to the epic. Shakespeare is Schelling's example, and like August Wilhelm Schlegel he decides that in Shakespeare character replaces ancient fate, character *becomes* fate for the Shakespearean hero.[42] Shakespeare appears as the greatest inventor of the "characteristic," and is thus considered deficient in beauty and too close to realism. Schelling shares the view of the Schlegels that Shakespeare was a highly conscious artist, and supports it by a reference to Shakespeare's poems in which he finds tender subjective feelings, clearly and consciously elaborated. There is nothing left of the Storm and Stress view of Shakespeare as a divine savage.

Schelling puts Calderón even higher than Shakespeare: especially the *Devoción de la Cruz* which he read in A. W. Schlegel's translation. Everything there happens through Providence, through Christian fate, according to which there must be a sinner to demonstrate the power of Divine Grace.[43] The fall of man is the involuntary fault of the hero: he must be sacrificed in order to be saved. Likewise in form and execution Calderón seems perfect to Schelling. Only Sophocles is his equal.[44]

Faust is treated, surprisingly, as modern comedy in the highest style. Schelling recognized that Faust (though he knew then only the fragment of 1790) must and will be saved and raised to higher spheres.[45] Schelling ends his lectures expressing hope for a union of the arts, for a revival of the Greek drama, of which modern opera is only a caricature.[46] He points, like many Germans of the time, toward the ideal proclaimed by Wagner. But generally speaking, Schelling's ideal of poetry is by no means a romantic confusion of the arts: rather it is a highly stylized collective art, Greek in its austere taste for sculpture and the sculpturesque. In practice, however, Schelling's Hellenism is modified by his appreciation of Dante, Cervantes, Calderón, and Goethe, by his praise of Christian tragedy, by his hope for a new philosophical poem, and his constant recognition of man's continuous myth-making power.

Schelling's *Philosophie der Kunst* is not always organized with due proportion and shows signs of haste, understandable in writing for lectures. Unfortunately it was not published until 1859, when it could no longer have any direct effect. Yet it had circulated in MS and a Schellingian, Friedrich Ast (1778–1841), in his *System der Kunstlehre* (1805) gave currency to his ideas. Though Hegel may not have read Schelling's lectures, he starts from Schelling's position and in their different ways so do Schopenhauer and Solger. Coleridge, for a period, was a Schellingian and considered himself chiefly an expounder of Schelling. Emerson sometimes sounds like Schelling, and so does Bergson, who apparently drew on Ravaisson as an intermediary.

NOVALIS

Saintsbury called Novalis (Friedrich von Hardenberg, 1772–1801) not only the "greatest critic among the German romantics," preferring him to the Schlegels, but also, "in a sense the greatest critic of Germany." [1] But this seems extravagant, for Novalis in his theory of poetry is clearly dependent on Schelling, and his concrete criticisms hardly ever go beyond mere aphoristic statements of opinions. Saintsbury, as usual, confuses well phrased pronouncements of literary taste with criticism—forgetting that criticism always demands analysis, explanation, and substantiated evaluation.

Still, Novalis has something personal to say also on poetry; he gives a more mystical twist to Schelling's theory and connects it more clearly with the special conception of poetry as dream and fairy tale. Poetry in Novalis is virtually identified with religion and philosophy, and the poet is exalted beyond any other human being. A sense of poetry, he recognizes, has much in common with a taste for mysticism. [2] It is thus, like the mystical state, undescribable and undefinable. "Who does not immediately know and feel what poetry is cannot be taught any idea of it." [3] At the same time Novalis identifies poetry with free association and with play [4] (evidently in Schiller's sense) as well as with thinking—since both thinking and writing poetry are the free productive use of our organs [5]—and ultimately with truth itself. "Poetry," he is able to say, "is the truly, absolutely real. That is the core of my philosophy. The more poetic, the truer." [6]

If we accept these identifications and expansions of terms, we can understand why Novalis (through the mouth of his poet Klingsohr) can deplore the notion that "poetry has a special name and that poets make up a special guild. It is nothing special. It is the peculiar mode of action of the human spirit. Does not man poeticize and aspire every minute?" [7] Poetry, then, is thought, play, truth, aspiration, in short, all of man's free activity. Novalis can then say that "love is nothing but the highest natural poetry," [8] and that "the best poetry is quite near to us and an ordinary object is frequently its favorite material," [9] and even that "poetry rests wholly upon experience." [10] But it would be a total misunderstanding, of course, to interpret these passages as a defense of realism. They merely mean that everything is poetry, that everything can be transformed into poetry and assume poetic and thus cosmic significance. Actually, Novalis expressly condemns "imitation of nature." His view of poetry is just the opposite.[11] In practice he exalts the fairy tale as the highest poetic form and wrote totally unrealistic prose himself.

The poet is a priest. "The genuine poet . . . is always a priest" and the original union of priest and poet should be restored in the future.[12] The poet is the servant of man's first gods, "of the stars, spring, love, joy, fertility, health and happiness." [13] He alone deserves the name of sage. The "genuine poet is omniscient—he is a real world in miniature." [14] We should understand that the division of poet and thinker is deceptive. "It is a sign of disease and a diseased constitution." [15] The poet is the voice of the universe,[16] and the representative of the genius of humanity.[17] These are all old themes of the Platonic tradition, fervently and extravagantly phrased.

Novalis' views seem to me more interesting and more distinct when he defines his conception of poetry and of genres more concretely. Poetry is conceived of as thoroughly symbolical, dreamlike, musical. We must not be deceived by such pronouncements as "the more personal, the more local, the more temporal, the more peculiar a poem, the nearer it is to the center of poetry." "A poem must be as inexhaustible as a person or a good proverb." [18] He refers here only to the peculiarly exact ritual of poetry, the individual and multiple meaning of its symbols, and does not defend local color, realism, or mere personal idiosyncrasy. It is a protest against neoclassical abstractionism and generality. But Novalis speculates that there might be and suggests there should be "stories without connection, but with association, like dreams—poems merely euphonious and full of beautiful words, but without sense and connection. At most, single stanzas would be comprehensible. They must be only fragments of the most diverse things. At most, true poetry can have a broad allegorical meaning and an indirect effect like music." [19] Might poetry, he asks, be nothing but "inward painting and music, modified of course by the nature of the mind"? [20] This idea must not, however, be confused with the poetic music and painting in Tieck and Goethe,[21] for these poets want descriptive poetry and poetry to imitate music, while Novalis asks for a poetry that would be somehow more musical and more pictorial in the peculiar manner of poetry.[22]

This obscure idea becomes clearer when we examine in detail what Novalis thought the central genres, the fairy tale and the novel, should be. "The fairy tale is, as it were, the canon of poetry . . . everything poetic must be fairytale-like. The poet worships Chance." [23] A fairy tale, as he defines his notion of it, is actually like a dream picture without connection, an assemblage of marvelous things and events, e.g. a musical fantasy, the harmonic sequences of an Aeolian harp, or Nature herself.[24] After saying "I believe I am able to express my mood best in the fairy tale," Novalis adds ingenuously that "everything is a fairy tale," [25] since the world is obviously a mystery and a dream. The poet of fairy tales is also a prophet of the future, because in the fairy tale the original world, the world before time and history, the age of freedom, the golden age of the past, foreshadows the golden age to come.[26]

The novel (*Roman*) is only a variant of the fairy tale (*Märchen*), as Novalis' own novel *Heinrich von Ofterdingen* shows. The term *romantisch*, apparently not yet stabilized in the Schlegelian sense, is derived by Novalis from *Roman,* a "kind of fairy tale." Romantic poetics is thus the "art of making an object strange and yet familiar and attractive." [27] Since everything is strange, he can say that "nothing is more romantic than what we usually call the world and fate. We live in a colossal novel [*Roman*]." [28] The novel is also free history, as it were, the mythology of history.[29] *Romantiker* (Novalis seems to have coined the word) is used by him as synonymous with novelist.[30] The novel must be poetry through and through.[31] "Romantic," in Novalis, can assume even a mystical sense, as when a "personal God" is called a "romanticized universe" or personality the "romantic" element of the ego.[32] If we interpret these baffling shifts of meaning in the light of the whole system, "romantic" here means the essential, the truly real, what today it has become the fashion to call "existential." We see why Novalis declares the annihilation of contradiction "as perhaps the highest task of the higher logic," [33] since in his dialectics everything turns into everything else just as things do in a fairy tale. Poetry is metamorphosis in the sense in which the poem "Die Vermählung der Jahreszeiten" ("The Marriage of the Seasons") [34] prophesies the fusion of future, present, and past, spring, autumn, summer and winter, youth and age. "Philosophy is the theory of poetry. It shows what poetry is, that it is one and all." [35] The *En kai pan* of mystical pantheism is here directly invoked for poetics.

While holding such extreme monistic views, it is surprising that Novalis can make any distinctions at all and that he is quite aware of the part the rational and the linguistic play in poetry and the poetic process. Poetic creation is described as a "double activity of creating and comprehending, united in one moment; a mutual perfecting of image and concept." [36] Especially "the young poet cannot be cool, cannot be conscious enough." [37] "Nothing is more indispensable to the poet than insight into the nature of every trade, familiarity with the means to reach every goal, and presence of mind to make the most appropriate choice according to time and circumstances. Enthusiasm without understanding is useless and dangerous, and the poet will work few miracles who himself is surprised by miracles." [38] "Poetry must be practiced as a strict craft." [39] We may well imagine that Novalis felt no contradiction between this view of the poet as craftsman and his view of the poet as magician and prophet. He is both, just as a humble medieval painter would ply his craft and at the same time feel the inspiration of religion.

Novalis is also perfectly aware of the difference between "real, perfected, achieved art, working through outer organs, and imaginary art." [40] He can say, and Croce would support him, "We know something only insofar as we can express, i.e. make, it." [41] This emphasis on the union of the conscious and the unconscious and on the role of language and expression needs to be interpreted in the context of Novalis' general philosophy. Consciousness is certainly not Cartesian rationalism but rather a state which must have passed through the unconscious; it is in fact identical with "irony," which he defines as "genuine consciousness, true presence of mind." [42] This highest consciousness is not reason, ratiocination, but illumination. Similarly, language is not merely the tool of the poet's craft which he must know and cherish [43] but a world of signs and sounds,[44] of hieroglyphics, which allows us to read the great book of nature, to decipher its mysteries.[45] Words to Novalis are not general signs,[46] but "magic words," "tones," "incantations." [47] "As the garments of a saint still preserve miraculous powers, so many a word is hallowed by some sublime memory and has become almost in itself a poem. For the poet language is never too poor, but it is always too general. He needs frequently recurrent words, played out by use," [48] presumably in order to revive them, to make them over into magic words. "The world is a universal metaphor of the spirit, its symbolic image." [49] Thus Novalis can wish for a "tropology that comprises the laws of the symbolic construction of the transcendental world." [50] Language is magic, just as poetry and science are magic; they are all to "raise man above himself," reconcile him again with nature, lead him back to the golden age, transform the world into paradise. "Through poetry arise the highest sympathy and cooperation, the most intimate union of the finite and infinite." [51]

One can understand that in such a view of the world there is really no room for criticism. "Criticism of poetry is monstrous. The only possible decision (and that is difficult) is whether anything is poetry or not." [52] This is a reasonable attitude if poetry is actually divine and revelatory. At most, Novalis would admit "productive criticism," the "ability to produce the very product to be criticized." [53] But this makes the critic a poet and at the same time abolishes criticism. Actually, there is still some hope for criticism. Novalis concludes that we should

censure nothing that is human. Everything is good, but not everywhere, not always, not for everybody. In judging poems e.g. one must beware not to censure anything which, taken strictly, is not a real artistic mistake, a false tone in every connection. We should assign to every poem, as exactly as possible, its precinct, and that is enough criticism for the vanity of its author. For we must judge poems only in this respect, whether they should have a wide or narrow, near or distant, dark or bright, high or low place. Thus Schiller writes for the few, Goethe for the many. Today we have paid little attention to advising the reader how to read a poem—under what circumstances alone it can please. Every poem has its relations to all kinds of readers and diverse circumstances. It has its own environment, its own world, its own God.[54]

Criticism thus seems a strategy of finding the place of a work of art, discovering its proper readers, defining its position in the world of poetry. A book, Novalis realizes, causes thousands of sensations and activities, some determined and defined, some free. An ideal review would be a complete extract or essence of everything that can be written or said about it.[55]

In this sense Novalis wrote no review and very little criticism. But he described and defined his own relation to several authors in some detail. His judgment of Shakespeare is not unrelated to what he says of poetry. He protests against the Schlegels' emphasis on Shakespeare's artistry. After all, art in his conception belongs to nature. Shakespeare is "no calculator, no scholar"; his works, "like products of nature, bear the imprint of a thinking mind"; they are throughout full of "correspondences with the infinite structure of the universe, coincidences with later ideas, affinities with the higher powers and senses of mankind. . . . They are symbolic and ambiguous, simple and inexhaustible as these, and nothing more senseless can be said about them than to call them works of art in that limited, mechanical sense of the word." [56] Earlier, Novalis, under the influence of A. W. Schlegel's essay on *Romeo and Juliet,* saw Shakespeare in terms of unreconcilable contrasts: poetry and antipoetry; harmony and disharmony; the vulgar, low, and ugly next to the romantic, lofty, and beautiful; the real next to the fictional.[57] The history plays especially exemplify this struggle between poetry and nonpoetry.[58] But *Hamlet,* strangely enough, is called a satire on a modern civilized age, an expression of English national hatred for Denmark,[59] and Shakespeare's poems are considered similar to the prose of Cervantes and Boccaccio, quite as "elegant, pedantic, and complete." [60] Late in his short life Novalis expressed puzzlement at Shakespeare, who, he says, is darker to him than Greece. "I understand the wit of Aristophanes, but I am far from understanding that of Shakespeare. On the whole, my understanding of Shakespeare is very imperfect." [61]

Novalis necessarily felt nearer to his German contemporaries and predecessors. He worshiped Schiller as a person and as a moral force, prophesying that he would be "the educator of the coming century." [62] He endorsed his review of Bürger, finding it even too mild.[63] He made a few shrewd remarks which show that he recognized some of the limitations of the Schlegels and Tieck. But his reaction to Goethe and especially to *Wilhelm Meister* is more fully stated and most characteristic. At first he saw in *Meister* the ideal romantic novel: its philosophy and morals are romantic, everything is presented with romantic irony.[64] But then he discovered— and he wonders that he could have been blind so long—that the novel is pretentious and precious, unpoetic in the highest degree, a satire on poetry, religion, etc. It is a *Candide* directed against poetry.[65] It is throughout prosaic and modern.[66] The romantic perishes there, as well as natural poetry and the marvelous. Nature and mysticism are forgotten. Novalis, himself a nobleman, also feels resentment at what he considers its glorification of the hunt for the patent of nobility. One does not know who comes off worse, poetry or nobility, since Goethe considers poetry as belonging to nobility and nobility as belonging to poetry.[67] In contradistinction to the Schlegels, who had exalted *Wilhelm Meister* as *the* romantic novel, Novalis feels its prosiness, its Philistinism, its snobbishness. It is "odious," even "silly" (*albern*). His own *Heinrich von Ofterdingen* was, in effect, written against this. It is an apotheosis of poetry,[68] which celebrates the union with the universe, with nature, with the one and the all, with death and the dream:

Die Welt wird Traum, der Traum wird Welt.[69]

WACKENRODER AND TIECK

Wilhelm Heinrich Wackenroder (1773–98) and his friend Ludwig Tieck (1773–1853) are usually associated with Novalis, but their aesthetic thought and intellectual background were actually very different. Novalis stems from Hemsterhuis, Schiller, and Schelling. Wackenroder derives from Hamann and Herder. Tieck is an eclectic who reflects, almost year by year, the aesthetic theories of his contemporaries, beginning with Wackenroder and ending with a long attachment to the theories of his friend Solger.

Wackenroder was hardly a *literary* critic. One could collect some literary opinions from his correspondence or note the rather severely critical paper on Hans Sachs's plays which he wrote for one of the first antiquarian historians of German literature, Erduin Julius Koch. But the aesthetic theories propounded in *Herzens-ergiessungen eines kunstliebenden Klosterbruders* (1797) and *Phantasien über die Kunst* (1799), though ostensibly devoted to painting or music, are nevertheless relevant, because in them Wackenroder expresses his attitude toward art in general and his own art in particular, under the mask of his "art-loving lay brother" and the musician Joseph Berglinger. His view of art and indeed the whole tone of his writing are too important and novel to be ignored in a history of criticism.

Clearly Wackenroder thinks of art primarily as serving religion, as being a religion, as being revelation. All good artists are inspired, they wait and pray for "immediate Divine assistance." [1] In his naive style Wackenroder tells a story of Raphael, to whom, in a dream, the finished picture of the Madonna appeared; when he awoke he was able to copy it from memory. In support of this invention Wackenroder quotes an actual letter by Raphael to Castiglione in which he said that "in the absence of beautiful women, he availed himself of a certain idea which came to his mind." But Wackenroder, ignoring the fact that Raphael was not speaking of the Madonna but of Galatea,[2] translates "idea" as "Bild" and "mente" as "Seele," and thus gives the neo-Platonic passage about an internal idea the quite unwarranted interpretation of a "dream picture."

Art as divine inspiration is one of the two languages of God; the other is nature. "Art speaks to man through images and uses thus a writing in hieroglyphics, whose signs we know and understand externally. But art fuses the spiritual and the non-sensual into visible shapes." Art and Nature "move together our senses and our spirit; or rather, it is as if all parts of our incomprehensible being

would melt into a single new organ, which grasps and comprehends the heavenly miracles in this double fashion." [3] Ciphers,
the double language of nature and art—these are ideas which
we met before in Hamann but which appear in Wackenroder in a
new context and with a new sentimental fervor. For the same
idea he can also use the neo-Platonic and Leibnizian image of
nature and art as "two magic concave mirrors . . . which for
me reflect all things in the world symbolically, through whose
magic pictures I learn to know and understand the true spirit of
all things." [4] Ostensibly, in this conception of art, poetry is excluded, since "words" are expressly disparaged. "It is only the
Invisible hovering above us that words do not draw down into
our minds." [5] But surely words here must mean rational words,
everyday words, or the language of science, and not poetry, which
is one of the arts, Wackenroder's own art.

With this view of art as inspiration, the proclamation of a mysterious sign language of God, it is not surprising that Wackenroder disparages all criticism and all thought about art. "Whoever
with the divining rod of searching understanding wants to discover
what can be felt only from inside, will always discover only
thoughts about feeling and never the feeling itself. An eternal
hostile gulf is fixed between the feeling heart and the investigations
of research. Feeling can only be grasped and understood by feeling." [6] Thus there should not and cannot be any comparison between works of art. "The true touchstone of the excellence of a
work of art is if one forgets all other works because of it, and not
even thinks of wanting to compare it with others." [7]

If works of art cannot be compared, because all genuine works
show the same quality of inspiration, universal toleration must be
the consequence. While Wackenroder is usually classed as the in-
spirer of artistic medievalism and the movement of the Nazarenes
(which began some ten years after his death in 1798), actually his
view of art is broad and eclectic: Gothic and Renaissance painting
please him equally well, as does 18th century music, and in theory
he recommends universal toleration. "To God a Gothic temple is
as pleasing as a temple of the Greeks; the crude war music of
savages is to Him just as charming a sound as artful choruses and
church songs." [8] Why damn the Middle Ages for not building like
Greece? We must "feel ourselves into" all strange beings, shed the

intolerance of the understanding. "Beauty: a marvelously strange word! First invent new words for every single artistic emotion, for every single work of art!" [9] Superstition is better than belief in a system, adoration better than dogmatism. The advantage of our age is our elevation: we stand as if on the summit of a mountain: many lands and peoples lie around us and at our feet. "Let us then enjoy this happiness and stray with serene glances over all times and peoples and let us always try to feel what is human in all their manifold feelings and works of feeling." [10] The voice of Herder speaks here again, even more fervidly: each work of art is unique, and good in its place, and we must enjoy the world of art in all its wonderful variety. There is still piety and genuine humanistic fervor in Wackenroder. It was in later historicism and eclectic antiquarianism that they disappeared.

Since art consists in inspiration from above and the communication of emotion, no place is left in it for technique or craft. Joseph Berglinger, the musician who had felt its inspiration like a divine intoxication (the more potent the darker and more mysterious its language), is indignant when he discovers that art is craft, that all melodies are based on a single mathematical law, that "instead of flying freely" he "had to climb around in the clumsy scaffolding and cage of the grammar of art" and learn its laborious mechanics.[11]

Wackenroder thus feels, perhaps more strongly than any of his contemporaries, the alienation of the artist from society and the conflict between art and life, poetry and prose, reality and dream. Berglinger perishes in this conflict "between ethereal enthusiasm and the low misery of the earth." [12] He gradually comes to accept "the idea that an artist must be artist only for himself, for the exaltation of his own heart and for one or a few people who understand him." [13] But we must not forget that Wackenroder puts these sentiments into the mouth of a fictional figure, that he himself feels a certain distance to them, and that he sees the human deficiency of those who feel so strongly the gulf between reality and art. Berglinger (and possibly this was Wackenroder's bitter self-criticism of his own limitations) was one of those created rather to "enjoy art than to practice it." [14] There is, Wackenroder recognizes, a difference between *Phantasie* and the incomprehensible creative power of the greatest artists. Berglinger perishes in this conflict with the world: he is the "divided" artist, ambitious and finally frustrated and impotent, the precursor of Kapellmeister Kreisler in E. T. A. Hoffmann's stories. The ideal artists are Dürer or Raphael, men who lived humbly in the service of their Maker, in a time when enthusiasm for art and divine inspiration were general, when art and religion were identical, one life-giving stream.[15]

In the last chapters Wackenroder wrote for the *Phantasien über die Kunst,* shortly before his death in his twenty-sixth year, a perceptible change in his view of art may be observed. His early religious piety and trust seem to have deserted him. He now doubts whether our feelings, "sometimes so sublime and grand that we enclose them like relics in costly monstrances, and joyfully kneel before them," really come from our Creator, or whether we are not selfishly adoring our own heart.[16] Poetry (*Dichtung*) is now, by a fanciful etymology common at the time, the art of condensing the emotions (*Verdichten*) which wander forlornly in life. Art in general is the preservation of feelings, with no hint of any metaphysical significance. At most, art is something stable in the incessant, monotonous alternation of days and nights, in that "uninterrupted, queer chess game of white and black squares, in which no one finally wins but grievous Death." [17]

Art lends us a helping hand; it keeps us hovering over the vast, empty abyss, suspended between heaven and earth. Art, the "Oriental Legend of a Naked Saint" [18] suggests, is the way to salvation from the incessant deafening roar of the wheel of Time, which the saint had to imitate compulsively with ecstatic mad gestures until he was freed by the sounds of a song. This saint's legend seems almost to anticipate Schopenhauer, who celebrated the effect of art in "stopping the wheel of Ixion" and temporarily and illusorily alleviating the pain of existence. But this hope of salvation through art, especially through music, through its "criminal innocence, its terrible, oracular ambiguous obscurity" [19] has now a desperate sound, far different from the cheerful piety of Wackenroder's early German artists. Wackenroder died too soon to elaborate his new point of view. Only his identification of religion and art, his simple trust in inspiration and genuine feeling, his sense of the divorce between art and life, of the artist's solitude in an unfriendly society, are remembered today.

Ludwig Tieck is usually considered the head of the German romantic school. As critic he cannot, however, be ranked with the Schlegels. His mind was too loose, too incoherent to contribute to a theory of literature; his taste, though well-defined, was rarely expounded in arguments substantial enough to make him a good practical critic. His work as a literary scholar, however meritorious at its time and place, is now hopelessly obsolete. It would be easy to dismiss him on all three counts. Yet something can be said for Tieck as a critic.

Tieck is an eclectic who reflects the influences of his time and of his friends. He passed through several fairly distinct stages: an early preparatory period which reflects his reading in English aesthetics and in Herder; a period (mainly between 1797–99) in which he adopts his friend Wackenroder's religion of art; a later period (mainly between 1800–03) which shows the influence of the Schlegels; and then, after a pause, a new period (after about 1810) when he accepts the guidance of his friend F. W. Solger.[20] We can trace all the key concepts of the time in Tieck's writings, though they are used uncertainly and shiftingly. For example, he oscillates disconcertingly between a conception of "genius" as pure inspiration and a Schlegelian stress on the share of consciousness in creation.[21] So "irony," which Tieck employed profusely and originally in his satirical comedies, is used in his critical writings sparingly and vaguely. Only much later, under the influence of Solger, does Tieck arrive at distinctions between "lower" and "higher," and "positive" and "negative" irony. He then condemns "vulgar" irony and accepts an interpretation which makes it identical with objectivity, with the poet's power over his material.[22] Tieck did much to popularize the term "romantic," but he himself used it quite loosely, in the old sense of anything marvelous or medieval. Late in life he insisted that all poetry since antiquity is "romantic" and that it is impossible to draw a distinction between the "romantic" and the "poetic." [23] Clearly, not much in the way of theory can be learned from Tieck.

In Tieck's many writings we can find, of course, a mass of literary opinions: indeed much of his fiction and drama is literary satire and parody, against the group of surviving rationalists in Berlin, against the tremendously successful playwrights, Kotzebue and Iffland, against many of his fellow romanticists, and late in his

life against the Young Germans. From his last years we have recorded conversations in which Tieck pronounces on almost every
writer of world literature.[24] But little of this is elaborated and
substantiated, analyzed and argued. It is merely stated, for Tieck
wants criticism to convey an immediate feeling of his personality.[25]

The mass of editorial labors, translations from Elizabethan
dramatists, the translation of *Don Quixote,* the collaboration and
supervision of the German Shakespeare, after August Wilhelm
Schlegel had given it up—all this has only historical interest today. Research has shown that Tieck's translations and revisions
are often grossly inaccurate.[26] Today we would have no sympathy
for his enthusiasm for the Shakespearean *apocrypha.* At one time,
at least, Tieck took the extravagant position of assigning as many
as 62 plays to Shakespeare. The English who did not agree only
earned his scorn: they had not read Shakespeare "in his context." [27]
His praise of such plays as the *Pinner of Wakefield* or *Locrine*
seems especially extravagant, since he thought Marlowe and Webster overrated. But he praised and analyzed Middleton's *Change-
ling* and was an admirer and close student of Ben Jonson.[28]

However, nothing came of Tieck's great book on Shakespeare,
which he had worked on all his life. What has been published as
its remains, in 1920, is no more than a pathetic heap of notes,
annotations, and remarks, most of which date back to about 1794.
The two chapters of an introduction (1815) contain merely general reflections on the Middle Ages, Christianity, chivalry, etc. The
theory behind the project was the historical approach: not to look
at Shakespeare as an "isolated phenomenon" but to "deduce him
from his time and environment and especially his own mind." [29]

Of his published papers on Shakespeare the earliest one, written
when he was only twenty, "Shakespeare's Treatment of the
Marvelous" (1793), is critically the most interesting. It is an excellent exercise in psychological criticism in the English manner.
Tieck knows that Shakespeare is interested in theatrical effect, in
creating illusion. He shows how this is achieved in different ways
in comedies such as the *Tempest* and *Midsummer Night's Dream*
and in tragedies such as *Hamlet* and *Macbeth.* In the "romantic"
plays a whole consistent world of the marvelous is evoked, while
all powerful emotions are toned down in order not to disturb the

illusion. In the tragedies the spirit world appears more remotely
in the background and hence much more mysteriously and fright-
eningly. The paper shows traces of 18th-century rationalistic mis-
conceptions: Shakespeare's handling of the marvelous is thought
to be an attempt at hiding the lack of rules, at making us forget
the laws of aesthetics. Hamlet seeing the ghost in the closet scene
or Macbeth seeing Banquo's ghost at the banquet is action supposedly capable of natural explanation, of an allegorical sense.[30]
Yet on the whole the piece is full of sensitive observations and is
surely superior to earlier discussions of the same topic by Mrs.
Montagu and Joseph Warton. Compared with it, Tieck's next
published piece, "Letters on Shakespeare" (1800), is rambling and
diffuse. He announces bardolatry on principle: one cannot criticize a work of art, just as one cannot scold nature. He boasts that
nobody before him, certainly no "printed Englishman," has understood Shakespeare, but he says little that is concrete beyond praising the advantages of Shakespeare's age (familiar since Hurd and
Thomas Warton), the variety of Shakespeare's plays, and the freedom imagination was allowed by the physical make-up of the Elizabethan theater.[31]

Tieck was intensely occupied with the revival of Elizabethan
stagecraft. He directed performances purged of the usual 19th-
century encumbrances; and in a late novel, *Der junge Tischler-
meister* (1837), he described in great detail a fictional amateur performance of *Twelfth Night*, with close attention to the staging in
Elizabethan style.[32] There is much other evidence for Tieck's grasp,
rare among his contemporaries, of Shakespeare as man of the
theater, and of the art of acting. From his visit to London in 1817
we have shrewd criticisms of John Phillip Kemble, Macready, and
Kean.[33] But one can only doubt Tieck's profound understanding
of Shakespeare if one reads his paradoxical theories of Shakespeare's characters: Lady Macbeth is called a "delicate and loving
soul," King Claudius is defended and praised as a ruler and as a
strong character, Polonius is called a "true statesman," Hamlet's
behavior to Ophelia is explained by her supposed pregnancy, and
the monologue "To be or not to be" is argued *not* to be about
suicide.[34]

Tieck's failure as a Shakespeare critic seems most clearly demonstrated by the novel *Dichterleben* (1825, 1829), in which Shake-

speare, Greene, Marlowe, Nashe, Florio, the Earl of Southampton, the Dark Lady of the Sonnets, etc. appear as fictional figures. The book is curious for being one of the earliest novelistic treatments of the death of Marlowe and of the triangle between Shakespeare, Southampton, and the Dark Lady. As a picture of Elizabethan England, however, it is incredibly sentimental and false. It has no historical accuracy or atmosphere and little narrative interest. Southampton recites "This royal throne of Kings, this sceptered isle" to the tearful father of Shakespeare, and Shakespeare, a sentimental weakling, talks like a German romanticist: through writing *Romeo and Juliet* he feels himself "created" and his "own essence brought to life." [35]

Likewise, Tieck's interest in Spanish literature leaves us with a similar sense of disappointment. There is hardly any criticism of Cervantes in Tieck's writings, though he translated *Don Quixote* and suggested that his daughter translate *Persiles* (1837). Only his defense of the insertion of the novella "El Curioso Impertinente" may be quoted as an illustration of the Schlegelian method of finding organic unity in a great work at all costs. He sees it as an illustration of the destructive folly of a man who wants his ideal verified, contrasting with Don Quixote's own unperturbed illusionism. [36]

Tieck was the first German deeply interested in Calderón, and was the first to imitate his meters and devices in German drama. He infected August Wilhelm Schlegel with his enthusiasm; but when Schlegel's translation created a vogue of Calderón in Germany, Tieck moderated his earlier admiration. He saw in Calderón contrivance, rigid conventionality, bombast, and cruelty, and developed an opposing interest in the more realistic Lope de Vega, questioning whether he is not the greater poet of the two. [37] Tieck also knew many of the other less known Spanish dramatists of the Golden Age: Moreto, Rojas, Montalván, etc. and engaged in erudite researches which today would be called "comparative literature." [38]

Tieck also played a certain role in the revival of older German literature. In 1803 he brought out a badly modernized collection of *Minnelieder*. Its introduction proved very influential. Jakob Grimm tells us that he caught his enthusiasm for the study of German antiquities from it. It is, however, no monument of erudition, but rather a popular rehearsal of some of the Schlegels' opinions. It tells us that there is only one poetry, one art. He praises his age for understanding all kinds of poetry, Shakespeare, the Italians, and the Spaniards. He paints a sentimental picture of chivalry and courtly love and describes the 12th and 13th centuries as the great age of the flowering of "romantic" poetry. As for the German *Minnesang* itself, Tieck has hardly anything to say beyond commending the poems for their sweet sound, skillful rhyme schemes, and naiveté.[39]

Furthermore, Tieck initiated the study of the early German drama by publishing a collection, *Deutsches Theater* (1817), which reprinted for the first time the 16th century dramatist Jakob Ayrer, some plays of the English comedians, and dramas of Andreas Gryphius.

But all these activities are completely overshadowed, in critical importance, by Tieck's editions of Lenz, Novalis, and Heinrich von Kleist,[40] and by his discussions of Goethe, in which a coherent and original taste emerges. Tieck has a strong feeling in favor of the German Storm and Stress and the early Goethe. He greatly prefers the young Goethe to the later: *Goetz von Berlichingen* and *Werther* are extolled. Still, his whole attitude even to the early Goethe is by no means uncritical. He emphasizes the weakness of Goethe's fictional protagonists. Even Faust is passive in his relation to Gretchen. Goethe's plays are undramatic, he has no historical sense, and is not a good critic: especially his Shakespeare criticism finds no favor with Tieck. Goethe's later classicism seems to Tieck an aberration. The association with Schiller was detrimental to both. Tieck finds the second part of *Faust* repellent and he has no use for Goethe's other writings. Yet he interprets the early Goethe with sympathy and insight. To him Goethe is the problematic artist, not unlike Goethe's own Tasso or Goethe's friend Lenz or Kleist, in their revolt against society and in their nearness to madness and suicide.[41] Thus Tieck could edit the writings of the then almost forgotten Lenz, though he made no claims for his greatness and recognized that he was a mere caricature of Goethe.[42] The same fellow feeling attracted him also to Kleist, whom he had barely met during his lifetime but whose writings he rescued and published. To modern Kleist enthusiasts the introductory essay on Kleist will appear vague in its biographical information and excessively cool in its appreciation of the works. Tieck's interest is clearly psychological and personal. He is attracted by the "dark force" inside Kleist which destroyed him and by his "sudden, baffling desire to leap over both truth and nature and to put the empty and nothing above reality." He likes in Kleist's writings the German historical element and the romantic fairy tale touches; but he is repelled by the mystical and bizarre and can see in Kleist, ultimately, only a "sublime mannerist." [43] The same interest in the *poète maudit* accounts for Tieck's sympathy for Grabbe, for whose *Herzog von Gothland* he wrote an introduction and whom he tried to help personally.[44] It was inevitable that Tieck should prefer the *Robbers* to all the other plays of Schiller and that he condemn his later development, especially the *Bride of Messina,* for its contrived classicism, its operatic lyricism, and its conception of irrational fate. Schiller, who founded the German stage, was also, in Tieck's eyes, the first to destroy it.[45]

Later in his life Tieck tried to forget his romantic past. He wrote to Friedrich Schlegel that he had "no pleasure in all the things we have instigated." He resented being considered the "head of the so-called romantic school." [46] He judged his own younger contemporaries severely and unsympathetically: Brentano and his sister Bettina seemed to him histrionic and insincere, E. T. A. Hoffmann a writer of mere grotesques, a "scribbler." [47] Tieck also had no use for Young Germany, whose political radicalism went against his grain. In speaking of Heine he gave vent to his anti-Semitism; but he also thought him only a poor imitator of Goethe and complained of his impertinence, vulgar irony, and monotony.[48]

In all of Tieck's criticism the discussions of Goethe, Lenz, and Kleist have the most personal tone. They suggest that Tieck was profoundly involved in the problem of the artist in society, in the danger of poetry to a poet's mental health. Personally Tieck had escaped the danger and could interpret his own evolution as one toward sanity and truth. At the same time he preserved an interest and sympathy for the artist "at the brink" of the abyss, since as a young man he had experienced this feeling on his own pulses. Now, in retrospect, knowing his studies of his fellow artists, the young Goethe, Lenz, and Kleist, we can find added interest in scattered pronouncements of the early Tieck which occur in a fictional context and yet are revealing, not only biographically but also critically, as extreme formulations of problems and ideas which only much later received systematic discussion. Freud could not have stated more clearly the association of art and lust than did Tieck in his early novel *William Lovell* (1796). "Poetry, art, and even devotion are only disguised hidden lust . . . sensuality and lust are the spirit of music, of painting and of all art . . . the feelings for beauty and art are only other dialects and ways of pronunciation; they mean nothing beyond man's urge for sensual pleasure." [49] In *Dichterleben* Marlowe, the artist who suffers shipwreck because he could not restrain himself, says the same thing, associating poetry with lust and cruelty, with the desire "both to create and to destroy." Now, however, Tieck rejects this view. His spokesman, Shakespeare, denies that it is true of the highest poetry and talks romantically and conventionally of the "desire for the Invisible," the union of "the eternal with the earthly." [50]

The early Tieck, contributing to Wackenroder's *Phantasien,* found the formula for the most extreme aestheticism, both its dangers and attractions. He wants us to "change our life into a work of art." The artist is an actor who looks on life as on a part to play. He has no firm convictions. He knows that art is a "seductive, forbidden fruit; whoever has once tasted its innermost, sweetest juice, is irrevocably lost to the active, living world. . . . And in the middle of the tumult he sits quietly like a child in its baby chair and blows compositions into the air like soap bubbles." [51] This is Tieck speaking through a fictional mask; yet he is speaking his own deepest mind, characterizing himself and what he feels to be the curse and plight of the artist. Even death should appear as part of a work of art. "Oh you weak, fragile human life! I want always to consider you as a work of art, which delights me and which must have a conclusion in order to be a work of art and to delight me. Then I shall always be content, then I shall be equally far removed from vulgar joy and oppressive melancholy." [52]

Tieck himself had the actor's temperament, the gift of mimicry, the plastic impersonality which made Brentano say that he was "the greatest acting talent who *never* trod the stage." [53] Tieck himself recognized this trait in his character, saying, "I am the more an individual the more I can lose myself in everything." He even admitted that he would act out ideas for a whole year before he actually came to believe them. At times his talent along with his love for poetry seemed to him the most evil thing in him, which might destroy him completely.[54] He is afraid of the dream world which he has tapped in his writings, of the eerie world of the *Blonde Eckbert,* the *Runenberg,* and *Pokal.*[55] Tieck himself escaped into historical realism and irony. But he preserved a taste for the problematical, broken, and antisocial artist, which is only imperfectly overlaid with admiration for the versatility, sanity, and impersonality of Shakespeare. Tieck was no metaphysician like Friedrich Schlegel, no mystic like Novalis, no theorist like August Wilhelm Schlegel. But he contributed importantly to a description and criticism of the romantic artist.

JEAN PAUL

Jean Paul (Johann Paul Richter, 1763–1825) is the author of an *Introduction to Aesthetics* (*Vorschule der Aesthetik,* 1804) which deserves attention in our history, since it is not an aesthetics but rather a poetics or, more correctly, a series of chapters on aspects of literary theory: poetry in general, imagination, genius, Greek and romantic poetry, the comic, humor and wit, characters and plot, the novel and style. Though the book is written in a florid, highly metaphorical style, full of recondite comparisons and allusions and unending displays of pedantic wit, it propounds a sane theory of literature and adds something new and personal on questions rarely discussed at that time: the technique of the novel, characterization and motivation, and the theory of the comic, humor, and wit.

It is not easy to define Jean Paul's general position. He is very satirical about Schelling and the Schellingians, "polarization," "the indifference of the subjective and objective pole," and so on.[1] He attacks the Schlegels for their Fichtean idealism (which to Jean Paul was pernicious solipsism and egoism), their violent partisanship, their self-conceit, and their limited, exclusive taste; [2] he has little use for Schiller's aesthetics, which he considers formalistic and frivolous, misunderstanding the play concept.[3] His personal and philosophical associations were with Herder and F. H. Jacobi. At times we might think that Jean Paul was simply a good 18th-century empirical psychologist: he could even say that Kames's *Ele-*

ments of Criticism is of a "higher critical school than the high one at Jena," i.e. Schiller and the Schlegels.[4] The avowed purpose of his book is, in part at least, self-analysis and self-observation in a very concrete way. Jean Paul has most to say about the kind of novel he was writing himself: the sprawling humorous romance, his own strange mixture of the fantastic, dreamy, and sentimental with the odd and grotesque.

But while Jean Paul preserved a considerable independence among the literary parties of the time and also his ties with an earlier past, he agreed with the romantics on fundamental issues of poetics. In spite of his reservations against the Schlegels and Schelling, his main position is the same: the proclamation in the preface to the first edition that "the newer school is right in the main"[5] must be taken as final. Not only is Jean Paul dependent on Friedrich Schlegel for a number of specific points,* but their basic views of poetry are identical. Though Jean Paul tried to keep a dispassionate balance between the classical and romantic in his theory, there cannot be any doubt where his preference lay in practice. But as opposed to the Schlegels he kept his admiration for the English humorous novel of the 18th century, for Richardson, Sterne, Fielding, and even Smollett, from whom his own art, at least in part, was derived.

Poetry, Jean Paul argues, does not imitate reality, nor is it a pure expression of personal emotion. Naturalistic art is attacked as "materialism"; too lyrical, emotional, or thinly fantastic art is labeled "nihilism." The one is too particular, the other too general. Art should be the union of the particular and the general.[6] It does not copy and it must not annihilate the world. Rather it should decipher its mysterious language. Thus poetry cannot be teaching. It offers signs. "The whole world, all time is full of signs; the reading of the letters is what is missing; we need a dictionary and a grammar of the signs; poetry teaches reading."[7] In interpreting the world in its own terms, poetry creates a miniature world, a second world, reborn by mind.[8]

The poet achieves this interpretation by imagination. Like Schelling and August Wilhelm Schlegel, Jean Paul distinguishes

* E.g. *Sämtliche Werke,* ed. Berend, *11,* 113–4, 233, 56–7, 157, 215. Jean Paul e.g. endorses Friedrich Schlegel's saying that all poetry must be romantic; *SW, 11,* 113; cf. Friedrich Schlegel, fragment 116.

between the lower power he calls "Einbildungskraft," which is only a more powerful, more vivid memory, and the higher "Phantasie" or "Bildungskraft," which makes all parts a whole, which "totalizes everything." [9] The great poet has genius which Jean Paul distinguishes sharply from mere talent. Talent is partial, genius requires the whole man: "all his powers are in bloom at the same time." [10] He depicts all life, not merely its parts. He draws on the unconscious, which is the mightiest power in a poet, since poetry is kindred to dreaming and dreaming is involuntary poetry.[11] The poet must *hear* his characters, not merely *see* them: the character must tell him—as happens in a dream—what he has to say, not the poet the character. "A poet who has to reflect whether a character in a specific situation is to answer yes or no should discard him. He is a stupid corpse." [12] But while Jean Paul at times can speak of genius as if it were identical with instinct and writing identical with dreaming, he also stresses the role of consciousness in the creative process. He draws a doubtful distinction between the whole as produced by inspiration and the parts which can be "cultivated in peace." [13] Jean Paul very emphatically rejects the "fever of passion" as poor inspiration and constantly insists that all art is and should be self-conscious.[14] He himself prominently used the theme of the "double" in his novels, as he had a vivid consciousness of man seeing himself, doubling, splitting up into two egos, the one acting, the other observing. In his novels a man is terrified by his own image in a mirror, meets his double, makes his wax figure, looks at his own body and asks: "Somebody is sitting there and I am in him. Who is that?" [15] So also in his poetic theory he feels the dualism between the dream life on which he draws and the transformation accomplished by art, which cannot be anything but a conscious manipulation of language. A novelty in Jean Paul's discussion of genius and talent is his recognition of an intermediate type: the "passive" genius, the feminine man who lacks the true creativity of the greatest but is as universal as genius himself. Jean Paul gives Moritz and Novalis as examples.[16] Similarly, while consciousness is necessary to the artist, there is also a "sinful" consciousness which destroys and dissolves the world of imagination and the instinct of the unconscious.[17]

From the Schlegels Jean Paul draws the main division of poetry into classical and romantic. But Jean Paul avoids the term "classical," as he associates it with excellence and perfection of every kind. He prefers to speak of Greek or plastic poetry in contrast to romantic or musical poetry.[18] The fervid hymn to Greece and the Greeks, "this beauty-intoxicated people with their serene religion in eye and heart," [19] the view of Greek poetry as sculpturesque, objective, morally graceful, joyfully peaceful, is not new to readers of Winckelmann and Friedrich Schlegel's earliest writings, but it is surprising in Jean Paul, who had nothing of the Greek spirit. In him the nostalgia for Greece seems an even more romantic dream than in the other Germans, for surely there were few less serene and objective minds than his. Romantic poetry is described as the direct result of Christianity, from which chivalry and courtly love are derived. "A Petrarch who would not be a Christian is an impossibility: Mary alone ennobles all women romantically." [20] In the second edition of *Vorschule* (1813) Jean Paul, in response to criticisms, somewhat modified his account of the Christian romantic: he now recognizes that there are romantic traits in Homer and Sophocles,[21] long before Christ, and that there is a Nordic, Indic, and Near Eastern romanticism which is based on their non-Christian religions. He now adds also the distinction between the romanticism of the North and that of the South, in line with concepts elaborated by Bouterwek and Madame de Staël. Surveying modern poetry, he observes sensibly that "every century is differently romantic." [22] He even doubts the value of all such dichotomies; it is as if we divided all nature into straight and crooked lines. The crooked, he observes slyly, as well as the infinite line, is romantic poetry. But what can one gain for the understanding of "dynamic life" from such distinctions? Naive and sentimental, subjective and objective do not help us to distinguish between the different romanticism of Shakespeare, Petrarch, Ariosto, and Cervantes, or the different objectivity of Homer, Sophocles, Job, and Caesar.[23]

The distinction between the genres is handled by Jean Paul with a like measure of levity. In the first edition he has nothing to say about the lyric. In the second edition he adds a meager section on the lyric, where he makes, in passing, the fateful suggestion that "the epic presents an event which develops from the past, the drama an action which extends into the future, the lyric an emotion which is enclosed in the present." [24] This association of the main genres with the dimensions of time and tense has since caught the fancy of many writers on poetics from Dallas to Staiger.[25] But Jean Paul elsewhere ignores it and even contradicts it when he associates epic with the past and drama with the present.[26] In practice he distinguishes the epic and the drama but at length discusses the novel, which to him holds an intermediate position between the two. He can thus distinguish an epic novel from a dramatic novel: the epic novel includes the romantic novel, which is similar to a dream or a fairy tale and thus needs no beginning or end and allows any number of episodes (as does the epic in the Schlegels' theory). The dramatic novel is more closely plotted and seems to Jean Paul the preferable form. But on the whole Jean Paul thinks of the novel as some kind of "poetic encyclopedia," a genre allowing great freedom.[27]

Plot and motivation, in comparison to character, are minimized. Plot assumes meaning only in terms of character and is thought of as following the invention of character. Motivation is considered dangerous if over-rigid and excessive. Jean Paul sees many relations between plot, motivation, and character. For instance, he points out that very rigid characters are not good for a novel because they decide every action beforehand and thus make it predictable, while purely passive characters do even more damage because they shift the burden to the plot, which then disintegrates easily into a series of chance events.[28] In discussing characters Jean Paul applies his ideal of the union of the particular and universal: every humorous character, even a Walter Shandy and Uncle Toby, must have something to make him universal and symbolic, and every universal character must be individualized to become a speaking and memorable figure. Still, Jean Paul defends perfect, idealized characters, though they may be very difficult to handle, since generality increases with ideality.[29] Yet the poet must depict a complete world, a pandemonium and a pantheon, both his particular devils and his particular angels.[30] He must depict the gamut of human types, the "races of the inner man," the "mythology of souls," [31] in order to create his second world. Jean Paul argues that poets need not know these situations and characters in real life; in each man there are all forms of humanity and the poet knows them as if by anticipation; he knows both Caliban and Ariel. The reader will find the characters true and right, even though he could not have met them in real life, since it is the poet who gives speech and awareness to humanity.[32] Each character, Jean Paul pleads, needs a *punctum saliens,* a "dominant tone," though he admits that a great poet can convincingly reconcile the most discordant traits.[33] Characters should have "rootwords," their own vocabulary, but they should also be characterized by physical traits—sometimes only one physical trait—and even by their names.[34] Jean Paul must have been one of the first novelists to reflect at length on the naming of novelistic figures. His standards of judgment, of course, are never those of verisimilitude and sheer illusion. He allows the novelist to endow his characters with his own wit and imagination, even though they should speak their own language of will and passion.[35] Some of these distinctions seem not very convincing or at most seem confined to very specific types of the novel. Also, Jean Paul's observations on style are often little more than defenses of his own practice: he prefers "optic" to "acoustic" figures, defends catachresis and rhythmic prose, and, of course, loves puns and learned allusions, since verbal art is closely related to wit and wit to imagination.[36]

In many ways the sections devoted to wit, humor, and the comic are the most original in the *Vorschule.* They were among the first attempts to deal with these concepts speculatively in the context of a poetics and have proved extraordinarily influential. F. T. Vischer's discussion comes from Jean Paul; Coleridge reproduced his views; and Meredith used him.[37] But while one must grant the historical merit of Jean Paul's classifications and the ingenuity of some of his formulas, it seems impossible to be satisfied with his distinctions today. One reason for Jean Paul's failure is his lack of clear distinction between psychology and poetics. Definitions of the comic, the witty, the humorous can be simply a matter of descriptive psychology, just like definitions of love, hate, joy, despair, or any other emotion.[38] The question becomes aesthetic only if it is centered on the use to which the comic or the humorous is put in a work of art, or on its function in particular forms such as comedy or satire, or on the ways it defines the pervasive attitude of a particular author. Jean Paul does not draw these distinctions but rather tries elaborately to describe the varieties of the comic, interpreting the words to make their meaning conform with his ideals.

Thus "wit" for Jean Paul is a psychic power entirely apart from the comic. Wit is the discovery of similarities between incommensurable entities.[39] Jean Paul distinguishes then between a wit of understanding and a graphic, visual wit. Graphic wit is important in art: it can either animate a body or embody a soul.[40] It is thus the metaphorical power in general, the poetic power itself, which is in the service of the symbolic view of the world. Puns thus can be defended as a technique for discovering remote similarities, producing surprise by coincidences and "wild pairings without priest," [41] and also (an interesting point) for displaying our freedom from subservience to the sign by drawing attention to the sign itself.[42] Wit is a great liberator and equalizer. Jean Paul writes eloquently how necessary it is for the Germans to cultivate wit, since wit would give them freedom and equality just as these would give them wit.[43] Wit is thus basic to poetry and needed in a healthy and free society. But it can do these things only because Jean Paul does not distinguish between social wit and wit in literature. The term is conceived in psychological and linguistic and not in aesthetic terms. Wit is completely divorced from the comic and so becomes hardly distinguishable (in spite of Jean Paul's efforts) from "ingenuity," "acumen," and even "invention," with which the term has been associated historically. If wit and ingenuity were the same, works of great combinatory power such as the *Critique of Pure Reason* would be witty.

The comic is likewise seen as a general phenomenon of life, but here Jean Paul gets involved in metaphysics. The comic is "sensually intuited infinite Unreason"; there is an "objective contrast between the striving or being of the ludicrous beings with the sensuously intuited relation"; [44] and there is also a subjective contrast which Jean Paul explains by a "lending" of our insight to the subject, the ludicrous being. To note Jean Paul's example: Why is it comic that Sancho Panza spends a whole night suspended over a shallow ditch? His action is not unreasonable because he could not know that there was no deep abyss and sensibly enough did not want to risk a fatal drop. Still, "lending our insight" to Sancho Panza does not describe what actually happens. If we "lent" our knowledge to Sancho his action would be merely absurd and silly.[45] Besides, even if "imputation"—a term later taken up by Vischer and Lipps [46]—occurs, it seems unable to account for all the varieties of the comic. Nonetheless, Jean Paul is surely right in rejecting Hobbes's (and implicitly Bergson's) theory of laughter as derived from a feeling of superiority, a "sudden glory." * He knows that laughter may be childish and good-natured; we do not mind if hundreds and thousands laugh with us.

Though examples are drawn from literature, the question of the comic is not focused on its aesthetic use. It is different with humor, a more narrowly definable phenomenon which Jean Paul was able to describe in terms of artistic values. He starts with Kantian concepts; humor is for him a species of the comic, the romantic comic. It is the "sublime in reverse," it does not "annihilate the individual, but rather the finite by contrast with the Idea. Humor knows no individual foolishness, no fools [as in satire] but only folly and a mad world." [47] Jean Paul here brings to a climax the evolution which this term had been previously undergoing in England. At first "humor" was associated with "humors," with oddities, "humorous characters," riders of hobby horses. Only in the 18th century did it begin to take on a serious or sentimental undertone.† With Jean Paul it becomes a peculiar form of the comic in which a philosophy of toleration, a serious conception of the world, is implied: an insight into its contradictions and a forgiveness for its follies. Jean Paul's humor is closely allied to hypochondria. The most serious, the most melancholy nation, the English, are the most humorous, and the most tragic times in history gave birth to the greatest humorists. As opposed to the older notion that humor is a distorted view, Jean Paul finds humor just the opposite, the largest and freest view of the world, *sub specie aeternitatis*. In the language of Schellingian metaphysics, which Jean Paul here adopts, the finite *is* here annihilated by the eternal Idea.[48]

* *Sämtliche Werke, 11*, 108. Addison, Voltaire, Beattie, and Goethe had used such arguments against Hobbes. For a modern statement directed against Hobbes and Bergson, see Max Eastman, *Enjoyment of Laughter,* New York, 1936.

† See a history of the term in "Les Définitions de l'humour" in Fernand Baldensperger, *Études de l'histoire littéraire* (Paris, 1907), pp. 176 ff. Kames, *Elements of Criticism* (9th ed. Edinburgh, 1817), *1,* 332, says: "This quality [of humor] belongs to an author, who, affecting to be grave and serious, paints his objects in such colors as to provoke mirth and laughter." Cf. Vol. *1* of this *History*, p. 120.

Obviously, Jean Paul's concept of humor is very near that of romantic irony as elaborated by Friedrich Schlegel.[49] Jean Paul, like Schlegel, defends the complete consciousness of the humorist. He recognizes, for example, that Sterne is a highly conscious artist: he argues that conscious manipulation allows even the use of the dirty and obscene because it is neutralized by humor. Swift's Yahoos or his "Lady's Dressing-room," which shocked Thackeray, did not shock Jean Paul.[50] The clown in drama is defended as the chorus of comedy. But irony in the narrow sense is confined by Jean Paul to the "semblance of the serious" and is, in general, suspected of frivolity, cynicism, and mere aestheticism.[51] Jean Paul has a deep suspicion of aestheticism: his novel *Der Titan* (1800–1803), written just before his book on aesthetics, depicts its dangers in the demonic self-destroying figure of Rocquairol. The double consciousness of the actor and the spectator was for Jean Paul a great personal temptation against which he fought all his life.[52] His elaborate distinctions between the comic, the ironic, the witty, and the humorous serve, at least in part, to establish his own ideal, which is both aesthetic and moral, a vision of the world which sees its incongruity and folly but views it with concern and sympathy.

Jean Paul was hardly a good practical critic. It is possible, of course, to collect a mass of opinions from his varied writings about most German writers and a few foreign ones.[53] They would throw light on his general theoretical position, such as his veneration for Herder, his coolness to Schiller and Goethe, and his generous praise for many contemporaries: Tieck, Novalis, Fouqué (whom he grossly overrated), and E. T. A. Hoffmann, whom he introduced into literature but with whose later writings he seems to have been disappointed.[54] We could collect a number of appreciative remarks about the English novelists of the 18th century. Jean Paul has the usual romantic admiration for Shakespeare but condemned *Paradise Lost*.[55] His praise of Molière seems to oppose August Wilhelm Schlegel's low opinion, but he also endorses Schlegel's preference for the farces.[56] Little of all this, however, is argued or based on any analysis or characterization. Jean Paul did do some formal reviewing, but most of it is slight. The two extensive pieces on Madame de Staël's *De L'Allemagne* and *Corinne* are shrewd and penetrating. They show up her sentimentality and the superficiality of her understanding of German literature and philosophy.[57]

A feather in Jean Paul's cap was the favorable paragraph (1825) on Schopenhauer's *Welt als Wille und Vorstellung* which at the time was almost completely ignored by reviewers and public.[58] Still, one is hardly prepared for Jean Paul's high regard for practical criticism. He remarks that a collection of reviews would be of more use to an artist than the newest aesthetics. "In every good review is hidden or revealed a good aesthetics, and more than that, one that is applied and free and the briefest of all and, by examples, the clearest." [59] He can say that the best poetics would be to characterize all poets.[60] He makes some efforts of this kind, surveying, for instance, the prose style of the main German authors,[61] but the characterization itself is almost always only metaphorical, of the sort which was later called "impressionistic." It agrees with his views that the critic should only point out beauties and that criticism is only a new poetry of which the work of art is the subject.[62] It is the logical consequence of the extreme view of totality which Jean Paul formulated: "The best in every author is what is not in the particular and which cannot be shown at all, because the splendor of the context does not tolerate the pointing to a detail." [63] But this would be critical paralysis and all that we have said about Jean Paul's literary theory must have shown that it is not a mere poetry about poetry but a serious intellectual construct, the strength of which is precisely in its distinctions, definitions, and descriptions, not of authors or works but of categories and devices, of the technique of the novel, and the nature of humor.

In England, as opposed to the Continent, there was no "romantic" movement, if we limit the meaning of such a term to a conscious program and consider the precise name as crucial. Though the term "romantic" had spread to the Continent from England in the 17th century and had in England assumed the literary meaning pertaining to medieval romances and the epics (Ariosto, Tasso) descended from them, nevertheless the elaboration of the contrast between romantic and classical belongs to the Schlegels. When Coleridge used the distinction, in his 1811 lectures, he obviously derived it from A. W. Schlegel. But as these lectures were not printed at that time, the distinction was popularized in England only through Madame de Staël's *De l'Allemagne* (1813), which was published first in London and quickly appeared in an English translation. The book was widely and favorably reviewed and the distinction between classical and romantic often repeated. Madame de Staël's remarks drew attention to Schlegel, and the *Dramatic Lectures* soon appeared in an English translation by John Black (1815). Schlegel's distinctions and views were then used and quoted, especially by Hazlitt and Scott, but also by many minor writers.[1]

None of the English poets of the time, however, recognized himself as a romanticist or admitted the relevance of the debate to his own time and country. Neither Coleridge nor Hazlitt made such application. Byron definitely rejected it: though he knew and disliked Schlegel personally and had read *De l'Allemagne,* he considered the distinction "romantic-classical" as merely a Continental debate. He certainly was not conscious of belonging to the romantics. An Austrian police spy in Italy knew better. He reported that Byron belonged to the *Romantici* and had "written and continues to write poetry of this new school."[2]

The terms "a romantic," "a romanticist," "romanticism" were

used in England for the first time by Carlyle in reference to the Germans, but an English romantic school did not become established in textbooks of literary history until the 50's, obviously under Continental influence.* The absence of the terms in England, however, should not obscure the fact that English writers had early a clear awareness that there was a movement under way which rejected the critical concepts and poetic practices of the 18th century, that it formed a unity, and that it had its parallels on the Continent, especially in Germany. Without the term "romanticism" we can trace, within a short period, the shift from the earlier conception of the history of English poetry as one of a uniform progress from Waller and Denham to Dryden and Pope, still accepted in Johnson's *Lives of the Poets*, to the opposite point of view, strongly phrased in 1807 by Southey: "The time which elapsed from the days of Dryden to those of Pope is the dark age of English poetry." [3] But this was not merely the view of a revolutionary group, the little company of Wordsworth, Southey, and Coleridge. It was the concept of English literature which was accepted and welcomed also by the highly influential *Edinburgh Review* and its critical spokesman, Francis Jeffrey (1773–1850).

It is an irony of history that Jeffrey should be remembered today largely for his hostility to Wordsworth and for opening his review of the *Excursion* with the schoolmasterly "This will never do." Jeffrey is thus often considered a neoclassicist, a survival of the 18th century, or, by his defenders, a forerunner of the American neohumanists, an apostle of antiromanticism.[4] The first sentences of his review of Southey's *Thalaba* in the first number of the *Edinburgh Review* (1802) are quoted in support. "Poetry has this much, at least, in common with religion, that its standards were fixed long ago, by certain inspired writers, whose authority it is no longer lawful to call in question." [5]

But if we examine Jeffrey's concrete critical opinions we must

* "A romantic," in 1827, refers to the Italian Grossi. *Two Notebooks,* ed. C. E. Norton (New York, 1898), p. 111. "Romanticist" in 1827, in "State of German Literature"; "Romanticism" in 1831, in article on Schiller. *Works,* Centenary ed. (London, 1890), *26,* 53; *27,* 172. The OED gives much later first occurrences of these terms: for "a romantic," 1882; for "romanticist," 1830; for "romanticism," 1844. On textbooks see article quoted in note 1.

conclude that this is quite misleading. Actually he disparaged English neoclassicism as much as did Southey. He gives a picture of the age which would satisfy the most extreme romanticist. Its poets "had no force or greatness of fancy—no pathos, and no enthusiasm. . . . They are sagacious, no doubt, neat, clear, and reasonable; but for the most part cold, timid and superficial. They never meddle with the great scenes of nature, or the great passions of man. . . . Their inspiration, accordingly, is little more than a sprightly sort of good sense; and they have scarcely any invention but what is subservient to the purposes of derision and satire." [6] Dryden is censured for his lack of pathos and his "brutal obscenities," Addison and Swift for the "tameness and poorness" of their serious style. Swift, in general, is rated low. "Almost all his works are libels," and *Gulliver,* his greatest work, seems, even in most of the reflective and satirical passages, "extremely vulgar and commonplace." [7] Pope is "a satirist, and a moralist, and a wit, and a critic, and a fine writer, much more than he is a poet." "There are no pictures of nature or simple emotion in all his writings." [8] Jeffrey is thus obviously pleased that the "wits of Queen Anne's time have been gradually brought down from the supremacy which they had enjoyed, without competition, for the best part of a century." Nor does he see any improvement soon afterward: the reign of the first two Georges was an "interregnum of native genius." [9]

Jeffrey's greatest admiration goes out to Shakespeare and his time. The Elizabethan age is "by far the brightest in the history of English literature,—or indeed of human intellect and capacity." "In point of real force and originality of genius, neither the age of Pericles, nor the age of Augustus, nor the times of Leo X, nor of Louis XIV, can come at all into comparison." [10] Jeffrey not only admires Shakespeare and defends him against the strictures of Madame de Staël, almost without reservation, but also interests himself in minor figures of the 17th century and bestows great praise on John Ford and Jeremy Taylor. "We will venture to assert, that there is in any one of the prose folios of Jeremy Taylor more fine fancy and original imagery—more brilliant conceptions and glowing expressions—more new figures, and new applications of old figures—more, in short, of the body and the soul of poetry, than in all the odes and the epics that have since been produced in Europe." [11] Nor is this admiration for pre-Restoration literature an antiquarian or patriotic foible. Jeffrey welcomes the revival of the Elizabethan style in the drama and in poetry. "That imitation of our older writers, and especially of our older dramatists, to which we cannot help flattering ourselves that we have somewhat contributed, has brought on, as it were, a second spring in our poetry." [12] Jeffrey lauds Keats, tracing his derivation from Fletcher, the pastoral Ben Jonson, and the young Milton, and recognizing in him "the true genius of English poetry," with imagination "paramount and supreme." [13] He is also deeply impressed by Byron, a "poet of the very first order," by his tragedy, *Sardanapalus,* and especially by *Manfred,* which he prefers to Marlowe's *Faustus* and to Aeschylus' *Prometheus.* [14] Jeffrey was also one of the first critics who extolled *Waverley,* comparing Scott to Shakespeare and recognizing that the novels establish an era in literature "casting sensibly into the shade all contemporary prose, and even all recent poetry." [15] Logically enough, he admired Burns and Cowper as the writers who prepared the change toward genuine "imitation of nature," original poetry, toward a "revolution in our literature." Jeffrey describes its causes well: the influence of the French revolution, Burke and the Germans, and the rise of Evangelicalism. [16]

How is it possible then that Jeffrey persecuted Wordsworth (and to a lesser degree Coleridge and Southey) in sarcastic and sometimes brutal reviews? Jeffrey's attacks on the Lake School have been put down to mere political partisanship and even to sheer personal malice. [17] It is true that political antagonism played its part, and increasingly so as the Lake poets became champions of all Tory causes. Jeffrey's attack on Coleridge, after his death, for his disparagement of Sir James Mackintosh exploits Coleridge's hatred of the Reform Bill and his other conservative social ideas. [18] Southey, when he had become poet laureate, was an obvious butt for satire, especially when the re-publication of his early Jacobinical play, *Wat Tyler,* made it easy to document his apostasy from the liberal cause. [19] But this is surely not the whole story in the case of Wordsworth. The elaborate criticism of Wordsworth is not (or only very rarely) political and not personal. Rather, it follows logically from certain basic assumptions and theories of Jeffrey, which are not clear from our survey of his tastes. There are other strands in Jeffrey's thought which may be incompatible with his praise of the imaginative tradition of English poetry.

We must turn to his "Essay on Beauty" (1811), originally a review of Archibald Alison's *Essays on the Nature and Principles of Taste* (1790), which was re-published in the *Encyclopaedia Britannica* and continued to figure there as the authoritative treatment of aesthetics till 1875.[20] It is not a great original performance: it is rather an exposition of Alison, with some reservations, and a historical survey of the British tradition of aesthetics. Jeffrey resolutely embraces the view that beauty is purely subjective, "nothing more than the reflection of our own inward emotions, and is made up entirely of certain little portions of love, pity, or other affections, which have been connected with these objects." Beauty has nothing to do with harmony, proportion, etc., pure sound or color, it has no cognitive or metaphysical significance. "The sensations which we receive from objects that are felt to be beautiful, and that in the highest degree, do not differ at all from the direct movements of tenderness or pity towards sentient beings." Thus Jeffrey is compelled to conclude that "all men's perceptions of beauty will be nearly in proportion to the degree of their sensibility and social sympathies," and that "all tastes are equally just and correct." But he balks at the implication that the best taste would be that which feels beauty in everything. Unexpectedly he pleads the cause of "common sense," of universal human nature, by making a distinction between a purely personal taste and the taste which the artist wants to impose upon his public. The artist must be careful to "employ only such objects as are the *natural* signs, or the inseparable concomitants of emotions, of which the greater part of mankind are susceptible; and his taste will *then* deserve to be called bad and false, if he obtrude upon the public, as beautiful, objects that are not likely to be associated in common minds with any interesting impressions."[21] The application to Wordsworth, who does not make common associations, is obvious.

We have stated Jeffrey's argument in some detail because it shows that he had a critical theory in mind and did not merely indulge his whims. His description and his application of Scottish aesthetics show up best the limitations and even the basic falseness of this psychological approach to criticism. Obviously Jeffrey and his models are completely unable to distinguish between aesthetic experience and experience of "sympathy." They have no criterion to set off enjoyment of a peaceful landscape, or sudden insight into character from experiences derived from art objects. Jeffrey and his forerunners are inevitably reduced to only one kind of critical standard, that of a morality of sympathy, derived from Adam Smith or Hume, and in practice to an expansive sentimentalism. There is this streak in Jeffrey. But just as Hume or Kames could not be satisfied with mere subjectivism of taste, so Jeffrey also has to appeal to the universal standard of taste, to tradition, to majority opinion, to common sense. The artist, by implication, is asked to speak the common mind, to be a common man. But common sense, in practice, is susceptible of many interpretations: to Jeffrey it means an appeal not to the neoclassical tradition but to the English tradition which had absorbed Shakespeare and Jeremy Taylor and managed to absorb much of what we would call romantic sensibility. It also implied, however, other elements: a mild realism, a suspicion of mysticism and metaphysics, and a strict regard for propriety. In short, the common man is somebody like Jeffrey; and Jeffrey, as his wide audience shows, was the spokesman of a large middle class.

Thus we can understand Jeffrey's case against Wordsworth. In his eyes Wordsworth tries to foist purely private associations on the public. Mysticism, or what Jeffrey considered mysticism, was simply incomprehensible to him. The "Intimations" ode is called "illegible and unintelligible," and even fairly simple passages in the *Excursion* such as the address to Duty, "elude all comprehension." [22] Not only philosophical or meditative passages puzzle Jeffrey: he completely misses the point of so simple a poem as "Strange fits of passion have I known" and he can refer to "stuff about dancing daffodils." [23] Wordsworth not only deviates "from the eternal and universal standard of truth and nature" by odd associations and extravagant speculations but also violates the standards of realism and neoclassical "decorum." There are no schoolmasters like Wordsworth's Matthew or sea captains such as the teller of the "Thorn," nor are there philosophical peddlers.[24] But this appeal to documentary social truth is combined, however illogically, with a rejection of the consequences of the implied realistic standards. Wordsworth's language is low, and a "household tub" must not be referred to in poetry.* Besides, the social feeling expressed in Wordsworth's poems seems to Jeffrey "a splenetic and idle discontent with the existing institutions of society." [25] Jeffrey was a Whig who believed in progress, though moderate and slow progress. He argued sensibly against the "perfectibility" creed of Madame de Staël, for he knew that men love war and that the industrial revolution would lead to terrible conflicts and abuses.[26] But he could not understand Wordsworth's glorification of dalesmen and could not see any practical proposals in his agrarian conservatism. If one holds Jeffrey's creed of liberalism, agrees with his suspicion of mysticism, and cannot, as Jeffrey could not even in theory, distinguish between art and life, one must arrive at such conclusions. Jeffrey's honesty need not be doubted, though he might have phrased his resentment less harshly and rudely. Especially inexcusable is the jeering review of the *White Doe of Rylstone,* because it completely misreads the tone and theme of a simple and grave poem.

Jeffrey treated the other poets of the time with much greater consideration, though he applied to them the same standards of common sense, propriety, and morality. He regrets Byron's "dreadful tone of sincerity" in his autobiographical poems and declares flatly that a topic such as incest is "not a thing to be brought at all before the imagination." [27] He is shocked by Byron's cynicism, his tendency to destroy all belief in virtue. The standard of trueness to life is immediately abandoned as soon as the morals to be drawn seem false to him. Thus Jeffrey is upset that Donna Inez, in the first Canto of *Don Juan,* being a "shameless and abandoned woman," should write an "epistle breathing the very spirit of warm, devoted, pure and unalterable love," or that the gruesome scene of the shipwreck is disturbed by levity and fun.[28] Tragicomedy, the mixing of moods, and Byron's anticlimaxes run counter to Jeffrey's

* *Edinburgh Review, 11* (1808), 225, on the household tub: "This, it will be admitted, is carrying the matter as far as it will well go; nor is there any thing—down to the wiping of shoes, or the evisceration of chickens,—which may not be introduced in poetry, if this is tolerated." Wordsworth removed the household tub from the "Blind Highland Boy" and, at the suggestion of Coleridge, substituted a turtle shell. Lamb protested against the change; see notes in Wordsworth's *Poetical Works,* ed. Selincourt, *3,* 447–8.

straightforward morals and also violate what remained in him of neoclassical prejudice in favor of purity and unity of effect. It is not surprising Jeffrey ranks Byron below Scott in genius and in morals.[29]

Jeffrey admires the spirit of kindliness and humanity he finds in Scott's works and generously and prudently acknowledges his fairness in describing the conflict of Cavaliers and Puritans in *Old Mortality*, though he disagreed with his Tory politics.[30] But Jeffrey was not entirely content with Scott on purely literary grounds. He never could stomach medievalism and the introduction of the marvelous and superstitious. He disliked the impish dwarf Horner in the *Lay of the Last Minstrel*, and criticized *Ivanhoe* as a mere "fantastical pageant." [31] He ranks the *Waverley* novels very well, applying his criteria of realism: he rightly prefers the Scottish topics and the humorous and homely figures. He sees, however, something of the shoddiness of Scott's poetry and is sorely tempted to abandon his trust in popularity and the verdict of the people. How is it that one must grant good taste only to the few? His answer does not admit a real cleavage between the public and the critic. Jeffrey grants only that the critic is better equipped to discern originality and to see the merits of difficulty overcome and rarity of achievement, while the general public has no such standards of comparison.[32] But it is not clear how this is applied to the poem under review. Scott's *Lady of the Lake* is not particularly original, nor can its difficulties be hidden from any reader.

A preference for accurate pictures of manners accounts for Jeffrey's high praise of Cowper and Crabbe. Crabbe, "one of the most original, nervous, and pathetic poets," is contrasted expressly with Wordsworth. Crabbe appeals to "familiar and long remembered emotions, to common human nature and common human feelings"; his poetry is made up of an "infinite multitude of little fragments of sympathy," a phrase which almost literally agrees with Jeffrey's definition of beauty. Still, he has his objections to Crabbe for too repulsive detail and too much "Chinese accuracy." [33] Cowper is extravagantly admired for "boldness and originality," as a great master of English, though he sometimes seems to Jeffrey too "colloquial and familiar." [34] Burns is also a "great and original genius." Jeffrey prefers his humor to his pathos and understands very well that he was neither uneducated nor illiterate.[35] But

Jeffrey has strong moral objections to Burns: he dislikes his contempt for prudence, decency, and regularity, his boasts of independence, his harsh invectives; and he objects to his erotic poetry. It has an "indelicate fervor," is "seldom accommodated to the timidity and 'sweet austere composure' of women of refinement." "Instead of suing for a smile, or melting in a tear, his muse deals in nothing but locked embraces and midnight rencontres." [36] There is a streak of pre-Victorian prudery in Jeffrey. He manages not to mention the title of Ford's *Tis a Pity She's a Whore,* though he praises the play and quotes it at length.[37] He waxes extremely indignant at the loose morals depicted in Goethe's *Wilhelm Meister* and is particularly shocked by its vulgarity, a term he applies to all references to food and eating, to "combs and soap and towels." [38] Diderot is not only indecent, profane, but has a "tone of blackguardism." [39] The common obverse of this prudishness is sentimentality, in which this judge of the Court of Sessions could indulge to an incredible degree. One could quote the late letters to Dickens which drip with tears shed over Dickens' books,* but even if one confines oneself to his public pronouncements, the evidence of mawkish taste seems to me overwhelming. Jeffrey praised Campbell extravagantly and quotes absurdly sentimental passages from *Theodric* with approval. He is moved to tears by the ridiculous *Trials of Margaret Lindsay* by John Wilson.[40] The poems of Felicia Hemans excite his admiration for the "sober and humble tone of indulgence and piety" which should "allay the apprehension of those who are most afraid of the passionate exaggerations of poetry." He prophesies her "enduring fame" in contrast to the poets of his youth who at the time of the review (1829) were "melting fast from the field of our vision": Southey, Keats, Shelley, Wordsworth, Crabbe, Byron, and Scott. "The two who have longest withstood this rapid withering of the laurel, and with least marks of decay on their branches, are Rogers and Camp-

---

* Lord Cockburn, *Life of Jeffrey,* 2, 406: "I have so cried and sobbed over it [i.e. the death of Paul Dombey] last night and again this morning; and felt my heart purified by those tears." *Ibid.,* 2, 292: "I have read all Burns' life and works—not without many tears, for the life especially. . . . I could lie down in the dirt, and cry and grovel there, I think, for a century to save such a soul as Burns from the suffering and the contamination and the degradation."

bell." [41] Jeffrey here wants to describe the actual state of reputation of these poets and, in part, he does not approve of it. He specifically remarked in reprinting his essays (1843) that Keats is wrongly forgotten. Still, his satisfaction with the high standing of Rogers and Campbell is unmistakable. Jeffrey's praise for Keats is, however, not merely a lucky chance. Jeffrey liked "pure poetry," images, beautiful sounding verse. He quotes fine things from Keats, such as the *Ode to Autumn,* though he cannot relish *Hyperion.*[42] "Pure poetry," however, seems to him a "very dangerous species," as "it is apt to run into mere mysticism and extravagance." [43] He enjoyed it in Hogg, in Moore's *Lalla Rookh,* in Leigh Hunt's *Story of Rimini,* and in Keats, where nothing offended his morals and his politics. But one suspects that Keats was to him another Hogg, Hunt, or Moore: a fanciful writer of no great consequence. He preferred to him, at any time, a poet such as Rogers, from whom he quotes commonplace reflections and sentimental descriptions of the married life of a country squire with great admiration and approval, or Campbell, whose *Gertrude of Wyoming* came nearer than anything else to his "conception of pure and perfect poetry." [44]

It seems impossible, therefore, to consider Jeffrey a great critic. The claim for "a philosophical foundation" of his criticism is vitiated by the fact that the theory on which he leans is unable to distinguish between literature and life, love and beauty, aesthetics and ethics. The claim that Jeffrey himself made of "combining Ethical precepts with Literary Criticism" [45] is nothing new or extraordinary and must be scaled down if we think how limited, prudish, and partisan these morals were and how narrowly the standard was applied from the outside without a clear conception of the working of moral ideas in poetry. But one must not deny to Jeffrey very considerable historical merit. The *Edinburgh Review,* soon followed by rivals and imitators, did much to raise the status of periodical criticism and its financial rewards.* Jeffrey was greatly influential, even on the Continent, in expounding a moderate romanticism. In the English-speaking world he played a role in consolidating a historical view of literature. His literary nationalism with its stress on the glories and independence of the

* The reviewer for the *Monthly* or *Critical Reviews* received about two guineas per sheet, while the average pay in the *Edinburgh* was 20–25 guineas. See Lewis Gates, *Three Studies in Literature,* pp. 48, 53.

English tradition emanating from Shakespeare and its complete rejection of French taste was important, though Jeffrey combined these views incongruously with Scottish nationalism and many survivals of the neoclassical faith in "decorum" and purity of genre. He also did something to popularize the views of the dependence of literature on society which he drew in part from Madame de Staël. In the *Wilhelm Meister* essay, where he emphasized the divergences of national tastes, he even tried to theorize on their causes, distinguishing between the two which Taine later called "milieu" and "moment": between the influence of government, climate, early models, etc. and the rate of evolution, the position in an assumed cycle of progress "from mere monstrosity to ostentatious displays of labor and design" and then, "to the repose and simplicity of graceful nature." [46] But these ideas, distant echoes of Vico and Winckelmann, Herder and Madame de Staël, are not applied concretely; they actually introduce a sermon on the low taste of the Germans who can admire Goethe's novel, which to Jeffrey seems "eminently absurd, puerile, incongruous, vulgar, and affected." [47]

Jeffrey's deficiencies cannot be seen by those who are impressed by his judicial tone, the skill he shows in exposition and summing up, the sureness of his claim to authority. This, however, is only the surface which covers the many conflicts and tensions, contradictions and compromises of his critical position. Survivals of neoclassicism clash with romantic tastes, hard-headed realism with tearful sentimentality, worldly sophistication with old-maidish prudery. While Jeffrey resembles (though on a lower plane) Johnson and his attempts to reconcile the irreconcilable, he also anticipates the Victorian compromise. After the death of Coleridge and Hazlitt English criticism was to undergo a slump of some thirty years, in which theories of romantic sentimentalism, combined with moralism, ruled almost unchallenged.[48]

While Jeffrey, whatever his shortcomings, was a genuine critic, the main contributors to the rival *Quarterly Review* (founded in 1809) will be remembered largely as antiquaries and historians of literature. Robert Southey (1774–1843) developed the new view of the history of English literature which we found also in the supposedly neoclassical Jeffrey. Southey was an even more pronounced literary nationalist. In the introduction to the *Specimens of the Later English Poets* (1807), in which he disparaged the age of Dryden and Pope, he asserted also that "at all times we have preserved a costume and character of our own." We must not speak of foreign schools in English literature, as has been the accepted convention since Gray.[49] In "Sketches of the Progress of English Poetry from Chaucer to Cowper," which introduce a *Life of Cowper* (1836), Southey reaffirms his belief in the "homegrowth" of English literature, in poetry as "colored by the national character, as the wine of different soils, has its raciness." The development of English literature appears to him as a "succession of heresies" against this gospel of nature with intervals of orthodoxy during the great ages, the Elizabethan and his own. Southey speaks of fashions in literature which supply a real or supposed defect, "and in both cases the spirit of antagonism has generally given rise to the opposite error."[50] While Southey believes in "convention and revolt" as a necessary historical process, he always sides with convention as he understood it. The English convention is the free Elizabethan taste, while neoclassicism is a deviation from the national norm.

Southey was a learned antiquary who did much to stimulate interest in medieval romances (he edited *Morte d'Arthur*), and in Spanish and Portuguese literature but he was not an important critic. He was too generous, too uncritical to be a good judge of his contemporaries: he extolled Kirk White, lauded several "uneducated poets," and praised Joanna Baillie to the sky, placing her next to Shakespeare.[51] Southey has no power of characterization, no edge, no critical personality, no theory. Saintsbury speaks of the "critical gold" in Southey's late miscellany, *The Doctor,* but it is impossible to discover criticism even in the sensible protest against the bowdlerization of Spenser.[52] Southey's announced principles of criticism are only moralistic and political. "Has it [the book] induced you to suspect that what you have been accustomed to think unlawful may after all be innocent, and that that may be harmless which you have hitherto been taught to think dangerous? Has it tended to make you dissatisfied and impatient under the control of others? . . . If so—throw the book in the fire."[53] No criticism can come from such a test.

It is equally difficult to consider Sir Walter Scott (1771–1832) an important critic. He was a widely read antiquary and there are passages in his writings which are attempts at literary history. *The Life of Dryden* (1808), an early example of the "Life and Times" type, sketches the literary situation of Dryden's youth very skillfully. There is some rather rudimentary criticism in the *Lives of the Novelists* (1821). Scott preferred Smollett to Fielding and praised Jane Austen, as he should. But he praised almost everybody of whom he wrote. He thought that Southey's *Madoc* would "assume his real place at the feet of Milton" and he considered Joanna Baillie "now the highest genius of our country." [54] Scott lacked discernment, and even critical pretensions and principles. The compilations on the history of chivalry, romance, and the drama for the *Encyclopaedia Britannica* are quite undistinguished. In the long piece on the drama (1818) he conveys much information and reproduces critical opinions, Johnson's on the unities or A. W. Schlegel's on French drama, but does not set forth a point of view of his own. Scott comes nearest to genuine criticism in his discussion of folk poetry: especially do the essays added to a new edition of the *Minstrelsy of the Scottish Border* (1830) expound freshly a Herderian view of "primeval poetry" and give good first-hand accounts of the history of ballad collecting, [55] in which Scott himself keeps an honored place.

If we except the great figures discussed in the following chapters, we must conclude that the positive achievement of the age was primarily its adoption of the historical point of view. The harsh dogmatic tone of much reviewing, divided as it was by acrimonious political feelings, should not mislead us into believing that there were sharply drawn critical issues at that time. The general temper of the age was rather that of increased tolerance for the wide variety of literature.

The *Essay on English Poetry* (1819) by Thomas Campbell (1777–1844) is just such a broad sketch, in a tolerant spirit, of the history of English poetry which keeps the focus on art and deplores mere antiquarianism and out-and-out romantic dogmatism. Campbell defends Pope, extends his welcome to such baroque works as Chamberlayne's *Pharonnida,* and concludes by saying, "But in poetry there are many mansions. I am free to confess that I can pass from the elder writers and still find charm in the correct and equable sweetness of Parnell." [56] Campbell knows that poetry is a universal human need and will not perish from the earth. "A world inhabited by active, impassioned, and perishable beings, must forever be an inexhaustible emporium of the materials to the poets." [57]

At first sight Lord Byron (1788–1824) seems a defender of an eternal standard of art. Today his defense of Pope and his curious confession of the errors of his own poetic ways is the only thing remembered of his criticism. He tells us, "we are upon a wrong revolutionary poetic system or systems, not worth a damn in itself, and from which none but Rogers and Crabbe are free." "I have been amongst the builders of this Babel," and "I am ashamed of it." The highest of all poetry is ethical poetry. Pope is the moral poet of all civilization, and should be the "national poet of mankind." Byron defended the unities and wanted to re-establish the "regular English drama." He thought of it as modeled on the Greeks, as "simple and severe as Alfieri." [58]

All this may have been Byron's dream and ideal, his reaction against the "Lakers" whom he detested and the "Cockneys" he sometimes tolerated. But actually Byron in his theories shares the emotionalism and historicism of his time. He frequently tells us that "poetry is the expression of excited passion," "the lava of the imagination," that it is "in itself passion," a personal need which he feels "as a torture," an ecstasy, or *estro*. [59] The polemics defending Pope against Bowles's strictures are hopelessly entangled in the puerile contrast between "natural" and "artificial" subjects in poetry: Bowles arguing that the sun and the sea are more poetic than a ship and Byron countering that the sea without a ship is only an empty desert, and so on. But Byron concludes, at last, that the poet "who executes best is the highest," that a hierarchy of subject matters is doubtful, and that there are no "invariable principles of poetry," such as were proclaimed by the Rev. W. L. Bowles, the supposedly romantic enemy of Pope:

> So far are these principles of poetry from being "invariable," that they never were nor ever will be settled. These principles mean nothing more than the predilection of a particular age; and every age has its own, and a different from its predecessor. It is now Homer, and now Virgil; once Dryden, and since Walter Scott; now Corneille, and now Racine; now Crébillon,

now Voltaire. The Homerists and Virgilians in France disputed for a half a century. Not fifty years ago the Italians
neglected Dante—Bettinelli reproved Monti for reading "that
barbarian"; at present they adore him. Shakespeare and Milton have had their rise, and they will have their decline.
Already they have more than once fluctuated, as must be the
case with all the dramatists and poets of a living language.
This does not depend upon their merits, but upon the ordinary vicissitudes of human opinions.

And then he adds, somewhat cryptically: "Schlegel and Madame
de Staël have endeavored also to reduce poetry to two systems,
classical and romantic. The effect is only beginning." [60] Clearly,
Byron would not be satisfied with only two systems: he wants more,
he sees the whirligig of taste, the fluctuations of fame. Everything
passes, nothing matters finally, as everything will be engulfed by
change.

No greater contrast can be imagined than that between Byron
and Shelley (1792–1822). Shelley's entire faith in the imagination
and its eternal truths should not, however, obscure the fact that
he shares a historical point of view with his friend and his other
contemporaries. The most original insights of the *Defence of
Poetry* (1821) are historical. In Shelley the Platonic vision is at the
center of the argument. It is asserted without misgivings, eloquently, even stridently. Shelley draws from Plato, directly or indirectly, the view of poetry as the creative principle in man. Poets
are "not only the authors of language and of music, of the dance,
and architecture, and statuary, and painting; they are the institu-
tors of laws, and the founders of a civil society, and the inventors of
the arts of life," the teachers of religion. "Poetry is the record of the
best and happiest moments of the happiest and best minds." The
poets are "men of the most spotless virtue, the most consummate prudence, the most fortunate of men." Poets are also "philosophers of the very loftiest power," and poetry is "the center
and circumference of knowledge," "that which comprehends all
science." [61] The historical role of poetry is exalted to that of the
primary civilizing factor in the dim past, in the present age, and
in the future. In the concluding words of the *Defence of Poetry*,
"poets are the unacknowledged legislators of the world."

It must be obvious today that this kind of defense of poetry defeats its own purpose. Poetry loses its identity completely in a loose synthesis of philosophy, morality, and art. What can be ascribed to all three together or to any one of the other two will not be seriously credited to poetry alone. Shelley's rhetoric was dated even in his own time; its arguments belong rather to the Renaissance; he often sounds like Sidney (whose *Defence* he had read just before writing his own and whom he frequently follows) and like Tasso, whom he quotes to the effect that the poet is the only creator other than God.[62] Shelley's piece might fit into a cultural situation in which the union of scholar, teacher, and prophet could still be asserted in religious terms. The description of the poetic act as sheer inspiration, however justified by Shelley's own experience, is made in the rapturous tones of the singer Ion, of Tasso, and Giordano Bruno. The poet's mind, according to Shelley, is completely passive: "the mind in creation is as a fading coal, which some invisible influence, like an inconstant wind, awakens to transitory brightness." Thus, "when composition begins, inspiration is already on the decline, and the most glorious poetry that has ever been communicated to the world is probably a feeble shadow of the original conceptions of the poet." [63] Poetry is not art but vision, incommunicable vision, an inexpressible state of mind. The poet cannot *will* to compose: at most, he can carefully observe his inspired moments. He cannot have an audience and apparently does not need one. Poetry is sheer self-expression, self-consolation for the alienating curse and blessing of his mysterious gift. "A poet," Shelley says, without apparently realizing the contradiction to his claims for the tremendous social and moral effects of poetry, "is a nightingale who sits in darkness and sings to cheer its own solitude with sweet sounds." [64] The moral effect of poetry is conceived by Shelley in classical terms: the poet depicts "beautiful idealisms of moral excellence," as Shelley defines his aim in the preface to *Prometheus Unbound,* and in more didactic terms, in the earlier preface to the *Revolt of Islam:* the poet "excites a generous impulse, an ardent thirst for excellence," and celebrates love as the law which should govern the moral world.[65] Poetry is to present the ideal hero, on whom we are to model ourselves. Shelley thinks that "Prometheus is a more poetical character than Satan," and prompted, of course, by his theological aversions, he defends Satan in *Paradise Lost* as a "moral being far superior to Milton's God." [66]

These claims for poetry, excessive as they must appear in their very grandiosity, were provoked, in part, by Thomas Love Peacock's *Four Ages of Poetry,* a rationalistic, cynical, and humorous description of the decay and final disappearance of poetry in an age of utility. Shelley's very extravagance is, in part, polemical. Even his exaltation of inspiration must be taken with some reserve. Shelley himself, of course, revised his work continually and did not entirely rely on his first inspiration. But taken literally, many of Shelley's statements have contributed to the discredit of what today is usually considered the romantic theory of poetry: the extravagance of the prophetic claim, the complete trust in inspiration, the sentimental or Utopian idealizing of the mere communication of kindness and love.

Fortunately there is more to the essay than these most often quoted purple passages. Though the distinction between poetry and almost any other creative human activity remains unclear, Shelley speaks well of poetry once he has focused on it. What modern theory would describe as "realization" is well phrased when Shelley speaks of poetry as "purging from our inward sight the film of familiarity." "It compels us to feel that which we perceive, and to imagine that which we know." [67] He understands the kind of superiority which may be claimed for the poetic medium over that of the other arts. Language itself is "arbitrarily produced by the imagination," language itself is "poetry" (in his wide sense), while paint or marble appear to him inert matter, an obstacle, a "cloud which enfeebles." [68] Though one could argue that the materials of sculpture and painting are also an inspiration and spur to the artist, Shelley correctly sees that language is not inert and external, like stone or paint, but is pre-formed by man and thus continuous with poetic creation. Shelley has also a strong feeling for the role of rhythm in poetry: like Coleridge he tries to minimize the distinction between metrical verse and rhythmic imaginative prose. Plato and Bacon are to him poets, not only in the wide sense of poet-philosophers, but because of their rhythmic language and imagery.[69] His sense of the specificity of language is so strong that he denies the possibility of translation, though he himself was a very successful translator, especially of passages from *Faust.* "It were as wise to cast a violet into a crucible that you might discover the formal principle of its color and odor, as seek to transfuse from one language into another the creations of a poet." [70]

But the most remarkable feature of the essay seems to me the sketch of a general social history of literature. It is not referable to the Platonizing eloquence and has a different intellectual background. It is directly inspired by Peacock's *jeu d'esprit*. Peacock had developed the old idea of a golden and silver age of poetry into a cycle of four ages in this unusual order: the classical age of iron, that of gold, that of silver, and that of brass, all four of these repeated in the modern period. The age of iron was the dim origin of poetry, the age of gold that of Homer, Aeschylus, and Pindar, the age of silver that of Virgil and the Augustans, and the age of brass the late Roman decadence, for which Nonnus is Peacock's representative. In English poetry the iron age was the Middle Ages, the golden age that of Shakespeare, the silver age that of Dryden and Pope, and the age of brass Peacock's own time. The whole scheme allows a ridicule of the primitive and medieval on the one hand, and of the contemporaneous on the other. Peacock laughs at the "egregious confraternity of rhymesters, known by the name of the Lake Poets" and alludes to Shelley when he speaks of "querulous, egotistical rhapsodies, to express the writer's high dissatisfaction with the world and every thing in it." The scheme also allows the argument, known earlier to Vico and later to Hegel, that the "poet in our times is a semi-barbarian in a civilized community," that poetry is a thing of the past, "the mental rattle that awakened the attention of intellect in the infancy of civil society." Peacock pleads that it is high time to settle down to the real business of life. "Mathematicians, astronomers, chemists, metaphysicians, moralists, historians, politicians, and political economists, who have built into the upper air of intelligence a pyramid . . . see the modern Parnassus far beneath them." [71]

Shelley retorts to these semiserious arguments with a similar 18th-century scheme of speculation. The exact source of Shelley's conception is difficult to determine, but it is the kind of schematic history encountered in the Scottish primitivists, in Rousseau or in Herder. Shelley's source was apparently French, as he speaks of the "Celtic" conquerors of the Roman Empire and the predominance of the "Celtic" nations after the fall of Rome. Such a confusion of

Celtic and Teutonic occurs in Paul-Henri Mallet, the Swiss propagandist of things Nordic, and among the *celtomanes* of the late 18th century. It could hardly have been found in Germany, and in England was early refuted by Bishop Percy, the English editor of Mallet. Shelley describes the origins of poetry quite in the naturalistic manner of Rousseau, Herder, Monboddo, or John Brown.[72] Poetry is connate with the origin of man: the savage first expressed his emotions about surrounding objects, and then about man in society. All occurred in neat sequence. In the youth of the world every man was a poet, men danced and sang and spoke a language "vitally metaphorical." Poets were both legislators and prophets. Poetry is closely linked with moral progress; it embodies the ethical ideals of its age. Shelley argues that what we would consider vices in the Homeric epics, the ferocity of Achilles, the cunning of Ulysses, were actually ideals set up for emulation. The drama especially is a faithful mirror of the history of manners: its decline goes always hand in hand with the decline of society. Restoration comedy is Shelley's example, as it was that of many other romantic critics, though Shelley argues that the depiction of sensuality is preferable to no art at all. The erotic and bucolic poets, during the late Roman empire, addressed themselves to the last emotions still felt vividly when human heroism had died. Later, presumably, a torpor of even the ordinary low passions and feelings paralyzed all poetry and fine writing.[73]

Shelley's conception of evolution is cyclical, and for the fierce individualist that he was, surprisingly collectivist. Original language is called "the chaos of a cyclic poem"; the erotic poems of late antiquity are "episodes to that great poem, which all poets, like the co-operating thoughts of one great mind, have built up since the beginning of the world." Even the history of the Roman empire, though that empire was without poets, is a series of "episodes of that great cyclic poem written by Time upon the memories of men." Homer, Dante, and Milton are the three genuine epic poets (and there are no others), because they "bore a defined and intelligible relation to the knowledge and sentiment and religion of the age in which they lived." [74] The title of epic poet in this highest sense must be denied to Virgil, Tasso, Ariosto, and Spenser, presumably because they were too individualistic, not sufficiently representative of their culture. Speaking of Dante, Shelley finely formulates the inexhaustible potentiality of a great poet and the process of accretion and varied interpretation which he inspires. "A great poem is a fountain for ever overflowing with the waters of wisdom and delight; and after one person and one age has exhausted all its divine effluence which their peculiar relations enable them to share, another and yet another succeeds and new relations are ever developed, the source of an unforeseen and an unconceived delight." [75] This feeling for the stream of history of which poetry is a part helps to explain Shelley's repeated assertion of his own contemporaneity and participation in the spirit of his age, though he did not subscribe to any contemporary poetic doctrine (Wordsworth's, for instance, or Keats's).[76] It explains the peculiar glorification (peculiar if we consider Shelley's personal isolation and the unfriendliness of his reviewers) which he confers upon his own age in the conclusion of the *Defence*. His age was a "new birth," of which Shelley considered himself a herald, a trumpet, a legislator, but even those who did not know that they were prophets of a new age were unconsciously contributing to the spiritual and political revolution which Shelley could foresee. "Poets are the hierophants of an unapprehended inspiration." They utter "words which express what they understand not." They are "trumpets which sing to battle, and feel not what they inspire." [77] Shelley believed in the "grand march of intellect" (like Keats when he preferred Wordsworth to Milton),[78] in some mysterious scheme which he would not ascribe to Divine Providence. Of this scheme poetry was part and parcel. The poet and the art of poetry had almost lost their identity, but they had newly found a social role which was so exalted and so secure in its very inevitability that no contemporary neglect and no isolation could affect it. Poetry was re-established as part of the fabric of society and of the process of history: potent even when scarcely visible. This was Shelley's true defense of poetry, surely more convincing than the arguments confusing philosophy, morality, and art in one common mixture. It was the defense of poetry which came to dominate the 19th century.

5 : WORDSWORTH

THE LITERARY criticism of William Wordsworth (1770–1850) is usually considered the manifesto of the English romantic movement, the signal for the break with the age of neoclassicism. All the emphasis is put on Wordsworth's rejection of 18th-century diction, on his identification of the "language of prose" with that of metrical composition, and of the language of poetry with the language spoken by the "middle and lower classes of society." This plea for a kind of naturalism—the poet reproducing the speech of "humble and rustic life"—is seen as combined with "emotionalism," the view that poetry, in Wordsworth's famous phrase, is the "spontaneous overflow of powerful feelings." [1]

These ideas do appear in Wordsworth's theory and they proved historically most important, but if we examine the whole range of Wordsworth's literary criticism—the Prefaces of 1800 and 1815, the Appendix of 1802, the Supplementary Essay of 1815, the three essays upon epitaphs and the correspondence [2]—we must come to the conclusion that Wordsworth modified these ideas considerably and that they actually need reinterpretation as elements of a coherent body of thought with very different assumptions. The disapproval of poetic diction, the idea of imitating rustic speech, the concept of poetry as the overflow of feelings do not particularly appeal to our time and cannot be reconciled with a rational conception of literary theory. They could be quickly dismissed, but we would not have brought out what is most peculiar and valuable in Wordsworth's theory.

Wordsworth's objection to 18th-century poetic diction and his reaction in favor of colloquial speech excited an immense debate which in the perspective of the historical process of which Wordsworth's theory was a symptom hardly appears called for. At the end of the 18th century the poetic devices of the tradition beginning with Dryden had become outworn stereotypes. Wordsworth's reaction was the more violent, as his own early poetry was completely steeped in the most extravagant diction of descriptive poetry.[3] In the course of his highly individual emotional and intellectual evolution he came to realize that this diction was "vicious," "adulterated," "distorted," "glossy," "unfeeling," [4] while he felt that his own new style was "natural," just as every innovator in the history of English poetry has felt that he was reviving the spoken language. Donne thought his style more natural and colloquial than Spenser's, Dryden reacted against the artificialities of metaphysical wit, and T. S. Eliot and Ezra Pound in our own day advocate spoken language in poetry. Also in France such a reaction is common. Malherbe felt his "reform" to be one in favor of the spoken language, and Delille in the preface to his translation of Virgil's *Georgics* (1769) defended common words against the exclusions of French classical diction.*

Wordsworth's own rejection of 18th-century diction is based on such numerous and heterogeneous reasons that a systematic analysis is very difficult. He rejects "poetic diction" in a narrow sense, i.e. a fixed sacred vocabulary with its exclusions of what it considers low or trivial. He objects to specific stylistic devices, such as personification, periphrasis, Latinisms, and grammatical licenses; to syntactical features like inversions and frequent antitheses; and to structures which are merely enumerative and hence similar to some kind of *catalogue raisonné*.[5] These objections might extend to the use of classical mythology, or to the "pathetic fallacy" if it seemed uncalled for and too violent; on some occasions he was merely applying common-sense standards of truth and accuracy. Thus he disliked the line of an epitaph on a lady who had died after taking the waters at Bristol:

> She bow'd to taste the wave—
> And died,

on the ground that one does not actually "bow" in drinking bath waters, that bath waters should not be called a "wave," as they are

---

* See Eliot's own comments on Wordsworth in *The Use of Criticism and the Use of Poetry* (London, 1933), pp. 69 ff. Delille and his preface was well known to Wordsworth. See a note to line 759 of *An Evening Walk* in Wordsworth, *Representative Poems*, ed. Arthur Beatty (New York, 1937), 31–2.

drunk from a goblet, and that there was no causal relation between her drinking and her death.[6] The objections to Dryden's description of the night or to Pope's moonlight scene in the *Iliad* are based on similar grounds: mountains do not nod their heads, and the astronomy of Pope is obviously vague and even absurd.* At times Wordsworth's criticisms are directed against what we would call 17th-century characteristics: quaintness, conceits, extravagant hyperboles, verbal wit, elaborate obscurity. For reasons not always discernible in the text Wordsworth tolerates these devices if they seem to indicate that there was an "undercurrent" of genuine emotion and that the poet only succumbed to the vices and fashions of the age.† Thus Wordsworth praises Donne's sonnet "Death, be not proud" as "weighty in thought, and vigorous in the expression, though to modern taste it may be repulsive, quaint and labored." [7]

The phrasing of many of Wordsworth's objections is too loose and incautious, his use of the term "language" so uncertain that he left himself wide open to Coleridge's refutation from his own practice. Wordsworth himself uses many devices against which he objected. His syntax can be very involved; he sometimes uses very bookish polysyllabic words; his poems are full of the pathetic fallacy; and even many instances of 18th-century types of periphrasis can be found in his poems. Wordsworth in his critical writings was incapable of defining the difference between what was to him a legitimate and even central animating metaphor and a false and artificial one. Neither could he describe theoretically why certain inversions are right and others wrong.‡

---

* *Wordsworth's Literary Criticism,* ed. Smith, pp. 185–6. Wordsworth knew the discussion of the Dryden passage in Thomas Warton's *Observations on the Fairie Queene* and apparently drew the objections to Pope's passage from Coleridge's oral comments, later published in *Biographia Literaria,* ed. J. Shawcross (2 vols. Oxford, 1907), *1,* 26–7.

† E.g. Smith, pp. 165–6, 107, 109, 110, 111, 113, 115, 117. Wordsworth admired Sir Thomas Browne (see letter to J. Peace, April 8, 1844; *Letters: Later Years, 3,* 1203), but he alluded only in passing to Herbert and Marvell. He praised Shakespeare's *Sonnets* but censured many for "sameness, quaintness, and elaborate obscurity." See Coleridge, *Miscellaneous Criticism,* ed. T. M. Raysor (London, 1936), p. 454.

‡ The contrast between Wordsworth's theory and practice has been discussed by many: Coleridge, Sir Walter Raleigh, Miss Barstow,

But Wordsworth's recommendation of the "natural language" of man needs interpretation. If it means the actual language of rustics, even Wordsworth himself could not have thought of it as applying to more than a few of his *Lyrical Ballads*. He himself defended these only as "experiments," and in later editions he recognized that his "observations" on diction had "so little application to the greater part, perhaps, of the collection, as subsequently enlarged and diversified, that they could not with any propriety stand as an Introduction to it," and he relegated them, therefore, to an appendix.[8] Besides, Wordsworth himself considerably modified his recommendation of rustic speech. At times, he has the social distinction in mind. He contrasts the speech of the "dalesmen" of the Lake country with that of "London wits and witlings," of people who have "to do with routs, dinners, morning calls, hurry from door to door, from street to street, on foot or in carriage."[9] At times, he thought of some of his poems as ballads which might be hawked about as broadsheets and ought to replace the ones actually sold, as these were frequently either superstitious or indelicate. But if he harbored such illusions, he must have abandoned them very soon. The "Essay Supplementary to the Preface" (1815) is a self-consoling, reassuring history of English poetry, arguing that all the great poets were unappreciated at first and "have the task of creating the taste by which they are to be enjoyed." Wordsworth has now to make a distinction between the public which ignored or rejected him and the People, whose voice will finally pass the right verdict which he confidently expects.*

At times, Wordsworth's "rustic speech" becomes difficult to distinguish from generally human speech, emotional language, purified for the purposes of the poet. He speaks about a "selection of

---

Frederick A. Pottle, and others. Wordsworth's criterion was apparently a distinction between "ornament" and "incarnation of thought" (see Smith, p. 129, and De Quincey's report of conversation with Wordsworth in "Style," *Collected Writings,* ed. Masson, London, 1896, *10,* 229–30, and sometimes between truth and falsehood.

* Smith, pp. 195, 201; letter to Wrangham, June 5, 1808. Cf. Wordsworth's complaint that not a single copy of his poems was sold by one of the leading booksellers in Cumberland (letter to Moxon, August, 1833; *Letters: Later Years, 2,* 664). The phrase about "creating the taste" is ascribed to Coleridge by Wordsworth (Smith, p. 195).

the real language of men," about expression, "simple and un-elaborated," but "purged from causes of dislike or disgust." Words-worth recognizes that "selection" alone will "separate the composi-tion from the vulgarity and meanness of ordinary life." The poet must remove what is painful and disgusting. He "selects from the real language of men, or which amounts to the same thing, com-poses accurately in the spirit of such selection." [10] This surely leaves all the leeway anybody could demand. Wordsworth actually ends in good neoclassicism when he requires "the general language of humanity" and when he appeals to the "common principles which govern first-rate writers in all nations and tongues." [11] He con-tinuously assumes that there is a core of language common to all men, comprehensible to all, from which the learned and artificial poet deviates at his peril.

But Wordsworth has other positive recommendations than mere naturalness and universality. Poetic language must be language in a "state of vivid sensation," and hence, "if selected truly and judi-ciously, must necessarily be dignified and variegated, and alive with metaphors and figures." [12] To be "dignified and variegated" seems an odd pair of requirements, but these are the traditional demands of ancient rhetoricians for the "high" style.* We have in Words-worth, as many times before in the history of rhetoric, not merely a demand for vividness. Metaphor is associated with passion, for in passion we are supposed to use figures spontaneously. Passionate figurative language has often been thought to have been the lan-guage of primitive man. Like many 18th-century authors Words-

---

* See Klaus Dockhorn, "Wordsworth und die rhetorische Tradition in England," *Nachrichten der Akademie der Wissenschaften,* Göt-tingen, 1944. Dockhorn gives further examples of Wordsworth's use of rhetorical terms and ideas and shows his knowledge of Quintilian. Wordsworth certainly knew Longinus (see letter to J. Fletcher, April 6, 1825; *Letters: Later Years, 1,* 194), and the very Longinian John Dennis; see letter to Mrs. Clarkson, 1814, in *Correspondence of Crabb Robinson with the Wordsworth Circle,* ed. Morley, *1,* 78; also Smith, p. 224 (letter to Southey, 1815) and De Quincey's letter to A. Blackwood, June 30, 1842, telling about his collecting Dennis' pamphlets to "oblige Wordsworth who (together with S. T. C.) had an absurd 'craze' about him"; quoted in John Dennis, *Critical Works,* ed. E. N. Hooker (Balti-more, 1943), *2,* lxxiii.

worth tells us that "the earliest poets wrote naturally, feeling powerfully, in a figurative language." * The rhetorical figures of learned 18th-century poetry appear to Wordsworth as a distortion, a misapplication of this original language, which was spontaneous expression. Wordsworth believes apparently that the poet's language is really inferior to what men in passion, especially in former days, had said. "The language of the poets falls short of that which is uttered by men in real life, under the actual pressure of those passions." The poet's words are inferior to these "emanations of reality and truth." The language of the early poets differed from ordinary language, Wordsworth admits, but it differed legitimately because it was the language of extraordinary, presumably heroic occasions. Still, it was a language really spoken by men.[13]

Wordsworth thus seems well on the way toward some kind of primitivism similar to that of certain Scotch critics or Herder. This naturalism consists of a recommendation of the poetry of strong passions and heroic occasions, written in an elevated metaphorical language which the primitive bard was supposed to have used. Paradoxically, Wordsworth does not differ here from Gray, who wrote his turgid, highly figurative, "elevated" odes, *The Progress of Poesy* and *The Bard,* with such a theory in mind.

But Wordsworth does not take this point of view consistently. He is, one must admit, affected by the contemporary concern for folk poetry: we know that he thought highly of Burns and Bürger and considered English poetry "absolutely redeemed" by the publication of Percy's *Reliques*.[14] He himself wrote much in ballad stanzas and in folk song forms. But Wordsworth keeps aloof from many implications of this view. He suspects and ridicules the craze for Ossian, that "phantom begotten by the snug embrace of an impudent Highlander upon a cloud of tradition";[15] and he never, of course, rejects the tradition of learned Latin poetry as Herder and many other Germans did. This may have had something to do with his classical training, his firm regard for ancient Rome, which also had its political reasons. He never ceased admiring Lucretius, "a far higher poet than Virgil," Virgil himself, whom

* Smith, p. 41. The idea of early figurative language comes from Lucretius and is common in Blackwell, Blair, Kames, and Hartley. The influence of Vico is obscure. See Wellek, *Rise*, pp. 87 ff., and my review of Vico's *Autobiography* in *PQ, 24* (1945), 166–8.

he began to translate, and even Horace, his "great favorite." [16] If he despised French literature, we must ascribe his sweeping and ignorant condemnation to the violence of his patriotic and religious feelings, and not to any critical objection to the tradition of French poetry.* Wordsworth's great hero in poetry and life was Milton, and not far below him was Spenser; both are the most learned, even bookish, poets of the English tradition. Thus in a curious way, the wheel has come full circle: at first sight Wordsworth sounds like a naturalist defending the imitation of folk ballads and rustic speech; or at least as a primitivist of the same sort as Herder, favoring simple passionate "nature" poetry and condemning "art" and the artificial. But actually Wordsworth assimilates Spenser, Milton, Chaucer, and Shakespeare to his concept of "nature" without making them over into primitives, as the Germans for a certain period tried to do. Wordsworth expressly endorsed the Germans for exalting the judgment of Shakespeare.†

Also, the criticism of the Augustan tradition made by Wordsworth was by no means indiscriminate. Wordsworth knew Dryden and Pope intimately and had a great admiration for the Georgic tradition of descriptive and reflective poetry of the 18th century. There is a continuity in style and ideas between Thomson, Akenside, Dyer, and Wordsworth which can hardly be exaggerated.‡ Wordsworth merely shared the view of Joseph Warton that Pope "unluckily took the plain when the heights were within his reach." [17] The heights must mean the higher genres of sublime

* Cf. the sonnet "Great Men" with the astonishing lines, "But equally a want of books and men," about France (1802). Wordsworth called *Candide* "this dull product of a scoffer's pen" (*Excursion*, 11, 484), but he seems to have admired Racine's *Athalie*, and Béranger—of all poets! See Thomas Moore's *Diary*, p. 27, entry of October 24, 1820; and letter to J. Gibson, December, 1848; *Letters: Later Years*, 3, 1321.

† Smith, p. 178. This passage caused offense to Coleridge because it ignored his own endeavors to justify Shakespeare as an artist. See *Shakespearean Criticism*, 1, 18; 2, 306.

‡ Cf. "To this day I could repeat, with a little previous rummaging of my memory, several thousand lines of Pope." *Letters of the Wordsworth Family*, ed. W. Knight (Boston, 1907), 3, 122. On the continuity with the ideas in English descriptive poetry see esp. H. N. Fairchild, *Religious Trends in English Poetry* (New York, 1949), 3, 186 ff., and A. F. Potts, *Wordsworth's Prelude* (Ithaca, 1953), pp. 244 ff.

poetry, "the plain" must refer to the colloquial verse of the *Satires* and *Epistles*. The language spoken by men came to mean something very different from naturalism. It finally meant the language of Milton and Shakespeare, the impassioned language of the great poet.

We see here the bridge to an emotionalism which apparently is quite incompatible with the imitation of rustic speech. Wordsworth again seems to recommend an extreme position: the "spontaneous overflow of powerful feelings," the view that poetry is self-expression, release of personal emotions. The *Prelude* is a versified autobiography of 8500 lines; the poet himself recognized it as "a thing unprecedented in literary history that a man should talk so much about himself." [18] "Sincerity" is Wordsworth's constant standard for judging poetry, including his own. In the curious three essays "Upon Epitaphs" (1810), he assumes that the composer of an epitaph must "give proof that he himself has been moved," that he is a "sincere mourner," that his heart was not cold, that his soul labored. "If the unction of a devout heart be wanting everything else is of no avail." Wordsworth knows that this is a "criterion of sincerity," that the "sensations and judgments depend upon our opinion or feeling of the author's state of mind." If he senses what he calls an "under feeling," he can forgive errors of style and manner. Even fantastic images and bad taste need not stain the soul. [19]

Wordsworth argues at times as Dr. Johnson argued against *Lycidas:* a writer who is going out of his way in search of supposed beauties cannot be truly moved. But when for some purely instinctive reason Wordsworth feels that the poet is sincere, he forgives him the quaintest conceits. Even the line in an epitaph on a wife:

> God pluck'd my rose that He might take a smell

is condoned as coming from a "sincere mourner," whose "heart, during the very act of composition, was moved." [20] Yet Wordsworth could not have been certain whether the poem was composed by the husband, by the local curate, or by a professional rhymester. The goodness or badness of poetry has nothing to do with sincerity. The worst love poetry of adolescents is the most sincere. With no talent for the drama himself, Wordsworth could not understand a poet's assuming a mask or entering the mind of a fictional figure.

If the standard of sincerity were taken seriously, the critical problem would shift to the examination of the psychology and biography of the author. Nevertheless, Wordsworth very well recognized the limitations of such an approach. In the "Letter to Friend of Burns" he tells us that "our business is with their books —to understand and to enjoy them. And, of poets more especially it is true—that, if their works be good, they contain within themselves all that is necessary to their being comprehended and relished." [21] Wordsworth draws the distinction between two types of poetry which we might call "objective" and "subjective." It is, he thinks, "comparatively of little importance, while we are engaged in reading the *Iliad,* the *Æneid,* the tragedies of *Othello* and *King Lear,* whether the authors of these poems were good or bad men," though he assumes, rather rashly, that they *were* both good and happy. In Burns, however, he recognizes a subjectivity which makes it impossible to forget the author. He even admits that "genius is not incompatible with vice," for in Burns he could not very well ignore the evidence for drunkenness and lechery.* He suggests that Burns on the basis of his human character had reared a poetic one, or "constructed a poetic self." This excellent insight and the human charity he extended to Burns should have saved him from much unctuous moralizing about Goethe and Byron and from such rash generalizations as, "in the mind of the truly great and good . . . all is stillness, sweetness, and stable grandeur." †

Wordsworth cannot be put down as an advocate of emotional-

---

* Smith, pp. 212–3, 215. Wordsworth called Landor "a madman, a bad man, yet a man of genius, as many a madman is." See letter to W. R. Hamilton, April, 1843; *Letters: Later Years, 3,* 1164.

† See Peacock, *The Critical Opinions of William Wordsworth,* pp. 264–6, for a collection of Wordsworth's violent pronouncements about Goethe, his "inhuman sensuality," etc. based on a reading of the beginning of *Wilhelm Meister* and the "Bride of Corinth." On Byron see Peacock, pp. 202 ff. "All is stillness" in Smith, p. 124. Wordsworth can say that "poets are the happiest of men"—To Mary and Sara Hutchinson (1802), *Early Letters,* p. 305—a view which is connected with his emphasis on joy as necessity for the creation of poetry and thus with the depreciation of satire.

ism in the raw. When he repeated the famous phrase about the
"overflow of feelings," he modified it by saying, "it takes its origin
from emotion recollected in tranquillity; the emotion is contemplated till, by a species of reaction, the tranquillity gradually disappears, and an emotion, kindred to that which was before the
subject of contemplation, is gradually produced, and does itself
actually exist in the mind." [22] The process of creation here described sounds like the deliberate evocation of a past emotion
which reappears only as "kindred," and not identical with what it
was in the past. In many passages Wordsworth acknowledged the
share of consciousness in poetic composition. In his list of the
poetic faculties reflection and judgment take up third and sixth
place in what seems a hypothetical temporal order; observation
and sensibility precede reflection, which defines "the value of
actions, images, thoughts and feelings." Imagination, fancy, and invention precede judgment, which makes a choice between the
faculties to be asserted (whether imagination or fancy) and determines the species of composition, the genre.[23] One need hardly
cite the overwhelming evidence of Wordsworth's constant meticu-
lous revisions of his verse and his own statement: "my first expression I often find detestable; and it is frequently true of second
words as of second thoughts, that they are best." [24] Especially in
later life Wordsworth recognized "rules of art and workmanship"
and advised a friend that the "composition of verse is infinitely
more of an art than men are prepared to believe; and absolute
success in it depends upon innumerable minutiae. Milton talks of
'pouring easy his unpremeditated verse,' " but this tends to mislead
and must be taken with a grain of salt.[25] Wordsworth surely appreciated the virtues of formal discipline when he wrote in praise of
the sonnet "Nuns fret not at their convent's narrow room."

This recognition of the importance of revision and technique
was quite reconcilable in Wordsworth's mind with a reliance on
the initial inspiration, the "inward impulse." Many times Wordsworth says that the numbers "came spontaneously," that they
"came in such a torrent that he was unable to remember it," that
he "poured out a poem truly from the heart." Or he can say that
"these truths," in epitaphs, "should be instinctively ejaculated,"
"not spoken by rote, but perceived in their whole compass with
the freshness and clearness of an original intuition." [26]

Like many poets, he vacillates in deciding about the origins of this inspiration or intuition. Sometimes inspiration seems to come from above as "visitings of imaginative power"; at other times, more characteristically, it seems to rise from the inner life, from the buried past.

> A shy spirit in my heart
> That comes and goes—will sometimes leap
> From hiding-places ten years old.[27]

Much of his best poetry seems such a leaping from hiding places, or a search for the "spots of time," the gleam of childhood. But this evocation and expression of emotion is in Wordsworth's theory never, I believe, justified by purely personal needs of catharsis or by the joy of making for its own sake. Wordsworth always feels the need to justify poetry by the effect on the reader or to look in poetry for a means to knowledge.

Poetry to Wordsworth is primarily a manipulation of human feelings for a purpose: for man's mental and moral health and happiness. "A great poet ought to rectify men's feelings, to give them new compositions of feeling, to render their feelings more sane, pure, and permanent, in short, more consonant to nature, that is, to eternal nature, and the great moving spirit of things." [28] "Nature" here means in part an ideal humanity living close to outdoor nature, simply and frugally on the land, away from the evils of urban civilization, and in part, "nature" as the 18th century meant it: a consciousness of our common humanity, of the bond among all people and the unity between man and external nature. The emotional effect of poetry in arousing sympathy for other men, animals, and even inanimate objects is crucial: poems should delineate feelings "such as all men may sympathize with, and such as there is reason to believe they would be better and more moral beings if they did sympathize with." [29] One of the functions of poetry is that of jolting people out of their emotional indifference, making them realize the nature and the mystery of the world. Poetry serves as a stimulant against the "savage torpor" of our present age. But it must, of course, serve as a stimulus to *right* feelings and to the *right* kind of awareness. Frantic novels, German tragedies excite us wrongly. The poet must "bind together by passion and knowledge the vast empire of human society."

Readers must be "humbled and humanized, in order that they may be purified and exalted." [30] Thus poetry effects a catharsis: partly of false feelings, such as the prejudices arising through false refinement and social snobbery, and partly of bad and vicious feelings such as hatred or malice. The poet "widens the sphere of human sensibility, for the delight, honor, and benefit of human nature," he produces an "accord of sublimated humanity." [31] It all anticipates Tolstoy, On Art, though Tolstoy had never read Wordsworth. The common denominator is their Rousseauism, their enmity toward urban civilization, their trust in emotional spontaneity and sincerity, their concern for the effect of literature on humanity, as an instrument of unification in a spirit of love. Neither can escape the obvious difficulties raised by the criterion of sincerity and the attendant impossibility of drawing any kind of boundary between art and emotional persuasion, propaganda. Nor did they face the fact that in limiting the emotions to be aroused by art to those they considered good and right they shifted the criterion of evaluation to ethics, politics, and religion and ran into the constant danger of mere didacticism, judgment by good intention and right subject matter.

Unfortunately, Wordsworth takes his theory very literally, applying it to every single poem and every line. The cultivation of good feelings, of the "joy of that pure principle of love" * becomes the one central aim of poetry. That is why he condemns satire and all revolutionary or reform propaganda. Satirical attacks even on real abuses would divide men, tend to widen the class divisions, and weaken the "vital power of social ties." [32] Though one has to admit a certain overstatement for the occasion, Wordsworth's letter to Charles James Fox, accompanying a copy of Lyrical Ballads, must be taken seriously. He sends it to the statesman because he feels

* Excursion, IV, 1213. This passage, originally in "The Ruined Cottage" (1797), was quoted by Coleridge in the letter to George Coleridge in which he "snapped his squeaking baby-trumpet of sedition" and promised not to "encroach on the anti-social passions—in poetry, to elevate the imagination and set the affections in right tune by the beauty of the inanimate impregnated as with a living soul by the presence of life" (Letters, 1895, I, 243), a statement obviously in complete consonance with Wordsworth's aims. On satire see Peacock, p. 142.

that his poetry offers a remedy against "the rapid decay of the domestic affections among the lower orders of society." Family ties and the ties of property which bind the dalesman to his little plot of land are expressly set against the effects of industrialization and urbanization.[33] Wordsworth considered poems such as "Michael" or "The Brothers" as moral and political achievements in favor of a true agrarian democracy of freeholders, the "perfect republic of shepherds" in the Lakes.[34]

In these early pronouncements poetry is still largely thought of as a manipulation of feelings, not as the conveyance of moral propositions or truths. With the years Wordsworth's point of view became, however, more and more simply didactic and instructive. "Every great poet is a teacher: I wish either to be considered as a teacher, or as nothing." [35] Poetry even draws blueprints for Utopia. It is to be employed

> In framing models to improve the scheme
> Of Man's existence, and recast the world.[36]

But in spite of even clumsier moralistic or didactic formulas Wordsworth understood that poetry is not merely an inculcation of moral truths. In the inadequate vocabulary of the time he stresses the share of pleasure. "We have no sympathy but what is propagated by pleasure." [37] Meter is one of the elements of increasing pleasure. Wordsworth's discussion is frequently marred by his tendency to speak of meter as a "superadded charm," obviously because he wants to guard against the argument that meter "paves the way for other artificial distinctions" of diction or syntax. Meter, he recognizes, raises the mind as if to a new plane of consciousness and enhances what we would call aesthetic distance. It "tempers and restrains the passions." It has the tendency to "divest language, in a certain degree, of its reality, and thus to throw a sort of half-consciousness of unsubstantial existence over the whole composition." The reader of poetry has an "indistinct perception perpetually renewed of language closely resembling that of real life, and yet, in the circumstance of meter, differing from it widely." Wordsworth appeals to the ancient notion that meter induces a perception of similitude in dissimilitude, and this he interprets very broadly. Even sexual appetite is cited as an analogy.[38]

Wordsworth knew that poetry is not merely a means of conveying truth. He opposed it to matter of fact or science quite sharply.[39]
His general anti-intellectualism and hostility to science emphasized
the distinction between poetry and the intellect. We need not
quote the well-known passages about the "meddling intellect,"
"the false secondary power by which we multiply distinctions," or
the "dull eye, dull and inanimate" of science which, at the most,
is but a "succedaneum, and a prop to our infirmity." [40] Less well
known is the saying that science "waged war with and wished to
extinguish Imagination" and that he would much rather be a
"superstitious old woman" than a scientist without imagination
and without God.[41] It is thus a little surprising to read the passage
in the 1800 *Preface* which seems to envisage a collaboration between poetry and science. In foreseeing a material revolution
brought about by science Wordsworth predicts that the poet will
be at the side of the man of science, "carrying sensation into the
midst of the objects of the science itself." "The remotest discoveries
of the Chemist, the Botanist, or Mineralogist will be proper objects
of the Poet's art." "If the time should ever come when what is
now called science, thus familiarized to men, shall be ready to put
on, as it were, a form of flesh and blood, the Poet will lend his
divine spirit to aid the transfiguration." [42] This has been called
"an absurd fiction, undesirable and impossible," [43] but means, I
suggest, partly something very simple and concrete: a hope that
new scientific words and ideas will become material assimilable to
poetry in the same way that Copernican astronomy and Newtonian
optics had become; and partly a vaguer hope, similar to that of the
Naturphilosophen and to his friend Coleridge's, that science will
cease to be mechanistic and become reconcilable with a qualitative
and even aesthetic view of the world. It certainly shows that at this
point at least Wordsworth had given up some of his primitivism—
which, of course, never put complete reliance in a past golden age
—and that he kept his trust in man's creativity and the basic continuity of human feelings, predicting that poetry will be necessary
to humanity at all times. He has no use for theories of the inevitable extinction of poetry by science, though his association of poetry with childhood and an agrarian state of society might suggest
such an alignment. There is no nonsense in saying that poetry is
"the impassioned expression which is in the countenance of all

science" [44] if we think of poetry as an emotional way to knowledge, as Wordsworth thought of it many times. If Wordsworth's antipathy to science became stronger with time and his hope for "transfiguration" faded, to understand this we need only refer to the growing triumphs of technology and utilitarianism and the defeat of Coleridge's hope in a symbolic "philosophy of nature."

True knowledge, as we might expect in the later Wordsworth, is identical with religious insight. But Wordsworth refrains very carefully from an identification of poetry and religion. They are paralleled when he recognizes that both rely on symbols and "substitutions." "Poetry—ethereal and transcendent, yet incapable to sustain her existence without sensuous incarnation," [45] seems to be poetry in the Platonic sense, a spirit diffused through the world, a usage which has little support in Wordsworth's other writings. Commonly, all his emphasis is on the sensuous incarnation. He concedes that his own poetry is "not sacred in the highest acceptation of the word." In discussing epic poetry he agrees with John Dennis "that no subject but a religious one can answer the demand of the soul in the highest class of this species of poetry," and he endorses the subject of Tasso's *Gerusalemme liberata.* He himself, however, felt "unworthy to deal with matters high and holy." He apparently did not consider the *Ecclesiastical Sonnets* strictly religious poetry, and he carefully avoided controversial theological questions because he was afraid of error. [46] As religion moved in his mind more and more into a purely supernatural realm, outside of knowledge and even imaginative knowledge, poetry was kept to its own presumably lower station. But had not imagination been conceived as a way to knowledge, to insight into the nature of reality? Wordsworth, it seems, wavers on this point, or rather seems to hold two conceptions which he considers continuous with each other.

In many pronouncements imagination is substantially the 18th-century faculty of arbitrary recall and willful combination of images. In others it is the neo-Platonic intellectual vision. There is apparently no chronological progress from one conception to the other. The idea of imagination as vision occurs both early and late. There seems to be a distinction between statements in prose and statements in verse. The neo-Platonic metaphysical conception permeates the last books of the *Prelude* and the *Excursion,* the psy-

chological the *Preface* of 1815. The discussion in the *Prelude*, and
The Excursion, in verse, can hardly be treated as literary theory
without falsifying its tone and implication. The distinctions there
between imagination in general and the poetic imagination are so
fluid and obscure that it seems impossible to extract a coherent doctrine for poetics. Wordsworth disconcertingly vacillates among
three epistemological conceptions. At times he makes imagination
purely subjective, an imposition of the human mind on the real
world. At other times he makes it an illumination beyond the control of the conscious mind and even beyond the individual soul.
But most frequently he takes an in-between position which favors
the idea of a collaboration,

> An ennobling interchange
> Of action from within and from without.[47]

The many passages which suggest an extreme subjectivism, an
activity of the imagination exerting itself against the world, must
be always interpreted in the light of the other conceptions which
assume a continuity between mind and nature. When Wordsworth speaks of throwing a "certain coloring of imagination"
over "incidents and situations from common life," he justifies his
choice of subject matter. Even when he says that the duty of
poetry is "to treat things not as they *are*, but as they *appear*, not
as they exist in themselves, but as they *seem* to exist to the *senses*,
and to the *passions*," he defends the poet's emotion and transfiguration of reality and not psychological solipsism or illusionism,[48] which may seem to follow if we press the terms "appear" and
"seem."

The famous vision on Mount Snowdon suggests a parallelism
between the workings of nature and imagination: nature, represented by the moon, "moulds, endues, abstracts, combines." It has
a "genuine counterpart" in the imaginative faculty of "higher
minds" (geniuses, especially poets) who, like nature, can "create a
like existence." These higher minds can hold "communion with
the invisible world." They have genuine liberty, genuine free
will. This imagination is identified with

> absolute strength
> And clearest insight, amplitude of mind,
> And reason in her most exalted mood.[49]

It is then associated very closely with intellectual love. Imagination is here conceived as intellectual intuition, as a higher faculty of knowing, as reason, *nous, Vernunft,* which demands the association of love, the love of mankind and of God.* On occasion Wordsworth adopts the language of idealism and calls imagination "the faculty by which the poet conceives and produces—that is, images—individual forms in which are *embodied universal ideas* or *abstractions.*" † But such an approximation to the idea of poetry as a symbolism of abstractions is rare. More common is the view that imagination "turns upon infinity," "incites and supports the eternal," and thus suggests religion or, at least, religious feelings.[50]

Only the 1815 *Preface* brings the concept of imagination into closer relation with actual literary texts. There Wordsworth defends the ordering of his poems by explaining imagination and fancy in psychological terms. He objects to the usual definitions as making imagination and fancy only modes of memory and then tells that it rather means "processes of creation or of composition." His illustrations are, however, curiously inept: they merely cite very ordinary metaphorical transfers. Thus the samphire gatherer in *King Lear* "hangs" on the cliff, which, according to Wordsworth, shows imagination, because "hanging" is not to be understood as actual support from above but refers, presumably, to the precariousness of the man's hold on the rocks. Other examples are drawn from Wordsworth's own poetry. The stock-dove's voice is described as "buried among trees"; the phrase is not literally ac-

---

* I find unconvincing the attempt by R. D. Havens to deny that imagination in Wordsworth is a faculty of knowing. See *The Mind of a Poet,* esp. pp. 230–1.

† Crabb Robinson's Diary, September 11, 1816; a similar explanation in Diary, May 31, 1812; *H. C. Robinson on Books and Their Writers,* ed. E. J. Morley (London, 1938), *1,* 191. *Ibid.,* p. 89: "The poet first conceives the essential nature of his object and strips it of all casualties and accidental individual dress, and in this he is a philosopher; but to exhibit his abstraction nakedly would be the work of a mere philosopher; therefore he reclothes his *idea* in an individual dress which expresses the essential quality, and has also the spirit and life of a sensual object, and this transmutes the philosophic into a poetic exhibition." It is perhaps significant that these most intellectualist formulations come from Robinson, who knew German idealism and its vocabulary.

curate but suggests the love of seclusion of the bird and the effect
of the "voice being deadened by the intervening shade." Similarly,
calling the cuckoo a "wandering voice" is an instance of imagination, as "voice" is here a substitution depriving the creature almost
of a corporeal existence, while "wandering" suggests seeming
ubiquity. Wordsworth then proceeds to an analysis of more complex instances and discusses his own leechgatherer, who is compared to both a "huge stone" and a "sea-beast." The stone is given
some measure of life to make it similar to the beast, and the sea-
beast is deprived of some life to assimilate it to the stone. Thus
imagination is defined, in a quotation from Charles Lamb, as
"drawing all things to one," as "consolidating numbers into
unity" but also as "dissolving and separating unity into number." [51]
It seems thus both a unifying and an analyzing power. Elsewhere
Wordsworth discusses his sonnet "With ships at the sea" as another
example of the mind fastening on an individual object (a ship)
among a multitude of others, as if the poem were an elementary
lesson in the psychology of attention.[52] Wordsworth here seems not
to go beyond the idea that imagination dissolves, endows, modifies, and abstracts, and when he speaks of imagination as shaping
and creating, he seems to think of nothing more than "consolidating numbers into unity."

Next comes the distinction between fancy and imagination, for
which Wordsworth quotes Coleridge's passing reference in *Omniana*.* Wordsworth argues that Coleridge's definition of fancy as
the "aggregative or associative power" (in contrast to imagination
as the "shaping or modifying power") is too general. He maintains
that imagination, as well as fancy, aggregates and associates, evokes
and combines, and that fancy, as well as imagination, is a creative
faculty. But actually Wordsworth's own theory is well in agreement
with Coleridge's, at least, as that theory was developed or put on

* *Omniana* (London, 1812), 2, 13. It might be added that the earliest
distinction in Wordsworth between fancy and imagination comes from
the note to "The Thorn" in the 1800 edition of *Lyrical Ballads*. It
differs in emphasis. "Imagination [is] the faculty which produces impressive effects out of simple elements; . . . fancy, . . . the power by
which pleasure and surprise are excited by sudden varieties of situation
and an accumulated imagery." *Poetical Works,* ed. de Selincourt, 2,
512.

paper a little later.* Both Wordsworth and Coleridge make the distinction between fancy, a faculty which handles "fixities and definites," and imagination, a faculty which deals with the "plastic, the pliant and the indefinite." [53] The only important difference between Wordsworth and Coleridge is that Wordsworth does not clearly see Coleridge's distinction between Imagination as a "holistic" and fancy as an associative power and does not draw the sharp distinction between transcendentalism and associationism which Coleridge wanted to establish. His own examples lead to a rather naive revival of the difference between the beautiful and sublime. We are in the presence of fancy when definite sizes are indicated, in the presence of imagination when we hear that the Archangel's "stature reached the sky" or when the firmament is called "illimitable." [54] Chesterfield's conceit of referring to the "dews of the evening" as the "tears of the sky" is dismissed as fancy, while Milton's sky weeping "sad drops" at the completion of Adam's fall is approved as imagination because "the mind acknowledges the justice and reasonableness of the sympathy in nature." [55] In practice this amounts to a rating of imagery in terms of seriousness. Fancy is disparaged because it is based on some kind of deceit. Fancy is recognized by the rapidity with which she scatters her thoughts and images, and by the "curious subtilty and the successful elaboration with which she can detect the lurking affinities" of thoughts and images.[56] Fancy is thus a sleight of hand and an intellectual exercise. Combinatory power, intellectual subtlety are unpoetic compared to the slow workings of imagination dealing with indefinite illimitable objects. The distinction serves to devalue the whole line of wit—both 17th and 18th century poetry—though Wordsworth concludes by quoting an "admirable composition," Cotton's *Ode upon Winter,* as an example of fancy.

The distinction between fancy and imagination is parallel to a distinction between the animating metaphors or personifications of the 18th century of which Wordsworth disapproves and the metaphors which he himself uses. This is not very clear theoretically

---

* I am not convinced by Clarence D. Thorpe's argument that on this point there is a deep disagreement between Wordsworth and Coleridge. See "The Imagination: Coleridge versus Wordsworth," *PQ, 18* (1939), 1–18.

but is apparently based on some final test of truth. Chesterfield is wrong, because the "dews of the evening" are not the "tears of the sky." Milton is right because it is spiritually true that the sky should weep at Adam's fall. "I have never given way to my own feelings in personifying natural objects," says a late letter, "without bringing all that I have said to a rigorous after-test of good sense." [57] But surely Wordsworth's good sense is not that of other men: it includes the belief in a profound identity of man and nature, in the good heart of the ass, in the flower enjoying the air it breathes, and in the "unutterable love in the silent faces of the clouds." [58] Imagination is thus linked and fused with Wordsworth's view, or rather feeling, of the world as a unity and community of living beings.

Wordsworth rarely uses what is the critically most fruitful element in the theory of imagination: the insight into the wholeness and totality of a work of art. After alluding to August Wilhelm Schlegel, he praises Shakespeare's "judgment in the selection of his materials, and in the manner in which he has made them, heterogeneous as they often are, constitute a unity of their own, and contribute all to one great end." [59] His objections to 18th-century poetry are frequently directed against something which could be called its atomism: the "glaring hues of diction" which show no appreciation of a "pure and refined scheme of harmony"; or the imagery of Macpherson, "defined, insulated, dislocated, in absolute independent singleness." [60] A standard of unity or rather of continuous flow is also at the basis of his criticism of *ottave rime* in an epic poem such as Tasso's, or behind his praise of the sonnet for its "pervading sense of intense unity." "Instead of looking at this composition as a piece of architecture, making a whole out of three parts, I have been much in the habit of preferring the image of an orbicular body, a sphere, or a dewdrop." [61] The analogy from building is rejected in favor of an analogy, not from an organism but from the roundness of a geometrical sphere.

Wordsworth thus holds a position in the history of criticism which must be called ambiguous or transitional. He inherits from neoclassicism a theory of the imitation of nature to which he gives, however, a specific social twist; he inherits from the 18th century a view of poetry as passion and emotion which he again modifies by his description of the poetic process as "recollection in tranquillity." He takes up rhetorical ideas about the effect of poetry but extends and amplifies them into a theory of the social effect of literature, binding society in a spirit of love. But he also adopts, in order to meet the exigencies of his mystical experiences, a theory of poetry in which imagination holds the central place as a power of unification and ultimate insight into the unity of the world. Though Wordsworth left only a small body of criticism, it is rich in survivals, suggestions, anticipations, and personal insights.

THE REPUTATION of Samuel Taylor Coleridge (1772–1834) as a philosopher and critic stands today higher than ever. Saintsbury eliminated one after another of possible contenders for the title of greatest critic and concluded: "So, then, there abide these three, Aristotle, Longinus, and Coleridge." [1] Arthur Symons called *Biographia Literaria* "the greatest book of criticism in English." [2]
Since then—in spite of occasional demurrers—Coleridge's stature,
at least in the English-speaking world, has grown even greater. J. H.
Muirhead has proclaimed Coleridge the founder of the voluntaris-
tic form of idealistic philosophy, of which "he remains to this day
the most distinguished representative." [3] I. A. Richards has hailed
Coleridge as a forerunner of the modern science of semantics. Coleridge's "step across the threshold of a general theoretical study of
language was of the same type as that which took Galileo into the
modern world." [4] Herbert Read considers Coleridge "as head and
shoulders above every other English critic" and sees him anticipating existentialism and Freud.[5] Most recent American literary critics
discuss no older critic except Aristotle, Coleridge and Arnold.
Constant references are being made to Coleridge's principle of the
reconciliation of opposites, to his definition of the imagination, to
the idea of the organic whole and to his distinction between symbol
and allegory.[6]

But if we look at Coleridge from an international perspective,
fresh from our reading of Kant, Schiller, Schelling, the Schlegels,
Jean Paul, Solger, and all the others, we must, I think, come to a
considerably lower estimate of his significance, however great and
useful his role was in mediating between Germany and England.
It is not simply a question of plagiarism or even of direct dependence on German sources, though these cannot be so easily dismissed
or shirked as it has become the custom of a good many writers on
Coleridge to do. We need not reopen the question of plagiarism as

an ethical issue and psychological problem. One should grant much to Coleridge's defenders. Coleridge's memory may have been weakened by ill health and opium; his habits of note-taking were such that he could have mistaken a translation of his own for original reflections; there are scattered acknowledgments in Coleridge's printed and unprinted writings; there was no need or even opportunity for citation of sources in public lectures, the notes for which were never meant for print and might never have been claimed by Coleridge as his own work. Besides, Coleridge held a theory of truth as the "divine ventriloquist," speaking from whatever mouth it chose. He was genuinely anxious to receive support from the agreement of other men, and often could justly feel that he had arrived at ideas and conclusions on his own, even though in his exposition he buttressed them with phrases from his German contemporaries.[7]

Nevertheless, there remains a residue of indebtedness which cannot be eliminated. At crucial points in his writings Coleridge used Kant, Schelling, and A. W. Schlegel, reproducing the very pattern of sentences and the exact vocabulary. Whatever the ethics or psychology of the situation, it seems impossible to give Coleridge credit for ideas simply quoted literally. This is particularly true of the long passages from Schelling in chapters 12 and 13 of *Biographia Literaria* (1817) which lead up to the distinction between imagination and fancy and represent the most sustained attempt at an epistemological and metaphysical foundation for his theories. Much that has impressed I. A. Richards and Herbert Read—the discussion of the subject-object relation, their synthesis and identity, and the appeal to the unconscious—is simply the teaching of Schelling and cannot be made the basis of a claim for Coleridge's philosophical greatness. Coleridge's lecture "On Poesy or Art" (1818), which has been used by several expositors of his aesthetics as the key to his thought, is with the exception of a few insertions of pious sentiments little more than a paraphrase of Schelling's Academy Oration of 1807.[8] The series of papers "On the Principles of Genial Criticism" (1814), which Coleridge considered "the best things he had ever written,"[9] follow the distinctions drawn in Kant's *Critique of Judgment* at times so closely that Coleridge takes over even Kant's anecdotes and illustrations.[10] In discussing the contrast between ancient and modern literature Coleridge reproduces a crucial passage from Schiller's *Naive and Sentimental Poetry*.[11] The manuscript notes for the lecture on "Wit and Humor" are a patchwork of quotations from Jean Paul's *Vorschule*.[12] In many instances Coleridge borrowed from A. W. Schlegel. A lecture on Greek drama is simply a translation from Schlegel and "ought not to be included in Coleridge's works at all." [13] Many crucial distinctions are derived from Schlegel. Thus the formula for the distinction between "mechanical regularity" and "organic form" is a literal translation.[14]

These are the main examples of direct quotations or paraphrase in Coleridge's aesthetic and critical writings. Many more could be drawn from his philosophical and scientific speculations. *Theory of Life* is merely a mosaic of passages from Schelling and Steffens; the lecture on Aeschylus' *Prometheus* paraphrases Schelling's *Gods of Samothrace*.[15] The big two-volume "Logic," still unpublished for the most part, is largely an elaborate exposition of the *Critique of Pure Reason* with all its architectonics, tables of categories, and antinomies taken over literally.[16] The history of association psychology in *Biographia Literaria* comes from Maass, an obscure German writer on imagination.[17] The newly published *Philosophical Lectures* draw most of their information and learning from Tennemann's *History of Philosophy*.[18] Even among the poems are unacknowledged translations: the most serious is the case of the "Hymn Before Sunrise," where it is impossible to deny the evidence for deliberate concealment.[19] In all the cases cited Coleridge must have had the actual texts in front of him or used detailed notes taken directly from them. It seems to me a matter of intellectual honesty not to credit Coleridge with ideas distinctly derived and even literally transcribed from others.

Coleridge himself defined his relations to Schelling and A. W. Schlegel. In the *Biographia Literaria*, Coleridge makes a general acknowledgment to Schelling and even says that "it will be happiness and honor enough, should I succeed in rendering the system itself intelligible to my countrymen." [20] But marginalia of uncertain date are severely critical, accusing Schelling even of "gross materialism," and, late in life, Coleridge expressly condemned the metaphysical disquisition at the end of the first volume of the *Biographia Literaria* (i.e. the argument taken from Schelling) as "unformed and immature;—it contains the fragments of the truth, but it is not fully thought out." [21] In a public lecture on March 22, 1819, Coleridge virulently attacked Schelling as a "Roman Catholic pantheist," and there is plenty of other evidence of Coleridge's disapproval.* Yet it would be a misunderstanding of the workings of Coleridge's mind to conclude that adherence to Schelling's views was only a passing phase: Coleridge simply wanted to separate himself from pantheism and disapproved of conversions to Rome. This did not prevent him from absorbing and using Schelling's ideas and vocabulary elsewhere: they can be found in *Theory of Life* (1816), in *Aids to Reflection* (1825), and all over the late theological writings.[22] Also the criticism of Kant, in the MS "Logic," is largely drawn from the writings of the young Schelling,[23] and we shall see that Coleridge's literary theory is deeply indebted to Schelling's central ideas. One need not even assume that any special revulsion occurred between March 10, 1818, when Coleridge treated his audience to a paraphrase of Schelling's oration on the fine arts, and the lecture almost exactly a year afterward denouncing him as a Roman Catholic. Coleridge could approve and absorb the aesthetics, the *Naturphilosophie*, and even the analysis of the subject-object relation, and still want to draw a sharp line to exclude anything that seemed incompatible with his own Anglican orthodoxy.

Coleridge did not live to defend himself against the accusations of plagiarism from Schelling.[24] He did defend himself against similar accusations with regard to Schlegel and did so rather effectively.[25] He is surely right in saying that he did not need a knowledge of Schlegel to declare Shakespeare's judgment equal to his genius. The arguments against the conception of Shakespeare as the noble savage violating all the rules are spelled out in Lessing and are implied in many early English discussions of Shakespeare's art, e.g. in Webb, Morgann, and others. Also Coleridge could very well feel that his conception of Hamlet as an intellectual was original with him and differed widely from the character sketch in A. W. Schlegel's *Lectures*. Actually, Friedrich Schlegel was the

* *PL*, pp. 390–1. Coleridge repeats malicious gossip, with no foundation in fact. Schelling never was converted. Miss Coburn's transcription must be at fault in telling of a call of Schelling to "Geneva." It might be "Jena." There were negotiations in 1816 about a recall to Jena. See Schelling's *Werke*, ed. Otto Weiss (Leipzig, 1907), *1*, lxxvii.

first to suggest such an interpretation, but Coleridge is not in any way verbally dependent on his brief passage.[26] Yet while Coleridge is right on these most important points, he gives an entirely misleading account of the chronology of his relations to A. W. Schlegel.* He himself acknowledges that he read Schlegel late in

---

* Coleridge asserts that he had never heard of Schlegel's *Lectures* before December 12, 1811, when a German auditor of his, one Bernard Kruse (T. M. Raysor reads the name "Krusve," but this seems a most unlikely form), brought a copy to his desk and told him that "it was just published as he left Germany, scarcely more than a week since" (*SC, 2,* 236–7). As Coleridge first lectured on Shakespeare in Jan., 1808, the charge of dependence on Schlegel seems refuted. But two facts are to be noted. For one thing, Schlegel's first two vols. were actually published in 1809 and the third (which contains the discussion of Shakespeare) in December 1810 (with a title-page date of 1811), a whole year before the conversation with Kruse. See, J. Körner, *Die Botschaft der deutschen Romantik an Europa* (Augsburg, 1929), p. 24. Secondly, it is not true that Coleridge had not heard of Schlegel's *Lectures* before December 12, 1811. On January 29, 1811, Coleridge was discussing "Schlegel's idea of the Greek chorus" with Henry Crabb Robinson, clear proof that he had read the first vol. (*SC, 2,* 212). On Nov. 6, 1811, he wrote to Robinson: "I am very anxious to see Schlegel's *Werke* before the lectures commence" (*SC, 2,* 222), an expression which can hardly be interpreted as a desire for first acquaintance with Schlegel's writings. In the third lecture on Nov. 24, 1811, Coleridge is reported to have discussed "the unity of interest," a term which must be derived from the first vol. of Schlegel's *Lectures,* as it seems highly improbable that Coleridge could have known Schlegel's own source, the early 18th-century French critic, De La Motte (*SC, 2, 82*).

The considerable similarities between Coleridge's discussion of *Romeo and Juliet* and Schlegel's (*SC, 1, 6–7, 11; 2, 144*) can best be explained if we assume that Coleridge knew Schlegel's famous essay in *Charakteristiken und Kritiken* (1801), or in its first printing in Schiller's *Horen* (1797), a magazine widely known and fresh from the press when Coleridge was in Germany. The argument which makes Coleridge's acquaintance with Schlegel begin on December 12, 1811, ignores the ample opportunities which Coleridge had of knowing German criticism from other books, periodicals, and personal contacts. Coleridge knew Tieck in Rome in 1806 and talked with him about Shakespeare's doubtful plays. *MC,* p. 287; *L., 2, 670*; E. K. Chambers, *Coleridge* (Oxford, 1938), p. 190. Tieck's sister, Sophie Bernhardi, reported enthusiastically

1811 and certainly after 1811 Coleridge's Shakespeare lectures draw heavily on Schlegel. Coleridge even took the volumes with him to the 1812–13 lectures and asked again for them for the 1813–14 lectures.[27] The later lectures do not tread on the same ground, probably because Schlegel had been translated by John Black in 1815 and could thus be known to the audience.

One has to conclude that Coleridge's assertions about dates of acquaintance with specific texts and his professions of hostility to German authors and their religious or philosophical views are of little relevance to the discussion of influence. In the case of Schelling and Schlegel the evidence for direct borrowings is irrefutable. It must be stated, of course, that it affects only certain parts of Coleridge's philosophical and critical writings.

But beyond verbal reproductions and close paraphrases, we must also realize that many or even most of Coleridge's key terms and distinctions are derived from Germany. The general aesthetic position—the view of the relation between art and nature, the reconciliation of opposites, the whole dialectical scheme—comes from Schelling. The distinction between symbol and allegory can be found in Schelling and Goethe, the distinction between genius and talent in Kant, the distinctions between organic and mechanical, classical and modern, statuesque and picturesque in A. W. Schlegel. Coleridge's particular use of the term "Idea" comes from the Germans, and the way in which he links imagination with the process of cognition is also clearly derived from Fichte and Schelling. It is true, of course, that some of these ideas have their ultimate source in antiquity and can be found occasionally in the English neo-Platonists. Coleridge was acquainted with Plato, Plotinus, Cudworth, Henry More, and others, but still he draws on the

_____

to August Wilhelm (then at Coppet) about the "wonderful Englishman" (she had forgotten his name!) who had studied Kant, Fichte, Schelling, and the Old German poets and admired Schlegel's translation of Shakespeare "unbelievably." Letter, Feb. 6, 1806, in *Krisenjahre der Frühromantik. Briefe aus dem Schlegelkreis*, ed. J. Körner (Brünn, 1936), *1*, 291–2. Coleridge knew Wilhelm von Humboldt in Rome well enough to read Wordsworth's *Intimations Ode* to him (*Fr.*, p. 337). He constantly borrowed German books from De Quincey and Robinson. Coleridge, we must conclude, was an omnivorous reader well abreast of German aesthetics and philosophy.

Germans, for only they use the same dialectical method as he, the same epistemology and the same critical vocabulary. The neo-Platonists remained essentially scholastic mystics.* Coleridge could not have been known to Schopenhauer, Hegel, De Sanctis, or Belinsky, and still most of the concepts, theories, and ideas which in the English-speaking world are today ascribed to Coleridge can be found in them. In Germany there was a large body of aesthetic thought which slowly radiated to France, Italy, Spain, and Russia. In England Coleridge stood quite alone, sharply distinct even from his close associates, Wordsworth, Lamb, and Hazlitt, who had only very slight German contacts. The vocabulary, the dialectical scheme, the whole intellectual atmosphere sets Coleridge apart. The difference is explainable only by Coleridge's adaptation and importation of the Germans. This in itself constituted an important historical merit which should not be minimized. Coleridge was the main source, in this respect, not only for a long line of English critics but also for the American transcendentalists and for Poe, and thus indirectly for the French symbolists.

What has just been said and needed to be said might be interpreted as implying that Coleridge was a mere echo of the Germans with no originality and no independence. This is not the case.

* All this is ignored by those who make Coleridge completely independent of the Germans, thus flying in the face of all evidence, e.g. most recently R. L. Brett, "Coleridge's Theory of the Imagination," in *English Studies 1949,* ed. Sir Philip Magnus (London, 1949), pp. 75–90. One important piece of evidence is that Coleridge introduced many terms and pairs of terms, common today, into English from the German: psychological, aesthetic, objective—subjective, organic—mechanical, Reason—Understanding, transcendent—transcendental, symbol—allegory, statuesque, classical—romantic, etc. See J. Isaacs, "Coleridge's Critical Terminology," *Essays and Studies,* 21 (1936), 86–104. In a few cases others were picking up these terms a little earlier. Coleridge himself sometimes tried to trace them far back into history and argued that these distinctions existed in the schoolmen and English divines. But he produced no convincing evidence. Even "sensuous," though used by Milton once, seems to me suggested by "sinnlich." "Atmosphere" in a literary sense, which Isaacs considers original with Coleridge, is used by Herder and others before. Even "potence" was suggested by Schelling's use, though the term occurs in John Brown's *Elementa medicinae* (1780) before and can be traced back to Giordano Bruno.

Rather, Coleridge combines the ideas he derived from Germany in a personal way, and he combines them moreover with elements of the 18th-century tradition of neoclassicism and British empiricism. We shall try to analyze these different strains and see how well Coleridge's system stands up under close inspection.

Coleridge differs from almost all preceding English writers by his claim to an epistemology and metaphysics from which he derives his aesthetics and finally his literary theory and critical principles. He aimed at a complete systematic unity and continuity even though in practice he left wide gaps. But he made an attempt and he insisted rightly on the significance of the attempt. He sometimes speaks of his "disease of totalizing and perfecting" and tells a story about his fanciful impulse to complete the perishable architecture of some smoldering pieces of wood in a fireplace, late at night.[28] But usually he states earnestly and with conviction that the "end and purpose of all reason is unity and system," that the "ultimate end of human thought and human feeling is unity."[29] We must aim at "fixed canons of criticism, previously established and deduced from the nature of man," at a "science of reasoning and judging concerning the productions of literature."[30] Method is Coleridge's constant watchword: it inspired his interests in encyclopedias and the classification of all knowledge. Method means "unity with progression," "that which unites, and makes many things *one* in the mind of man," the "keynote," the "initiative."[31] Coleridge goes to the extravagant length of saying that poetry "owes its whole charm, and all its beauty, and all its power, to the philosophical principles of Method."[32] The statement assumes meaning if we know that method means unity and unifying power and that method is hence identical with the workings of the creative imagination.

These principles, Coleridge argues, must be based on "human nature," i.e. must follow from an analysis of the human mind. Coleridge disconcertingly wavers between a psychological and an epistemological foundation for such an analysis. It is the same basic uncertainty we shall find elsewhere, the same conflict between the tradition of empirical psychology and the dialectics of the German idealists. Coleridge says of himself in the 1790's that "according to the faculty or source, from which the pleasure given by any poem or passage was derived, I estimated the merit of such a poem or passage." [33] In the famous definition of poetry in *Biographia Literaria* an appeal is made to the psychic effect on the reader. The poet "brings the whole soul of man into activity, with the subordination of its faculties to each other, according to their relative worth and dignity." [34] Coleridge never elaborated such a psychological scheme; yet he ranked the faculties, beginning with the senses and ascending to reason, in a fairly clear scale, and he used the distinction between imagination and fancy as a value criterion. Elsewhere he more ambitiously tried to "deduce" the position of the arts (and of poetry) from an analysis of the epistemological situation, very much like Fichte's or Schelling's analysis. He proclaims that it is "the office and object of his philosophy" to "demonstrate the identity of subject and object." [35] He conceives of nature as identical with that which exists in man as intelligence and self-consciousness. Being is identified with knowing and truth.[36] Art assumes its place as a "mediatress between, and reconciler of, nature and man," as a "union and reconciliation of that which is nature with that which is exclusively human." [37] But this exaltation of art to a metaphysical role which makes it the center of philosophy is merely a reproduction from Schelling and remains isolated in Coleridge's writings. He gives up the attempt to bridge the gap between the subject-object relation and the imagination, either because he remains unconvinced by Schelling's elaborate deduction or because he genuinely feels that he cannot impose the long argument from the *System of Transcendental Idealism* on his readers. He thus adopts the clumsy expedient of introducing a letter from a friend protesting against the abstruseness of the argument, and he summarizes his conclusion in the famous passage on the primary and secondary imagination. This distinction, again derived from Schelling, asserts the existence of a power of imagination which constitutes perception and is thus unconscious, while artistic imagination, though continuous with the all-human primary imagination, differs by "co-existing with the conscious will." [38] Coleridge never again, I believe, used the distinction between primary and secondary imagination and never again discussed the function of art in the exalted terms of Schelling's oration.

Coleridge usually ignores the problem of art and discusses beauty. At times he uses the Schellingian vocabulary: Beauty is "the shorthand hieroglyphic of truth—the mediator between truth and feeling, the head and the heart, a silent communion of the Spirit with the Spirit in Nature."[39] But elsewhere he adopts ideas common in Schiller about the union of life and shape as the essence of beauty.[40] In other contexts he lapses into a neo-Platonic mystical terminology; he can speak of "supersensuous beauty, the beauty of virtue and holiness," and of its immediate perception as "light to the eye."[41] Most often he repeats the ancient theory of beauty as harmony, as the one in the many.[42] At other times, he reproduces Kant's arguments for the distinction of the beautiful from the useful and the agreeable. Like Kant, Coleridge insists that beauty must give "immediate pleasure," which is his odd way of translating Kant's "interesseloses Wohlgefallen," i.e. a pleasure where nothing comes in between (*inter-est*) or mediates between us and the object.[43] But all these speculations on beauty in Coleridge are undigested and uncorrelated: they do not lead to a theory of literature and play no role in it, though Coleridge, one must assume, sees in the principle of unity in variety the bridge between general beauty and poetry.

Coleridge's speculations on the sublime, though various enough, do not hang together and hardly enter his theory of literature.[44] As in Kant, the sublime is considered as subjective: "No object of sense is sublime in itself, but only as far as I make it a symbol of some Idea." Coleridge gives an example: "the circle is a beautiful figure in itself; it becomes sublime, when I contemplate eternity under it."[45] Elsewhere the sublime is considered "neither whole nor parts, but unity as boundless and endless allness," a "total completeness."[46] At other times Coleridge accepts a close relation between the sublime and infinity and like Schelling and the Schlegels applies it to a distinction between ancient and modern literature. Greek literature is finite, Christian romantic literature strives for the infinite. Thus Coleridge can deny sublimity to the Greeks and quote passages from the Bible and Milton as examples of the sublime.[47] But little is made of these conceptions in practice, nor is anything made of such related terms as the "grand" and the "majestic."

In like manner Coleridge's pronouncements on taste hardly go beyond the issues raised in Kant's *Critique of Judgment*. Coleridge is worried by the analogy drawn from tasting and is careful to emphasize that taste is not merely a sense of pleasure and pain but implies "an intellectual perception of the object," which is "blended with a distinct reference to our own sensibility of pain and pleasure." [48] Elsewhere he makes observations in the style of 18th-century discussions: he approves Reynolds' view that taste must be acquired by a study of the best models and should be based on an acquaintance with the principles of grammar, logic, and psychology, "rendered instinctive by habit." [49] At times he simply adopts Kant's analysis of taste; he calls it an intermediate faculty between intellect and the senses and ascribes to it the role imagination plays elsewhere: it elevates the images of senses and realizes the ideas of the intellect. [50] Coleridge also raises the central problem of the *Critique of Judgment* concerning the universality of taste and decides it in the Kantian way: "we involuntarily claim that all other minds ought to think and feel the same." Each man at the moment "legislates for all men." Like Kant, Coleridge draws the distinction between the judgment of taste, in which we "*expect* that others should coincide with us. But we *feel* no right to demand it," and the judgment of moral action, which is compulsory and thus categorical. [51]

These different fragments on aesthetics derived from a variety of sources, from Schelling, from Kant, and from 18th-century psychologists, do not give Coleridge an important position in a history of general aesthetics. His specific theory of poetry is far more important, for in it he made a genuine attempt at synthesis. Coleridge tried to work out a scheme that would unify a description of the poet, his equipment and faculties, with a description of the work of art itself and its effect on the reader. Within these three main divisions he tried to apply one and the same logical principle. There is a principle of unity, he argues, but within it there is distinction which must not, however, be complete contradiction and separation. The logic is that of the whole being the sum of the parts but more than the sum of the parts. This "holistic" logic alternates disconcertingly, however, with the application of a triadic scheme of dialectics: the reconciliation of opposites, thesis, antithesis, and synthesis. At other times the elaborate scheme is abandoned and Coleridge comfortably solves his problem by being on both sides at once.

There is first the poet or (almost identical in meaning) genius, e.g. Shakespeare, who is the ideal poet. A long list of qualifications is required in the poet: sensibility, passion, will, good sense, judgment, fancy, imagination, etc. He must be also a good man and *"implicite,* if not *explicite,* a profound metaphysician," a profound philosopher. A poet "is also an historian and naturalist in the light as well as the life of philosophy." Furthermore, he is a religious man. "An undevout poet," Coleridge proclaims, is "mad, is an impossibility." [52] This assertion seems to fly in the face of evidence but makes sense if interpreted freely as meaning that the poet must be struck by wonderment at the mystery of the universe. These pronouncements sound like those of Renaissance poetics and are open to the charge of the intellectualist error. On occasion, Coleridge seems to have fallen into it. He describes the desired preparation of the poet even in anatomy, hydrostatics, metallurgy, fossilism, and so on. He himself studied all the sciences for his projected hymns on the sun, the moon, and the elements, and, pressed the role of a systematic philosophic poet on Wordsworth.[53] But mostly, Coleridge recognizes that there is a diversity in the identity between philosopher and poet. While he could not describe it theoretically, he himself acutely experienced the conflict in his own life.

The inclusiveness of such philosophic requirements is clarified if we realize that genius for Coleridge is always objective, impersonal, directed toward a grasp of the whole universe. A poet is not excited by personal interests. "To have a genius is to live in the universal, to know no self but that which is reflected not only from the faces of all around us, our fellow-creatures, but reflected from the flowers, the trees, the beasts, yea from the very surface of the waters and the sands of the desert. A man of genius finds a reflex to himself, were it only in the mystery of being." [54] In Shakespeare's early poems Coleridge sees the promise of genius in a "choice of subjects very remote from the private interests and circumstances of the writer himself." The highest praise is given to Shakespeare for the "utter aloofness of the poet's own feelings, from those of which he is at once the painter and the analyst." [55] Shakespeare is like "the Spinozistic deity—an omnipresent creativeness." [56] This impersonality, this contemplative absorption in rendering reality by creating a new one, requires judgment. Coleridge is tireless in insisting on Shakespeare's genius revealing "itself in his judgment, as in its most exalted form." This genius is so consummate that it reveals itself "not only in the general construction, but in all the detail." [57]

From these pronouncements we might conclude that the poet is a philosopher, an impersonal observer, a self-conscious, judicious maker. But Coleridge, with his view of the poet as the whole man, can at the same time say that the poet works "unconsciously." "There is in genius itself an unconscious activity; nay, this is *the* genius in the man of genius." [58] As in Schelling or the Schlegels the poet is both conscious and unconscious. But in Coleridge the poet is also the man of sensibility and the man of passion. He creates in "an unusual state of excitement," in a "steady fervor" of the mind.[59] Not only is the poet thus a man of intense feeling: he has preserved this feeling from his childhood. "The poet is one who carries the simplicity of childhood into the powers of manhood." [60] Coleridge does not think the gifts he heaps upon the poet contradictory; the poet is simply everything: both conscious and unconscious, both a philosopher and a child, both constructive and emotional. Coleridge claims for himself an unusual union of intellect and feeling; Wordsworth, another example of a genius not quite so perfect as Shakespeare, is praised for a "union of deep and subtle thought with sensibility," for his "meditative pathos," a quality which combines philosophy and emotion.[61]

Still, while the poet is the whole man, he has a specific faculty which is his alone or is at least shared only by other creators. This faculty is imagination, which is the power of unifying things, of being all things. Coleridge misinterpreted the ordinary German word *Einbildungskraft* to mean "In-eins-Bildung," which he then translated into Greek as "esemplastic" or "coadunating" power.[62] Imagination is the power of objectifying oneself, the Protean self-transforming power of genius. "To become all things and yet remain the same, to make the changeful God be felt in the river, the lion and the flame—this is, that is true Imagination." [63] But within the scale of powers of the poet's mind the imagination has also this unifying function: it mediates between reason and understanding. It is, like reason, independent of space and time and thus gives the poet the faculty of disposing with space and time.[64] Imagination is also the power of changing the possible into the real, "the potential into the actual," the "essence into existence." [65] This notion seems to be derived from Leibniz and provides the bridge between the conception of the poet and the poetry itself. In his famous definition of the imagination as the balance or reconciliation of opposites Coleridge can indiscriminately mix traits descriptive of the poet with contraries observable only in the work of art. "What is poetry?" is, in Coleridge's mind, "nearly the same question with, what is a poet?" [66]

Genius and imagination in the poet are distinguished from corresponding lower faculties, talent and fancy. These are not opposites in the sense that genius excludes talent, or imagination excludes fancy. Rather, genius needs talent and imagination needs fancy. Still, they are distinct and widely different faculties. Genius and imagination are unifying, reconciling: they belong to the level of Coleridge's holistic and dialectical thought, while talent and fancy are only combinatory and thus mechanistic, associationist. Genius is a gift, talent is manufactured; genius is creative, talent mechanical. It is the contrast "between each part separately conceived and then put together as the pictures on a motley screen," with a landscape behind which is "a single energy, modified *ab intra* in each component part." [67] The preservation of fancy and talent is another attempt to keep empirical and associationist thought undisturbed in a subordinate position below an idealistic system.

The distinction between genius and talent has become common since Kant. The distinction between imagination and fancy seems to come from the Scottish 18th-century psychological tradition: it is found in William Duff, Dugald Stewart, Arthur Browne and Robert E. Scott.[68] But only in the Germans is it definitely connected with the whole act of knowing. In Tetens' *Philosophische Versuche über die menschliche Natur* (1777), a book known to Kant and Coleridge, a distinction is drawn between "bildende Dichtkraft," which is artistic, and *Phantasie;* [69] Kant himself distinguishes reproductive, productive, and aesthetic imagination. In Schelling there is a distinction between *Phantasie* and *Einbildungskraft* which is different from Coleridge's in that it differentiates between original conception and externalization but is similar in its stress on unification and in the same etymology of the German word *Einbildungskraft.*[70] In Jean Paul and A. W. Schlegel the ranking of these terms is reversed. *Phantasie* is higher, associated with reason; *Einbildungs-*

kraft is only a form of memory.[71] Nowhere, I think, can a use of these terms be found identical with Coleridge's use, for Coleridge in a unique manner combined the psychological tradition with the dialectics of the Germans.

Fancy is described by Coleridge as "the aggregative and associative power," as "the arbitrary bringing together of things that lie remote, and forming them into a unity. The materials lie ready formed for the mind and the fancy acts only by a sort of juxtaposition." [72] Fancy, in the concluding definition of the first volume of *Biographia,* has "no other counters to play with, but fixities, and definites. The Fancy is indeed no other than a mode of Memory emancipated from the order of time and space." But while Coleridge insists on the distinction, he can recognize shadings. Spenser, for instance, has "fancy under conditions of imagination. He has an imaginative fancy, but he has not imagination." [73] Thus the many discussions of whether Coleridge is right in distinguishing these faculties seem not very useful. There is no reason today to take faculty psychology literally. We must, as Coleridge did at his best, recognize the fundamental unity of the mind and grant that Coleridge distinguished different types of poetic gifts which are observable in the works themselves.

Coleridge does not always recognize the distinction between the poet and his poetry. Sometimes he wants to reduce the problem of defining poetry to that of describing the poet. He says that "the most general and distinctive character of a poem originates in the poetic genius itself" and that a just definition of poetry is possible "only so far as the distinction still results from the poetic genius, which sustains and modifies the emotions, thoughts, and vivid representations of a poem by the energy without effort of the poet's own mind." [74] We would thus abolish the distinction between psychic processes and capacities and the finished product, the work of art, which, in literature, is a structure of linguistic signs. But happily Coleridge *does* in other places discuss the differentia of poetry without the poet.

In the wake of Schiller, the Schlegels, and Schelling Coleridge sometimes extends the term "poetry" to all the arts and even to all human creativity. This use has the authority of Plato's *Symposium,* but even in Plato it blurs the distinction between the poet and the philosopher, the legislator and the warrior. Occasionally,

Coleridge will speak of a child's scolding a flower as "poetry," or will call Luther "one of the greatest poets that ever lived," not referring, however, to his hymns or the translation of the Bible, but meaning that he "acted poems not wrote them." He can say that through the observations of a group of chemists "poetry was, as it were, substantiated and realized." [75] This vague Platonic use of the term underlies his proposal to write a treatise on poetry which will "supersede all the books of metaphysics and all the books of morals too," which will in reality be a "disguised system of morals and politics." * Poetry is in such passages an all-inclusive, all-conquering, all-absorbing term.

In one place Coleridge tries to introduce a distinction between "poesy" and "poetry": poesy is to be a "generic name of all fine arts"; poetry is to be limited to works whose medium is words.[76] Usually, however, he abandons this terminological innovation and talks about music as the poetry of the ear and painting as the poetry of the eye or adopts the ancient view that all the other arts are "mute poesy." [77]

In general, however, Coleridge is not much interested in enforcing a view of poetry as basically identical with the other arts. He is not even much concerned with parallelisms and analogies among the arts. He takes from Schlegel the comparison of romantic poetry with Gothic architecture, and ancient poetry with a Greek temple.[78] He draws a parallel between recent poetry and painting, both interested in depicting the minutiae in the background, while Renaissance poetry and painting were supposedly more interested in the beauty and harmony of the whole.[79] Once he pleads for what today would be called synaesthesia, a community of the senses, "the latency of all in each, and more especially as by a magical *penna duplex,* the excitement of vision by sound and the exponents of sound." [80] But these are isolated insights which show that Coleridge accepted the unity of the arts but paid no particular attention to the problems of their relationship and distinction.

Usually Coleridge speaks of poetry as an art of "articulate language" and attempts to determine its differentia from other

* *L.,* pp. 347, 338. These passages cannot be interpreted to mean, as I. A. Richards suggests in *Coleridge on Imagination* (p. 20), that Coleridge wanted to dismiss philosophical and metaphysical problems. He was no logical positivist.

forms of discourse. He tries to distinguish it from science and morality in terms of its end and function. The immediate end of poetry is pleasure, "immediate" implying the lack of practical interest, the aesthetic distance which Kant had described. "The poet must always aim at pleasure as his specific means"; [81] he must not aim at the useful and good directly, but through pleasure aim at these only as an ultimate end. This end is, on occasion, defined as that of "cultivating and predisposing the heart of the reader," of "moralizing" the reader.[82] In theory Coleridge holds firmly to this distinction, though it seems only another attempt to keep the empirical tradition intact in an idealistic scheme where the pleasure principle has no place at all. One sees Coleridge's difficulties when he tries to include Plato, Jeremy Taylor, Burnet's *Theoria sacra*, and the first chapter of Isaiah as "poetry in the most emphatic sense," while recognizing that truth, and not pleasure, was the immediate aim of these writers.[83] Once he objects to Wordsworth's introducing characters from low life as a recommendation of equality among men, because it violates the existing state of association and thus substitutes truth for pleasure. But with a characteristic gesture Coleridge refers to the "blessed time, when truth itself shall be pleasure," [84] when the Platonic utopia of *kalokagathia* will abolish the distinction he has so laboriously drawn. Actually, in practice Coleridge forgets this distinction between means and ends and quickly succumbs to moralistic preconceptions. It would be easy to assemble many highly moralistic judgments from Coleridge's practical criticism. To name but a few instances: his "horror and disgust" at Gay's *Beggar's Opera*, his strange suggestions for the rewriting of *Volpone*, his willingness to exclude the porter's soliloquy in *Macbeth* from the genuine work of Shakespeare, his revulsion at the idea of homosexuality in Shakespeare's *Sonnets*, and many others.*

Poetry must be passion. Coleridge draws, not always clearly, a distinction between a "state of excitement" expressed immediately and crudely (this he rejects), and the role of excitement in stimulating the two main techniques of poetry, figurative language and meter.[85] On this point Coleridge, curiously enough, accepts the

* *Omniana,* 2, 20; *MC,* p. 55; *SC, 1,* 75, 77–8; *MC,* p. 455. Cf. *SC, 2,* 119, where he speaks of "Shakespeare's purity, innocence, and delicacy of an affectionate girl of eighteen."

naturalistic and primitivistic theories of the 18th century. "Strong passions command figurative language." "Figures of speech are originally the offspring of passion." Strong passion "has a language more measured than is employed in common speaking." [86] Meter itself implies passion. Coleridge even speaks of "nature the poet," alludes to the passionate speech of distressed mothers, and uses *Deborah's Song* as an example of lyrical repetitions and sublime tautology.[87] On occasion he seems to accept the historical scheme of primitivism: he reflects on "the ever-increasing sameness of human life" which has led to the decay of strong emotions and the disuse of forceful language.[88] He endorses, on the whole, Wordsworth's view of the history of poetic diction: its decay from a "natural language of empassioned feeling" to mere "artifices of connection and ornament." [89] It is true that he rejects Wordsworth's idealization of the Lake Country rustics and that he ridicules the Scottish professor who "cannot write three minutes together upon the Nature of Man but must be dabbling with his savage state, with his agricultural state, his hunter state, etc." [90] But this does not prevent Coleridge from expounding a very similar "conjectural" sequence of the arts, following Herder, and from suggesting a similar history of the origin of language. "Passion was the true parent of every word in existence in every language," and hence the "elder languages are fitter for poetry." [91] Shakespeare appears as standing midway between the use of natural language expressing reality and modern arbitrary sign language.[92] It is hard to see how Coleridge could have clung to these emotionalist theories and standards when he otherwise described the poet as an objective impersonal contemplator and creator. Apparently he thought of poetic "passion" as something rather different from mere emotion. Passion seems identified with one of his most personal requirements for the production of poetry; with joy, with happiness, or as he can say, the peace of God. In joy individuality is lost.[93] *Dejection : An Ode* is the most impressive declaration of an intimate connection in Coleridge's experience between the loss of joy and the drying-up of the powers of creative imagination.

Coleridge thus tried to define poetry with very traditional terminology: as pleasure for the reader and passion in the author during composition. But he also wanted to differentiate between poetry and verse and thus to recognize poetry outside of metrical compositions. He argues that there is poetry of the highest kind without meter, and he quotes Plato, Jeremy Taylor, Burnet, and Isaiah as examples.[94] But how does this prose-poetry differ from other prose? Coleridge quickly rejects the idea that fictionality makes poetry what it is. "It is not merely invention: if it were, *Gulliver's Travels* would be poetry." [95] We do not call "novels and other works of fiction" poems.[96] These are the passages in which Coleridge disposes of a solution which would find much favor today. *Gulliver* is poetry, it is imaginative literature, we would answer without hesitation. Poetry, in a more narrow sense, is only distinguishable by meter.

At the same time, Coleridge tries to draw a line between poetry and verse. He cannot recognize meter itself as the distinguishing characteristic of poetry. He tries to find a tortuous circumlocution for a concept which in effect includes both meter and rhythmical prose. In poetry, as distinct from fiction, "each part shall also communicate for itself a distinct and conscious pleasure," or "the greatest immediate pleasure from each part should be compatible with the largest sum of pleasure on the whole." [97] Though Coleridge repeats this definition with great emphasis several times, it surely offers no solution. Either it is a surreptitious introduction of the pleasures of meter and rhythm or it says merely that poetry is more highly organized than prose, which may not be true in many cases. One must, of course, admit that Coleridge could not have foreseen later developments toward closely patterned poetic fiction. He was content that his criterion of close organization allowed him to group poetic passages in the Bible, Plato, and Taylor with Shakespeare and Milton on the one side, and to put Scott, Defoe, and Richardson on the other. His later attempts at defining the difference ("prose is words in their best order;— poetry is the best words in the best order"; or "good prose is— proper words in their proper places, good verse—the most proper words in their proper places") [98] are even less convincing. They seem to say that poetry is simply better than prose, or that select "best" words are most proper for poetry. These are theories quite untenable on Coleridge's own premises. One must conclude that Coleridge failed in his attempts to define poetry.

While Coleridge hardly succeeds in defining the difference between poetry and verse, he writes an excellent defense of meter against Wordsworth's comparative disparagement of it as a mere "superadded charm." He abandons his own derivation of meter from passion and explains the effect of meter as a stimulant to the attention of the reader, as a "continued excitement of surprise," an "aggregate influence" which acts as "medicated atmosphere, or as wine during animated conversation." [99] Coleridge glimpses here the "heightening," distancing power of meter, its capacity to remove us from ordinary emotion. He also describes the manner in which poetry works, by a "distinction without disjunction," a harmony or fine balance of two opposite (not contrary) forces, "meter" and rhythm.[100] Meter here apparently means metrical pattern, and "rhythm" is the rhythm of ordinary speech. He observes the same double effect in the metrical time sequence. The pleasure of poetry is in part derived from the preparation and previous expectation of the reader: there are attractions in the "journey" itself; a regressive-progressive advance which Coleridge compares to the motion of a serpent. He sees that meter is not only an ornament; it must also be organic, and all other parts must be made consonant with it.[101]

Coleridge's insistence on the unity of the work of art yields a much more convincing analysis of poetry than his attempts to make either the pleasure principle or the emotion of the poet his criterion. The work of art forms a whole: "language, passion, and character must act and react on each other." [102] Totality works also in the direction of time: "the common end of all narrative, nay, of all poems, is to convert a series into a whole: to make those events, which in real or imagined history move in a straight line, assume to our Understanding a circular motion." [103] Thus conceived, the relation between whole and parts is a version of unity and variety, or as Coleridge prefers to say, of "unity in multeity," and thus an illustration of the workings of the imagination. It may mean a "tone and spirit of unity," "some one predominant thought or feeling"; [104] it may mean, in drama, the one "unity of interest" [105] which in Coleridge, as in Schlegel, replaced the old three unities of time, space, and action. It may depend on the ruling passion of a fictional character like Capulet, whose anger affects a whole scene, or Lear, whose despair extends to the heavens.[106] It may be a unification of images, the bringing out of multiple relations, as in a favorite passage from Venus and Adonis:

> Look! how a bright star shooteth from the sky,
> So glides he in the night from Venus' eye.

"How many images, and feelings," Coleridge comments, "are here
brought together without effort and without discord—the beauty
of Adonis—the rapidity of his flight—the yearning yet hopeless-
ness of the enamored gazer—and a shadowy ideal character thrown
over the whole." [107]

This criterion of wholeness works also negatively: it allows
Coleridge to ask whether the passages in Wordsworth's poems
affected by the bad parts of Wordsworth's theory "are inwoven
into the texture of his works, or are loose and separable." He
can disparage some of Wordsworth's descriptions as a jig-saw puzzle.[108] He can criticize the Senecan prose style as "merely strung
together like beads, without any causation or progression." [109] He
can object to the "distinct couplets" in Ben Jonson, Dryden, and
Pope; [110] to the "aphoristic style of the Oriental nations" and to
modern choppy prose.[111] The standard of wholeness is responsible for his ranking Beaumont and Fletcher far below Shakespeare and for rejecting *Hudibras* as lacking in "fusion." [112] Coleridge rings constant changes on this one principle, sometimes
adopting a slightly different terminology. "Interfusion" and "separateness" mean the same as wholeness and individual parts when
he praises Shakespeare's will as an "interfusion, a continuous
agency, no series of separate acts." [113] Massinger's *Maid of Honor*
is disparaged because all its characters are planned each by itself,
while in Shakespeare "the play is a *syngenesia* [a kind of flower]—
each has indeed a life of its own and is an *individuum* of itself, but
yet an organ to the whole." [114] Similarly, Coleridge can think of
this unity in a temporal sequence, as a union of the successive and
the instantaneous. There must be "a union of the liveliest image
of succession with the feeling of simultaneousness." [115] In Shakespeare, he can say, "all is growth, evolution, *genesis*"; but again, in
apparent contradiction, in Shakespeare there is "neither past nor
future, but all is permanent." [116] Even Shakespeare's women are
praised for having "a feeling of all that continuates society, a sense
of ancestry and sex." [117]

In most cases Coleridge keeps hold, so to speak, of both handles:
the unity and the things unified, the whole and the parts. The

effect depends on the tension, on the reconciliation of opposites, not on sameness or unity in the sense of indistinct totality. There is no contradiction between the reconciliation of opposites, the dialectics of whole and the parts, and the analogy of organism, if the latter is interpreted moderately. They allow Coleridge the contrast between Shakespeare and Beaumont and Fletcher. A play by Shakespeare is like a real fruit, while a play by the two friends is like "a quarter of an orange, a quarter of an apple, and the like of a lemon and of a pomegranate." [118] And again he uses the analogy of a real garden compared with a child's garden of stuck flowers which will wither overnight.[119] Yet such an emphasis on totality can be pushed to superstitious extremes. If we say, as Coleridge does, that "you can't alter a word, or the position of a word, in Milton or Shakespeare" without damage,[120] an impossible ideal of coherence and perfection is postulated. The onus might be put on something totally mysterious and obscure, as when Coleridge says of Dante that "the wholeness is not in vision or conception, but in an inner feeling of totality, and absolute being." [121] Coleridge's anxiety to defend the work of art as a tightly organized whole contributed thus to his Shakespeare idolatry. When he did not see how he could fit a passage into the presumed ideal whole, he simply declared it to be an interpolation of the actors, as he did with the Porter's speech in *Macbeth* or the wooing of Lady Anne by Richard III.[122] Still, for the most part, the principle of organic unity sharpened Coleridge's appreciation and allowed him to see continuities, to remove apparent contradictions in works of art, and to justify seeming superfluities.

Whole, organism, unity, continuity are the key terms for the structure of the work of art. But the work of art also represents the world of reality and projects its own fictional world. In what relation is this other world to the great world, and how does art suggest this relation? Coleridge answers again in two ways, keeping the traditional account and adding a new theory. Art is imitation in Coleridge but it is also symbolization. Imitation is, of course, not copying, not naturalism. Imitation is described in terms of the audience reaction as a recognition of likeness in the dissimilar, or, in the terms of the share of the author, as an infusion of the author's own knowledge and talent into external objects.[123] All this is traditional enough: Coleridge himself appeals to such diverse authorities as Petrarch and Adam Smith.[124] What is imitated is not nature but general nature, universal nature. So Coleridge can say that "the essence of poetry is universality." [125] "It was Shakespeare's prerogative to have the universal which is potentially in each particular, opened out to him in the *homo generalis*." [126] Similarly, Robinson Crusoe is praised as the universal representative, as Everyman.[127] "Whatever is not representative, generic, may be indeed most poetically expressed, but it is not poetry." [128] Coleridge thus disparages the merely particular and local. "Poetry is essentially ideal, it avoids and excludes all accident." [129] Wordsworth is criticized for "matter-of-factness," and dramatists other than Shakespeare for depicting transitory manners.[130] At times Coleridge sounds like a good neoclassicist and he himself appeals to Aristotle and Davenant.[131] But of course he sees the problem of the union of the particular with the general, of the concrete with the universal, which is another case of the reconciliation of opposites. "The characters of a poem, amid the strongest individualization, must still remain representative." [132] Lady Macbeth, like all characters in Shakespeare, is a "class individualized"; Shakespeare's characters are "genera intensely individualized." [133] Coleridge emphasizes that he is recommending not abstraction but rather "an involution of the universal in the individual." [134]

The same tension of interpretations can be found in Coleridge's use of the term "nature." Nature is sometimes the spirit of nature, *natura naturans,* the creativity of nature. "The artist must imitate that which is within the thing, which is active through form and figure, and discourses to us by symbols—the *Naturgeist,* or spirit of nature." [135] This "productive power which is in nature, as nature, is essentially one with the intelligence which is in the human mind above nature." [136] Art is not imitation but self-revelation, as mind and nature are profoundly identical. "Shakespeare worked in the spirit of nature, by evolving the germ within by the imaginative power according to an idea." [137] This statement assembles all the favorite terms: spirit of nature, the germ from within, imagination, idea.

Idea and symbol are the two main instruments by which the poet represents this spirit of nature. As in many other writers, "idea" is a slippery term. Coleridge uses it sometimes as the English empiricists do to mean sense datum. At other times he allows the term to assume a supernatural Platonic meaning. But wnen Coleridge has literary theory in mind, he usually thinks of the "idea" as an instance of the union of the universal and the particular. Idea is the same as essence, is "the inmost principle of the possibility of any thing, as that particular thing." [138] Idea "never passes into an abstraction and therefore never becomes the equivalent of an image." [139] It is neither concept nor image. It cannot be generalized, it cannot be seen, it can only be contemplated. It is a form of being but above form; it is a law contemplated subjectively. It is made accessible, visible to us by symbols. [140]

Law is in the objects; Idea is their essence; it can even be the essence of an individual object (as law could not be). Symbol is the device by which idea is presented. Symbol in Coleridge is contrasted with allegory, in the same way that imagination is contrasted with fancy, the organic with the mechanical. On occasion Coleridge lapses into the old use of "symbol" to mean conventional sign, [141] but usually symbol is to him the union of the universal and the particular. Symbol is characterized by a "translucence of the special [the quality of the species] in the individual; or of the general [the quality of genus] in the special, or of the universal in the general." [142] It partakes of the reality of what it symbolizes; it enunciates the whole. "Symbol is a sign included in the idea, which it represents." It is always itself "a part of that, of the whole of which it is representative." [143] In contrast, allegory is a translation of abstract notions into a picture language. [144]

These formulas which could be paralleled in Goethe, Schelling, and Creuzer must, however, have remained rather obscure to Coleridge. Strangely enough, when he quotes examples, he seems to confuse symbol and synecdoche. A symbol of a man, he tells us, is "a lip with a chin prominent." An expression like "Here comes a sail" [i.e. a ship] Coleridge considers symbolical, while "Behold our lion!" in speaking of a gallant soldier, is allegorical. [145] But the examples of symbol would seem to be mere instances of synecdoche, a figure of contiguity from which symbol cannot even develop. Symbol comes from metaphor, but Coleridge considers metaphor rather a fragment of an allegory. [146] The modern use of the terms is reversed. It is thus not surprising that Coleridge often treats allegory with great sympathy * and gives it a tinge of individuality of which it is deprived in the original dichotomy devised by the Germans in order to disparage it. We must conclude, then, that Coleridge (whatever his poetic practice) was not really a symbolist in the sense in which we could speak of the Schlegels and Schelling as symbolists. Furthermore, he differs from these Germans in not sharing in the glorification of myth which seems a consequence of the symbolist point of view. There is one passage where Coleridge takes refuge behind an unknown Greek philosopher, saying that "the material universe is but one vast complex *mythus*, [i.e. symbolical representation], and mythology the apex and complement of all genuine physiology." [147] But the Greek philosopher sounds suspiciously like Schelling, and his mythology like the complement of Schellingian *Naturphilosophie*.

In his practical criticism Coleridge rarely uses the term "symbol." Yet in speaking of Wordsworth's "Intimations" ode he refers to the "modes of inmost being," which "yet cannot be conveyed save in symbols of time and space." [148] These remarks seem to refute, out of Coleridge's own mouth, the common-sense ridicule he has poured, a few pages before, on the address to the child as "Mighty Prophet! Seer blest." Yet on the whole, Coleridge seems most disappointing on the question of imagery and symbolization. The distinction between imagination and fancy is used to disparage rhetorical figures which today we would classify as "witty" or metaphysical or simply as figures in which there is only one point of similarity between tenor and vehicle, as in Coleridge's examples:

> And like a lobster boil'd, the morn
> From black to red began to turn, [from *Hudibras*]

and

> Full gently now she takes him by the hand,
> A lily prison'd in a gaol of snow [from *Venus and Adonis*] [149]

Coleridge criticizes the metaphysicals for "fantastic out-of-the-way thoughts," for sacrificing "the passion and passionate flow of poetry, to the subtleties of intellect, and to the starts of wit," "the heart to

---

* E.g. his appreciation of Spenser and Bunyan; his view of Dante as only quasi-allegorical (*MC*, p. 150); and his conception of *Don Quixote* as a "substantial living allegory" (*MC*, p. 102).

the head." [150] A conceit in Cowley is rejected as an *"apparent
reconciliation of widely different and incompatible things."* It
shows a lack of inward vision, and of "any sympathy with the
modifying powers with which the genius of the poet had united
and inspirited all the objects of his thought." It is therefore "a
species of *wit*, a pure work of the *will*, and implies a leisure and
self-possession both of thought and of feeling, incompatible with
the steady fervor of the mind possessed and filled with the grandeur
of its subject." [151] While one may not admire Cowley's particular
conceit (hills reflecting the image of a voice), the standard applied
by Coleridge is the commonplace romantic view of poetry as pictorial vision, self-forgetting rapture and fervor. But Coleridge *did*
appreciate Donne: he certainly had an unusual sense of his rhythm,
a sympathy for his ideas and, if rarely, an appreciation of his wit
and even of his metaphors. He praises, for instance, the figure of
the compass in "A Valediction: Forbidding Mourning." * He admires Herbert and Crashaw.[152] Unfortunately we do not have
Coleridge's projected apology for conceits, though we have his
apology for puns, at least in outline. But this shows that Coleridge
had no very deep appreciation of the symbolist view. His defense
is not that of Schlegel's in terms of correspondences in the universe
and the free play with language but is made on psychological
grounds: it labors to show that punning is a "natural expression of
natural emotion," that it arises out of a mingled sense of injury
and contempt.[153] It would be hard to illustrate this theory with
more than a few examples, and it seems irrelevant to the uses of
punning in poetry.

Coleridge understands one part of the symbolic, linguistic point
of view. He realizes that the emphasis, inherited from the 18th
century, on "imagination" as purely visual realization is mistaken.
He quotes Kant in support of his distinction between the conceivable and the picturable; he protests against the "despotism of
the eye" and the "delusive notion that what is not imageable is
likewise not conceivable." [154] Yet he rarely draws the consequences
from these insights. Rather he emphasizes imagery which might
be called "animating," the kind of figure which Ruskin was later
to condemn as "pathetic fallacy." He says that some images are po-

---

* *MC*, pp. 131 ff., esp. pp. 133, 138. "Nothing was ever more admi-
rably made out than the figure of the Compass."

etic only, "when a human and intellectual life is transferred to
them from the poet's own spirit," and he illustrates this by adding
to lines about a row of pines the idea of their *"fleeing* from the
fierce sea-blast." [155] Imagery serves largely to corroborate the view
that man is identical with nature. "A poet's heart and intellect
should be combined, intimately combined and unified with the
great appearances of nature." [156] Coleridge thus accomplishes a
justification of romantic anthropomorphism but fails to see the
uses of the symbolic view as a justification of other types of meta-
phoric expression.

Coleridge has least to say about the affective aspect of the aesthetic situation. His clinging to the term "pleasure" prevents him
from facing the problem of the ugly or tragic in art. He is content
to discuss illusion. He solves the problem much as Mendelssohn had
solved it.[157] Art—he is here mainly thinking of drama on the stage
—is not delusion, not a deception such as naturalistic standards
require; nor is it, on the other hand, complete consciousness of the
artificiality of art. Coleridge accepts a compromise for which he
finds the famous phrase, "that willing suspension of disbelief for
the moment which constitutes poetic faith." [158] Sometimes he speaks
of "negative faith," of voluntary acquiescence in the fiction which
shuts out everyday reality. The poet "solicits us to yield ourselves
to a dream; and this too with our eyes open; . . . and meantime,
only, not to *dis*believe." [159] Sometimes he argues that there is a
distinction between our knowing and our feeling. We know, for
instance, that Othello and Desdemona are actors, but we do not
feel it. Otherwise, we would not say in praise of a good actor that
he was "lost in his character; that he appeared and became the
very man." It is not true that fiction is known to be always fiction.
"It is not felt to be fiction when we are most affected. We know
the thing to be a representation, but we often feel it to be a
reality." [160] Coleridge suggests that stage-properties diminish illusion, while good acting increases it, an observation which helps
to explain his aversion to seeing Shakespeare on the stage of his
time.[161] Yet it is hard to see how, even on Coleridge's own terms,
knowing could be kept separate from feeling. Dr. Johnson seems
to have been more nearly correct when he said that we always know
that we are in the theater. The events on the stage, one might say
in modern terms, are neither real nor unreal, but another reality

which we compare with everyday reality. Coleridge perhaps succeeds in suggesting the effect of "framing," which occurs in the act of watching a play.

The problem of theatrical illusion as discussed by Coleridge is not very different from that of probability or plausibility in an epic or a novel. Coleridge rather frequently uses this criterion, which in a system like Schelling's is quite superfluous. He points out an improbability in Scott's *Rob Roy* which "awakens one rudely out of the day-dream of negative faith." [162] Elsewhere he tries to distinguish between a temporary belief in strange situations and a rejection of moral miracles. [163] A variation of the problem occurs in his discussion of Klopstock's *Messiah,* where he complains of the breakdown of illusion through the conflict of "words and facts of known and absolute truth," [164] the truth of the biblical account. He tries to show that there is no such clash in Milton. In discussing Wordsworth he feels a diminution of our sense of probability because of the frequent interpolations of the author's own personal voice and views, his "ventriloquism" as Coleridge calls it. [165] He observes the same phenomenon in Beaumont and Fletcher and Massinger: subjectivism appears here as breaking down and disturbing dramatic illusion. Coleridge's general preference is always for objective presentation, for characters speaking in their own tone of voice. In the novel he finds the height of successful illusion in the reproduction of the workings of the minds of the characters. He prefers the method of Richardson to that of Fielding. Richardson has talent for reproducing meditation, Fielding only for external observation, though Coleridge prefers Fielding for his saner morality. [166] A novel by John Galt, *The Provost,* impresses Coleridge because it is a fictional autobiography which dramatically succeeds in conveying the "natural irony of self-delusion." [167]

Coleridge thus ascribes little importance to story or plot. It is continually disparaged as merely "interesting." There is, he says, no story interest in *Don Quixote,* Ariosto, the Greek tragedies, or Milton. Indeed, plot is merely a canvas, [168] a scaffolding for a work of art. In enumerating the parts of the drama—language, passion, character—Coleridge leaves out plot, which Aristotle would have put first. [169] His criticism of Shakespeare is largely character analysis. The play as a play is either ignored or minimized. Psychology of character or of situation, at most the pervading emotional tone of a play, not the play as a piece of stagecraft, is what interests Coleridge.

All that we have been saying explains why Coleridge is quite disappointing on the level of genre criticism or anywhere in the realm between general theory of poetry and practical criticism. He is of two minds on the central question: whether genre is a standard of criticism. Once he disparages the whole concept of genre. "It is absurd to pass judgment on the works of a poet on the mere ground that they have been called by the same class-name . . . or on any ground indeed save that of their inappropriateness to their own end and being, their want of significance, as symbol and physiognomy." [170]

Elsewhere he thinks that it is "far better to distinguish poetry into different classes" and to ascertain whether a poem is perfect within its genre.[171] On occasion he reflects on these distinctions and even invokes standards of purity. Thus Wordsworth is criticized for his predilection for the dramatic, i.e. the dialogue in the lyric; and Beaumont and Fletcher are charged with constantly slipping into lyricisms.[172] Against Wordsworth, Coleridge argues that detailed biographical material must not be introduced into a poem, but in discussing Shakespeare's histories he tries to show that "pure historic drama" has its own laws, allowing a violent interruption of the succession of time.[173]

On the related question of the hierarchy of genres Coleridge seems also to be of two minds. At times he seems to identify the lyrical and the poetical. This identification is behind the famous passage in which he anticipates Poe on the impossibility of a long poem. "A poem of any length neither can be, or ought to be, all poetry." [174] The subordinate nonpoetic (that is narrative) parts must merely be in keeping with the poetry. Coleridge argues that meter is the right means for this. On the other hand, he cannot escape the traditional concentration of interest on the epic and drama. He adopts the German theories: the lyric is subjective, the epic objective. The essence of the epic is "the successive in events and characters." Epic, he suggests fancifully, comes from *epomai, sequi*, "to follow." [175] Drama, as in Schiller and Schlegel, is seen largely as tragedy and thus in terms of the relation between man and fate. "In the drama, the will is exhibited as struggling with fate." [176] In ancient tragedy there is "the lofty struggle between irresistible fate and unconquerable free will, which finds its equilibrium in the Providence and the future retribution of Christianity." [177] Like the Germans Coleridge has no use for poetic justice and disparages sentimental and pathetic tragedy, which lacks the "power of destiny and the controlling might of heaven." [178] He defends tragicomedy with Schlegel's argument that the Fool and Lear mutually heighten both the tragic and the comic.[179] Later Coleridge seems to have had some qualms about these theories. When he read Solger's *Erwin* he referred to "all the doctrine of resistance to Fate and Nature, and the rest of the hyper-tragic histrionic stoicism." [180]

Coleridge has little to say about historical types of literature. He uses the dichotomies of the Germans, classical versus modern or Gothic or romantic, but these ideas do not occupy the central position they do in the Schlegels. They occur primarily when Coleridge has to lecture on the Middle Ages or on the contrast between the ancient and the modern drama.[181] He refers to Shakespeare as romantic and echoes from Schlegel the opinion that the romantic mind is inward and picturesque and leans toward a mixture of genres, while the ancient is outward and statuesque and strictly observes the genres.[182] From Schiller Coleridge takes the distinction between the musical and the pictorial poet.[183] Once he draws a distinction similar to that drawn by Schiller between naive and sentimental, when he said that the poetry of the ancients reflects the world without, while the allegorizing fancy of a modern poet (the Polish humanist, Casimir Sarbieski) is striving to project the inward.[184]

Yet one can hardly say that Coleridge shares the Germans' historical point of view. This is most strikingly proved by his constant attempt to take Shakespeare, the exemplary poet, out of his time. He calls him "least of all poets colored in any particulars by the spirit or customs of his age," and he even says that "there is nothing common to Shakespeare and to other writers of his day—not even the language they employed." [185] When Coleridge uses the historical argument, when, for instance, he defends Milton's coarse polemical manners by the "genius of the times," [186] he uses this argument merely as an excuse. He never sees a positive virtue in historicity, as the Germans do.

Several times in his life, it is true, Coleridge planned to write histories of literature. In 1803 he conceived the scheme of a huge general history of literature. The 1808 lectures are an outline history of English poetry. In 1816 he proposed a full-scale history of German literature.[187] But surely external obstacles were not the only causes which prevented the realization of these plans. If we examine Coleridge's proposals, we must conclude that they do not show an advanced grasp of the problems of literary historiography. The scheme of 1803 envisages eight to ten volumes, of which only one was to be devoted to belles lettres but several to the history of metaphysics, theology, and even law. The volume devoted to poetry and poets was to be divided into two halves. The first was to contain essays on the great single names, Chaucer, Spenser, Shakespeare, Milton, Taylor, Dryden, Pope, etc. The second half of the volume "should be a history of poetry and romances, everywhere interspersed with biography, but more flowing, more consecutive, more bibliographical, chronological, and complete" than the first.[188] The history of German literature would have included natural history, comparative anatomy, and even chemistry. It would be hard to imagine a worse hodge-podge of methods and topics.

Coleridge was not profoundly affected by the antiquarian and medieval movement of his time. He studied Old German when he was in Göttingen, but with the exception of some passages from Otfried he quotes no German text before Luther.[189] In English he seems to have known only Chaucer and Ritson's *Metrical Romances*.[190] In Italian he had first-hand knowledge of Dante and Petrarch and knew some Boccaccio and Pulci,[191] but when he talked about the Middle Ages, he indulged in vague generalizations about the Gothic mind and even found a "Gothic soul" in Roman dress in the troubadours.*

Coleridge knew, of course, much more about the Elizabethans, but even his excursions into Shakespearean scholarship are none too happy. His chronology of Shakespeare's plays, his views on the doubtful plays, and his textual emendations are of little value. His

---

* *MC*, p. 19. Coleridge also adopts the German view of a "dilution of Gothic blood" in France, Descartes, Malebranche, Pascal, and Molière being "the *ultimi Gothorum,* the last in whom the Gothic predominated over the Celtic." *MC*, p. 286.

comments on individual passages often suffer from his prudishness and his fanciful etymologies and, curiously enough, from a very 18th-century common-sense taste. Like Dr. Johnson he could not tolerate such figures as the "blanket of the dark." *

His Shakespeare criticism belongs almost wholly to the tradition of character studies inherited from such 18th-century writers as Richardson, Mackenzie, Morgann, and Goethe.[192] Like them Coleridge mostly remarks on the psychology of Shakespeare's figures. In method he anticipates Bradley, but only in a sketchy way. On occasion he confuses fiction and reality, as Bradley does so frequently. Thus the much admired observations on Hamlet's wassail speech concern the unknown and unascertainable state of Hamlet's mind. "The momentum had been given to his mental activity, the full current of the thoughts and words had set in, and the very forgetfulness, in the fervor of his argumentation, of the purposes for which he was there, aided in preventing the appearance from benumbing the mind." [193] To say that "Polonius is the skeleton of his own former skill and statecraft" [194] is a similar confusion, since a fictional character has no past beyond the statements of the author.

The most admired and most influential of Coleridge's character sketches is that of Hamlet. The idea of making Hamlet an intellectual seems to have been Friedrich Schlegel's; [195] still, Coleridge worked it out in more detail and tried to relate it to his theory of imagination. "In Hamlet," he says, "I conceive Shakespeare to have wished to exemplify the moral necessity of a due balance between our attention to outward objects and our meditation on inward thoughts—a due balance between the real and the imaginary world." [196]

In much of Coleridge's Shakespeare criticism there are observations which show that he had his principles in mind. Hamlet talking with Ophelia is "sporting with opposites." [197] Othello cannot be a real negro, as Desdemona's love for him "would argue a disproportionateness, a want of balance," [198] and so on. But if we strip the vocabulary of its pretensions, the meaning amounts to the

---

* The funniest emendation is that of "Doll Tearsheet" into "Tearstreet," supposedly from *terere stratum,* "walk the street" (*SC, 1,* 158). Cf. the derivation of *tuch* (touch, black quartz) from German *Tuch* (cloth) (*MC,* p. 248). "Blanket of the dark" is changed to "blank height"! (*SC, 1,* 73).

belief that Shakespeare "surveyed all the great component powers
and impulses of human nature, and showed their harmony by the
effects of disproportion, either of excess or deficiency." [199] Shakespeare is thought of as a kind of purveyor of the Nicomachean
Ethics in dramatic disguise, or as the ideal sane and normal man
who has warned us against excess and *hybris,* as every tragedian
should.

Coleridge's remarks on the plays and characters of Shakespeare
are often disappointing: either trite and moralizing or, when ingenious, unconvincing. Even some of the more famous dicta, such
as that about Iago's "motive-hunting of motiveless malignity," are
misleading.[200] The view that the Pyrrhus' speech in Hamlet is not
burlesque would find few defenders today.* Whatever the merits
of these observations, they are not in any way integrated into a
theory or even into a unified conception of a play.

There is little of distinction in the fairly extensive comments
on Milton, Cervantes, and Dante. The characterization of Don
Quixote and Sancho Panza leads up to a Coleridgean contrast and
synthesis. Don Quixote becomes a "substantial living allegory, or
personification of the reason and the moral sense, divested of the
judgment and the understanding," while Sancho is the converse,
"common sense without reason or imagination." "Put him and his
master together, and they form a perfect intellect." Despite this
disconcerting conclusion, detailed comments show acute perception. Coleridge notices Don Quixote's "entire featurelessness, face
and frame," indicated by the hesitation about his name. His "lean-
ness and featurelessness are happy exponents of the excess of the
formative or imaginative in him." †

The lecture on Dante is much inferior. It lists examples of style,
of images, of profundity, of picturesqueness, of topographical reality, of Dante's power over the pathetic and of his fault of becoming

* *SC, 1,* 28. "The fancy that a burlesque was intended, sinks below
criticism." Bradley makes a tortuous defense of Coleridge (*Shakespearean Tragedy,* pp. 413–4). I agree with S. L. Bethell, *Shakespeare and the
Popular Dramatic Tradition* (Durham, N.C., 1944), pp. 181, 185–6.

† *MC,* pp. 102, 100. On p. 100 "featureliness" must be a misreading
of "featurelessness." Don Quixote's instability of name is brilliantly
pursued by Leo Spitzer in "Linguistic Perspectivism in the *Don
Quixote," Linguistics and Literary History* (Princeton, 1948), pp. 41–86.

grotesque. Still, it is superior to the commonplace reflections on Milton's universal subject, the character of Satan and the "exquisitely artificial" style of *Paradise Lost*. More interesting is Coleridge's appreciation of Sir Thomas Browne and Jeremy Taylor, "the great patterns or integers of English style," whom he exalts over the overrated authors of the age of Queen Anne.[201] Among much that is trivial on 18th-century literature the comment on the last voyage of *Gulliver* stands out. "Critics in general complain of the Yahoos; I complain of the Houyhnhnms." But Coleridge does not see that Swift's satire embraces also the rational horses. In speaking of Sterne, Coleridge recognizes that "the digressive spirit is not wantonness, but the very form of his genius. The connection is given by the continuity of the characters." [202] This is an insight which might have put Sterne criticism on the right road long ago.

Many of Coleridge's comments on his contemporaries are shrewd and sensitive. To my mind, he is surely right in his comparatively low estimate of Sir Walter Scott and Byron.* He is right on second-rate contemporaries like his friend Southey, on Gothic romances and on melodramas. He is right in his criticism of Wordsworth. Though he has to protest against the naturalism of Wordsworth's theories of poetic diction, he knows that Wordsworth is the greatest poet of his time. But the famous chapter on Wordsworth's poetry violates the cardinal principle of Coleridge's theory in being a good old-fashioned recital of beauties and defects. In its detail, much of the criticism against the "Daffodils" or the "Intimations" ode is surprisingly literal minded, "common sense" in the style of Dr. Johnson.[203] Coleridge read Blake's *Songs of Innocence and Experience* and in a letter graded the poems according to an elaborate scale. As far as one can judge from the meager remarks, he liked "The Little Black Boy" best and deplored "The Little Girl Found" on doctrinal grounds. But there was merit in the friendly attention to the unknown Blake.[204] Throughout Coleridge's criticism one can find striking formulas and here and there finely phrased poetic appreciations in the

* *MC*, pp. 321–42, 338–42. *UL*, 2, 37–41, 402, 420–1, *MC* 285, 401–2. Coleridge had actually two sets of opinions on Scott and Byron: one more favorable, in public pronouncements, and one full of violent disparagement in private letters to close friends. There is no doubt which was his real view.

manner of Lamb,[205] but the modern reader will again and again
be disconcerted by evidences of amazing prudishness, bigotry, and
chauvinism. In these respects Coleridge seems very provincial both
in time and in place. His absurd judgments on French literature
can be explained by his hatred for Napoleon and the French revolution,* the prudishness by his own unhappy personal life and the
growing pressure of what is wrongly called Victorianism; the bigotry, displayed for instance in his comments on Goethe's *Faust*,
resulted no doubt from his increasing anxiety for complete orthodoxy.†

We have to conclude on a note of disappointment. Coleridge as
an aesthetician is fragmentary and derivative. He does not succeed
in bridging the gap between his aesthetics and his theory of literature. His theory of literature is his most impressive achievement:
it is an attempt to work out a variable, many-sided scheme; it is
extremely rich in the number of elements he tries to fuse into a
unity. But the attempt is ultimately not successful and cannot be
so on his terms. On the one hand we have his holistic arguments
about structure and his symbolist view of the poet embodying
"ideas," and on the other his pleasure principle and his emotionalism, which he tries to preserve in spite of everything. The poet
as philosopher and "knower" (the principle of imagination) cannot be combined with the poet as the man of passion aiming at
immediate pleasure. Fancy, talent, the mechanical, the separate,

---

* "He could not tolerate the French Telemachus, nor indeed anything that was French, excepting Gresset's *Vert-Vert*" (*SC*, 2, 39). The
French are said to be incapable of poetry (*SC*, 2, 101; *Inquiring Spirit*,
pp. 155–6), but this is modified in *AP*, pp. 119–20. French tragedy is
constantly disparaged (*BL*, 2, 158; *SC*, 1, 206). Rabelais is admired by
Coleridge (*MC*, pp. 127–8, 407). Cf. *AP*, p. 152. "But spite of Pascal,
Madame Guyon and Molière, France is my Babylon, the mother of
whoredoms in morality, philosophy and taste."

† *MC*, p. 416: "I debated with myself whether it became my moral
character to render into English . . . much of which I thought vulgar,
licentious, and blasphemous" (1833). In 1820, refusing to write captions
to Retzsch's illustrations to *Faust*, Coleridge refers to Goethe's work as
"in bad repute with the religious part of the community," containing
"passages morally and prudentially untranslatable." Letter in *Yale University Library Gazette*, 22 (1947), 6–10.

and the like are all concepts designed to disparage what has survived from associationist psychology, but Coleridge refuses to cast them out: he tries to preserve everything in an all-embracing eclectic scheme.

If we look at the famous passage on imagination [206] as the reconciliation of opposite or discordant qualities, we can see in miniature all the random eclecticism of Coleridge's mind. "Sameness, with difference" must refer to the reader's recognition of imitation. "The general, with the concrete," refers to what happens in the work itself when a character or a situation, while remaining particular, implies the general reference of poetry. "The idea with the image, the individual, with the representative," says the same thing in a slightly different vocabulary. But "the sense of novelty and freshness, with old and familiar objects" refers to the reader's surprise and recognition. "A more than usual state of emotion, with more than usual order" moves back to the poet's mind, as does the next pair of items, "judgment ever awake and steady self-possession, with enthusiasm and feeling profound or vehement." And then we are told that imagination, "while it blends and harmonizes the natural and the artificial, still subordinates art to nature." This implies a refusal to admit a reconciliation of art and nature, as envisaged in Schiller and Schelling, in favor of submission to nature which, besides, is very difficult to see as a function of the imagination. Imagination is then said to subordinate "manner to matter": a concession designed apparently to avert the suspicion of formalism. Finally, "our admiration of the poet" is to be subordinated to "our sympathy with the poetry," an admirable sentiment but hardly coordinated with what precedes and quite unrelated to the role which Coleridge usually assigns to imagination. After a quotation on the soul from Sir John Davies, Coleridge concludes this chapter, in which he professes to give his conclusions on the nature of poetry, by saying: "Finally *Good Sense* is the *Body* of poetic genius, *Fancy* its *Drapery, Motion* its *Life,* and *Imagination* the *Soul* that is everywhere, and in each; and forms all into one graceful and intelligent whole." These bombastic personifications where a concept "Motion," not otherwise used, appears as the "life" of poetry, surely cannot withstand closer inspection. The desire for a "graceful and intelligent whole" seems defeated at almost every point.

Yet we must recognize that this very eclecticism allowed Coleridge to be something to almost all English critics who came after him. His importance for the transmission of German literary ideas to the English-speaking world is very great, especially today when the German romantics have almost disappeared from the horizon and seem to have become almost incomprehensible in their specific philosophical suppositions. Coleridge carries enough of the Aristotelian and empirical tradition to make the idealistic elements palatable. His very looseness and incoherence, the wide gaps between his theory and his practice, his suggestiveness, his exploratory mind, his "inquiring spirit"—these will always appeal to certain apparently permanent features of the Anglo-Saxon tradition.

WILLIAM HAZLITT (1778–1830) is usually considered a follower of Coleridge: Coleridge's prestige stands so high that the relationship is conceived as one of dependence, especially in questions of literary theory. Hazlitt himself gave countenance to this view when he described his "First Acquaintance with the Poets," with Wordsworth and Coleridge in 1798, idealizing it by the nostalgia for his youth. In the *Lectures on the English Poets,* he said in public that Coleridge is "the only person from whom I ever learnt anything." [1] But this first impression is misleading; actually Hazlitt's critical thought is based on philosophical assumptions very different from those of Coleridge. What is more important, the critical methods and procedures of the two are utterly different. Coleridge is primarily a theorist handling general ideas even when he discusses specific works of art: Hazlitt is primarily a practical critic interested in evoking the specific impression of a work of art. Coleridge, even when he writes for a periodical, meditates almost oblivious of his audience. Hazlitt is primarily a journalist who addresses and woos a new public. Moreover, Hazlitt himself rejected any intellectual allegiance to Coleridge. The savagery of some of Hazlitt's reviews of Coleridge is mainly due to Hazlitt's bitter disappointment with Coleridge's political development, but the disagreements in criticism and philosophy cannot be ascribed merely to party prejudice and warfare. Hazlitt definitely rejected Coleridge's philosophical and critical position not only in the polemics directed against him but implicitly in the bulk of his writings. In one long sentence, a *tour de force* of malice, Hazlitt ridicules Coleridge's tortuous course through all intellectual history, his spasmodic adherence to one creed after another, his eclecticism, and specifically his commendation of Kant. [2] Hazlitt, who knew no German, was for a short time attracted to what he then understood to be Kant's position. In 1807 he believed with Kant in the "unity of consciousness, or 'that the mind alone is formative.' " [3] But on closer acquaintance with unfortunately very inaccurate second-hand accounts, irritated by what he considered the Kantian conclusions in Coleridge, Hazlitt turned violently against Kant. Kant's system appeared to him "the most willful and monstrous absurdity that ever was invented." He disapproved especially of the role of practical reason and of the *apriori;* he interpreted them as a revival of a philosophy of faith and innate ideas, a defense of religious obscurantism.[4]

Whatever the particular deficiencies of Hazlitt's misinterpretation of Kant's philosophy may be, there can be no doubt of his disapproval of Coleridge's "Principles and Ideas" and the genuineness of his conclusion that Coleridge was a "bad philosopher."[5] Nor was he sympathetic with Coleridge's criticism: he disapproved of the discussion of Wordsworth and considered the question of poetic diction completely mishandled.[6] He thought that Coleridge bewildered himself sadly with the definition of poetry. He did not know what to make of the discussion on the imagination.[7] In his book *On the Characters of Shakespeare's Plays* (1817) Hazlitt kept significantly silent on Coleridge's Shakespeare lectures, while he was generous and explicit in recognizing the merits of August Wilhelm Schlegel's *Dramatic Lectures.*[8] The motives of the silence were undoubtedly in part "political," but they were surely prompted also by a recognition of Schlegel's priority and the falsity of Coleridge's pretensions. Though Hazlitt did not attend any of Coleridge's lectures, he read the newspaper accounts and must have heard about them from others who attended: there are scattered covert references to Coleridge's views on Shakespearean matters in Hazlitt's lectures; and there is one piece, also based on a newspaper report, which specifically attacks Coleridge's view that Caliban represents the spirit of Jacobinism.[9] While it would be rash to deny that Hazlitt learned something from Coleridge, enough has been said to show that Hazlitt's rejection of Coleridge went far beyond politics into the fundamentals of philosophy and criticism.

Neither, of course, can Hazlitt be considered a follower of August Wilhelm Schlegel. He did not read the *Dramatic Lectures* until 1815, in English translation, when his own style of writing was well developed and his opinions almost settled. In reviewing the *Lectures* Hazlitt censured Schlegel's love of theory and spirit of partisanship, his horror of the obvious, his idolatry of Shakespeare, and his mysticism and affectation so sharply that Stendhal used this very review as a confirmation of his aversion to German romanticism.[10] But the harshness of some of Hazlitt's pronouncements on Schlegel, excited by his superior airs and intellectual arrogance as well as by a profound suspicion of German mysticism, should not obscure the fact that Hazlitt reproduced Schlegel's outline of the history of the drama (with its implication for a general history of poetry and civilization) and that in the *Characters of Shakespeare's Plays* he calls the *Lectures* "the best account of the plays of Shakespeare that has hitherto appeared." [11] He quotes Schlegel at length and with obvious approval, especially in the first part of the book, though later on he disagrees frequently about details of the plays, rejects Schlegel's fantastic ascription of several doubtful plays to Shakespeare, and defends the Restoration dramatists against his low estimate. Hazlitt could hardly have understood the complete position of Schlegel: he wards off its metaphysical implications, which smack to him of mysticism, but adopts the general view of literary history implied: the distinction between romantic and classic and the description of the different types of drama, though these terms and ideas could not, in Hazlitt's scheme of things, play the central role they do in Schlegel's. Still, much that seems Coleridgean in Hazlitt is due to the affinity between Coleridge and Schlegel.

On many points Hazlitt is nearer to Wordsworth than to Coleridge. He is, like Wordsworth, rooted in the English empirical tradition, and like Wordsworth he inherits the emotionalism and Rousseauism of the later 18th century. It is true that Hazlitt disparaged Wordsworth's conversation as egotistical and asserted that he never "got any ideas at all from him, for the reason that he had none to give." [12] But on the other hand, Hazlitt reported a very fine discussion by Wordsworth of Poussin's "wholeness," and his many generous tributes to Wordsworth's greatness as a poet testify that Hazlitt kept his basic admiration in spite of the personal and political conflict between them.* The prefaces to *Lyrical Ballads*,

---

* *Complete Works*, ed. Howe, *11*, 93; esp. *5*, 156; *11*, 86 ff. The actual break between Hazlitt and Wordsworth was *not* due to an erotic adventure of Hazlitt's during his visit to the Lakes in 1803. See C. M. Maclean, *Born under Saturn* (New York, 1944), pp. 359 ff. for a full discussion of the mystery.

though rarely referred to, are clearly basic texts from which much
of Hazlitt's own theory is derived.

The affinity to Charles Lamb (1775–1834) is even more obvious.
Coleridge, late in life, said: "Compare Charles Lamb's exquisite
criticisms on Shakespeare with Hazlitt's round and round imitations of them." [13] There is much truth in this maliciously exaggerated statement. In method and procedure Lamb anticipates
Hazlitt, though Lamb cannot compare with Hazlitt in range and
scope, systematic application and theoretical awareness. What is
common to Lamb and Hazlitt are three methods of criticism which
were apparently new at that time: evocation, metaphor, and personal reference. The methods are ultimately Longinian, but there
are no examples in English 18th-century criticism which even
approximate what Lamb and Hazlitt were doing. In Germany
Winckelmann, Herder, Jean Paul, and on occasion the Schlegels
achieved similar effects, and in France Chateaubriand was almost
simultaneously introducing such methods. But it would be, I
think, impossible to prove any direct "influence," as neither Lamb
nor Hazlitt read any German or cared for Chateaubriand.* We
have to ascribe the profound change in critical methods to a general change of sensibility or, if we are not content with such a
vague gesture toward underground forces, we can look at art and
theatrical criticism, where attention was paid to physical, concrete
detail earlier than it was in literary criticism, which was preoccupied with theory. Hazlitt knew something of Diderot's similar art
criticism, and he may have read Winckelmann.† It seems no
chance that both Hazlitt and Lamb early cultivated these fields.
Whatever the obscure origins of these procedures may be, Lamb

* But note that Hazlitt, probably for financial reasons, suggested to
a publisher in 1810 the project of translating Chateaubriand's *Les
Martyrs*. See Howe, *Life of William Hazlitt* (1949), p. 140. His other
references to Chateaubriand are all unfavorable.

† Hazlitt probably knew Diderot's *Essai sur la peinture* (ed. 1795,
containing the 1765 *Salon*), and he certainly knew the Grimm-Diderot
Correspondance littéraire, though the one specific reference (Howe, *4*,
66–67n.) is to the English abridgment, *Historical and Literary Memoirs
and Anecdotes* (2 vols. London, 1814), *1*, 185. Winckelmann is mentioned in Howe, *16*, 199.

was the original initiator in England. It seems hard, however, to agree to the extravagant claims which have been made for his general importance in a history of criticism. A. C. Bradley called Lamb flatly "the best critic of the nineteenth century," [14] and E. M. W. Tillyard has said that "of English masters of theoretical criticism Coleridge is the greatest, of applied, in a sense, Lamb." [15] We can see the germs of Lamb's method in early informal letters dating back to 1801. Speaking of Walton's *Angler* he says: "Don't you already feel your spirit filled with the scenes?—the banks of rivers—the cowslip beds—the pastoral scenes—the neat alehouses —and hostesses and milkmaids." [16] As we have read so much of this kind of evocative criticism, we may not be impressed, but it would be hard to find earlier instances in English. Nor could one find pure instances of criticism by metaphor earlier than in Lamb. Thus, speaking of Jeremy Taylor, Lamb enumerates the similes and allusions "taken, as the bees take honey, from all the youngest, greenest, exquisitest parts of nature," and then calls Taylor's imagination "a spacious garden, where no vile insects could crawl in; his apprehension a *Court* where no foul thoughts kept 'leets and holydays.' " [17]

These casual pronouncements become a method in the remarks commenting on individual plays and passages in Lamb's *Specimens of English Dramatic Poets* (1808) and in scattered essays, of which two, "On the Tragedies of Shakespeare Considered with Reference to Their Fitness for Stage Representation" (1811) and "On the Artificial Comedy of the Last Century" (1822), are the best known and most admired. But these essays are not impressive for their general arguments. The view that the "plays of Shakespeare are less calculated for performance on a stage, than those of almost any dramatist whatever" [18] can hardly be taken seriously except as a means of drawing our attention to the greatness of Shakespeare's poetry and the diverse shortcomings of the stage in the time of Lamb. Nor are we likely to be convinced by the argument that Restoration comedy leads us into the "land of cuckoldry, the Utopia of gallantry" which "has no reference whatever to the world that is." [19] We must take it as a protest against the literalminded moralism of the time, as an assertion of the conventionality of the stage, not as a serious argument against relations between literature and life, drama and society. Lamb, on occasion, can drive

home a single well-taken point: he argues against strict stage-
illusion in comedy, "for a judicious understanding, not too
openly announced, between the ladies and gentlemen—on both
sides of the curtain." [20] He is good in praising the sanity of true
genius, an argument of peculiar poignancy in his own case.[21] But
for the most part Lamb's criticism must be described as "detached
thoughts on books and reading," as *marginalia*. They deserve our
admiration because they are finely phrased and reveal a literary
taste new at that time, shared only by Coleridge and a few others:
a taste for the 17th century, its quaintness and baroque grandeur,
for Browne and Burton, for Fuller and Jeremy Taylor. But it
seems impossible to claim for these marginalia great significance in
a history of criticism.

Specimens of English Dramatic Poets was an influential anthology of the non-Shakespearean drama, which at that time had been
only partially reprinted and had elicited mostly antiquarian interest. Lamb was one of the very first to appreciate these plays for
their poetry.[22] His enthusiasm for Webster was new, and one can
understand the feelings of a discoverer that led Lamb to call
Thomas Heywood "a sort of prose Shakespeare" and to place John
Ford in the "first order of poets." [23] But as criticism the comments
are usually little more than exclamation marks, mere assertions of
enthusiasm. Even such a longer passage as the comment on the torture scenes in the *Duchess of Malfi* amounts to little more than an
enumeration of the details of the action and the doubtful claim
that Webster has conveyed the horror with dignity and decorum.
It is the kind of personal unargued criticism whose irrelevance to
the text becomes most obvious when Lamb speaks of the *Reveng-
er's Tragedy*. "I have never read it but my ears tingle, and I feel a
hot blush overspread my cheeks." [24] It is the criterion of the thrill
down the spine, the bristling of the beard, the rise in the pit of the
stomach, which A. E. Housman has in our time proclaimed to be
the test of true poetry. This exclamatory criticism has its function
in the notes to an anthology: it serves in lieu of the inverted
commas used by Pope to mark off the "beauties of Shakespeare."

Much of the rest of Lamb's criticism is a kind of pointing to
fine passages: the essays on Thomas Fuller and George Wither
especially are little more than anthologies. Only in the piece on
the sonnets of Sidney is there an attempt at actual criticism: in

opposition to Hazlitt, who thought them frigid and cumbrous, Lamb considers them "full, material and circumstantiated." But it seems doubtful whether the verse of these sonnets "runs off swiftly and gallantly," or whether "it might have been tuned to the trumpet; or tempered (as he himself expresses it) to 'trampling horses' feet.' " [25] There is small relation between such a metaphor derived from a knowledge of Sidney's life and martial experiences, as suggested by Sidney's remarks on *Chevy Chase,* and the sonnets which Lamb himself quotes as his favorites: "With how sad steps, O Moon, thou climb'st the skies"; "Come, Sleep, O Sleep, the certain knot of peace." What have such lines to do with trumpets and trampling horses' feet? This is impressionistic criticism which has lost all contact with the text.

Lamb's formal reviews, such as that of Wordsworth's *Excursion* and of Keats's *Lamia* volume, are largely strings of extracts with pronouncements of preferences. The much admired review of Keats, which selects fine passages from a poet then quite unrecognized, still comes to the false conclusion that *Isabella* is better than *Lamia, The Eve of St. Agnes,* and the odes on the ground that "an ounce of feeling is worth a pound of fancy." [26] This and many other judgments show Lamb's emotional romanticism, the view that passion is "the all in all in poetry." [27]

Lamb, of course, *wanted* to point out fine passages and convey his own enthusiasm to his readers. He knew that he was no theorist and not even a regular critic; with his usual modesty he speaks of his "inability of reviewing, of giving account of a book in any methodical way." "I can vehemently applaud, or perversely stickle, at *parts:* but I cannot grasp at a whole." [28] At the same time he recognized the deficiencies of all selections, all snippets: "how beggarly and how bald even Shakespeare's princely pieces look when thus violently divorced from connection or circumstance! . . . Everything in heaven and earth, in man and in story, in books and in fancy, acts by Confederacy, by juxtaposition, by circumstance and place." [29] Lamb also understood Wordsworth's and Coleridge's theory of the imagination, of which he said (earlier than any of their extensive discussions in print) that it "draws all things into one . . . makes things animate and inanimate, beings with their attributes, subjects and their accessories, take one color, and serve to one effect." [30]

Some of Lamb's *obiter dicta,* scattered over the essays and letters, may seem to us mistaken, but his dislike of Shelley and Byron, his description of Goethe's *Faust* as "a disagreeable canting tale of seduction," his approval of Wordsworth's opinion about the dullness of Voltaire's *Candide* cannot surprise if we know the political and social context.[31] Nevertheless, we must agree with him when he praises the *Ancient Mariner* or chides Wordsworth for his overt didacticism and for "continually putting a sign post up to show where you are to feel." [32] Lamb's most "creative" criticism is his most indirect. His pastiches and imitations of Burton and Sir Thomas Browne's "beautiful obliquities" show that he had a true feeling for their style even though he was unwilling or unable to define or analyze it intellectually.[33]

Hazlitt has no such untheoretical and unself-conscious mind. He makes a direct defense of what later was to be called "impressionist criticism." "I say what I think: I think what I feel. I cannot help receiving certain impressions from things; and I have sufficient courage to declare (somewhat abruptly) what they are." [34] This reliance on personal feeling makes him conceive that the task of criticism is precisely to communicate such feelings. He would want "to read over a set of authors with the audience," when giving his public lectures, "as I would do with a friend, to point out a favorite passage, to explain an objection; or if a remark or a theory occurs, to state it in illustration of the subject, but neither to tire him nor puzzle myself with pedantic rules and pragmatical formulas of criticism that can do no good to anybody." Hazlitt thus also disparages antiquarianism: "I do not think that is the way to learn 'the gentle craft' of poesy or to teach it to others:—to imbibe or to communicate its spirit." At least by implication, however, Hazlitt readmits theory in his final declaration of faith. "In a word, I have endeavored to feel what is good, and to 'give a reason for the faith that was in me,' when necessary, and when in my power." [35]

Hazlitt's practice develops and elaborates that of Lamb. Many of Hazlitt's best known passages could be called evocations. Some, like the description of Restoration comedy, try to conjure a picture of people and costumes: "What a rustling of silks and waving of plumes! what a sparkling of diamond ear-rings and shoe-buckles!" [36] Others are skillful enumerations, recitals of scenes or characters from books read, such as the catalogue of Scott's characters and the lists of topics in the *Tatler* and scenes in Rabelais.[37] Others are little fanciful variations suggested by the theme of the book. Speaking of Thomson's *Seasons,* Hazlitt can descant on the "glow of summer, the gloom of winter, the tender promise of the spring," and so on.[38] Ossian can be described by evoking his landscape: "the cold moonlight, the thistle, the strings of his harp sighing and rustling like the dry reeds in the winter's wind." [39] At its worst the method degenerates into gushing rhetoric. *Romeo and Juliet* evokes the "purple light of love, the silver sound of lovers' tongues by night, the voice of the nightingale from the pomegranate tree." [40] At its best the method can suggest some characteristics of the writer discussed. Thus Jeremy Taylor is said to "mix up death's heads and amaranthine flowers; make life a procession to the grave, but crown it with gaudy garlands, and 'rain sacrificial roses' on its path." [41]

The procedure works almost entirely by metaphor even if the attempt is not to recall a specific scene or character but rather to define a style or mind. Thus, Ben Jonson's laboriousness and effort is several times imagined as that of a grub or a mole.[42] Shakespeare's humor is described as bubbling, sparkling, while Ben Jonson's is, "as it were, confined in a leaden cistern, where it stagnates or corrupts; or directed only through certain artificial pipes and conduits, to answer a given purpose." [43] A little further on, the idea of effort is elaborated in relation to Ben Jonson's plots. "The author, in sustaining the weight of his plot, seems like a balance-master who supports a number of people, piled one upon another on his hands, his knees, his shoulders, but with a great effort on his own part, and with a painful effect to the beholders." [44] When the strain and effort seems to Hazlitt even greater, he has recourse to the figure of a Caesarean operation: Donne's "muse suffers continual pangs and throes. His thoughts are delivered by the Caesarean operation." The same metaphor is applied, in another book, to Sidney: "All his thoughts are forced and painful births, and may be said to be delivered by Caesarean operation." [45] Clarity of style combined with lack of content can be illustrated by a comparison with wines. Southey's style "has not the body or thickness of port wine, but is like clear sherry," while Lamb's "runs pure and clear, though it may often take an underground course, or be conveyed through old-fashioned conduit pipes." [46] The conduit pipes, which, before with Ben Jonson, were used to illustrate forcing, illustrate here Lamb's predilection for archaisms.

The concreteness and particularity of the method is increased by frequent appeals to the author's personal memory.[47] Hazlitt tells us how on Salisbury Plain, he was preparing his lectures on the Age of Elizabeth, and how the characters from the books seem to accompany him on his walks. Returning "I can 'take mine ease at mine inn,' beside the blazing hearth, and shake hands with Signor Orlando Friscobaldo, as the oldest acquaintance I have. Ben Jonson, learned Chapman, Master Webster, and Master Heywood, are there; and seated round, discourse the silent hours away." [48] The happy Endymion in Lyly's play provokes in Hazlitt the wish that he could pass his life in "such a sleep, a long, long sleep, dreaming of some fair heavenly Goddess." Quoting a passage from Beaumont and Fletcher's *A False One,* he breaks out enthusiastically: "It is something worth living for, to write or even read such poetry as this, or to know that it has been written, or that there have been subjects on which to write it!" [49]

Such criticism serves to convey what Hazlitt called the "gusto" of literature: the feeling of personal enjoyment, of intimacy, of concrete knowledge of the text. The ideal of criticism implied is hardly one of knowledge or judgment, system or theory. The critic, rather, serves as an enthusiastic guide through a picture gallery, or as host in a library who pulls out his books and points to favorite passages or recalls incidents and scenes in them and remembers when and where he read them. When Hazlitt wants, as he frequently does, to characterize and judge (and thus to advance the actual task of the critic), he proceeds by indirection. Like any other critic, he seizes some general quality, but he proceeds to play variations on it by drawing out a whole string of metaphors and associations. Thus Crabbe is the target of Hazlitt's ridicule for what could be called his literal naturalism. Crabbe "gives you," Hazlitt says, "the petrifaction of a sigh, and carves a tear, to the life, in stone." His characters remind us of anatomical preservations, of a stuffed cat in a glass-case; his poetry is like a museum, or curiosity shop.[50] Here what might have been an abstract opinion becomes concrete and memorable. In short, Hazlitt is an artist who attempts the task of translating a work of art into a completely different set of metaphors. At times the result seems only a superfluous duplication, in a looser and inevitably inferior medium. At other times Hazlitt actually succeeds at the genuine critical task of characterization and evaluation by metaphorical analogies which it would be wrong to dismiss as *mere* analogies. Obviously the method has its dangers and drawbacks: it is highly individual, like all artistic talent, and thus does not allow the incremental growth from critic to critic which builds up a living body of critical thought. It is in constant danger of loss of contact with the object. For instance, talking of Pope, whom he appreciated much more than the other Romantics, Hazlitt epitomizes the contrast between natural and artificial poetry. Pope, he says, "could describe the faultless whole-length mirror that reflected his own person, better than the smooth surface of the lake that reflects the face of heaven—a piece of cut glass or pair of paste buckles with more brilliance and effect, than a thousand dew-drops glittering in the sun." [51] But this, of course, is positively misleading, for Pope never described himself in a mirror and did speak finely of the "lakes that quiver to the curling breeze" or of the "glittering textures of the filmy dew." [52]

At times Hazlitt recognizes that the method of evocation has its dangers: he criticizes Coleridge's impressionistic account of Thomas Browne's *Urn Burial,* pointing out that it is totally unsupported by the text.[53] But the method was to spread far and wide and seemed to triumph toward the end of the 19th century in the purple passages of Walter Pater and Oscar Wilde and in the deliberate personalities of Anatole France and George Saintsbury. It lingers on in the vignettes of a Van Wyck Brooks.

Hazlitt's critical work, however, is not exhaustively described by this analysis of his methods of anthologizing, evocation, metaphorical characterization, and personal appeal. There is more theory in Hazlitt than is generally recognized. One must keep in mind that in contrast to Coleridge he was very much the journalist who had to live from the proceeds of his pen. He had, too, a constant awareness of the needs and limitations of the middle-class audience to which he addressed his lectures. When speaking of the nature of poetry, he must have felt strongly the difficulty of the abstract subject and made it purposely palatable by digressions, illustrations, repetitions. It is not quite fair to judge Hazlitt's capacities for theoretical thinking from these loose and popular pronounce-

ments. He learned a lesson from the ill success of his early abstract
book, *On the Principles of Human Action* (1805), and later determined to be nontechnical, unsystematic, and semipopular. He has
a different relation to his audience than has Dr. Johnson, Coleridge, La Harpe, or even August Wilhelm Schlegel. He is not the
judge, the authority pronouncing *ex cathedra,* the poet defending
his own practice, or the philosopher speculating in the privacy of
his notebooks (even when published in cold print). He is a middleman trying to persuade his audience of the importance and joy of
literature. He strongly feels his own social position. In an essay on
the "Aristocracy of Letters" he ridicules the inflated reputation of
scholars (that is, people knowing Latin and Greek) who have not
written anything and never had to commit themselves. Learning,
Hazlitt feels, is something impersonal: a transferable property,
while genius and understanding are "a man's self, an integrant
part of his personal identity." [54] He claims such personality for
himself and fiercely defends himself against the pontifical condemnation of Gifford and others who denied him the right to
speak of classical authors and constantly alluded to his low social
standing and supposed lack of education and breeding. The consciously cultivated popularity of Hazlitt's writings suited his
theory. He demanded particularity and distrusted abstraction and
system so far as, on occasion, to proclaim a complete pluralism of
truths. "It is said, I know, that truth is one, but to this I cannot
subscribe, for it appears to me that truth is many." [55]

If truth is many, then poetry is many. There is an endless variety
of excellence. "It is ridiculous to suppose that there is but one
standard and one style." [56] Taste is subjective. On occasion, Hazlitt
appeals to the analogy of tasting, and there is an end of it. "There
are people who cannot taste olives—and I cannot much relish Ben
Jonson." [57] But when he had to consider the question of taste more
closely, he admitted that there is a universal standard. "But it must
be that, not which does, but which *would* please universally, sup-
posing all men to have paid an equal attention to any subject and
to have an equal relish for it." [58] Hazlitt here seems unworried by
the question-begging term "relish" or by the difficulties of the
view that "each age or nation has a standard of its own" and that
literature is "confined within local and temporal limits," [59] views
which would put an end to all criticism of works lying outside of

one's own time. On one occasion Hazlitt seems to disclaim any certainty for criticism. He voices his doubts whether "any body twenty years hence will think any thing about any" of the living poets of his time.[60] But this must have been in a specially skeptical and self-disparaging mood.

Hazlitt's concept of poetry is usually wide and varied enough to accommodate diverse conceptions. In the defense of his lecture on poetry, *A Letter to William Gifford,* who had ridiculed it for the looseness and all-inclusiveness of his definition, Hazlitt himself recognized that he had used the term "poetry" to mean three different things: "the composition produced, the state of mind or faculty producing it, and, in certain cases, the subject-matter proper to call forth that state of mind." The common something which belongs to these several views was "an unusual vividness in external objects or in our immediate impressions, exciting a movement of imagination in the mind, and leading by natural association or *sympathy* to harmony of sound and the modulation of verse in expressing it." [61] He could also use the word "poetry" in a Platonic sense which seems almost meaningless in its wideness. "Wherever there is a sense of beauty, or power, or harmony, as in the motion of a wave of the sea, in the growth of a flower . . . there is poetry, in its birth." Even "fear is poetry, hope is poetry, love is poetry, hatred is poetry. The child is a poet in fact, when he first plays at hide-and-seek . . . the miser, when he hugs his gold." All beauty, all passion, all excitement is poetry, and hence we are all poets. The poet only expresses what he and all feel alike.[62]

Thus poetry has to be described largely in terms of the emotional life of the poet and the reader infected by him. Poetry is excitement, stimulation, the joy of exercising one's emotional powers. We like to indulge our hatred and scorn, we like to have a sense of power gratified, an explanation which Hazlitt finds sufficient to account for our pleasure in tragedy. But elsewhere Hazlitt finds a somewhat different theory: Tragedy "exhausts the terror or pity by an unlimited indulgence of it." [63] In this dubious rephrasing of Aristotle the excitement of poetry serves a psychic need for release, compensation, or self-delusion. Hazlitt, in a way which might please Freudians, reflects that poets are usually weak in constitution, sedentary, nervous, melancholy and thus look for "speculative comforts." [64] They seek compensation for the handi-caps inflicted on them by nature: Byron for his misshapen foot, Pope for the curvature of his spine. Authors "sow their wild oats in their books, and take their swing in theory." [65] Poets are thus dreamers. "Poetry dwells in a perpetual Utopia of its own." Imag-ination "represents objects, not as they are in themselves, but as they are moulded by other thoughts and feelings, into an infinite variety of shapes and combinations of power." [66] Poetry is a fiction "made up of what we wish things to be," a "fanciful structure raised on the groundwork of the strongest and most intimate asso-ciations of our ideas." [67] So far these ideas make a coherent system which would interest our own time: poetry is compensation, re-lease, day-dreaming, wish-fulfillment. But Hazlitt also holds that art is imitation of nature, a way of knowledge, insight into reality. Especially in his writings on the art of painting does he constantly emphasize the subordination of art to nature and the necessity of submission to her. "Everything is in nature and the artist only finds it." "Man, instead of adding to the store, or creating any thing . . . can only draw out a feeble and imperfect transcript." [68] There is even an incredibly sentimental passage about a nightingale and the stream of joy pouring from its throat. This singing is preferred to that of a woman, and her singing in turn is considered more natural than instrumental music.[69]

Hazlitt is thus definitely hostile to Reynolds' theory of idealiza-tion, especially to his view that the painter must abstract some-thing like the representative mean from nature.[70] In his theory of painting Hazlitt comes close to a recommendation of exact nat-uralism, but his formulas constantly shift and change, and most frequently, especially in connection with literature, he advocates the view that art must aim at the reproduction of the "character-istic," the essential of a particular object. This essence of a single thing, however, is also conceived as imbedded in a web of asso-ciations and correspondences and even symbols. Thus we find in Hazlitt all the different answers traditionally given to the question about the relation of art and nature: naturalism, almost literal copying; insight by emotional sympathy into the particular char-acter of an object; or finally intuition into the whole system of na-ture, into its general meaning for man. Hazlitt defines original genius as the power of giving some feature of nature "its characteristic essence." Yet he rejects as a contradiction in terms the thesis that art can embody abstractions; he constantly attacks generalities in art in favor of an induction of particularities. He argues that the "ideal is not in general the stronghold of poetry." [71]

In Hazlitt's theory the term "gusto" applies not merely to the enthusiasm of the artist; it is also the "power or passion defining any object." It is the truth of character which arises from truth of feeling. For instance, Michelangelo's figures have "gusto," in Hazlitt's vocabulary.[72] Imagination is thus the faculty of intuition into the character of an object, the power of empathy we would say, the power of identification with other beings. While his pronouncements about poetry as release and compensation, dream, and fanciful structure would suggest the ideal of a subjective poet, Hazlitt at other times, and apparently even more emphatically, conceives the poet to be the all-sympathizer, devoid of any individuality and absorbed in his objects. Shakespeare is, of course, the great exemplar. Like Coleridge, Hazlitt compares Shakespeare's art to that of the ventriloquist. "He had only to think of any thing in order to become that thing. . . . He was nothing in himself, but he was all that others were, or that they could become." He was the "Proteus of the human intellect." [73] Hazlitt thus assigns a comparatively lower rank to the other type: the subjective poet, the egotist, who is to him best represented by Wordsworth. He even complains, in obvious contradiction to many other of his pronouncements, that the "great fault of a modern school of poetry [i.e. the romantic] is, that it is an experiment to reduce poetry to a mere effusion of natural sensibility." [74]

The contrast which he draws between Byron and Scott is also based on such a preference for the objective. Scott is praised because he "looks at nature, sees it, hears it, feels, and believes that it exists, before it is printed," while Byron thinks only of himself.[75] Scott is never "this opaque, obtrusive body getting in the way and eclipsing the sun of truth and nature," [76] while Byron's Giaour, the Corsair, Childe Harold, are all the same person, and they are apparently all himself. But the choice is not completely clear-cut. Scott is censured for his lack of feeling and Byron praised for having a "demon," "and that is the next thing to being full of the God." [77] Scott "has all the power given him from without—he has not, perhaps, any equal power from within. The intensity of the feeling is not equal to the distinctness of the imagery." [78] Thus poetry must be passion, but the best poetry is objective passion. "The greatest strength of genius is shown in describing the strongest passions," [79] he says, referring to *King Lear,* and *Lear,* which Hazlitt ranks highest among Shakespeare's plays, is not presumably an expression of personal emotions.

This conception of the poet as the sympathizer, the depictor of human passions, is, however, on occasion modified by more pretentious concepts of the role of the imagination. Hazlitt reduces to associationist vocabulary many notions about the imagination which Wordsworth and Coleridge could have uttered only in their most exalted moods. He can say, like Shelley, that "art may be said to draw aside the veil from nature." [80] He quotes "Tintern Abbey" on "seeing into the life of things" and applies this to "an inner sense, a deeper intuition into nature." [81] He speaks of the "intuitive perception of the hidden analogies of things, or, as it may be called, this instinct of the imagination" which "works unconsciously, like nature." [82] He even calls art a discovery of a web of associations. "Real poetry, or poetry of the highest order, can only be produced by unraveling the real web of associations, which have been wound round any subject by nature, and the unavoidable conditions of humanity." [83] This last phrase allows Hazlitt to side with Bowles in his quarrel with Byron and to endorse the view, hardly tenable on his own psychologist grounds, that there is a distinct poetical subject matter. Hazlitt can endorse the idea that "nature is also a language. Objects, like words, have a meaning; and the true artist is the interpreter of this language." Each object is a "symbol of the affections and a link in the chain of our endless being." [84] There is thus something like a symbolic language of nature. Hazlitt even arrives at an identification of "truth, nature, and beauty" as "almost different names for the same thing." If art is the perception of truth, "the development or the communication of knowledge," then beauty is truth, truth beauty. [85] The bearing on Keats's "Ode on a Grecian Urn" is immediate in these reflections: they serve as a commentary, if not as a source.

Thus Hazlitt combines emotionalism with a doctrine (if we can call it that) of imagination as sympathizing with the characteristic essence of things. In addition, we find even traces of the symbolic view of Hazlitt's fellow romantics. All the emphasis in these theories falls on the mental processes and equipment of the artist: the work itself hardly enters into the discussion.

But Hazlitt has also definite views on the importance of sound in poetry. Rather easily a bridge is made from the psychological process to the music of verse. In his defense against Gifford, Hazlitt imagines "a movement of imagination in the mind, leading by natural association or *sympathy* to harmony of sound and the modulation of verse in expressing it." [86] The music of the mind is answered and expressed by the music of language. "There is a near connection between music and deep-rooted passion. Mad people sing. As often as articulation passes naturally into intonation, there poetry begins." This impassioned raising of pitch is considered sufficient to account for verse, for the mingling of the tide of verse "with the tide of feeling, flowing and murmuring as it flows." [87] This vague physiological and psychological theory, derived from 18th-century primitivists, Hazlitt blandly offers to Coleridge as a substitute for the latter's definition of poetry.[88] But then we must not seek in Hazlitt analytical skill or even deep interest in the structure of a work of art.

On the whole, Hazlitt's attitude toward witty and conceited poetry is quite negative. He opens his excellent *Lectures on the English Comic Writers* with introductory reflections on wit and humor, trying to distinguish between three degrees: the laughable, the ludicrous, and the ridiculous. Wit is considered "the product of art and fancy." [89] But the distinctions remain fuzzy and groping: they are psychological and are not focused on the use of wit and humor in art, though once, in reviewing Butler's *Hudibras,* Hazlitt enumerates instances of wit according to rhetorical classifications.[90] When discussing the metaphysicals in general, Hazlitt criticizes them severely for obscurity and intellectual abstraction, and he expounds the standard neoclassical theory of metaphor. Comparison must be always with something more beautiful in nature, or with a more touching feeling, never apparently the other way around.[91] This argument is also used against Sidney's style in the *Arcadia,* a book Hazlitt constantly quotes as an example of artificiality, frigidity, and intellectual coxcombry.[92] But at other times Hazlitt recognizes that conceits are not necessarily contradictory to sentiment. Petrarch is defended by a historical argument: the scholastic style was natural to him. "All pedantry is not affectation." [93] If we would press for an explanation of Hazlitt's approval of Petrarch, compared to his condemnation of Donne and Sidney, we would, presumably, be referred to his subjective impression of sincerity or to a historical reflection that scholasticism was indigenous in the Middle Ages but was an affectation after the Reformation. In practice, Hazlitt quoted some lines of Donne with approval, liked much in Cowley, and was, after Bowles, one of the first to admire Marvell. Hazlitt quotes "To his Coy Mistress" and includes an ample selection from Marvell in his *Select British Poets* (1824).*

Hazlitt's main interests are not formal or stylistic. In his discussion of Shakespeare's plays everything is centered on the analysis of characters. *Characters of Shakespeare's Plays* (1817) is a comparatively immature work. Much is only quotations, with enthusiastic and personal remarks interspersed. There is little illumination in the declaration which, as if on purpose, confuses fiction and reality: "We have almost as great an affection for Imogen as she had for Posthumus." [94] The remarks on Desdemona which suggest lewdness as a motive for her marrying the Moor [95] might be appropriate if applied to a real life situation where Hazlitt's realistic insight into sexual relations might apply, but they are completely inapplicable to the Desdemona of the play,

> a maiden never bold:
> Of spirit so still and quiet, that her motion
> Blush'd at itself. [96]

She is not actual flesh and blood but a dramatic character. With Hazlitt we are not far from books like *The Girlhood of Shakespeare's Heroines* or discussions of the famous question "How many children had Lady Macbeth?" Because Hazlitt has an insufficient sense of the distinction between art and reality he teeters on the brink of such absurdities. His *Characters of Shakespeare's Plays* is partly vitiated by a view of art as a mere copy of reality. *Antony and Cleopatra* and *Hamlet* are pronounced, astonishingly enough, transcripts of real events. *Hamlet* is "an exact transcript of

* Howe, 6, 314. The anthology includes "Bermudas," "The Nymph to her Fawn," "The Garden," "On a Drop of Dew," "The Gallery," "To his Coy Mistress," "Upon the Hill and Grove at Billborow," and "The Horatian Ode," a very good choice indeed.

what might be supposed to have taken place at the court of Denmark, at the remote period of time fixed upon." [97] But then again we are told, "it is *we* who are Hamlet," and Hamlet is described as a tender-minded hero, similar to Goethe's or Mackenzie's, "full of weakness and melancholy, the most amiable of misanthropes." [98] This means bringing the figure into one's own time. There is sympathy and identification here, of a sort which also appears when Hazlitt, for the first time, I believe, in the history of Shakespeare criticism, rescues Shylock. He sides with him, pities him, and thinks him "hardly dealt with by his judges." [99] Hazlitt is at his best when he describes Iago as "an amateur of tragedy in real life" who has a "passion of hypocrisy," "a diseased intellectual activity." [100] Hazlitt's psychological acumen shines when he deals with a figure of very complex or obscure motivation. His character sketch of Iago is superior to Coleridge's description of his "motiveless malignity" or to Tucker Brooke's recent attempt to sentimentalize Iago into a basically likeable good fellow.

Hazlitt, more than any of his English contemporaries, has a strong awareness of the relations between literature and society and a strong historical sense. Though he is not quite ready to treat literature as a social document, he can say that *Joseph Andrews* is a "perfect piece of statistics," and praise the accuracy of the picture of manners we receive from 18th-century English novels.[101] At times Hazlitt sounds very deterministic about the causes of literature, in spite of his usual exaltation of genius. The statement that "the human mind floats on the tide of mighty *Circumstance*" taken by itself might be innocuous enough, but for Hazlitt it means that no single mind can resist "the vast machine of the world" and that the "poet can do no more than stamp the mind of his age upon his works." [102] *Être de son temps,* the later slogan of the French romantics, is conceived as both a duty and a necessity. "If literature in our day has taken this decided turn into a critical channel, is it not a presumptive proof that it ought to do so?" [103] The bias of abstraction as the reigning spirit of the age explains the decay of the drama.[104] The genius of the poet must cooperate with the mind of the age or country. "Whatever appeals to the imagination, ought to rest on undivided sentiment, on one undisputed tradition, one catholic faith." [105] This is a surprising pronouncement to come from a man who was such a nonconformist himself in life and politics.

In praising the Elizabethan age Hazlitt praises its Englishness, and exalts the effect of the Reformation because it gave a mind to the people. He speaks of the natural genius of the country, which gave unity and a common direction to all the different causes contributing toward the flowering of Elizabethan literature. Shakespeare is part of his age. "His age was necessary to him." "He overlooks and commands the admiration of posterity, but he does it from the tableland of the age in which he lived." He was "one of a race of giants, the tallest, the strongest, the most graceful, and beautiful of them." [106] He is not out of his age, as Coleridge would like to have him.

In two of Hazlitt's books, however, *Lectures Chiefly on the Dramatic Literature of the Age of Elizabeth* (1820) and *The Spirit of the Age* (1825), the latter containing portraits of his own contemporaries, there is little analysis of the reigning spirit of a time. The plan is static, and there is hardly any continuity between the essays. The main historical conception of the Elizabethan age is the same as Warton's. The "age of chivalry was not then quite gone." Man's life was fuller of traps and pitfalls. There were "more unhappy loves or matches," they were still "borderers on the savage state." [107] The implied assumption is that the "necessary advances of civilization are unfavorable to the spirit of poetry." [108] Hazlitt several times discusses the question: "Why are the Arts not progressive?" Advances in technology, political freedom, and manners are one thing, but the greatest poets, the best painters, "appeared soon after the birth of these arts, and lived in a state of society, which was, in other respects, comparatively barbarous." [109] The appeals to genius, to feeling as independent of social advance, to the advantages of the first comer, to nearness to nature, to the lack of encumbering tradition, are commonplaces for at least a century. But such a primitivistic evolutionary scheme is not really entertained by Hazlitt in his other writings. He canvasses different schemes of evolution, only vaguely envisaging that of a steady decline in imagination. Hazlitt's scheme in the *Lectures* of the history of English poetry is an elaboration of Warton's. He sees a succession from a poetry of imagination (under Elizabeth) to one of fancy (under Charles I), to one of wit (under Charles II and Queen Anne), to one of commonplaces (under the first Georges), and finally to a poetry of paradox supposedly flourishing since the French Revolution.[110] In discussing the novel he tries to account for its changes by social influences: the Hanoverian succession gave a more popular taste to literature and genius. The age of George II was the age of hobby-horses. "The whole surface of society was cut out into square enclosures and sharp angles which extended to the dresses of the time, their gravel walks, and clipped hedges." The novel under George III partakes of the disorder of the times.[111]

The most elaborate of Hazlitt's theories is his attempt to account for historical changes in the style of English comedy. Shakespeare's comedy gently ridicules "solitary excrescences growing up out of their native soil without affectation." The butts of Shakespeare's wit are not really dangerous, and thus his comedy is "social and humane," really "too good-natured for comedy." English comedy changed when "individual infirmities passed into general manners," [112] when vices became, as in Restoration comedy, social evils which deserved to be exposed to ridicule and satire. Such ridicule, however, had the effect either of driving vices underground or of destroying them. A general leveling of character followed, a spread of uniformity which had killed genuine comedy. "It is not the criticism which the public taste exercises upon the stage, but the criticism which the stage exercises upon public manners, that is fatal to comedy, by rendering the subject-matter of it tame, correct, and spiritless." [113] Hazlitt's preference goes to Restoration comedy. Shakespeare is too romantic and serious a writer in his comedies, where even deformed characters claim our personal forgiveness. Modern sentimental comedy sins also against the purity and purposes of the genre. Comedy must not be an affair of the heart or the imagination.[114] Hazlitt's theory seems to be suggested by Hugh Blair's attempt to account on similar grounds for the superiority of English over French comedy. Such an explanation has, of course, the flaw of excessive simplicity. The democratization and the increase of social uniformity observed by Hazlitt does not mean the extinction of human individuality as the raw material of comedy. It is a naturalistic theory too much in the style of the "conjectural" histories of the 18th century.

Whatever one may think of Hazlitt's causal explanation of

comedy, he successfully described types of comedy. He similarly distinguished and described four types of tragedy: classical, Gothic (Shakespearean), bourgeois, and German or paradoxical.[115] But here he is closely following Schlegel's *Lectures*, just as he is dependent on Schlegel for his distinctions between the ancients and moderns, the classical and the romantic.* But the Schlegelian contrasts do not interest Hazlitt deeply. His perspective does not extend to the Middle Ages and antiquity. He disparaged the tragedies of Sophocles as "hardly tragedies in our sense of the word," and he had no use for Aristophanes' "monstrous allegorical pantomimes, —enormous practical jokes." [116]

This kind of rash judgment lays Hazlitt wide open to the charge of ignorance and provincialism. He clearly was not a classical scholar, but one should not underrate the width of his modern reading, in English and French literature primarily, with excursions into Italian, Spanish, and German.[117] Hazlitt is by no means provincial in his judgments. He has a genuine liking for and knowledge of a few medieval authors: Chaucer, Boccaccio, Dante, and Petrarch. He knows Montaigne and Rousseau intimately, and he has read all the main texts of English literature from Sidney and Marlowe on. He had a very wide knowledge of stage plays from Shakespeare to the most commonplace farces. His grasp of philosophy was technically accurate, though confined to the English empirical tradition and kindred French authors.

There is, however, some truth in the charge that Hazlitt was a "facile eulogist." [118] It is consonant with his theory of gusto and his whole conception of the role of the critic as a middleman between poet and reader that Hazlitt should suffer from a certain lack of discrimination, an excessive catholicity of taste. But one cannot say that he had no scale of values, no standards. Lecturing on the age of Elizabeth, he wanted to interest its auditors in a literature still little appreciated outside of Shakespeare, but he did not share Lamb's enthusiasm for Ford; [119] he was always hostile to Ben Jonson and was positively repelled by Sidney's *Arcadia*. In writing of the characters in Shakespeare's plays Hazlitt conceived his function as that of a discoverer of beauties in the less known plays. But he was very cool to the *Merry Wives of Windsor, Love's Labour's*

* E.g. Howe, *16*, 64–5; *6*, 347–8. There Hazlitt uses Schlegel's contrast between a Doric temple and Westminster Abbey.

Lost, and the *Comedy of Errors.* He did not share the new admiration for Shakespeare's poems: he called *Venus and Adonis* and *Lucrece* "ice houses" and was frankly puzzled by the sonnets.[120]

Hazlitt wrote much on his contemporaries. He meets the difficult test of recognizing the best of his time remarkably well—a test so difficult that it is in fact rarely met even by the greatest critics. Though Hazlitt's political outlook embittered his relations with Wordsworth and Coleridge, he always recognized their greatness as poets. His limitations—his basic empiricism and skepticism, his distrust of anything he considered mystical—come out only in his incomprehension of *Kubla Khan* and *Christabel.** His praise of Scott seems excessive, but then there were few authors with whom Scott could be properly compared at that time. Besides, one has the feeling that Hazlitt leaned backward in order to be fair to a writer whom he hated as the power behind the Tory journalists.† Hazlitt was surely not far wrong in his comparatively low opinion of Byron, whom he criticized not only as a moralist but for the "slovenliness" of his style and the triteness of his reflections. He seems only rather obtusely unappreciative of *Don Juan.*[121] To the present writer at least Hazlitt seems also right in his moderate estimate of Shelley. He points out the weakness of his longer compositions, his "shadowy or glittering obscurity," and praises only his translations very highly.[122] He admired and liked Keats, though he overstated his effeminacy and delicacy.[123] Such judgments were not offset by excessive praise for inferior writers: Rogers, Campbell, Southey, Moore, and even Crabbe and Landor are judged fairly and we may even say with detachment, if we allow for the context of political warfare. Hazlitt felt free even to criticize his admired friend Lamb for the caprices, exclusions, and vagaries of his taste.[124] That Hazlitt thought too highly of Jeffrey is comprehensible, as Jeffrey was his breadgiver and patron, the model of success in his own journalistic criticism.

* Howe, *19,* 32–4. A review in the *Examiner* of June 6, 1816. Hazlitt did not write the notorious review of *Christabel* in the *Edinburgh Review,* September, 1816. Elisabeth Schneider has produced convincing evidence that it was written by Thomas Moore. *PMLA* 70 (1955), 417–32.

† Howe, *11,* 68. Cf. Howe's note (*11,* 335) which shows that Hazlitt's violence was not unprovoked. Cf. also *10,* 325, and *19,* 95.

Hazlitt has none of the defects which infected his nearest critical rivals, Johnson and Coleridge: chauvinism, prudery, and unctuous sermonizing. Though he can be very conscious of the English tradition, it seems to him Gothic, grotesque, inspired rather by Pan than by Apollo,[125] and he does not engage in the contemporary vilification of the French. Rather, he defends them against Wordsworth and Coleridge and shows a genuine admiration for Montaigne, Molière, and even Voltaire and Rousseau. He is blind only to the merits of French tragedy: the comments on Racine do not show any deep understanding of his art. He is free of the prudery which in his day pervaded English culture; when he does expurgate his text, he honestly refers to the "change in manners": * he discusses and quotes *Romeo and Juliet* with side glances at Bowdler's *Family Shakespeare*,[126] and he gives straightforward accounts of Boccaccio and Chaucer without deploring their immorality. He is free of the crude didacticism and moralism common among English critics and has nothing of the tone of preaching which is so prominent in many of Coleridge's writings.

This does not mean, however, that Hazlitt was an aesthete or even that he had a clear grasp of the distinctly aesthetic in literature. He was too much interested in politics and the social effects of literature to believe in any separate realm of art. Literature was communication of emotion and thus hardly distinguishable from persuasion, propaganda, and rhetoric. Hazlitt grasped simply that "the most moral writers are those who do not pretend to inculcate any moral," [127] that Shakespeare—the model of all poets—"was the least moral of all writers; for morality (commonly so called) is made up of antipathies, and his talent consisted in sympathy with human nature, in all its shapes, degrees, elevations, and depressions." [128] These phrases could be applied also to Hazlitt's basic method and could describe his special merit: sympathy, "a masterly perception of all styles and of every kind and degree of excellence." [129]

Hazlitt practiced the criticism of beauties, the communication of the pleasures of literature to a new and eager audience by means which frequently were far from intellectual analysis and theoretical clarity. But he held firm to the British empirical tradition and to its instinctive tastes, and he can scarcely be considered responsible

* Howe, *6*, 56. Hazlitt cannot quote Suckling's "Ballad upon a Wedding" in full.

for all the subsequent developments in that tradition, the arbitrary "adventures among masterpieces" of our belletristic professors, the indiscriminate praise and the huckstering practiced by our middlemen and advertisers of the Sunday and Saturday reviews. The immediate effect of his methods was good and fine. Sainte-Beuve wrote his fictitious sonnet by Hazlitt, and the title of his first collection—*Portraits contemporains*—seems to be a translation of the subtitle of Hazlitt's *Spirit of the Age.** In England De Quincey, Leigh Hunt, and Macaulay developed popular criticism along lines suggested by Hazlitt's writings. Among the poets Keats became a close disciple.

In a history of criticism John Keats (1795–1821) must be dealt with in an appendix to Hazlitt. Keats was hardly a professional critic, though he wrote one review, published criticism of two performances by Kean, left some marginalia in copies of Milton, Shakespeare, and Burton, and pronounced on poetry and poets in his private letters.[130] Intellectually, Keats was dependent on Hazlitt and Wordsworth. Taken purely abstractly, his sayings do not contain anything substantially new. But some of his scattered statements formulate his creed about the nature of the poet and poetry so memorably that they ought to be recalled in any history of criticism. Keats has his own personal voice, which should not be drowned in the general romantic chorus.

Keats admired Hazlitt immensely: he read his writings, annotated a copy of the *Characters of Shakespeare's Plays,* went to his lectures on the English poets, spoke of the "depth of his taste" as among the "three things to rejoice in his age," and was impressed by his "demon." He demurred, however, at his low estimate of Chatterton and felt that he had been ill-humored about Wordsworth's "Gipsies" and ill advised in alluding to Southey's grey hairs.[131] But the style of Keats's fervent appreciations of Kean's acting is a mere pastiche of Hazlitt's, and his central views of poetry are in complete agreement with Hazlitt's.

The best known and most striking passages in Keats's letters are those on the impersonality, the "negative capability" of the poet.

* See *Portraits contemporains* (Paris, 1870), 2, 515: "J'ai voulu surtout . . . rendre l'espèce d'entrain que accompagne et suit ces fréquents articles improvisés de verve et lancés à toute vapeur."

"Negative capability" means to Keats something quite specific, the capability of "being in uncertainties, mysteries, doubts, without any irritable reaching after fact and reason." By this standard the poet (and Keats always has Shakespeare as a model for himself in mind) should not be committed, should not be, like Coleridge, a philosopher "incapable of remaining content with half knowledge." [132] "Negative capability" is thus a phrase which defines Keats's grasp of the nature of an aesthetic which is not the same as the intellectual or the didactic. Keats condemns the overtly didactic many times: "we hate," he says speaking of Wordsworth, "poetry that has a palpable design upon us," "we do not want to be bullied into a certain philosophy." [133] Shelley seems to Keats too much of a propagandist in verse: in the only letter he wrote him he advised him to "curb his magnanimity" and be more of an artist and "to load every rift of his subject with ore." [134] But this recognition of the special workings of poetry does not mean the later 19th-century aestheticism, the view that the poet is a maker of merely beautiful and useless decorative things. It means that Keats "never wrote a single line of poetry with the least shadow of public thought," [135] that poetry should come (as Keats felt that it did to him in his best moments) as "naturally as the leaves of a tree." [136] The "genius of poetry must work out its own salvation in a man: it cannot be matured by law and precept, but by sensation and watchfulness in itself. That which is creative must create itself." [137] Thus poetry is to Keats mainly self-expression and an expression of feeling rather than of ideas or moral precepts.

In different moods, and increasingly toward the end of his brief life, Keats recognized the claim of humanity on the poet. In a curious note on Milton's *Paradise Lost* he discovers a contrast between Milton's "exquisite passion for poetical luxury" and the "ardors of song" which made the mature Milton "break through the clouds which envelope so deliciously the Elysian fields of verse to write sublime religious and political poetry." [138] He cannot regret that Milton did not curb his magnanimity. In the *Fall of Hyperion* a new contrast is drawn, between the poet and the dreamer.

> Diverse, sheer opposite, antipodes,
> The one pours out a balm upon the world,
> The other vexes it.

The poet has become one of those

> . . . to whom the miseries of the world
> Are misery, and will not let them rest.[139]

But this recognition is hardly, in Keats's mind, contradictory to
the earlier insight that the poet should not be a self, an egotist such
as Wordsworth, who stands apart as an impressive but odd exception from humanity. The poetical character "has no self—it is
everything and nothing. . . . It has as much delight in conceiving
an Iago as an Imogen. What shocks the virtuous philosopher, delights the chameleon poet. . . . A poet is the most unpoetical of
any thing in existence; because he has no Identity—he is continually [informing] and filling some other body." [140] Chameleon,
Proteus—these were the exact metaphors used by Coleridge and
Hazlitt for Shakespeare: like Coleridge and Wordsworth, Keats
felt that being such a poet is supreme happiness. "Shakespeare was
the only lonely and perfectly happy creature God ever formed." [141]
But Keats, on occasion, is not free from a certain regret and self-
disparagement, a reluctant resignation of ordinary humanity and
its privileges before the awful task of the poet. There is something
like envy for the men of power. However, this is rather a question
of Keats's biography and psychology than of critical theory.

Keats's preoccupation is with the poet, his character and function, not with poetry as a structure and meaning. Fine craftsman
that he was, he must have thought about it and felt these problems. But he left very few formulas: his interest in an alternation
of open and closed vowels is known only by the report of a friend.[142]
From his description of Kean's enunciation we know how strongly
Keats felt about the euphonic texture of verse. He reflects that a
"melodious passage in poetry is full of pleasures both sensual and
spiritual. The spiritual is felt when the very letters and points of
charactered language show like the hieroglyphics of beauty, the
mysterious signs of our immortal freemasonry." [143] But this, with
its use of the term "hieroglyphics" that we met in Diderot, is only
a tantalizing bit. Usually Keats speaks of poetry in terms of the
poetic qualities praised by Wordsworth and Hazlitt: intensity, invention, fancy, or imagination. There are in Keats only rare
glimpses of the Platonic conception: an early letter proudly claim-

ing that "what the Imagination seizes as Beauty must be Truth" [144]
and the conclusion to the "Ode on the Grecian Urn"

> Beauty is Truth, Truth Beauty—that is all
> Ye know on earth, and all ye need to know.

We must not try here to interpret these words as part of the poem,
as a dramatic speech of the Urn, though this would be necessary for
a complete reading. Even out of context, *pace* Mr. T. S. Eliot, the
identification of truth and beauty means something perfectly comprehensible and definite, as similar passages in Hazlitt do. Art is
perception of truth. Everything real (and thus true) is beautiful.*

* There are many elaborate discussions of this passage. The best are
Middleton Murry, in *Studies in Keats*, Oxford, 1930; James R. Caldwell, in *Keats' Fancy*, Ithaca, 1945; and Cleanth Brooks, in *The Well
Wrought Urn*, New York, 1947. Eliot's "I fail to understand it" occurs
in n. to sec. 2 of the Dante essay, *Selected Essays* (London, 1932), p.
256.

8: MADAME DE STAËL AND CHATEAUBRIAND

In France neoclassicism, not only as a sharply defined "good taste" but also as a system of rules and prescriptions, held out longer than in any other major country. The French revolution, though breaking with the past very radically in many respects, inaugurated a new revival of neoclassicism, and Napoleon protected the neoclassical creed, even officially. The turning point came only in 1814, after the downfall of Napoleon, when Schlegel's *Dramatic Lectures* and Madame de Staël's *De l'Allemagne* were first published in France. But even after the Restoration of the Bourbons the defenders of the *ancien régime* in literature, supported by the government, the Academy, and the political feelings of the time which saw in the breakup of the neoclassical system an analogue to the downfall of French political and cultural hegemony, could put up a strong fight. In 1814 a satirical journal, *Le Nain jaune*, drew up a mock treaty of a Romantic Confederation for the utter defeat of French literature and language, a treaty signed by Madame de Staël, Schlegel, etc.* In 1822 a mob chased English actors from the theater and shouted, allegedly, "A bas Shakespeare! C'est un aide de camp du duc de Wellington." [1]

In the 20's, however, the new point of view prevailed more and more: it is fully stated in Stendhal's *Racine et Shakespeare* (1823), in the moderate discussions of the *Globe* (1824–31), and finally in Hugo's preface to *Cromwell* (1827). French dramatic conventions changed definitely after the triumph of *Hernani* in February, 1830. In general literary criticism, the rise of the young Sainte-Beuve

---

* Printed in Eggli, *Le Débat romantique en France*, pp. 261–2. The same journal printed another article drawing a parallel between the invasion of the allied armies and the offensive of romantic theories on January 30, 1815, Eggli, pp. 264–7.

marks the break. He had collaborated in the *Globe,* but his critical physiognomy became defined only with his book on French poetry of the 16th century (1828) and the series of articles on the French classics which began to appear in the same year in the *Revue de Paris.*

Thus the process was long and painful: it was enormously important for the history of French literature and, as France was still the model for the other Romance, and in part for the Slavic, nations, it was a process of international importance. England and the United States were directly affected mainly by Madame de Staël's *De l'Allemagne,* which stimulated both Carlyle and Emerson in their search for new ideas in Germany. But if we look at the French process from the perspective of a general history of critical ideas, its significance will shrink considerably. The discussions about the North and the South, the classical and the romantic, the Christian and the pagan, the three unities, reason and feeling, and so on, which fill the debates of the time, hardly put anything forward that had not been said in England and Germany before. Stendhal rehearses the arguments of Dr. Johnson against the unities, even quoting them literally without acknowledgment. Genius, spontaneity, lyricism; in the drama the necessity of breaking with the rules in favor of looser structures; the historical drama, with strong local color; and later, increasingly, the mixture of styles, tragi-comedy in the sense in which Shakespeare juxtaposed mirth and pathos: these were the main issues. In criticism the debate raged around the abandonment of the old certainties about genres and rules. The replacement of the older, judicial criticism by a criticism of beauties rather than faults and an increasing sense of the historical setting and the variety and even relativity of taste—these were achievements long anticipated in England and Germany. The historical merit, within the context of French literature, of figures such as Madame de Staël and Chateaubriand was very great, but in a general history of criticism the thirty odd years under review seem of little intrinsic importance. French criticism, which led European criticism in the 17th century and profoundly influenced it in the first half of the 18th, fell behind the English and Germans in initiative and originality. It came to the fore again after it had assimilated the new ideas: it vigorously reasserted itself with Sainte-Beuve in the 30's and Taine in the 50's of the century, and slowly recaptured something of its old hegemony.

But before discussing Madame de Staël, we must glance at the so-called Empire critics (Geoffroy, Féletz, Hoffmann, Dussault). Among them Julien-Louis Geoffroy (1743–1814) is clearly the most distinguished. He was the originator of the *feuilleton* and between 1800 and 1814 wrote theatrical criticism for the *Journal des débats* which was collected after his death as *Cours de littérature dramatique* (1818). When Geoffroy started the feuilleton he was 57, a veteran critic who from 1779 to 1790 had been chief editor of *Année littéraire*. In that post he had been the successor of Elie Fréron (1718–76), the doughty fighter for religion against Voltaire. Geoffroy's critical position was fixed long before he attempted the feuilleton. It is basically neoclassicist, violently *antiphilosophe,* antirevolutionary. Corneille, Racine, and Molière are his heroes; but in contrast to La Harpe, even after his conversion, Geoffroy has no use for Voltaire as a dramatist. He detests Diderot, his theories and his comedies, as well as the "subversive" Beaumarchais. He recognizes the decadence of French tragedy, the rise of the *melodrame,* and the contemporary middle class comedy as symptoms of a new period which fills him with anxiety. At the same time his dogmatism is tempered and modified by a recognition of historical necessity and some insight into the social conditions of literature. Geoffroy becomes extremely violent when he feels that society and religion are threatened. Criticism, his kind of "harsh" criticism, he claims, serves the government, "good taste, sound morals, and the eternal foundations of the social order." [2] He calls for the police to punish bad authors, though at times he shares Rousseau's view that the moral influence of the theater is very small.[3] Still, he studies the drama mostly as an indication of the spirit and manners of his time. He has shrewd insights into the relations between society and the social picture on the stage. He suspects sentimentalism and grandiloquent celebrations of virtue, as he is acutely conscious that the Terror came after the age of sentimentalism. "The scoundrels are in society, and virtue reigns on the stage." [4] The theater always flatters the accepted passions and vices, even in the ideals it presents or the manners it ridicules.

At times Geoffroy's historical sense reaches heights of objectivity: reviewing Lessing's *Hamburgische Dramaturgie* in French translation, he preaches tolerance to Lessing. He should have recognized that the French cannot have a strictly Aristotelian tragedy, that the moving and pathetic is purely a matter of national taste.[5] Nevertheless he himself condemned Shakespeare with Voltairian standards and violence. *Hamlet* is a heap of nonsense, *Lear* a series of absurdities, *Macbeth* a monument of English barbarism. Geoffroy wants Shakespeare raw and undiluted as a historical document and resents Ducis' adaptations of Shakespeare's plays to French taste. He wants his Hottentot (still, he *is* a Hottentot) naked, not imprisoned in European clothes.[6]

Geoffroy's reviewing of plays is largely confined to a discussion of the characters, the morals, and the acting, so that he neglects the dramatic craft and does not give any artistic impression of the whole. He holds fast to the rules as symbols of order and yet is not averse to some innovations of subject matter. Chivalry and religion are dramatic themes which can replace ancient mythology.[7] At times he formulates skillfully the leading sentiment of an author he likes, the sense of duty which becomes a passion in Corneille's heroes and heroines, the recurrent "surprise by love" in Marivaux's plays; [8] but mostly he fights sentimentality, the melodramatic, the horrible, mere suspense on the stage—convinced, as early as 1787, that good taste is necessary for the maintenance of order.[9] Though Geoffroy died just before the Restoration, he belongs to it spiritually: tradition, religion, and the classics of the 17th century are his values. His firm hold on absolutes did not preclude a recognition of the actual historical variety of literature and an insight into its social conditions. Whatever his limitations, this combination is rare and not illogical. It is certainly representative of this moment in history. He belongs to the old world, but is uneasily and resentfully aware of the new.

In France the new historicism arrives with the *De la Littérature considerée dans les rapports avec les institutions sociales* (1800) of Madame de Staël (Germaine Necker, 1766–1817). Her second book, *De l'Allemagne* (1813), opened the way to German literature and started the French romantic polemics after 1814. Madame de Staël attracted and still attracts an enormous amount of attention which seems out of proportion to the intrinsic value of her writings. She was undoubtedly a great political figure engaged in the struggle with Napoleon: she was the first woman critic (with the possible exception of Madame Dacier) of any prominence in history; she was the mistress of a salon and a castle where she assembled her little court of famous men (Benjamin Constant, A. W. Schlegel, Sismondi, etc.). Her erotic life excites curiosity even today. In her time her brilliant conversational powers and her financial generosity (backed by huge investments in American real estate) were sufficient to command attention to her views. But we must try to judge her books apart from her personality and her historical prominence.

De la Littérature is much inferior to *De l'Allemagne*. Its program is, however, excellent; it attempts to show the "influence of religion, manners, and laws on literature, and what the influence is of literature on religion, manners, and laws." [10] She thus resumes a subject treated before by Dubos, Marmontel, the Scotch sociologists, and Herder, and she does so resolutely by putting the central historical question on the title page. Unfortunately the book does not come up to the expectations raised by its program. Much of it has hardly anything to do with literature but is just one more survey of Western history in the speculative manner beloved by the 18th century. Much else is nothing but abstract declamation about virtue, glory, liberty, and happiness, fuzzy and pompous and so empty of concrete content that it is difficult to summarize. Yet there is a kernel of literary theory in the book; her conception of poetry stands out very clearly. It is in essence the conception of the early Diderot: poetry is emotion, sensibility, pathos, melancholy, sweet sorrow, somber reflection. With rashness, for which history has since punished her, Madame de Staël embraced the phantom of Ossian and set him up as the great parent of her favorite kind of poetry and imaginative prose. Rousseau, Bernardin de Saint-Pierre, Young, and Gray are grouped—rightly as it proved—with him and exalted as the masters of genuine poetry which moves the soul to tears and thus to virtue. Passages which seem to defend the novel of manners (as she had done before in her *Essai sur les fictions*, 1795, in which she disparaged the marvelous in fiction) are also a recommendation of sensibility, of a Rousseauistic analysis of emotions. Even her new defense of the supernatural, of witches and ghosts in Shakespeare, is prompted by her desire for emotional upheavals: for the effects of terror and awe and the thrills of the horrible.

This emotionalist theory is combined, rather incongruously, with a belief in perfectibility, a frantic faith in progress, which clashes oddly with her taste for melancholy and her admiration for Ossian. Madame de Staël displays the double point of view that we described in Warton, Hurd, and Blair, in so obvious a juxtaposition that its contradictoriness would seem apparent. In theory, Madame de Staël tries to preserve a division between the arts of imagination, which are not progressive, and the inventions, sciences, politics, morals, and even sensibility, shown especially in the improved position of women, which are progressing steadily and uninterruptedly. But the two beliefs, the primitivistic applicable to poetry and the intellectualistic applicable to social life, cannot be kept separate by her. In spite of compliments to the earliest writers for their pictures of manners and nature Madame de Staël cannot help seeing the history of literature as a constant progress of refinement, of sensibility and pathos, leading up directly to Rousseau and Young. She thus consistently disparages the Greeks in favor of the Romans, who seem to her not only more philosophical, i.e. enlightened and rationalistic, but also more sensitive, more delicate, more refined than the Greeks. Also, the Middle Ages are worked into the scheme of progress insofar as Christianity brought about an intensification of the inner life and an improvement in the position of women. Madame de Staël draws from Dubos and Blair the idea of a contrast between the South and North and clearly states her sympathy for the North.[11] The theories about the influence of climate current since Montesquieu and Dubos allow her to describe the literature of the North in terms of the "passionate sadness of the inhabitants of a foggy climate" and to contrast it with the South, whose literature is supposedly full of "images of freshness, limpid streams, and the shade protecting us from the burning rays of the sun." [12]

Details in Madame de Staël's literary history are often vague, wrong, or simply absent. Her discussion of Greek literature is almost grotesque. The Greeks were supposed to lack a "more moral philosophy," a "profounder sensibility." There is no moral conclusion in Aeschylus. Plato lacks method and propounds a bizarre metaphysics. The Greek historians trace only events and neglect characters and causes.[13] The main offense of the Greeks is the low status granted to women: Telemachus ordering Penelope to be silent must have conjured the vision of some man giving the same order to Madame de Staël.[14] Latin literature is treated with more sympathy and knowledge, but medieval writings seem hardly known to her at all. Dante, though he shows energy, has the innumerable faults of his time.[15] Even English literature cannot be known to her except for some 18th-century writings and some of Shakespeare and Milton. She blithely refers to the English who "rejected their national character in order to imitate the Italians" and enumerates as examples Waller, Cowley, "Downe" (apparently Donne), and Chaucer.[16] Also, the German chapter is very meager. Only two books are discussed: *Werther* and Wieland's *Peregrinus Proteus.* Among the Italians she praises Ariosto most, calling him "possibly the greatest modern poet"; [17] but she has little use for Petrarch, who introduced tasteless *concetti,* for the indecent Boccaccio, and for the artificial, though properly melancholy Tasso.

Shakespeare, whom she discusses in some detail, must also conform to her preconceptions. He is the great melancholiac, a master of pathos. His deviation from the rules is defended by the familiar argument that they are merely local, temporal rules which Shakespeare need not have kept. But she admits that he also violates the eternal principles of taste: his mixture of the tragic and comic and his display of horrors are condemned as genuine faults. Madame de Staël tolerates the marvelous in Shakespeare, if it is emotionally effective, but she thinks that *Macbeth* would be better without the witches, even though she gives them an allegorical interpretation.[18] She has, however, no appreciation of Shakespeare's comedy. Falstaff is called a "popular caricature." [19]

Restoration comedy is judged almost as Lamb judged it later. It seems to her completely divorced from English reality. English audiences, she asserts, enjoy Congreve as fairy tales, as fantastic images of a world which is not theirs.[20] Such an art seems to her very inferior to Molière's, which requires life in a genuine society. Madame de Staël admires most the didactic and reflective poetry of Pope's *Essay on Man,* of Young's *Night Thoughts,* and of Gray's *Elegy.* She quotes Thomson's praise of conjugal love from *Spring* and considers Young's somber imagination "the general color of

English poetry." [21] She also admires Richardson and Sterne as leading up to the greatest of all prose writers, Rousseau.

Thus admiration for the vein of pathos and sensibility in English 18th-century literature (which includes her favorite Ossian)
goes well with her taste in French letters. She admired Racine and
Fénelon for their delicacy, but she goes into throes of ecstasy only
at Voltaire's *Tancrède,* which produces emotions greater than
Racine, "all kinds of rapture [*volupté*] of the soul." [22] Rousseau,
to whom she had devoted her first critical (or rather uncritical)
treatise, is again exalted. Even if as a thinker he had not discovered
anything, he "set everything on fire." [23] Setting on fire is her main
view of the function of literature: it is emotionalist and rhetorical,
but also moralistic and utilitarian. The masterpieces of literature
produce an agitating transport of admiration in us. "Virtue becomes an involuntary impulse, a movement which passes into the
blood." [24]

At this stage Madame de Staël has no means of distinguishing
between imaginative literature and eloquence. She hesitates about
the value of verse and clearly favors the impassioned prose of
Rousseau above all other forms of style. Yet she cannot distinguish
between such writing and the eloquence of an advocate or even a
conversation. When she discusses the future of literature—she was
writing under the Republic, just at the beginning of the rise of
Napoleon—she sees its effects as eminently social and practical.
While older literature was only indirectly useful, the new Republican writer "can save innocence, overthrow despotism, devote
himself to the happiness of mankind." [25] Obviously the new writer
is mainly an orator, even though in print, who would expound
philosophical (in the French sense) ideas and at the same time convey a sense of profound melancholia "in the most corrupt century." [26] She believes that conviction and sincerity are a guarantee
of truth, that sentiment cannot err. Thus she manages to combine
an ardent faith in progress and republicanism with a sense of
melancholy about human life, which to her is both sad and delicious. When she specifically refers to the traditional genres, tragedy, epic, and lyric, she recognizes that the decay of taste and manners was brought about by the Revolution. But very timidly she
recommends only such innovations for the French stage as would
allow it to move in the direction of historical tragedy.[27] In poetry

she sympathizes with Delille, Fontanes, and Saint-Lambert, the imitators of English descriptive poetry; for the novel she wants poetic prose in the style of Rousseau or Bernardin de Saint-Pierre, or a feminine novel of sensibility. Literature must have a social effect. Its emotions must lead us to virtue, meaning Republican virtue, enlightenment, liberalism. It is not difficult to relate this effect to her critical terms: virtue is for her emotion, enlightenment is sympathy, liberalism, primarily a feeling of the heart. She thus manages to reconcile the contradictions between what might be described as her arid intellectualism and her Rousseauistic emotional expansiveness. But the contradiction did not escape contemporary criticism: Fontanes and Chateaubriand pointed it out very sharply,[28] and the rapid rise of Napoleon soon made obsolete her plea for a special Republican literature. The book remained ineffective in France.

It was different with *De l'Allemagne*. The mere facts of its history gave the book enormous publicity: in 1810, though completely printed, it was suppressed by the French police. The Duke of Rovigo, Napoleon's minister, told Madame de Staël in a famous letter which she printed in her preface, that her work was "not French." *De l'Allemagne* was published in London by John Murray in October, 1813, just about the time of the battle of Leipzig. The English translation came out in December. A Paris edition was published immediately after the occupation by the allies in May, 1814. It constituted a political event, in purpose comparable to Tacitus' *Germania*. The French were shown the picture of a good, sincere, pious nation of thinkers and poets with few political ambitions and little national feeling: an idyll which already had been refuted by the history of the years between the writing and publication. The image created by Madame de Staël, though attacked by Heine and many others, lingered on in France till 1870. Thus the book cannot be judged as primarily a work of literary criticism. It is the picture of a whole nation, a sketch of national psychology and sociology, and also something of a personal travel book. The discussion of literature in a narrow sense takes up about a third of the book and is constantly pursued with a view toward a general characterization of the nation and interspersed with personal impressions.

From our point of view these parts are greatly superior, as poetics and criticism, to *De la Littérature*. The vague rhetoric, the factual ignorance are gone. The bulk of the book conveys solid information on the texts known to Madame de Staël, whatever her lapses and gaps in knowledge may be from the point of view of a modern student of German literature. The information, ideas, and criticism in these parts have often been ascribed to Madame de Staël's sources. She has been considered a mere mouthpiece of August Wilhelm Schlegel and her other numerous informants. The precise degree of her indebtedness cannot, however, be determined, for much of her information was oral. She had distinguished acquaintances and friends, many of whom tried to impress their views on her. Wilhelm von Humboldt was her first teacher of German and gave her a French abstract of his book on *Hermann und Dorothea* as early as 1799.[29] Charles Villers, as French émigré settled in Germany, whom she met in Metz in 1803, was her informant on Kant. In Weimar, during her stay in the winter of 1803–04, she saw Wieland, Goethe, Schiller, and a young Englishman, Henry Crabb Robinson, who was brought in to instruct her in German philosophy and actually gave her several papers on Kant;[30] in Berlin she saw Fichte, and there she met August Wilhelm Schlegel, whom she took with her to Coppet as part of her household. There was ample opportunity to talk with him: in 1808–09 Madame de Staël also attended his Vienna lectures on the drama. She met other German celebrities. She saw Schelling in Munich in 1807. Friedrich Schlegel came to Coppet and later to Acosta and lectured to her there on German philosophy in the winter 1806–07.[31] Zacharias Werner was a visitor to Coppet in 1809. The sources of printed information flowed even more abundantly. A reading of the text of *De l'Allemagne* must convince us, however, that surprisingly little trace can be found of all these informants and that the independence of her judgment was hardly affected. One might grant that her conception of Kant is largely derived from Villers and that the later parts on German metaphysics and mysticism reflect her association with Friedrich Schlegel and Schelling. But in the literary criticism there seems no doubt that Madame de Staël largely relies on her actual knowledge of the texts and cannot in any sense be described as an exponent of August Wilhelm Schlegel's theories.

There are, of course, agreements with Schlegel's opinions: e.g.

she has a low opinion of Goethe's success as a dramatist on the stage and she considers Jean Paul a small-town provincial in outlook. In a few cases one can speak of actual echoings of Schlegel's views, as when she complains about Schiller's superfluous concern for poetic justice in punishing Queen Elizabeth after Mary Stuart's execution.[32] But only on one point, though historically a very important one, did she definitely follow Schlegel. The term "romantic" replaces the older "Nordic." A whole chapter (the 11th of Part 2) summarizes Schlegel's views that romantic poetry is Christian, medieval, and chivalrous and is associated with painting rather than sculpture. Like Schlegel, Madame de Staël contrasts the ancient tragedy of event with the modern tragedy of character, ancient fate with Christian Providence. The contrast between German literature, which has popular and national roots, and French literature, which is upperclass, is also Schlegel's and Herder's. But the very same chapter shows a conception of poetry entirely foreign to Schlegel's. "Ancient poetry," she says, is "purer as art, modern poetry makes us shed more tears." It uses our personal impressions to move us; genius addresses our heart immediately.[33]

Madame de Staël, in short, has kept her emotionalist conception of poetry. She shows no sympathy for the symbolist view of poetry, or even for a mystical view, as an access to a higher reality, though there are a few traces of these doctrines in the book.* On several occasions she alludes unfavorably to the teachings of the "new school" of the German romantics, especially to the Schlegels' exaltation of objectivity and irony, to their disparagement of tears as an effect of literature, to their minimizing of mere subject matter, and to their general intolerance. To her mind A. W. Schlegel's criticism shows an undue preference for the simple and even the rude.[34] Her discussion of Friedrich Schlegel shows not an

* Cf. Œuvres, 10, 264: "il faut, pour concevoir la vraie grandeur de la poésie lyrique . . . considérer l'univers entier comme un symbole des émotions de l'âme." This sounds German but might also be Rousseau. "C'est cette alliance secrète de notre être avec les merveilles de l'univers qui donne à la poésie sa véritable grandeur. Le poète sait rétablir l'unité du monde physique avec le monde moral: son imagination forme un lien entre l'un et l'autre" (10, 316). This sounds almost like an echo of Schiller's Briefe zur aesthetischen Erziehung. But these are isolated passages.

inkling of his specific doctrines, though she alludes to his early book on Greek poetry.* Besides, her tastes and preferences are by no means identical with those of the Schlegels. She was deeply stirred by Schiller, whom the Schlegels constantly disparaged. She did not share August Wilhelm's cult of Goethe and was obviously repelled by Goethe's coldness, objectivity, and impartiality, vastly preferring *Werther* to any of his later writings. She praised Wieland, alluding to the Schlegels' low opinion of his writings, and paid far more attention to Werner and Kotzebue than Schlegel could have felt any warrant for.[35] The historian Niebuhr was surely right when he remarked that Schlegel could not have even seen her manuscript.[36]

Madame de Staël did not change her basic view of literature and poetry: *De l'Allemagne* is completely continuous with *De la Littérature*. But she had greatly improved as a literary critic, especially in analyzing and characterizing individual works of art. "The animated description of masterpieces" [37] is her critical ideal, an ideal that she achieves rather often. She gives a good account, with interspersed translations into prose, of many German plays, poems, and novels. She knew, no doubt, nothing of early German literature. Though she could have learned a great deal about the *Nibelungenlied* from August Wilhelm Schlegel, she alludes to it only very briefly and vaguely.[38] One must suspect that the neat and just classification of older German literature as successively written by monks, knights, artisans, and scholars comes from Schlegel.[39] Madame de Staël begins to have an opinion of her own when she discusses Wieland, Klopstock, and Lessing. These are good and sympathetic characterizations based on a first-hand knowledge. She catches the undertone of sentiment in Wieland and defines Lessing's success as critic and dramatist well and not uncritically. In discussing Winckelmann she shows a grasp of the historical point of view: the necessity of knowing the country and the age of a work of art, of using both imagination and learning to compensate for the lapse of time, and to bring to life what seems to be dead.[40] But her characterization of Herder is disap-

* *Ibid., 11,* 139–40. The review of Jacobi's *Woldemar* (*11,* 370 ff.) generally voices Friedrich's opinions on the book. Friedrich was much annoyed by this treatment. See letter to his brother, Jan. 17, 1813, in *Briefe an seinen Bruder, A. W. Schlegel* (Berlin, 1890), p. 539.

pointingly thin and completely second hand. Schiller is her hero, in that he lived up to her ideal of a "great soul which the storm has lashed"[41] and impressed her by his pathos and eloquence. She describes the plays sympathetically and fully, voicing occasional criticisms which are well taken though hardly new. Thus she disapproves of the romantic ending of the *Maid of Orleans* or the double choruses in the *Bride of Messina*.[42] Her treatment of Goethe is far less satisfactory: she describes the plays rather fully, objecting to the loose structure of *Goetz* and the ending of *Egmont* and arguing at some length that *Tasso* has little to do with the historical figure.[43] She gives well selected translations of some of Goethe's finest ballads.[44] But the account of *Faust* (she could know only the first part) is completely muddled: the order of the scenes is jumbled, and the comments about the "intellectual nightmare" show her puzzlement, as those on Gretchen show the social and intellectual snobbery of a great bluestocking. *Faust* is considered a dream, a "delirium of the mind," something that must not be imitated or repeated.[45] She is equally baffled by *Wilhelm Meister*, praising only the figure of Mignon, and even more so by *Die Wahlverwandtschaften,* which seems to her completely obscure in its aim.[46] In discussing the latter she shrewdly accuses Goethe of "laziness of the heart" and of throwing aside half of his talent out of fear of making himself suffer in moving his readers.[47] Goethe lacks enthusiasm, a firm and positive philosophy and faith, an accusation which was more and more insistently leveled against Goethe by an increasing number of Germans.

Madame de Staël's sympathy with the actual German romantic literature was very limited. Jean Paul seems to her provincial, too innocent for our age. Speaking of him, she made the often quoted demand that "in modern times, one must have a European spirit."[48] Wieland is to her too little German, too little national; Jean Paul seems too purely German, too local. She quotes a few passages such as the "Dream about the Dead Christ" from *Siebenkäs,* but by dropping the conclusion she changes its whole tenor. Jean Paul protested, but the dream became the great showpiece of German atheism and impressed Vigny and Hugo.[49] Madame de Staël knew, of course, something of Tieck. She praises *Sternbald,* enjoying its Bohemian atmosphere, and she discusses some of the comedies as examples of the Aristophanic fantasy favored by German theory.[50] But her interest seems only lukewarm. Strangely enough, Madame de Staël was most impressed by Zacharias Werner, who seemed to her, after the death of Schiller, the first of the German dramatists. She describes his plays so sympathetically, including *Attila,* that many found allusions to Napoleon in her portrait of the Scourge of God.[51] She recounts the *24th of February,* a play she had seen on her private stage with Schlegel and Werner as actors, admiring its great theatrical effect and poetical coloring. Yet she resents Werner's mystical propaganda and distrusts his liking for physical horrors.[52] She always comes back to her sound in-between position: there must be neither cloudy idealism and mysticism nor horrifying and disgusting naturalism.

Thus her sympathy for German literature is always tempered by her almost instinctive adherence to the principles of French taste. She does not hold them rigidly; she draws comfort from the distinction between eternal and temporal principles and is quite ready to give up the rules. But the eternal principles are constantly interpreted as following closely the specific taste of French neoclassicism. She seems frequently of two minds. Granting certain irregular beauties, she deplores bad taste and extravagancies. She would like to have it both ways: German literature more regular, more tasteful, and French literature less circumscribed by rigid conventions, freer to indulge in flights of imagination. She hopes that Frenchmen would be more "religious," Germans a little "more worldly." [53]

But this desire for a reconciliation on middle ground, for a harmonious European spirit, is counteracted by her other wish that each nation should express its national character as clearly and freely as possible. Wieland, whom she admired personally, is surrendered to the German nationalists: "national originality is worth more and, though one recognizes Wieland as a great master, one must wish he had no disciples." [54]

Lessing is praised for establishing the right of the Germans to a national taste. Her exposition of the contrast between the classical and the romantic culminates in her avowal of preference for romantic literature because it alone can be improved, "because, having its roots in our own soil, it alone can grow and revive; it expresses our religion; it recalls our history." [55] The literature of the ancients is with us a transplanted literature: romantic or chivalrous literature is indigenous.

Her conception of the epic is completely primitivistic, Ossianic.

"An epic poem is almost never the work of a single man and the ages themselves, so to speak, work at it . . . the characters of an epic poem must represent the original character of a nation." [56] Madame de Staël finds the differences of national taste most pronounced in the drama. She can say that "nothing would be more absurd than wanting to impose the same system on all nations." [57] But she does not really keep her own advice and makes concrete proposals for the liberalizing of the French system, criticizing German plays for their lack of conformity to French standards. She shares Johnson's and Schlegel's views on the unities. Only the unity of action is indispensable; change of place and extension of time are allowed if they increase the emotion and make the illusion stronger. She disapproves of the uniform solemnity of French alexandrines, obviously preferring prose, and she recommends historical tragedy as the natural tendency of the century, the main remedy against the threatening sterility of French drama. Yet she constantly disclaims recommending the adoption of German principles and can be very severe on German lapses from taste. For example, she is shocked by the confession scene in *Mary Stuart* and by the erotic themes of Goethe's ballads and elegies, she shows a strong prejudice in favor of upper-class characters in her remarks on Klärchen and Gretchen, and she is horrified by Valentine's dying speech that curses Gretchen: it violates the dignity of tragedy.[58] She also shakes her head at Mephistopheles, though she grants that a devil is less ridiculous on the stage in Germany than in France. She even wants to give "famous names" to the characters of an 18th-century tragedy, Klinger's *Zwillinge* (1775), in order to enhance its effect. "In tragedy, historical subjects or religious traditions are necessary which will awake great memories in the souls of the spectators." [59] In comedy, she prefers Molière to any other playwright because of his knowledge of society. A whole chapter, "De la declamation," is devoted to the praise of French acting, especially of Talma in a horribly mangled adaptation of *Hamlet* by Ducis. Talma achieves the right union of Shakespeare and Racine. "Why would dramatic authors not attempt also to combine in their compositions what an actor has succeeded so well in amalgamating by his art?" [60]

Thus cosmopolitanism wins out at the end over nationalistic theories. "Nations must serve as guides for one another." In every country one should "welcome foreign ideas, for hospitality in this way makes the fortune of those who receive it." [61] *De l'Allemagne* contributed importantly to that "world literature" which Goethe envisaged later as a synthesis of the European spirit. The very limitations of Madame de Staël's taste and sympathy enhanced the effect of her book. Her literary theory hardly went beyond Rousseauistic emotionalism. Her taste is mildly preromantic, in favor of historical tragedy, descriptive poetry, and the novel of sensibility. She constantly rejected what she considered the *bizarrerie* of the Germans: of *Faust,* of Jean Paul. But this very rootedness in the French past made her voice audible, even far beyond the confines of France.

In France the book elicited a heated polemic in which one party charged her with lack of patriotism, while the other welcomed her and, on occasion, even criticized her for timidity. One of her defenders, Alexandre Soumet, in *Scrupules littéraires de Madame de Staël* (1814), violently attacked French neoclassicism and pleaded for a criticism of beauties.[62] He admired Klopstock most and Schiller's *Mary Stuart,* defending even the confession on the stage. In England, the book excited a huge volume of praise, Jeffrey not excluded. It became the standard source of knowledge on Germany till the advent of Carlyle and was widely read in the United States also, for instance by Emerson. The Germans were understandably flattered by the success of *De l'Allemagne.* Goethe, who was not pleased by her discussion of his writings, generously acknowledged its historical merits; [63] Jean Paul somewhat mockingly yet good-naturedly pointed out the limitations of her knowledge and understanding,[64] and Count Otto von Loeben criticized her violently for ignoring Novalis and Fouqué and not sharing the German romantic point of view.[65] Though much said by the German critics was true, nothing can diminish the merit of the book. It really made a breach in the Chinese wall between the countries. It was enormously important for the spread of the term and concept of the "romantic." It was an early step in the history of French emancipation from the tenets of neoclassicism and a manifesto of the new literary cosmopolitanism.

François René, Vicomte Chateaubriand (1768–1848) is apparently the exact opposite of Madame de Staël. On his return from his English exile Chateaubriand began his literary career in France by attacking the newly published *De la Littérature*.[66] He points out the contradiction between melancholy and belief in perfectibility; he tells Madame de Staël that Ossian is a forgery, that its spirit is Christian, and that it depicts an ideal morality inconceivable in third-century Caledonia. He smugly formulates the contrast between himself and Madame de Staël by saying that his "folly is to see Jesus Christ everywhere, just as Madame de Staël sees perfectibility."[67] The Catholic nobleman of ancient lineage who wants to restore the religion and the dynasty of his fathers seems to have nothing in common with the Protestant lady from Geneva who believes in progress and liberalism.

Yet if we limit ourselves, as we must, to literary theory, criticism, and taste, the contrast will appear less violent. Chateaubriand's concepts of poetry and literary taste are really not so far from Madame de Staël's. As with her, his nearest models are Rousseau, Bernardin de Saint-Pierre, and Ossian. Rhythmic prose about man's (and woman's) yearning for infinity and the vanity of human existence is their concrete idea of the essence of true poetry. Like hers, his literary taste is circumscribed by the system of French classicism. Both make some allowance for what might liberalize it if it could assimilate Milton and parts of Shakespeare and Dante. Like her, Chateaubriand contributed to an increased feeling for history and to an understanding of the historical setting of literature. His most important contributions to criticism are suggestions about literature's relationship to the development of religion and sensibility. In a wide perspective Chateaubriand and Madame de Staël belong together.

Le Génie du Christianisme (1802) is a general apologetics of Christianity (and mainly of Roman Catholicism) directed against the skepticism and atheism of the 18th century and the Revolution. What interests us and what appealed to the time was its plea in favor of the beauties of Christianity. Christianity, Chauteaubriand tries to show, is not only the one true religion but "the most poetic religion and the religion most favorable to the arts."[68] The literary argument consists of a confrontation of passages and figures from Greek and Latin poetry with analogous passages and figures from modern writers. It is a restatement of the quarrel between the ancients and moderns, with a bias in favor of the Christian moderns. But it is hard to see what could be the critical value of showing that Milton's Adam is more "majestic and noble" than Homer's Ulysses; that Lusignan in Voltaire's *Zaïre,* because he exhorts his daughter to martyrdom, is a more heroic father than Homer's Priam, who humbles himself before Achilles, the killer of his son, in asking for the body of Hector; that the Andromaque of Racine is a more tender mother than the Andromache of antiquity; that the Guzman of Voltaire's *Alzire* is not as docile and passive a son as the Telemachus of Homer, and so on.[69] In most cases the passages and characters are not comparable critically, since sonship and motherhood, outside the context of a work of art, are no criteria of excellence. The standard imposed is inevitably quite external, applicable to a comparison of figures in life and history but not in literature. Literary success and greatness is in no way connected with the moral preference expressed. Chateaubriand himself recognized that the scene of Priam before Achilles is incomparably greater than the speech from *Zaïre.* Whatever the abstract superiority of Adam and Eve may be, Ulysses and Penelope are a far more convincing "married couple." As argument the whole scheme of these parallels seems mechanical and even puerile.

Nevertheless, Chateaubriand has genuine critical insights. He was apparently the first who interpreted French 17th-century literature not as a revival of classical antiquity but as a Christian literature, sharply set off from the decadent period of the unbelieving 18th century. Chateaubriand had a taste for what today we would call "baroque," an insight into the tensions and conflicts between love and duty, body and soul, which seemed to him basically Christian even when dressed in the costume of classical antiquity. Thus Iphigénie in Racine's tragedy is a Christian girl who obeys the call of Heaven. Thus Phèdre is a "Christian woman reproved, a sinner fallen alive into the hands of God." [70] Even Voltaire, who persecuted the Church, built his tragedies on sentiments and conflicts unthinkable without the Christian tradition.

When Chateaubriand goes beyond parallels and abandons his purpose of disparaging classical mythology, he can give fresh interpretations of the great French writers of the past. Pascal and Bossuet, La Bruyère and Massillon are his Christian heroes. Even Molière and La Fontaine are seen as touched by melancholy, by a recognition of the vanity of vanities which is the great theme of Chateaubriand's writings. The exaltation of the Christian classics of the 17th century serves, besides, to support the general thesis: without religion there can be no beauty or art. Unbelief is the main cause of decadence. The reasoning spirit, in destroying imagination, saps the foundations of the fine arts. Thus "the 18th century diminishes every day in the perspective, while the 17th seems to rise the more we recede from it: the one sinks to the bottom, the other soars to the skies." [71]

Chateaubriand also has a feeling for nature and a gift for description new at that time. He thought that his own feeling differed from that of antiquity and tried to establish its pedigree. Antiquity, he argues, did not know descriptive poetry in his sense, the poetry of solitude, of deserts, of the infinite skies in which man disappears before the grandeur of God. Ancient mythology of nature with its naiads and nymphs makes nature small and pretty, habitable, and merely human. Only with Christianity does there come a feeling for landscape in itself, apart from man. Though the attempt to trace this descriptive poetry back to the anchorites is fanciful, Chateaubriand succeeds in distinguishing stages of descriptive writing in modern literature: the 17th-century reaction against Renaissance pastoral, the British group beginning with Thomson, the French imitators of the English. He sets himself off from these contemporaries, such as Delille, who seem to him too minute practitioners of the Georgic vein, by claiming derivation from travelers and accounts of Jesuit missionaries in the 17th century and by appealing to Bernardin de Saint-Pierre, who "owed his talent for describing scenes of solitude to Christianity." [72] The thesis is pushed too far, but it adds a further item to the great issue of moderns versus ancients.

The critical section of the *Génie* culminates in elaborate parallels between Virgil and Racine, Homer and the Bible.[73] Sainte-Beuve praised the first piece as the greatest passage in French criticism, comparable to anything in Lessing and Herder.[74] But as little more than a mechanical weighing and pronouncing of preferences it hardly seems to deserve such praise. Racine is superior in the invention of characters. Phèdre is more passionate than Dido. Virgil's lyre is more plaintive than Racine's. Virgil is the friend of the lonely man, the companion of the secret hours of life. Racine has lived too much at court. In Racine we seem to wander through the abandoned park of Versailles. In Virgil there is all nature: the depth of forests, the view of mountains, the shore of the sea where the exiled women gaze weeping at the immensity of the waves. The choice between this Virgil, the Virgil of *lachrymae rerum,* and Racine is difficult: they were really brothers and Racine has to be preferred, only for the sake of the thesis, because he wrote *Athalie,* "the most perfect work of genius inspired by religion." [75] The decision in favor of the Bible is easier, for Chateaubriand can describe the style of the Bible, in terms derived from Lowth, as simple and sublime, while Homer's is depicted as a much looser, more flowing, improvised pattern. The section concludes with a travesty of Homer: a rewriting of a passage from the book of Ruth in a flowery pseudo-Homeric manner.[76]

Chateaubriand, in a famous essay on Dussault (1819), advises us to "abandon the petty and easy criticism of faults in favor of the great and difficult criticism of beauties." [77] His own method is mostly that of quotation, appreciation, and confrontation, accompanied by occasional remarks on versification and the use of vowels and consonants. It is never that of a characterization of a single author or work, nor is it ever a speculative, theoretical argument. When he appeals to general principles, he can think only of the commonplaces of classicism. Thus the essay on Shakespeare (1801) must be classed with a criticism of faults. In it Chateaubriand recognizes that Shakespeare had great historical merits in his time, that he has insight into human nature and depicts lively and impressive scenes, but despite this he insists that Shakespeare had no art. Like the earlier French and English critics of Shakespeare, Chateaubriand is completely blind to Shakespeare's constructive skill and insensitive to his verbal texture, which seems to him only bombast. Chateaubriand thus can argue that "writing is an art, that art has genres and that every genre has rules." He thinks he can turn the tables on the admirers of Shakespeare's nature: "Racine, in the whole excellence of his art, is more natural than Shakespeare; just as Apollo, in all his divinity, has more human forms than a crude Egyptian statue." [78]

All of Chateaubriand's critical pronouncements are thus full of the clichés of classicism. The *beau idéal* hides the ugly and low; beautiful nature must not imitate monsters; taste is the good sense of genius, and without it genius is only sublime folly; the rules, even of the three unities, are valid at all times and places because they are founded in nature.[79] These are the standards to which Chateaubriand constantly appeals in introducing, explaining, and defending his own works. In an elaborate defense of *Les Martyrs* he worries about the purity of its genre, quotes strings of authorities, and refutes, step by step, the most pedantic objections. He declares that he wants no change, no innovation in literature, and that he completely adopts the principles formulated by Aristotle, Horace, and Boileau.[80] *Le Génie du Christianisme* might suggest a sympathy with the symbolic concept of poetry, but actually Chateaubriand allows only allegories of qualities and affections and has a most literal-minded conception of the allegorical and figurative meaning of the Bible.[81]

The one point of theoretical innovation, beyond the not unconventional defense of the Christian marvelous, is the emphasis on the author's share in his own creation. Chateaubriand is convinced that great writers have "put their history into their work," that "they paint nothing so well as their own heart." [82] Without quite identifying Milton and Satan, Chateaubriand suggests that Milton depicts his own spirit of perdition in Satan and that the loves of Adam and Eve reflect Milton's marital experiences. Virgil's sadness comes from his stuttering, his physical weakness, and disappointments in love.[83] But this view is not imposed on everything, and the general scheme of classicism is never abandoned.

With the passage of years Chateaubriand somewhat modified his critical position. On the one hand, he became even more conservative, deploring the consequences of his own writings. Just as Goethe disowned Werther, Chateaubriand denounced the brood of René.[84] Though he had accepted early the role of the founder of a new school,* which he imagined as a return to the true principles of the 17th century, he later became more and more disgusted with the excesses of the actual French romantics. He was very cool

---

* See the letter to Fontanes, September 23, 1802, after a visit to La Harpe; *Correspondance générale, 1*, 66: "Je sors de chez la H. Il est sous le charme. Il dit que vous finissez l'antique école et que j'en commence une nouvelle." In the review of DeBonald (1802) Chateaubriand foresees changes and yet the victory of those who lean on the great traditions. *Œuvres, 17*, 109–10.

to Lamartine and Hugo, and he severely condemned the drama of blood and horrors.* He lectured George Sand about morality, hoping that old age, "the blast of the North," would teach her the vanity of passion.[85] He could admire Béranger for political reasons, as Chateaubriand did not fear comparison with a popular song writer.[86]

His most sustained critical work is the *Essai sur la littérature anglaise* (1836). It is, in many ways, a disappointing book, full of lacunae and errors, heavily padded with digressions on Luther, Lammenais, Danton, and others. The discussion of the early periods is all second hand, a compilation from out-of-date English sources, without discernment and sense of proportion. The remarks on Chaucer and Spenser are grotesquely inadequate and erroneous. Actually only Shakespeare, Milton, and Byron are handled at any length and with any elaboration. The chapters on Shakespeare open promisingly. Chateaubriand recognizes that he "had measured Shakespeare with a classical spy glass." But that is a "microscope inapplicable to the observation of the whole." [87] The section ends with a eulogy in which Shakespeare is ranked with the five or six *génies-dominateurs* or *génies-mères* of literary history, alongside Homer, Dante, and Rabelais, who are all now included in this new proclamation of tolerance. But in between, Chauteaubriand reproduces, word for word, his criticism of thirty-five years before, and adds a disparagement of Shakespeare's comedy and his supposedly "ossianesque shadows" of women who cannot stand comparison with Racine's Esther.[88] The point of view remains the same: romantic writers, e.g. Shakespeare and Dante, gain by being quoted in extracts, while the monuments of classical ages have the merit of "perfection of totality and the just proportion of its parts." [89] Shakespeare's work, Chateaubriand concludes, lacks dignity, just as his life lacked it. He had no taste: the kind of taste which appears at very rare moments of the world's history, presumably mainly in the age of Louis XIV.

* On Lamartine see A-C. Comte de Marcellus, *Chateaubriand et son temps* (Paris, 1859), pp. 113–4. On Hugo see Gillot, *Chateaubriand*, pp. 286–7; and Louis Barthou, "Chateaubriand et Victor Hugo," *Annales romantiques*, 9 (1912), 49. Barthou quotes a letter congratulating Hugo on the success of *Hernani*. On romantic drama see *Œuvres*, 22, 268–70 (*Essai sur la littérature anglaise*).

Milton was by far the closest of all English poets to Chateaubriand's heart and taste. He is quoted as a witness throughout the *Génie du Christianisme*. Late in life Chateaubriand published a complete translation of *Paradise Lost* into prose, and the *Essai* adds a fairly full description of Milton's other works. Chateaubriand had a surprisingly sympathetic attitude toward even the most criticized parts of *Paradise Lost:* he defends the last books as not inferior to the earlier ones, he praises even Sin and Death and saw the point of the artillery in heaven. He wrote two remarkable pages on the theology of *Paradise Lost* which distinguish the conflicting strands of Milton's ideas in the light of a good knowledge of theological and philosophical trends. He repeats the autobiographical interpretation of Milton. "The republican can be found in every verse of *Paradise Lost;* the speeches of Satan breathe a hatred of dependence." [90] We hear nothing of the earlier view that Milton should have been born in France with the taste of Racine and Boileau.[91] Even Milton's politics appeal now to Chateaubriand, who assumes the mood of a desperate and gloomy prophet of universal democracy.

The parallel between Milton and Chateaubriand in the service of Cromwell and Napoleon seems strained. More plausibly Chateaubriand compares himself with Byron, both aristocrats, both carrying the "pageant of their bleeding heart" through Europe to the Orient. But Chateaubriand has to establish his priority and superiority. Byron is an ungrateful imitator; he strikes an insincere attitude; he lacks faith, always a sign of superficiality.[92] Walter Scott is dismissed as the initiator of a false genre, who also remained on the surface of things.* The view that *Les Martyrs* is an epic probably for Chateaubriand obscured the fact that he had himself written something very like a historical romance. *Les Martyrs,* based on a multitude of sources painstakingly pieced together, annotated and defended, is, after all, a precursor of nothing better than *Quo Vadis?*

Chateaubriand's criticism thus never emancipates itself from

---

* *Œuvres, 23,* 333 ff. *(Essai, 2).* Chateaubriand prefers Manzoni (p. 334) and alludes disparagingly to Hugo's *Notre Dame de Paris:* "Il me restait pour dernière illusion une cathédrale; on me la fait prendre en grippe" (p. 333).

the fixed canons of the rules and taste as formulated in French neoclassicism. In its methods it is still circumscribed by techniques of rhetorical comparisons or detailed comments on individual beauties. While it cannot be given a high place in a history of literary theory or of critical methods, it nevertheless reflects the shift of sensibility to which Chateaubriand's own creative writings are an eloquent testimony. While he hardly knew or cared for actual medieval literature (with the possible exception of Dante), his writings directed attention to the feudal past, to chivalry and to Gothic churches. While one cannot say that Chateaubriand was himself a serious historian of literature (the *Essai sur la littérature anglaise* is a mere compilation), his grasp of history in general, his strong sense of the flow of time, contributed to the awakening of the historical sense in France. His emphasis on the Christian element in the French classics of the 17th century was apparently new and helped to establish them as the source of a permanent tradition even after adherence to strict neoclassical theory had weakened. His admiration for Milton and his very qualified interest in Shakespeare parallel Madame de Staël's more enthusiastic efforts on behalf of German literature. But most personally, Chateaubriand was one of the initiators of romantic aestheticism, not only in the attitude he took toward the beauties of Christianity, especially the Catholic ritual, but also in the fervent exaltation of the eternity of art and in the cult of the superiority and apartness of the genius. There is the well attested story of his aesthetic attitude toward a storm at sea: when as a mere youngster he crossed the ocean to America, he found he preferred the description of a storm in Homer.[93] And there is the passage in the *Mémoirs* where he calls the roll of twenty-one famous people, participants with him at the Congress of Verona, who had died in the meantime. "The Emperor of Russia, Alexander?—dead. The Emperor of Austria, Francis I?—dead. The King of France, Louis XVIII?—dead. . . . Nobody remembers our speeches at the table of Prince Metternich: but, oh power of genius! no traveler will ever hear the song of the lark in the fields of Verona without recalling Shakespeare." [94] Yet this seems doubtful today when the memory of the past and of great literature has weakened as never before and the "immortality" of even the greatest works seems precarious. The

THE STORY of the French romantic movement culminating in the triumph of *Hernani* in 1830 has often been told and has been investigated in great detail. It is only partially a struggle between rival critical systems: much of it is a story of cliques and groups, the formation of *cénacles* and, inevitably, of political alignments, desertions, and conversions. The two names, Madame de Staël and Chateaubriand, alone suffice to indicate that the early romantics had the possibility of two political affiliations: either liberal or Catholic royalist. After the Restoration of 1814 the Catholic association of the romantics seemed natural. With the growing opposition to the Bourbon regime many romantics moved slowly into the camp of Liberalism (which, for a time, was identified with the cult of Napoleon). Others, like Alexandre Soumet, "deserted" to the classical camp and got themselves elected to the Academy. Stendhal stands somewhat apart, as he had been a Liberal, an admirer of Napoleon, and a romantic, consistently since his early years of youthful classicism. But all these alignments are of little importance for our central subject, criticism. The growth of the French romantic movement in general belongs rather to a history of French literature or to a social history of the times. As for actual critical ideas, the debate stayed within very narrow bounds and the issues were drawn very simply. Until Hugo's preface to *Cromwell* (1827), which launched out boldly into the history of poetry and general aesthetics, little was said in all these debates that would show any awareness of basic problems. Classicism was combated as an ossified system of rules which needed liberalization. But this liberalization was conceived for the most part in purely technical terms. In the lyric, verse was to become freer; in the drama the right to violate the unities was to be established. The claims to an earth-shaking literary revolution, made so extravagantly by Victor Hugo,

Je fis souffler un vent révolutionnaire,

are belied by his own admission,

Je mis un bonnet rouge aux vieux dictionnaire.
Plus de mot sénateur! Plus de mot roturier!
Je fis une tempête au fond de l'encrier.[1]

The French had to fight for the use of such words as *poulet,
mouchoir,* or *pistolet* on the stage. It *was* a tempest in an ink-
pot.

But one cannot say that this technical liberalization implied a
really new concept of poetry. The practice of the French romantic
poets does not show any radical break with the rhetorical tradition
of neoclassicism. Lamartine and Vigny and Hugo were hardly true
innovators. The regeneration of French poetry came only with
Baudelaire and Rimbaud. "Romantic" drama seems today an
episode of little importance which produced no works of enduring
value. The revolutionary wind blows only in the new realistic
novel: in Stendhal and Balzac. The romantic debate merely re-
vived a concept of poetry which can be described as that of the
emotionalism of Dubos, Diderot, and Madame de Staël. Enthusiasm, inspiration, the depth of the human heart, genius, are the
slogans, even at that time pretty hackneyed in the history of criticism. Hugo asks in 1819: "What indeed is a poet? A man who
feels strongly and expresses his feelings in a more expressive language." He adds, quoting Voltaire, of all people: "poetry is almost
nothing but feeling." [2] Stendhal, also, believes in the myth of
sincerity and spontaneity, at least when he talks about poetry.
"One cannot depict what one has not felt" is one of his early
aphorisms, which he fortifies by quoting the Horatian tag: "Si vis
me flere." [3] But at bottom, Stendhal did not care for poetry and
rejected verse for the drama.

Besides this emotionalism, there are traces of a Platonic conception of poetry in several writers. But it is usually the vague and
broad idea that poetry is almost everything, an idea we found at
times in the Germans or in English writers such as Hazlitt and
Shelley. Lamartine can say that "there is more poetry in the smallest corner of nature than in all our human poetry," but he conceives of his own writings as "relief of his heart," as a "sigh or a cry

of the soul." [4] Hugo, in the 1822 preface to *Odes et ballades*, tells us that poetry is at the heart of everything: nature, religion, man.[5]

Only one writer of the time, and he stood completely apart, had an insight into an imaginative conception of poetry: Joseph Joubert (1754–1824). But he was hardly a critic in a public sense; he was rather a writer of aphorisms in the great French tradition. His papers were published only in 1838—and then only in a small selection—and thus could not affect the development of critical ideas at that time.[6] Many of the admired sayings of Joubert on poetry formulate the usual emotional reaction to 18th-century rationalism. "There is no poetry without enthusiasm." "The lyre is, so to speak, a winged instrument." "Beautiful verses are exhaled like sounds or perfumes." "Anybody who has never been pious shall never become a poet." [7] Joubert is exceptional only when he speaks of the poet as "purging and emptying the forms of matter" with the help of certain rays. "He makes us see the universe as it is in the mind of God." [8] This Platonism is based on an insight into the role of imagination in art and life. "Imagination is the faculty of making sensuous what is intellectual, of making corporeal what is spirit: in a word, of bringing to light, without depriving it of its nature, that which in itself is invisible." [9] Here the problem of the symbol in art is glimpsed without the term; the synthesis of the particular and the universal, the task of rendering in material language what is mental and spiritual. Joubert distinguished—as did Rivarol, many Germans, and Coleridge—between two kinds of imagination. "The imaginative, the animal faculty, [is] very different from imagination, the intellectual faculty." The first is "passive." The second is "active and creative." [10] Most of his remarks are about imagination as a "species of memory," on "memory as the storehouse on which imagination draws," on imagination as a "painter." "It paints in our soul and outside for the soul of others. It clothes with images." [11] It is substantially the visual imagination of Addison and the whole of the 18th century, with a glimpse, here and there, of its creativeness.

There are other remarkable sayings in Joubert's commonplace books: The poet should return the physical and primitive meaning to words, "polish, remint the money and renew its original markings." [12] Another saying shows that Joubert understood the conciseness of poetry and its difference from rhetoric. "The character of the poet is to be brief, that is to say, perfect, *absolutus* as the Latins said; that of the orator is to be flowing, abundant, spacious, extended, varied, inexhaustible, immense." [13] Joubert speaks of the poet "making words light and giving them color, making them fly about," though he can also speak of the "architecture of words" or the "pure essence" with which verse should be seasoned.[14] All these are occasional metaphorical sayings which show that Joubert had learned from Diderot, whom he knew personally.

In spite of these theoretical insights, Joubert's literary opinions (we cannot speak of criticism) are not particularly coherent or independent. He disliked Racine, who seems to him sufficient only "for poor souls and poor spirits." Racine "made poetic the most middle-class sentiments and the most mediocre passions." Of all French poets Joubert admired La Fontaine most, calling him "our real Homer; the Homer of the French." [15] His horror of reality was such that he frequently sided with the conventional and even inane. He preferred the Abbé Delille to Milton and defended Corneille's grand style by saying, "We should rise above the trivialities of the earth, even if we have to mount on stilts." Delicacy, even preciosity, his valitudinarian's shrinking from issues, will always impede a deeper impact of Joubert's fine observations. He knew himself well. "I can sow, but I cannot build." [16]

Joubert died in 1824. The year before, the Romantic debate had come to a head. The term "romantisme" emerges for the first time in these discussions.* Stendhal, just returned from Milan, intervened with his *Racine et Shakespeare* (1823), still using the Italianate form "romanticisme." *Racine et Shakespeare,* as published that year, was only a thin pamphlet of three short chapters. The first presents an argument against the three unities, drawn in part from a dialogue by Ermes Visconti in *Il conciliatore* and in part from Johnson's *Preface* to Shakespeare and Marmontel's article on illusion.[17] Like Johnson, Stendhal argues that we always know that we are in the theater and thus have no difficulties in following changes of place or time. But Stendhal concedes that there are

* I am not sure who used the word first. Possibly François Mignet, in *Courrier français* (October 19, 1822), saying that Scott "a résolu selon moi la grande question du romantisme." Lacretelle calls August Wilhelm Schlegel "le Quintilien du romantisme" in *Annales de la littérature et des arts, 13* (1823), 415.

moments of perfect illusion which induce a special state of emotion in the mind of the spectator. The second chapter on laughter is a restatement of Hobbes's theory of "sudden glory," the unexpected sight of our superiority over another. Thus comedy must be directed against actually existing abuses. Molière is not funny or is not funny any more. The third chapter begins with the famous definition of romanticism as "the art of giving to the people literary works which in the present state of their customs and beliefs are capable of giving the most pleasure possible," while "classicism, on the contrary, gives them the literature which yielded the most pleasure possible to their great-grandparents." [18] "Romantic" thus means simply modern, contemporaneous, and Stendhal has to grant that Racine and Dante were romantic in their time. The definition can hardly be taken seriously. It is a mockery of the imitators who have lost touch with their time, and a proclamation of modernity.

The second part of *Racine et Shakespeare,* published in 1825, is also a small polemical pamphlet directed against the French Academy which, in the meantime, had taken action against the rising tide. Auger, its director, had attacked romanticism at a solemn session in 1824. Stendhal jeers at him cruelly and wittily, repeating the plea for modernity which specifically means a recommendation of a historical French drama, in prose, with no unity of place and time. The alexandrine is only "un cache-sottise." The tirades of a French tragedy are even worse than the unities. Prose is preferable because it allows the "proper, unique, indispensable, necessary word." [19] Though Shakespeare is the great object of Stendhal's admiration, he is not recommended as a model in every respect: he must not be imitated for his speeches, his metaphors, or even for his mixture of the comic and tragic. Rather, Stendhal seems most impressed by the *Théâtre de Clara Gazul,* the pseudo-Spanish dramas of his friend Mérimée, and expects most from dramatizations of episodes from Froissart, Brantôme, or other old French historians. To those who know the originals it seems a bad anticlimax that Stendhal described and recommended Zacharias Werner's *Luther* as superior to Schiller and that elsewhere he could say that the very mediocre Austrian dramatist Josef von Collin represents best what the French drama can hope for. [20] The last reference is probably only a *boutade* typical of Stendhal, based on no further knowledge than the enthusiasm A. W. Schlegel showed for Collin in the concluding pages of the *Dramatic Lectures*. Stendhal's two pamphlets were strictly polemical writings in favor of a special kind of drama not yet allowed on the regular French stage. Stendhal was disappointed when he witnessed the further development of the French stage: Hugo's dramas, which rejuvenated the alexandrine and disregarded historical truth, were not to Stendhal's taste, since he always hated rhetoric and bombast.[21]

The two small pamphlets, which had little effect in their time, assume a much greater interest if we think of them as a part of Stendhal's voluminous literary criticism, an episode in his long struggle for self-expression, a small specimen of his peculiar literary taste. Stendhal's mind is surely one of the most interesting and possibly oddest minds of the time. We know it now better than any contemporary could know it, since a large mass of letters, diaries. drafts of articles, marginalia, and thinly disguised autobiographical narratives have been unearthed. All through this mass of papers are scattered pronouncements on literature and books. They are most formal, though still light in tone, in the large number of reviews printed in English in three English magazines: the *New Monthly*, the *London Magazine*, and the *Athenaeum*.[22] Stendhal, who is usually known for the slight piece *Racine et Shakespeare*, emerges in that as a critic of considerable intrinsic interest; he represents an attitude toward literature which could hardly be elsewhere documented so well and so entertainingly.

Stendhal was not an aesthetician and theorist of great consequence. Partly, he simply distrusted system and theory, because, in his mind, they were associated with the poetics of neoclassicism, with the pedantries of La Harpe and Marmontel. Partly he thought of aesthetics as the theories of ideal beauty formulated by Winckelmann and his disciples, and he had no use for their absolutism. In his *Histoire de la peinture en Italie* Stendhal tried rather dilettantishly to formulate his own theory of ideal beauty, using the temperament types of Cabanis and endorsing a historical relativism.[23] Partly, he considered theory as the baneful pedantry of the new German romantics, especially A. W. Schlegel whom he heartily disliked.[24] Stendhal is frankly and simply an Epicurean, a hedonist who judges and wants us to judge art by the pleasure it gives us. "Whoever we are, king or shepherd, on the throne or in a hovel, one has always reason to feel as one feels and to find beautiful that which gives pleasure." [25] Thus, the "quantity of pleasure felt seems to [him] the only reasonable thermometer to judge of the merit of the artist." [26] Also in music, "in order to be happy we don't have to be reduced to examining it: this is what the French will not understand; their manner of enjoying the arts is to judge them." [27]

This does not promise well for criticism, but actually Stendhal's search for happiness is too self-consciously intellectual ever to deprive him of the strong framework of convictions and norms of taste which he holds almost instinctively. Harry Levin's telling definition of the essence of Beylism, "to keep one's head while losing one's heart," [28] applies also to Stendhal's literary opinions. Stendhal has a deep suspicion of mere emotionalism and a positive horror of the mystical and vague. His pleasure must be an intellectual pleasure, not the all-too-easy one of tears and laughter. It should be rather the delicious smile kindled by a Cervantes or a Lesage or a Mérimée. [29] Thus we can easily predict his dislikes. He had no use for the expansive sentimentality of Madame de Staël, though he acknowledged the justness of many of her views. He despised the aesthetic religion of Chateaubriand, his florid style, his gross insincerity. [30] He abominated most of his contemporaries for their pompous, loud, emphatic style and pretended, at least, to take the *Code civil* as the model of his own writing. He was sincerely shocked when Balzac, in his eulogy of the *Charterhouse of Parma,* thought that the weak part of the book was its style. He defended himself, saying that he may write badly only "out of an exaggerated love of logic." [31]

We can understand why Stendhal had no use for German philosophy and ridiculed Kant and Schelling from hearsay. [32] Plato was another writer he would not understand, as everything mystical and high flown smacked to him of obscurantism. Religion of any sort was a closed book to him, and anticlericalism was a basic instinct to a man who hated the Bourbon Restoration and the Austrian rule of Italy. Thus Lamartine cannot excite his admiration and Vigny is ridiculed for *Eloa.* The loves of the devil and the incarnation of a divine tear must have been inspired by "too copious potations of that famous Italian wine *Lachryma Christi*." [33]

It may be surprising that Stendhal showed much sympathy for one pronouncedly Catholic writer: Manzoni. He thought of him primarily as the author of the *Lettre à M. Chauvet,* from which he drew some arguments against the unities. He admired *Il cinque maggio* as one of the summits of modern poetry, surely also because it expressed his own feelings about Napoleon. He praised the tragedies, though they seemed to him to make too many concessions to classical conventions. He praised the *Inni sacri,* though he added that they have an antisocial, poisonous tendency. He thought the *Promessi sposi* much overrated. [34] But there is always in Stendhal a special tenderness for his Italian contemporaries, particularly the romantic group in Milan from which he had originally learned to associate liberalism, patriotism, and romanticism.

Stendhal had no such restraints toward the Germans. He did not know their language and disliked the people. He admired Schiller and their historical tragedy on doctrinal grounds but usually joined in the disparagements of Goethe that he read in the *Edinburgh Review*.* He disliked A. W. Schlegel most, though this may seem a paradox considering Schlegel's own exposition of dramatic romanticism. But Stendhal wanted to prove to himself and others that romanticism was not reactionary, not mystical, not German, and thus minimized his considerable agreement with many of Schlegel's theories. All the marginalia preserved are extremely uncomplimentary. Every other note calls Schlegel a "ridiculous pedant," empty, mystical, vague. Stendhal objects most to the disparagement of Molière and to the idolatry of every word in Dante, Shakespeare, and Calderón. [35] He eagerly reproduced Hazlitt's introductory reflections to his review of Schlegel's *Lectures,* which criticized German scholarship and its desire for eminence at any price, but he apparently did not note that Hazlitt actually agreed with Schlegel's basic tenets. [36] Stendhal saw in Jeffrey and Hazlitt,

---

* See *Rome, Naples et Florence,* ed. D. Muller (Paris, 1919), 2, 224. There, Stendhal ridicules *Dichtung und Wahrheit,* drawing on Jeffrey's review. See *Correspondance,* 5 (Oct. 20, 1816), 7 ff. On Goethe see *New Monthly,* 1 (June 1826), 602.

and even in Johnson, the expounders of the true romantic creed, which to him was largely a rejection of the French dramatic system. The new literature meant the historical drama, the modern satirical comedy, and it came to mean the new psychological novel which Stendhal was to write. Poetry is not in the center of things at all. At most Stendhal appreciated Byron when he was satirical and liberal, and Béranger because he was the singer of the French opposition. His admiration for Jeffrey and Johnson, whom he called the "father of romanticism," [37] is thus not so surprising as it may seem. Stendhal knew Johnson's *Preface* to Shakespeare and could agree with his polemics against the unities and his conception of Shakespeare as a painter of men, a creator of characters rather than a poet or a playwright. Stendhal could admire Byron for personal and political reasons, but he was not too seriously interested in his poetry. He found the tragedies boring and too similar to the manner of Racine and Alfieri. He did not care for *Lara* or the *Corsair,* as they were foreign to French taste, his own taste, which preferred the delicate vein of satire (the *Lettres persanes, Candide,* Molière, and Beaumarchais) to pathos and passion. Stendhal remarks well that Byron tried to be both a lord and a great poet and that one must choose one of these two irreconcilable merits. Byron lacked the will to make the choice. Stendhal liked only the satirical poetry of the later Byron, which reminded him of Ariosto and the Venetian poet Buratti.[38] If Stendhal had any poetical taste it was for the dialect poets of Italy, partly for reasons which were not literary. As a self-appointed Milanese, Stendhal sided violently in the *questione della lingua* with those who fought the exclusive dominance of Tuscan. He most enjoyed Tomasso Grossi, Carlo Porta from Milan, Giovanni Meli from Sicily, and Pietro Buratti from Venice. Stendhal thought of them as popular, "natural," and liberal poets, Italian Bérangers.[39]

The center of Stendhal's literary interest was in the two genres he attempted himself: comedy and the novel. At first he put high hopes in comedy as a socially effective type and studied its technique closely, hoping to produce comedies himself. He commented on most of Molière's plays, went to performances, observing and counting the passages which aroused laughter, ranked them elaborately, and tried to fit them into a theory of laughter and into a scheme of evolution of literature in relation to society.[40] Stendhal

analyzed the sources of the comic in a court society and arrived at
the conclusion that there are two: to be mistaken in the imitation
of what is good taste at the Court, and to have some similarity in
one's manners and conduct with a bourgeois. With the rise of the
bourgeoisie around 1720 a third source of the comic appeared: the
imperfect and awkward imitations of courtiers by the bourgeois
themselves. The French comedy writers are fitted into this scheme;
but Molière is condemned as immoral, in that his art is inspired
by a horror of being different from the ruling society, by a desire
for complete conformity. His *Femmes savantes* is immoral because
it teaches women to beware of ideas. *Le Misanthrope,* though a
great play, is not comic: the hero is a misplaced republican. The
comedies ridiculing the physicians are not truly comic either, because the victims of the satire are made odious and arouse rather
indignation than laughter. *Tartuffe* is not comic, because he ex-
poses a danger and engages us too passionately to make us laugh:
Jesuitism was still very much an issue of the day. Thus Molière is
paradoxically shown to be neither moral nor truly comic. Regnard,
on the other hand, is both, as he excites neither hatred nor indignation.[41]

The social scheme of evolution which frames Stendhal's history
of comedy forces him, as it did Hazlitt before, to the conclusion
that our own time is not a good time for comedy. A republic kills
laughter, because men seriously occupied cannot laugh. Modern
society becomes uniform; class distinctions and thus distinctions
of manners disappear. The sources of comedy dry up.[42] But in
practice Stendhal enjoyed the comedies of Picard and Scribe and
many obscure playwrights of the time and reported about them
with gusto to the English magazines. His own ambition to become
a new Molière was dead by then.

All his hopes were put in the novel. The 19th century, he
thought, will distinguish itself by its accurate depictions of human
passion. In his own copy of *Le Rouge et le Noir,* Stendhal noted
that the head of the *idéologues,* Destutt de Tracy, had told him
"that truth could only be attained by means of the novel." [43] The
novel is the comedy of the 19th century. It is to be social and psychological, contemporaneous, even topical, but also universal,
probing into the nature of man. At times Stendhal seems to speak
like an advocate of photographic naturalism. The famous epigraph

of a chapter in *Le Rouge et le Noir,* which defined the novel as a
"mirror walking down a road," might give rise to such an interpretation, especially if we confront it with the earlier use of the
same figure in the Preface to *Armance:* "is it the fault of the mirror
that ugly people have passed in front of it? On whose side is a
mirror?" [44] But surely this emphasis on objectivity and on the need
for inclusion of the ugly in the novel must be modified by Stendhal's frequent rejections of the horrible and dull. In refusing to
describe the election in *Lucien Leuwen* he admits that "it is true,
but true like the morgue, which is the kind of truth we leave to
novels in duodecimo for chambermaids." [45] Stendhal even defends
the need for idealization in the novel. It must be the kind Raphael
used to make his portraits more like the subject. Especially the
heroine needs such treatment, as the reader has seen the woman
he has loved only by idealizing her. [46] At first, Stendhal welcomed
the historical novel, such as Scott's, for Scott seemed "romantic,"
i.e. more real, more alive than the current productions of the
sentimental or horrible novelists. But Stendhal was not blind to
Scott's shortcomings. He recognized that he has no true historical
imagination and always wrote only from the point of view of his
own time. "He studies love in books and not in his own heart." [47]
In a manuscript piece entitled "Walter Scott et *La Princesse de
Clèves,*" Stendhal expresses preference for the method of Madame
de La Fayette, because it is "easier to describe the dress and the
leather collar of a serf of the Middle Ages than the movements of
the human heart." [48] Still, he can ask elsewhere whether "the action
of things on man is the particular domain of the novel," [49] and
surely his own practice of drawing on court documents and memoirs and calling his books "chronicles" seem to point in the direction of the later "documentary" novel. But this is again contradicted by his protest against the principle of imitation of nature
and his bold assertion that "a work of art is always a beautiful
lie." [50] Hugo's *Han d'Islande* seemed to him "the most extraordinary and *ultra* horrible production of a disordered imagination,"
but Balzac's realistically pictured *Médecin en campagne* is also
called "a dirty pamphlet." [51]

There are many surface contradictions in Stendhal's pronouncements which, after all, were made over a long period of time, often
on some polemical occasion, to score a point and to display his

wit. But one should recognize the basic unity of his taste and see his peculiar and possibly unique position in a history of criticism. By his instinct for clarity, his rationalism in philosophy, his irony, his distrust of sentimentalism, and his love for understatement Stendhal derives from the 18th century, in spite of all his attacks on the courtly forms of French classicism. He engages in the romantic debate as an outsider, bringing from Italy the identification of romanticism with modernity and liberalism. Only his fierce individualism and his cult of passion associate him with the other romantics. He ignores or rejects the symbolic and mystical view of literature: he has no use for medievalism or even for Christianity. At times he anticipates the theories of realism, but he lacked the theoretical equipment to define more closely the great and astonishing novelty of his own practice.

The main romantic debate was carried to its victorious conclusion by Victor Hugo. It has been the fashion to dismiss Hugo as an intellect and as a critic, but this understandable reaction against the excesses of his rhetoric has surely gone too far, as has the wholesale dismissal of his poetry. Both need rectification. Much has been done for the reinstatement of his last "apocalyptic" poems; something can be done for his criticism, which among much verbiage, contains profound insights and brilliant formulas for age-old problems.

In the 1824 preface to the *Odes* Hugo refused to engage in the romantic debate. He professed not to understand what is meant by "classical" and "romantic" genres, but it is hard to believe that he misunderstood so badly as to think that "classical" refers to literature the subject matter of which is pre-Christian and "romantic" to literature with a post-Christian subject matter, on which basis *Paradise Lost* would be classical and Voltaire's *Henriade* romantic. Hugo simply avoids the debate by asserting (what Croce and many others would endorse) that in literature there is only the good and the bad, the beautiful and the ugly, the true and the false, and that historical styles do not exist.[52] The 1826 preface to the same collection shows, however, a complete change of attitude. It contains a radical pronouncement against the hierarchy and very existence of literary genres. Hugo again professes not to understand what is meant by the dignity of this genre, the conventions of that, the limits of another, and the latitudes of a third. He asks what is meant by saying "tragedy forbids what the novel allows; the song tolerates what the ode will not permit." Hugo repeats that the only valid distinction between works of the mind is that of good and bad. But what seems an assertion of complete liberty and even anarchy is modified by a brief statement of the distinction between order and regularity. Order comes from the nature of things and is perfectly reconcilable with freedom. Regularity is something external. The classical is the worship of rules, and hence of mediocrity, while the romantic is the establishment of order according to the rules of nature and the taste of genius. It is the kind of theory pronounced by a good classicist such as Lessing, or by A. W. Schlegel when he spoke of organic unity.[53]

The Preface to *Cromwell* (1827) is the fullest statement of Hugo's early critical views and is deservedly regarded as the main critical text of the French romantic debate. It is easy to find anticipations and sources for many of its views. Hugo had read Madame de Staël, Chateaubriand, Stendhal, Manzoni's *Lettre à M. Chauvet*, and Schlegel's *Dramatic Lectures*. The preface, in part at least, is a skillful summary of their arguments. But it is much more. Hugo, unlike other French writers of his time, went far beyond the debate about the rules and the unities. He drew up a scheme of the history of literature and reinterpreted poetry in dialectical and symbolical terms. Only in Germany and in Coleridge can we find parallels; but Hugo is not dependent on any German text and adds something of his own. First he develops a historical scheme, very much in the 18th-century manner of conjectural history, of which Vico is today the best known example. In detail it can hardly withstand inspection, for history is seen from too far and lofty a perspective. Primitive man is first supposed to sing a hymn, compose an ode (as Herder and others had argued). Genesis (surely not an ode and not even lyrical in tone) is quoted as the representative work of early man who lived in a theocratic society. In the second stage the epic arises. Homer dominates classical antiquity. With Christianity comes the drama and Shakespeare is the representative of the modern age. Only Christian dualism, the conflict between body and soul, makes the drama possible. It is true poetry, complete in its harmony of contraries. Christianity is thus at the basis of tragi-comedy, of a union of the sublime and comic, the beautiful and ugly. Hugo's special contribution is the emphasis on the grotesque as the opposite of the sublime. He describes the Christian grotesque in Dante and Milton and the folklore grotesque, the gnomes and witches, as the sources of modern art. He sees their effect not in isolation but in their place in a whole. "Can one believe that Francesca da Rimini and Beatrice would be so enchanting if the poet had not locked us up in the Hunger Tower and forced us to partake of the revolting meal of Ugolino?" [54] The beautiful has only one type; the ugly has a thousand. "What we call ugly is part of the great whole which escapes us and which harmonizes, if not with man, then with the entire creation." [55] The old idea of a world harmony in which evil and ugliness have their place is made here the justification of a total art in which all genres and moods would be united. The distinction between genres is abolished, as is the distinction between levels of style. There is only total freedom, no rules, no models. Specifically, the unities in the drama are attacked: there is no justification for the unities of time and place, only for that of action or totality, but even this needs to be interpreted freely in order to allow secondary actions, which should, however, gravitate toward a central action and always be subordinate to it.

Many of these ideas are either familiar or formulated extravagantly and loosely. Especially is the sketch of literary history, with its simple sequence of the lyric, epic, and drama, open to criticism. One should say in defense of Hugo's scheme, however, that he uses these terms in a very wide sense. For instance, both the *Divina Commedia* and *Paradise Lost* are interpreted as dramas, that is, dualistic conflicts.[56] Hugo also tries to take account of obvious objections. The predominance of the epic in antiquity is argued from the prevalence of Homeric themes in the drama and from the epic tone of Herodotus and Pindar. Hugo, however, is on thin ice when he minimizes the role of the comic and grotesque in antiquity and dismisses Aristophanes and Plautus or argues that even grotesque mythological figures such as the Furies, satyrs, tritons, and sirens are not really ugly. Pluto, one must admit, is no devil with horns and hooves.[57]

Still, whatever reservations we have as to the exact truth of Hugo's scheme, the emphasis on the grotesque was new and important and fits into a theory of poetry which allows a complete rendition of reality, a union of opposites, a harmony of contraries. It fits in with the breakdown of the distinct levels of style which Hugo helped to accomplish. Also a modern specialist, Erich Auerbach, has ascribed to Christianity and the model of the biblical narrative of Christ's suffering the origins of a tragic style dealing with low characters and trivial events.[58] Hugo can phrase this as a good formalist when he says: "A thing well made, a thing badly made; that is the beautiful and the ugly in art." "An ugly, horrible, hideous thing transported with truth and poetry into the realm of art, becomes beautiful, admirable, sublime, without losing anything of its monstrosity; on the other hand, the most beautiful things of the world, falsely and systematically arranged in an artificial composition, will be ridiculous, burlesque, hybrid, ugly." [59]

Hugo, of course, was no formalist or aesthete in the later sense of cutting off art from life and social purpose. He simply understood that form and content cannot be divided and that the moral and political (in a wide sense) effects of art follow from its being art. He varies this idea frequently: he speaks either of an internal order that "results from the intelligent disposition of the intimate elements of a subject," [60] or of a central idea, a mother-idea whose development constitutes the proper and essential character of the work. He well understands that this central idea is not an intellectual concept. "An idea," he argues, "has always only one form which suits it, which is its essential form. . . . With the great poets nothing is more inseparable, nothing more consubstantial than the idea and the expression of the idea. Kill the form, and you almost always kill the idea." [61] Late in life Hugo found the sharpest formulas for this union: "Form and content are as indivisible as flesh and blood." "The form is essential and absolute: it comes from the very vitals of the idea." "In reality there is neither content nor form but only the powerful gushing of the thought, the immediate and sovereign eruption of the idea." [62] This last phrase emphasizes spontaneity, inspiration, for Hugo usually exalted genius and the poet to superhuman heights. But in more sober moments he does not believe in mere inspiration. He reflects well on the need for meditation, seclusion, calm, silence, retirement into self, and he recognizes the poet's ability almost at will to call up inspiration by meditation.[63]

Hugo understood also that the poet's business is with words. In a sketch of the history of French style he recognizes the intimate dependence of poetry on the development of the language. He explains the expansion of the French vocabulary during the Renaissance, and its later contraction, which he describes as having passed through three distinct stages. The earliest, represented by Mathurin Regnier, left the language intact. The second, in the later 17th century under Louis XIV, and the third, during the 18th century, meant, however, an impoverishment of the original resources of French poetry which France was rediscovering only in Hugo's own time.[64] Thus Hugo can say that style determines the life of a work and the fame of a poet. He rejects the direct utility of art, its immediate service to political truths. "Art should, above all, be its own proper aim, and it should moralize, civilize, edify along the way but without deviating from its path." [65]

With the years, when Hugo's fame had grown to enormous proportions, when his political role had increased and he himself was an exile on Guernsey, he came to think of literature more and more in terms of its social function. The civilizing power of art, we are told, imposes on the writer the duties of an intentional reformer; the poet's function is to change "charity to fraternity, laziness to utility, iniquity to justice, the crowd to a people, the mob to nation, the nations to humanity, war to love," etc., etc. Art for progress, beauty as the servant of the truth—these are now the slogans, and the poets are exalted as great luminaries of humanity on its way to a social and vaguely socialistic Utopia.[66]

William Shakespeare (1864), Hugo's major work of criticism in later years, is an extremely exasperating series of incoherent, flamboyant meditations full of incredible verbiage and ecstatic rhetoric. As a book on Shakespeare it can be easily dismissed, since only a small part is concerned with Shakespeare at all and since the information on Shakespeare's life and times is grossly uncritical and even fantastically wrong.* The occasional comments on the plays can also be ignored, as it is hard to see what is meant by saying oracularly and solemnly that "Macbeth *is* hunger" or "Othello *is* Night." [67] The lack of critical spirit, the complete negation of discrimination is proclaimed complacently by the author himself. "Genius is an entity like nature and must, like her, be accepted

* Hugo draws heavily on Guizot and Chasles; cf. J. H. Thomas, *L'Angleterre dans l'œuvre de Victor Hugo* (Paris, 1933), pp. 143 ff.

purely and simply. We must take or leave a mountain." "I admire everything like a fool." "I admire Aeschylus, I admire Juvenal, I admire Dante, in the mass, in the lump, all." "What you call a fault, I call accent." [68] The words remind us of Herder's quotation from Leibniz, the acceptance of the universe *in toto* as good even in its contradictions, and the whole 19th-century victory of the historical spirit over the critical.

But among all the welter of names, exhortations, declamations against stupid critics, persecutors of poets, and so on, there are a few pages which show a remarkable insight into a mythic concept of poetry and anticipate the Jungian view of literature as a creation of "archetypal patterns." Hugo calls them "types," "Adams" which he well distinguishes from mere universals. "A type does not reproduce any man in particular . . . it sums up and concentrates under one human form a whole family of characters and minds. A type does not abbreviate, it condenses. It is not one, it is everybody." Don Juan and Shylock are his first examples; Harpagon, Iago, Achilles, Prometheus, and Hamlet appear later. The type is "a lesson which is man, a myth with a human face so plastic that it looks at you, a parable which nudges you with the elbow; a symbol which cries out 'Beware!', an idea which is nerve, muscle and flesh." [69] We understand what is meant when Hugo calls Hamlet "Orestes in the image of Shakespeare" and when he speaks of Nimrod as the ancestor of Macbeth.[70]

Hugo's conceptions of imagination and the history of poetry fit in with this view of art as a re-creation of the very deepest patterns of humanity. Imagination is the great "plunger into the deep," the reconciler of everything with everything.[71] There is thus no progress in art. Decadence and renaissance are meaningless terms: there is no rise and no fall in art.[72] Contraries do not exclude each other. Everything mirrors everything. Antithesis, contrast, mirroring are Hugo's obsessive metaphors for his observations on art. He comes nearest to concrete insights into Shakespeare's plays when he describes their mirror scenes, the parallelisms of the actions, the relationship between Hamlet and Laertes, Lear and the Fool, or Lear and Gloucester, or when he rapturously evokes the last scene of *Lear,* "Cordelia's young breast next to the white beard of her father." [73]

Hugo has such a tremendous desire for synthesis, for reconciliation, that he finally abolishes all barriers and ends in what must be described as grandiose confusion. "The masterworks," he says, "are so immense that they are eternally present at the acts of humanity. Prometheus on Caucasus is Poland after 1772, is France after 1815, is the Revolution after Brumaire." [74] He himself, he thinks, is such a Prometheus, sitting on Guernsey and spurning the offers of Mercury-Napoleon III. He joins Homer and Shakespeare as the third and greatest. Self-conceit could not go further. The abolition of all distinctions between literature and life, literature and history, is complete.

But even these later developments should not obscure what is valuable in Hugo's insights. No doubt he was not a good practical critic, for he had no patience, no power of analysis, and little discrimination. One can hardly imagine that a theory of literature could be built on his pronouncements, for they lack system and continuity. But granting all the faults of loose phrasing and rash generalization, Hugo, of all the French writers of the time, seems to have by far the profoundest insights into the nature of poetry. He found many striking formulas for central problems: the internal order of a work of art, the identity of form and content, the union of the opposites, the transformation of the ugly and grotesque in a higher synthesis. Moreover, his later view of "types" or patterns is of far greater consequence than the battle against the rules and unities, which had been long since decided in other countries. Even as a polemicist Hugo was extremely important, at least in France: the rejection of the rules and the abolition of the old distinctions of genres and levels of style were a historical necessity which made the development of modern literature possible. It is true, of course, that Hugo formulated his theory of the drama largely under the impact of the performances of Shakespeare he witnessed just before writing the preface to *Cromwell*,[75] and it is also true that several German writers had expounded a symbolic, antithetical conception of poetry more systematically and philosophically before him. But this hardly diminishes Hugo's merit, especially for the West of Europe, where his voice carried much further than that of the Germans.

36 hours equal 3. Berchet knew the *Dramatic Lectures* of A. W. Schlegel and Bouterwek's *History,* which he reviewed in 1818.[5] He is hardly a good critic, yet he is an important intermediary between Germany and Italy. He also was the first to formulate the issue clearly as one between conservatism and modernism, reaction and liberalism.

The romantic group then crystallized around the periodical *Il Conciliatore* (1818–19), in which Ludovico di Breme, Silvio Pellico (later to become the almost legendary martyr of the Italian *Risorgimento*), Ermes Visconti, and others discussed the question at great length. Though constant precautions against Austrian censorship (which very soon suppressed the sheet anyway) conceal political implications, we must always keep in mind that "modernity," "romanticism," meant for these Italians a renovation not only of literature but of Italian life in general, that the rebirth of literature was to them a preparation for the future independence and unity of Italy. From the point of view of literary theory they had nothing original to contribute. The most systematic statement in the *Conciliatore,* Ermes Visconti's *Idee elementari sulla poesia romantica* (1818), is a reproduction of Schlegel's and Madame de Staël's distinctions between classicism, based on ancient mythology and manners, and romanticism, based on Christianity, chivalry, and modern discoveries. But the distinction is weakened by his admission of a neutral, mixed sort of poetry and by the astonishing declaration that there are no "essentially romantic or essentially classical styles." [6] The difference is all in the subject matter. Ancient religion and life are past and gone, and hence classical, while, for instance, America, discovered in modern times, is romantic. Visconti and the other Italian romantics especially attack the use of classical mythology in poetry, for they are tired of gods, Amors, nymphs, and satyrs inherited from 18th-century Arcadia. They recommend themes from Italian history, treated in a Christian spirit. The new poetry must be patriotic, Christian, and useful. This is the burden of Pellico's articles, which come to extremely relativistic conclusions as to the possibility of standards of criticism but escape complete skepticism by proclaiming the civic effect and utility of literature as its only measure.[7] Visconti, in a sprightly dialogue, attacked the unities of time and place with arguments drawn from Johnson and Schlegel: there is never complete illusion; Racine is badly handicapped by the observance of the rules, while Shakespeare, in his *Macbeth,* has the freedom to develop convincingly the psychology of his central figures. Characteristically, Visconti, in retelling *Macbeth,* leaves out the witches.[8] The argument in favor of the new dramatic system is one for psychological realism, truth to life and history.

This is also Manzoni's ideal. Alessandro Manzoni (1785–1873) was not a member of the *Conciliatore* group but was closely associated with it. Actually he became the one great Italian who expressly proclaimed himself a romanticist. Outside of Italy it is not generally realized what position of authority Manzoni eventually assumed in his nation. *I Promessi sposi* in Italy is constantly—despite protests such as Croce's—placed beside the *Divine Comedy,* and the weight of Manzoni's austere moralism and poetic fame has given great prominence also to his views on literary criticism.

Manzoni began as a literary critic with a defense, in the *Preface,* of his tragedy *Il Conte di Carmagnola* (1820), which exactly fulfilled the demands of Visconti: it violated the unities and was based on Italian history. Manzoni quotes Schlegel and argues like Visconti against the unities of time and place and the inconveniences of the French system. He adds a general defense of the stage as an instrument of moral improvement. Manzoni, who by that time had been converted to a strict observance of Catholicism, was deeply impressed by the attacks on the stage made by Nicole, Bossuet, and Rousseau but hoped to refute them by his reform of the drama, which was to adhere very strictly to historical truth and by imaginative reconstruction was to supply the psychological truth implied in the historical events. To bolster his interpretation of the Carmagnola conspiracy Manzoni wrote an elaborate historical commentary and even divided his characters into "historical" and "invented." [9] The *Preface* elicited in France a defense of the unities by a little known writer, Victor Chauvet, to which Manzoni replied in a long piece, *Lettre à M. C— sur l'unité de temps et de lieu dans la tragédie* (1820). This is a very sober, dignified, well-reasoned statement of the case against the unities of time and space. In part Manzoni repeats the arguments known to Johnson and in part adopts Lessing's and Schlegel's argument that French tragedy, by adhering to the unities, violates the very principle of classicism, namely probability. The French sacrifice probability to the rules though the rules were supposedly made to preserve probability. Manzoni comes to a complete rejection of rules by asking, "If the great geniuses violate the rules, what reason is there to presume that they are based on nature and that they are good for anything?" Still, he insists strongly on the unity of action and on the purity of genre, rejecting tragi-comedy as "destroying the unity of impression necessary to the production of emotion and sympathy." [10]

The question of the unities is not, however, Manzoni's central concern. It is merely one instance of his interest in truth. The essence of poetry, he argues, is not invention of fact. All great works of art are based on events of history or on national traditions considered true in their time. Poetry is thus not in the events but only in the sentiments and discourses which the poet creates by entering sympathetically into their minds. Dramatic poetry aims at explaining what men have felt, willed, and suffered because of their actions. The poet is, we might draw the conclusion, a historian who, like Thucydides or Plutarch, invents the appropriate speeches and details for the events supplied by medieval chronicles.

Goethe, who reviewed the *Conte di Carmagnola* with high praise, knew that "for the poet no person is historical" and that all of Manzoni's characters should be and are ideal.[11] In a letter to Goethe Manzoni recognized that the division of characters into historical and ideal is a "mistake caused by his excessive adherence to the historical," [12] and in the next tragedy, *Adelchi* (1822), the division disappeared. But Manzoni could not really have changed his attitude, since he added a long discourse on Langobard history, justifying every detail of the play.

In 1823 he wrote a letter to Marchese Cesare d'Azeglio, another statement in defense of romanticism, which again revolves around the concept of truth. Manzoni there distinguishes negative and positive sides of romanticism. On the negative side his distinction means the rejection of classical mythology (as false and idolatrous), of servile imitation, and of the rules and unities. On the positive side Manzoni admits that romanticism is a vague term, but it is so for an excellent reason. "In proposing that system of abolishing all the norms that are not truly general, permanent, and in every way reasonable, it makes their number much smaller and their selection much harder and slower." [13] Manzoni can think of only one common aim for the romanticists: poetry must propose truth as its object. Truth for Manzoni is, first of all, historical truth, the conquest by literature of a new theme, modern history, and then, though hardly distinguishable to his mind, the truth of Christianity, its ethics, its spirituality. Manzoni rejects as false the idea that romanticism has anything to do with witches, ghosts, and systematic disorder. Poetry was to him history, truthful history, and the novel, at which he was then working, *I Promessi sposi* (1827) was to be a conscientious re-creation of the past, based on extensive research, in a Christian, Catholic spirit.

But soon after the novel had become the new Italian classic, Manzoni began to feel increasing scruples about the very possibility of a historical novel. *Del Romanzo storico* (1845) is Manzoni's quiet, closely reasoned argument against the mixture of truth and fiction and thus against his own life work. He presents first the difficulties encountered by the reader who wants only historical truth. The very narrative form makes the demand impossible. But those who want fiction, a continuity of impression and total effect, cannot be satisfied either, because they can never abolish the distinction between the historical "consent" we give to a real figure such as Mary Queen of Scots or Bonnie Prince Charles or King Louis XI of France, and the other, "poetic consent" we give to probable events.[14] History and fiction are irreconcilable. The historical novel is a hybrid which must yield to the light of truth. To show that this is an inevitable process Manzoni seeks support in the history of the other comparable genres, the epic and tragedy. He believes that they were originally based on events considered and felt as true (like those of the Homeric epics or the Greek tragedies), but that late in the process of enlightenment they became increasingly involved in the conflict between fiction and reality and thus have become impossible in modern times. Manzoni's history of the epic and tragedy runs into great difficulties, however, since it is hardly convincing to think even of Homer's listeners as having been interested merely in truth in Manzoni's literal sense; and it is hardly possible to take the appeal to historical sources in medieval romances very seriously. How can Manzoni approve of Virgil, whom he greatly admires, without approving of the modern historical novel? But he makes good analyses of the difficulties of Tasso's *Gerusalemme liberata* and

Voltaire's *Henriade* and everywhere finds support for his conclusion that a historical novel cannot be written, since it requires the author to supply the original and the portrait at the same time, both history and its fictional probable imitation.

One can dismiss Manzoni's troubles by means of Goethe's argument against his distinction between historical and fictional figures. All characters in a novel or play are ideal; the view that two kinds of consent are required is false. Even for a historical figure we need only poetic acceptance, the "willing suspension of disbelief," in Coleridge's phrase for illusion. At most, one could grant that Manzoni has proved that the historical novel cannot fulfill its professed task of recreating the past truthfully and that historical truth belongs in history and nowhere else. Manzoni clings to an interpretation of Aristotelian "verisimilitude" which, by definition, excludes history, and since he worships only "fact," he must end in rejecting even poetic truth and misunderstanding the very nature of art. Manzoni, quite honestly and logically, ceased to write fiction. But this abandonment of art in favor of truth should not be confused with the naturalism or realism of the 19th century which was then becoming vocal around him. Manzoni's faith in truth and historical fact is religious, as is obvious also from his late dialogue *Dell' invenzione* (1850), which propounds a theory, based on Rosmini's philosophy, that the artist does not create but merely finds the ideas existing eternally in the mind of God. Here Manzoni outlines a new apologetics of art which might have toned down his condemnation of fiction. But what is remembered today is Manzoni's honest grappling with the problem of a dual allegiance to history and fiction, which he could personally resolve only by repudiating art in favor of history. His preference was obvious in his early pronouncements on romantic tragedy, but the dilemma was then still concealed by his artistic instincts.

Thus it seems hardly surprising that a modern student could argue that there really was no Italian romanticism.[15] The group that called itself romantic had a concept of art which we could call rather realistic, moralistic, patriotic. Neither Manzoni nor the polemicists had a grasp of art as imagination, of the symbolic concept which we have seen expounded by the great romantic critics in Germany and England. But of course there are linkages and common sympathies: Schlegel was the propounder of the historical drama, as was Manzoni. Still, excessive attention to the professedly romantic group is misleading. Paradoxically, the two greatest Italian poets of the time, Ugo Foscolo and Giacomo Leopardi, who expressly attacked the theories of the romantic group, themselves best represent the turn in Italy toward doctrines which were the basis of European romanticism.*

Ugo Foscolo (1778–1827), in the last year of his life, wrote an essay on the "New Dramatic School" attacking Manzoni's theories and his play *Il Conte di Carmagnola*.† The sharpness of the polemical tone is due to the old personal rivalry between the two men, to Foscolo's own disappointment with the stage and to the offense his Venetian patriotism took at the representation of the Doge and Senate in Manzoni's tragedy. Foscolo can argue in great detail that Manzoni is quite mistaken in his favorable view of the hero, the Count of Carmagnola, who was executed for treason by the Venetians, and he can show convincingly that Manzoni makes historical mistakes and commits anachronisms even in small verbal matters. The attack strikes more deeply when Foscolo argues against Manzoni's distinction of ideal and historical figures. "In any work of imagination everything depends on the incorporation and identification of reality and fiction." Illusion is achieved only when "truth and fiction, facing each other and in contact, not only lose their natural tendency of clashing but aid each other mutually to unite and fuse and to appear a single thing." [16] Foscolo holds up Shakespeare's *Othello* as an example of the poet's power of emancipating himself from history. Italian romantic theory is suspect to him as an attack on the rights of imagination, as a turn toward the

* I thus completely disagree with the thesis of Borgese, *Storia della critica romantica in Italia*, which makes Italian romantic criticism merely a liberal neoclassicism.

† "Della nuova scuola drammatica in Italia," *Opere edite e postume*, ed. Mayer and Orlandini, *4*, 293–338. The editor says that the article reprinted from the Italian MS was published in the first number of the *Foreign Quarterly Review*, 1826. But the article there on Manzoni has nothing to do with Foscolo's. I do not know the English review. The Italian text was first published in 1851.

actual, the dreary reality which the poet should escape. German romanticism, which Foscolo knew only from Schlegel's *Lectures,* excites his distrust as mysticism and system-mongering. Foscolo even rejects all genre and school distinctions, saying that "every great production is an individual object which has different merits and distinct characteristics." He protests against the lumping together of different, supposedly classical schools of drama: the Greeks, the French, and the Italians (Alfieri). They seem to him all perfectly distinct. Even "each drama of the same poet, if he has genius, is more or less different from every other." [17]

The fine insights of this essay, its assertion of the power of imagination and the individuality of the work of art, are, however, the most brilliant flash of Foscolo's critical activity. The high level of the essay was never or very rarely reached before. Coming from it to an examination of the other critical writings, one must express a keen sense of disappointment. In part this is due simply to the external circumstances in which Foscolo's writing was produced. Much of his early criticism is in small prefaces or in formal orations at the University of Pavia which are full of fervid but bombastic academic oratory; much of the later writing, done in exile in England, sometimes preserved only in a wretched English translation, is heavily weighed down by a display of inert learning which Foscolo apparently felt to be demanded by the English periodicals or publishers for whom he was writing. His individuality is constantly cramped by his regard for the audience on which he felt dependent for his precarious living; he sometimes masks his personal remarks by attributing them to a "foreigner of great literary distinction." [18] He even supplied a rather lengthy description of the "Present State of Italian Literature," to John Hobhouse for publication under Hobhouse's name in *Historical Illustrations of the Fourth Canto of Childe Harold* (1818).* Foscolo's many grandiose schemes for a history of Italian literature and for a *European Review* which would be devoted to "comparative criticism" and to tracing "the reciprocal influence of literature and manners," [19] came to nothing, though fragments of his plans are realized in his *Essays on Petrarch* (1823)—his only book-form pub-

* That Foscolo wrote this part of Hobhouse's book is proved conclusively by Vincent, *Byron, Hobhouse and Foscolo.*

lication in English—in his editions, with long introductory dissertations, of the *Divine Comedy* and the *Decameron* (1825), and in
scattered articles on Dante, Tasso, and the "narrative and romantic
poets of Italy." [20]

But the fragmentariness and incompleteness, the heavy admixture of patriotic oratory and inert obsolete antiquarianism, are
not the only causes of disappointment. It is rather a certain lack
of coherence and sharpness in the choice of ideas which make
Foscolo an eclectic, a figure of transition who, however great his
importance in the history of Italian criticism, will never acquire
great stature in a European context. One could even make a case
for Foscolo's criticism as a repertory of neoclassical commonplaces.
He can talk about "instruction by delighting," about *Ut pictura
poesis* as the "chief rule of poetry." He can define imagination in
terms of 18th-century psychology as a power of visual recall.[21] But
most frequently Foscolo wavers between two concepts of poetry:
one of them emotionalist, deriving from Dubos and Diderot, the
other Platonic, deriving from a reading of Plato himself and from
the 18th-century tradition of idealizing aesthetics. In the self-
portrait he wrote for Hobhouse, Foscolo claims "he would tear his
heart from his bosom if he thought that a single pulsation was not
the unconstrained and free movement of his soul." [22] The "flame of
the heart" is his common phrase, and the purpose of poetry is defined as "making us strongly and fully feel our existence." [23] But
this view exists side by side with Platonic idealism. The early
Pavia lectures (1809) expound a curious concept of "eloquence"
as the animating force behind all the arts and behind both prose
and verse, which is identified with genius and inspiration in terms
drawn from the polemics of Socrates against the sophistical rhetoricians.[24] Later Foscolo can also say that the poet does not imitate
but selects, combines, and perfects the scattered beauties of the
world; he abstracts and embellishes in order to create the ideal.
The ideal is the "universal secret harmony, which man strives to
find again in order to strengthen himself against the burdens and
pains of his existence." Poetry thus satisfies our need to "veil the
unpleasant reality of life with the dreams of imagination." [25] The
poet is the man of feeling who expresses himself freely, and at the
same time he is the creator of a world of ideals. He is also the total

man who proceeds not by analysis but by synthesis. "The poets," he says in the *Essays on Petrarch*, "transform into living and eloquent images many ideas that lie dark and dumb in our mind, and it is by the magic presence of poetical images that we are suddenly and at once taught to feel, to imagine, to reason, and to meditate." [26]

Foscolo is saved from the consequences of mere emotionalism or Platonic idealism by his intense consciousness of the word, of the role of language and style in poetry. Many subtle comments on individual passages in Dante and Petrarch discuss the effect of single words. The detailed analyses of translations, either from Homer into Italian or Tasso into English, show Foscolo to be a true philologist, a "lover of words," whatever his technical shortcomings as an editor were. Foscolo knows the value of the study of revisions. "To develop the beauties of a poem the critic must go through the same reasonings and judgments which ultimately determined the poet to write as he has done. But such a critic would be a poet." He adds, with a self-irony which could not have been apparent to the readers of an anonymous essay in the *Edinburgh Review*, "his ardent and impatient genius would never submit to the cold labor of criticism." [27] But Foscolo did submit and produced many textual and bibliographical investigations, learned and whimsical discussions of Catullus' *Hair of Berenice*, of the Greek *digamma*, of emendations in Dante, or of expurgations in various editions of the *Decameron*. Foscolo knew that "literature is joined to language" and that style is joined to "the intellectual faculty of every individual." Words have a long history which is a "confluence of minor and accessory meanings," [28] of feelings and images, which differ with every language and which the poet knows and uses for his purposes.

Foscolo's chief importance, especially for Italy, lies in his attempt to see this conception of poetry as part of history, of a philosophy of human development, and thus as the basis of a scheme for Italian literary history and a program for his own time. Foscolo's concept of history is, no doubt, influenced by Vico, but more directly it derives from 18th-century primitivism in the mode of Rousseau and Herder. An early age of mythic, bardic, heroic poetry is imagined when all the kinds were mixed and the poet was a prophet and philosopher. Foscolo does not envisage this original poetry very clearly, though he reported, at length, on the ancient British druids and bards, drawing on a dissertation by William Owen.[29] Still, enough is known to Foscolo for him to justify the view that poetry was originally lyrical, lyrical-epic, and heroic and that it should become so again. Reviewing Monti's epic, *The Bard of the Black Forest,* he defends it with such historical arguments; his own *Grazie* he views as a mixture of the didactic, the lyric, and the epic. "Such perhaps was the first poetry." Such lyrical poetry is "the very summit of art." The ode celebrates gods and heroes and thus does not materially differ from ancient epic poetry.[30] Heroic and lyric are confused or identified, since the aim of poetry is the exaltation of our existence and the poet is a hero himself.

In his criticism Foscolo always makes the genre distinction between "romantic" and "heroic" poetry to the disadvantage of "romantic." Thus in his mind Tasso surpasses every other Italian poet except Dante. The burlesque tradition of Italian poetry, especially its last stage in Casti, is constantly disparaged, and even Ariosto, though greatly admired, is to Foscolo only the master of an inferior, less noble kind of poetry. Tasso is definitely separated from Ariosto by emphasis on the historical character of his theme, which to Foscolo is a history of the Crusades written as an example for Tasso's own time. The main point of many of Foscolo's acute observations on Wiffen's English translation of Tasso is in the charge that Wiffen ignores Tasso's historical accuracy and makes him over into a poet of romance in the style of Spenser. Foscolo, for the sake of his lofty conception of the heroic, here runs counter to the evidence of the text and to the taste established since Hurd's plea for the Italians' "world of fine fabling." [31]

The historical scheme which follows from primitivism is that of the decay of imagination with the progress of civilization. Foscolo sees this process in antiquity. Homer and Pindar are the great ancients, while Virgil and Horace are artificial, derivative, and courtly. The process is seen repeated during the Middle Ages. There Dante is the exemplar of the free, heroic poet, while Petrarch and Boccaccio indicate the beginnings of decadence. Foscolo's conception of Dante is, in its detail, untenable, for he ascribes to him heretical ideas and sees him as a reformer of the Church not only in morals but also in ritual and dogma. Nevertheless, Foscolo, in his article on Dante and the long dissertation on the text, makes a real effort, remarkable for the time, to place Dante in his historical and intellectual context. He pays close attention to Dante's theology and political ideas, to his life and to the tradition of the text. The theories are frequently mistaken or based on insufficient information, but the comments are often sensitive and new: for instance, the discussion of the Francesca da Rimini episode makes much of the silence of her lover Paolo and interprets Dante's attitude toward the lovers persuasively and, on the whole, in agreement with most recent commentators.[32]

Foscolo also studied Petrarch very closely, not only the Italian poetry but also the Latin prose. He expounds his concept of courtly love and interprets his relation to Laura less sentimentally than was then the custom. But Petrarch is considered the representative of a new age of refinement which prepared the way for the later servitude of Italy. In an elaborate parallel between Dante and Petrarch Dante appears as the man of imagination and Petrarch the man of feeling. "Dante interests us for all mankind; while Petrarch is only interested in himself." [33] Dante is thus, as in Vico, the great primitive poet who serves as the foil to modern poetry, which has ceased to be so free, so original, and so individual. Molière and Pope are cited as examples of poetry which can trace shades of individuality for purposes of fine comedy; but comedy, in Foscolo's scheme can only seize "the exterior of character" which is determined by fashion and thus changes with every age, while genuine poetry, "whose business is with the human heart, is coeval and coextensive with human nature." [34] In general Foscolo complains that "when, in times of a more advanced civilization, the faculties of the critic and the poet tend to meet in the same minds, there arises a new poetry, less candid, less pure, more brilliant, mixed with metaphysics and a knowledge of the world. This is the poetry of Pope, Horace, Voltaire; mediocre minds prefer it; and the highest imaginations despise it." [35] Foscolo must have realized that he himself belonged to this union of poet and critic, but he deplored it as a necessity of the time and tried to escape it.

If Italian decadence begins with Petrarch, Boccaccio will appear as an even greater corrupter. Foscolo, in spite of his erudite interest in the history of the text of the *Decameron*, professes to be shocked by its morals and disapproves of the influence of its style as a model of Italian prose. The humanistic 16th century seems to him an arid time, though he exempts Tasso and the much admired Machiavelli. The 17th century and the Arcadia appear to him periods of the deepest decadence. Baretti, though praised rather illogically for his general good influence, is judged very severely as a mere "ape" of Dr. Johnson.[36] Parini is to Foscolo the new Italian Virgil, and Alfieri seems to him greater than Corneille or Shakespeare. He is to him the model of the strong and free man, the poet of passion and power. Foscolo shared the high admiration of his contemporaries for Monti, but he disapproved of his shifting political allegiance and under cover of Hobhouse's name attacked him as a turncoat, drawing a parallel in Dryden.[37]

French literature is usually slighted in Foscolo's writings, though his admiration for Bayle, "a very great critic," stands out.[38] He wrote disparagingly of Rousseau and Madame de Staël, though his intellectual debt to both was very great.[39] He distrusted the Germans as mystics and scoffs at Goethe and Schlegel.[40] He admired only *Werther,* which was at least the technical model of his own *Jacopo Ortis*.

It is difficult to judge how much Foscolo knew of English literature. In England he conversed and wrote in French, but later he must have learned English well, since his reviews show appreciation of fine shades in English translations. But his comment on English literature is very limited. His admiration for Shakespeare is qualified by his neoclassical prejudices. He explains that seeing Shakespeare on the stage always increases his resistance, because in the theater he cannot follow the verbal beauties and sees only the action and business.[41] The reservation against Milton for lack of human interest is also conventional. Foscolo gives fervid praise to Gray's *Bard,* which seems to him both Pindaric and biblical in style.[42] He loved Sterne and translated the *Sentimental Journey*. His interest in his English contemporaries seems quite perfunctory: for example, he was shocked by the impiety of Byron's *Cain*.[43] There is a curious streak of the conventional and prudish in Foscolo's criticism which contradicts his own tumultuous erotic life and his exaltation of the strong and free man. But one must not forget that Foscolo had to struggle to keep his head above water in England and tried to make many adjustments to English respectability. He did not succeed, as witness the contemptuous comments in Sir Walter Scott's *Journal* or the quarrel with Hobhouse.* Nobody in England knew then that the exile hunted by bailiffs would become the symbol of the Italian *Risorgimento,* would be solemnly reburied in Florence's Santa Croce alongside Michelangelo, Machiavelli, Galileo, and Alfieri, and would be, even more recently, exalted and closely studied as one of the very greatest Italian poets. In the history of Italian criticism Foscolo will keep an important position as the first critic who broke with neoclassicism and introduced a historical scheme for the writing and criticism of Italian literature. But in a European context Foscolo is a latecomer, an eclectic somewhere in the transition from a preclassical Platonic idealism to a romantic view of history.

In critical ideas and temperament Leopardi seems to me much more original and striking. Giacomo Leopardi (1798–1837), a young man of eighteen and already a seasoned classical philologist, tried to intervene in the romanticism debate. He wrote a letter to the periodical which had published Madame de Staël's recommendations to translate Nordic literature, but the review refused to print it. Two years later in 1818, when the debate was again in full swing, Leopardi sent a long dissertation on romantic poetry to another review and was again rejected.[44] The first letter is a proud assertion of Italian patriotism. "If Europe does not know Parini, Alfieri, Monti, and Botta, the fault, it seems to me, is not Italy's."[45] Leopardi also argues against imitation, against any hope in the effect of translations, and, somewhat illogically, calls on Italians to read the Greeks and Romans and to ignore the Nordic writers. The later "Discourse of an Italian on Romantic Poetry," though diffuse and wordy, states the essence of the critical position he held for the remainder of his life. The romanticists (and Leopardi knew

* *The Journals* (Edinburgh, 1890), *1,* 14: "Talking of strangers, London held, some four or five years since, one of those animals who are lions at first but by transmutation of two seasons become in regular course boars. Ugo Foscolo by name, a haunter of Murray's shop and of literary parties. Ugly as a baboon, and intolerably conceited he spluttered, blustered and disputed without even knowing the principles upon which men of sense render a reason, and screamed all the while like a pig when they cut its throat." On the affair with Hobhouse see Vincent.

then only the Italians and Madame de Staël) are wrong because
they do not understand that poetry is illusion, imaginative illusion which needs myth, ancient mythology, and the dream of the
golden age. "See, then, manifest and palpable in us, and manifest
and palpable to anyone, the overwhelming inclination toward the
primitive; I mean in us ourselves, that is, in the men of this age,
in those very ones whom the romantics try to persuade that the
ancient and primitive manner of poetry does not do for them.
Therefore, by the genius we all have from the memories of childhood, one should judge how great is that [genius] we all have from
unchanged and primitive nature, which is, neither more nor less,
that nature which reveals itself and reigns in children; and the
childish images and the fantasy we were speaking of are precisely
the images and the fantasy of the ancients." [46] Poetry thus is rooted
in our nostalgia for "nature," childhood, the youth of mankind.
Our poets sing of nature and of the eternal and changeless matters
and forms and things of beauty, in short, of the works of God;
while the romanticists treat of civilization, of what is transitory
and mutable—of the works of men. [47] Leopardi sees the contradiction between the recommendation of topicality, utility, and
modernity in their manifestoes and the Nordic medievalism they
want to introduce. But he did not see (and hardly could do so)
that his own fervid Hellenism, with its identification of childhood,
antiquity, and the age of poetry, was at the very center of much
that elsewhere was called romanticism.

It cannot be denied that Leopardi's critical reflections are full
of the doctrines and terms of neoclassicism. The several thousand
pages of his commonplace books (*Zibaldone*) show an intense study
of classical languages and authors, a technical, almost professional
interest in classical scholarship. They are crowded with the names
of German editors and commentators and many pages are taken
up with quotations from Wolf and Müller on the Homeric question. Much of Leopardi's theorizing moves along well-worn
grooves: imitation, delight as the end of poetry, style as the test of
good art, and verisimilitude are the concepts that occur again and
again. When Leopardi drew up the outline of an unwritten treatise, "On the Present Condition of Italian Literature," he filled
it with recommendations to supply the various deficiencies of
Italian literature in the different genres: he deplores the lack of

an unaffected fluid harmonious prose, he wants to have Italian eloquence, a new comedy, a prose epic in the style of Fénelon's *Télémaque,* and so on.[48] It is hard to imagine anything more external and more "practical," even mechanical in its faith in corporate activity and the distinction of the kinds—even Leopardi's speculations on the relativity of beauty and taste hardly go beyond 18th-century skepticism.

Nor could one argue that Leopardi is sympathetically inclined to authors we would call romantic today. He admired *Werther* and *Corinne.*[49] Occasionally he has words of praise for Byron, though usually he considered him cold and affected, devoid of genuine feeling.[50] There is hardly a contemporary author whom Leopardi really admired. Foscolo and Manzoni come in only for very mild praise.* More and more, Leopardi thought of himself as alone in a period of decadence, and with the increase of his illness and isolation his bitterness found outlet in satires against modern progress and the century in general. Leopardi lived in the past, his own past, in ancient Italy, and in antiquity.

But if we go through the *Zibaldone,* we come across, among the welter of philological notes and reflections on the vanity of life and the need of illusion, a series of most remarkable pronouncements on literature which should change any superficial first impression of Leopardi's conventionality and neoclassical orthodoxy. Indeed, in these few pages, written mostly around 1827, Leopardi asserts more radically than anybody else in contemporary Europe the view that poetry is lyrical, "sentimental," and nothing else. Not only is the lyric called "the summit of poetry," "true and pure poetry in all its extension," "the eternal and universal kind because first in time," [51] but the consequences of this view are very boldly drawn. Poetry, says Leopardi in a crucial entry, "consisted from the beginning in this kind alone, and its essence is always mainly in this kind, which almost becomes confused with it, and it is the most truly poetic [kind] of all poems, which are not poems except insofar as they are lyrical." [52] The lyric quality derives from

* *Zibaldone, 1,* 1425, speaks of "glimmer" of genius in Alfieri and Foscolo. Leopardi met Manzoni in 1827 and liked him as a person (*Lettere,* pp. 784, 826, 849), but his judgment of *I Promessi sposi* is lukewarm (*Lettere,* pp. 783, 825, 849).

sensibility or sentiment. But sentiment to Leopardi is not immediate emotion, as in the false simplicity of folk songs,[53] but rather
reminiscence, memory, that recall of childhood and the past which
made him a worshiper of antiquity. Mere excess of enthusiasm
rather hinders poetry. His own poetry is conceived in a flash of
inspiration lasting two minutes, but even the shortest poem takes
two or three weeks to elaborate and revise. Yet without inspiration
he could not have written, "Water could sooner flow from a tree
trunk than a single verse from my brain." [54] Thus, Leopardi says,
anticipating Poe, the "labors of poetry desire by their very nature
to be short." [55]

Poetry, Leopardi argues, in flat contradiction to earlier pronouncements, is not and cannot be imitation. "The poet imagines:
the imagination sees the world not as it is; it fabricates, invents."
"The poet is a creator, an inventor," who writes "from his own
intimate sentiment" because he has a "need to express the sentiments which he really experienced." [56] In these passages "imagination" and "sentiment" are identified, or at least juxtaposed. Yet
often Leopardi draws a historical distinction between them: imagination belongs to antiquity and to childhood and is thus irrevocably past and gone, while sentiment which is reminiscent or even
frankly called "the capacity of feeling pain" is the privilege and
curse of the moderns.[57] The historical scheme implied is a simple
one, Rousseauistic in implication, somewhat similar to Schiller's
contrast between naive and sentimental. The ancients are nature;
they lived in nature and created through imagination a beautiful
world of illusion which made the darkness of this world tolerable.
"The works of genius," Leopardi reflects, "serve always as con-
solation, even when they depict the nothingness of things, even
when they show us and make us feel the inevitable unhappiness of
life, even when they express the most terrible despair." [58] Even
the knowledge of the falsity of all beauty and greatness is itself
beautiful and great. But with the progress of civilization and the
spread of the enlightenment man has been thrown into an even
deeper misery: the sources of imagination have dried up, the world
of illusion has withered, and nothing is left for the poet but to
express the feeling of sadness and despair. "The creative force of
the imagination was exclusively the property of the ancients. Since

then man has become permanently unhappy and what is worse has recognized the fact and thus caused and confirmed his unhappiness." [59]

Leopardi sees a confirmation of his historical scheme in his own personal history. He went through an early period of unconscious imaginative creation and then underwent a crisis in 1819 from which he learned to feel the misery of the world. "One can even say that, strictly speaking, only the ancients were poets and that today only the children and young men are, and that the moderns who have this name are nothing but philosophers. I, at least, became sentimental only when I lost imagination and became insensible to nature and dedicated to reason and truth, in short, a philosopher." [60] This self-condemnation to philosophy was not, however, final. It rather posed Leopardi's problem: can there be a poet in this modern age? Becoming a philosopher is obviously a denial of poetry. "The more poetry is philosophical, the less it is poetry." [61] Philosophy wants truth, poetry falsity and illusion. "Philosophy harms and destroys poetry. . . . There is an unsurmountable barrier, a sworn and mortal enmity between them, which cannot be abolished, reconciled or disguised." [62] If philosophy is hostile to poetry, so is science. Poetry has not improved since the time of Homer,[63] while science makes discoveries every day.

The process of fatal rationalization is illustrated also in the evolution of language. Original language is poetic, rich in connotations, metaphorical, vague, imprecise. Modern language tends toward the abstract, the technical term rather than the word. Leopardi thus constantly disparages the French language (and poetry) as mere prose and can exhort the poet to restore the original meanings of words, to preserve archaisms and to use poetic, indefinite, mysterious words.[64]

The emphasis on the lyric which we have met in Herder or Foscolo becomes much more startling in Leopardi when we see him draw the consequences and disparage the epic and the drama. This was far from the thought of Herder, who at most wanted to assimilate all genres into one. Leopardi makes similar attempts to deny the distinction between the lyrical and the epic. He calls the epic "a hymn in honor of heroes and peoples and armies: only a drawn-out hymn." [65] The epic "insofar as it conforms to nature and true poetry, that is, consists of short songs like the Homeric and Ossianic poems and of hymns, etc., rejoins the lyric." [66] Leopardi looks for support in Wolf's theory of the origin of Homer in songs, alludes even to Lachmann's transfer of Wolf's scheme to the *Nibelungenlied,* and notes down information on the lyrical meters of the oldest Roman epics.[67] But Leopardi speaks his mind more freely when he gives up such compromises and says that "an epic poem runs against the very nature of poetry. It demands a plan conceived and arranged in completely cold blood. What can a work which demands many years for its completion have to do with poetry? Poetry consists essentially in an impetus." [68]

The drama comes off even worse. It belongs even less to poetry than does the epic. "To pretend to have a passion, a character which he does not have (a necessity in the drama) is completely foreign to the poet: no less than the exact and patient observation of someone else's characters and passions. The more a man is a genius, the more he is a poet, so much the more has he sentiments of his own to expound, the more will he refuse to put on another personality, to speak in the person of another, to imitate." [69] Leopardi recognizes that "the novel, the story, etc. are much less alien to a man of genius than the drama, which is to him the most alien of all the genres of literature, because it requires the greatest closeness of imitation, the greatest transformation of the author into other individuals, the most complete renunciation and the most complete surrender of his own individuality, to which a man of genius clings more firmly than anybody else." [70] In a preface to an unfinished pastoral, *Telesilla* (1819), Leopardi had already rejected the "miserable trick of extremely intricate nodes and twists" of plot to keep the attention and curiosity of the spectators,[71] because plot was for him the lowest and least poetic of all the elements of poetry. Even Greek tragedy, which can hardly be condemned for sinning by excessive plot interest, seems to Leopardi material and external. The Greeks wanted strong effects, fierce, energetic sensations. Their favorite subjects were horrible and singular misfortunes, unique characters, unnatural passions; they were sensation hunters: something Byron and the romanticists liked and wanted. Neither does Aristophanes find grace in Leopardi's eyes: his comedies are full of unnatural fantastic inven‑ tions, allegorical figures, frogs, clouds, and birds.[72]

Given Leopardi's view of poetry, it is not surprising that finally there remained for him little to admire. There were the ancients, of course, Homer, Pindar, Anacreon, Virgil, Lucretius, and even Lucian, who remained the gods of his Parnassus. There was Dante, whose *Divine Comedy,* consistently enough, is called a "long lyric where the poet and his feelings are always in evidence." [73] There was Petrarch, who alone among the moderns has pathos and who obviously was the model of Leopardi's own early style. But he finally came to the conclusion that there are only very few poetic beauties in him to admire.[74] There was Tasso, for whose fate Leopardi had a personal tenderness, and there were a few fine things in Chiabrera and Testi. But Metastasio was the last singer of Italy, perhaps the only poet since Tasso. Parini did not have enough passion to be a poet, and even Alfieri was rather a philosopher (a reasoner in Leopardi's sense) than a poet.[75]

Leopardi's taste contracted more and more: his personal brand of poetry increasingly seemed to him the only genuine one. Such dogmatism is the right of every artist. After all, Leopardi was a poet first and foremost and a critic only intermittently. He had nothing of the tolerance, the curiosity for the creative world around him, which the great romantic critics had. In spite of his historical scheme of the decay of imagination, he is hardly imbued with a genuine historical spirit. Nevertheless the most original entries in *Zibaldone* must be singled out, for they represent the most complete reversal of the neoclassical hierarchy of genres. Drama and plot, which in Aristotle are the essence of poetry, are banned by Leopardi to its periphery. The lyric, which had been excluded by Bacon and Hobbes from poetry, and the expression of personal feeling, are the only poetry, the highest kind. The wheel has come to a full circle.

We must not forget that Leopardi's pronouncements remained in the privacy of his notebooks till the last decade of the 19th century and thus remained without influence in their time. The reconstruction of Italian criticism had to await the arrival of De Sanctis who loved and studied Leopardi, but drew his critical ideas from Hegel and the other Germans.

ABOUT 1806 a marked change in the German intellectual atmosphere becomes noticeable. The rise of Napoleon and the downfall of Prussia in the battle of Jena excited a fervent patriotism which turned against the ideas of the French Revolution and the whole gospel of humanity and reason associated with the 18th century and the German classics. The older romantic writers were good German patriots: both Schlegels took active part in the struggle against Napoleon. But those of the younger group, around twenty or twenty-five years of age in 1806, were obsessed with the question of nationality to a degree quite foreign to the theoretical mind of the Schlegels. The literary theories and criticism of the group show this change: they all turned to the study of origins, the Teutonic past, folk songs, folk tales, legends, the *Nibelungen,* the *Edda,* and in general to everything they thought was indigenous, aboriginal, pristine, "German," untouched by the blight of modern civilization, and thus contributory to a recovery of the nation. Two of the most important achievements of the group were editions: the collection of German folk songs, *Des Knaben Wunderhorn* (1805–08) by Achim von Arnim and Clemens Brentano, and the universally famous *Kinder- und Hausmärchen* by the brothers Jakob and Wilhelm Grimm (1812–15). Moreover, the Grimms were the founders of what was substantially a new branch of learning, Germanic philology, which was interpreted by them very broadly as the science of Germanic civilization. Jakob Grimm, especially, laid its foundation with tireless labor and brilliant combinatory power. His *Deutsche Grammatik* (1819–37) revolutionized not only the study of Germanic philology but all linguistics, with its discovery of phonetic laws, consonant and vowel shifts, etc. The Grimms' other books, such as the collection of German local and historical legends, the studies of Teutonic mythology and

Teutonic legal antiquities, and the German historical dictionary initiated by them, created "Germanistics" almost single (or rather double) handed. In the course of the 19th century Germanistics took over almost all literary studies—not merely the academic kind—in Germany, and later profoundly influenced the course of literary studies in England, the United States, and all the Slavic and Scandinavian countries. Even today the emphasis on Anglo-Saxon and *Beowulf* in American graduate programs of English is a survival of this German romantic outlook.

From our point of view, focused as it is on literary theories and criticism, the oldest of the group, Joseph Görres (1776–1848) comes nearest to being a literary critic. His life was primarily devoted to the politics of the Catholic Restoration, but he started (except for a short period of intoxication with the French Revolution) as a Schellingian *Naturphilosoph* who also engaged in speculations about aesthetics. *Aphorismen über die Kunst* (1802) contains dichotomies and polarities which try to modify Schiller's distinction between the naive and sentimental by means of distinction between "productive" and "eductive" art.[1] Also, his contributions to the periodical *Aurora* (1804–05) are in part speculations about the contrasts of ages and types. French and German literature are supposed to compare as plains with mountains. But the other critical essays in this group show more of Görres' ability: his sureness of recognition and his brilliance of characterization by analogies and metaphors expressed in a style which reminds one of Jean Paul's fireworks. The admiration for Jean Paul, Herder, and Novalis is to be expected; but the fervent praise of Hölderlin's *Hyperion* and of Kleist's first tragedy, *Die Familie Schroffenstein*, was novel and right. Görres' most interesting piece is that on Goethe, which attempts to distinguish the stages of his style by analogy with the development of Greek sculpture, from the naturalistic, early period through the idealization of the middle years to the elegant, mannered style of his latest writings such as *Die natürliche Tochter*.[2]

These early critical articles were little known. Görres' historical role begins only with his arrival at Heidelberg in 1806 and his association with Brentano and Arnim. His book, *Die deutschen Volksbücher* (1807), concerns us most. It is a description of German chapbooks, such as *Faust* and *Die Haimonskinder*, mostly of the

16th century, with elaborate studies of their sources and analogues in medieval romances, oriental legends, and so on. This central part of the book would have made it an early document in the study of comparative literature, of the migration of themes which today would necessarily be obsolete. But the introduction and conclusion make it a manifesto of the new outlook on literature. These chapbooks, though their foreign sources are established in many instances by Görres himself, are proclaimed to be folk literature, the expression of the "genuine inner spirit of the German nation," objects of highest devotion, "sacred antiquities." Folk songs, folk legends, folk superstitions and customs, all "works of nature such as plants," are considered relics of the dimmest Middle Ages, and the Middle Ages are in turn extolled as the "garden of poetry, the Eden of romanticism." [3] In this blessed age history was a religious epic, poetry flowered, the nation was united in one people without class distinctions. No imitation of the ancients blighted native creativity. Since then Görres sees only decay into rationalism and prose. Herder's contrast between *Natur-* and *Kunstpoesie* is redrawn here very sharply and all the light falls on natural poetry, which alone is genuine.

Görres' enthusiastic review of *Des Knaben Wunderhorn* (1809–1810) defines his position most clearly. "We believe poetry preceded art, and enthusiasm preceded discipline. We believe frankly in the existence of a special natural poetry which to those who practice it comes as if in a dream, which is not learned and not acquired in school, but which is like the first love that even the most ignorant knows in a flash and without effort practices best when he has least studied it, and likewise worst, the more he has examined it." Every exemplary work of art "is let out into the day as Nature lets out animals and plants." [4] Natural poetry is simple and grand; it produces its own forms necessarily, its form and content are grown together in organic life like soul and body. Recognizing that the folk songs collected by Arnim and Brentano do not live up to this ideal, Görres treats them simply as debased survivals of a more glorious past. He considers them as one single poem, "one faithful mirror of the people," and in an astonishing *tour de force* he enumerates and characterizes a great number of them in a certain order according to themes: from birth to death, from sensual love to religious ecstasy. Though individually they are "lyrical ejaculations," they form a "dramatic epic whole" since "an invisible bond goes through all things." Though at times Görres recognizes that poets who never composed anything else might have been the authors of individual poems, in general he thinks of them as the common property of the nation. They guarantee the excellence of the nation: the folk poet and the nation are one.[5]

If folk poetry forms one poem, despite the fact that the songs in Arnim and Brentano actually come from different centuries and contain much that is late and highly artificial, we can well imagine that remote epic poetry is considered as part of the aboriginal myth. Görres' articles on the *Nibelungenlied* (1808) were the first to examine the parallels in Old Norse sagas and to state the conclusion that the *Nibelungenlied* is the one surviving fragment of a colossal poem or myth.[6] His largest book, *Die Mythengeschichte der asiatischen Welt* (1810), then tries to establish more fully that there is only one natural poetry and that it is identical with myth and that all myth came from the East. In time Görres' theories, based on wide but uncritical reading, became more and more fantastic. The introduction culminates in a pretentious comparison between the Indian epics, Homer, Ossian, *Titurel,* and the *Nibelungen.* The plan of a history of universal myth, however, never materialized, partly because Görres became more and more absorbed in political journalism.

Only a few of his later writings discuss what he would call "art poetry." A review of Jean Paul's writings (1811) cleverly uses the distinctions of the *Vorschule* in a survey categorized according to genius, humor, irony, wit, characters, plot, landscape painting, and style. In a way similar to his review of the *Wunderhorn,* Görres weaves into one pattern his characterizations of almost all the figures in Jean Paul's novels, evoking a whole world of humor and sentimentality by ingenious and fanciful analogies and metaphors. He even returns to his early interest in the contrast between ancient and modern and draws a distinction between the Greek world view based on Euclidean geometry and the modern world which has invented differential and infinitesimal calculus. His comparison between a Christian church and a differential formula can equal anything recent analogizing German *Geistesgeschichte* has invented to prove the complete parallelism of all human activities.[7]

A late review of Bettina von Arnim's *Goethes Briefwechsel mit einem Kinde* (1835) defines very shrewdly the attitude of the Catholic Restoration to Goethe. Goethe appears as the pagan and Philistine who, at the appearance of the "child," was temporarily quickened back to life. Görres did not see through the sham of Bettina's fiction, surely because his own temperament was similar to her own high-pitched hysteria.[8] His whole critical method consists in a constant analogizing and metaphorizing which remind one of the worst purple passages in so-called "impressionist" criticism of the 1890's. What he says of Jean Paul could be applied to him: "He makes the Samoyedes ride swiftly on camels, the Arabs drive through the desert in a carriage with reindeer, flying fish sing high up in the tops of linden trees, so that the nightingales listen, and the monkeys attentively leaf through sentimental novels." [9] It is not surprising that Görres considered any attempt at defining poetry "materialistic," since "poetry, like everything holy, is concealed in the darkness of mysticism." [10]

THE BROTHERS GRIMM

What in Görres is put forward with great emotional fervor, in a cascade of metaphors, was simultaneously elaborated more soberly and scientifically by the Grimm brothers. On the central issue, the difference between natural and artificial poetry, there was, however, some disagreement between the brothers. Jakob Grimm (1785–1863), who was the greater scholar of the two, formulated the more extreme view of natural poetry as composing itself, quite unconsciously, far in the dim past and as gradually deteriorating with the distance from the divine source of Revelation, the childhood of mankind, which shone for him in the bright light of paradisaical reminiscence. Wilhelm Grimm (1786–1859), had a greater trust in human nature and was prepared to admit that even contemporary poets can and should achieve "nature." Wilhelm was the more artistic of the two brothers: he translated verse very well and to him we owe, apparently, the stylistic form of the fairy tales. Jakob, who wrote in a terse and often crabbed style, had hardly any interest in modern literature. He lived completely in the past, among the Teutonic myths, the *Nibelungen*, the *Edda*, fairy tales, legends, fables, everything that seemed to him ancient and Germanic. But though his writings are permeated by a fervent

pan-Teutonic patriotism, one must beware of thinking him ignorant or uninterested in other nations. Jakob studied and admired
folk poetry wherever he found it: he published, in Spanish, a collection of old Spanish romances *Silva de romances viejos* (1815).
He was one of the earliest students of the French *Roman de
Renard,* of Grail histories and *chansons de geste.*[1] He learned
Serbian in order to study and translate some of the Serbian folk
epics.[2] His faith in Ossian remained unshaken even late in his life.[3]
He thought of natural poetry as universal, though he ascribed to
the Teutonic nations great prominence in producing and preserv-
ing it. Especially old French poetry can always be traced back to
some supposed Teutonic source.

While many of Jakob's early reviews and articles define his general position, the correspondence with Arnim gives the clearest
statement. There is, Jakob Grimm asserts, an eternal distinction
between nature poetry and art poetry. They are so different that
they cannot exist simultaneously. Ancient nature poetry is based
on myth, and our standard of judging it must be whether the
poetry is more or less faithful to this basis.[4] Grimm expressly chides
those who would make aesthetic distinctions in the study of Old
Germanic poetry: whatever is to be studied is the myth and the
myth itself makes a totality dependent on its time, which thus
can be recognized even from misshapen and dead forms. The historian of nature poetry must explain and describe the different
shapes in which the myth appeared and trace it back as far as possible to its origins.[5] History, in the sense of factual truth, seems to
Grimm always subordinated to myth and poetry, but great historical events are necessary as a stimulus to the creation of heroic
myth.[6] In defending his position against Arnim, Grimm repeats
that "poetry is what comes pure out of the mind into the word.
. . . Folk poetry arises from the mind of the whole; what I mean
by art poetry arises from that of the individual. That is why ancient poetry cannot call its poets by name: it has not been made
by one or two or three, but is the sum of the whole. . . . It seems
to me unthinkable that there should ever have been a Homer or
an author of the *Nibelungen.* History proves the distinction also
by the fact that no civilized nation is able to produce an epic, and
has never done so."[7] Nothing seems to him more perverse than

the idea of writing epic poetry today, as epics can only compose themselves. The failure of Klopstock's *Messiah* and Goethe's wise abandonment of an *Achilleis* are further proof. "The ancient men were greater, purer, and holier than we; the glory of the divine dawn still shone on them. Thus I consider old epic poetry (= legendary, mythic history) purer and better than our witty, i.e. knowing, refined, and complex" poetry. "Ancient poetry has an inner form of eternal validity." Art poetry is a "preparation, nature poetry a making of itself." [8] Folk poetry does not reflect on its meters, just as a singing bird who wants to produce a tone does not reflect on how to adjust his bill, tongue, and throat. Nature poetry is definitely past, just as the youth of mankind is past. Its forms, the source of rhyme, and alliteration are in the whole: "no workshops or reflections of individual poets can be admitted." [9]

The exact way this original poetry composed itself remains, however, quite mysterious. Collective creation is pushed so far into the past that the origins of poetry and myth become fused and we are brought up against something ultimate whose source is Divine Revelation.[10] The whole process since then has been one of decay, in exact parallel to the history of language, which Grimm conceives of as decaying from its pristine stage by shedding cases, verbal forms, suffixes, and so on. Only in 1893 did Otto Jespersen succeed in reversing this view by arguing for progress in language toward simplicity and lack of inflection. At times Grimm tries to define the process more closely and to distinguish between several stages. He speaks e.g. of a triad in which the epic (objective, collective art) comes first, the lyric (subjective, individual) comes second, and the drama (their synthesis) comes last.[11] Or he speaks of poetry as an intermediary stage between the Divine Idea and human events (history). "This bread of life [is] wider and freer than the present, more narrow and confined than revelation." [12] The epic, fairy tales, local legends, folk songs, even animal fables are thus looked at as hallowed relics of the divine youth, the golden age of humanity. Grimm argued vigorously for considering the *Renard* stories as remains of a genuine old epic cycle of primitive antiquity when men lived with animals and recognized their human features as a matter of course. Grimm stresses the folk element in the Renard stories, deriving the name from the Germanic *Reginhald* (adviser); he fails to see the satirical, ironical, and definitely clerical tone of the early medieval versions.[13]

We know only very little of what Jakob Grimm thought of modern literature. Late in his life he delivered a centenary oration on Schiller (1859) which celebrates him, considering the official occasion, not uncritically. Again the poet, however artificial and philosophical, is conceived of as the voice of the people, as one who "expresses, as it were incarnates, the full nature of the nation." [14] But otherwise, Grimm is always cool to art poetry. In reflections occasioned by a trip to Italy (1844) he condemns all Italian literature as artificial. The contents of Dante are dead, Petrarch is a derivative of the troubadours, Ariosto ridicules the ancient epic, Tasso is a sentimentalist. Only Boccaccio, presumably because he is nearest to the people, finds favor in Grimm's eyes. Grimm does not fail to single out Tommaseo among all the modern Italians for his collection of folk songs.[15] It agrees with his aversion to art poetry that he expressly denies genuine poetry to Horace and all his followers.[16] Even translations, adaptations, and modernizations of ancient myths are viewed with complete lack of enthusiasm. Tegnér's *Frithiofs-Saga* is ranked very low.[17] Though Grimm's judgments will appear extravagant to anybody raised in the Western tradition of literature, his taste is by no means exceptional. Admirers of Horace, Virgil, Racine, Voltaire, and Pope are still rare in Germany.

Wilhelm Grimm shares in most respects his brother's views and tastes. His discussion of the origin of Old Germanic poetry (1808) also asserts that history and poetry were originally the same and that the two together made the epic. The scalds, he confidently argues, were not the authors of these songs but merely their transmitters. Like Jakob he delights in the comfortably vague reflexive verbs. He can speak of the "innocence and unconsciousness in which the whole composed itself." [18] The *Nibelungenlied* is denied any definite form: it would have been different in different mouths and, if it had been recorded earlier, it would have been preserved in a grander and severer style, since "all evolution tends toward polish and grace, in which the greatness of the original idea gradually declines and at last completely disappears." [19] Wilhelm Grimm sets off very sharply (far too sharply, we would say today)

this Old German epic, which is completely indigenous and shows
no foreign trait, against the courtly poetry of the time, which does
not "directly concern the essence of genuinely German poetry." It
was the product of a class, and since national poetry was then still
alive, it was not merely art poetry but "mannered" poetry, "completely outside the spirit of the nation." [20]

But Wilhelm, in spite of these pronouncements, has more understanding for art poetry than his brother, and has a greater trust in
the continuity of human creativeness. While Jakob deplores even
his brother's translations from the *Edda* and the Danish ballads and
resigns himself to the fact that ancient poetry is completely irre-
coverable, except to the historical scholar,[21] Wilhelm defends
modernizations and adaptations and even grants that the distinction between nature and art poetry need not be completely rigid.
He agrees that there is consciousness in the *Nibelungen* and in
Homer and grants that Goethe's poems in the popular manner
(such as the "King of Thule") are as good as anything in the *Wunderhorn*.[22] In theory he admits that art poetry is as excellent as
natural or national poetry. But in practice he judges art poetry also
from a collectivist point of view: it must express the spirit of the
nation. Even what is wholly unexpected and individual must be
based on a national idea. All knowledge and recognition of poetry
is collective; it is the voice of the people, to which Grimm appeals
even when ranking, in a survey, the main German 18th-century
writers.[23] He praised the novels of Arnim and defended an adaptation of the Sigurd legends by Fouqué. "We are modern, and what
is good in us is also modern. Why should not what our age has
achieved be allowed to express itself? And would it be possible to
deny our age?" There is this distinction, however: the ancient ages
lived in innocent unconsciousness, the modern age lives in consciousness.[24]

In most details the general structure of the Grimms has since
crumbled. The reaction against their views has gone far. Much
evidence has been accumulated to show that a great deal of what
they considered folk literature is the composition of a single author
in the Western tradition and not unacquainted with antiquity.
The *Nibelungen,* the *Edda,* even *Beowulf,* are neither primitive
nor purely Teutonic. The *chansons de geste* have been shown to be
monkish compositions. Folk songs, fairy tales, and chapbooks are

frequently quite late in origin, traceable even to specific authors and full of the devices and traditions of artificial poetry. Much that is supposedly folk poetry is rather "gesunkenes Kulturgut," i.e. it has descended socially to the "lower classes" and its simplicity and naiveté are rather a reduction than an origin. One may still, as Croce does, object to any bifurcation of poetry, to any attempt to break up its unity,[25] but the reaction against the Grimms' point of view has clearly run its course. Granted the exaggeration of their position, there is much in it that is basically sound. Medieval poetry has ultimate roots in folk poetry and folk traditions. Scholars are even coming back to the view that the courtly love lyric has its origins in folk forms.[26] Myth is almost palpably discernible behind much poetry even of modern times, and the "archetypal patterns," derived from Jung and expounded by Maud Bodkin, do not differ substantially from what the Grimms meant by myth. While the dichotomy of natural and artificial poetry is indefensible if it implies different aesthetic standards, undoubtedly folk poetry does have its own specific ways of creation and specific problems of transmission and social setting, which are very different from those of written literature and can still be observed today in many countries.[27] The study of oral literature is an indispensable part of literary scholarship. The Grimms were wrong only in pushing it too far into the past and thus preventing clear discriminations between myth and actual poetry. Finally, nobody need sympathize with their very influential dislike for the tradition of complex learned poetry of the West.

ARNIM AND KLEIST

Achim von Arnim (1781–1831), as coeditor of *Des Knaben Wunderhorn* (1805–08), belongs to the initiators of the folk song vogue. His supplementary essay "Von Volkliedern" (1806) is as enthusiastically vague about them as possible. He even suggests that the decay of folk song made the French revolution possible.[1] In an earlier letter Arnim proposed the founding of a poetry and singing school in Switzerland which would spread poetry among the people and finally make the German language accepted by all the nations of the earth.[2] But Arnim soon sobered and in his correspondence with the Grimms defended a very sensible point of view. He tells them that he has felt enthusiasm for folk poetry not because it was produced by a different nature and art than today's but because it has stood the test of time, as many things of our own time will stand it. Arnim "swears," in the name of the Homerides, the singers of folk songs, that nobody who has sung more than one verse is without some artistic intention, even if it be small compared to what he achieves unconsciously.[3] Arnim admitted the contrast of nature and art poetry but argued that it was drawn far too sharply by the Grimms. There is a slow evolution from the communal to the individual. There is conscious art in old poetry and old poetry is not always perfect: good Homer sometimes naps and there are plenty of empty fillers and artificialities in the *Nibelungen.* The anonymity of folk poetry is also not always strict. Arnim found a song sung in many villages within a hundred miles of each other and only afterward discovered that its author was a poet of the late 18th century. Nor is all art poetry contrived: he himself asserts that he has written verse without thinking of the meter and, on the other hand, many folk poems, e.g. the Danish heroic ballads, were written to a set metrical pattern. The eternal sources of poetry flow at all times, even at times when no verse is written. Thus Arnim defends modernizations and pastiches of folk songs.[4] He felt himself primarily a poet who wanted to mingle with the people and become a folk poet himself.

In the later years of his life Arnim arrived at a more realistic, historical conception of literature. The preface to the *Kronenwächter,* a historical novel, proclaims the earth, the past, truth, and reality as the eternal sources of poetry.* Arnim's criticism, however, never achieved real coherence. Occasional pronouncements show that he shares the anti-intellectualist bias of his group. He was, after all, an imaginative artist first and foremost and thus could write to A. W. Schlegel: "one work of art is better than the whole history of literature." [5] When defending a play by Oehlenschläger he could appeal only to feeling: "Whoever has no sense of it, won't learn it by the most extensive explanations and who has, won't need them." [6]

This new group of romantics had given up the theoretical achievements of the Schlegels: the recognition of the cooperation

---

* *Sämtliche Werke,* ed. Grimm, *3,* 7. Still, I don't understand why Albert Béguin calls this page "l'une des plus belles qu'on ait jamais écrites sur la poésie." *L'Âme romantique et le rêve* (Paris, 1946), p. 256.

of the conscious and unconscious in creation, the insight into the organic unity of content and form, the view of poetry as one universal whole developing in history. The Grimms most vigorously denied the last in their dichotomy between art and nature poetry. When we look only for myth regardless of the specific poetic form it assumes, we abandon the unity of form and content. The insight into the share of the conscious and unconscious was obscured by a revival of inspiration theories. To document this we can glance briefly at passages from other famous writers of the time who did not leave a body of criticism sufficient to merit special discussion. Bettina Brentano (who married Arnim) proposed a "direct revelation of poetry, without the firm limits of form, which would impress the mind more quickly and more naturally." [7] Heinrich von Kleist (1777–1811) also wanted poetry without form. "Language, rhythm, euphony: these are real, though natural and necessary, obstacles; and art, in respect to them, must aim at nothing else but making them disappear," he tells in an open letter to a young poet.[8] His most remarkable essay, "Über das Marionettentheater" (1811), finds a striking image in defense of unconscious creation. A great dancer who frequents the puppet theater, explains to the interlocutor that the puppet has the blessing of automatism and unconsciousness, saying that reflection spoils the dancer and the poet. In order to show what disorder is caused by self-consciousness, he tells an anecdote of a handsome young man who in attempting to pull out a sliver from his foot happened to see himself reflected in a mirror and realized the similarity of his posture to the famous ancient bronze representing the same action. The young man was henceforth unable to repeat the graceful movement, try however he might. "In the degree that reflection becomes darker and weaker, gracefulness always shines forth more brightly and powerfully." Only a dim hope is held out that whoever falls from the state of innocence may in the end, in the last chapter of world history, regain it and become at one with God, the infinite consciousness.[9]

The theme of the loss of unconsciousness is common in Kleist's writings: Alkmene in *Amphitryo*, Penthesilea at the sight of Achilles' corpse, Kohlhaas before Luther's proclamation. We can understand how Kleist can say, "All movement, everything involuntary is beautiful; but crooked and distorted is everything as soon as it understands itself. Oh the understanding! The unhappy understanding!" [10] This basic irrationalism, which has been curiously denied by critics who look only at Kleist's complex dramatic dialectics, prevented Kleist and many of his contemporaries from becoming critics and theorists. While the actual poetic achievement of the earlier romantics, with the exception of Novalis, seems small today, the newer generation has far greater works of art to its credit: Brentano and Arnim, Kleist and E. T. A. Hoffmann created genuine worlds of imagination. But they suffer from a lack of self-criticism, from a fundamental lack of form which prevents them from ranking with the greatest writers. Their anti-intellectualism came back at them with a vengeance. Only one of them (and he was no artist) stands out as a real and, I believe, important critic: Adam Müller.

ADAM MÜLLER

Among the younger German romantic critics, Adam Müller (1779–1829) is close to the Schlegels and to the speculative metaphysics of Schelling and Novalis. Apart from his achievement in adapting their general ideas on criticism and the nature of poetry and art, with a new personal emphasis, to a new context, Adam Müller seems to me a practical critic of great perception and eloquence. Today he is hardly known even in Germany, though two of his books were reprinted in 1920 and there was at that time some interest in him as a political philosopher. His conversion to Roman Catholicism in 1805 and his later association with Metternich's Austria contributed to his obscurity, since reputations in Germany were largely determined by Protestant liberal historians. But there is no such reason for ignoring him today; as a matter of fact his literary views are rarely colored by specifically Roman Catholic teachings. He belongs definitely with the speculative monists and pantheists of his time, whatever private means he may have found to reconcile this outlook with his religious professions.

Müller very persuasively draws the consequences from the historicism of the Schlegels. He decides at least theoretically in favor of a "mediating," relativistic criticism. In the *Vorlesungen über deutsche Wissenschaft und Literatur* (1806) he expounds the view that there are no eternal models, no absolute perfection in literature, that there must be no despotism of golden ages. The great

merit of the German critical movement, which had its beginning
in Winckelmann and culminates in Friedrich Schlegel, is the conception of a totality of art or literature, which develops like the
natural history of an organism: the individual works of art are
viewed as if they were limbs or nervous or muscular systems of
one great body. Friedrich Schlegel is criticized by Müller for not
seeing this complete continuity of literary tradition, for his inability to resolve the dualism of Greek and Germanic art, and for
his dogmatic decision in favor of one of the two, namely romantic
art. We must not, Müller argues, because of a single poet forget the
greater poet, Humanity, or because of a single poem, the greater
poem, History. There is a higher criticism, an eternal mediating
criticism, which knows not only how to fight but also how to reconcile while fighting.[1] According to Müller this mediating criticism
does not imply a complete abdication of all judgment; every work
of art is to be judged by its place in the whole of literature; it has
its place as a weight, or at least as a counterweight. No work is
without significance; each, in its place, contributes to the whole
and in so doing modifies the whole.[2] Criticism need not lose its
severity even though it combine with the freedom and tolerance of
history.[3] Its goal is to achieve the dialectical reconciliation of judgment and history.[4] Müller, however, nowhere faces the problem
of how this "weight" or place can be ascertained without extra-
historical standards.

Müller draws a scheme for his convictions from the all-
pervading dialectics of the reconciliation of opposites which he
derived from Fichte and Schelling and expounded in his first publication, *Die Lehre vom Gegensatz* (1804). This dialectics of reconciliation seems to him also an inspiration for Germany to be a
mediator, a synthesizing nation, to be the middle, the center of
Europe.

The reconciliation of opposites is also the key concept in Müller's idea of beauty and poetry as expounded in *Von der Idee des
Schönen* (1809). Beauty is neither wholly subjective nor wholly
objective. It is a rhythmical movement, a harmony, a reciprocity
between man and man. Poetry is not merely the art of writing in
verse, nor is it the spirit of the world, the poetry of youth, of love,
the poetry of poetry about which Friedrich Schlegel had spoken. It
is not mere technique, a mere selection from a list of fixed words,

nor is it identical with a feeling for the universe. Poetry is the union of both: it is an artful presentation of life in words; it is a whole, a closed, a *made* world. The poet's intention does not matter: his desire to present the world can never be completely achieved. Life, the creation of life, is a sufficient aim.[5] All opposites are reconciled in poetry: the universal and the particular, the individual and the general, the characteristic and the ideal. The poet cannot combine too many contradictory elements: his work cannot be too rich, great, particular, if it is to be generally comprehensible, truly simple, truly significant, truly universal. Moreover, the individual work of art is such a contradictory identity; it is both soul and body, form and matter. One can consider a part of a work of art only with a view to the whole, and vice versa, the whole only with a view to the part.[6] A work of art is an organism, grown and growing. The standpoint of the artist is where idealism and realism, freedom and necessity, art and nature, unite.[7] Polarity, the union of the opposites, is Müller's central idea. He rings the changes on these formulas, polarizing and analogizing all creation. At times the metaphor of the opposition of the sexes, the constant parallelizing of the poles with the feminine and masculine is so obsessive that one cannot help suspecting Müller's motives. The pedantic eloquence addressed to an audience, largely of ladies, sounds like the celebration not only of cosmic unity but of sentimental pan-sexuality.

Whatever the excesses of this dialectical point of view, it meant a rejection in Adam Müller's critical practice of the usual either/ or in favor of a clearly conscious both/and. While most Germans of his time recognized only one ideal, Teutonic romantic poetry, Müller was one of the very few to have an understanding of the Latin ideal of poetry, of French good taste, of rhetorical poetry, of Racine. Both in the lectures *Über dramatische Kunst*[8] and in *Zwölf Reden über die Beredsamkeit und deren Verfall in Deutschland*,[9] there are defenses of French literature. Müller protests against the German contempt for French poetry. "Nobody can say that he understands the Greeks and the romantic poets if he puts the Romans and the French contemptuously aside, or vice versa. There is only one meaning, one eternal meaning of art, and that must be able to pass gently and animatingly through the art forms of all times."[10] Müller contrasts the representative character

of French and Roman poetry with the personal character of Greek
and German poetry. He knows what the French theater aims at:
measure, totality, closed form, artifice, clarity, universality.[11]

This discussion of French tragedy widens in the *Lectures on
Eloquence* into a defense of good taste. Good taste must not be
dismissed as shallow: the ages of good taste, those of Pericles,
Augustus, Leo X, and Louis XIV always follow upon the ages of
great original poets, those of Homer, Dante, Shakespeare. But we
must not be blind to the greatness of both the original and the
"tasteful" poets; we must enter into the condition under which
they wrote, and must be governed by the sentiments and opinions
at the origin of a work.[12] Müller even defends the unities (something unheard of in Germany at that time), though not of course
with the naturalistic arguments of the French neoclassical theorists; their talk about probability and "nature" seems to him all
nonsense. The French audience, on the contrary, did not care for
naturalness and even wanted art to stand out sharply. They put up
with exaggeration just as the Greeks put up with masks on the
stage. The real reason of the unities cannot be naturalistic. Rather,

> The French tragic stage is an unfolded rostrum, set up for
> this particular place, for this particular time, for this court,
> for this genuine popular assembly of talents which gathered
> during the century of Louis XIV. French tragedy . . . aims
> at a very definite effect . . . Racine has in front of his writing
> desk the portrait of his great monarch, and his whole train of
> heroes and beauties is present in his mind . . . he desires to
> please France and thinks of nothing else . . . *Britannicus*
> must appear in the costume of this French court; to retain
> the Roman costume would be tasteless, because the speaker
> would transgress his own bounds; to change the setting would
> be tasteless, because it would mean a pretense at naturalness
> which would destroy all the rest of the work and its character.
> The French tragic stage requires in the tone of all the actors
> a kind of chant which is common to them all: one wants to
> be reminded that there is really only one speaker, the poet,
> the rhetorical poet. If every actor spoke in his own tone and
> rhythm, it would be just as tasteless as if an orator wanted to
> change his voice to imitate his opponent when he introduces

him in a speech. French tragedy will not tolerate death on the stage, just as likewise the rhetorical action must not be interrupted by any show, by any spectacle at all, by any superfluous stage properties.[13]

Taste thus is the ability to act, speak, and live according to the aim, the circumstances, the proprieties, in brief, the conditions which the society imposes. It means avoiding excess, supplementing what is deficient; in a word, taste means justice.[14]

Müller could make such a defense of French tragedy and taste because he had an unusual sense of the place of literature in society. He conceived of the writer (at any rate, one type of writer) as a man acting on society, as an orator, and even as a politician in a high sense. He himself was an orator and politician and admired the great orators of history, especially Edmund Burke, with whose ideas he felt in complete sympathy.

Just as he sees the writer as acting on society, so also does he see the crippling influence of society on the writer. He comments on the limitations of a burgher poet such as Hans Sachs,[15] recognizing that "political, economic, and poetic existence condition each other." The poet cannot be indifferent to the social condition of his country. German literature suffers from its bookishness; its learned writings are not addressed to a specific public, and its poets sing for themselves in complete isolation. As a remedy, Müller recommends reading aloud, recitation, oratory, and drama, which is the social art *par excellence*. Thus Müller, unlike the two Schlegels, is appreciative of Schiller, in whom he sees an orator *manqué*. This is not blame but praise: Schiller was a man of sound political and social instincts, for which, in the Germany of his time, he could find no other expression than the drama.

Drama itself could and should be made more social by appealing more directly to the audience. Müller therefore commends the breaks in dramatic illusion, the attempts to draw the spectator into the action. He accepts the address to the audience (such as Harpagon's at the end of Molière's *L'Avare*), the Greek chorus, the Shakespearean fool, and even the complete abolishment of the barrier between stage and audience in Tieck's romantic comedies. Drama should return to its original form and become a community celebration, not remain merely a pageant or a poor mirror of manners.[16] Following Friedrich Schlegel, Müller is a great admirer of Aristophanes' irony, which he likewise interprets as a "manifestation of the freedom of the artist." [17]

More surprising and most unusual for that time is Müller's appreciation of even the low comic and blasphemous scenes in the medieval mysteries of Christ's passion. Müller approves of them because he recognizes that they do not scoff at religion itself (as Voltaire does) but at man's inadequate, unworthy faith.[18] Similarly, Socrates and Euripides could see themselves parodied on the stage and could laugh with the audience, because a God presided over the stage. Müller admires Holberg and Gozzi and recommends the devices of Italian comedy, improvisation and the masks, which are in effect social. They create the close contact between poet, actor, and public. The masks remind us of yesterday's performance. Pantalon, Brigella, Tartaglia, and Truffaldino accumulate, as it were, a "capital of pleasure" on which they can draw.[19] Clearly, here is the source of Müller's unusual appreciation of Viennese folk comedy, of Casperl, Tadädl, Tinterl.[20]

Comedy cannot be too contemporaneous or too topical, for comedy without a true society is impossible. Indeed, a history of comedy would stress those periods when true political life was astir.[21] In a true society Harlequin would be as much at home among the spectators as on the stage. A speaker from the audience might take part. There might even come a time when the curtain would rise in order not only for the audience to see the actor but also for the actor to see the audience.[22] Only very recently, "expressionist" dramas have fulfilled Müller's ideal of such a cooperation between audience and stage.

There are other motifs in Müller's drama criticism which are of considerable interest, though we may have misgivings about the truth of his views. Müller, like the later Friedrich Schlegel, formulates very sharply the difference between ancient and modern literature in terms of the superiority of Christianity over Paganism. In this matter Müller belongs to German anti-Hellenism, which was not simply "modern" in an 18th-century sense but was anti-Hellenic out of Christian fervor. Müller hoped for a more religious stage than the Greeks could accomplish.[23] Greek tragedy remained for him a tragedy of fate: the crushing idea of fate is inexorable; the ancients teach us to despise death, not to overcome it.[24] But unlike the Schlegels and Schelling, Müller, though a convert to Catholicism, sees the serious limitations of Calderón, whom his fellow romanticists exalted as the great Christian tragedian. Calderón is allegorical, musical, picturesque—and is thus not comparable to the truly dramatic Shakespeare.

The extended discussion of Shakespeare (which, we must remember, preceded the *Dramatic Lectures* of August Wilhelm Schlegel) is, however, disappointing in that it lacks a unified conception beyond the usual stress on Shakespeare's creativity. It does contain many interesting and, I believe, original remarks: *Midsummer Night's Dream* is discussed in terms of a figure dance, and the analysis of *Hamlet,* though still romantic in its conception of Hamlet's character, points to what Müller calls the "mirror scenes," [25] such as the presentation of the play within the play and the scene at Ophelia's grave, which mirror for Hamlet the effect on him of his father's murder or his own murder of Polonius on other children.

Strangely enough, Müller finds his conception of religious tragedy best exemplified in Goethe's *Egmont* and *Tasso.* In them quiet submission to fate is at the end rewarded by a vision of "eternal freedom." Müller considers what he calls the motif of the "ascension" necessary to Christian tragedy.[26] He also had hopes for the future: his friend, Heinrich von Kleist fulfilled the promise of a new German-Christian tragedy. Kleist's *Amphitryo* (for which Müller wrote an enthusiastic preface) accomplishes a successful union of the classical and the Christian. Furthermore, Müller holds out hope for a rebirth of a true Christian eloquence, which he extolls above French conversation and English parliamentary oratory as the art of the future. In these passages we hear the voice of the anti-Napoleonic Restoration, the new European Conservatism. It is the side of Müller which is of only historical interest today. It has obscured what seems to me the extraordinary merit of his insights into the social art of the drama and into the living tradition of rhetorical "Latin" poetry.

KARL WILHELM FERDINAND SOLGER (1780–1819) appears at first
sight another aesthetician in the wake of Schelling, somewhere on
the way to Hegel. Solger criticized Schelling severely for what he
considered his false abstract idealism and his setting aside a separate realm for beauty of which all individual beauty is only a
reflection.[1] But such a criticism of Schelling is justified only in
regard to one stage of his development, the neo-Platonic passages
in *Bruno* (1802); furthermore Solger himself frequently lapses into
a mystical worship of supernatural beauty. But Solger's central
argument is that the beautiful is only in its concrete appearance,
in its separateness, limitation, and presence, that art is our immediate, real existence, known and experienced in its essentiality.[2]
From his deep sense of the contradictions of existence Solger drew
the bold conclusion that irony is the principle of all art and from
that was able to give a novel interpretation of tragedy, which he
buttressed with considerable practical criticism, mainly of ancient
tragedy and Shakespeare and Calderón.

The central position in art given to irony is itself so striking
an idea that Solger deserves resurrection today, when "irony,"
though in a different sense, has again been exalted to a central
position in a theory of poetry. But the difficulties of expounding
Solger's position are unfortunately very great, for his main work,
Erwin (1815), is a series of Platonic dialogues so awkwardly, pre-
ciously, and obscurely composed that few works even of German
philosophical thought can compare with it in denseness and in-
communicability. Of the four interlocutors, Adalbert speaks with
the voice of Solger, Anselm with that of Schelling, Bernhard with
that of Fichte, and Erwin appears as the learner and interrogator.
But the dialogue form, complete with fictional framework, an
allegorical vision, and much polite banter, though modeled on

Plato and on Schelling's *Bruno,* suits Solger badly and aggravates the faults of his groping mind and lumbering sprawling exposition. Fortunately the *Vorlesungen über Aesthetik,*[3] though lecture notes taken by a pupil and thus not completely authentic, help considerably to clarify Solger's position, and much besides can be learned from his minor writings, from the introduction to his translation of Sophocles (1808), from the very elaborate and extensive review of A. W. Schlegel's *Lectures on Dramatic Art and Literature* (1819), and from the correspondence, especially with Ludwig Tieck.[4]

We need not enter into a technical discussion of Solger's general aesthetics. For our purposes it is sufficient to know that the beautiful (and Solger, like Schelling, does not recognize beauty outside of art) is a union of the general and the particular, of concept and appearance, essence (*Wesen*) and reality. All art is hence "symbolical," another term for defining this union. "The symbol is the existence of the Idea itself. It is really what it signifies. It is the Idea in its immediate reality. The symbol is thus always true in itself: not a mere copy of something true." [5] What is said here of beauty and art has its parallel in the activity of the artist. The artist's imagination acts to fuse the unity of the Idea of beauty with the contradictions of reality.[6] Imagination (*Phantasie*) is distinguished in Solger, as in Schelling, from fancy (*Einbildungskraft*); the latter belongs to ordinary cognition and is nothing but human awareness, while artistic imagination is an analogue of divine creation in which act and achievement are one and the same. At times, especially in *Erwin,* this affinity between divine and artistic creation is assumed to be an almost complete identity and is made the occasion for the most extravagant glorification of the artist as prophet and creator. In Solger's more sober moods, imagination merely means creation in the sense that will and execution are one in art. A mere plan, a mere intention can never make a work of art; the work of art is activity itself. Only through the work of art does the artist learn what he had willed by his activity.[7] Croce and Collingwood would be content with this complete identification of art with the inner imaginative act.

The central position of irony follows from this concept of the imagination. The term irony occurs for the first time prominently toward the end of *Erwin* [8] as the name for our sense of the transitoriness or, as Solger often says, the "nothingness" of this momentary unity of universal and particular, essence and reality, which differs from divine creation by being aesthetic illusion. Irony, Solger expressly says, has nothing to do with cynicism, as he finds it in Lucian and his modern imitators (he mentions Wieland).[9] It is not irresponsible subjectivity or mere playful superiority, though Solger approves the breaking of illusion as one of the devices of dramatic art and enjoyed the romantic comedies of his friend Tieck.[10] Solger's irony is the irony of Sophocles and Shakespeare: it is the highest objectivity of the artist, and the reconciliation of opposites,[11] of the conscious and the unconscious, of "wit" and "contemplation."[12] Solger can thus speak of irony as the "essential center of art" and accept the statement of one of the interlocutors of his dialogue that he "dissolves the nature of art into irony."[13] In the *Lectures* we are told several times that "without irony there is no art,"[14] that irony constitutes the "nature of art, its innermost meaning."[15] It is not an individual, contingent mood of the artist but the innermost vital germ of all art.[16] Irony means the artist's consciousness that his work is symbol, that he is aware of the Divine and at the same time aware of our own nothingness.[17]

These general statements are considerably clarified in Solger's practical criticism and polemics. His review of August Wilhelm Schlegel's *Lectures on Dramatic Art* (1819) is especially illuminating. Solger was particularly dissatisfied with Schlegel's distinction between tragedy and comedy as a contrast between seriousness and mirth. There must be something common to both, and that, Solger says, is the "whole conflict between the imperfect in man and his higher destination," in other words the insight into the vanity of human affairs.[18] Irony is the mood in which these contradictions destroy themselves. What would dramatic poetry and theatrical representation be without irony? The bitterness of Aeschylus and the cruelty of Shakespeare would lacerate us if the irony did not raise us above everything. We would be disgusted by the naturalness of Aristophanes if it were merely a joke and did not bring us back to a pure feeling of innocence in the midst of the wildest sensuality.[19] Solger complains that Schlegel mentions irony only once and that he forbids its interference with the tragic. With genuine irony the opposite holds true: "it begins with the contemplation of the world's fate in the large."[20] It is thus at the center of tragedy and comedy in Shakespeare as well as in Sophocles *and* Aristophanes.

Solger's criticism of August Wilhelm Schlegel is directed against his neglect of irony and against his whole theory of the drama, which to Solger appears superficial and not properly philosophical. This is, however, not a convincing criticism of Friedrich's concept of irony, despite Solger's attempt on other occasions to distinguish his own irony from the buffoonery, mere subjectivism, and irresponsible cynicism which he attributed to Friedrich Schlegel's concept. Solger ignores the "objective" side of Friedrich's theory, though this is actually the source of his own conception. Hegel sided with Solger [21] and thus exaggerated the gulf between Friedrich Schlegel, whom he despised, and Solger, whom he admired. To Hegel romantic irony, as derived from Friedrich Schlegel, is mere frivolity, mere "probabilism" (he always thought of Friedrich Schlegel's conversion as opportunistic), while Solger's irony is to him "mysticism," seeing things *sub specie aeternitatis.* Kierkegaard, in his dissertation on irony (1844), shares Hegel's view and calls Solger's irony a "kind of contemplative prayer." [22] But both Hegel and Kierkegaard put too much weight on certain passages in Solger which lend support to this mystical interpretation. They ignore the fact that Solger takes his view of the reconciliation of opposites in art seriously and sees irony both in tragedy and comedy. It is not one mode but the union and reconciliation of modes.

This becomes obvious when we examine Solger's discussion of the history and main types of drama. Reviewing the Greek concept of tragedy, Solger rejects Schiller's concept of tragedy as the revolt of man's freedom against necessity. According to Solger, tragedy requires the death of the individual in order that the species may flourish in the reflection of eternal laws. [23] In *Antigone* the eternal power of sacred custom triumphs over the harsh verdict of purely human origin. Both sides, Antigone and Creon, together expiate the irreconcilable break between the Eternal and the Temporal. [24] In analyzing Oedipus Solger stresses *Oedipus at Colonus.* Oedipus, whom the hand of fate has stricken, has become a consecrated person: he is transfigured and dies a blessed death. [25] Tragedy thus is not pity for the hero, nor is it the spectacle of man's physical defeat and moral triumph. It is not true that Oedipus spiritually revolts against the cruel power of fate. Rather, Sopho-

cles crowns him "as a martyr of sacred laws" and glorifies his very
perdition.[26] Greek tragedy is thus the "truest representation of the
species as the first born and of the individual as the second." [27]
Solger anticipates Hegel's theory of tragedy as well as that of
Hebbel, who voiced his agreement with Solger,[28] though both
Hegel and Hebbel formulate the tragic conflict in more purely
ethical and even social and political terms.

With regard to comedy Solger rejects Schlegel's interpretation
of Aristophanes, as well as his stress on the comic ideal as purely
sensual and on the rule of chance and caprice in ancient comedy.
He tries to show, rather, that it cannot be mere caprice or anarchy, but that a higher order, a fantastic world order comprehended only by irony must be recognizable.[29] Also, the later Greek
comedy and modern comedy (such as Molière's) is defended against
Schlegel's antirealistic prejudice: the real must be presented in its
fullness and its contradictions, the whole meaning of life in its in-
tricacies and their resolutions.[30]

Modern drama is discussed with reference to Shakespeare, and
Solger elaborates the common contrast, derived from Schlegel, between the Greek tragedy of fate and the modern tragedy of character. But unlike Schlegel, Solger does not see in Shakespeare's
dramas a new neutral form of the *Schauspiel,* a mixture of comic
and tragic, but recognizes that Shakespeare's plays are easily divis-
ible into two genres, comedy and tragedy, which are related as
essence is to appearance. In comedy Shakespeare plays with illusion and leads us from the trivial to the deeper and more significant. Solger attempts to grade Shakespeare's comedies according
to his theory, with some strange results. *Measure for Measure* appears among the light comedies; *Love's Labour's Lost* is put, together with *Midsummer Night's Dream,* in the highest place.[31] The
role of the comic, the importance of the fools and buffoons in the
historical plays and tragedies, is then defended by means of the
theory of opposites, of the real and illusion. Hamlet, Solger comments, needs no fool around, for he has the fool in himself; he
parodies and mirrors himself.[32] Fortinbras is necessary in that he
opens the concluding vista into a new life, as is the ironical reconciliation between the families at the end of *Romeo and Juliet.*

Calderón, glorified by Schelling as the model of romantic religious tragedy, is viewed much more critically.[33] His mythology is

abstract; he is basically an allegorical and conventional writer, for whom everything is settled beforehand; his world order of love, honor, and religion is mere subject matter. Solger, the Protestant, protests against the imitation of Calderón, which can be only external and empty.

The Germans are treated very severely throughout Solger's criticism. He defends Lessing's plays as genuine and German, but dismisses *Nathan the Wise* as preachment. He praises Goethe's *Tasso* and *Faust* but remarks that the mental state of Faust which drives him through spiritual insatiability to magic and to the compact with the devil has little connection with the specific action, that is, the affair with Gretchen.[34] Schiller, though highly admired as a person, is severely criticized for his idealized abstract plays. *Wilhelm Tell* seems to him one of the weakest because of the confusing and skeptical view of the hero's deed.[35] Solger, however, praises Tieck consistently, especially *Blaubart* and *Der gestiefelte Kater,* and recognizes the greatness of Heinrich von Kleist.[36] This praise contrasts oddly with the contempt Solger conceived for Grillparzer: *Die Ahnfrau* is "trash" and *Sappho* is a vulgar and absurd love romance.[37]

It is not easy to pin down Solger's critical position. His sympathies and admiration are focused on Sophocles and Shakespeare. His interest in his contemporaries is limited (Tieck chides him for his coolness to Novalis).[38] Solger thus is hardly a romanticist in the ordinary sense. He seems to have no interest in the lyric or the novel, except for Goethe's *Elective Affinities,* which he praised very much according to the terms of his theory of tragic drama.[39] Rather, with his philosophy of irony, his dialectical union of opposites, his emphasis on the concrete presence of beauty, his tragedy of reconciliation, he belongs to the group of critics who favor a fundamentally symbolic view of art as imagination.

SCHLEIERMACHER

Friedrich Schleiermacher (1768–1834), the most important Lutheran theologian of the century, the German translator and interpreter of Plato, was almost unknown as an aesthetician before Croce rediscovered his system and described it in laudatory terms in his *Estetica* (1901). Schleiermacher had lectured on aesthetics first in 1819, then in 1825, and again in 1832–33. The last lecture course was published from student transcripts in 1842 but attracted mainly hostile notices from Hegelian and Herbartian historians of aesthetics.[1] In 1931 Rudolf Odebrecht published the notes for the earlier courses and analyzed them thoroughly, arguing that they represent a version far superior to the later lectures.[2] One should indeed recognize that the 1842 edition is an extremely diffuse, repetitious compilation. Nevertheless, it represents, contrary to Odebrecht's opinion, a somewhat more mature stage of Schleiermacher's thinking. The changes between 1819 and 1832–33 seem to me, in any case, not really fundamental. I shall use both versions almost indiscriminately.

Schleiermacher's aesthetics differs radically from the systems of his contemporaries. Its antecedents are to be found in the ideas of Baumgarten (a follower of Baumgarten, Johann August Eberhard was Schleiermacher's teacher), and Herder rather than of Kant and Schiller or of his great rivals, Schelling and Hegel. It is true that Schleiermacher, in his early years, was a close friend of Friedrich Schlegel and Novalis: he contributed to the *Athenaeum,* defended in *Vertraute Briefe* (1800) Schlegel's novel, *Lucinde,* against the charge of obscenity, and in his *Reden über die Religion* expounded a highly emotional and aesthetic version of religion which he called *Kunstreligion.*[3] But in his later lectures on aesthetics when Schleiermacher is elaborating a system of ethics, dialectics, and metaphysics, few traces are left of his associations with the romantic circle. He now definitely rejects the view that art is a way to the Absolute, that it has any metaphysical function or pretension. The arts of acting and dancing, rather than the art of poetry, form the starting-point of aesthetics. Art, with Schleiermacher, is "self-awareness," self-expression.[4] The act of creation is expression, self-manifestation, a definition and externalization of feeling. Art is approached purely from the side of the artist, through his mental process. The work of art as an object and the effect on its audience is minimized, or rather considered as a mere consequence of the crucial act of free expression. The act of composition in words or stone or paints or sounds is an act of communication which is morally and socially demanded of the artist but is not the geninue work of art itself. There are many more acts of art than works of art. With a slightly different emphasis

Schleiermacher can say, "The inner image is the work of art proper." [5]

We shall be misled, however, if we interpret a phrase like the last to mean that Schleiermacher stresses a Platonic "inner vision" of the artist. He uses the word "image" only in the context of poetry and painting. Art in general he calls "self-awareness," even "feeling," "mood." [6] This self-awareness is a consciousness without object or concept. Art is thus not imitation of nature or intellectual knowledge. Art does not represent external beauty or even create beauty. Artistic self-awareness is rather a purely individual, subjective, intuitive cognition, which has nothing to do with pleasure or pain, and which becomes organized, perfected precisely in the process of definition. Art is thus a constant activity, related to day dreaming, "a dark background, from which emerges clearly only what drove the artist to external production." [7] The term "feeling" must not be interpreted to mean any immediate overflow of feeling or any revery as such. That is not enough for art. Rather the element of "collection," the overcoming of the moment of excitement, is decisive. Self-awareness is really identical with "productive imagination," which Schleiermacher distinguishes sharply from the common associative imagination, related to memory. [8]

From this point of view Schleiermacher can dismiss many ancient problems of aesthetics. He never speculates about genius, for all men are artists, in his sense, though in different degree; he does not argue about taste except to say that it is the obverse of self-awareness, a rudimentary productivity. [9] Nor does he need to speculate about a specific audience for art. "An artist," he says, "would not be content to produce the same experience in all people. The full measure of a work of art can be achieved only in infinite modifications of effects. The effect cannot even be an object of the artist's consideration." [10] There is no hierarchy of subject matters, no hierarchy of the arts or genres. "Each work of art must be looked at absolutely in itself, must have its absolute value." [11] By putting everything into the interior act of the artist Schleiermacher must also minimize the distinctions between the arts. They are actually one, as there is one "Kunstsinn." He takes up motifs of romantic speculation when he alludes to the unity of the senses, traces the transitions between the arts, and hopes for an ultimate union of them all.[12]

Schleiermacher has considerable trouble with the finished work of art, the diverse worlds of the different arts, and the social effect of art. Unlike Croce, he lacks the complete courage of his convictions to deny the whole problem of the classification of the arts or to solve the question of "externalization" by boldly declaring that intuition and expression are identical. At times he may approach such an identification. He will say that "the original work of art is the purely interior one, and the putting-forth into appearance is a second act," but on the other hand, he recognizes that these two stages may be indistinguishable, that the poet "within himself, can produce only in the form of language." [13] He even suggests that this identity of internal conception and language may be used as a standard of wholeness and thus of value. The perfect poem will be produced at one stroke.[14] Yet he considers this situation to be peculiar to one art—namely poetry—while in the plastic arts the distinction between conception and execution seems to him insuperable.

Usually he labors somewhat to distinguish and describe the different stages of the act of production—mood, free play of imagination, "original image," elaboration [15]—and tries to classify the arts, after all, even though he always admits ultimate defeat. Schleiermacher proves his intellectual integrity when he frankly recognizes the difficulties with which his theory is confronted and sees that he cannot overcome them within his scheme.

This seems particularly true of his discussion of poetry. Poetry is defined as "free productivity in language." [16] The relation to reality is minimized: historical truth and descriptive accuracy are inessential. But Schleiermacher in his time could hardly think of developing a theory of poetry as mere dreaming or nonsense words or music. He has to recognize a "direction toward truth," though this cannot, of course, be the truth of science. He solves the problem by breaking language into two functions: its musical sound and its logical meaning. Poetry is, first of all, sound, a "totality of euphony" which Schleiermacher conceives, on the analogy of music, as expressing the stream of self-awareness, the "inner changeability of being," the "pure subjectivity of the inner mood." [17] At the same time poetry utilizes the meaning of language by forcing language, which is always general, to represent the individual. The poet evokes an individualized, completely single, definite image. Poetry is thus double: it is plastic, representing the "pure objectivity of the image," and it is musical, representing the inner mood.[18] This dichotomy serves to buttress the old genre distinctions: the lyric is musical, the epic and drama plastic. Drama is poetry in combination with the art of acting, epic tends toward sculpture, the lyric toward music. Schleiermacher recognizes that in his day these historical distinctions were being blurred—there is closet drama, lyric without music, unsculpturesque epic. But he does not mind the blurring. "We cannot expect strict distinctions in art any more than in anything else alive." [19]

In his detailed discussion of the forms and functions of poetry he deviates more and more from his basic theory and is compelled to introduce ideas alien to his basic assumptions. Faced with the obligation of producing a poetics, he becomes dependent on current theories hardly related to his personal insights. Thus he makes much of "types" in poetry, and most surprisingly he embraces a highly nationalistic view of art. In part this relates to a recognition that every language has its own metrical system.[20] But he will go so far as to say, "Only fellow countrymen understand each other with immediate vivacity." [21] He draws a distinction between social and religious art. On the one hand he makes a spirited defense of erotic poetry (which he distinguishes from obscene writing),[22] and on the other he reintroduces the religious role of art which can overcome national boundaries and fulfill a moral function. He can define the use of art in good classical terms. "Art must effect the purification of the passions." [23]

In his poetics he thus struggles with many heterogeneous ideas, not always successfully. His greatest contribution to concrete literary study was in the science of interpretation, in "hermeneutics," where, together with Friedrich Schlegel, he was one of the first theorists. His hermeneutic speculations parallel and illustrate his aesthetics and are a concrete exemplification of the same approach and its difficulties. Schleiermacher argues that interpretation is not the exclusive prerogative of classical philology or biblical studies or even literary studies in general, but that it applies to all acts of human expression, even conversation.[24] Just as in his aesthetics Schleiermacher minimizes the act of communication, so here in hermeneutics he dismisses the distinction between "understanding" and "interpretation." They differ only as inner speech from speaking aloud.[25] The main emphasis falls on feeling, intuition, "divination," as he calls it, of the mind of the author or speaker.[26]

Schleiermacher conceives this "divination" mainly as an immediate grasp of the whole, but he also first clearly described what has been since called the circle of understanding. "The detail can be understood only by the whole, and any explanation of detail presupposes the understanding of the whole." [27] The relation between work and creator, between meditation and composition, must be understood by such a circle. It is not "vicious" at all but basic to all understanding of human expression.[28] Besides this "divinatory" procedure, Schleiermacher recognizes the "comparative" method, which studies a text in the light of the other works of an author and of the literary tradition. However contradictory this may seem to Schleiermacher's emphasis on individual feeling, in practice he had a strong sense for what he calls the "morphology" of genres, the shaping influence of conventions and patterns.[29] But even the comparative method is ultimately reduced to some irrational intuition, to a feeling, an insight, which like every individual thing is indescribable, "ineffable."

Schleiermacher's theories of interpretation deeply influenced those of Boeckh and Dilthey, who built them into elaborate structures of methodological speculation. But as an aesthetician Schleiermacher remained without influence. His system tries to assimilate too many contradictory strains of thought to recommend itself. Yet even today it ought to command attention. Schleiermacher was apparently the first to attempt, with any speculative power, an aesthetics of feeling, of the creative act, of expression. In a sense Schleiermacher is *the* aesthetician of romantic expressionism.

SCHOPENHAUER

The philosophical system of Arthur Schopenhauer (1788–1860) was published in 1819 with the title *The World as Will and Idea*, but the book was little reviewed and hardly read until the 50's and 60's. Only then did Schopenhauer's fame and influence spread rapidly. In the meantime a second, supplementary volume of *The World as Will and Idea* (1844) and a collection of shorter pieces, *Parerga and Paralipomena* (1851), had elaborated, though hardly changed, the original insights of the young man. In a history of literary theory, in spite of the delayed effect, Schopenhauer definitely belongs to the early decades of the 19th century. His furious attacks on Fichte, Schelling, and Hegel as "windbags" and "charlatans" should not obscure the fact that his aesthetics is actually quite similar to Schelling's. Schopenhauer, on occasion, showed a little indulgence to Schelling, though he could dismiss his theory of tragedy as "completely confused drivel." [1] But one need not assume much direct influence, since many similarities between Schelling and Schopenhauer are easily explainable by their common derivation from Kant and Plato.

Schopenhauer's aesthetics is a part of his metaphysics and thus not really comprehensible without it. For our purposes it will be sufficient to remind ourselves that Schopenhauer asserts the essence of the world, "the thing-in-itself," to be Will, and that this Will "objectifies itself" in the world of appearance or idea, in stages leading from the inorganic world of matter to man. There is no God and Will is evil and can be overcome only by a revolt, a reversal of the Will, a recognition of the abyss, its negation through complete identification with others in pity and asceticism. Art is a second, inferior (because less permanent) way of negating the Will. In contemplating the world and thus recognizing its nature, the artist gives us a means of escaping the treadmill of the Will. Schopenhauer's ordinarily sober language becomes charged with emotion when he describes this blessed release through art. "It is the painless state which Epicurus prized as the highest good and as the state of the gods; for we are for the moment set free from the miserable striving of the will; we keep the Sabbath of the penal servitude of willing; the wheel of Ixion stands still." [2] Beauty thus is, as in Kant, completely disinterested contemplation. Everything that appeals to our practical interests must be eliminated from art, not only still-life paintings, arousing our appetite, or lascivious nakedness in pictures, but also everything subjective and *any* appeal to mere plot or intrigue. Schopenhauer thus has difficulty with the subjective lyric and with action in drama and epic. He draws up an ascending scale of the genres of poetry: song, ballad, idyll, novel, epic, and drama, with the drama as the most objective kind at the top.[3] He distinguishes between poets of the first rank, such as Shakespeare and Goethe, who are objective, are "ventriloquists" of their characters,[4] and poets of the second rank, like Byron, who speak only of themselves even through the mouth of fictional figures.

Still, Schopenhauer tries to make allowances for the subjective lyric and the "interesting" novel or drama. The lyrical poet must be a universal man, not merely an individual. There is a sharp distinction between the author, the "representer," and what is "represented." [5] Moreover, song is not simply the expression of either joy or sorrow: the genuine poet becomes simultaneously aware of himself as "the subject of pure will-less knowing, whose unshakable blissful peace contrasts with the stress of the will, which is always limited and always needy. The feeling of this contrast, this alternation, is expressed in a song and constitutes the lyrical state of mind." [6] Schopenhauer makes an effort to document this double point of view by analyzing some of Goethe's lyrics and referring to some German folk songs. Thus in the lyric the "miracle of an identity of the subject of knowing and willing" is achieved, or in popular language, the head and heart are reconciled. But Schopenhauer does not quite recognize the consequence of the abolition of his basic dualism in the lyric. The lyric remains for him a rudimentary form of poetry, because he prefers the more explicit, more intellectual art of the novel and drama.

A somewhat later paper, "On the Interesting" (1821, published posthumously in 1864) [7] introduces some recognition of the appeal of plot in epic and drama. But it is definitely relegated to an inferior position, inasmuch as a concatenation of events is subject to the law of sufficient reason (the laws of causality, time, and space), while genuine art must take us beyond ordinary reality into the realm of ideas. The greatest works of literature, says Schopenhauer, are not "interesting": even Shakespeare's plays excite little interest by their plots and therefore do not appeal to the big crowd.[8] In the greatest novels, *Don Quixote, Tristram Shandy, La Nouvelle Héloïse, Wilhelm Meister,* there is little plot. But Schopenhauer admits that there is plot interest in some good works: in Schiller's plays, in Sophocles' *Oedipus Rex,* in Ariosto, and in Sir Walter Scott. He admits that the interesting is compatible with the beautiful and even necessary in dramatic and narrative works as a kind of cement or binder. In long works technique and routine must fill the gaps between moments of inspiration. Like Poe, Schopenhauer thinks that there is inevitably something insipid and boring in long works such as *Paradise Lost* or the *Aeneid*.[9] He concludes that the interesting, as a necessary property of the action, is the matter, while the beautiful is the form. The form needs the matter to become visible.[10]

This emphasis on complete disinterestedness and objectivity in art is combined in Schopenhauer with a theory of Ideas, which also develops, in a Platonic manner, Kantian suggestions about the eternal ideas in art. Art "repeats the eternal Ideas grasped through pure contemplation, the essential and abiding in all the phenomena of the world." [11] These Ideas are not, of course, general concepts but are the essences of things. In art they are intuited, perceived, and not merely thought about. On many points Schopenhauer tries to guard against an intellectualistic misinterpretation of his theory. The Idea, he emphasizes over and over again, is intuitive and not conceptual: although representing an infinite number of particular things, it is nevertheless thoroughly determined. It is never known by an individual as such, but only by one who has risen above all willing and individuality to become a pure subject of knowing.[12] Concept is thus "eternally barren" in art and Schopenhauer is most emphatic in condemning allegory and symbol (in the sense of conventional sign) in the plastic arts. Still, he makes the interesting attempt to defend allegory in poetry. There, he argues, the concept is the material, the immediately given, and the task of the poet is to elicit the concrete, the visual from language which is made up of universals. The poet must combine the concepts, given by language, in such a way that their spheres intersect each other and that none of them remains within their abstract quality. Poetry is thus an art of precipitating the concrete and the individual from the general.[13]

Schopenhauer describes the means and devices to this end: epithets, metaphors, similes, parables, allegories. Works of a pervasive allegorical character, *Don Quixote, Gulliver's Travels,* and Gracián's *Criticón* are highly praised.[14] Rhythm and rhyme are considered also devices of concretization. Schopenhauer prefers rhythm to rhyme because rhythm is in time alone and thus according to Kantian epistemology belongs to "pure sensibility," while rhyme appeals to the ear and thus to a merely empirical sense.[15] While this distinction seems hardly tenable, the effect of rhyme is clearly explained: it serves as a binder, it strongly induces agreement, and it suggests that the idea expressed by the poet is, so to speak, predestined, preformed in the language and thus true.[16] Sound in poetry is generally important in that it suggests that poetic language is not merely a sign of something signified, in a one-to-one relation to an object as in ordinary language, but that it is there for its own sake.[17] Thus Schopenhauer argues that poetry is untranslatable.[18] Unfortunately, these fine suggestions, which show a considerable analytical grasp of the nature of poetry, are not followed up.

However, it is no contradiction to Schopenhauer's concept of poetry when, in his most famous pronouncements on writing and style, those of the second volume of the *Parerga,* he recommends an unadorned, simple, clear style in the manner of the 18th century. Schopenhauer can do so because he distinguishes sharply between rhetoric, which seeks to achieve practical ends or expound concepts, and genuine poetry. Poetry as the disinterested contemplation of Ideas is quite remote from rhetoric: "the less rhetorical, the better the poetry." [19] Hence Schopenhauer violently disapproves of French tragedy and prefers Goethe to the rhetorical Schiller.[20] He can analyze the devices of poetry which remove it from ordinary language and can still appeal to intellectualist and rhetorical standards in judging expository prose. Schopenhauer himself represents the paradox of holding and expounding a highly mystical philosophy with the clarity and simplicity of an 18th-century French moralist, of combining in his teaching an ultimate "o altitudo" with the toughness of a worldly-wise Stoic or even Cynic. So also in his theory of literature he can fully recognize the role of rhythm, rhyme, metaphor, and allegory in poetry, and at the same time recommend a purely intellectual ideal of prose. Schopenhauer found striking formulas against incomprehensibility, vagueness, and looseness, and for simplicity, clarity, and compactness in style. "The Unintelligible is related to the Unintelligent," "the first rule of style is to have something to say," "use ordinary words and say extraordinary things," "the leading principle of stylistics should be that one can think of only one idea at a time," etc.[21] The style of German philosophy and scholarship is Schopenhauer's main target: he condemns their endless, formless sentences, their love for parentheses, which he considers as impolite as an interruption of a conversation, their indistinct, ambiguous, "squinting" expressions. Schopenhauer wrote as he wanted others to write, but he knew that he was not writing poetry, since otherwise he could not have constantly recommended the necessity of planning, of forethought, of conscious awareness, and of regard for the reader, with whom the author is to carry on a dialogue. The famous distinction between the three classes of writers, those who write without thinking, those who think while writing, and those who have thought before writing, is only applicable to prose.[22]

In genuine imaginative art genius decides, and genius, according to Schopenhauer, is inspired, unconscious, even instinctive. Genius is related to madness, as Schopenhauer tries to show with detailed psychiatric knowledge. Poets are dreamers and children or, at least, young men.[23] Schopenhauer can say that we are all perfect poets when dreaming, that the *Divine Comedy* has the truth of dreams,[24] and that the poetic gift is confined to the time of youth.[25] Genius, of course, is always an exception: a lone wanderer to eternity, misunderstood, ignored and maligned by his contemporaries, rewarded at most by posthumous fame. Schopenhauer displays, more so than almost any writer, an overbearing self-conceit, an entire trust in his own immortality, yet also, one should admit, an admirable intellectual independence and sturdy honesty. His character has some kinship with that of Dr. Johnson, whom he read but disparaged for his "stupid and brute-headed bigotry." [26] Knowing the enmity of the world to the artist, Schopenhauer proposes a "tragic literary history," [27] yet despises ordinary literary history as a mere "catalogue of stillbirths." [28] Great men stand out as giants in lonely isolation. History shows no progress, no real moral change. There is no progress in art, for "art is everywhere at its goal." [29]

In spite of all the safeguards against intellectualism one cannot help concluding, however, that the vision of the artist is for Schopenhauer the same as that of the philosopher, and the conclusion seems inevitable that the artist is only an inferior (because partial) philosopher. Art is distinguished from philosophical vision only

by one very insufficient criterion which conceals the whole problem of aesthetics: accessibility, facility. "The work of art," says
Schopenhauer, "is only a means of facilitating [intuitive] knowledge." "We are most easily put into the state of pure will-less contemplation when the objects come to meet it, i.e. when by their
manifold and yet distinct and definite shape they easily become
representatives of their Ideas, in which beauty in an objective
sense consists." [30] But surely form is not sufficiently described by
such "facility" of apprehension. Nor is much achieved by drawing
a distinction between philosophy and poetry which is almost that
between the universal and the particular. Poetry, says Schopenhauer, wants us to be acquainted with the Ideas of being by means
of individuals and examples. Poetry is to philosophy as experience
is to science. [31] It is a quite special way of knowing, in that the poet
wants to know the "what" and not merely the "where, when, why,
and wherefore" of things which the scientist and the practical man
are after. [32] But how then does the poet differ from the philosopher,
who also asks for the "what"? Art is a cognition of Ideas and these
Ideas are still essences outside of time and space. [33] It remains unclear how there can be individual Ideas at all in his system, and
even a multitude of them, when the essence of the world is just one
Will. How can there be, one could ask, any object of knowledge without being in space and time? How can these Ideas
be "forms" at all, if they are out of space and time? In practice
Schopenhauer minimizes concreteness and individuality and ignores the process of artistic creation and the work of art as an
artifact. It is not surprising that with his theory he has to come to
the conclusion that everything is beautiful, [34] that there is really
no difference between the beautiful and the ugly, because everything has its essence, which the artist has to intuit. There is in
Schopenhauer no distinct realm of aesthetics and art, just as there
is no distinct aesthetic response and no theory of criticism, for
there cannot be approval and disapproval, only contemplation,
grasping of essences, insight into the nature of the world. Schopenhauer has to identify the beautiful with the "characteristic," a
term which Friedrich Schlegel had originally reserved for romantic
beauty, and even with the organic principle of a being. [35]

But in spite of these deceptively romantic terms and his insights
into devices for concreteness in poetry, Schopenhauer usually uses

beauty and the characteristic to mean the ideal, the typical, the general, in a good neoclassical sense, sometimes dangerously near to dreary idealization. Poetry, he says, leaves out all "disturbing contingencies," [36] and it deals only apparently with the particular, really with what exists everywhere and at all times. [37] Schopenhauer approves only of Greek architecture and condemns Gothic; he disapproves of romanticism, in which he sees only medievalism, obscurantism, and an absurd cult of women. [38] He condemns the overrating of the *Nibelungen* and is very cool to the German romantic school, though he has some good words for Zacharias Werner (whom he knew personally), for A. W. Schlegel (whose learning impressed him) and even for Heine, "a buffoon but a genius." [39] Like any good neoclassicist, Schopenhauer recommends strict observance of decorum. There must be no contradiction in fictional characters. [40] The supernatural in poetry is condemned completely, though a feeble apology for the ghost in *Hamlet* is attempted.* Works which are definitely fantastic, based on a suspension of the laws of nature, such as *Midsummer Night's Dream*, are considered second rate, as they show only the dream world and not real life. [41] That we are perfect poets in dreaming is forgotten. Like any neoclassicist, Schopenhauer disapproves of the mixture of the arts and genres. He did not like Richard Wagner, who was his great admirer, and lauded Rossini's operas, maintaining that they are pure sound and words don't matter in music. [42]

Still, there is something very distinctive in Schopenhauer's interpretation of tragedy. Tragedy teaches resignation: it affects us as a sedative of the will; it suggests the surrender not only of life but of the very will to life. [43] It is the genre which preaches Schopenhauer's own philosophy. There are three kinds of tragedies according to his scheme: those in which the catastrophe is due to the malice of a villain, those in which it is caused by some chance or error, and those in which it is caused merely by the situation, the relationship of the persons. The last is, of course, the highest kind. "It shows us the greatest misfortune as something not occasioned by rare circumstances or monstrous characters but arising easily and of itself out of the doings and characters of men." [44] By

* *Philosophische Vorlesungen*, Deussen, p. 335n. Schopenhauer thinks that communications from dying people are not out of nature. But what has this to do with Hamlet's ghost?

this highest kind of tragedy we are taught that life itself is a curse, that, as Calderón expressed in lines Schopenhauer loved to quote,

> Pues el delito mayor
> Del hombre es haber nacido.[45]

The demand of poetic justice is thus based on a complete misunderstanding of the nature of tragedy and even the nature of the world. Dr. Johnson is condemned for complaining about Shakespeare's disregard for poetic justice. His demand implies a "shallow, optimistic, Protestant-rationalist and peculiarly Jewish view of the world." [46]

When Schopenhauer returned to the discussion of tragedy in the second supplementary volume of *World as Will and Idea* (1844), he drew the consequences of his view more clearly. He made an apparent concession to the view of Schiller and Kant by associating tragedy, as they did, with the sublime. He recognized now that tragedy is not merely a depressing horrible spectacle of the "misery of mankind, the reign of chance and error, the fall of justice, the triumph of evil," which is to teach us negation of the will to life, as he again described it; it also demands a completely different existence, another world, which we can know only indirectly, by such a demand. Tragedy gives us "a peculiar feeling of elevation" by making us know "that the world, that life cannot truly satisfy us and is not worth our allegiance." [47]

In contradiction to his usual staunch classicism Schopenhauer recognizes that there is little resignation in Greek tragedy. Hippolytus dies resigned to fate and the will of the gods, but he has not given up the will to life itself. Thus Christian tragedy is nearer to Schopenhauer's ideal. Calderón's *Steadfast Prince* moved him deeply. Shakespeare he ranks far higher than Sophocles. Compared to Goethe's *Iphigenie* Euripides' play on the same theme seems to him almost crude and vulgar. The *Bacchae* is "a revolting concoction in favor of the heathen priests." *Antigone* and *Philoctetes* have repulsive, even disgusting, themes.[48]

If the highest tragedy is one in which the catastrophe is brought about without monsters, or chance, Schopenhauer should defend bourgeois tragedy, tragedy without villains and heroes. He argues against too noble characters. In Shakespeare, he says, though hardly correctly, there are only two completely noble characters: Cordelia and Coriolanus. Marquis Posa in Schiller's *Don Carlos* has more nobility, he observes mockingly, than can be found in Goethe's complete works. Schopenhauer considered Goethe's *Clavigo*, in this respect at least, as a model tragedy because, according to his interpretation, no single figure in it is completely bad or completely good. Corneille's *Cid* also is praised for such a balance.[49] But Schopenhauer's approval of bourgeois tragedy, which we could expect, is very reluctant because he misses what any good neoclassicist missed in it: the "height of fall" [50] which impresses us in the catastrophes of kings and princes. On the one hand Schopenhauer wants identification with the hero, "pity" in the sense of fellow suffering and not of commiseration, and recognizes that this is easiest to achieve when we feel that we could get into the same predicament; yet on the other hand he wants distance and idealization, and he objects to bourgeois tragedy because its catastrophies are not inevitable and could often have been prevented by some small (for instance, financial) assistance. Thus Schopenhauer should not be described as he often has been, as a defender of bourgeois drama.[51] His merit lies rather in the statement of a clear view of tragedy which contradicts that of most Germans before him. Tragedy to Schopenhauer is not a theodicy, as in Lessing and Schiller, but a revelation of the contradictions, the disorder in the world, of guiltless, unjust suffering. Yet in Schopenhauer the opposition to the optimism of the current theory of tragedy, his total rejection of any transfiguration and spiritual victory, has led again to a leveling of everything tragic. If the world is evil throughout, tragedy seems a somewhat superfluous and monotonous confirmation of an established fact.[52] Neither the optimistic defense of God's perfect order, in which Lessing saw the aim of tragedy, nor Schopenhauer's unrelieved gloom describes the nature of tragedy.

The existence of comedy must have been an embarrassment to Schopenhauer. He puts it down as an "incitement to a continued affirmation of the will to life." It tells us that life, on the whole, is good, and especially that it is always amusing. Schopenhauer adds sardonically: "certainly it must hasten to drop the curtain at the moment of joy, so that we may not see what comes after." [53]

But comedy is troublesome to him, as is the idyll, which he either ignores or simply declares to be impossible. Permanent happiness does not exist and thus cannot be the subject of art.[54]

The difficulties of Schopenhauer's position in aesthetics (as in metaphysics) seem unsurmountable. He is close to Kant, Schelling, and Goethe in his conviction that poetry is a disinterested knowledge of ideas. But on other crucial issues he differs from his contemporaries. He has little to say on imagination, which he recognizes as useful mainly for the extending of the poet's limited experience;[55] he is silent on irony and myth and the novel. But he can be surprisingly concrete in his theory of the lyric, observant on poetic devices, and original in his theory of tragedy. His actual taste in literature was that of German classicism, and his literary opinions thus do not stand out as unusual. Schopenhauer's aesthetics assumed great historical importance only late in the 19th century, because he carried these Platonic ideas into a time when Schelling and Hegel had become discredited. Especially his aesthetic of music, the art which in his system is set apart as the direct expression of the Will without the mediation of Ideas, proved enormously influential on Nietzsche, Wagner, and Thomas Mann. But in the theory of literature, though we have picked out penetrating observations and even theoretical insights, only his concept of tragedy proved a sharply distinctive contribution.

HEGEL

The aesthetic of Hegel (1770–1831) is the culmination of the whole astonishing development of German speculation on art. Hegel sums up, though with a difference, what had been said by Kant, Schiller, Schelling, and Solger, to mention only his most obvious predecessors, and works it all into a system of aesthetics which in its turn is only a small part of an all-embracing philosophy of mind, history, and nature. Hegel, we now recognize, is one of the most influential figures in the history of mankind. In political philosophy Marxist dialectical materialism, as well as much conservative and liberal theorizing on the state, is descended from him, even though he would not have recognized many of his heirs. Hegel's role in the history of logic is enormous. He wrote the first history of philosophy that was more than a repertory of books. His philosophy of history and religion had even more far-reaching repercussions. In the history of aesthetics his role is hardly less significant if we think of the long line of Hegelians in Germany, of his influence on Taine and De Sanctis, on Belinsky, Pater, Croce, and any number of others. This influence is usually one of method and a few central ideas. It rarely means close disciple-ship, as apparently the structure of the *Aesthetic* proved unaccept-able in its detail to most succeeding thinkers. Hegel's literary theory, in distinction from his general propositions on beauty, art, and the ideal, is hardly known today as a distinct body of thought, though the *Lectures on Aesthetics* devote a long concluding section to Poetics and are elsewhere studded with reflections on literary theory and comments on particular works of literature.

The *Lectures on Aesthetics* are, considered as a book, rather un-satisfactory: there is a great deal of repetition, much unevenness in the elaboration of details, much descriptive matter which seems not strictly relevant (especially on Oriental myth), and occasional traces of a jocular concern for his audience of German students. These shortcomings are due to the fact that the Lectures were published after Hegel's death by his pupil, Heinrich Gustav Hotho, in 1835, and are based on several sets of lecture notes taken down by students in the 1820's. They were combined, revised, and heavily edited by Hotho and thus do not represent Hegel's final formulas.[1] Unfortunately, the writings printed in Hegel's lifetime contain very little material useful as a check on the Lectures: the much briefer expositions of aesthetics in the *Phenomenology of the Spirit* (1807) and the *Encyclopaedia* (1817) present an earlier stage of Hegel's thought and the series of critical articles on Hamann, Solger, and one note on Schiller's *Wallenstein* supple-ment the lectures only on minor points.[2] Still, the Lectures have a great advantage for most modern readers: though less rigid sys-tematically, less final in their phrasing, they are more attractive just because of their digressions, the frequent use of concrete illustra-tion, the display of wide historical knowledge.

But the difficulties with the transmission of Hegel's aesthetic are slight compared to the difficulties of its interpretation and evalua-tion. There is, it seems, a fundamental contradiction at its center. On the one hand it is the most impressive system of the time, in which history and theory are blended successfully and all the main ideas of the German aestheticians are assimilated into one system, clearly defining the nature and delimiting the realm of art. On the other hand Hegel's theory, especially his literary theory, appears in part as a relapse into older rationalistic attitudes and concepts, which, when seized upon by his literal-minded followers, brought about a return to the old intellectualistic misinterpretation of art and a judgment of literature by standards of mere content and even moral and religious message.

Hegel's central aesthetic concepts will be familiar to us from Kant, Schiller, and Schelling. Like them Hegel insists that art "makes the sensuous spiritual and the spiritual sensuous," that in art the universal must be individualized, the general particularized, the idea and form identified.[3] Hegel's most famous formula, "the sensuous semblance of the idea," [4] is just such a reformulation of the dialectical unity of the sensuous and the idea which we met with in Schelling and Solger. Beauty is the concrete universal itself. A work of art is a totality, organized in every detail, creating a self-enclosed world, lacking external purpose. This concept, which is common to Hegel's predecessors, is interpreted originally. The Hegelian idea is not a Platonic Idea above the world of things and persons, nor is it, of course, an abstract concept. It is made completely historical, identified with the historical process itself. Art theory and art history are thus implicated with each other even more closely than in the Schlegels, who are nearest to Hegel in this matter.

Unfortunately, Hegel's fusion of theory and history makes him press the classification of the arts into the sequence of the historical stages of art. One can defend Hegel's three stages of art, symbolic, classical, and romantic. By "symbolic" Hegel means what we today would call "allegorical," art in which there is no concrete togetherness of meaning and form.[5] Such art would be, in Hegel's strict sense, really non-art, some preliminary of art, of which he sees examples primarily in the Orient, India and Egypt. There he finds only a vague relationship between form and content, a cleavage between the abstract ideal and the manifold reality of nature.[6] Classical art, the art of the Greeks in particular, is the union of content and form, their fusion and identity, while romantic art, which to Hegel means all art since antiquity, is art with a new division of the inner and outer, with subjectivity making the outer form again fortuitous and arbitrary.[7]

The addition of "symbolic" art to the classical-romantic double of the Schlegels can be considered an improvement of their scheme in that it recognizes a third (though inferior or at least preliminary) stage and in that it brings Oriental art into the world-wide pattern. Hegel, however, goes on to identify these stages with the different arts. The symbolic stage has architecture as its coordinated art; the classical has sculpture; the romantic stage has all three modern arts: painting, music, and poetry. This seems an awkward and artificial system, though it can be interpreted to mean that at certain periods one particular art was dominant or most characteristic. It certainly seems to establish that sculpture, the classical art, is the most perfect art; yet this conclusion is contradicted by many other passages in which poetry is exalted as the highest and ultimate art. This new scheme prevails at the end: it is a disguised intellectualism or rather, as Hegel would not have the "idea" confused with an abstract concept, an "idealism" in which art assumes merely the role of a stepping stone to religion and finally to philosophy. Hegel conceives this order of degrees of consciousness from art on up to religion and thence to philosophy not as a series of merely coordinated values but as a historical order, in which the older form must be replaced by the newer and higher. Hegel's aesthetic thus becomes an anti-aesthetic, a funeral oration on art. Art is past, transcends itself, has ceased to be "the highest need of the spirit." [8] According to this scheme, poetry will come last as the most spiritual art, since there is according to Hegel no sensuous element in it. It is made up entirely of signs, which are meaningless in themselves and receive meaning only through mind.[9] Poetry is thus put into its position as the highest art because it is most similar to thought. At times Hegel himself recognizes the danger of poetry losing itself in the spiritual and thus ceasing to be art, but in general he cannot escape the logic of his scheme.[10]

Still, the death of art, its pastness, its self-transcendence must not apparently be interpreted literally as a prophecy of the imminent extinction of all art or even of all good art. Hegel has, above all, a very strong feeling for the complete implication of art in its own time, for its being part and parcel of a particular age and society. Thus no epic is possible today, nor is satire in the Roman sense, which requires "firm principles in disagreement with their age, a wisdom which remains abstract, a virtue which clings only to itself with rigid energy," nor can we properly write poems about Venus, Jupiter, and the other gods, or even paint Madonnas.[11] Hegel rejects the romantic conversions to Catholicism as an artificial means of inducing belief. "The artist must not be in need of coming to terms with his own soul and of having to worry about his own salvation. His great, free soul must, before it starts creating, know what it is about, must be sure of itself and full of confidence." [12]

Hegel thus can defend anachronisms in art. On the stage the costuming of Chinese and Peruvians as Frenchmen of the age of Louis XIV shows rather the strength than the weakness of the civilization.[13] Hegel has little use for artificial revivals such as the German Nazarene painters attempted by imitating the Italian primitives, though he makes some good-humored concessions to their usefulness and merit.[14] With this sense for the "organicity" of historical development, for a complete parallelism not only of the arts but of all activities of man, he has to describe his time as one of artistic decadence, as a late stage in the history of art. He sees the decline largely as a lapse into naturalism on the one hand, and into the artificial resurrection of historical styles on the other, but also he sees it as a deviation into the merely fantastic and grotesque, into subjective destructive humor, and irresponsible aestheticism. As a diagnosis of the further development of 19th-century art these observations are remarkably shrewd, especially when one remembers that they were made in the 1820's. Hegel thinks of Kotzebue and the German realistic drama, of E. T. A. Hoffmann, Kleist, Tieck, and Jean Paul as romantic writers, displaying these decadent features of the time.[15] Yet twice he makes the curious suggestion— a reminiscence of Schelling's speculations—that there is still one great topic left for the moderns: a world epic, a *Légende des siècles*, with "Humanus" as its hero.[16] Thus Hegel sounds like a rationalist who foretells the supersession of art by science, philosophy, and aesthetics; he goes so far as to say, "Art finds its true justification only in science," presumably his own aesthetics.[17] On the other hand he also accurately described the 19th-century dissolution of styles, the confusion of art and reality in naturalism, and thus implied a reactionary position, an advocacy of classicism, which he held out as a model to the moderns.

Just as Hegel's historical and evaluative scheme of art, religion, and philosophy leads to an intellectualization of poetry as the last of the arts, so, within poetry, the Hegelian hierarchy leads to the exaltation of the most philosophical genre, the drama. Hegel consistently minimizes the sound stratum of poetry as an "accidental externality" and decides that the aesthetic surface (as we would say today) of literature is not language but the "inner representation and intuition itself." [18] The linguistic element is only a means, indifferent to the properly poetical element. Poetry can without substantial harm to its value be translated into another language, transferred from verse to prose and thus brought into completely different sound-relations. Poetry thus, in its most essential parts, is finished in the mind and its essence is brought to consciousness without sensual intuition and without appeal to the ear. [19]

In spite of this general position Hegel shows a remarkable grasp of the role of linguistic features (diction, word order, sentence structure) in poetry and eloquently expounds the effects and charms of versification and rhyme. [20] He makes the true observation that a "genuine artistic talent moves in his sensuous materials as in his most proper native element, which lifts and carries it rather than hinders and oppresses." [21] He suggests that verse is implicated in the rhythm of the ideas, that it is a "music which, though in a distant way, echoes the dark yet definite direction of the course and character of the representations." He asserts the need for rhythm but not for exact measure in poetry and describes well the clash between the metrical pattern and the rhythm of prose which "gives the whole a new peculiar life." [22]

We would misunderstand Hegel (as he was misunderstood by many Hegelians who discussed literature as if it were a didactic treatise) if we thought that he put philosophical poetry highest. Hegel maintains a hold on the concrete universal, the nature of art. He even plays a neat trick with didactic and descriptive poetry: he banishes them completely from his scheme of poetic genres. For Hegel the main kinds of poetry are the traditional three: the epic, the lyric, and the drama. They follow the order of objective, subjective, and their synthesis, with the epic, in an ingenious but artificial involution, corresponding to sculpture, the lyric to music, and the drama to a union of music and sculpture. [23] The order of the main kinds is also historical: the epic is the first in time, as it belongs to the heroic age, to the past, while the lyric follows. All subjectivism, self-consciousness, introspection comes later in the history of man. The drama combining the objective with the subjective, the epic with the lyric is then the latest form. Within the drama comedy is later than tragedy and nearer the dissolution of art, for comedy implies the superiority of the artist over his materials, supreme self-consciousness.[24] The scheme is obviously modeled on the sequence Homer, Pindar, Sophocles, Aristophanes—and the final position of comedy also agrees with Schiller's theory. It seems to imply an interpretation of comedy which is similar to that of the romantics and their emphasis on irony. But one must beware of identifying Hegel's point of view with that of Friedrich Schlegel or even Solger. Hegel always disparaged Friedrich Schlegel, partly because of his conversion, and he felt that his friend Solger had not quite freed himself of the influence of Tieck and had not reached the proper objectivity.[25] Still, Hegel's conception of comedy is really not so different from romantic irony if we interpret it objectively. Hegel merely condemned the destructive negative irony that lacks all seriousness and makes fun only for fun's sake. He severely criticized what he considered the lack of character, the inconsequence, irresponsibility, and arbitrary mysticism of the Schlegels, Tieck, Novalis, and E. T. A. Hoffmann, but he did not abandon the idea that the highest art is complete objectivity and superiority.[26]

This general scheme of a sequence of genres is supplemented by an attempt to assign some minor kinds and devices of art to a particular stage of its development and thus to deny them any proper place in the scheme itself. Under symbolic art, the first and lowest stage of art, we find a discussion of the kinds which, to Hegel's mind, illustrate the external relation of content and form and thus are peculiarly characteristic of that stage. Hegel there discusses the animal fable, the parable, the proverb, the apologue, the riddle, the epigram, and didactic and descriptive poetry. It is denied that these minor forms are art, as they all show an unreconciled dichotomy of content and form. In descriptive poetry the external content remains in its unspiritual particularity; in didactic poetry it remains in conceptual generality.[27]

Hegel, in this context, treats not only of these minor forms but also of poetic devices such as allegory, metaphor, "image" (an extended metaphor), and simile, which he also assigns to this "symbolic" stage of art. One can understand why in Hegel's scheme allegory should be ranked low as an abstract form and why the simile with its two separate sides, image and meaning, should fit into "symbolic" art. But it is hard to see why metaphor and image should be ranked here and thus implicitly condemned, since they precisely represent the union of meaning and form, the fusion (as we would say) of tenor and vehicle, which to Hegel is the essence of all art.[28] Hegel can do so because he interprets metaphor as a rudimentary form of the simile, in which meaning and image are "not yet" confronted, with the consequence that metaphor is considered only an external ornament of a work of art, as an interruption of the course of representation, as a continuous diversion.[29] Hegel is not blind to the great role of figuration in poetry: he quotes many examples from Shakespeare and recognizes that the Spanish dramatists, Jean Paul, and Schiller are also very rich in metaphors.[30] But in Hegel's mind figurative language is apparently so firmly associated with Oriental, "symbolic" poetry that it must remain characteristic of that stage and that stage alone. Consistently enough Hegel asserts, somewhat rashly in view of Homeric similes, that Homer and Sophocles "are founded on the whole almost throughout on direct expression." [31] One must assume that he thought this true of all great art.

Classical art is the center of art, the middle, the "moment" of beauty, which for Hegel is exemplified primarily in Greek sculpture and Greek mythology.[32] Here, as elsewhere in the Lectures, the distinctions between art and religion or myth become blurred, and art is identified with religion or at least used as an illustration of religious concepts. In Hegel's earlier discussions of art, in the *Phenomenology* and the *Encyclopaedia,* the identity of art and religion is asserted as part of the general philosophical scheme. The term "Kunstreligion," derived from Schleiermacher, is used as a compound to assert such a complete union.[33] But in the Lectures a distinction between art and religion is maintained, or sometimes merely circumvented by a Platonizing use of the word "poetry" in the sense of imaginative activity in general.[34] In practice, however, Hegel constantly discusses myth and religion, at least outside Christianity, as if they were art. Indian, Persian, Hebrew, and Egyptian religious conceptions are used to illustrate symbolic art, even if there is no question of an artistic monument or a piece of literature; in classical art the Greek gods, whether as in Homer or as represented in sculpture or simply as a system of mythology, are considered the main theme of art, and in romantic art the religious themes, Christ, his Passion, the Virgin Mary, the martyrs and saints, are all examined as if they were a part of aesthetics. A proviso is, however, introduced: Christ as the incarnation of God is more real than any ancient God and thus actually transcends art.[35] Christ himself, because he is flesh, needs no art, makes art superfluous. Also, the God of the Jews, in his very grandeur and sublimity, cannot be successfully represented in human and thus in artistic terms. The Psalms and other parts of the Bible, metaphorically celebrating the grandeur of God, are considered symbolic art which is not yet art and is not yet ideal because in it the inner and the outer do not interpenetrate. Hebraism is "sublime" and thus symbolic, Christianity is romantic. Greek religion is classical.[36]

Thus the Greek gods are in Hegel the center of art, almost as much as in Schelling. Ideal, Greek, and classical are the same and the general discussion of the ideal in art is closely parallel to the treatment of classical art. In both places constant changes are rung on the central theme of Hegel's aesthetics: beauty is the sensuous representation of truth. This is not, as Hegel reminds us, the Platonic classicism of Winckelmann, whose ideal seems to him inane and empty.[37] The ideal itself is not apart from the reality; it is not, as in Platonism, the beautiful itself. It appears, it *seems* only to us, it is subjective in a Kantian sense. The ideal is not general or abstract, but concrete, individual, "characteristic," and, at the same time, universal and general.[38] Now and then Hegel speaks like an 18th-century classicist who stresses art's purifying effect, its harmony, serenity, its freedom from the contingent and factual.[39] Hegel always condemns mere imitation, mere personal expression, any appeal to "interest." He shares the specific prejudices of the classicist when he rejects illness or hunger as subjects of art, declares flatly that anxiety for a living or work for gain has no place in art, or condemns all evil and the devil as unaesthetic.[40] Hegel has no tolerance for the grotesquely supernatural in art. In order to accept the witches in *Macbeth* or the ghost in *Hamlet* he has to allegorize them, reduce them to projections of inner states. No magic, no magnetism, nothing occult must be allowed in art, for there "everything is clear and transparent " [41]

Hegel has no use for modern middle-class realism: either for Kotzebue or the modern novel of manners. He even draws a subtle distinction between the coffee-drinking clergy of Voss's *Luise* and the wine-drinking tavern-keeper and his guests in Goethe's *Hermann und Dorothea*. The first are *Philister* who consume imported goods, coffee, and sugar; the second are figures of an epic and heroic setting, closed in itself, consuming the local product.[42] Likewise, satire is not really poetry. With a new break in the usual triad of genres, satire is put into a historical position at the end of classical art. It is a transitional form in the dissolution of the classical ideal, neither epic nor lyric, well in place with the prosaic Romans, near the fall of their empire.[43]

Classical art is serene, but not sublime. Still, an "eternal seriousness, an unchanging peace makes its throne on the forehead of the gods and is poured out over their entire figure." [44] This very serenity of the gods is, however, somehow melancholy. "The blessed gods sorrow over their blessedness"; a breath and perfume of sadness is in their very beauty, as the gods sense their overthrow and art knows its transience before thought.[45] The classical ideal is a precarious equilibrium rarely achieved and easily destroyed. In poetry it seems exemplified only in Homer and Sophocles.

But when Hegel comes to discuss romantic art, he cannot keep to his implied rejection of everything which is not ideal. Romantic art is seen as art which incorporates realism, though it must never become complete imitation of nature. Hegel makes a spirited defense of Dutch genre-painting and defends the place of the low and grotesque, the trivial and commonplace in Shakespeare. The sentries in *Hamlet,* the servants in Juliet's household, the fools and clowns, the taverns, chamberpots, and fleas are parallel to medieval religious pictures of the birth of Christ and the Adoration of the Magi. "Oxen and asses, manger and straw must not be missing." Even in art "the word must be fulfilled, that the humble shall be exalted." [46] Hegel here shows his fine historical insight into the relation of the rise of realism and Christianity, just as he associates the special realism of the Dutch with their Protestantism.[47]

As always, Hegel's attitude is ambivalent. From the point of view of his Hellenic ideal modern art is inferior. But he sees its historical necessity, its implication in the social process moving toward a middle-class society. He is not without sympathy for the humor of Hippel and Sterne, for the view that the smallest thing, a tree, a mill race, might be vivified and magnified by poetry.[48] There is poetry which is "pure pleasure in objects, an inexhaustible indulgence of the fancy, a harmless game," and Hegel is prepared to admire it until, in conclusion, he pulls himself up and pronounces that "content decides in art," since art has no other aim than to show forth the "significant in adequate, sensuous presentment." [49] Unfortunately, the term "Gehalt" assumes philosophical connotations in Hegel: it is identified with truth, the Idea, the Absolute, the Divine. "Art discharges its highest task in realizing and expressing the Divine, the deepest interests of man, the broadest truths of the spirit." [50] It is an easier road for penetrating to the Idea. "The hard crust of Nature and the everyday world offer more difficulty to the mind in breaking through to the Idea than do the works of art." [51] Art has thus again become a popular substitute for philosophy and religion.

The emphasis not only on the religious roots of art but on art as illustrating the basic religious conceptions of an age also permeates Hegel's theory of genres and many individual judgments of authors. The conflict between the concept of the "concrete universal," of art as ideal with its exaltation of Greek sculpture and Greek mythology, and the other view which stresses the Idea and the concealed Divine in art, remains unreconciled and unreconcilable. In the scheme of genres the lyric is minimized. The comments, shorter and more perfunctory than on the epic and drama, are also less distinguished. The principle of subjectivity is made the key to the lyric, but Hegel constantly warns that this subjectivity must not be a passing mood; it must have general validity.[52] The classification of the lyric subgenres is not based on any clear principle except in the case of obvious mixture with the epic, such as ballads and romances. The purely lyrical, the expression of internal moods and reflections, is rated low. The folk song, which to Hegel shows a "lack of explication," expresses a "merely popular sentiment," is "national" in a sense which Hegel finds to be limiting. He even makes the odd assertion that we cannot "completely feel with" the songs of any other nation than our own. The lyric is tied to the present, to sound, to music and imagery, all traits of early symbolic art.[53] The sketch of the evolution of the lyric is rather thin: it culminates in a generous appreciation of Klopstock's odes, which is tempered, however, by Hegel's strong disapproval of any revival of Teutonic mythology. It seems to him a false and artificial archaism.[54]

The discussion of the epic is far more detailed and sympathetic, despite the fact that the epic precedes the lyric, as an earlier art, in Hegel's scheme. Epic is primarily Homeric, the expression of an heroic age, a national spirit, the Bible of a nation. But unlike most of his contemporaries Hegel, who was impressed by Wolf's theories, holds fast to the individual origin of the epic. "However much an epic expresses the cause of a whole nation, the people itself as a totality cannot compose, but only individuals." [55] The view that an epic has no beginning and no end and could be continued indefinitely is firmly rejected as destroying the very nature of the work of art, which is always a whole.[56] Hegel makes an elaborate plea for the unity of the *Iliad*, arguing that there is no falling off after the death of Hector. "The games at Patroclus' pyre, the heart-rending pleas of Priam, the reconciliation of Achilles, who returns to the father the corpse of his son so that honor to the dead may be done, join with all the previous events and contribute to the supreme and satisfying beauty of the conclusion." [57]

Hegel is, however, cool to the *Nibelungenlied:* he misses the evocation of concrete reality, so successful in Homer. "We don't get to see the things, we only sense the impotent struggle of the author." The attempt to make the *Nibelungenlied* a national book meets his disapproval, as "the story of Christ, Jerusalem, Bethlehem, Roman law, and even the Trojan war have much more present reality for us than the events of the Nibelungen." [58] Its characters are hard, wild, and cruel. In their abstract stiffness, they remind him of crude wooden images. The *Nibelungenlied* cannot be put by the side of Homer.

Hegel similarly disparages the *Edda* for its obscure and confused myths and censures Ossian, whom he considers genuine, as lyrical, vague, indeterminate.[59] Yet it will not do to say that Hegel simply indulges in classical prejudices. He appreciates the Spanish *Cid* very warmly, calling it epic, plastic, comparable to the best things produced by antiquity. And he wrote two superb pages on

Dante which elaborate a central theme of Hegel's aesthetics: the eternization, the divinization accomplished by art. Dante "plunges the living world of human action and suffering or, more closely, that of individual acts and destinies into this changeless existence . . . as the individuals were in their life and sufferings, their intentions and accomplishments on earth, so are they set before us, for ever consolidated, as images of bronze." Dante's characters do not exist in our imagination; they are themselves essentially eternal. The passage through Hell, Purgatory, and Paradise undertakes to give us "a picture and a report of what has actually been seen, an account full of energetic movement, yet plastic in the rigidity of its tortures: rich in the flashes of its horror, yet plaintively mitigated in Hell by Dante's own pity; more gracious in Purgatory, but none the less fully and completely realized; and finally translucent as light in Paradise, and forever without material form in the eternity of thought." [60] The central paradox of Dante's scheme, its union of the human and the eternal, the this-worldly with the other-worldly, is here formulated, probably for the first time.

Hegel has little to say of Ariosto, Tasso, and Camoës; he sees the last two as imitators of Virgil, as "artificial." He ranked Virgil's *Aeneid* low, as mere "invention," full of coldly contrived marvels and artificial machinery.[61] The passage on Milton suffers from Hegel's obsession with purity of genres. In discussing Dante he admitted without qualms that the *Divine Comedy* is not exactly an epic. But *Paradise Lost* is criticized for being too dramatic, too lyrical, and too didactic, and is put far below Dante.[62] Hegel, of course, disparages Klopstock's *Messiah* as inflated rhetoric and of modern epics praises only Goethe's *Hermann und Dorothea* as a classical idyll with an epic background.[63]

The epic to Hegel is definitely past. It belongs to a heroic or at least a romantic age. The present state of the world, with well organized administrative and police systems, cannot be used as the ground for truly epic action, just as industrialization, the division of labor, tears men away from the living contact with nature required in the epic.[64] Hegel recognizes that the modern world has found a substitute in the novel, the "middle class epic," but as it lacks the support of a poetic state of the world, he considers it prose, non-art, mere imitation.[65] He slyly ridicules the German educational novel which always ends with the young man marrying his girl, achieving a position, and finally settling down as a *Philister,* just like everybody else.[66]

Hegel is most intensely interested in the drama, especially in tragedy. Drama is the synthesis of the epic and the lyric, of sculpture and music, so that it lends itself best to interpretation in terms of the Hegelian dialectic. Tragedy, to Hegel, is conflict, collision. Its theme is the divine, the great moral forces in which the divine is embodied: what Hegel, confusingly in our usage, calls "ethical substance." The collisions between two substances, both of which must be real moral forces and thus both justified, leads to tragedy, which must end in reconciliation. To give Hegel's favorite example, which he had discussed before in the *Phenomenology,* Sophocles' *Antigone* represents a clash between two obligations, to state and to family. Both Antigone and Creon are guilty in their exclusive devotion to their ideal. Antigone perishes, and Creon is punished by the death of his son and wife. Antigone's death, in Hegel's mind, is subordinate to the establishment of a final harmony, a resolution of the conflict. Hegel even considers Antigone's allegiance as one to lower principle: "the gods she worships are the lower gods of Hades, the 'inner ones' of sentiment, love, blood, not the gods of day, the gods of a free self-conscious life of a nation and people." [67] Physical death of the hero is not a requisite for tragedy in Hegel's mind. In the *Eumenides* of Aeschylus there is a collision between love for the father and love for the mother. The solution is forced by the decision of the goddess Athene, and Orestes survives purged of his guilt of matricide. There is an "inner reconciliation" at the end of *Oedipus at Colonus,* when Oedipus, in Hegel's curious terminology, is transfigured into "the unity and harmony of the ethical substance." [68] In modern literature there are examples of similar clashes of moral forces, such as the conflict between love and honor in Corneille's *Cid,* or between the rights of love and family in *Romeo and Juliet.* But Hegel, in general, criticizes modern tragedy (which means to him Shakespeare, Goethe, and Schiller) for not posing such a conflict clearly, indeed for obscuring it by the contingencies of individual character. Thus Hegel sees a failure in Schiller's *Wallenstein.* "Life against life: but only death rises up against life, and unbelievably, repulsively, Death triumphs over life. It is not tragic but appalling; it lacerates the soul." [69] So in Goethe's *Tasso* the rights of ideal life are not really asserted. Tasso is merely an object of the poet's sympathy and pity, not a truly tragic hero. [70]

Hegel has the same difficulties with Shakespeare's heroes. He considers them too individual, too characteristic, their aims too personal and egotistical, and frequently even evil. Macbeth, Othello, Romeo pursue their own personal ends, however much they may be absorbed by one overpowering passion—ambition, jealousy, or love. [71] In *Hamlet* the collision is not between two moral powers. There is no question that Hamlet's revenge would be moral. The conflict is transferred into Hamlet's noble soul, "which is not created for this kind of energetic activity and is full of disgust with the world and life." Hamlet's death, Hegel recognizes, is only superficially a chance event. "In the background of his mind Death lies from the beginning on; the sand bar of finitude will not content it." [72] So in *Romeo and Juliet* love is broken like a "tender rose in the valley of this world of chance." Our feeling, at the end of the play, is not one of tragic resolution, but of pain, of an "unhappy blessedness in misfortune." [73] Hegel objects to what he considers the untragic sadness of Shakespeare's endings. In *Lear, Hamlet,* and *Romeo,* the good and the innocent perish, and by chance. In *Macbeth* and *Richard III* the heroes are criminals who cannot elicit true sympathy. Hegel's reading of *Macbeth* makes the title character far harder, much more unwavering, with far less hesitation, uncertainty, compunction, than the text warrants. [74] One must conclude that Hegel fails to assimilate Shakespeare to his concept of tragedy because he has rejected the idea of an incomprehensible universe and any sympathy for an evil though heroically insurgent protagonist.

It seems easy to raise doubts about Hegel's specific interpretations of the plays he discusses: everyone will protest against his balancing between Creon and Antigone. We may doubt his conception of Hamlet's character, inherited from Goethe, or that of Macbeth as a hardened criminal. But this matters little compared to the basic objection to Hegel's theory. Tragedy, with him, is reduced to a conflict in which the characters, as mere carriers of ideas, are only accidental. It is hardly true, even of *Antigone,* that tragic heroes are "the individual representatives of the gods." [75] There is, even in *Antigone,* no equality between the clashing moral forces. Hegel's concept of tragedy obscures the hero and glosses over the irrationality and cruelty of fate. With Hegel we are back at a *theodicée,* as in Lessing, at a cosmic optimism in which the "real is the rational and the rational the real." * In seeing the tragic hero perish, we are to say "It is so," for in all art sorrow must for Hegel be beautiful, serene.[76]

Hegel thus succeeds in assimilating tragedy into his philosophy by making it a grandiose example of dialectics and the world order. Poetry passes into philosophy, with Aeschylus or Sophocles, at the point in time which Hegel recognizes as the highest in the history of art. From there on it is really only a story of decline. Shakespeare and the other moderns are either mere character painters, portraitists, or they excite feelings of horror and gloom which Hegel refuses to recognize as tragic and even as art.

If all art has the divine as its theme, comedy must have it too. But it has it only negatively: it starts with the reconciliation that is the aim of tragedy but leads by its very aloofness and freedom to the dissolution of art itself.[77] It stands at the end, both in Greece, with Aristophanes, and in Hegel's own time; with the self-destructive humor of Jean Paul; with romantic irony. Hegel casts only a passing glance at the comedy of manners. Molière's *Tartuffe* is called not really comic. It is the unmasking of a villain.[78] The Spanish comedies of intrigue also, and the modern French and German sentimental comedies—these are not comic in Hegel's sense. Shakespeare is the only example in modern times he seems to be able to approve unreservedly. A figure like Falstaff, though "sunk in vulgarity," is still an "intelligence," a "free existence." "There is no justification, no condemnation in Shakespeare, only a contemplation of universal fate." [79] Shakespeare thus is again the "right popular philosopher," who exemplifies the superiority of genius, its objectivity, its acceptance of the world as it is. Serenity, wisdom, reconciliation is the sum of Hegel's ethical *and* aesthetic wisdom.

Hegel thus presents a curious double face, a Janus head: one side looking back into the past, yearning for the Greek ideal of serenity and ideal art, the complete fusion of form and content

---

* In the article on *Wallenstein* (SW, *17,* 411), the fact that the play does not end as a *theodicée* is deplored. The famous identification of the rational and real comes from *Rechtsphilosophie, SW, 8,* 17.

CONCLUSION

THE YEARS around 1830 brought a deep break in literary history and in the history of criticism. A great generation passed away: in Germany Friedrich Schlegel (1829), Hegel (1831), and Goethe (1832) died in quick succession; in England Hazlitt (1830), Coleridge (1834), and Lamb (1834); in Italy Foscolo (1827) and Leopardi (1836). Those who survived fell silent, at least as critics. August Wilhelm Schlegel had become a specialist in Sanskrit; Wordsworth revised his poetry; Manzoni ceased to write at all. In France the triumph of *Hernani* and the July revolution, both in 1830, indicate the change in atmosphere.

A new generation became vocal. Germany, the country which at that time had contributed most to aesthetics and criticism, went through a period of rapid intellectual decline. After Hegel's death, his followers soon fell out with each other: a Hegelian Right and Left, divided by political and religious issues, were formed. The more or less orthodox Right continued to produce a flood of writings on aesthetics, poetics, and literary history, exploiting, applying, and cheapening Hegel's ideas. Hegelianism became a dreary shadow play of concepts, Hegelian interpretation of literature a game of extracting the "general idea" from a work of art. Especially the German Shakespeare commentators of the time, Gervinus, Ulrici, Roetscher, and others are full of clumsy didacticism and intellectualism. Hegelian aesthetics was systematized and modernized in F. T. Vischer's bulky series of volumes, *Aesthetik* (5 vols. 1846–57), which may be considered as something like a tombstone of German aesthetic speculation. At least, one important dramatist, Friedrich Hebbel, formulated a theory of tragedy under Hegel's and Solger's influence. The Hegelian Left showed more life: Arnold Ruge was a sharp critic of romanticism, and Marx and Engels, though hardly themselves literary critics, were to exert long after their death a profound influence on literary criticism in the 20th century, even in distant countries. Marx and Engels adopted the Hegelian dialectic but rejected his metaphysics. Their literary interests and opinions, still deeply colored by the taste of German classicism, were, however, quite subordinate to their political and social concerns.[1] One cannot speak of Marxist literary criticism before Plekhanov and Mehring, in the last decade of the 19th century.

The turn toward politics, the newly proclaimed subservience of the arts to social purpose, the rejection of speculative aesthetics, the ridicule of romantic mysticism, and the attack on Goethe as the representative (or supposed representative) of the aesthetic way of life are the common features of the literary movement which in 1834 took the name of *Young Germany*. Its spokesman in aesthetics, Ludolph Wienbarg, in *Aesthetische Feldzüge* (1834), had not yet broken all ties with the past.[2] His admiration for Jean Paul and Solger is outspoken, but his aim is very different; it is social, political, liberal. Heine, now the best remembered of the group, was a self-styled *romantique défroqué*, who laughed at romanticism, though with nostalgia and sadness at its demise.[3] *Die romantische Schule* (1833) is a satirical reckoning with the Schlegels and Madame de Staël's idealized picture of Germany. The reaction against Goethe is another sign of the times; it comes from both political camps, the conservative national and the radical liberal. Wolfgang Menzel, in a sensational book on German literature (1828), lashed out at Goethe for his supposed sympathy with national weakness and political decadence. The radical journalist Ludwig Börne criticized Goethe's flight from politics and proclaimed the end of the German *Kunstperiode*. The gulf between daily reviewing, practical, mostly political, criticism, and the Academy became deeper. When the disillusion with Hegelianism and all speculative philosophy also penetrated into the universities, the professorial critics turned to mere antiquarianism. They were skeptics and relativists in theory, or at most repeaters in a diluted form of the doctrines of German classical idealism. Germany, in the later part of the 19th century, lost its leadership in literary theory and criticism completely.

In Italy the situation was similar to Germany. There also political preoccupations absorbed literary interests more and more. Giuseppe Mazzini, the greatest moral force of the Italian *Risorgi-*

mento, was a critic of wide interests who preached art for social improvement, art as expression of the progressive thought of the time. Only Francesco De Sanctis, who had been involved in the 1848 revolution in Naples, combined national and social fervor with an insight into Hegelian aesthetics and Schlegelian romantic theory. But De Sanctis—though among the greatest critics of the 19th century, and not only in Italy—remained a lonely figure. His ideas, which were a restatement of the romantic creed, were not immediately effective, and just as in Germany, Italian criticism settled down to the fatal divorce between partisan reviewing and academic factualism.

In England and Scotland the years after the death of Hazlitt and Coleridge must also be described as years of decadence. The one impressive new figure, Thomas Carlyle, who soon deserted criticism, fulfilled the function of a purveyor of German ideas.[4] Also, De Quincey, dependent on Coleridge and the Germans, has little to say that is new.[5] In critical theory we see a turn toward sheer emotionalism, the view that poetry is an overflow of feelings, mere personal self-expression. John Stuart Mill, associated today with hard-headed utilitarianism, formulated this view most clearly and extremely in his youth,[6] and John Keble, the poet of the *Christian Year,* applied it even to Homer. "Poetry," he said, "is a kind of medicine, which gives relief to secret emotion, yet without detriment to modest reserve."[7] The bulk of criticism became didactic, sentimental, moralistic. Macaulay, though hardly sensitive to poetic values, sharpened at least a feeling for the past. Poetic theory was almost nonexistent: only Matthew Arnold brought about a sorely needed critical revival in the 1860's.

France, which had been the country of criticism in the 17th century and by its standard of taste had dominated most of the 18th, produced comparatively little of enduring significance early in the century. But French criticism awakened rather suddenly in the late 20's and early 30's, at the very end of our story. A group of historians and philosophers, Guizot, Cousin, and in literature Fauriel (writing little for print), the voluble Villemain, and the earnest Ampère, created modern French literary history. A young man, Sainte-Beuve, whose first book was published in 1828, joined them but went beyond them, combining, virtuoso fashion, all possible methods: literary history, characterization, psychological explanation, impressionistic subjectivism. He came to dominate the time, and by his long labors he restored the critical prestige of France. For many people in France and outside he is still *the* critic.

Sainte-Beuve occupies a middle ground, for in France during the years immediately following the July revolution criticism was pushed in the most diverse directions. There was an impressive revival of the neoclassical view which found an eloquent spokesman in Désiré Nisard. At one extreme Gautier formulated the theory of art for art's sake, and at the opposite extreme a doctrine of realism began to emerge which was to become a public force only in the 50's, when Champfleury spread the word and slogan.[8] Simultaneously, the symbolist point of view was restated in France. It had filtered through from German romanticism and from its new versions in Carlyle, Emerson, and Poe.[9] Baudelaire, a great critic in his own right, is its first exponent. Even profounder changes came with the rise of scientific determinism in the 60's, when Hippolyte Taine demonstrated its theories on literature. France, by sheer talent and by the diversity of critical viewpoints her critics represented, regained the leadership of Europe.

After 1830 new countries joined the ensemble of the Western world. Russia, which had echoed French theories in the 18th century, found a powerful critic in Vissarion Belinsky (1811–48). At first imbued with the ideas of Schelling and Hegel, he preached the general romantic creed, but later he moved on to a social view of art.[10] He provided the starting point for a group of radical critics, Chernyshevsky, Dobrolyubov, Pisarev, who can be seen as the forerunners of Marxism. But Belinsky, in contrast to many of his successors, knew what art was. He established and weighed the reputations of Pushkin, Gogol, and Lermontov, as well as the young Dostoyevsky, Turgenev, and Goncharov. Just as in Germany and Italy, however, the breach between the journalistic, largely political reviewing and the historicism of the Academy became irreparable.

The other Slavic countries also adopted the German romantic doctrines in their own way. In general the Poles were full of mysticism and Messianism, highly emotional versions of romanticism, even though their first important formal critic, Kazimierz Brodziński, was a remarkably sober and sane propagandist of the new views.[11] The Czechs were hardly touched by the mystical and symbolist side of romanticism. Their poetic theory was largely Herderian; it preached the return to the folk and to folk poetry and drew its inspiration from nationalism. Only František Palacký, the great historian of Bohemia, engaged, in his youth, in aesthetic speculation under the influence of Kant and Fries.[12]

Like the Slavic countries, the Scandinavian people drew their literary ideas largely from Germany once the French vogue had passed. Sweden late in the 18th century had a brilliant exponent of Herder's position in Thomas Thorild.[13] A Schellingian kind of mystical romanticism triumphed there early in the century with Atterbom and his group. Denmark's most prominent critic, J. L. Heiberg, was a Hegelian. Still, on the whole, all the Scandinavian countries were more interested in the nationalistic and folkloristic implications of German romantic criticism than in the dialectical position.

Cultural and geographical reasons explain why romanticism came to Spain and Portugal from France and Italy. But the Spanish and Portuguese romantic movements, which were late and of short duration, produced no prominent criticism and little that does more than rehearse the great French debate.[14]

The doctrines of romantic criticism also crossed the ocean to the United States. Nothing original was produced before the 1830's. The writings of Bryant are only echoes of Alison and Jeffrey.[15] The historian W. H. Prescott was among the first to recommend the introduction of German critical ideas. But Emerson was the first to formulate a definitely personal aesthetic, dependent though he was on Coleridge, Carlyle, and some Germans; [16] and Edgar Allan Poe found bright and extreme phrases to fit ideas derived from Coleridge into a scheme of magic idealism.[17] Thus the realm of romantic criticism reached literally from Baltimore to Petersburg, from Naples to Edinburgh.

Nevertheless it crumbled quickly: realism and naturalism were the strongest forces of the later 19th century; in England (Arnold), France (Nisard, Brunetière), and Italy (Carducci) one can soon speak of a revival of classicism. Romanticism itself lost in many countries its central force, the symbolic concept of poetry, and became only a justification of emotionalism and nationalism. But the bridges to the 20th century were not entirely dismantled: in Germany even a scholar as imbued with ideals of natural science as Wilhelm Scherer kept in contact with the tradition of the great age; and Wilhelm Dilthey, in his own long life, spanned the gap.[18] In the 20th century there is everywhere a return to the ideas of the years we have surveyed. In Italy De Sanctis became the intermediary for Croce, who himself went directly to Hegel and Schleiermacher. In France the symbolist movement recaptured the essence of romantic criticism and transmitted it to the 20th century. In England and the United States the French symbolists, Croce, and certainly those responsible for the revival of Coleridge have profoundly stimulated the rebirth of criticism which we have witnessed in the last thirty years.

We should now have established the vitality of the criticism in the eighty years under review, proved its continuity with our own time, and demonstrated its relevance to us. We need not be blind to the profound changes of more than a century since 1830. To describe, to explain and to judge them will be the task of our later volumes.

ABBREVIATIONS AND SHORT TITLES

For titles not listed here refer to the chapter bibliographies for full reference.

ELH: English Literary History
JEGP: Journal of English and Germanic Philology
JHI: Journal of the History of Ideas
MLQ: Modern Language Quarterly
MLR: Modern Language Review
MP: Modern Philology
PMLA: Publications of the Modern Language Association
PQ: Philological Quarterly
RR: Romanic Review
Saintsbury: George Saintsbury, *History of Criticism and Literary Taste in Europe*, 3 vols. Edinburgh, 1900–04
SP: Studies in Philology

BIBLIOGRAPHY: INTRODUCTION

There is no general treatment of romantic criticism and theory on an international scale, except in Saintsbury. Meyer Abrams, *The Mirror and the Lamp* (New York, 1953) pursues several themes mostly through English literature, with side glances at Germany.

I know of no history of German literary criticism in the romantic age. On aesthetics see the general histories by Zimmermann, Schasler, Bosanquet, Croce, and Gilbert-Kuhn, all quoted in Vol. *1*, and Hermann Lotze, *Geschichte der Aesthetik in Deutschland,* Munich, 1868; Eduard von Hartmann, *Die deutsche Aesthetik seit Kant,* Berlin, 1886. P. Reiff, *Die Aesthetik der deutschen Frühromantik* (Urbana, Ill., 1946) is a mere compilation.

General books on German romanticism and German literature of the age contain discussions of the aesthetic and poetics, mostly interspersed with discussions of the philosophy, ethics, literary texts, etc. Among these books the following seem most valuable for our purpose:

Marie Joachimi-Dege, *Die Weltanschauung der deutschen Romantik,* Jena, 1905.

Oskar Walzel, *Deutsche Romantik,* 2 vols. 4th ed. Leipzig, 1918; Eng. trans. A. E. Lussky, *German Romanticism,* New York, 1932.

Oskar Walzel, *Grenzen der Poesie und Unpoesie,* Frankfurt, 1937; a mistitled book, mostly about German romantic aesthetics, on organism, sign theory, etc.

Hermann A. Korff, *Der Geist der Goethezeit,* 4 vols. Leipzig, 1923–48; a general history which pays attention to poetics and aesthetics.

BIBLIOGRAPHY: FRIEDRICH SCHLEGEL

Friedrich Schlegel's works are quoted from *Sämtliche Werke,* 2d ed. 15 vols. Vienna, 1846 (cited as *Werke*). Besides, I quote *Philosophische Vorlesungen aus den Jahren 1804 bis 1806,* ed. C. J. H. Windischmann, 2 vols. Bonn, 1837.

Because Schlegel either suppressed or materially changed his early writings, these are quoted from Jakob Minor's re-edition, *Friedrich*

Schlegel 1794–1802: seine prosaischen Jugendschriften, 2 vols. Vienna, 1882 (cited as Minor).

A few reviews not found elsewhere are quoted from Oskar Walzel's selection from August Wilhelm and Friedrich Schlegel in Kürschner's series, Deutsche Nationalliteratur, *143,* Stuttgart, 1892.

The very important introductions to *Lessings Geist aus seinen Schriften* are quoted from the original ed., 3 vols. Leipzig, 1804; unchanged reprint, 1810.

Notes on "Beauty in Poetry" were published from MS by Josef Körner in Friedrich Schlegel, *Neue philosophische Schriften,* Frankfurt, 1935. Notes "Zur Philologie" were published by the same scholar as "Friedrich Schlegel's Philosophie der Philologie," *Logos, 17* (1928), 1–72.

Scattered critical pronouncements can be found in the many publications of Friedrich Schlegel's letters, e.g. in Oskar Walzel's ed. of the *Briefe an seinen Bruder August Wilhelm,* Berlin, 1890; in Josef Körner's *Briefe von und an Friedrich und Dorothea Schlegel,* Berlin, 1926; and in the same editor's *Krisenjahre der Frühromantik. Briefe aus dem Schlegelkreis,* 2 vols. Brünn, 1936. Josef Körner, with Ernst Wienecke, edited also *Die Brüder August Wilhelm Schlegel und Friedrich Schlegel im Briefwechsel mit Schiller und Goethe,* Leipzig, 1926. Henry Lüdeke edited *Ludwig Tieck und die Brüder Schlegel: Briefe mit Einleitung und Anmerkungen,* Frankfurt, 1930.

There is a large literature on Friedrich Schlegel, mostly devoted to his life, morality, "existence," conversion, and philosophy. The following I found most useful for my purposes: Rudolf Haym, *Die romantische Schule,* Berlin, 1870—a sober descriptive account which is still valuable; Josef Körner, *Romantiker und Klassiker, Die Brüder Schlegel in ihren Beziehungen zu Schiller und Goethe,* Berlin, 1924—which quotes unpublished MSS; and Carl Friedrich Enders, *Friedrich Schlegel. Die Quellen seines Wesens und Werdens,* Leipzig, 1913. Two French books, which supplement each other, do not go much beyond Haym and Enders: I. Rouge, *Frédéric Schlegel et la genèse du romantisme allemand (1791–1797),* Paris, 1904; and Alfred Schlagdenhauffen, *Frédéric Schlegel et son groupe. La doctrine de l'Athenaeum (1798–1800),* Paris, 1934. Important points are raised in the writings of Oskar Walzel, especially in *Romantisches* (Bonn, 1934) and *Grenzen von Poesie und Unpoesie* (Frankfurt, 1937). There are useful materials in Margaret Gröben, *Friedrich Schlegels Entwicklung als Literarhistoriker und Kritiker,* Essen, 1934. A good general essay on Friedrich Schlegel is in Friedrich Gundolf's *Romantiker* (Berlin and Wilmersdorf, 1930), pp. 9–140. In English, A. O. Lovejoy's two papers, "The

Meaning of Romantic in Early German Romanticism" and "Schiller and the Genesis of German Romanticism," in *Essays in the History of Ideas* (Baltimore, 1948), and Raymond Immerwahr's "The Subjectivity or Objectivity of Friedrich Schlegel's Poetic Irony," *Germanic Review*, *26* (1951), 173–91, settle some points conclusively. See also H. Henel, "Friedrich Schlegel und die Grundlagen der modernen literarischen Kritik," in *GR, 20* (1945), 81–93; E. R. Curtius, "Friedrich Schlegel und Frankreich," in *Kritische Essays zur europäischen Literatur* (Bern, 1950), pp. 78–94; Howard Hugo, "An Examination of Friedrich Schlegel's 'Gespräch über Poesie,' " *Monatshefte, 40* (1948), 221–31.

English translation: *Lectures on the History of Literature, Ancient and Modern,* trans. J. Lockhart, 2 vols. Edinburgh, 1818.

NOTES: FRIEDRICH SCHLEGEL

1. *Prosaischen Jugendschriften,* ed. Minor, *1,* 143: "Die griechische Bildung überhaupt war durchaus originell und nazional, ein in sich vollendetes Ganzes, welches durch blosse innre Entwicklung einen höchsten Gipfel erreichte, und in einem völligen Kreislauf auch wieder in sich selbst zurücksank."

2. *Ibid.,* p. 146: "eine ewige Naturgeschichte des Geschmacks und der Kunst."

3. *Ibid.,* pp. 312–3.

4. *Deutsches Museum, 1* (1812), 283: "Die beste Theorie der Kunst ist ihre Geschichte."

5. Minor, 2, 424: "Die Quelle objektiver Gesetze für alle positive Kritik."

6. *Lessings Geist, 1, 13:* "ein grosses durchaus zusammenhängendes und gleich organisiertes, in ihrer Einheit viele Kunstwelten umfassendes Ganzes und einiges Kunstwerk."

7. *Briefe an seinen Bruder,* ed. Walzel. Letter to A. W., March, 1798: "Mich ekelt vor jeder Theorie die nicht historisch ist."

8. MS quoted in *Neue Philosophische Schriften,* p. 342: "die Vollendung [einer Wissenschaft] ist oft nichts als das philosophische Resultat ihrer Geschichte."

9. Minor, 2, 48: "Die Methode jede Blume der Kunst, ohne Würdigung, nur nach Ort, Zeit und Art zu betrachten, würde am Ende auf kein andres Resultat führen, als dass alles sein müsste, was es ist und war."

10. Review reprinted in Kürschner, Nationalliteratur, *143,* 412–13: "dass alles aber kommen musste, grade so wie es kam, nach der bei unsern Zeitgenossen so beliebten Philosophie des Königs Gorboduc:

dass alles, was ist, ist. . . . Nur können wir uns nicht entschliessen, die Bücher unter die Zahl der ursprünglichen Kreaturen zu setzen."

11. Minor, 2, 11: "Das einzige Geschäft [des kritischen Genies] ist, den Wert oder Unwert poetischer Kunstwerke zu bestimmen."

12. We have fragments and drafts for a "Philosophie der Philologie" (1797), published by J. Körner in *Logos, 17* (1928), 1–72, and a piece never reprinted, "Vom Wesen der Kritik," introducing his Lessing anthology (1804).

13. Minor, 2, 273: "Aus reiner Philosophie oder Poesie ohne Philologie kann man wohl nicht lesen."

14. *Ibid.*, p. 186: "Ein Kritiker ist ein Leser, der wiederkäut. Er sollte also mehr als einen Magen haben."

15. *Ibid.*, p. 125: "Man sollte sich ordentlich kunstmässig üben, eben sowohl äusserst langsam mit steter Zergliederung des Einzelnen, als auch schneller und in einem Zuge zur Übersicht des Ganzen lesen zu können."

16. *Ibid.*, p. 423, and *Lessings Geist, 1*, 29–30: "Die erste Bedingung alles Verständnisses, und also auch das Verständniss eines Kunstwerks, ist die Anschauung des Ganzen."

17. Minor, 2, 170: "dem nachspähn, was er unserm Blick entziehen, oder doch nicht zuerst zeigen wollte . . . die geheimen Absichten, die er im Stillen verfolgt, und deren wir beim Genius . . . nie zu viele voraussetzen können."

18. *Ibid.*, pp. 11, 275.

19. *Ibid.*, pp. 131, 147, 376: "in der Kunstgeschichte nur eine Masse die andre mehr erklärt und aufhellt. Es ist nicht möglich einen Teil für sich zu verstehen."

20. *Lessings Geist, 1*, 34: "Diese Konstruktion und Erkenntniss des Ganzen ist . . . die eine und wesentlichste Grundbedingung einer Kritik."

21. *Neue Philosophische Schriften*, p. 382: "Die Karakteristik erfodert 1) gleichsam eine Geographie. . . . 2) eine geistige und ästhetische Architektonik des Werks, seines Wesens, seines Tons; und endlich 3) eine psychologische Genesis, die Entstehung aus seiner Veranlassung, durch Gesetze und Bedingungen der menschlichen Natur."

22. *Lessings Geist, 1*, 40–1: "Und doch kann man nur dann sagen, dass man ein Werk, einen Geist verstehe, wenn man den Gang und Gliederbau nachkonstruieren kann. Dieses gründliche Verstehen nun, welches, wenn es in bestimmten Worten ausgedrückt wird, Charakterisieren heisst, ist das eigentliche Geschäft und innere Wesen der Kritik."

23. Minor, 2, 11, 273.

24. *Lessings Geist, 1*, 31–2: "Für die Kritik ist aber damit immer

nicht viel gewonnen, so lange man den Kunstsinn nur erklären will, statt dass man ihn allseitig üben, anwenden und bilden sollte."

25. Minor, *2, 229*: "Fast alle Kunsturteile sind zu allgemein oder zu speciell. Hier in ihren eignen Produkten sollten die Kritiker die schöne Mitte suchen, und nicht in den Werken der Dichter."

26. *Ibid.*, p. 191: "Wenn manche mystische Kunstliebhaber, welche jede Kritik für Zergliederung, und jede Zergliederung für Zerstörung des Genusses halten, konsequent dächten: so wäre Potz tausend das beste Kunsturteil über das würdigste Werk. Auch giebts Kritiken, die nichts mehr sagen, nur viel weitläuftiger."

27. *Ibid., 1, 309*:
   einen Widerschein des Werks selbst zu geben, seinen eigentümlichen Geist mitzuteilen, den reinen Eindruck so darzustellen, dass die Gestalt der Darstellung schon das künstlerische Bürgerrecht ihres Urhebers beglaubigt; nicht bloss ein Gedicht über ein Gedicht, um eine Weile zu glänzen; nicht bloss den Eindruck, welchen das Werk gestern oder heute auf diesen oder jenen macht oder gemacht hat, sondern den es immer auf alle Gebildete machen soll.

28. *Ibid., 2, 383*: "die fertige Ansicht eines Werks ist immer ein kritisches Faktum . . . die Einladung, dass jeder seinen eignen Eindruck eben so rein zu fassen und streng zu bestimmen suche."

29. *Ibid.*, p. 200: "Poesie kann nur durch Poesie kritisiert werden. Ein Kunsturteil, welches nicht selbst ein Kunstwerk ist, entweder im Stoff, als Darstellung des nothwendigen Eindrucks in seinem Werden, oder durch eine schöne Form, und einen im Geist der alten römischen Satire liberalen Ton, hat gar kein Bürgerrecht im Reiche der Kunst."

30. *Lessings Geist, 3, 10–11*: "Eine Kritik, die nicht so wohl der Kommentar einer schon vorhandnen, vollendeten, verblühten, sondern vielmehr das Organon einer noch zu vollendenden, zu bildenden, ja anzufangenden Litteratur wäre. Ein Organon der Litteratur, also eine Kritik, die nicht bloss erklärend und erhaltend, sondern die selbst produzierend wäre, wenigstens indirekt durch Lenkung, Anordnung, Erregung."

31. Minor, *1, 24*: "Das furchtbare und doch fruchtlose Verlangen sich ins Unendliche zu verbreiten; der heisse Durst das Einzelne zu durchdringen."

32. Kürschner, Nationalliteratur, *143*, 256–7; Minor, *1*, 89: "Sehnsucht."

33. *Ibid.*, p. 108: "Der Gipfel der modernen Poesie."

34. *Ibid.*, p. 115.

35. *Ibid.*, p. 300.

36. *Ibid.*, 2, 184: "ein manirierter Hymnus in Prosa auf das Objektive in der Poesie."

37. The complex history of the word "romantic" is traced in my article "The Concept of Romanticism in Literary History," *Comparative Literature, 1* (1949), esp. 2–17 and the literature there quoted.

38. Minor, 2, 220:

> Die romantische Poesie ist eine progressive Universalpoesie. . . . Ihre Bestimmung ist nicht bloss, alle getrennten Gattungen der Poesie wieder zu vereinigen, und die Poesie mit der Philosophie und Rhetorik in Berührung zu setzen. Sie will, und soll auch Poesie und Prosa, Genialität und Kritik, Kunstpoesie und Naturpoesie bald mischen, bald verschmelzen . . . die romantische Dichtart ist noch im Werden; ja das ist ihr eigentliches Wesen, dass sie ewig nur werden, nie vollendet sein kann. . . . Die romantische Dichtart ist die einzige, die mehr als Art, und gleichsam die Dichtkunst selbst ist: denn in einem gewissen Sinn ist oder soll alle Poesie romantisch sein. . . . Aussicht auf eine gränzenlos wachsende Klassizität.

39. *Ibid.*, p. 352: "die romantische Grundlage des modernen Drama."

40. *Ibid.*, p. 372: "unaussprechlich modern und doch im geringsten nicht romantisch . . . das eigentliche Zentrum, der Kern der romantischen Fantasie . . . in jenem Zeitalter der Ritter, der Liebe und der Mährchen, aus welchem die Sache und das Wort selbst herstammt."

41. *Ibid.*, p. 368: "die einzigen romantischen Erzeugnisse unsers unromantischen Zeitalters."

42. *Ibid.*, p. 381.

43. *Ibid.*, 2, 189.

44. *Ibid.*, 2, 364: "wir fordern, dass die Begebenheiten, die Menschen, kurz das ganze Spiel des Lebens wirklich auch als Spiel genommen und dargestellt sei."

45. *Ibid.*, p. 190: "Ironie ist die Form des Paradoxen. Paradox ist alles, was zugleich gut und gross ist."

46. *Ibid.*, p. 222.

47. *Ibid.*, p. 187: "Um über einen Gegenstand gut schreiben zu können, muss man sich nicht mehr für ihn interessieren . . . So lange der Künstler erfindet und begeistert ist, befindet er sich für die Mitteilung wenigstens in einem illiberalen Zustande."

48. *Ibid.*, p. 195: "sich selbst über ihr Höchstes zu erheben."

49. *Ibid.*, p. 296: "Ironie ist klares Bewusstsein der ewigen Agilität, des unendlich vollen Chaos."

50. *Ibid.*, p. 189: "transzendentale Buffonerie . . . die Stimmung

welche alles übersieht, und sich über alles Bedingte unendlich erhebt, auch über eigne Kunst, Tugend, oder Genialität."

51. *Ibid.*, p. 171: "auf sein Meisterwerk selbst von der Höhe seines Geistes herabzulächeln scheint."

52. *Ibid.*, p. 189.

53. *Ibid.*, p. 361: "ein hieroglyphischer Ausdruck der umgebenden Natur."

54. *Ibid.*, p. 361: "diese künstlich geordnete Verwirrung, diese reizende Symmetrie von Widersprüchen, dieser wunderbare, ewige Wechsel von Enthusiasmus und Ironie . . . eine indirekte Mythologie."

55. *Ibid.*, p. 362: "die schöne Verwirrung der Fantasie, das ursprüngliche Chaos der menschlichen Natur, für das ich kein schöneres Symbol bis jetzt kenne, als das bunte Gewimmel der alten Götter." The last queer phrase alludes to Goethe's "Brant von Korinth," line 57.

56. *Ibid.*, p. 364: "alle Schönheit ist Allegorie. Das Höchste kann man eben weil es unaussprechlich ist, nur allegorisch sagen."

57. *Philosophische Vorlesungen*, 2, 244: "ein Zweig der göttlichen Magie."

58. Cf. Kant's *Kritik der reinen Vernunft*, 2d ed., p. 106.

59. *Neue philosophische Schriften*, p. 376.

60. Minor, 2, 364: "Alle heiligen Spiele der Kunst sind nur ferne Nachbildungen von dem ursprünglichen Spiele der Welt, dem ewig sich bildenden Kunstwerk."

61. *Philosophische Vorlesungen*, 2, 244: "Die Kunst ist eine sichtbare Erscheinung des Reichs Gottes auf Erden."

62. *Ibid.*, 2, 46: "Schön kann nur sein, was eine Beziehung auf das Unendliche und Göttliche enthält."

63. *Werke*, 8, 192: "die Poesie selbst [ist] nichts andres als der reine Ausdruck dieses innern ewigen Wortes."

64. Minor, 2, 294, 200.

65. Kürschner, Nationalliteratur, *143*, 300: "ein andrer Ausdruck derselben transzendentalen Ansicht der Dinge . . . nur durch die Form von ihm verschieden."

66. *Werke*, 2, 247.

67. Minor, 2, 339: "die formlose und bewusstlose Poesie, die sich in der Pflanze regt, im Lichte strahlt, im Kinde lächelt, in der Blüthe der Jugend schimmert, in der liebenden Brust der Frauen glüht?"

68. *Ibid.*, p. 354: "Ist denn alles Poesie?"

69. *Ibid.*, *1*, 284, 215 n., 229 n.

70. *Ibid.*, p. 287, 222–3.

71. *Ibid.*, p. 288.

72. *Ibid.*, 2, 368.

73. *Ibid.*, p. 369: "weil seine Fantasie weit kränklicher, also weit wunderlicher und fantastischer ist."

74. *Ibid.*, pp. 374–5.

75. *Ibid.*, p. 381.

76. *Ibid.*, p. 223: "Wenn man einmal aus Psychologie Romane schreibt oder Romane liest, so ist es sehr inkonsequent, und klein, auch die langsamste und ausführlichste Zergliederung unnatürlicher Lüste, grässlicher Marter, empörender Infamie, ekelhafter sinnlicher oder geistiger Impotenz scheuen zu wollen."

77. *Ibid.*, *1*, 37.

78. *Ibid.*, p. 142: "schwingt sich endlich frei empor."

79. *Ibid.*, p. 107: "vor der ewigen kolossalen Dissonanz, welche die Menschheit und das Schicksal unendlich trennt."

80. *Werke*, 2, 85: "wo die Welt und das Leben in ihrer vollen Mannigfaltigkeit, in ihren Widersprüchen und seltsamen Verwicklungen, wo der Mensch und sein Dasein, dieses vielverschlungene Rätsel, als solches, als Rätsel dargestellt wird. . . . das Ewige aus dem irdischen Untergange hervorgeht."

81. Minor, *1*, 89, 102.

82. *Lessings Geist*, *1*, 34: "wie jedes Ding, so auch jedes Werk nur in seiner Art und Gattung vortrefflich sein soll, oder sonst ein wesenloses Allgemeinding wird."

83. Minor, 2, 355: Die Fantasie des Dichters soll sich nicht in eine chaotische Ueberhauptpoesie ergiessen, sondern jedes Werk soll der Form und der Gattung nach, einen durchaus bestimmten Charakter haben. Die Theorie der Dichtungsarten würde die eigentümliche Kunstlehre der Poesie sein. [Addition in *Werke*, 5, 191:] Die wesentliche Form der Poesie liegt in den verschiedenen Dichtungsarten und ihrer Theorie; so weit gebe ich ihre Behauptung zu. Nicht aber das Wesen selbst; dieses ist einzig und allein die rastlos sinnende und schaffende, ewige Fantasie.

84. *Lessings Geist*, *1*, 336–40:

> . . . aus ewigen Verhältnissen der Harmonie gleichsam stolze Tempel erbaut, so dass, wenn die Töne auch schon äusserlich verklungen sind, das Ganze noch fest wie ein Denkmal in der Seele des Hörers stehen bleibt . . . wenn nicht am Schluss eines Gedichts das Ganze wie Ein Bild in Einer Anschauung klar vor den Augen des Hörers, oder selbst des Lesers stände . . . Dieses ist aber der Tod alles Kunstgefühls, als welches zuerst und zuvörderst auf der Anschauung des Ganzen beruht.

85. Minor, 2, 185, 353: "erst eine Sage der Helden, dann ein Spiel der Ritter, und endlich ein Handwerk der Bürger war, nun auch bei eben derselben eine gründliche Wissenschaft wahrer Gelehrten und eine tüchtige Kunst erfindsamer Dichter sein und bleiben."

86. Cf. Friedrich Gundolf, *Romantiker* (Berlin, 1930), p. 55.

87. Minor, 2, 293: "Ein isolierter Egoist." *Ibid.*, p. 305: "Selbst in den äusserlichen Gebräuchen sollte sich die Lebensart der Künstler von der Lebensart der übrigen Menschen durchaus unterscheiden. Sie sind Braminen, eine höhere Kaste, aber nicht durch Geburt, sondern durch freie Selbsteinweihung geadelt."

88. *Ibid.*, p. 122.

89. *Ibid.*, p. 139.

90. *Lessings Geist, 1,* 149–51.

91. Kürschner, Nationalliteratur, *143,* 361–9. A violent condemnation of *Des Knaben Wunderhorn* is in a letter to A. W., November 11, 1805 (*Krisenjahre, 1,* 246).

92. *Werke, 2,* 54.

93. *Ibid., 1,* 239: "doch ist es an sich immer nicht das rechte Verhältniss, wenn die Poesie, welche den Geist der gesamten Nation ergreifen, rege erhalten, und weiter entwickeln soll, dem Volke allein überlassen bleibt."

94. *Ibid., 2,* 65: "Ich bin übrigens weit entfernt, jenen nationalen Gesichtspunkt für den einzigen zu halten, aus dem der welthistorische Wert einer Literatur zu beurteilen ist."

95. Minor, *1,* 118: "Die sinnbildliche Kindersprache der jugendlichen Menschheit."

96. *Ibid.*, p. 120.

97. *Ibid.*

98. *Werke, 2,* 84.

99. Minor, *1,* 121; *2,* 220.

100. *Die romantische Schule,* sec. on "Die Gebrüder Schlegel": "Friedrich Schlegel übersieht hier die ganze Litteratur von einem hohen Standpunkte aus, aber dieser hohe Standpunkt ist doch immer der Glockenturm einer katholischen Kirche."

101. Minor, *1,* 243–4: "Wir sollten die hellenischen Orgien und Mysterien also nicht als fremdartige Flecken und zufällige Ausschweifung, sondern als wesentlichen Bestandteil der alten Bildung, als eine notwendige Stufe der allmähligen Entwicklung des hellenischen Geistes mit Ehrfurcht betrachten."

102. 1794. Minor, *1,* 11.

103. *Ibid.*, p. 140: "die göttliche Trunkenheit des Dionysos, die tiefe Erfindsamkeit der Athene, und die leise Besonnenheit des Apollo."

104. *Werke, 1,* 32: "im gewaltigen Kampf zwischen dem alten Chaos und der Idee des Gesetzes und der harmonischen Ordnung."

105. *Ibid.,* p. 34: "bewunderswerte Ahnung des Göttlichen."

106. Minor, 2, 396 ff.

107. *Ibid.,* p. 411.

108. *Ibid., 1,* 98.

109. *Werke, 2,* 7.

110. *Ibid., 8,* 56 ff.

111. *Ibid., 1,* 212.

112. *Ibid., 8,* 65.

113. *Ibid., 2,* 181.

114. *Ibid.,* pp. 71–2: "vom Geist des Altertums durchdrungen, und selbst in der Form gross und edel, wie das Drama der Griechen."

115. Minor, *1,* 106–7.

116. *Ibid.,* 2, 315, 393: "einer der absichtlichsten Künstler."

117. *Ibid.,* p. 352: "Der Gipfel seiner Kraft."

118. *Werke, 8,* 88: "in welcher unermesslichen Weite von der Bühne."

119. *Ibid.,* 2, 93: "vielmehr ein altnordischer Dichter, als ein christlicher."

120. *Ibid., 8,* 89: "eine allgemein nordische und wahrhaft deutsche Poesie."

121. *Ibid.,* 2, 74–5.

122. *Ibid.,* p. 67.

123. *Ibid., 8,* 41.

124. Minor, *1,* 176: "nur eine leere Formalität ohne Kraft, Reiz und Stoff, sondern auch ihre Form selbst ist ein widersinniger, barbarischer Mechanismus, ohne innres Lebensprinzip und natürliche Organisation."

125. *Ibid.,* 2, 352–3.

126. *Werke, 2,* 108.

127. *Ibid.,* p. 110.

128. *Ibid.,* pp. 122, 126.

129. *Ibid.,* p. 145.

130. *Ibid.,* p. 101.

131. Minor, 2, 273: "Denn vom Sinn für die Poesie findet sich in Harris, Home und Johnson, den Koryphäen der Gattung, auch nicht die schamhafteste Andeutung."

132. *Werke, 8,* 185–200.

133. *Ibid.,* p. 198.

134. *Ibid.,* 2, 147: "Ein Mosaik aus einzelnen Bruchstücken der romantischen Sage."

135. *Ibid.*, pp. 24, 31, 33.

136. *Ibid.*, pp. 184, 182.

137. Minor, 2, 416: "diese Mischung von Literatur, Polemik, Witz und Philosophie."

138. See Josef Körner, *Romantiker und Klassiker. Die Brüder Schlegel in ihren Beziehungen zu Schiller und Goethe*, Berlin, 1924.

139. Minor, *1*, 177: "Die Stärke der Empfindung, die Hoheit der Gesinnung, die Pracht der Phantasie, die Würde der Sprache, die Gewalt des Rhythmus, die *Brust und Stimme*."

140. *Ibid.*, 2, 4.

141. *Ibid.*, pp. 5–6: "der Krampf der Verzweiflung . . . mit einer, ich möchte fast sagen, erhabnen Unmässigkeit . . . Die einmal zerrüttete Gesundheit der Einbildungskraft ist unheilbar."

142. *Ibid.*, p. 40.

143. Körner, *Romantiker und Klassiker*, p. 78: "ein rhetorischer Sentimentalist . . . ein poetischer Philosoph, aber kein philosophischer Dichter."

144. *Werke*, 2, 229: "der wahre Begründer unsrer Bühne . . . ganz und gar dramatischer Dichter. . . . leidenschaftliche Rhetorik."

145. Körner, pp. 165, 156.

146. Minor, *1*, 116: "eine unwiderlegliche Beglaubigung, dass das Objektive möglich, und die Hoffnung des Schönen kein leerer Wahn der Vernunft sei."

147. *Ibid.*, p. 114.

148. *Ibid.*, 2, 13.

149. *Ibid.*, pp. 22–3.

150. Körner, pp. 90–1: "Goethe ist ohne Wort Gottes . . . *Meister* ist deshalb unvollkommen, weil er nicht ganz mystisch ist."

151. *Ibid.*, p. 103: "den mechanischen Kunstwerken viel ähnlicher, wie die Alten und Shakespeare und die romantischen . . . In Goethes Werken keine Einheit, keine Ganzheit; nur hie und da ein Ansatz dazu."

152. *Werke*, 8, 150: "Jeder Roman, jedes Lehrgedicht, das wahrhaft poetisch ist, bildet ein eignes Individuum für sich." Cf. *ibid.*, p. 147.

153. *Ibid.*, p. 136.

154. *Ibid.*, 2, 228.

155. Körner, p. 188; letter dated January 16, 1813: "seine innere Schlechtigkeit." Friedrich speaks also of his "innre Ruchlosigkeit" and calls him "der alte Fratz" (to August Wilhelm, July 15, 1805; *Krisenjahre, 1*, 214); "der alte Grasaffe" (September 6, 1805; *ibid.*, p. 230).

156. Minor, 2, 278–80: "pikante Geschmacklosigkeit . . . anziehende Schwerfälligkeit."

157. *Werke*, 2, 230.

BIBLIOGRAPHY:

AUGUST WILHELM SCHLEGEL

There is an excellent edition by Eduard Böcking of A. W. Schlegel's *Sämtliche Werke*, 12 vols. Leipzig, 1846–47 (cited as *SW*). Unfortunately, it is unfinished and today virtually unprocurable. Apart from the works cited only by volume and page, I cite as Vienna the second edition of the Vienna lectures on dramatic art, *Über dramatische Kunst und Litteratur* (3 vols. Heidelberg, 1817) and as Berlin *Vorlesungen über schöne Litteratur und Kunst,* ed. J. Minor; Deutsche Literaturdenkmale des 18. and 19. Jahrhunderts, *17–19,* Stuttgart, 1884. *Vorlesungen über philosophische Kunstlehre,* ed. August Wünsche (Leipzig, 1911) is cited as 1798 Lectures. *Geschichte der deutschen Sprache und Poesie,* ed. Josef Körner; Deutsche Literaturdenkmale, *147* (Berlin, 1913) is cited as Bonn. These can be supplemented (though slightly) by an English account: *A. W. Schlegel's Lectures on German Literature from Gottsched to Goethe Given at the University of Bonn and Taken Down by George Toynbee in 1833,* ed. H. G. Fiedler, Oxford, 1944. The main French writings are in *Essais littéraires et historiques,* Bonn, 1842. The MS of the 1803 lectures on *Encyclopaedia* is still unprinted. There is a brief description in R. Haym's *Romantische Schule* (Berlin, 1870), pp. 846–52; and a section is in W. Jesinghaus, below. Scattered articles like those on the *Nibelungenlied* in Friedrich Schlegel's *Deutsches Museum* (Vols. *1* and 2, 1812, Vienna) must be searched for in the original files. I have not had access to A. W. Schlegel's *Vorlesungen über Theorie und Geschichte der bildenden Kunst,* Berlin, 1827. To judge from Minor's account (in introduction to *Vorlesungen,* above, *1,* xxxi ff.) the several portions follow the earlier Berlin lectures very closely.

Most of the publications of letters listed under Friedrich Schlegel contain also letters of his brother. To those listed there must be added Josef Körner's ed., *Briefe von und an A. W. Schlegel* (2 vols. 1930, with a checklist of published letters) and Comtesse Jean de Pange, *Schlegel et Madame de Staël* (Paris, 1938), which contains the letters to Madame de Staël.

There is no biography of A. W. Schlegel except a thin sketch by Bernhard von Brentano (1943). Josef Körner, *Romantiker und Klas-*

siker (Berlin, 1924) and Madame de Pange's book listed above discuss episodes and provide a wealth of materials.

There is, also, surprisingly no extended discussion of the critic and literary historian. Rudolf Haym, *Die Romantische Schule* (Berlin, 1870), which describes the early career to about 1803, is still most useful. A short general sketch is in Walter F. Schirmer, *Kleine Schriften* (Tübingen, 1950), pp. 153–200.

Of special studies I found the following useful: Josef Körner, *Die Botschaft der deutschen Romantik an Europa*, Augsburg, 1929 (on Schlegel's *Dramatic Lectures* and their influence); Hans Zehnder, *Die Anfänge von August W. Schlegels kritischer Tätigkeit*, Mulhouse, 1930; Wilhelm Schwartz, *A. W. Schlegels Verhältnis zur spanischen und portugiesischen Literatur*, Halle, 1913; E. Sulger-Gebing, "Schlegel und Dante," in *Germanistiche Abhandlungen Hermann Paul dargebracht* (Strasbourg, 1902), pp. 99–134 (mostly on the translation); Walter Jesinghaus, *A. W. Schlegels Meinungen über Ursprache*, Düsseldorf, 1913; J.-J. Bertrand, "Guillaume Schlegel, Critique de Molière," *Revue de littérature comparée*, 2 (1922), 201–37; Philarète Chasles, "Euripide et Racine," in *Études sur l'antiquité* (Paris, 1847), pp. 245–53; and August Emmersleben, *Die Antike in der romantischen Theorie: Die Gebrüder Schlegel und die Antike*, Berlin, 1937.

English translation: *A Course of Lectures on Dramatic Art and Literature*, trans. John Black, 2 vols. London, 1815; revised by A. J. W. Morrison, London, 1846.

NOTES: AUGUST WILHELM SCHLEGEL

1. Berlin, *3*, 211.
2. *SW*, 7, 3–23.
3. *Ibid.*, *10*, 115.
4. *Ibid.*, p. 376.
5. *Ibid.*, *11*, 183.
6. Paris, 1807.
7. 1795; see *SW*, *11*, 71.
8. *SW*, *3*, 200: "Hingegen in die Zusammensetzung eines fremden Wesens eindringen, es erkennen, wie es ist, belauschen, wie es wurde."
9. Vienna, *1*, 5–6: "Aber ein ächter Kenner kann man nicht sein ohne Universalität des Geistes, d.h. ohne die Biegsamkeit, welche uns in den Stand setzt, mit Verläugnung persönlicher Vorliebe und blinder Gewöhnung, uns in die Eigenheiten anderer Völker und Zeitalter zu versetzen, sie gleichsam aus ihrem Mittelpunkte heraus zu fühlen."

10. Berlin, 2, 38: "es fehlt gänzlich an der zur Kritik so nothwendigen Kenntniss der universellen Geschichte der Poesie."

11. *Ibid.*, p. 85: "Da wir nun in der menschlichen Bildungsgeschichte überhaupt das Naturgesetz einer wechselnden Flut und Ebbe . . ."

12. *SW, 8*, 209: "Wir sind, darf ich wohl behaupten, die Kosmopoliten der europäischen Kultur."

13. Paris, 1818.

14. 1833–34.

15. See *Deutsches Museum,* ed. F. Schlegel, Vols. *1, 2*.

16. *SW, 7*, 98.

17. *Ibid.*, p. 133.

18. *Ibid.*, p. 146.

19. *Ibid.*, p. 104.

20. *Ibid.*, p. 99.

21. See passage from 1803, "Privatvorlesungen über Encyclopädie," quoted in W. Jesinghaus, *A. W. Schlegels Meinungen über Ursprache,* p. 61.

22. Berlin, *1,* 92.

23. *Ibid.*, p. 93.

24. *Ibid., 3,* 74: "Die Poesie kann nicht zu fantastisch sein, in einem gewissen Sinne also auch nicht übertreiben. Keine Vergleichung des entferntesten, des grössten und kleinsten, wenn sie sonst nur treffend und bedeutsam, ist ihr zu kühn."

25. *Ibid., 1,* 292: "Alle Dinge stehn in Beziehungen auf einander, alles bedeutet daher alles, jeder Teil des Universums spiegelt das Ganze."

26. *Ibid.*, p. 93: "In jenen schrankenlosen Übertragungen des poetischen Styls liegt also, der Ahndung und Anforderung nach, die grosse Wahrheit dass eins alles und alles eins ist."

27. *Ibid.*, p. 93: "die Fantasie räumt dieses störende Medium hinweg und versenkt uns in das Universum, indem sie es als ein Zauberreich ewiger Verwandlungen, worin nichts isoliert besteht, sondern alles aus allem durch die wunderbarste Schöpfung wird, in uns sich bewegen lässt."

28. *Ibid.*, p. 292: "Die Poesie ist, wenn ich so sagen darf, Spekulation der Fantasie."

29. *Ibid.*, p. 293: "Allein die wahrhaft schönen Bilder sind unsterblich, und mögen sie noch so oft gebraucht worden sein, unter der Hand eines echten Dichters verjüngen sie sich immer von neuem."

30. *Ibid.*, pp. 284–5.

31. *Ibid.*, pp. 327–8. Cf. *SW, 11,* 422; Vienna *3*, 63 f.

32. *SW*, *3*, 226: "Wir treten überall auf festen Boden, umgeben von einer Welt der Wirklichkeit und des individuellen Seins."

33. Vienna, *1*, 153–4: "Allegorie ist die Personifikation eines Begriffes, eine lediglich in dieser Absicht vorgenommene Dichtung; sonderlich aber ist das, was die Einbildungskraft zwar auf andere Veranlassungen gedichtet, oder was sonst eine von dem Begriff unabhängige Wirklichkeit hat, was aber dennoch einer sinnbildlichen Auslegung sich willig fügt, ja sie von selbst darbietet."

34. *SW*, *12*, 346.

35. 1798 Lectures, p. 23.

36. Vienna, *1*, 45.

37. *SW* 7, 30 (1796): "und folglich kann in seinen Schöpfungen nicht wohl ein andre Art von Dunkelheit stattfinden, als die Unergründlichkeit der schaffenden Natur, deren Ebenbild er im Kleinen ist."

38. Berlin, *1*, 103: "Jedes schöne Ganze aus der Hand des bildenden Künstlers ist daher im Kleinen ein Abdruck des höchsten Schönen im grossen Ganzen der Natur." Cf. Vol. *1* of this *History*, p. 209.

39. *Ibid.*, p. 103.

40. *Ibid.*, 2, 291.

41. *Ibid.*, p. 292.

42. *Ibid.*, *1*, 90: "Das Schöne ist eine symbolische Darstellung des Unendlichen."

43. *SW*, *8*, 144–5; letter to Fouqué, 1806: "Was ist es denn, was im Homer, in den Nibelungen, im Dante, im Shakespeare die Gemüter so unwiderstehlich hinreisst, als jener Orakelspruch des Herzens, jene tiefen Ahnungen, worin das dunkle Rätsel unseres Daseins sich aufzulösen scheint?"

44. Berlin, *1*, 330.

45. *Ibid.*, pp. 332–3.

46. *Ibid.*, p. 337.

47. *Ibid.*, 2, 83.

48. *SW*, *10*, 400.

49. *Ibid.*, *11*, 198; 1798 Lectures, p. 111; and Berlin, 2, 206.

50. Berlin, *3*, 200: "Die wesentlichsten Naturkräfte werden dem Dichter Symbole des geistigen Seins, und so geht aus der Vereinigung seiner Physik mit seiner Theologie eine scientifische Mythologie hervor, so dass, wenn man die Möglichkeit bezweifelt, dass die Poesie Organ des Idealismus werden könne, man sie hier schon realisiert findet."

51. *Ibid.*, pp. 194–5.

52. *Ibid.*, 2, 92: "Idealismus jetzt in seiner strebendsten Entwicklung. Dem Dichter, der ihn zu brauchen versteht, ist dadurch der Zauberstab

in die Hand gegeben, mit Leichtigkeit den Geist zu verkörpern, und das Materielle zu vergeistigen, da die Poesie ja eben zwischen der sinnlichen und intellektuellen Welt sich schwebend erhalten muss."

53. *Ibid.*, p. 315.

54. *Ibid.*, p. 119.

55. *Ibid.*, p. 119.

56. *Ibid.*, p. 119.

57. *SW, 8,* 77.

58. Vienna, *3,* 48: "fand ich bei näherer Betrachtung, wenn sie wirklich vortreffliche Werke geliefert, ausgezeichnete Kultur der Geisteskräfte, geübte Kunst, reiflich überlegte und würdige Absichten."

59. Berlin, *3,* 161.

60. *SW, 8,* 75.

61. Berlin, *1,* 82.

62. *Ibid.*, p. 83.

63. *Ibid.*

64. *Ibid.*, p. 84.

65. *Ibid., 2,* 84: "Man muss nur wissen, dass die Fantasie, wodurch uns erst die Welt entsteht, und die wodurch Kunstwerke gebildet werden, dieselbe Kraft ist, nur in verschiednen Wirkungsarten."

66. *Ibid., 1,* 102: "Das heisst nämlich, sie soll wie die Natur selbstständig schaffend, organisiert und organisierend, lebendige Werke bilden."

67. *Ibid., 2,* 90: "So muss auch der heutige Dichter über das Wesen seiner Kunst mehr im klaren sein, als es ehemalige grosse Dichter konnten, die wir daher besser begreifen müssen, als sie sich selbst; eine höhere Reflexion muss sich in seinen Werken wieder in Unbewusstsein untertauchen."

68. *SW, 7,* 33: "Wie aber, wenn ein dramatisches Gedicht dieser Art noch mehr Ähnlichkeit mit höheren Organisationen hätte, an denen zuweilen die angeborne Missgestalt eines einzigen Gliedes nicht geheilt werden kann, ohne dem Ganzen an's Leben zu kommen?"

69. Berlin, *2,* 358:

Wenn Kunstwerke als organisierte Ganze zu betrachten sind, so ist diese Insurrektion der einzelnen Teile gegen die Einheit des Ganzen eben das, was in der organischen Welt die Verwesung, welche um so scheusslicher und ekelhafter zu sein pflegt, je edler das durch sie zerstörte organische Gebilde war, und daher eben bei dieser vortrefflichsten aller poetischen Gattungen, mit dem grössten Widerwillen erfüllen muss. Freilich sind die meisten Menschen für den Eindruck dieser geistigen Verwesung nicht so empfänglich als für den der körperlichen.

70. Vienna, *3*, 8:

Mechanisch ist die Form, wenn sie durch äussre Einwirkung irgend einem Stoffe bloss als zufällige Zutat, ohne Beziehung auf dessen Beschaffenheit erteilt wird, wie man z.B. einer weichen Masse eine beliebige Gestalt giebt, damit sie solche nach der Erhärtung beibehalte. Die organische Form hingegen ist eingeboren, sie bildet von innen heraus, und erreicht ihre Bestimmtheit zugleich mit der vollständigen Entwickelung des Keimes. . . . Auch in der schönen Kunst wie im Gebiete der Natur, der höchsten Künstlerin, sind alle ächten Formen organisch, d.h. durch den Gehalt des Kunstwerkes bestimmt. Mit Einem Worte, die Form ist nichts anders als ein bedeutsames Äussres, die sprechende durch keine störenden Zufälligkeiten entstellte Physiognomie jedes Dinges, die von dessen verborgnem Wesen ein wahrhaftes Zeugniss ablegt.

71. *SW*, *8*, 122: "Einheit und Unteilbarkeit."

72. *Ibid.*, *11*, 187: "Nur durchgängige Vollständigkeit und innere Wechselbestimmung des Ganzen und der Teile kann die Vernunft befriedigen . . ."

73. Berlin, *1*, 49–50.

74. *Ibid.*, p. 291.

75. *Ibid.*, *1*, 79–80: "So kann man auch ein Gedicht oder sonst ein Kunstwerk mit Recht idealisch nennen, wenn sich in ihm Stoff und Form, Buchstabe und Geist bis zur völligen Ununterscheidbarkeit gegenseitig durchdrungen haben."

76. *Ibid.*, *3*, 209: "Solche Menschen haben freilich keinen Begriff, wie die Form vielmehr Werkzeug, Organ für den Dichter ist, und gleich bei der ersten Empfängniss eines Gedichts, Gehalt und Form wie Seele und Leib unzertrennlich ist."

77. *SW*, *10*, 134: "Wir müssen nun betrachten, in wiefern sie die poetische Form, den Stil, den Ton, die Farbe der Darstellung der homerischen Gesänge getroffen oder verfehlt hat, was eigentlich das Wichtigste ist, weil es sich über das Ganze erstreckt, und weil auch aller Inhalt eines Gedichts doch nur durch das Medium der Form erkannt wird."

78. Vienna, 2, 97: "fordere ich eine weit tiefer liegende, innigere, geheimnissvollere Einheit."

79. *Ibid.*, p. 95.

80. *Ibid.*, *3*, 366.

81. Berlin, 2, 303.

82. *Ibid.*, *3*, 183: "Allein die ächten Formen muss man betrachten wie Gattungen von Organisationen, in welchen das Leben erst ge-

bunden ist, die aber noch einen grossen Spielraum für Individualität zulassen."

83. *Ibid.*, p. 69: "Allgemein betrachtet, ist ein gewisses Gesetz der Form sogar Bedingung freier Individualität in der Kunst wie in der Natur, denn was zu keiner Gattung von Organisationen gehört, ist monströs."

84. *Ibid.*, 2, 163.

85. *SW, 11,* 188, 190, 208, 219.

86. *Ibid.*, p. 190.

87. 1798 Lectures, p. 125.

88. *SW, 11,* 195. E.g. *Aeneid,* iv, 408 ff.

89. Berlin, 2, 179–80.

90. 1798 Lectures, p. 216.

91. *Ibid.*, p. 217.

92. E.g. Diderot's, *SW, 8,* 7.

93. Berlin, *3,* 17.

94. *Ibid., 1,* 43.

95. *Ibid., 2,* 319.

96. *Ibid., 1,* 43.

97. *Ibid., 2,* 319.

98. *Ibid.*, p. 319.

99. *Ibid.*, p. 319.

100. *Vienna, 3,* 224: "dass Shakspeare die poetische Gerechtigkeit im echten Sinne des Wortes, wo es nämlich die Offenbarung des unsichtbaren Segens oder Fluches, der auf menschlichen Gesinnungen und Taten ruht, auf das genaueste beobachtet hat."

101. *Ibid., 1,* 62–3.

102. Berlin, 2, 320; Vienna, *3,* 112–3.

103. Lectures, p. 161; Vienna, *1,* 63.

104. *Ibid.*, pp. 63–4.

105. *Ibid.*, p. 273.

106. *Ibid.*, pp. 277–8: "sie sucht die buntesten Gegensätze, und immerfort sich kreuzenden Widersprüche."

107. *Ibid., 3,* 72.

108. *Ibid., 2,* 60–1: "Hier nur so viel, dass es ein in die Darstellung selbst hineingelegtes mehr oder weniger leise angedeutetes Eingeständniss ihrer übertreibenden Einseitigkeit in dem Anteil der Fantasie und Empfindung ist."

109. *Ibid., 3,* 72: "sondern frei über ihm schwebe, und dass er den schönen, unwiderstehlich anziehenden Schein, den er selbst hervorgezaubert, wenn er anders wollte, unerbittlich vernichten könnte."

110. *Ibid. 1,* 58–9:

Das lyrische Gedicht ist der musikalische Ausdruck von Gemütsbewegungen durch die Sprache. Das Wesen der musikalischen Stimmung besteht darin, dass wir irgend eine Regung, sei sie nun an sich erfreulich oder schmerzlich, mit Wohlgefallen festzuhalten, ja innerlich zu verewigen suchen. Die Empfindung muss also schon in dem Grade gemildert sein, dass sie uns nicht durch Streben nach der Lust oder Flucht vor dem Schmerz über sich selbst hinausreisse, sondern dass wir, unbekümmert um den Wechsel, welchen die Zeit herbeiführt, in einem einzelnen Augenblick unsers Daseins einheimisch werden wollen.

111. 1798 Lectures, pp. 130 ff.

112. Berlin, *1*, 15.

113. *Ibid.*, p. 17: "Sonst aber muss ein jedes Kunstwerk aus seinem Standpunkte betrachtet werden; es braucht nicht ein absolut höchstes zu erreichen, es ist vollendet, wenn es ein Höchstes in seiner Art, seiner Sphäre, seiner Welt ist; und so erklärt sich, wie es zugleich ein Glied in einer unendlichen Reihe von Fortschritten, und dennoch an und für sich befriedigend und selbstständig sein kann."

114. *Ibid.*, pp. 19, 18, 21.

115. *Ibid., 3,* 9: "Unser Bestreben hingegen ist darauf gerichtet, die Kunstkritik so viel als möglich auf den historischen Standpunkt zu führen, d. h. wiewohl jedes Kunstwerk nach innen zu in sich beschlossen sein soll, es als zu einer Reihe gehörig nach den Verhältnissen seiner Entstehung und Existenz zu betrachten, und aus dem, was zuvor gewesen und was darauf gefolgt ist oder noch folgt, zu begreifen."

116. *SW*, 7, 107: "Sie kann sie annehmen: denn indem man erklärt, wie die Kunst wurde, zeigt man zugleich auf das einleuchtendste, was sie sein soll."

117. *Ibid., 10, 379.*

118. *Ibid., 8,* 70:

Mit dem Hinstellen für die äussere Anschauung ist das Gedicht oder sonstige Erzeugniss des Geistes von der Person des Hervorbringers eben so abgelöst, wie die Frucht, welche genossen wird, vom Baume; und wenn gleich die sämmtlichen Gedichte eines Mannes seinen poetischen Lebenslauf darstellen, und zusammen gleichsam eine künstlerische Person bilden, in welcher sich die Eigentümlichkeit der wirklichen mehr oder weniger, unmittelbar oder mittelbar offenbart: so müssen wir sie doch als Erzeugnisse der Freiheit, ja der Willkür, ansehen, und es dahin gestellt sein lassen, ob der Dichter sein Inneres nicht auf ganz andere Weise in seinen Werken hätte abspiegeln können, wenn er gewollt hätte.

119. Berlin, *1*, 23.

120. *SW, 12, 39*: "auch giebt es in jeder Kritik, sie mag noch so förmlich sein, irgend einen Punkt, wo das Motivieren ein Ende hat, und wo es nur darauf ankommt, ob der Leser mit dem Beurteiler übereinstimmen kann und will."

121. Berlin, *2, 31*: "Weit entfernt ein solches im Ganzen nach seinem Bau und Wesen konstruieren zu können."

122. *SW, 7, 26*.

123. Berlin, *1, 25*.

124. *SW, 10, 285*: "ist es viel leichter, mit Verstand zu tadeln, als geistvoll zu loben. Jenes kann man tun, und doch bei der Aussenseite, gleichsam bei dem technischen Gerüste eines Geisteswerkes, stehen bleiben; dieses setzt voraus, dass man wirklich in das Innere gedrungen, und zugleich Meister im Ausdruck sei, um die dem blossen Begriffe entfliehende Eigentümlichkeit des geistigen Gepräges zu fassen."

125. Berlin, *2, 26*.

126. *Ibid., 1, 28*: "Es können verschiedne Menschen wirklich denselben Mittelpunkt vor Augen haben, aber weil jeder von einem verschiednen Punkte des Umkreises ausgeht, so beschreiben sie auch dahin verschiedne Radien."

127. 1798 Lectures, pp. 217, 221, 214: "ein vollendetes Meisterwerk der höheren romantischen Kunst."

128. *Ibid.*, p. 151.

129. *SW, 8, 80*: "unmittelbar aus reinen Kunstgesetzen."

130. Berlin, *1, 22*: "So kann man sich die antike Poesie als den einen Pol einer magnetischen Linie denken, die romantische als den andern, und der Historiker und Theoretiker, um beide richtig zu betrachten, würde sich möglichst auf dem Indifferenzpunkte zu halten suchen müssen."

131. *Ibid.*, pp. 356–7 (1802).

132. *Ibid., 2, 6*.

133. *Ibid., 3, 13*: "Übrigens liegt unserm Geist und Gemüt unstreitig die romantische Poesie näher als die klassische."

134. *Ibid.*, p. 240.

135. Vienna, *1, 14*: "in der Musik hat Rousseau den Gegensatz anerkannt, und gezeigt, wie Rhythmus und Melodie das herrschende Prinzip der antiken, Harmonie der modernen Musik sei."

136. *Ibid.*, p. 16: "Das Pantheon ist nicht verschiedener von der Westminster-Abtei oder der St. Stephans-kirche in Wien, als der Bau einer Tragödie des Sophokles von dem eines Schauspiels von Shakespear."

137. *Ibid.*, p. 25: "In der griechischen Kunst und Poesie ist ursprüngliche bewusstlose Einheit der Form und des Stoffes; in der neueren,

so fern sie ihrem eigentümlichen Geiste treu geblieben, wird innigere Durchdringung beider als zweier Entgegengesetzten gesucht."

138. *Ibid., 3,* 14.

139. *Ibid.,* pp. 14–5:

so ist die gesamte alte Poesie und Kunst gleichsam ein rhythmischer Nomos, eine harmonische Verkündigung der auf immer festgestellten Gesetzgebung einer schön geordneten und die ewigen Urbilder der Dinge in sich abspiegelnden Welt. Die romantische hingegen ist der Ausdruck des geheimen Zuges zu dem immerfort nach neuen und wundervollen Geburten ringenden Chaos, welches unter der geordneten Schöpfung, ja, in ihrem Schoosse sich verbirgt. . . . Jene ist einfacher, klarer, und der Natur in der selbständigen Vollendung ihrer einzelnen Werke ähnlicher; diese, ungeachtet ihres fragmentarischen Ansehens, ist dem Geheimniss des Weltalls näher.

140. *SW, 11,* 183.

141. Berlin, 2, 126 ff.

142. *Ibid.,* pp. 333 ff.

143. *Ibid., 1,* 76 ff.

144. Vienna, *1,* 179; Berlin, 2, 345.

145. *Ibid.,* pp. 351 ff.; Vienna, *1,* 198 ff.

146. Berlin, 2, 378; Vienna *1,* 268 ff.

147. Berlin, 2, 189.

148. *Ibid.,* p. 299.

149. *Ibid.,* p. 295.

150. *Ibid.,* p. 282.

151. *Ibid.,* pp. 282, 285, 300–1.

152. *Ibid.,* pp. 260, 306.

153. Vienna, *1,* 326 ff.

154. *Deutsches Museum* (1812).

155. Berlin, 2, 222: "Jenes ist ein Werk von kolossalem Charakter, nicht nur von unerreichbarer sinnlicher Energie sondern von erstaunenswürdiger Hoheit in den Gesinnungen; es endigt wie die Ilias, nur in weit grösserem Masstabe, mit dem überwältigenden Eindrucke allgemeiner Zerstörung."

156. *SW, 3,* 207, 224.

157. Berlin, *3,* 191 ff.

158. *Ibid.,* pp. 203 ff.

159. *Ibid.,* pp. 238 ff.

160. *SW, 12,* 275. Cf. Berlin, *3,* 251–2.

161. Vienna, *3,* 344.

162. *SW, 11,* 409: "In dieser Rücksicht beruht Alles auf dem grossen

Kontrapost zwischen parodischen und romantischen Massen, der immer unaussprechlich reizend und harmonisch ist, zuweilen aber, wie bei der Zusammenstellung des verrückten Cardenio mit dem verrückten Don Quixote, ins Erhabne übergeht."

163. *Ibid., 10,* 54.

164. *Ibid., 7,* 31: "Man kann sich recht gut denken, dass Shakspeare mehr von seinem Hamlet wusste als ihm selbst bewusst war."

165. *Ibid.,* p. 71: "Er hatte also feinere, geistigere Begriffe von der dramatischen Kunst, als man gewöhnlich ihm zuzuschreiben geneigt ist."

166. *Ibid.,* p. 87: "ein harmonisches Wunder"; p. 97: "Durchhin eine grosse Antithese."

167. *Ibid.,* p. 97.

168. *Ibid.,* p. 77.

169. *Ibid., 11,* 281: "Gegen unsre Konvenienz, das möchte sein, aber gewiss nicht gegen die seines Zeitalters und Volkes, und selten gegen die in der Natur gegründete Schicklichkeit."

170. *Ibid., 8,* 29 (1798):

So ist er auch systematisch wie kein andrer: bald durch jene Antithesen, die Individuen, Massen, ja Welten in malerischen Gruppen kontrastieren lassen; bald durch musikalische Symmetrie desselben grossen Masstabes, durch gigantische Wiederholungen und Refrains; oft durch Parodie des Buchstabens und durch Ironie über den Geist des romantischen Drama, und immer durch die höchste und vollständigste Individualität und die vielseitigste, alle Stufen der Poesie von der sinnlichsten Nachahmung bis zur geistigsten Charakteristik vereinigende Darstellung derselben.

171. Berlin, *2,* 376: "Den Shakespeare aber, der ein Abgrund von Absichtlichkeit, Selbstbewusstsein und Reflexion ist."

172. Vienna, *3,* 70. "Man wäre übel beraten, wenn man die Aeusserungen der Personen über sich selbst und andre immer für baare Münze nähme."

173. *Ibid.,* p. 54.

174. *Ibid.,* p. 90.

175. *Ibid.,* p. 52.

176. *Ibid.,* p. 46.

177. *Ibid.,* p. 111.

178. *Ibid.,* p. 165.

179. *Ibid.,* p. 156.

180. *Ibid.,* pp. 174–75.

181. *Ibid.,* p. 108.

182. *Ibid.,* p. 142.

183. *Ibid.*, p. 149: "er hat einen natürlichen Hang dazu, krumme Wege zu gehen."

184. *Ibid.*, pp. 229 ff.

185. *Ibid.*, p. 238: "Die drei letzten Stücke sind nicht nur unbezweifelt von Shakespeare, sondern sie gehören, meines Erachtens, unter seine reifsten und vortrefflichsten Werke."

186. *Ibid.*, p. 243.

187. *Ibid.*, p. 269.

188. *Ibid.*, p. 271.

189. *Ibid.*, p. 307.

190. *Ibid.*, 2, 138.

191. *Ibid.*, p. 159.

192. *Ibid.*, p. 200.

193. *Ibid.*, p. 198.

194. *Ibid.*, 2, 250: "Kammerdiener-moral."

195. *Ibid.*, p. 256.

196. *Ibid.*, pp. 262–3.

197. *Ibid.*, p. 275.

198. Berlin, p. 206.

199. *Ibid.*, p. 208.

200. *Ibid.*, p. 209.

201. Vienna, *3*, 314.

202. *Ibid.*, p. 373.

203. *Ibid.*, p. 374.

204. Berlin, 2, 213 ff.

205. Vienna, 2, 218.

206. *Ibid.*, p. 284.

207. Berlin, 2, 286: "frostig."

208. *Ibid.*, pp. 309–11.

209. *Ibid.*, p. 229.

210. *Ibid.*, p. 126: "der Gipfel der Verkehrtheit."

211. *SW*, 7, 86: "Dickhäutige Fühllosigkeit."

212. Berlin, *1*, 58–64.

213. 1800; see *SW*, *8*, 58.

214. *SW*, *11*, 269.

215. Vienna, 2, 58.

216. *Ibid.*, *3*, 388 ff.

217. *SW*, *8*, 49.

218. Berlin, *3*, 80 ff.

219. Quoted in R. Haym, *Die romantische Schule* (1870), p. 848, from MS of lectures on *Encyclopaedia* (1803).

220. Berlin, 2, 21.

221. *SW, 8,* 64 ff.

222. Josef Körner, *Romantiker und Klassiker,* is a detailed history of the relationship.

223. E.g. Berlin, *2,* 375–6; *SW, 11,* 275.

224. *SW, 8,* 67; *12,* 67.

225. Vienna, *3,* 407–15.

226. See A. W. Schlegel, *Lectures on German Literature,* ed. H. G. Fiedler (Oxford, 1946), pp. 43–4. The student was George Toynbee in 1833.

227. Cf. *SW, 10,* 7, 16.

228. *Ibid.,* pp. 62–3.

229. *Ibid., 11,* 183.

230. *Ibid.,* p. 221: "Hermann und Dorothea ist ein vollendetes Kunstwerk im grossen Stil."

231. See *ibid., 9,* 231–66, "Schreiben an Goethe" (1805).

232. Vienna, *3,* 405: "Man muss wohl eingestehn, dass Goethe zwar unendlich viel dramatisches aber nicht eben so viel theatralisches Talent besitzt."

233. *Ibid.,* p. 406: "Das stärkste erschütternde Pathos findet sich im Egmont, aber der Schluss dieses Trauerspiels ist ebenfalls ganz aus der äussern Welt in das Gebiet einer idealischen Seelenmusik entrückt."

234. Fiedler, p. 40.

235. Vienna, *3,* 401–2.

236. *SW, 10,* 87–8.

237. *Ibid., 12,* 27; *11,* 136.

238. *Ibid., 10,* 363.

239. See H. Lüdeke, ed., *Ludwig Tieck und die Brüder Schlegel,* Frankfurt, 1930.

240. Cf. the letters in *Krisenjahre der Frühromantik,* ed. J. Körner (Brünn, 1939), *2,* 390–2, etc.

241. Novalis, *Werke,* ed. Selig, *5,* 293 (April 5, 1800): "Deins ist allemal eigentümlich—das seinige historisch und allgemein."

BIBLIOGRAPHY: THE EARLY ROMANTICS IN GERMANY

1. Schelling is quoted from *Sämtliche Werke,* ed. K. F. A. Schelling, 14 vols. Stuttgart, 1856–61. Letters and poems in *Aus Schellings Leben in Briefen,* ed. G. L. Plitt, 3 vols. 1869–70. From the extensive literature I use M. Adam, *Schellings Kunstphilosophie,* in Abhandlungen zur Philosophie und ihrer Geschichte, *4,* 1907; and Jean Gibelin, *L'Esthétique de Schelling d'après la Philosophie de l'art,* Paris, 1934.

2. Novalis is quoted from *Gesammelte Werke,* ed. Carl Seelig, 5 vols. Zürich, 1945. Eduard Havenstein, *Friedrich von Hardenbergs aesthetische Anschauungen,* Palaestra, *84* (Berlin, 1909) is of little use. Helmut Rehder, "Novalis and Shakespeare," *PMLA, 63* (1948), 604–24, interprets Novalis' pronouncements well.

3. Wackenroder is quoted from *Werke und Briefe,* Berlin, 1938; reprint [1948]. There are three good essays on Wackenroder, of which the last is easily the best: Heinrich Wölfflin, "Die Herzensergiessungen eines Kunstliebenden Klosterbruders," in *Studien zur Literaturgeschichte: Michael Bernays gewidmet* (Hamburg, 1893), pp. 61–73; I. Rouge, "Wackenroder et la genèse de l'esthétique romantique," in *Mélanges Henri Lichtenberger* (Paris, 1934), pp. 185–203; and Gerhard Fricke, "Bemerkungen zu Wilhelm Heinrich Wackenroders Religion der Kunst," in *Festschrift Paul Kluckhohn und Hermann Schneider gewidmet* (Tübingen, 1948), pp. 345–71.

4. Tieck's criticism is quoted from *Kritische Schriften,* 4 vols. Leipzig, 1848–52 (cited as *Kri. Schr.*) and from *Das Buch über Shakespeare,* ed. Henry Lüdeke, Halle, 1920. Full discussions are in Robert Minder, *Un poète romantique allemand: Ludwig Tieck,* Paris, 1936; and in Edwin H. Zeydel's *Ludwig Tieck, the German Romanticist,* Princeton, 1935. On his relations to English literature see H. Lüdeke, *L. Tieck und das alte englische Theater,* Frankfurt, 1922; and Edwin H. Zeydel, *Ludwig Tieck and England,* Princeton, 1931. On Calderón and Tieck: J.-J. Bertrand, *Tieck et le théâtre espagnol,* Paris, 1914. Incidental discussion of criticism in Raymond M. Immerwahr, *The Esthetic Intent of Tieck's Fantastic Comedy,* St. Louis, 1953. More specialized articles, etc. are quoted in Minder's bibliography.

5. Jean Paul's *Vorschule der Aesthetik* is quoted from Vol. *11* of *Sämtliche Werke,* ed. Eduard Berend, Weimar, 1935 (cited as *SW, 11*) Eduard Berend's *Jean Pauls Aesthetik* (Berlin, 1909) is the best study.

NOTES: THE EARLY ROMANTICS IN GERMANY

SCHELLING

1. See "Das älteste Systemprogramm des deutschen Idealismus," in Hölderlin, *Werke,* ed. Pigenot (3d ed. Berlin, 1943), *3,* 623–5:

> Ich bin nun überzeugt, dass der höchste Akt der Vernunft, der, indem sie alle Ideen umfasst, ein ästhetischer Akt ist, und dass Wahrheit und Güte nur in der Schönheit verschwistert sind. Der Philosoph muss ebensoviel ästhetische Kraft besitzen, als der Dichter. Die Poesie bekommt dadurch eine höhere Würde, sie

wird am Ende wieder, was sie am Anfang war—Lehrerin der Menschheit; denn es gibt keine Philosophie, keine Geschichte mehr, die Dichtkunst allein wird alle übrigen Wissenschaften und Künste überleben.

I accept the view that this MS was written by Schelling and not by Hölderlin. Cf. Ludwig Strauss, "Hölderlins Anteil an Schellings frühem Systemprogramm," *Deutsche Vierteljahrschrift für Literaturwissenschaft und Geistesgeschichte,* 5 (1927), 679–747.

2. In *Kritisches Journal der Philosophie,* ed. Schelling and Hegel, 2 (Tübingen, 1803), 35–50.

3. *Sämtliche Werke, 3,* 628.

4. *Ibid.,* pp. 620, 627.

5. *Ibid.,* p. 619.

6. *Ibid.,* p. 626.

7. *Ibid., 4,* 227.

8. *Ibid., 5,* 348–9.

9. *Ibid.,* p. 348: "Ineinsbildung."

10. *Ibid., 7,* 292–3.

11. *Ibid.,* p. 301: "nur wie durch Sinnbilder redender Naturgeist"; p. 300: "diese unverfälschte Kraft der Schöpfung und Wirksamkeit der Natur wie in einem Umrisse."

12. *Ibid.,* p. 316: "Die Gewissheit, dass aller Gegensatz nur scheinbar, die Liebe das Band aller Wesen, und reine Güte Grund und Inhalt der ganzen Schöpfung ist."

13. *Ibid., 3,* 628: "Was wir Natur nennen, ist ein Gedicht, das in geheimer wunderbarer Schrift verschlossen liegt. Doch könnte das Rätsel sich enthüllen, würden wir die Odyssee des Geistes darin erkennen, der wunderbar getäuscht, sich selber suchend, sich selber flieht."

14. *Ibid., 5,* 405, 390–1.

15. *Ibid.,* p. 395.

16. *Ibid.,* p. 411.

17. *Ibid.,* p. 432: "Insofern war Christus zugleich der Gipfel und das Ende der alten Götterwelt."

18. *Ibid.,* p. 433.

19. *Ibid.,* p. 436.

20. *Ibid.,* p. 437.

21. *Ibid.,* p. 439.

22. *Ibid.,* p. 441.

23. *Ibid.,* p. 442.

24. *Ibid.,* p. 445.

25. *Ibid.,* p. 446.

26. *Ibid.,* p. 447.

27. *Ibid.*, p. 667.

28. *Ibid.*, p. 577.

29. *Ibid.*, p. 593: "wenn die Architektur überhaupt die erstarrte Musik ist."

30. *Ibid.*, p. 640.

31. *Ibid.*, p. 646.

32. *Ibid.*, p. 667.

33. He refers to the "famous Meda," apparently an error for Medoro; *ibid.*, p. 671.

34. *Ibid.*, p. 683.

35. *Ibid.*, p. 683.

36. *Ibid.*, p. 685.

37. *Ibid.*, pp. 686–7.

38. *Kritisches Journal*, 2, 57–62. Not in collected edition.

39. See *La poesia di Dante* (Bari, 1948), pp. 180–1.

40. *Sämtliche Werke*, 5, 690.

41. *Ibid.*, p. 710.

42. *Ibid.*, p. 720.

43. *Ibid.*, p. 729.

44. *Ibid.*, p. 729.

45. *Ibid.*, p. 732.

46. *Ibid.*, p. 736.

NOVALIS

1. Saintsbury, *3*, 386–7.

2. *Gesammelte Werke*, ed. Seelig, *4*, 302.

3. *Ibid.*, p. 301: "Wer es nicht unmittelbar weiss und fühlt, was Poesie ist, dem lässt sich kein Begriff davon beibringen."

4. *Ibid.*, p. 167.

5. *Ibid.*, p. 219.

6. *Ibid.*, *3*, 141: "Die Poesie ist das echt absolut Reelle. Dies ist der Kern meiner Philosophie. Je poetischer, je wahrer."

7. *Ibid.*, *1*, 260: "Poesie einen besondern Namen hat und die Dichter eine besondere Zunft ausmachen. Es ist gar nichts Besonderes. Es ist die eigentümliche Handlungsweise des menschlichen Geistes. Dichtet und trachtet nicht jeder Mensch in jeder Minute?"

8. *Ibid.*, p. 260: "oder die Liebe ist selbst nichts als höchste Natur-poesie."

9. *Ibid.*, p. 258: "Die beste Poesie liegt uns ganz nahe, und ein gewöhnlicher Gegenstand ist nicht selten ihr liebster Stoff."

10. *Ibid.*, p. 259: "Die Poesie beruht ganz auf Erfahrung."

11. *Ibid.*, *5*, 294.

12. *Ibid.*, *2*, 41: "Der echte Dichter ist aber immer Priester, so wie die der echte Priester immer Dichter geblieben—und sollte die Zukunft nicht den alten Zustand der Dinge wieder herbeiführen?"

13. *Ibid.*, *1*, 231: "Es sind die Dichter, diese seltenen Zugmenschen, die zuweilen durch unsere Wohnsitze wandeln und überall den alten, ehrwürdigen Dienst der Menschheit und ihrer ersten Götter, der Gestirne, des Frühlings, der Liebe, des Glücks, der Fruchtbarkeit, der Gesundheit und des Frohsinns, erneuern."

14. *Ibid.*, *3*, 98: "Der echte Dichter ist allwissend—er ist eine wirkliche Welt im kleinen."

15. *Ibid.*, p. 320: "Die Trennung von Poet und Denker ist nur scheinbar und zum Nachteil beider. Es ist ein Zeichen einer Krankheit und krankhaften Konstitution."

16. *Ibid.*, *4*, 314.

17. *Ibid.*, *2*, 41.

18. *Ibid.*, *4*, 286: "Je persönlicher, lokaler, temporeller, eigentümlicher ein Gedicht ist, desto näher steht es dem Zentro der Poesie. Ein Gedicht muss ganz unerschöpflich sein wie ein Mensch und ein guter Spruch."

19. *Ibid.*, p. 266: "Erzählungen ohne Zusammenhang, jedoch mit Assoziation, wie Träume. Gedichte, bloss wohlklingend und voll schöner Worte, aber auch ohne allen Sinn und Zusammenhang, höchstens einzelne Strophen verständlich; sie müssen wie lauter Bruchstücke aus den verschiedenartigsten Dingen sein. Höchstens kann wahre Poesie einen allegorischen Sinn im grossen haben und eine indirekte Wirkung wie Musik etc. tun."

20. *Ibid.*, p. 267: "Solle Poesie nichts als innre Malerei und Musik etc. sein? Freilich modifiziert durch die Natur des Gemüts."

21. *Ibid.*, p. 284.

22. *Ibid.*, *1*, 258–9.

23. *Ibid.*, *4*, 165: "Das Märchen ist gleichsam der Kanon der Poesie—alles Poetische muss märchenhaft sein. Der Dichter betet den Zufall an."

24. *Ibid.*, p. 172.

25. *Ibid.*, p. 126: "Poetik: Im Märchen glaub ich am besten meine Gemütsstimmung ausdrücken zu können. (Alles ist ein Märchen.)"

26. *Ibid.*, *3*, 262–3.

27. *Ibid.*, *4*, 301: "Die Kunst, auf eine angenehme Art zu befremden, einen Gegenstand fremd zu machen und doch bekannt und anziehend, das ist die romantische Poetik."

28. *Ibid.*, p. 43: "Nichts ist romantischer als was man gewöhnlich

Welt und Schicksal nennt. Wir leben in einem kolossalen Roman (im Grossen und Kleinen)."

29. *Ibid.,* p. 290.

30. *Ibid.,* p. 188.

31. *Ibid.,* p. 212.

32. *Ibid., 3,* 124.

33. *Ibid., 4,* 263: "Den Satz des Widerspruchs zu vernichten, ist vielleicht die höchste Aufgabe der höhern Logik."

34. *Ibid., 1,* 353.

35. *Ibid., 3,* 96: "Philosophie ist die Theorie der Poesie. Sie zeigt uns, was die Poesie sei, dass sie eins und alles sei."

36. *Ibid., 5,* 247–8:

> Das "Geheimnis der schönen Entfaltung" ist ein wesentlicher Bestandteil des poetischen Geistes überhaupt und dürfte im lyrischen und dramatischen Gedicht wohl auch eine Hauptrolle spielen, freilich modifiziert durch den verschiedenen Inhalt, aber ebenfalls sichtbar als besonnenes Anschauen und Schildern zugleich; zweifache Tätigkeit des Schaffens und Begreifens, vereinigt in *einen* Moment—eine Wechselvollendung des Bilds und des Begriffs.

37. *Ibid., 1,* 251: "Der junge Dichter kann nicht kühl, nicht besonnen genug sein."

38. *Ibid.,* p. 250: "Nichts ist dem Dichter unentbehrlicher als Einsicht in die Natur jedes Geschäfts, Bekanntschaft mit den Mitteln, jeden Zweck zu erreichen, und Gegenwart des Geistes, nach Zeit und Umständen die schicklichsten zu wählen. Begeisterung ohne Verstand ist unnütz und gefährlich, und der Dichter wird wenig Wunder tun können, wenn er selbst über Wunder erstaunt."

39. *Ibid.,* p. 252: " 'Die Poesie will vorzüglich,' fuhr Klingsohr fort, 'als strenge Kunst getrieben werden.' "

40. *Ibid., 3,* 89–90: "Die Kunst zerfällt, wenn man will, in die wirkliche, vollendete, durchgeführte, mittelst der äussern (Leiter) Organe wirksame Kunst—und in die eingebildete (unterwegs in den innern Organen aufgehaltene, in den innern Organen als Nicht-Leiter isolierte) und nur mittelst dieser wirksame Kunst."

41. *Ibid.,* p. 94: "Wir wissen etwas nur, insofern wir es ausdrücken—id est, machen können."

42. *Ibid., 2,* 41: "Was Schlegel so scharf als Ironie charakterisiert, ist, meinem Bedünken nach, nichts anderes als die Folge, der Charakter der echten Besonnenheit, der wahrhaften Gegenwart des Geistes."

43. *Ibid., 1,* 258.

44. *Ibid.,* p. 259.

45. *Ibid.,* p. 386. Cf. *3,* 72, on "Hieroglyphistik."

46. *Ibid., 3, 23.*

47. *Ibid.*, p. 12: "Jedes Wort ist ein Wort der Beschwörung. Welcher Geist ruft—ein solcher erscheint."

48. *Ibid.*, p. 23: "Wie Kleider der Heiligen noch wunderbare Kräfte behalten, so ist manches Wort durch irgendein herrliches Andenken geheiligt und fast allein schon ein Gedicht geworden. Dem Dichter ist die Sprache nie zu arm, aber immer zu allgemein. Er bedarf oft wiederkehrender, durch den Gebrauch ausgespielter Worte."

49. *Ibid.*, p. 107: "Die Welt ist ein Universaltropus des Geistes, ein symbolisches Bild desselben."

50. *Ibid.*, p. 26: "Von der Bearbeitung der transzendentalen Poesie lässt sich eine Tropik erwarten, die die Gesetze der symbolischen Konstruktion der transzendentalen Welt begreift."

51. *Ibid.*, p. 23: "Durch Poesie entsteht die höchste Sympathie und Koaktivität, die innigste Gemeinschaft des Endlichen und Unendlichen."

52. *Ibid., 4, 302:* "Kritik der Poesie ist Unding. Schwer schon ist zu entscheiden, doch einzig mögliche Entscheidung, ob etwas Poesie sei oder nicht."

53. *Ibid., 3, 24:* "Zur echten Kritik gehört die Fähigkeit, das zu kritisierende Produkt selbst hervorzubringen."

54. *Ibid., 2, 192:*

Tadle nichts Menschliches! Alles ist gut, nur nicht überall, nur nicht immer, nur nicht für alle. So mit der Kritik. Bei Beurteilung von Gedichten z.B. nehme man sich in acht, mehr zu tadeln als, streng genommen, eigentlicher Kunstfehler, Misston in jeder Verbindung ist. Man weise möglichst genau jedem Gedichte seinen Bezirk an, und dies wird Kritik genug für den Wahn ihrer Verfasser sein. Denn nur in dieser Hinsicht sind Gedichte zu beurteilen, ob sie einen weiten oder engen, einen nahen oder entlegnen, einen finstren oder hellen, einen hellen oder dunkeln, erhabnen oder niedrigen Standort haben wollen. So schreibt Schiller für wenige, Goethe für viele. Man ist heutzutage zu wenig darauf bedacht gewesen, die Leser anzuweisen, wie das Gedicht gelesen werden muss—unter welchen Umständen es allein gefallen kann. Jedes Gedicht hat seine Verhältnisse zu den mancherlei Lesern und den vielfachen Umständen. Es hat seine eigne Umgebung, seine eigne Welt, seinen eignen Gott.

55. *Ibid., 3, 66–7.*

56. *Ibid., 4, 262:*

Shakespeare war kein Kalkulator, kein Gelehrter—er war eine mächtige, buntkräftige Seele, deren Erfindungen und Werke wie

Erzeugnisse der Natur das Gepräge des denkenden Geistes tragen und in denen auch der letzte scharfsinnige Beobachter noch neue Übereinstimmungen mit dem unendlichen Gliederbau des Weltalls, Begegnungen mit spätern Ideen, Verwandtschaften mit den höhern Kräften und Sinnen der Menschheit finden wird. Sie sind sinnbildlich und vieldeutig, einfach und unerschöpflich wie jene, und es dürfte nichts Sinnloseres von ihnen gesagt werden können, als dass sie Kunstwerke in jener eingeschränkten, mechanischen Bedeutung des Worts seien.

57. *Ibid.*, p. 299.

58. *Ibid.*, p. 301.

59. *Ibid.*, p. 258.

60. *Ibid.*, p. 299: "Shakespeares Verse und Gedichte gleichen ganz der Boccazischen und Cervantischen Prosa: ebenso gründlich, elegant, nett, pedantisch und vollständig."

61. *Ibid.*, p. 293: "Shakespeare ist mir dunkler als Griechenland. Den Spass des Aristophanes versteh ich, aber den Shakespeares noch lange nicht. Shakespeare versteh ich überhaupt noch sehr unvollkommen."

62. *Ibid.*, 5, 156: "Der Erzieher des künftigen Jahrhunderts."

63. *Ibid.*, p. 163.

64. *Ibid.*, 4, 60.

65. *Ibid.*, p. 252.

66. *Ibid.*, p. 266.

67. *Ibid.*, 5, 291.

68. *Ibid.*, p. 290.

69. *Ibid.*, 1, 304.

WACKENRODER AND TIECK

1. *Werke und Briefe*, p. 15.

2. I owe this point to a note in H. H. Borcherdt's edition of *Herzensergiessungen* (Munich, 1949), p. 126.

3. *Werke und Briefe*, pp. 69–70:

Sie redet durch Bilder der Menschen und bedienet sich also einer Hieroglyphenschrift, deren Zeichen wir dem Äussern nach kennen und verstehen. Aber sie schmelzt das Geistige und Unsinnliche . . . in die sichtbaren Gestalten hinein . . . rühren unsere Sinne sowohl als unsern Geist; oder vielmehr scheinen dabei . . . alle Teile unsers (uns unbegreiflichens) Wesens zu einem einzigen, neuen Organ zusammenzuschmelzen, welches die himmlichen Wunder auf diesem zweifachen Wege fasst und begreift.

4. *Ibid.*, p. 147: "und es ist mir eine sehr bedeutende und geheimnis-

volle Vorstellung, wenn ich sie zweien magischen Hohlspiegeln ver-
gleiche, die mir alle Dinge der Welt sinnbildlich abspiegeln, durch
deren Zauberbilder hindurch ich den wahren Geist aller Dinge erkennen und verstehen lerne."

5. *Ibid.*, p. 67: "Nur das Unsichtbare, das über uns schwebt, ziehen
Worte nicht in unser Gemüt herab."

6. *Ibid.*, p. 222: "Wer das, was sich nur von innen heraus fühlen
lässt, mit der Wünschelrute des untersuchenden Verstandes entdecken
will, der wird ewig nur Gedanken über das Gefühl, und nicht das
Gefühl selber, entdecken. Eine ewige feindselige Kluft ist zwischen dem
fühlenden Herzen und den Untersuchungen des Forschens befestigt.
. . . So kann auch das Gefühl überhaupt nur vom Gefühl erfasst und
ergriffen werden."

7. *Ibid.*, p. 211: "Wie ich denn überhaupt glaube, dass das der
echte Genuss, und zugleich der echte Prüfstein der Vortrefflichkeit
eines Kunstwerks sei, wenn man über dies eine alle andern Werke
vergisst, und gar nicht daran denkt, es mit einem andern vergleichen
zu wollen."

8. *Ibid.*, p. 52: "Ihm ist der gotische Tempel so wohlgefällig als der
Tempel des Griechen; und die rohe Kriegsmusik der Wilden ist ihm
ein so lieblicher Klang, als kunstreiche Chöre und Kirchengesänge."

9. *Ibid.*, p. 54: "Schönheit: ein wunderseltsames Wort! Erfindet erst
neue Worte für jedes einzelne Kunstgefühl, für jedes einzelne Werk
der Kunst!"

10. *Ibid.*, p. 55: "So lasset uns denn dieses Glück benutzen, und mit
heitern Blicken über alle Zeiten und Völker umherschweifen und uns
bestreben, an allen ihren mannigfaltigen Empfindungen und Werken
der Empfindung immer das Menschliche herauszufühlen."

11. *Ibid.*, p. 124: "Das ich, statt frei zu fliegen, erst lernen musste, in
dem unbehülflichen Gerüst und Käfig der Kunstgrammatik herumzu-
klettern!"

12. *Ibid.*, p. 130: "Warum wollte der Himmel, dass sein ganzes Leben
hindurch der Kampf zwischen seinem ätherischen Enthusiasmus und
dem niedrigen Elend dieser Erde ihn so unglücklich machen und endlich sein doppeltes Wesen von Geist und Leib ganz voneinanderreissen
sollte!"

13. *Ibid.*, p. 128: "Er geriet auf die Idee, ein Künstler müsse nur für
sich allein, zu seiner eignen Herzenserhebung und für einen oder ein
paar Menschen, die ihn verstehen, Künstler sein."

14. *Ibid.*, p. 131: "mehr dazu geschaffen war, Kunst zu geniessen als
auszuüben?"

15. *Ibid.*, p. 147.

16. *Ibid.*, p. 206: "Es scheinen uns diese Gefühle, die in unserm Herzen aufsteigen, manchmal so herrlich und gross, dass wir sie wie Reliquien in kostbare Monstranzen einschliessen, freudig davor niederknieen, und im Taumel nicht wissen, ob wir unser eignes menschliches Herz, oder ob wir den Schöpfer, von dem alles Grosse und Herrliche herabkommt, verehren."

17. *Ibid.*, p. 217: "dass das ganze Leben des Menschen, und das ganze Leben des gesamten Weltkörpers nichts ist, als so ein unaufhörliches, seltsames Brettspiel solcher weissen und schwarzen Felder, wobei am Ende keiner gewinnt als der leidige Tod." Cf. *ibid.*, p. 226. *Dichten* comes from *dictare* and has nothing to do with *verdichten* (to condense).

18. *Ibid.*, p. 197.

19. *Ibid.*, p. 227: "Und eben diese frevelhafte Unschuld, diese furchtbare, orakelmässig-zweideutige Dunkelheit, macht die Tonkunst recht eigentlich zu einer Gottheit für menschliche Herzen."

20. A much fuller treatment is in Robert Minder, *Un poète romantique allemand: Ludwig Tieck,* esp. pp. 305 ff.

21. See the quotations and discussion in Marie Joachimi, *Die Weltanschauung der deutschen Romantik* (Jena, 1905), pp. 181 ff.

22. See Rudolf Köpke, *Ludwig Tieck* (Leipzig, 1855), 2, 173, 238; and *Schriften* (Berlin, 1828), 6, xxvii–xxix.

23. Köpke, *Tieck,* 2, 173, 237.

24. Köpke, "Unterhaltungen mit Tieck, 1849–1853," *Tieck,* 2, 167–256.

25. *Kritische Schriften,* 2, 183: "die unmittelbarste, nächste Empfindung meiner Persönlichkeit."

26. There is ample information in the books by Henry Lüdeke, ed. *Das Buch über Shakespeare,* and Edwin Zeydel, *Ludwig Tieck, the German Romanticist.*

27. *Kri. Schr. 1,* 237: "im Zusammenhange."

28. *Ibid., 1,* 230, 234, 283, 303; on Middleton see pp. 293 ff. Tieck translated *Volpone* (1798) and the *Silent Woman* (1800). On his studies of Ben Jonson see Walther Fischer, "Zu Ludwig Tiecks elisabethanischen Studien: Tieck als Ben Jonson-Philologe," *Shakespeare-Jahrbuch, 62* (1926), 98–131.

29. *Das Buch über Shakespeare,* ed. Lüdeke, p. 406: "den Dichter nicht mehr als eine isolierte Erscheinung zu betrachten, sondern ihn aus seiner Zeit und Umgebung abzuleiten, hauptsächlich aber ihn aus seinem eigenen Gemüt zu entwickeln."

30. *Kri. Schr., 1,* 37, 38, 65, 73, etc.

31. *Ibid.*, pp. 149, 152, 159: "kein gedruckter Engländer."

32. *Schriften* (28 vols. Berlin, 1828–54), *28,* 258 ff., esp. 265–9.

33. *Kri. Schr., 4,* 318 ff. See the full account of Tieck's visit in Zeydel, *Ludwig Tieck and England,* pp. 48 ff.

34. Cf. *Nachgelassene Schriften,* ed. R. Köpke (Leipzig, 1855), *2,* 154 ff.; *Dramaturgische Blätter* (Breslau, 1825–26), 2, 74, 118. Goethe in reviewing this book rejects Tieck's view of Lady Macbeth. *Werke, 38,* 22: "eine zärtliche liebevolle Seele." Also *Kri. Schr., 3,* 257: "ein wahrer Staatsmann"; cf. pp. 264, 277.

35. *Schriften, 18,* 265, 256: "als würde ich erst durch mein Gedicht erschaffen, und mein eigenstes Wesen zum Leben gebracht."

36. On Tieck's Spanish studies cf. the two books by J. J. Bertrand, *Tieck et le théâtre espagnol,* Paris, 1914; and *Cervantes et le romantisme allemand,* Paris, 1914. See *Schriften, 23,* 46 ff.; in "Eine Sommerreise."

37. *Kri. Schr., 2,* 194–5, 249. Letters to Solger, Nov. 10 and Dec. 17, 1818, in *Tieck and Solger. The Complete Correspondence,* ed. Percy Matenko (New York, 1933), pp. 476, 493–4.

38. *Kri. Schr., 2,* 61–92.

39. *Ibid., 1,* 185–214. J. Grimm, *Kleinere Schriften* (8 vols. Berlin, 1869–90), *1,* 6; *4, 7.*

40. The eds. of Lenz, 1828, Novalis, 1802 and 1846, and Kleist, 1826.

41. *Kri. Schr., 2,* 175 ff., esp. 187, 205, 207, 208, 230.

42. *Ibid.,* p. 243.

43. *Ibid.,* pp. 24, 34, 55: "eine dunkle Macht . . . ein plötzliches, grelles Gelüst, beide zu überspringen, und das Leere, Nichtige, dennoch höher als die Wirklichkeit zu stellen . . . ein grossartiger Manierist."

44. Köpke, 2, 22 ff.

45. *Kri. Schr., 2,* 309, 347, 349. Köpke, 2, 193 ff. In *Dramaturgische Blätter* there are several laudatory papers on Schiller's plays, e.g. on *Wallenstein.*

46. *Ludwig Tieck und die Brüder Schlegel,* ed. H. Lüdeke (Frankfurt, 1930), p. 169; letter of August 26, 1813: "Ich habe überhaupt keine Freude an allen den Sachen, die wir veranlasst haben." Köpke, 2, 173.

47. *Ibid.,* 206, 204, etc. On Bettina see letter of Tieck to Solger, May 5, 1818; *Tieck and Solger,* pp. 436–8.

48. Köpke, 2, 208. See letter to Brinckmann, Nov. 17, 1835, in *Euphorion,* Supplement *13,* p. 71.

49. *Schriften, 6,* 213: "Poesie, Kunst, und selbst die Andacht [ist] nur verkleidete, verhüllte Wollust . . . Sinnlichkeit und Wollust sind der Geist der Musik, der Malerei und aller Künste . . . Schönheitssinn und Kunstgefühl sind nur andere Dialekte und Aussprachen, sie be-

zeichnen nichts weiter, als den Trieb des Menschen zur Wollust."

50. *Ibid.,* 18, 60, 62; "zu schaffen und zu vernichten. . . . in Sehnsucht nach dem Unsichtbaren . . . das Ewige mit dem Irdischen."

51. Wackenroder, *Werke und Briefe,* Berlin [1948?], pp. 195, 232, 230, 231: "lasset uns darum unser Leben in ein Kunstwerk verwandeln . . . Das ist's, dass der Künstler ein Schauspieler wird, der jedes Leben als Rolle betrachtet . . . die Kunst ist eine verführerische, verbotene Frucht; wer einmal ihren innersten, süssesten Saft geschmeckt hat, der is unwiederbringlich verloren für die tätige, lebendige Welt . . . Und mitten in diesem Getümmel bleib' ich ruhig sitzen, wie ein Kind auf seinem Kinderstuhle, und blase Tonstücke wie Seifenblasen in die Luft."

52. *Schriften,* 5, 308, conclusion of Act I of *Verkehrte Welt* (1798): "Ach du schwaches, leichtzerbrechliches Menschenleben! Ich will dich immer als ein Kunstwerk betrachten, das mich ergötzt und das einen Schluss haben muss, damit es ein Kunstwerk sein und mich ergötzen könne. Dann bin ich stets zufrieden, dann bin ich von gemeiner Freude und von dem lastenden Trübsinne gleich weit entfernt."

53. Bettina von Arnim, *Frühlingskranz,* ed. W. Oehlke (Berlin, 1920), *1,* 371: "das grösste mimische Talent was jemals die Bühne *nicht* betreten."

54. *Ludwig Tieck und die Brüder Schlegel,* ed. Lüdeke, p. 144; letter to Friedrich Schlegel, Dec. 16, 1803: "ich bin un so mehr ein Individuum, um so mehr ich mich in alles verlieren kann." *Tieck and Solger,* ed. Matenko, p. 363; letter to Solger, March 24, 1817: "es ist mir schon sonst so gegangen, dass ich Gedanken, die nachher mein Leben wurden, vorher wohl ein Jahr in mir, ich möchte sagen, nur mimisch nachgemacht habe." *Ludwig Tieck und die Brüder Schlegel,* p. 146; to F. Schlegel: "Vorzüglich ängstigte mich Alles, was mir bis dahin das Liebste gewesen war: meine Liebe zur Poesie, mein Talent schienen mir recht eigentlich das Böseste in mir, was mich ganz zu Grunde richten musste."

55. See the discussion of Tieck's views of dreams and use of dreams in Albert Béguin, *L'Âme romantique et le rêve* (2d ed. Paris, 1946), pp. 217–38.

JEAN PAUL

1. *Vorschule,* in *Sämtliche Werke,* ed. Berend, *11,* 8, 14, 74.

2. See esp. "Jubilate-Vorlesung" in *Vorschule, SW, 11,* 377 ff. also note in "Clavis Fichtiana," *SW, 9,* 476. Unprinted notes on the Schlegels in Berend, *Jean Pauls Aesthetik,* pp. 37–8, and cf. p. 104.

3. E.g. *SW, 11,* 74–5, 75n., 80. The preface to the 2d ed. of *Quintus Fixlein* (1796) attacks Schiller's *Briefe über aesthetische Erziehung.*

4. In *Denkwürdigkeiten aus dem Leben von J. P. Richter,* ed. Ernst Förster (Munich, 1863), *3,* 39: "Eine höhere kritische Schule als in der hohen von Jena" (1799).

5. *SW, 11,* 19: "Meine innigste Überzeugung ist, dass die neuere Schule im ganzen und grossem recht hat."

6. *Ibid.,* pp. 22, 25, 37.

7. *Ibid.,* pp. 425, 234: "Blosse Zeichen geben; aber voll Zeichen steht ja schon die ganze Welt, die ganze Zeit; das Lesen dieser Buchstaben eben fehlt; wir wollen ein Wörterbuch und eine Sprachlehre der Zeichen. Die Poesie lehrt lesen."

8. *Ibid.,* pp. 235, 21.

9. *Ibid.,* p. 38: "Die Phantasie macht alle Teile zun Ganzen . . . sie totalisiert alles."

10. *Ibid.,* p. 46: "Im Genius stehen *alle* Kräfte auf einmal in Blüte." Cf. p. 53.

11. *Ibid.,* pp. 49, 196. There a note from *Jean Pauls Briefe und bevorstehender Lebenslauf* (Gera, 1799), p. 147. Albert Béguin, *L'Âme romantique et le rêve,* pp. 167 ff., has a good chapter on Jean Paul's dreams.

12. *SW, 11,* 196: "Er muss euch—wie ja im Traume geschieht—eingeben, nicht ihr ihm. . . . Ein Dichter, der überlegen muss, ob er einen Charakter in einem gegebenen Falle Ja oder Nein sagen zu lassen habe, werf' ihn weg, es ist eine dumme Leiche."

13. *Ibid.,* p. 48: "Die Teile werden von der Ruhe erzogen."

14. *Ibid.,* pp. 28, 46, on "Besonnenheit"; see pp. 123 and *passim.*

15. Especially Leibgeber in *Siebenkäs* and Schoppe in *Titan.* A history of the double in literature, with a section on Jean Paul, is in Otokar Fischer, *Duše a slovo* (Prague, 1929), esp. pp. 179 ff., and in Ralph Tymms, *Doubles in Literary Psychology,* Cambridge, 1949.

16. *SW, 11,* 41, 44.

17. *Ibid.,* p. 49.

18. *Ibid.,* p. 56.

19. *Ibid.,* p. 57: "Dieses schönheitstrunkne Volk noch mit einer heitern Religion in Aug' und Herz."

20. *Ibid.,* pp. 75–6, 79: "Ein Petrarch, der kein Christ ist, wäre ein unmöglicher. Die einzige Maria adelt alle Weiber romantisch."

21. *Ibid.,* pp. 76, 80.

22. *Ibid.,* p. 80: "Jedes Jahrhundert ist anders romantisch."

23. *Ibid.,* pp. 74–5.

24. *Ibid.,* p. 254: "Das Epos stellt die *Begebenheit,* die sich aus der

Vergangenheit entwickelt, das Dramo die *Handlung,* welche sich für und gegen die *Zukunft* ausdehnt, die Lyrik die *Empfindung* dar, welche sich in die *Gegenwart* einschliesst."

25. E. S. Dallas, *Poetics,* London, 1852; Emil Staiger, *Grundbegriffe der Poetik,* Zurich, 1946.

26. *SW, II,* 142.

27. *Ibid.,* p. 233: "Poetische Enzyklopädie." Cf. pp. 234–5.

28. *Ibid.,* p. 231.

29. *Ibid.,* p. 201.

30. *Ibid.,* pp. 202, 197.

31. *Ibid.,* p. 194: "Rassen des innern Menschen"; p. 206: "Seelen-mythologie."

32. *Ibid.,* p. 193.

33. *Ibid.,* pp. 208–9: "Dieser hüpfende Punkt . . . Hauptton (*tonica dominante*)."

34. *Ibid.,* p. 211: "Wurzelworte des Charakters." On naming see pp. 252–3.

35. *Ibid.,* p. 212.

36. *Ibid.,* pp. 260, 275, 303, 177 ff.

37. See Friedrich Vischer's *Aesthetik, I* (Reutlingen, 1846) on the objective comic (the farce), the subjective comic (wit), the absolute comic (humor); on Jean Paul, *ibid.,* e.g. pp. 354–5, 385, and *passim.* S. T. Coleridge, *Miscellaneous Criticism,* ed. T. M. Raysor, pp. 117–20, 440–6. George Meredith, *On the Idea of Comedy and the Uses of the Comic Spirit* (1877).

38. I accept here, though not completely, Croce's view. See "L'umorismo" in *Problemi di estetica* (1903; 4th ed. Bari, 1949), p. 281. See also *Estetica* (Bari, 1946), pp. 100, 385.

39. *SW, II,* 158.

40. *Ibid.,* p. 170.

41. *Ibid.,* p. 178: "Eine wilde Paarung ohne Priester."

42. *Ibid.,* p. 179.

43. *Ibid.,* pp. 184 ff.

44. *Ibid.,* p. 102: "Der sinnlich angeschaute unendliche Unverstand." "Den.Widerspruch, worin das Bestreben oder Sein des lächerlichen Wesens mit dem sinnlich angeschauten Verhältnis steht, nenn' ich den *objektiven* Kontrast."

45. *Ibid.,* p. 97: "Wir leihen *seinem* Bestreben *unsere* Einsicht."

46. *Ibid.,* p. 99: "Unterschiebung." Vischer, *Aesthetik, I,* 385. Theodor Lipps, *Komik und Humor* (Hamburg, 1898), pp. 60 ff.

47. *Ibid.,* p. 112: "Der Humor, als das umgekehrte Erhabene, vernichtet nicht das Einzelne, sondern das Endliche durch den Kontrast

mit der Idee. Es gibt für ihn keine einzelne Torheit, keine Toren, sondern nur Torheit und eine tolle Welt."

48. *Ibid.*, pp. 116, 113, 114–5.

49. See the chapter on Friedrich Schlegel, above, and literature on irony quoted in note on p. 15.

50. *SW, 11*, 124. On Yahoos, MS quoted in Berend, *Jean Pauls Aesthetik*, pp. 110–11: "Wie kann man Swift die Yahoos so übelnehmen, da sie doch nur die satirische Karikatur enthalten, wenn er auch im Leben über Menschen zürnte?—Warum soll jedes satirische, d.h. poetische Wort von ihm ein wahres sein?"

51. *SW, 11*, 134: "Schein des Ernstes."

52. On Jean Paul's fictional attack on aestheticism see K. J. Obenauer, *Die Problematik des aesthetischen Menschen in der deutschen Literatur* (Munich, 1933), pp. 182 ff.

53. Much is collected in Berend, *Aesthetik*, and in Paul Nerrlich, *Jean Paul und seine Zeitgenossen*, Berlin, 1876.

54. See the "lecture" on Herder concluding *Vorschule, SW, 11*, 420 ff.; reviews of Fouqué in *Kleine Bücherschau* (1825), and in *SW, 16*, 357, 360, 370. Jean Paul wrote an introduction to E. T. A. Hoffmann's *Phantasiestücke* (1814); in *ibid.*, pp. 288–93. On relations to Tieck, Novalis, etc. see Nerrlich, pp. 246, 250, 252, 253–6.

55. *SW, 11*, 200–1, 235; on Milton, p. 227. Shakespeare was "his God": *Wahrheit aus Jean Pauls Leben*, under March 21, 1805.

56. *SW, 11*, 133.

57. *Ibid., 16*, 297, 329. Carlyle translated Jean Paul's review of *De l'Allemagne* in *Fraser's Magazine* (1830). See Carlyle, *Works*, Centenary ed. (London, 1899), *26*, 476–501.

58. *SW, 16*, 468.

59. *Ibid.*, p. 6n.: "In jeder guten Rezension verbirgt oder entdeckt sich eine gute Aesthetik und noch dazu eine angewandte und freie und kürzeste und durch die Beispiele—helleste."

60. First ed. of *Vorschule* (Hamburg, 1804), pp. 805 ff.: "Die beste Poetik wäre, alle Dichter zu charakterisieren."

61. *SW, 11*, 259.

62. *Ibid.*, p. 343: "Denn alle echte positive Kritik ist doch nur eine neue Dichtkunst, wovon ein Kunstwerk der Gegenstand ist"; p. 350: "Fehler lassen sich beweisen, aber Schönheiten nur weisen."

63. MS quoted in Berend, *Aesthetik*, p. 77: "Das Beste in jedem Autor ist, was nicht im einzelnen liegt, und gar nicht zu zeigen ist, weil der Glanz des Zusammenhangs keinen einzelnen Fingerzeig verträgt." Cf. *SW, 11*, 355, 337–8.

BIBLIOGRAPHY:

FROM JEFFREY TO SHELLEY

On English criticism during the romantic movement, besides Saintsbury and Abrams, we have *The Romantic Theory of Poetry* by A. E. Powell (Mrs. E. R. Dodds), London, 1926; and Walter J. Bate, *From Classic to Romantic,* Cambridge, Mass., 1946. On the term see René Wellek, "The Concept of Romanticism in Literary History," *Comparative Literature, 1* (1949), 1–23, 147–72.

Jeffrey is quoted from *Contributions to the Edinburgh Review,* 4 vols. London, 1844 (cited as *Contributions*). Where this fails I quote from the files of the *Edinburgh Review.* There is an old-fashioned *Life* (with letters) by Lord Cockburn, 2 vols. Edinburgh, 1852; and a fervent plea for his greatness, *Francis Jeffrey of the Edinburgh Review,* by James A. Greig, Edinburgh, 1948 (cited as Greig).

Of the many essays, besides those of Hazlitt, Carlyle, and Leslie Stephen, one might consult G. Saintsbury's in *Essays in English Literature, 1780–1860,* London, 1890; Lewis E. Gates' in *Three Studies in Literature,* New York, 1899; Merritt Y. Hughes' "The Humanism of Francis Jeffrey," *MLR, 16* (1921), 243–51; and Byron Guyer's "Francis Jeffrey's Essay on Beauty," *Huntington Library Quarterly, 13* (1949–50), 71–85. On Jeffrey and Wordsworth see Russell Noyes, *Wordsworth and Jeffrey in Controversy,* Indiana University Publications, Humanities Series, *5,* Bloomington, 1941; and Robert Daniel, "Jeffrey and Wordsworth," *Sewanee Review, 51* (1942), 195–213.

I know of no extended discussion of Southey's criticism.

On Scott see Margaret Ball, *Sir Walter Scott as Critic of Literature,* New York, 1907; and the good remarks on Scott's *Life of Dryden* in James M. Osborn, *John Dryden: Facts and Problems* (New York, 1942), pp. 72–87.

Byron's critical writings can be found in *Letters and Journals,* ed. Lord Prothero (London, 1901), esp. Vols. *4* and *5.* On Byron see Clement Tyson Goode, *Byron as Critic,* Weimar, 1923.

Shelley's criticism is quoted from *Shelley's Literary and Philosophical Criticism,* ed. John Shawcross, London, 1909 (cited as Shawcross). The prefaces are from *The Complete Poetical Works,* ed. Thomas Hutchinson, Oxford, 1904. *Peacock's Four Ages of Poetry* is from the ed. by H. F. B. Brett-Smith (Boston, 1921), which includes also Shelley's *Defence.*

On Shelley's *Defence* see introductions and notes to the editions by Shawcross, Brett-Smith, and by Albert S. Cook, Boston, 1890. A. C.

Bradley wrote a fine essay in the *Oxford Lectures on Poetry,* Oxford, 1909. The fullest study of the Platonic sources is in James A. Notopoulos, *Shelley's Platonism,* Durham, N.C., 1950. Lucas Verkoren's *A Study of Shelley's Defence* (Amsterdam, 1937) is almost useless. Croce makes good remarks in "Difesa della poesia," *Ultimi saggi* (Bari, 1948), pp. 58–78.

NOTES: FROM JEFFREY TO SHELLEY

1. Fully documented in Wellek, "The Concept of Romanticism in Literary History," *Comparative Literature, 1* (1949), 1–23, 147–72.

2. There is a copy of *De l'Allemagne,* with a long note by Byron, in the Harvard Library. Madame de Staël sent Schlegel's *Lectures* to Byron. See Byron's *Letters and Journals,* ed. Lord Prothero (London, 1901), *2, 343*; on the police spy, *ibid., 4, 462.*

3. Introduction to *Specimens of the Later English Poets* (London, 1807), p. xxix.

4. See Merritt Y. Hughes, "The Humanism of Francis Jeffrey," *MLR, 16* (1921), 243–51; Byron Guyer, "Francis Jeffrey's Essay on Beauty," *Huntington Library Quarterly, 13* (1949–50), 71–85; James A. Greig, *Francis Jeffrey of the Edinburgh Review.*

5. *Edinburgh Review, 1* (1802–03), 63.

6. *Contributions, 1,* 160.

7. *Ibid., 2,* 290–1; *1,* 167, 209, 212.

8. *Ibid., 2,* 292.

9. *Ibid., 1,* 158, 165.

10. *Ibid., 2,* 284–5.

11. *Ibid.,* p. 287.

12. *Ibid., 3,* 102.

13. *Ibid.,* pp. 103–4.

14. *Ibid., 2,* 362, 388.

15. *Ibid., 3,* 466.

16. *Ibid., 1,* 167.

17. See Robert Daniel, "Jeffrey and Wordsworth," *Sewanee Review, 51* (1942), 195–213.

18. *Contributions, 4,* 520–7.

19. See the review of Southey, *Lay of the Laureate,* in *Edinburgh Review,* 26 (1816), 441–9, and of *Wat Tyler* in *ibid., 28* (1817), 151–74. But Jeffrey praised *Roderick* generously; see *Contributions, 3,* 133.

20. *Ibid., 1,* 3. There is a completely uncritical discussion in Guyer, "Francis Jeffrey's Essay on Beauty."

21. *1*, 30, 53, 75–7.

22. *Edinburgh Review*, *11* (1808), 227. *Contributions*, *3*, 245–6.

23. *Ibid.*, p. 9; 2, 421.

24. *Ibid.*, *3*, 9, 239.

25. *Edinburgh Review*, *1* (1802), 71.

26. *Contributions*, *1*, 93 ff., 104.

27. *Ibid.*, *3*, 198; 2, 386.

28. *Ibid.*, p. 370.

29. *Ibid.*, p. 372.

30. *Ibid.*, p. 372; *3*, 441, 457.

31. *Ibid.*, 2, 464; *3*, 474.

32. *Ibid.*, 2, 484–7.

33. *Ibid.*, *3*, 5, 6 ff., 27–8, 14.

34. *Ibid.*, *1*, 411–13.

35. *Ibid.*, 2, 397, 389.

36. *Ibid.*, p. 393.

37. *Ibid.*, pp. 302 ff.

38. *Ibid.*, *1*, 267–8.

39. *Ibid.*, p. 347.

40. *Ibid.*, *3*, 530.

41. *Ibid.*, pp. 283, 296–7.

42. *Ibid.*, pp. 102, 113–4, 119.

43. *Edinburgh Review*, *24* (1815), 163.

44. *Contributions*, *3*, 120 ff.; 2, 422.

45. *Ibid.*, *1*, ix, x (preface).

46. *Ibid.*, p. 257–8.

47. *Ibid.*, p. 263.

48. These further developments are described in Alba H. Warren, *English Poetic Theory 1825–1865*, Princeton, 1950.

49. *Specimens of the Later English Poets* (London, 1807), *1*, xvii.

50. *Works of Cowper* (London, 1836), 2, 114, 123, 129, 138.

51. *Critical Review*, 2d ser., *37* (1815), 212.

52. Saintsbury, *3*, 236. On Spenser see *The Doctor* (London, 1849), pp. 382 ff.

53. *The Doctor*, p. 99.

54. Lockhart, *Life of Scott* (London, 1902), *1*, 477; 2, 132.

55. "Introductory Remarks on Popular Poetry," in *Minstrelsy of the Scottish Border*, ed. T. Henderson (London, 1931), *1*, 501. See also "Essay on Imitations of Ancient Ballads," *ibid.*, pp. 535–62.

56. *Essay on English Poetry* (London, 1819), pp. 221–2. Originally the preface to *Specimens of the British Poets*, 7 vols.

57. "Lectures on Poetry," in *New Monthly Magazine, 1*, (1821), 139.

58. *Letters and Journals,* ed. Lord Prothero (London, 1901), *4*, 169; *5,* 559, 554, 560, 347, 323.

59. *Ibid.,* pp. 318; *3,* 405; *5,* 582, 215, 336; *4,* 11, 43.

60. *Ibid.,* 5, 553–4.

61. *Shelley's Literary and Philosophical Criticism,* ed. Shawcross, pp. 124, 154, 156, 128, 152.

62. On March 11 and 12, 1821, Mary read Sidney's *Defence* to Shelley. See Edward Dowden, *Life of Shelley, 2,* 384. Shelley quotes very loosely from Tasso's *Discorsi del poema eroico* (1594), III, 22 (Shawcross, p. 156).

63. Shawcross, p. 153.

64. *Ibid.,* p. 129.

65. *Poetical Works,* ed. Hutchinson, pp. 203, 33.

66. *Ibid.,* p. 201. Shawcross, p. 146.

67. Shawcross, p. 156.

68. *Ibid.,* p. 125.

69. *Ibid.,* p. 127.

70. *Ibid.,* p. 126.

71. H. F. B. Brett-Smith's ed. of the *Four Ages* (Boston, 1921), pp. 14, 18, 16, 19.

72. See Vol. *1* of this *History,* pp. 127, 187. Further comments are in Wellek, *Rise,* p. 126; *idem,* "De Quincey's Status in the History of Ideas," *PQ, 23* (1944), esp. 268.

73. Shawcross, pp. 123, 134–5; 137–9.

74. *Ibid.,* pp. 124, 139, 146.

75. *Ibid.,* p. 148.

76. *Poetical Works,* pp. 35–6, 202.

77. Shawcross, p. 159.

78. *Letters,* ed. M. B. Forman (4th ed. Oxford, 1952), p. 143 (May 3, 1818).

BIBLIOGRAPHY: WORDSWORTH

I quote from *Wordsworth's Literary Criticism,* ed. Nowell C. Smith, London, 1905 (cited as Smith); from *The Prelude,* ed. E. de Selincourt, Oxford, 1926; and from *Poetical Works,* ed. de Selincourt and H. Darbishire, 5 vols. Oxford, 1940–49. The letters are collected as *Early Letters* (Oxford, 1935), *The Middle Years* (2 vols. Oxford, 1939), and *The Later Years* (3 vols. Oxford, 1939), all ed. by de Selincourt. Besides these there is *The Correspondence of Crabb Robinson with the Wordsworth Circle,* ed. E. Morley, 2 vols. Oxford, 1927.

There is a good survey of the huge Wordsworth literature by E. Bernbaum in *The English Romantic Poets: A Review of Research,* ed. Thomas M. Raysor, New York, 1950.

The compilation *The Critical Opinions of William Wordsworth,* by Markham L. Peacock (Baltimore, 1950) is most useful.

Few discussions of Wordsworth ignore the theories, but few focus on it clearly. The following books and articles proved most relevant:

Marjorie L. Barstow, *Wordsworth's Theory of Poetic Diction,* New Haven, 1917.

J. C. Smith, *A Study of Wordsworth* (Edinburgh, 1946), pp. 49–65.

On Imagination:

D. G. James, *Scepticism and Poetry* (London, 1937), pp. 141 ff., esp. pp. 164 ff.

C. D. Thorpe, "The Imagination: Coleridge versus Wordsworth," *PQ 18* (1939), 1–18.

Raymond D. Havens, *The Mind of a Poet* (Baltimore, 1941), esp. pp. 203 ff.

Newton P. Stallknecht, *Strange Seas of Thought,* Durham, N. C., 1945.

On individual points:

T. S. Eliot, *The Use of Poetry and the Use of Criticism* (London, 1933), esp. pp. 6 ff.

Frederick A. Pottle, *The Idiom of Poetry* (2d ed. Ithaca, 1946), esp. pp. 51 ff.

Klaus Dockhorn, *Wordsworth und die rhetorische Tradition in England,* Nachrichten der Akademie der Wissenschaften, *11,* Göttingen, 1944.

Josephine Miles, *Pathetic Fallacy in the Nineteenth Century* (Berkeley, Calif., 1942), pp. 201 ff., 251 ff.

Florence Marsh, *Wordsworth's Imagery* (New Haven, 1952), pp. 111 ff.

NOTES: WORDSWORTH

1. *Wordsworth's Literary Criticism,* ed. Smith, p. 20; cf. pp. 19, 1, 14–5.

2. The three essays "Upon Epitaphs" were written in 1810, but only the first was published in that year in *The Friend,* the second and third not seeing the light until 1876.

3. See the analysis of *Descriptive Sketches* and *Evening Walk* (1793) in Eng. trans. of Émile Legouis, *Early Life of W. Wordsworth* (1921), pp. 127 ff.

4. Smith, pp. 46, 43, 42, 189.

5. *Ibid.*, pp. 45–6, 20, 114–5.

6. *Ibid.*, pp. 126–7.

7. *Ibid.*, pp. 246–7; letter to A. Dyce in 1833.

8. Preface to 1815 ed. of *Poems*, in *Poetical Works*, ed. de Selincourt, 2, 431.

9. Smith, pp. 47–9.

10. Smith, pp. 11, 13, 14, 21, 24, 30.

11. *Ibid.*, pp. 90, 117.

12. *Ibid.*, pp. 11, 22.

13. *Ibid.*, pp. 24, 43.

14. Smith, p. 193. on Bürger see *ibid.*, pp. 188 ff.; also letter to Coleridge, Feb. 27, 1799; *Early Letters*, p. 222. Also, the letter quoted in a letter by Coleridge to William Taylor (Jan. 25, 1800) in *Unpublished Letters of S. T. C.*, ed. Griggs, *1*, 133–4. On Burns the main locus is "Letter to Friend of Burns" (1816), in Smith, pp. 202 ff.

15. Smith, p. 190.

16. On Lucretius see Emerson, *English Traits*, dated August 28, 1833. On his translation of parts of the *Aeneid* see letter to Lord Lonsdale, February 17, 1819; *Letters: Middle Years*, 2, 840. On Horace see Christopher Wordsworth's report in Grosart's ed. of *Prose Works*, *3*, 459, 469.

17. Smith, p. 234; letter to Dyce, Jan. 12, 1829.

18. Letter to G. Beaumont, May 1, 1805; *Early Letters*, p. 489.

19. Smith, pp. 94, 103, 113, 125, 115, 108, 117.

20. *Ibid.*, pp. 113–4, 112.

21. *Ibid.*, p. 211.

22. *Ibid.*, pp. 34–5.

23. *Ibid.*, pp. 150–1.

24. Letter to Gillies, December 22, 1814; *Letters: Middle Years*, 2, 614.

25. Letter to A. Hayward, 1828, and letter of Nov. 22, 1831 (Smith, p. 243). Cf. "The logical faculty has infinitely more to do with poetry than the young and the inexperienced, whether writer or critic, ever dreams of" (letter to W. R. Hamilton, September 24, 1827; *Letters: Later Years*, *1*, 275).

26. "Inward impulse," to James Montgomery, Jan. 24, 1824; *Letters: Later Years*, *1*, 136, "came spontaneously" in *Prelude*, I, 51–2; "torrent," to Beaumont, May 1, 1805 (*Early Letters*, p. 488); "poured from the heart out," to Dora and I. Fenwick, April 7, 1840; *Letters: Later Years*, 2, 1016. See Smith, p. 121, for epitaphs.

27. *Prelude*, XII, 203. "The Waggoner," IV, 208–10.

28. Smith, p. 7.

29. *Ibid.*, p. 10.

30. *Ibid.*, pp. 17, 28, 196.

31. *Ibid.*, pp. 198, 202, 200.

32. *Prelude*, VII, 547, from the passage on Burke.

33. *Early Letters,* p. 259; letter to Fox, Jan. 14, 1801.

34. Wordsworth's own description from *Guide to the Lakes*, ed. E. de Selincourt (London, 1926), p. 67.

35. To Sir George Beaumont, Jan. or Feb., 1808; *Letters: Middle Years, 1,* 170.

36. *Excursion*, III, 335–7.

37. Smith, p. 26.

38. *Ibid.*, pp. 31, 21, 33, 35, 34.

39. *Ibid.*, p. 21. This distinction had been drawn by William Enfield in an article "Is Verse Essential to Poetry?" *Monthly Magazine,* 2 (1796), 452 ff.

40. "The Tables Turned," *Prelude*, II, 216–7, 214–5; *Excursion*, IV, 1254–5.

41. R. P. Graves, *Life of William R. Hamilton* (Dublin, 1882–89), *1,* 313. Interview dated August, 1829.

42. Smith, p. 28.

43. By James, *Scepticism and Poetry*, p. 167.

44. Smith, p. 27.

45. *Ibid.*, p. 173.

46. Robert Percival Graves, *Afternoon Lectures on Literature and Art* (Dublin, 1869), pp. 319–21. Letter to Southey (1815) in Smith, pp. 224–5. Letter to H. Alford, February 21, 1840, expresses fear that he "might err in points of faith . . . Even Milton, in my humble judgment, has erred, and grievously" (*Letters: Later Years, 3,* 1007).

47. *Prelude,* XIII, 375–6.

48. Smith, pp. 13, 169.

49. *Prelude* (1805 version), XIII, 79, 88–9, 94–5, 105, 121–2, 166–70.

50. Letter to Landor, January 21, 1824; Smith, p. 165.

51. Smith, pp. 157, 162. The quotation from Lamb comes from "On the Genius and Character of Hogarth" (1811), *Works*, ed. Hutchinson (Oxford, 1924), *1,* 95–6. The example of "hanging" comes from Goldsmith's essay "Poetry Distinguished from Other Writing." See J. L. Lowes, "Wordsworth and Goldsmith," *The Nation, 92* (1911), 289–90.

52. Smith, pp. 52–4; letter to Lady Beaumont, May 21, 1807.

53. Fancy's "fixities," in *Biographia Literaria*, ed. Shawcross, *1,* 202; "the plastic," in Smith, p. 164.

54. Smith, p. 164.

55. *Ibid.*, pp. 165–6.

56. *Ibid.*, p. 164.

57. To W. R. Hamilton, Dec. 23, 1829; *Letters: Later Years, 1,* 436–7.

58. Allusions to "Peter Bell," "Lines written in Early Spring," and *Excursion,* 1, 204–5.

59. Smith, p. 178.

60. *Ibid.*, pp. 171, 191.

61. *Ibid.*, pp. 224, 247; letter to Southey (1815); letter to A. Dyce (1833).

BIBLIOGRAPHY: COLERIDGE

Biographia Literaria, ed. J. Shawcross (2 vols. Oxford, 1907), *Shakespearean Criticism,* ed. T. M. Raysor (2 vols. London, 1930), and *Miscellaneous Criticism,* ed. T. M. Raysor (London, 1936) are the critical editions used, and cited respectively as *BL, SC,* and *MC.* The philosophical writings have to be quoted from the old Bohn and Pickering editions: *The Friend* (London, 1865) as *Fr.; Aids to Reflection* (London, 1913) as *AR; Lay Sermons* (London, 1839), as *LS;* and *Specimens of the Table Talk* (London, 1851) as *TT.* Three modern editions are used: *Treatise on Method,* ed. Alice Snyder (London, 1934) as *TM; Coleridge on Logic and Learning,* ed. Snyder (New Haven, 1929) as *LL;* and *The Philosophical Lectures,* ed. Kathleen Coburn (London, 1949) as *PL.* The notebooks from *Anima Poetae,* ed. E. H. Coleridge (London, 1895) are given as *AP;* and from *Inquiring Spirit,* ed. K. Coburn (London, 1951) as *IS.* I use the four volumes of letters: *Letters,* ed. E. H. Coleridge (2 vols. London, 1895) as *L.;* and *Unpublished Letters,* ed. E. L. Griggs (2 vols. London, 1932) as *UL.* Scattered marginalia are found in periodicals, quoted in the notes.

I have discussed the large literature on Coleridge in *The English Romantic Poets: A Review of Research,* ed. T. M. Raysor, New York, 1950. Here is a small selection:

J. H. Muirhead, *Coleridge as Philosopher* (London, 1930), is still the best review of his thought.

On German sources: Wellek, *Kant in England* (Princeton, 1931), pp. 65–135; Elisabeth Winkelmann, *Coleridge und die Kantische Philosophie,* Leipzig, 1933; Anna Augusta von Helmholtz (Mrs. Phelan), *The Indebtedness of Samuel Taylor Coleridge to August Wilhelm Schlegel,* Madison, Wis., 1907; A. C. Dunstan, "The German Influence on Coleridge," *MLR, 17* (1922), 272–81, and *18* (1923) 183–201; Joseph

Warren Beach, "Coleridge's Borrowings from the German," *ELH, 9* (1942), 36–58.

Discussions of aesthetics and criticism:

W. J. Bate, "Coleridge on the Function of Art," *Perspectives of Criticism,* ed. H. Levin (Cambridge, Mass., 1950), pp. 125–60.

P. L. Carver, "Coleridge and the Theory of Imagination," *University of Toronto Quarterly, 9* (1940), 452–65.

J. Isaacs, "Coleridge's Critical Terminology," *Essays and Studies by Members of the English Association, 21* (1936), 86–104.

F. R. Leavis, "Coleridge in Criticism," *Scrutiny, 9* (1940), 57–69; also in *The Importance of Scrutiny,* ed. Eric Bentley (New York, 1948), pp. 76–87.

F. L. Lucas, *The Decline and Fall of the Romantic Ideal* (Cambridge, 1936), 157–200.

G. McKenzie, *Organic Unity in Coleridge,* Berkeley, 1939.

E. Pizzo, "Samuel Taylor Coleridge als Kritiker," *Anglia, 40* (1916), 201–55.

A. E. Powell, *The Romantic Theory of Poetry* (London, 1926), pp. 73–121.

T. M. Raysor, "Coleridge's Criticism of Wordsworth," *PMLA, 34* (1939), 496–510.

Herbert Read, "Coleridge as Critic," *Sewanee Review, 56* (1948), 597–624. Also in *Lectures in Criticism: The Johns Hopkins University,* ed. H. Cairns (New York, 1949), pp. 73–116; and *The True Voice of Feeling* (London, 1953), pp. 157–88.

I. A. Richards, *Coleridge on Imagination,* London, 1934.

Alice D. Snyder, *The Critical Principle of the Reconciliation of Opposites as Employed by Coleridge,* Ann Arbor, Mich., 1918.

Clarence D. Thorpe, "Coleridge as Aesthetician and Critic," *JHI, 1* (1944), 387–414.

Clarence D. Thorpe, "The Imagination: Coleridge vs. Wordsworth," *PQ, 18* (1939), 1–18.

B. Willey, *Coleridge on Imagination and Fancy,* Warton Lecture, Oxford, 1946.

To these should now be added J. M. Moore, *Herder and Coleridge* (Bern, 1951), I. A. Richards' curious introduction to the *Portable Coleridge* (New York, 1950), and five articles: R. L. Brett, "Coleridge's Theory of Imagination," *English Studies 1949,* ed. Sir Philip Magnus (London, 1949), pp. 75–90; James Benziger, "Organic Unity: Leibniz to Coleridge," *PMLA, 46* (1951), 24–48; Charles Patterson, "Coleridge's Conception of Dramatic Illusion in the Novel," *ELH, 18* (1951), 123–

37; E. L. Stahl, "Zur Theorie der Dichtung bei Coleridge im Hinblick auf Goethe," and L. A. Willoughby, "English Romantic Criticism," both in *Weltliteratur: Festgabe für Fritz Strich,* Bern, 1952. I had overlooked a good German thesis: Elisabeth Raab, *Die Grundanschauungen von Coleridges Aesthetik,* Giessen, 1934.

NOTES: COLERIDGE

1. Saintsbury, *3,* 230.

2. Introduction to Everyman ed. (1906), p. x.

3. *Coleridge as Philosopher* (London, 1930), p. 117.

4. *Coleridge on Imagination* (London, 1934), p. 232.

5. "Coleridge as Critic," in *Lectures in Criticism* (New York, 1949), pp. 88, 103.

6. See the references in the Introduction to this *History,* Vol. *1,* p. 3.

7. Sarah Coleridge's introduction to the 1847 ed. of *Biographia Literaria* is an able defense. For the "divine ventriloquist" see *Biographia Literaria (BL),* ed. Shawcross, *1,* 105.

8. The evidence can be seen best in Sara Coleridge's ed. and in *BL.*

9. *Letters from the Lake Poets . . . to Daniel Stuart* (London, 1889), p. 233. Cf. *Table Talk* (Jan. 1, 1834), pp. 300–1.

10. See notes in *BL,* e.g. 2, 241, 313.

11. *Miscellaneous Criticism (MC),* ed. Raysor, pp. 148–9. *Notebooks 1,* 1705 (Dec. 1803) prove that Coleridge knew Schiller's treatise.

12. *MC,* pp. 11, 117, 440 ff., and Raysor's notes.

13. *Shakespearean Criticism (SC),* ed. Raysor, *1,* 167. Raysor's own view.

14. *SC, 1,* 224, with Vienna *Vorlesungen, 3,* 8. See above, p. 48.

15. Cf. H. Nidecker, "Preliminarium zur Neuausgabe der Abhandlung über Lebenstheorie [Theory of Life] von *S. T. C.,*" *Berichte der philosophisch-historischen Fakultät der Universität Basel* (pt. 5. Bâle, 1927), pp. 7–12. W. K. Pfeiler, "Coleridge and Schelling's Treatise on the Samothracian Deities," *MLN,* 52 (1937), 162–5.

16. As demonstrated in detail in my *Kant in England* (Princeton, 1931), pp. 116 ff.

17. Johann Gebhard Ehrenreich Maass, *Versuch über die Einbildungskraft,* 1792; 2d ed. 1797. Cf. with *BL, 1,* 70–3. Shawcross' notes.

18. *Philosophical Lectures (PL),* ed. Kathleen Coburn. See introduction and notes, *passim.*

19. See Adrien Bonjour, *Coleridge's "Hymn before Sunrise"* (Lausanne, 1942), for a detailed and fair examination.

20. *BL, 1*, 104.

21. See Sara Coleridge's ed. of *BL*, appendix I, p. 311, and *Specimens of the Table Talk (TT)*, p. 330. Cf. the full discussion in my *Kant in England*, pp. 78 ff.

22. See e.g. *Aids to Reflection (AR)*, pp. 117-9; the "Dialogue between Demosius and Mystes," the appendices to the *Statesman's Manual*, etc. Cf. my *Kant in England* and Elisabeth Winkelmann, *Coleridge und die Kantische Philosophie*, esp. p. 121, which differs from my present conclusions.

23. Shown in my *Kant in England*, esp. pp. 95 ff.

24. The charges of plagiarism were first made by De Quincey in *Tait's Magazine* (1839), reprinted in *Collected Writings*, ed. Masson, *2*, esp. pp. 145-6; and afterward by J. F. Ferrier in *Blackwood's Magazine, 47* (1840), 281-99.

25. *SC, 1*, 18-9; *2*, 164, 235-8, 306; *BL, 1*, 22n., 102.

26. *Die Prosaischen Jugendschriften*, ed. Minor, *1*, 106-7. See p. 27 above.

27. *SC, 2*, 260; *Unpublished Letters (UL), 2*, 94. The editor, E. L. Griggs, wrongly identifies "Schlegel's *Vorlesungen*" as Friedrich Schlegel's *Philosophische Vorlesungen*, not printed until 1836-37.

28. *Anima Poetae (AP)*, ed. Coleridge, p. 117, dating from 1805.

29. *BL, 1*, 187; *SC, 1*, 216.

30. *BL, 1*, 44; *Letters (L.)*, ed. Coleridge, *2*, 628.

31. *Treatise on Method (TM)*, ed. Snyder, p. 2.

32. *TM*, p. 36.

33. *BL, 1*, 14.

34. *BL, 2*, 12.

35. *BL, 1*, 178.

36. *BL, 1*, 176; also *1*, 182-3, 89-90. In *PL*, p. 114, this doctrine is ascribed to Pythagoras.

37. *BL, 2*, 253, 254-5.

38. *BL, 1*, 202. The clearest parallel not noticed before, I believe, is in Schelling's *System des transcendentalen Idealismus* (1800), *Sämtliche Werke, 3*, 626: "Es ist das Dichtungsvermögen, was in der ersten Potenz die ursprüngliche Anschauung ist, und umgekehrt, es ist nur die in der höchsten Potenz sich wiederholende produktive Anschauung, was wir Dichtungsvermögen nennen. Es ist ein und dasselbe, was in beiden tätig ist, das Einzige, wodurch wir fähig sind, auch das Widersprechende zu denken und zusammenzufassen—die Einbildungskraft." Clearly the term "first potence" suggested "primary." The distinction between unconscious perception and conscious imagination, e.g., is in *3, 271*.

39. MS quoted by Muirhead, *Coleridge as Philosopher*, p. 195.

40. *BL*, 2, 257; cf. Schiller, *Sämtliche Werke, 18*, 55; and Vol. *1* of this *History*, p. 234.

41. *BL*, 2, 246, 243.

42. E.g. *BL*, 2, 232.

43. *BL*, 2, 224.

44. There is an elaborate discussion by Clarence D. Thorpe, "Coleridge on the Sublime," in *Wordsworth and Coleridge. Studies in Honor of G. M. Harper* (Princeton, 1939), pp. 192–219.

45. Fragment printed by T. M. Raysor in *SP*, 22 (1925), 532–3.

46. *BL*, 2, 309.

47. Marginalia to Herder's *Kalligone*, in *NQ*, 10th ser. *4* (1905), 342; *UL*, *1*, 117. Cf. *SC*, *1*, 222; *MC*, pp. 7, 12, 148; *TT*, p. 188.

48. *SC*, *1*, 178–9; *BL*, 2, 248.

49. *BL*, 2, 26, 64.

50. *BL*, 2, 227.

51. *BL*, 2, 249, 242.

52. *L.*, p. 372; *BL*, 2, 18–20; *SC*, 2, 87, 230, 148; *MC*, p. 343.

53. *UL*, *1*, 71. On reading for hymns cf. J. L. Lowes, *The Road to Xanadu* (Boston, 1927), pp. 73–6.

54. *PL*, p. 179.

55. *BL*, 2, 14–6. Cf. *SC*, *1*, 218; 2, 17, 91; *L.*, p. 372.

56. *TT*, p. 71.

57. *SC*, *1*, 126; *BL*, *1*, 22.

58. *MC*, p. 210.

59. *BL*, 2, 56, 68. Cf. remarks on Bowles, *L.*, *1*, 404.

60. *SC*, 2, 148. Cf. *BL*, *1*, 59; *Fr.*, p. 65.

61. *L.*, *1*, 197; *BL*, *1*, 59; 2, 122.

62. *BL*, *1*, 107; *AP*, p. 199. *L.*, *1*, 405–6. See also Marginalia to Maass, quoted in Sara Coleridge's ed. of *BL* (1847), *1*, 1, 97n. "Einbilden" in German has nothing to do with "ein," one.

63. *Literary Remains* (London, 1836), 2, 59. Based on *SC*, 2, 81. Cf. *BL*, 2, 20; *SC*, *1*, 218; 2, 95–6.

64. *MC*, p. 286; *SC*, 2, 168; *1*, 198; *UL*, *1*, 268–9.

65. *AP*, p. 186. *BL*, *1*, 167.

66. *BL*, 2, 12.

67. *SC*, 2, 36; *SC*, *1*, 5; *BL*, *1*, 153.

68. See John Bullitt and W. J. Bate, "The Distinctions between Fancy and Imagination in Eighteenth-Century English Criticism," *MLN*, *60* (1945), 8–15.

69. Johann Nicolaus Tetens, *Philosophische Versuche über die menschliche Natur* (modern reprint, Berlin, 1913), e.g. pp. 103, 112.

70. Schelling, *Sämtliche Werke*, 5, 386, 395; *1*, 357.

71. See above, pp. 46, 102.

72. *BL*, *1*, 193–4; previously pub. in *Omniana*, 2, 13; *MC*, p. 387. Cf. *L.*, *1*, 405.

73. *MC*, p. 38.

74. *SC*, *1*, 166. Cf. 2, 78.

75. *AP*, p. 10; *PL*, p. 309; *TM*, p. 25.

76. *TM*, p. 85.

77. *BL*, 2, 220, 255.

78. *MC*, pp. 149–50.

79. *BL*, 2, 22–3.

80. *BL*, 2, 103. Suggested by Bacon, *Advancement of Learning*, II, v, 3.

81. *MC*, pp. 320–1.

82. *BL*, 2, 105.

83. *BL*, 2, 11.

84. *BL*, 2, 104–5.

85. *BL*, 2, 42. Cf. p. 68 for requirement of passion, and *Inquiring Spirit*, p. 207.

86. *SC*, *1*, 206; *BL*, 2, 50. Cf. *SC*, 2, 78. Cf. p. 103.

87. *L.*, p. 374; *SC*, *1*, 218, 96. Cf. 2, 136–7; *BL*, 2, 43.

88. *SC*, *1*, 209.

89. *BL*, 2, 28.

90. *Inquiring Spirit*, p. 193. *BL*, 2, 39, 44. Marginalia to R. P. Knight's *Analytical Inquiry into the Principles of Taste*, published by E. A. Shearer in *Huntington Library Quarterly*, *1* (1937), 73. There is some doubt whether these notes are by Wordsworth or Coleridge.

91. *SC*, 2, 15, from Herder's *Kalligone*. *SC*, 2, 103; *AP*, p. 5.

92. *SC*, *1*, 209.

93. *PL*, pp. 141, 179.

94. *BL*, 2, 11.

95. *SC*, 2, 65.

96. *SC*, *1*, 163.

97. *SC*, *1*, 164. Cf. 2, 67; *BL*, 2, 11.

98. *TT*, pp. 48, 264.

99. *BL*, 2, 51, 53.

100. *MC*, pp. 337–8.

101. *BL*, 2, 9–11; *SC*, *1*, 223.

102. *SC*, *1*, 205.

103. *UL*, 2, 128.

104. *BL*, 2, 12, 14.

105. *SC*, *1*, 50.

106. *SC*, 2, 131; *1*, 213; *2*, 73–4.

107. *BL*, 2, 18; *SC*, *1*, 213.

108. *BL*, 2, 95, 102.

109. *MC*, p. 217. Similarly, modern prose style is called "marbles in a bag which touch without adhering" (*TT*, p. 248).

110. *PL*, p. 290; *BL*, *1*, 11.

111. *PL*, p. 290.

112. *TT*, pp. 259, 264–5.

113. *MC*, p. 89.

114. *MC*, p. 95.

115. *BL*, 2, 18.

116. *MC*, pp. 88–9; *SC*, 2, 168.

117. *SC*, *1*, 133, 234.

118. *MC*, pp. 42–3.

119. *SC*, *1*, 221, 231; 2, 261; *MC*, pp. 88–9. The comparison comes from A. W. Schlegel, Vienna, *1*, 7.

120. *BL*, *1*, 15.

121. *MC*, p. 152.

122. *SC*, *1*, 75, 77–8; *MC*, p. 45; *SC*, 2, 16, 209.

123. *BL*, 2, 56; *SC*, pp. 127–8, 204–5.

124. *PL*, p. 442 (Miss Coburn's note); *SC*, *1*, 200.

125. *SC*, 2, 9.

126. *MC*, p. 44. Also *SC*, 2, 130.

127. *MC*, p. 300.

128. *L.*, 2, 645.

129. *BL*, 2, 33.

130. *BL*, 2, 101; *MC*, p. 50.

131. *BL*, 2, 101–2.

132. *BL*, 2, 106–7.

133. *SC*, *1*, 72, 137; 2, 33.

134. *BL*, 2, 33n., 159.

135. *BL*, 2, 259. This passage paraphrases Schelling's Oration. *Werke*, 7, 301. Cf. p. 76 above.

136. *Fr.*, p. 328.

137. *MC*, p. 43.

138. *BL*, 2, 47.

139. Marginalia in *Revue de littérature comparée*, 7 (1927), 139.

140. *Coleridge on Logic and Learning (LL)*, p. 136; *AR*, 119n.; *Fr.*, 345; *BL*, 2, 259.

141. *MC*, p. 31.

142. *Statesman's Manual*, p. 230.

143. *AR*, p. 173n.; *MC*, p. 99.

144. *Statesman's Manual,* p. 230.

145. *AR,* p. 173n.; *MC,* p. 99.

146. *MC,* pp. 28–9.

147. *Fr.,* p. 345.

148. *BL,* 2, 120.

149. *MC,* p. 436; *SC, 1,* 212.

150. *BL, 1,* 15.

151. *BL,* 2, 67–8.

152. *MC,* pp. 244 ff., 277 ff.

153. *SC,* 2, 103, 121–2, 137–8, 184, 190; also *1,* 38; on Gaunt see *SC, 1,* 149, 153; 2, 184.

154. *BL, 1,* 189, 74; *LL,* p. 126.

155. *BL,* 2, 16–7.

156. *L., 1,* 404.

157. See Vol. 1 of this work, p. 149.

158. *BL,* 2, 6.

159. *BL,* 2, 189.

160. Comments on Knight, in *Huntington Library Quarterly, 1* (1937), 83. Cf. n. 90 above.

161. *Ibid.,* pp. 81, 84.

162. *MC,* p. 325.

163. *MC,* p. 373. This refers to Lewis' *Monk.*

164. *BL,* 2, 107.

165. *BL,* 2, 109. Schopenhauer uses the term "ventriloquism" with exactly the reverse meaning. See above, p. 310.

166. *AP,* p. 166; *TT,* p. 332. *AP,* p. 167.

167. *MC,* pp. 344–5.

168. E.g. *SC,* 2, 18; *BL,* 2, 161; *SC, 1,* 226; 2, 192. The term "interesting" comes from Friedrich Schlegel. See above, p. 11.

169. *SC, 1,* 205–6.

170. *SC, 1,* 196. Coleridge here paraphrases Reynolds' paper, *Idler,* No. 82.

171. *MC,* pp. 170, 166.

172. *BL,* 2, 109; *TT,* p. 312; *MC,* p. 44n. Beaumont and Fletcher are called the "most lyrical of our dramatists."

173. *BL,* pp. 106–7; *SC, 1,* 139, 147.

174. *SC, 1,* 226; *BL,* 2, 11.

175. *SC, 1,* 138, 142. This etymology occurs in F. Creuzer's *Symbolik* (2d ed. 1819, p. 46) with references to Scheidius and Lennep.

176. *SC, 1,* 138, 142.

177. *MC,* p. 342.

178. *BL,* 2, 163–4.

179. *MC*, p. 179; *SC*, 2, 216, 73; *1*, 203.

180. Published by T. M. Raysor in *SP*, 22 (1925), 531. As *Erwin* was published in 1815, the note must be later.

181. *MC*, p. 7; *SC*, *1*, 196–7; 2, 265; *PL*, p. 291; *Inquiring Spirit*, p. 152.

182. *SC*, *1*, 176; 2, 262.

183. *MC*, p. 165.

184. *BL*, 2, 209.

185. *SC*, *1*, 244. Cf. 2, 140; *SC*, 2, 125. Similarly "Shakespeare is of no age. His is not the style of the age." *TT*, p. 311.

186. *MC*, p. 168.

187. *L.*, pp. 425–7; *UP*, *1*, 263–5; *Inquiring Spirit*, pp. 152–3; *L.*, p. 515; *UL*, 2, 175–6.

188. *L.*, p. 426.

189. *BL*, *1*, 139. Coleridge seems not to be acquainted with the *Nibelungen* or any of the chivalric romances. In Göttingen he read the *Minnesingers* (*BL*, *1*, 140).

190. *MC*, pp. 27–8. *Iwain and Gawain* is retold after Ritson. *MC*, pp. 15–6.

191. *MC*, pp. 145–57, 24–6, 22–4, 26–7. Petrarch is briefly discussed in *PL*, pp. 292–4, and frequently quoted, e.g. *AP*, pp. 262–3; *BL*, *1*, 151; *Fr.*, pp. 42–3. Coleridge had a remarkable knowledge of Petrarch's Latin works.

192. The evidence of Coleridge's knowledge and indebtedness is, however, very slight. See R. W. Babcock, *The Genesis of Shakespeare Idolatry* (Chapel Hill, 1931), pp. 233–9.

193. *SC*, *1*, 25.

194. *SC*, *1*, 26.

195. See above, pp. 20, 27.

196. *SC*, *1*, 37.

197. *SC*, *1*, 30.

198. *SC*, *1*, 47.

199. *SC*, *1*, 233.

200. *SC*, *1*, 49. See, however, A. C. Bradley's attempt to justify Coleridge's phrase, though he does not quite agree with it, in *Shakespearean Tragedy* (London, 1904), pp. 209 ff., esp. p. 228n.

201. *MC*, pp. 145–57, 157–90, 218.

202. *MC*, pp. 130, 126.

203. *BL*, 2, 110, 112.

204. *L.*, pp. 684–8 (A letter to C. A. Tulk, 1818). See R. B. McElderry, "Coleridge on Blake's *Songs*," *MLQ*, 9 (1948), 298–302.

205. On Browne's *Hydrotaphia*, *MC*, p. 271 (a letter dating from

1804). Cf. Hazlitt's sound criticism in Howe, pp. 6, 340–1. "What is Lear?—It is storm and tempest" (*MC,* p. 45n.—undated).

206. *BL,* 2, 12, 15.

BIBLIOGRAPHY:

HAZLITT, LAMB, AND KEATS

Hazlitt is quoted from *The Complete Works,* ed. P. P. Howe, 21 vols. London, 1930 (cited as Howe). There are two good modern lives: P. P. Howe's (London, 1922; later ed. 1949) and Catherine Macdonald Maclean's, *Born under Saturn,* New York, 1944. The best discussion is Elisabeth Schneider's *The Aesthetics of William Hazlitt,* Philadelphia, 1933. John Bullitt's "Hazlitt and the Romantic Conception of Imagination," *PQ, 24* (1945), 343–61, makes important suggestions. There is a good comment in *Criticism: The Major Texts,* ed. W. J. Bate (New York, 1952), pp. 281–92. Karel Štěpanik's *W. H. jako literárni kritik* (Brno, 1947), in Czech, is negligible. The essays by Garrod, Ker, Saintsbury, and Virginia Woolf are slight.

Lamb is quoted from the *Works,* ed. Thomas Hutchinson (Oxford, 1924), Vol. *1,* entitled *Miscellaneous Prose, Elia, Last Essays of Elia;* and the *Letters,* ed. E. V. Lucas, 3 vols. London, 1935 (cited as *Letters*). The standard books by E. V. Lucas and Derocquigny say little about the criticism. Interesting comments appear in E. M. W. Tillyard's brief introduction to his anthology, *Lamb's Literary Criticism,* Oxford, 1923.

Keats's *Letters* are quoted from M. B. Forman, 4th ed. Oxford, 1952 (cited as *Letters*); the essays from *The Complete Works,* ed. H. B. Forman (London, 1901), Vol. *3.* On Keats's criticism Clarence D. Thorpe, *The Mind of John Keats* (Oxford, 1926) and James R. Caldwell, *John Keats' Fancy* (Ithaca, N.Y., 1945) are most useful. Walter J. Bate, *Negative Capability* (Cambridge, Mass., 1940), has good suggestions, and C. D. Thorpe discusses "Keats and Hazlitt" in *PMLA, 62* (1947), 487–502.

NOTES: HAZLITT, LAMB, AND KEATS

1. Howe, 5, 167.
2. *Ibid., 11,* 32–3; 7, 115; *16,* 123.
3. *Ibid., 1,* 130.
4. *Ibid., 16,* 123. For a fuller discussion of Hazlitt's relations to Kant see my *Kant in England* (Princeton, 1931), 164–71.
5. Howe, *16,* 110, 137.

6. *Ibid.*, pp. 134–36.

7. *Ibid.*, p. 115.

8. *Ibid.*, *4*, 171.

9. E.g. *ibid.*, *5*, 48, 88; 6, 340n.; *9*, 255n.; *19*, 206.

10. *Ibid.*, *16*, 58–9, 76–7. On Stendhal see above, p. 248.

11. *Ibid.*, *4*, 171.

12. *Ibid.*, *9*, 5.

13. *Table Talk*, August 6, 1832, p. 192.

14. *Oxford Lectures on Poetry* (Oxford, 1909), p. 105.

15. In introduction to Lamb's *Literary Criticism* (Oxford, 1923), p. ix.

16. *Letters*, *1*, 243–4.

17. *Ibid.*, *1*, 257. The allusion is to *Othello,* IV, iii, 137–40.

18. *Works,* ed. Hutchinson, p. 127.

19. *Ibid.*, pp. 650–1.

20. *Ibid.*, p. 677.

21. *Ibid.*, pp. 704–7.

22. For details see Robert D. Williams, "Antiquarian Interest in Elizabethan Drama before Lamb," *PMLA, 53* (1938), 434; and Wellek, *Rise,* esp. pp. 99–101.

23. Hutchinson, pp. 59, 65.

24. *Ibid.*, pp. 63–4.

25. *Ibid.*, pp. 737 ff., esp. p. 743.

26. *Ibid.*, p. 259.

27. *Ibid.*, p. 70.

28. *Letters*, *1*, 362.

29. *Ibid.*, p. 285.

30. Hutchinson, pp. 95–6, in essay on Hogarth (1811).

31. *Letters*, 2, 437, 426, 411, 137.

32. *Ibid.*, *1*, 136–7, 240, 239.

33. Hutchinson, p. 566.

34. Howe, 5, 175.

35. *Ibid.*, *6*, 301–2.

36. *Ibid.*, *6*, 70.

37. *Ibid.*, *11*, 64; *6*, 96; *5*, 113.

38. *Ibid.*, *5*, 87.

39. *Ibid.*, *5*, 18.

40. *Ibid.*, *9*, 81.

41. *Ibid.*, *6*, 342.

42. *Ibid.*, pp. 38, 262, etc.

43. *Ibid.*, p. 39.

44. *Ibid.*, pp. 42–3.

45. *Ibid.*, pp. 51, 320.
46. *Ibid.*, *11*, 84, 179.
47. *Ibid.*, *6*, 235.
48. *Ibid.*, p. 247.
49. *Ibid.*, pp. 199, 254.
50. *Ibid.*, *5*, 97.
51. *Ibid.*, p. 70.
52. "Eloisa to Abelard," line 160. *Rape of the Lock,* Canto II, line 64.
53. Howe, *6*, 340–1. Hazlitt quotes a letter by Coleridge written to an unknown correspondent, dated March 10, 1804, which had been published in *Blackwood's Magazine, 6* (1819), 197–8. Cf. Coleridge, *Miscellaneous Criticism*, ed. T. M. Raysor (London, 1936), esp. p. 271.
54. Howe, *8*, 208.
55. *Ibid.*, *7*, 308.
56. *Ibid.*, *20*, 262–3, 391.
57. *Ibid.*, *6*, 39.
58. *Ibid.*, *20*, 387.
59. *Ibid.*, *16*, 215–6.
60. *Ibid.*, *5*, 145.
61. *Ibid.*, *9*, 44–5.
62. *Ibid.*, *5*, 1–2; *9*, 45.
63. *Ibid.*, *5*, 5.
64. *Ibid.*, *4*, 58.
65. *Ibid.*, *11*, 308, 236.
66. *Ibid.*, *4*, 151; *5*, 4. Is "other" a misprint for "our"?
67. *Ibid.*, p. 3; *20*, 211.
68. *Ibid.*, pp. 300, 298.
69. *Ibid.*, *19*, 77.
70. Esp. *ibid.*, *8*, 317 ff.; *18*, 77 ff.; *20*, 302 ff.
71. *Ibid.*, pp. 297, 303–5. Cf. *12*, 44 ff., for attack on abstraction.
72. *Ibid.*, *4*, 77–8.
73. *Ibid.*, *5*, 50, 48, 47; *8*, 42.
74. *Ibid.*, *8*, 44; *5*, 53.
75. *Ibid.*, *12*, 319–20.
76. *Ibid.*, *16*, 401.
77. *Ibid.*, *5*, 153.
78. *Ibid.*, *6*, 128.
79. *Ibid.*, *4*, 271.
80. *Ibid.*, p. 74.
81. *Ibid.*, *12*, 290.
82. *Ibid.*, *6*, 109. Cf. *16*, 8–9.
83. *Ibid.*, *19*, 75.

84. *Ibid., 8,* 82–3.

85. *Ibid., 4,* 75; *12,* 334.

86. *Ibid., 9,* 45.

87. *Ibid., 5,* 12.

88. *Ibid., 16,* 136.

89. *Ibid., 6,* 8, 15.

90. *Ibid.,* pp. 63–4.

91. *Ibid.,* p. 50.

92. *Ibid.,* p. 320.

93. *Ibid., 16,* 43–4.

94. *Ibid., 4,* 180.

95. *Ibid., 5,* 217; *20,* 401.

96. *Othello,* I, iii, 94–6. Quoted by Hazlitt himself, Howe, *4,* 205.

97. Howe, pp. 228, 233.

98. *Ibid.,* pp. 232, 237.

99. *Ibid.,* p. 320.

100. *Ibid.,* p. 207, 209.

101. *Ibid., 16,* 5–6; cf. *6,* 106.

102. *Ibid., 16,* 218; *5,* 96.

103. *Ibid., 16,* 212.

104. *Ibid., 18,* 305.

105. *Ibid., 19,* 29.

106. *Ibid., 6,* 175, 180.

107. *Ibid.,* p. 189.

108. *Ibid., 5,* 9.

109. *Ibid., 4,* 161. Cf. *18,* 5, 7.

110. *Ibid., 5,* 82–3.

111. *Ibid., 16,* 19–20.

112. *Ibid., 6,* 35–6.

113. *Ibid.,* p. 150.

114. *Ibid.,* pp. 33, 38.

115. *Ibid.,* p. 347.

116. *Ibid., 16,* 76; *6,* 35; *16,* 79.

117. Elisabeth Schneider's *The Aesthetics of William Hazlitt* contains an appendix on Hazlitt's reading.

118. J. M. Robertson, *Essays towards a Critical Method* (London, 1889), p. 81.

119. Howe, *6,* 268–9.

120. *Ibid., 4,* 358–60.

121. *Ibid. 11,* 70, 75–6.

122. *Ibid., 16,* 266, 270, 280.

123. *Ibid., 9,* 244–5; *18,* 368n.; *16,* 269; *8,* 254–5.

124. *Ibid., 11,* 178–83. On the "Occult" school of criticism see *8,* 225–6; *17,* 318.

125. *Ibid., 6,* 192.

126. *Ibid., 4,* 253.

127. *Ibid., 16,* 6.

128. *Ibid., 5,* 283.

129. *Ibid., 8,* 224–5.

130. The essays and marginalia can be found in Vol. *3* of H. B. Forman's *Complete Works* (1900–01). To these must be added those in *Keats' Shakespeare,* ed. Caroline Spurgeon, Oxford, 1929.

131. See full discussion by C. D. Thorpe, "Keats and Hazlitt," *PMLA, 62* (1947), 487–502. Keats's copy of Hazlitt's *Characters* is in the Harvard Library. Text in Amy Lowell's *John Keats* (Boston, 1925), *2,* 587–90. The other references are to *Letters,* pp. 79, 309, 106, 56, 23.

132. *Letters,* p. 71 (Dec. 21, 1817).

133. *Ibid.,* p. 95 (Feb. 3, 1818).

134. *Ibid.,* p. 507 (August, 1820).

135. *Ibid.,* p. 131 (April 9, 1818).

136. *Ibid.,* p. 107 (Feb. 27, 1818).

137. *Ibid.,* pp. 222–3 (Oct. 9, 1818).

138. *Works,* ed. Forman, *3,* 256.

139. Lines 199–202, 148–9.

140. *Letters,* p. 227 (Oct. 27, 1818). I adopt the emendation "informing" instead of "in for—," as suggested by G. Beaumont in *TLS,* Feb. 27, 1930.

141. *Works, 2,* 240.

142. Benjamin Bailey's letter to Lord Houghton, May 7, 1849. Quoted by W. J. Bate, *The Stylistic Development of Keats* (New York, 1945), p. 51.

143. *Works, 3,* 230.

144. *Letters,* p. 67 (Nov. 22, 1817).

BIBLIOGRAPHY:

MADAME DE STAËL AND CHATEAUBRIAND

On French criticism, see besides Michiels, Brunetière, Mustoxidi, and Van Tieghem, quoted in Vol. *1,* p. 274, Irving Babbitt, *The Masters of Modern French Criticism* (Boston, 1912), with chapters on Madame de Staël and Chateaubriand.

On Empire critics: Sainte-Beuve, "M. de Féletz, et la critique littéraire sous l'Empire," *Causeries du lundi* (1850), Vol. *1.*

Geoffroy's articles are reprinted in *Cours de la littérature drama-tique*, 5 vols. 2d ed. Paris, 1825. They are quoted by date of issue of *Journal des débats* (cited as *Débats*). On Geoffroy see Charles Marc Des Granges, *Geoffroy et la critique dramatique sous le Consulat et l'Empire*, Paris, 1897 (cited as Des Granges)—excellent, though diffuse and too laudatory.

Madame de Staël's writings are quoted from *Œuvres complètes*, 17 vols. Paris, 1820 (cited as *Œuvres*). Of the huge biographical literature the two books by David Glass Larg, *Madame de Staël. La Vie dans l'œuvre (1766–1800)* (Paris, 1924) and *Madame de Staël. La Seconde vie (1800–1807)* (Paris, 1928) are most relevant. Also, Comtesse Jean de Pange, *Auguste-Guillaume Schlegel et Madame de Staël*, Paris, 1938.

On the sources of *De l'Allemagne* cf. Oskar Walzel, "Frau von Staëls Buch de l'Allemagne und W. Schlegel," in *Forschungen zur neueren Litteraturgeschichte. Festgabe für Richard Heinzel* (Weimar, 1898), pp. 275–334; and Gertrude Emma Jaeck, "The Indebtedness of Madame de Staël to A. W. Schlegel," *JEGP*, *10* (1911), 499–534. Jean Gibelin, *L'Esthétique de Schelling et l'Allemagne de Madame de Staël* (Paris, 1934) fails to establish any relationship. Comtesse Jean de Pange, *Madame de Staël et la découverte de l'Allemagne* (Paris, 1929) tells the external story. On the influence see texts in ed. Edmond Eggli, *Le Débat romantique en France 1813–1830*, Vol. *1* (1813–16) Paris, 1933. Investigations: Gertrude Emma Jaeck, *Madame de Staël and the Spread of German Literature*, New York, 1915; Robert Calvin Whitford, *Madame de Staël's Literary Reputation in England*, Urbana, Ill., 1918; Ian Allan Henning, *L'Allemagne de Madame de Staël et la polémique romantique*, Paris, 1929; Carlo Pellegrini, *Madame de Staël: il gruppo cosmopolito di Coppet: influenza delle sue idee critiche*, Firenze, 1938.

Chateaubriand is quoted from *Œuvres complètes* (25 vols. Paris, 1836), and *Mémoires d'outre tombe*, ed. E. Biré and P. Moreau, 6 vols. Paris, 1947. Of the huge literature Sainte-Beuve's *Chateaubriand et son groupe littéraire* (2 vols. 1849) is still outstanding. Hubert Gillot, *Chateaubriand. Ses idées; son action; son œuvre* (Paris, 1934) pays attention to the criticism.

Special aspects are discussed in Meta Helena Miller, *Chateaubriand and English Literature*, Baltimore, 1925; and Carlos Lynes, "Chateau-briand—Critic of the French Renaissance," *PMLA*, *62* (1947), 422–35.

NOTES:

MADAME DE STAËL AND CHATEAUBRIAND

1. Stendhal, *Racine et Shakespeare,* ed. P. Martino (Paris, 1932), *1,* 141. Similar passages in *Courrier anglais,* ed. H. Martineau (Paris, 1935), *1,* 21; *3,* 134.

2. *Débats,* January 24, 1804; February 16, 1805: "le bon goût, la saine morale, et les bases éternelles de l'ordre social." Quoted by Des Granges, *Geoffroy,* pp. 173, 176.

3. *Débats,* January 25, 1804; October 11, 1803. Des Granges, pp. 179, 168.

4. *Débats,* January 23 and 29, 1805. Des Granges, pp. 169–70. *Débats,* June 26, 1807: "les fripons sont dans la société, et la vertu règne sur le théâtre." Des Granges, p. 166.

5. *Année littéraire* (1785), *1,* lettre 3. Des Granges, pp. 70–1.

6. *Débats,* April 11, 1803: "un amas de folies"; September 22, 1800: "une série d'absurdités"; June 4, 1804: "ce monument de la barbarie anglaise"; *ibid.:* "un Hottentot emprisonné dans des vêtements européens." Des Granges, pp. 327–8.

7. *Année littéraire* (1801), *3,* No. 18. Des Granges, pp. 88–9.

8. *Débats,* January 3, 1804; August 27, 1801. *La Surprise de l'amour* is the title of one of Marivaux's comedies. Des Granges, pp. 273, 369.

9. *Année littéraire* (1787), *1,* lettre 1. Des Granges, p. 56.

10. *Œuvres* (1820), *4,* 25: "L'influence de la religion, des mœurs et des lois sur la littérature, et quelle est l'influence de la littérature sur la religion, les mœurs et les lois."

11. *Ibid.,* pp. 4–5, 258.

12. *Ibid.,* p. 196: "La tristesse passionnée des habitans d'un climat nébuleux"; p. 259: "l'image de la fraicheur, des bois touffus, des ruisseaux limpides. . . . l'ombre bienfaisante qui doit les préserver des brûlantes ardeurs du soleil."

13. *Ibid.,* pp. 85, 104, 126, 129.

14. *Ibid.,* pp. 87–8.

15. *Ibid.,* p. 248.

16. *Ibid.,* pp. 284, 308: "un assez grand nombre de poètes anglais s'écarta du caractère national, pour imiter les Italiens."

17. *Ibid.,* p. 242: "L'Arioste est le premier peintre, et par conséquent peut-être le plus grand poète moderne."

18. *Ibid.,* p. 282.

19. *Ibid.,* p. 300: "caricatures populaires."

20. *Ibid.,* pp. 300–1.

21. *Ibid.,* p. 315: "cette sombre imagination . . . est cependant la couleur générale de la poésie anglaise."

22. *Ibid.,* p. 395: "tous les genres de volupté de l'âme."

23. *Ibid.,* p. 392: "Il n'a rien découvert, mais il a tout enflammé."

24. *Ibid.,* p. 31: "La vertu devient alors une impulsion involontaire, un mouvement qui passe dans le sang."

25. *Ibid.,* p. 404: "c'est l'homme alors qu'il peut sauver l'innocence, c'est l'homme alors qu'il peut renverser le despotisme, c'est l'homme enfin lorsqu'il se consacre au bonheur de l'humanité."

26. *Ibid.,* p. 511: "dans le siècle du monde le plus corrompu."

27. *Ibid.,* p. 498n.

28. Fontanes' review in *Œuvres* (Paris, 1859), *2,* 160–205; originally in *Mercure de France, 1800.* For Chateaubriand's review see n. 66 below.

29. In *Magasin encyclopédique, 5* (1799), 44–65, 214–35; reprinted in Wilhelm von Humboldt, *Gesammelte Schriften* (Berlin, 1904), *3,* 1–29.

30. These articles are described and the relationship discussed in my *Kant in England* (Princeton, 1931), pp. 143–58.

31. Friedrich Schlegel, *Neue philosophische Schriften,* ed. J. Körner (Frankfurt, 1935), pp. 223–57, contains notes (in French) of a private lecture for Madame de Staël.

32. *Œuvres, 10,* 464; *11,* 102; *10,* 462–63. A more extended list of parallelisms in Walzel's article, quoted in bibliography.

33. *Œuvres, 10,* 274: "La poésie des anciens est plus pure comme art, celle des modernes fait verser plus des larmes." *10,* 276: "la poésie des Germains . . . se sert de nos impressions personelles pour nous émouvoir: le génie qui l'inspire s'addresse immédiatement à notre cœur."

34. Cf. *Œuvres, 10,* 299–300; *11,* 45: "Depuis quelque temps on a prétendu que pleurer ou rire ne prouve rien, en faveur d'une tragédie, ou d'une comédie; je suis loin d'être de cet avis." See *11,* 48 on comic theory; *11,* 136: "Partisan d'un goût simple et quelquefois même d'un goût rude."

35. *Ibid., 10,* 217, on Wieland; *11,* 45, on Kotzebue; *11,* 2 ff., on Werner.

36. Dora Hensler, *Lebensnachrichten* (Hamburg, 1838–39), *1,* 579: "Er kann es nicht einmal vor dem Drucke eingesehen haben." Letter of Jan. 25, 1814.

37. *Œuvres, 11,* 133: "La description animée des chefs-d'œuvre."

38. *Ibid., 10,* 210, 303–4.

39. *Ibid.,* p. 209.

40. *Ibid.,* p. 234: "On ne peut donner de la vie aux objets de l'art que par la connaissance intime du pays et de l'époque dans laquelle

ils ont existé. . . . en s'aidant à la fois de l'imagination et de l'étude, on récompense le temps, et l'on refait la vie."

41. *Ibid.*, pp. 247–8: "Il faut avoir une âme que la tempête ait agitée, mais où le ciel soit descendu pour ramener le calme."

42. *Ibid.*, pp. 446, 447.

43. *Ibid.*, pp. 470–1; 484–5; 496–8.

44. E.g. "Die Braut von Korinth," "Der Gott und die Bajadere," "Der Fischer," "Der Zauberlehrling."

45. *Œuvres*, p. 544: "Le délire de l'esprit." *10*, 506: "Le cauchemar de l'esprit."

46. *Ibid.*, *11*, 89 ff., 93 ff.

47. *Ibid.*, p. 94: "Paresse de cœur."

48. *Ibid.*, p. 101: "Il faut, dans nos temps modernes, avoir l'esprit européen."

49. *Ibid.*, p. 107. Cf. Fernand Baldensperger, "Le Songe de Jean Paul dans le romantisme français," *Alfred de Vigny* (Paris, 1912), pp. 159–76. See also Albert Béguin, "Le Songe de Jean Paul et Victor Hugo," *Revue de littérature comparée*, *14* (1934), 703–13.

50. *Œuvres*, *11*, 97–8, 50 ff.

51. *Ibid.*, p. 2: "le premier des écrivains dramatiques de l'Allemagne." On *Atilla* see *11*, 11–12.

52. *Ibid.*, pp. 18–22.

53. *Ibid.*, *10*, 200: "Il faut . . . que le Français soit religieux, et que l'Allemand soit un peu mondain."

54. *Ibid.*, p. 218: "L'originalité nationale vaut mieux, et l'on devait, tout en reconnaissant Wieland pour un grand maître, souhaiter qu'il n'eût pas de disciples."

55. *Ibid.*, p. 276: "La littérature romantique est la seule qui soit susceptible encore d'être perfectionée, parce qu'ayant ses racines dans notre propre sol, elle est la seule qui puisse croître et se vivifier de nouveau; elle exprime notre religion; elle rappelle notre histoire."

56. *Ibid.*, p. 304: "Un poème épique n'est presque jamais l'ouvrage d'un homme, et les siècles mêmes, pour ainsi dire, y travaillent . . . les personnages du poème épique doivent représenter le caractère primitif de la nation."

57. *Ibid.*, pp. 340–1: "Rien ne serait donc plus absurde que de vouloir à cet égard imposer à toutes les nations le même système."

58. *Ibid.*, pp. 425, 226. On "Braut von Korinth" see *ibid.*, pp. 312, 483, 525.

59. *Ibid.*, *11*, 33: "Il faut pour la tragédie, des sujets historiques ou des traditions religieuses qui réveillent de grands souvenirs dans l'âme des spectateurs."

60. *Ibid.*, p. 82: "Pourquoi les écrivains dramatiques n'essaieraient-ils pas aussi de réunir dans leurs compositions ce que l'acteur a su bien amalgamer par son jeu?"

61. *Ibid.*, p. 145: "Les nations doivent se servir de guide les unes aux autres . . . On se trouvera donc bien en tout pays d'accueillir les pensées étrangères; car, dans ce genre, l'hospitalité fait la fortune de celui qui reçoit."

62. Reprinted in Eggli, *Le Débat romantique*, pp. 217–40.

63. *Tag- und Jahreshefte* (1804); *Werke, 30*, 134: "Jenes Werk über Deutschland . . . ist als ein mächtiges Rüstzeug anzusehen, das in die chinesische Mauer antiquierter Vorurteile, die uns von Frankreich trennte, sogleich eine breite Lücke durchbrach." Other less favorable letters and conversations are quoted in Henning, *L'Allemagne de Madame de Staël* (Paris, 1929), pp. 241 ff.

64. Jean Paul's review in *Heidelberger Jahrbücher* (1815), reprinted in *Kleine Bücherschau,* ed. Berend, *Sämtliche Werke, 16.* Carlyle translated the Jean Paul review for *Fraser's Magazine* (1830), reprinted in *Works,* Centenary ed., *26,* 476–502.

65. *Deutsche Worte über die Ansichten der Frau v. Staël von unserer poetischen Litteratur in ihrem Werk über Deutschland* (Heidelberg, 1814), 250 pp.

66. Ostensibly a letter to Fontanes in *Mercure de France,* December 22, 1800; *Œuvres, 13,* 289–315. Also in *Correspondance Générale,* ed. Louis Thomas (Paris, 1912), *1,* 23–43.

67. *Œuvres, 13,* 290: "Vous n'ignorez pas que ma folie est de voir *Jésus-Christ* partout, comme Madame de Staël la *perfectibilité.*"

68. *Ibid., 11,* 15: "La religion chrétienne est la plus poétique, la plus humaine, la plus favorable à la liberté, aux arts et aux lettres."

69. *Ibid.*, pp. 279 ff. (*Génie,* Pt. 2, Bk. II, chs. 2 ff.).

70. *Ibid.*, p. 342: "C'est la chrétienne réprouvée, c'est la pécheresse tombée vivante entre les mains de Dieu" (*Génie,* Pt. 2, Bk. III, ch. 3).

71. *Ibid., 12,* 222: "Que l'incrédulité est la principale cause de la décadence du goût et du génie" (*Génie,* Pt. 3, Bk. IV, ch. 5). *12,* 229–30: "Aussi le dix-huitième siècle diminue-t-il chaque jour dans la perspective, tandis que le dix-septième semble s'élever à mesure que nous nous en éloignons; l'un s'affaise, l'autre monte dans les cieux" (*Génie,* Pt. 3, Bk. IV, ch. 5).

72. *Ibid.*, p. 17: "C'est au christianisme que Bernardin de Saint-Pierre doit son talent pour peindre les scènes de la solitude" (*Génie,* Pt. 2, Bk. IV, ch. 3).

73. *Ibid.*, *11*, 317–20; *12*, 66–102 (*Génie*, Pt. 2, Bk. II, ch. 10; Bk. V, chs. 1–4).

74. In *Chateaubriand et son groupe littéraire*, ed. M. Allem (Garnier ed.), *1*, 257 ff. (Treizième leçon).

75. *Œuvres*, *11*, 318: "L'œuvre le plus parfait du génie inspiré par la religion." Cf. Voltaire's similar view, Vol. 1 of this work, p. 45.

76. *Ibid.*, *12*, 101. On the influence of Lowth cf. Madeleine Dempsey, *A Contribution to the Study of the Sources of the Génie du Christianisme*, Paris, 1928.

77. *Œuvres*, *17*, 277: "D'abandonner la petite et facile critique des *défauts* pour la grande et difficile critique des *beautés*" (*Mélanges littéraires*).

78. *Ibid.*, p. 53: "Écrire est un art. . . . cet art a nécessairement des genres, et chaque genre a des règles. . . . Racine, dans toute l'excellence de son art, est plus naturel que Shakespeare; comme l'Apollon, dans toute sa divinité, a plus les formes humaines qu'une statue grossière de l'Egypte."

79. On *beau idéal* see *ibid.*, *11*, 322–3 (*Génie*, Pt. 2, Bk. II, ch. 11). On "La belle nature": e.g. *10*, 5 (Preface to *Atala*): "Peignons la nature, mais la belle nature: l'art ne doit pas s'occuper de l'imitation des monstres." On taste: *17*, 34, review of Young (*Mélanges*): "Le goût est le bon sens du génie; sans le goût, le génie n'est qu'une sublime folie." On rules: *14*, 47 (preface to 3d ed. of *Les Martyrs*): "La règle des trois unités, par exemple, est de tout temps, de tout pays, parce qu'elle est fondée sur la nature."

80. *Ibid.*, *14*, 25 (preface to 3d ed. of *Les Martyrs*): "Je ne veux rien changer, rien innover en littérature; j'adore les anciens; je les regarde comme nos maîtres; j'adopte entièrement les principes posés par Aristote, Horace et Boileau."

81. *Ibid.*, *12*, 70–1 (*Génie*, Pt. 2, Bk. V, ch. 2).

82. *Ibid.*, *11*, 259–60: "Nous sommes persuadé que les grands écrivains ont mis leur histoire dans leurs ouvrages. On ne peint bien que son propre cœur, en l'attribuant à un autre; et la meilleure partie du génie se compose de souvenirs" (*Génie*, Pt. 2, Bk. I, ch. 3).

83. *Ibid.*, *12*, 37–8: "Milton lui-même avait partagé cet esprit de perdition" (*Génie*, Pt. 2, Bk. IV, ch. 9). *11*, 259 (Pt. 2, Bk. I, ch. 3). *11*, 318–9 (Pt. 2, Bk. II, ch. 10).

84. *Mémoires d'outre tombe*, *2*, 202–3: "Une famille de René poètes et de René prosateurs a pullulé."

85. *Ibid.*, *6*, 293: "Elle ne chantera *quand la bise sera venu*."

86. *Ibid.*, *5*, 307–10.

87. *Œuvres*, 22, 239 (*Essai sur la littérature anglaise, 1*): "J'ai mesuré autrefois Shakespeare avec la lunette classique . . . microscope inapplicable à l'observation de l'ensemble." On Chaucer see p. 110. On Spenser see p. 230: "glacé et ennuyeux."

88. *Ibid.*, pp. 286 ff. (*Essai, 1*): "les ombres ossianiques," "Génies mères," pp. 323–5.

89. *Ibid.*, p. 285 (*Essai, 1*): "la perfection de l'ensemble et la juste proportion des parties."

90. *Ibid.*, 23, 122, 128, 156, 164–5 (on theology), 159: "Le républicain se retrouve à chaque vers du *Paradis perdu:* les discours de Satan respirent la haine de la dépendance" (*Essai, 2*).

91. *Ibid.*, 12, 63: "Mais supposons que le chantre d'Eden fût né en France sous le siècle de Louis XIV, et qu'à la grandeur naturelle de son génie il eût joint le goût de Racine et de Boileau" (*Génie*, Pt. 2, Bk. IV, ch. 16).

92. *Ibid.*, 23, 365 ff. (*Essai, 2*). For a comparison with Byron, see pp. 380, 386.

93. Quoted by V. Giraud in intro. to *Atala. Reproduction de l'édition originale* (Paris, 1906), pp. xxiv ff.

94. *Mémoires d'outre tombe*, 6, 160–1: "L'empéreur de Russie Alexandre?—Mort. L'empéreur d'Autriche François I?—Mort. Le roi de France Louis XVIII?—Mort. . . . Personne ne se souvient des discours que nous tenions autour de la table du prince de Metternich; mais, ô puissance du génie! aucun voyageur n'entendra jamais chanter l'alouette dans les champs de Vérone sans se rappeler Shakespeare."

BIBLIOGRAPHY: STENDHAL AND HUGO

Joubert's *Pensées* are quoted from *Les Carnets,* ed. A. Beaunier, 2 vols. Paris, 1938; and in a few instances from *Pensées,* ed. P. Raynal, Paris, 1888. Joubert is discussed in famous essays by Sainte-Beuve, *Portraits littéraires, 2,* and *Causeries du lundi, 1;* by Matthew Arnold, *Essays in Criticism, 1,* and in a chapter of Babbitt's *Masters of Modern French Criticism;* and by M. Gilman, "Joubert on Imagination and Poetry," *RR, 40* (1949), 250–60.

Stendhal's works are quoted from the critical Champion editions, especially *Racine et Shakespeare,* ed. Pierre Martino, 2 vols. Paris, 1925. When these fail, I quote from the Divan edition 79 vols. Paris, 1926–37). The articles for English magazines are collected in French retranslations in Divan edition as *Courrier anglais,* 5 vols. Paris, 1935–36. I quote the English text from the files of the magazines. Gina Raya's *Stendhal* (Modena, 1943) has a chapter on the critic. The English articles were identified in Doris Gunnel, *Stendhal et l'Angleterre* (Paris, 1909) and are discussed in René Dollot, *Stendhal journaliste,* Paris, 1948. Robert Vigneron's "Stendhal and Hazlitt," *MP, 35* (1938), 378–414, and the chapter on Manzoni and Stendhal in P. Trompeo's *Nell'Italia romantica sulle orme di Stendhal* (Rome, 1924) illuminate Stendhal's sources. Harry Levin, *Toward Stendhal* (Murray, Utah, 1945) is a fine general essay.

On the romantic debate see especially the instructive *Chronologie du romantisme (1804–1830),* by René Bray (Paris, 1932), which lists the older works by Marsan, Séché, Souriau, etc.

Hugo's works are quoted from *Œuvres complètes,* ed. définitive, 43 vols. Paris, 1881. On Hugo see the edition of *La Préface de Cromwell,* by Maurice Souriau, n.d.; Ch.-Albert Rossé, *Les Théories littéraires de Victor Hugo,* Délémont, 1903; and John Hayward Thomas, *L'Angleterre dans l'œuvre de Victor Hugo,* Paris, 1933.

NOTES: STENDHAL AND HUGO

1. From *Contemplations* (1856): "Réponse à une acte d'accusation."

2. *Œuvres complètes, 17* (*Littérature et philosophie*), p. 130: "Qu'est-ce en effet qu'un poète? Un homme qui sent fortement, exprimant ses sensations dans une langue plus expressive. La poésie, ce n'est presque que sentiment, dit Voltaire."

3. *Pensées* (Paris, 1931), *2,* 283: "On ne peut peindre ce qu'on n'a pas senti." Cf. *1,* 120.

4. Letter to Mme la marquise de Raigecourt, May 21, 1819, in *Correspondance* (Paris, 1882), *2,* 36: "Il y a plus de poésie dans le plus petit coin d'un de ses tableaux que dans toutes nos poésies humaines."

5. *Œuvres complètes, 1* (*Odes et ballades*), 6.

6. In 1838 Chateaubriand published a small volume, *Recueil et pensées.* In 1842 a larger selection was published by Paul de Raynal, which has been frequently reprinted. In 1938 the full text of *Les Carnets,* with their dates, was published by André Beaunier. But 168 aphorisms in Raynal's *Pensées* cannot be found in *Carnets.*

7. *Carnets, 2,* 595: "La lyre est, en quelque manière, un instrument ailé." *Ibid.,* p. 604: "Les beaux vers sont ceux qui s'exhalent comme des sons ou des parfums." *Ibid.,* p. 861: "Et il est certain que quiquonque n'aura jamais été pieux ne deviendra jamais poète."

8. *Pensées,* p. 264: "A l'aide de certains rayons, il purge et vide les forces de matière, et nous fait voir l'univers tel qu'il est dans la pensée de Dieu même."

9. *Carnets, 2,* 493: "J'appelle imagination la faculté de rendre sen-

sible tout ce qui est intellectuel, d'incorporer ce qui est esprit, et en un mot, de mettre au jour sans le dénaturer ce qui est de soi-même invisible."

10. *Ibid.*, p. 563: "De ceux en qui l'imaginative (faculté animale fort différente de l'imagination, faculté intellectuelle) domine. L'imagination est l'imaginative de l'esprit. . . . L'imaginative se frappe. Elle est passive. L'imagination est active, créatrice" (1806).

11. *Ibid.*, *1*, 205, 260, 282: "Une espèce de mémoire . . . Un magasin ou l'imagination puise. . . . L'imagination est peintre. Elle peint dans notre âme et au dehors à l'âme des autres. Elle revêt d'images." Joubert calls Addison "le plus sage des critiques" (*ibid.*, *2*, 482).

12. *Pensées*, p. 275: "C'est les fourbir . . . c'est refondre cette monnaie . . . c'est renouveler, par le type, des empreintes effacées."

13. *Carnets*, *1*, 132: "Le caractère du poète est d'être bref, c'est-à-dire parfait, *absolutus*, comme disaient les Latins. Celui de l'orateur est d'être coulant, abondant, spacieux, épandu, varié, inépuisable, immense."

14. *Ibid.*, *2*, 478, 498: "le poète . . . les rend légers et leur donne de la couleur . . . Faire voltiger les mots . . ." Cf. Letter to Molé (March 10, 1805), *Pensées*, ed. Raynal, 340: "architecture de mots." *Carnets*, *2*, 646: "La pure essence dont il faut les assaisonner."

15. *Ibid.*, p. 679: "Ceux à qui Racine suffit sont des pauvres âmes et de pauvres esprits. . . . Admirable sans doute pour avoir rendu poétiques les sentiments les plus bourgeois et les passions les plus médiocres." *Ibid.*, p. 859: "Notre véritable Homère, l'Homère des Français."

16. *Ibid.*, p. 895: "Mais pour nous élever et pour ne pas être salis par les bassesses de la terre, il nous faut en tout des échasses."

17. See introduction and notes to Martino's critical ed., *Racine et Shakespeare*. On Visconti, see above, p. 260.

18. *Racine et Shakespeare*, *1*, 39: "Le *romanticisme* est l'art de présenter aux peuples les œuvres littéraires qui, dans l'état actuel de leurs habitudes et de leurs croyances, sont susceptibles de leur donner le plus de plaisir possible.

"*Le classicisme*, au contraire, leur présente la littérature qui donnait le plus grand plaisir possible à leurs arrière-grands-pères."

19. *Ibid.*, p. 86: "un cache-sottise." *Ibid.*, p. 97: "ce mot propre, unique, nécessaire, indispensable."

20. *Ibid.*, on Luther, *2*, 223; Collin, *Courrier anglais*, *1*, 212; Mérimée, *4*, 222 (in *London Magazine*, July, 1825).

21. F. C. Green, *Stendhal* (Cambridge, 1939), 165, 212, 214.

22. Identified in Doris Gunnell's *Stendhal et l'Angleterre*. Collected

in French re-translations in Divan edition as *Courrier anglais,* 5 vols. Paris, 1935–36.

23. *Histoire de la peinture en Italie,* ed. P. Arbelet (Paris, 1924), *1,* 269; *2,* 46 ff.

24. See below, n. 35.

25. *Racine et Shakespeare, 2,* 258: "Et, quel qu'on soit, roi ou berger, sur le trône ou portant la houlette, on a toujours raison de sentir comme on sent et de trouver beau ce qui donne du plaisir."

26. *London Magazine, 1* (1825), 280.

27. *Vie de Rossini,* ed. H. Prunières (Paris, 1922), *1,* 222: "Même en musique, pour être heureux, il ne faut pas en être réduit à examiner: voilà ce que les Français ne veulent pas comprendre; leur manière de jouir des arts, c'est de les juger."

28. So defined by Levin, *Toward Stendhal,* p. 27.

29. *Mélanges de littérature* (Paris, 1933), *3,* 397.

30. On Madame de Staël see letter to E. Mounier, March 26, 1803; *Correspondance,* Divan, *1,* 117; letter to Pauline, Sept. 19, 1810; *ibid., 3,* 278. On Chateaubriand see e.g. *Mélanges intimes* (Paris, 1936), *2,* 98; on *Itinéraire:* "Je n'ai jamais rien trouvé de si puant d'égotisme, d'égoïsme, de plate affectation et même de forfanterie."

31. Balzac's review in *Revue Parisienne,* Sept. 25, 1840; *Œuvres complètes* (Paris, 1873), *23,* 687–738; Stendhal's letter, Oct. 16, 1840; *Correspondance, 10,* 267: "Voilà sans doute, pourquoi j'écris mal: c'est par l'amour exagérée pour la logique."

32. In *London Magazine,* March, 1825, "Steding" seems a corruption of "Schelling"; also, *Correspondance, 6,* 37 (Dec. 4, 1822): "Quant à l'Allemagne, l'absurdité de sa philosophie et la prétension d'être originale la gâtent tout à fait."

33. *New Monthly Magazine, 12* ("1824 Historical Papers"), pp. 557–8.

34. On Manzoni see *New Monthly* (Pt. 1, 1827), p. 377; *Mélanges, 3,* 391.

35. On Schlegel see marginalia in *Mélanges intimes, 1,* 311; in *Histoire de la peinture en Italie, 2,* 54–5; long note on Molière criticism and idolatry of Shakespeare. Other references in *Racine et Shakespeare, 2,* 269–70; letters to L. Crozet in *Correspondance, 4* (Sept. 28, 1816), 371, "Schlegel reste un pédant ridicule"; *ibid., 4* (Oct. 1, 1816), 389, "pauvre et triste pédant"; *ibid., 5* (Oct. 20, 1816), 15, "un petit pédant sec, confit de vanité allemande, mais fort savant"; *ibid., 5* (Dec. 26, 1816), 28–9, "pédant pire que les La Harpe."

36. See above pp. 189–90.

37. *Racine et Shakespeare, 2,* 119: "le père du romanticisme"; on

Johnson's *Dictionary: ibid.*, *2*, 70–1; Johnson's *Preface* used, *ibid.*, *1*, 16, and *2*, 14; Johnson's comments on *Cymbeline* criticized in *Histoire de la peinture, 2*, 84n.

38. On Byron see *Racine et Shakespeare*, *1*, 35; *2*, 31; *London Magazine*, *2* (May, 1825), 136, 140; *New Monthly*, *1* (April, 1828), 376; *ibid.*, *1* (May, 1826), 514.

39. On Buratti see *Mélanges intimes*, *3*, 373 ff.; *London Magazine*, *3* (Sept., 1825), 36; *ibid.*, *4* (Jan., 1826), 23, 26; on Grossi see *New Monthly*, *1* (May, 1826), 516.

40. *Racine et Shakespeare, 2*, 165 ff., 193 ff.

41. *Ibid.*, *2*, 46, 62–3, 86, etc.

42. Article, "La Comédie est impossible en 1836," *Mélanges de littérature, 3*, 413 ff.

43. *Le Rouge et le noir,* ed. J. Marsan (Paris, 1923), *1*, 389: "On ne plus atteindre au vrai que dans le roman."

44. *Le Rouge et le noir, 1*, 133, ch. 13: "Un roman: c'est un miroir qu'on promène le long d'un chemin." Ascribed to Saint-Réal. Cf. *2*, 224. Préface to *Armance,* ed. R. Lebèque (Paris, 1925), p. 5: "Est-ce leur faute si des gens laids ont passé devant ce miroir? De quel parti est un miroir?"

45. *Lucien Leuwen,* ed. Martineau, *2*, 36: "cela est vrai, mais vrai comme la Morgue, et c'est un genre de vérité que nous laissons aux romans in-12 pour femmes de chambre."

46. *Mélanges intimes, 2*, 258–9: "En général, idéaliser comme Raphaël idéalise dans un portrait pour le rendre plus ressemblant."

47. *New Monthly Magazine* (Dec., 1822), p. 558. *Ibid.* (Feb., 1825), pp. 278–9.

48. *Mélanges de littérature, 3*, 306: "L'habit et le collier de cuivre d'un serf du moyen âge sont plus faciles à décrier que les mouvements du cœur humain."

49. MS quoted by Green, p. 268: "L'action des choses sur l'homme, est-elle particulièrement le domaine du roman?"

50. *Mélanges de littérature, 3*, 308: "Tout ouvrage d'art est un beau mensonge." Cf. *ibid.*, *2*, 106.

51. *Mélanges intimes, 2*, 162, "sale pamphlet." On *Han d'Islande* see *The New Monthly Magazine,* "1823 Historical Papers," p. 174.

52. *Œuvres complètes,* ed. Hetzel, *1* (*Odes et ballades*), preface to *Odes* (1824), p. 8.

53. *Ibid.*, preface to *Odes* (1826), p. 24: "la tragédie interdit ce que le *roman* permet; la *chanson* tolère ce que l'*ode* défend, etc."

54. *Œuvres complètes, 24*, 22; preface to *Cromwell* (1827): "Croit-on que Françoise de Rimini et Béatrix seraient aussi ravissantes chez un

poète qui ne nous enfermerait pas dans la tour de la Faim et ne nous forcerait point à partager le repoussant repas d'Ugolin?"

55. *Ibid.*, p. 23: "Le beau n'a qu'un type; le laid en a mille . . . Ce que nous appelons le laid, au contraire, est un détail d'un grand ensemble qui nous échappe, et qui s'harmonise, non pas avec l'homme, mais avec la création tout entière."

56. *Ibid.*, pp. 29–30.

57. *Ibid.*, pp. 19, 21.

58. In his *Mimesis* (Bern, 1946), *passim.*

59. *Ibid.*, p. 548:

> Une chose bien faite, une chose mal faite, voilà le beau et le laid de l'art; p. 547: Une chose difforme, horrible, hideuse, transportée avec vérité et poésie dans le domaine de l'art, deviendra belle, admirable, sublime, sans rien perdre de sa monstruosité; et, d'une autre part, les plus belles choses du monde, faussement et systématiquement arrangées dans une composition artificielle, seront ridicules, burlesques, hybrides, *laides.*

60. *Œuvres complètes, 1 (Odes et ballades)*, preface to *Odes* (1826), p. 26: "Ce qu'il est très important de fixer, c'est qu'en littérature comme en politique l'ordre se concilie merveilleusement avec la liberté; il en est même le résultat."

61. *Ibid., 17 (Littérature et philosophie)*, "But de cette publication" (1834), p. 16: "Une idée n'a jamais qu'une forme, qui lui est propre, qui est sa forme excellente, sa forme complète, sa forme rigoreuse, sa forme essentielle . . . Ainsi, chez les grands poètes, rien de plus inséparable, rien de plus adhérent, rien de plus consubstantiel que l'idée et l'expression de l'idée. Tuez la forme, presque toujours vous tuez l'idée."

62. *Postscriptum de ma vie* (Paris, 1901): "Le goût"; p. 46: "La forme et le fond sont aussi indivisibles que la chair et le sang"; *ibid.:* "Utilité de beau"; p. 18: "La forme est essentielle et absolue; elle vient des entrailles mêmes de l'idée"; p. 24: "En réalité, il n'y a ni fond ni forme. Il y a, et c'est là tout, seulement le puissant jaillissement de la pensée . . . l'éruption immédiate et souveraine de l'idée armée du style."

63. *Œuvres complètes, 17 (Littérature et philosophie)*, "Idées au hasard"; p. 284 ff.: "cette double puissance de méditation et d'inspiration."

64. "But de cette publication," pp. 17 ff.

65. *Ibid.*, p. 32: "Il faut, après tout, que l'art soit son propre but à lui-même, et qu'il enseigne, qu'il moralise, qu'il civilise, et qu'il édifie chemin faisant, mais sans se détourner, et tout en allant devant lui."

66. *Œuvres complètes, 18 (William Shakespeare)*, 410: "transformer la charité en fraternité . . . l'oisiveté en utilité . . . l'iniquité en

justice . . . la populace en peuple, la canaille en nation, les nations en humanité, la guerre en amour."

67. *Ibid., 18,* 254: "Macbeth, c'est la faim"; p. 257: "Othello est la nuit."

68. *Ibid.,* p. 294: "le génie est une entité comme la nature, et veut, comme elle, être accepté purement et simplement. Une montagne est à prendre ou à laisser"; p. 296: "J'admire tout, comme une brute . . . J'admire Eschyle, j'admire Juvénal, j'admire Dante, en masse, en bloc, tout . . . Ce que vous qualifiez défaut, je le qualifie accent."

69. *Ibid.,* p. 238: "Un type ne réproduit aucun homme en particulier . . . il résume et concentre sous une forme humaine toute une famille de caractères et d'esprits. Un type n'abrége pas; il condense. Il n'est pas un, il est tous"; p. 239: "Une leçon qui est un homme, un mythe à face humaine tellement plastique qu'il vous regarde, et que son regard est un miroir, une parabole qui vous donne un coup de coude, un symbole qui vous crie gare, une idée qui est nerf, muscle et chair."

70. *Ibid.,* p. 127: "Hamlet, c'est Oreste à l'effigie de Shakespeare"; p. 255: "L'aïeul de Macbeth, c'est Nemrod."

71. *Ibid.,* p. 211: "La grande plongeuse"; p. 214: *totus in antithesi.* Shakespeare contains Góngora as Michelangelo contains Bernini, etc.

72. *Ibid.,* pp. 109 ff., 125 ff.

73. *Ibid.,* pp. 291 ff., 257: "la jeune mamelle près de la barbe blanche."

74. *Ibid.,* p. 245: "Les chefs-d'œuvre ont cela d'immense qu'ils sont éternellement présents aux actes de l'humanité. Prométhée sur le Caucase, c'est la Pologne après 1772, c'est la France après 1815, c'est la Révolution après Brumaire."

75. Hugo's attendance at Shakespeare performances before writing preface to *Cromwell,* noted by Souriau in *La Préface de Cromwell,* p. 17. Also in *Œuvres complètes, 48 (Victor Hugo Raconté, 2,* 227).

BIBLIOGRAPHY: THE ITALIAN CRITICS

The pamphlets and articles of the "romanticism" debate are collected in *Discussioni e polemiche sul romanticismo (1816–1826),* ed. Egidio Bellorini, 2 vols. Bari, 1943. Berchet's contributions, however, must be seen in Giovanni Berchet, *Opere,* ed. Egidio Bellorini, Vol. 2 entitled *Scritti critici e letterari,* Bari, 1912.

Manzoni is quoted from *Opere varie,* ed. M. Barbi and F. Ghisalberti (Milan, 1943), Vol. 2.

Foscolo is quoted from *Opere edite e postume,* ed. E. Mayer and

L. S. Orlandini, 11 vols. Florence, 1939. But the writings which are there retranslated into Italian are quoted from the English versions.

Leopardi is quoted from *Tutte le opere*, Classici Mondadori, ed. F. Flora, 5 vols. Florence, 1949: *Le poesie e le prose* (2 vols.); *Le lettere;* and *Zibaldone di pensieri* (2 vols.).

The only general study is Giuseppe A. Borgese, *Storia della critica romantica in Italia*, Naples, 1905; reprinted Florence, 1949.

On Manzoni see Joseph Francis De Simone, *Alessandro Manzoni: Esthetics and Literary Criticism*, New York, 1946—a diffuse description of his opinions. There are good comments in F. de Sanctis, "La Poetica di Manzoni" (1872), in *La letteratura italiana nel secolo XIX* (Bari, 1953), pp. 19–39; G. A. Levi, "Estetica Manzoniana," in *Giornale storico della letteratura italiana, 108* (1936), 25–270; and Amado Alonso, *Ensayo sobre la·novela histórica*, Buenos Aires, 1942.

On Foscolo, three books discuss the criticism: Eugenio Donadoni, *Ugo Foscolo, pensatore, critico, poeta*, 2d ed. Palermo, 1927; and Mario Fubini, *Ugo Foscolo*, Torino, 1928. Nicoletta Festa, *Foscolo Critico* (Florence, 1953) is the fullest and most enthusiastic discussion. See also Fubini's introduction to Foscolo's *Saggi letterari*, Torino, 1926; reprinted in *Romanticismo italiano* (Bari, 1953), pp. 106–60. F. Viglione, *Ugo Foscolo in Inghilterra* (Catania, 1910). E. R. Vincent, *Byron, Hobhouse and Foscolo* (Cambridge, 1949), and *Ugo Foscolo, an Italian in Regency England* (Cambridge, 1953) are largely biographical. Emilio Santini, "Poesia e lingua nelle lezioni pavesi del Foscolo," *Giornale storico della letteratura italiana, 110* (1937), 58–105, analyzes the early Platonism.

On Leopardi see a chapter in Karl Vossler, *Leopardi* (Munich, 1923) and two articles: E. Bertana, "La mente di Giacomo Leopardi in alcuni suoi Pensieri di bella letteratura italiana e di estetica," *Giornale storico della letteratura italiana, 41* (1903), 193–283; and M. Fubini, "L'estetica e la critica letteraria nei Pensieri di Giacomo Leopardi," *op. cit., 97* (1931), 241–81. Romualdo Giani, *L'estetica nei Pensieri di Giacomo Leopardi* (Torino, 1904, 2d ed. 1929) tries to construe a system of Leopardi's aesthetics.

NOTES: THE ITALIAN CRITICS

1. Madame de Staël, "Sulla maniera e l'utilità delle traduzioni," in *Biblioteca italiana* (1816), reprinted in *Discussioni e polemiche*, ed. Bellorini, *1*, 7–8: "Dovrebbero a mio avviso gl' italiani tradurre diligentemente assai delle recenti poesie inglesi e tedesche; onde mostrare qualche novità a' loro citadini, i quali per lo più stanno contenti all'

antica mitologia, né pensano che quelle favole sono da un pezzo anti-
cate, anzi il resto d'Europa le ha giá abbandonate e dimentiche."

2. Lodovico di Breme, "Intorno all' ingiustizia di alcuni giudizi
letterari italiani," reprinted *ibid.*, *1*, 25–56, esp. 39.

3. In Giovanni Berchet, *Opere,* ed. Bellorini, *2*, 20: "Poesia de'
morti, poesia de' vivi."

4. *Ibid.*, p. 38: "L'uomo non può pensare all' uomo lontano e posto
in circonstanze diverse dalle sue con quell' interesse medesimo, con cui
egli pensa a se stesso ed a' vicini. Le lagrime del povero contadino,
l'angoscia del mandriano, la pace dell' eremita profanata ci faranno
pietá."

5. *Ibid.*, pp. 73–100.

6. In *Discussioni*, *1*, 436n.: "Non credo che sianvi stili essenzialmente
romantici o essenzialmente classici."

7. *Ibid.*, pp. 406–15.

8. "Dialogo sulle unitá drammatiche di luogo e di tempo." *Ibid.*, *2*,
29–45 (on *Macbeth*, p. 39).

9. *Opere varie,* ed. Barbi and Ghisalberti, pp. 219–25: "Personaggi
storici"; p. 236: "personaggi ideali."

10. *Ibid.*, p. 363: "Si ce sont les grands génies qui violent les règles,
quelle raison restera-t-il de présumer qu'elles sont fondées sur la nature,
et qu'elles sont bonnes à quelque chose?" P. 332: "détruit l'unité d'impression nécessaire pour produire l'émotion et la sympathie."

11. *Sämtliche Werke,* Jubiläumsausgabe, *37*, 166: "Für den Dichter
ist keine Person historisch."

12. Published by Goethe in Ger. trans., *ibid.* (January 23, 1821), pp.
182–4. Original in *Carteggio,* ed. G. Sforza and G. Gallavresi (Milan,
1912), *1*, 520: "un fallo tutto mio, e che ne fu cagione un attaccamento
troppo scrupuloso alla esattezza storica."

13. *Opere varie,* p. 615: "Proponendosi quel sistema d'escludere tutte
le norme, che non siano veramente generali, perpetue, ragionevoli per
ogni lato, viene a renderne più scarso il numero, o almeno più difficile
e più lenta la scelta."

14. *Ibid.*, p. 630. Manzoni alludes to the historical figures in Scott's
Monastery, Waverley, and *Quentin Durward.*

15. Gina Martegiani, *Il romanticismo italiano non esiste,* Florence,
1908.

16. *Opere edite, 4,* 297: "In qualunque lavoro della immaginazione
sta tutto nell' incorporare e identificare la realtà e la finzione"; p. 317:
"L'illusione . . . non acquista potere magico irresistibile, se non
allorchè la verità e la finzione ritrovandosi faccia a faccia e in contatto,
non solo perdono la loro naturale tendenza a cozzare fra loro, ma

s'ajutano scambievolmente a riunirsi e confondersi e parere una cosa sola."

17. *Ibid.,* p. 306: "Ma ciascuna produzione grande è un oggetto individuale che ha meriti diversi e caratteri distinti dalle altre"; p. 313: "Ciascun dramma dello stesso poeta, se ha genio, è più o meno diverso dall' altro."

18. *Edinburgh Review, 29* (1818), p. 465n.

19. *Opere edite, 4,* 7: "critique comparative," "l'influence réciproque de la littérature et des mœurs." A letter to John Murray, in 1817.

20. The two Dante articles are in *Edinburgh Review, 29* (1818), 453–74, and *30* (1818), 317–51. "Narrative and Romantic Poems of the Italians," in *Quarterly Review, 21* (1819), 486–556. The review of Wiffen's *Tasso* is in the *Westminster Review, 6* (1826), 404–45. Other less important pieces are in the *New Monthly Magazine,* the *London Magazine,* the *European Review,* and the *Retrospective Review.* See the list in F. Viglione's *Ugo Foscolo in Inghilterra,* pp. 319–21.

21. *Opere edite, 9,* 315: "La regola capitale della Poesia." *10, 541.*

22. *Historical Illustrations of the Fourth Canto of Childe Harold* (London, 1818), p. 479.

23. *Opere edite, 4,* 298: "La poesia tende a farci fortemente e pienamente sentire la nostra esistenza." Cf. *Essays on Petrarch* (London, 1821), p. 59.

24. See Emilio Santini, "Poesia e lingua nelle lezioni pavesi del Foscolo," *Giornale storico della letteratura italiana, 110* (1937), 58–107.

25. *Opere edite, 4,* 121: "Il poeta, il pittore e lo scultore non imitano copiando,—ma scelgono, combinano e immaginano perfette e riunite in un sola molte belle varietà che forse realmente esistono sparse e commiste a cose volgari." Cf. *4,* 122, 124: "Esiste nel mondo una universale secreta armonia, che l'uomo anela di ritrovare come necessaria à ristorare le fatiche e i dolori della sua esistenza"; p. 127: "Il genere umano ha bisogno di vestire de'sogni della immaginazione la nojosa realtà della vita."

26. *Essays on Petrarch,* p. 172. Cf. *Opere edite, 3,* 123.

27. *Edinburgh Review, 29* (1818), 460.

28. *Opere edite, 2,* 70: "La letteratura è annessa alla lingua"; p. 72: "La lingua è annessa allo stile, e lo stile alle facoltà intellettuali d'ogni individuo" p. 70: "conflato de' significati minimi ed accessorj."

29. "Dissertazione storica intorno ai druidi e ai bardi britanni" (1812), *Opere edite, 2,* 347–80.

30. On *Grazie* see *Opere edite, 9,* 208: "Tale fu forse la prima poesia." *9, 211:* "Il sommo dell' arte." *2, 337:* "La poesia lirica canta con entusiasmo le lodi de' numi e degli eroi."

31. On Wiffen's *Tasso* in *Westminster Review*. See above, n. 20. Hurd's *Letters on Chivalry and Romance* (1762), No. 10: "If it were not for these *lies* of Gothic invention, I should scarcely be disposed to give the *Gierusalemme liberata* a second reading."

32. *Opere edite, 3*, 370 ff.

33. *Essays on Petrarch*, p. 185.

34. *Edinburgh Review, 30* (1818), 345.

35. *Lezioni di eloquenza*, p. 197, quoted in Donadoni's *Ugo Foscolo*, pp. 221–2: "Allorchè, in tempi d'una più avanzata civiltà, le facoltà del critico e del poeta vengono a combinarsi nei medisimi spiriti, nasce allora una novella poesia, meno franca, meno schietta, più brillante, mista di metafisica e di conoscenza del mondo. Essa è la poesia di Pope, d'Orazio, di Voltaire; le mediocri intelligenze la preferiscono; e le più elevate immaginazioni la disdegnano."

36. *Opere edite, 10*, 464. Originally in *European Review, 4* (1824), 601–11.

37. *Historical Illustrations*, p. 448.

38. *Opere edite, 4*, 175. Also *3*, 275: "sommo critico."

39. Cf. E. Bottasso, *Foscolo e Rousseau*, Torino, 1941.

40. *Opere edite, 4*, 315, 305, 328.

41. *Edinburgh Review, 29* (1818), 465n.

42. *Opere edite, 1*, 519 (1808); on Milton, *Westminster Review, 6* (1826), 414.

43. A letter to Lady Dacre, March 1, 1822; *Opere edite, 8*, 60 f.; also *5*, 598 f.

44. "Lettera ai sigg compilatori della Biblioteca Italiana in risposta a quella di Mad La Baronessa di Staël Holstein ai medesimi," dated July 18, 1816, in *Poesie e prose, 2*, 597 ff.; and "Discorso di un Italiano intorno alla poesia romantica," *ibid.*, pp. 467–549. Both were published first in 1906.

45. *Ibid.*, p. 599: "Se Europa non conosce Parini, Alfieri, Monti, Botta, la colpa non parmi d'Italia."

46. *Ibid.*, p. 481:
Ecco dunque manifesta e palpabile in noi, e manifesta e palpabile a chicchessia la prepotente inclinazione al primitivo, dico in noi stessi, cïoè negli uomini di questo tempo, in quei medesimi ai quali i romantici proccurano di persuadere che la maniera antica e primitiva di poesia non faccia per loro. Imperocchè dal genio che tutti abbiamo alle memorie della puerizia si deve stimare quanto sia quello che tutti abbiamo alla natura invariata e primitiva, la quale è nè più nè meno quella natura che si palesa e regna ne' putti, e le immagini fanciullesche e la fantasia che

dicevamo, sono appunto le immagini e la fantasia degli antichi.

47. *Ibid.*, p. 486: "I nostri cantano in genere più che possono la natura, e i romantici più che possono l'incivilimento, quelli le cose e le forme e le bellezze eterne e immutabili, e questi le transitorie e mutabili, quelli le opere di Dio, e questi le opere degli uomini."

48. *Ibid.*, *1*, 694–7: "Della Condizione presente delle lettere italiane" (1819).

49. *Zibaldone*, *1*, 254, 86, 839; and 110, 113–6. Many passages are quoted from *Corinne* and commented upon.

50. *Poesie e prose*, 2, 539–40, comments on some verses translated from Byron; *Zibaldone*, *1*, 230, on *Corsair*; 2, 294n., 471, parallel with Monti; 2, 681–2, Byron cold and monotonous.

51. *Ibid.*, *1*, 243: "La lirica si può chiamare la cima il colmo la sommità della poesia." *Ibid.*, 2, 1063: "vera e pura poesia in tutta la sua estensione." *Ibid.*, p. 1283: "genere, siccome primo di tempo, così eterno ed universale."

52. *Ibid.*, p. 1284: "[La poesia] consistè da principio in questo genere solo, e la cui essenza sta sempre principalmente in esso genere, che quasi si confonde con lei, ed è il più veramente poetico di tutte le poesie, le quali non sono poesie se non in quanto son liriche."

53. *Ibid.*, *1*, 29; on sentiment, *ibid.*, 2, 1182; *Poesie e prose*, 2, 516–7.

54. *Zibaldone*, *1*, 505–6; *ibid.*, 2, 1037–8; on his creative process, *Lettere*, pp. 477–8: "se l'inspirazione non mi nasce da sè, più facilmente uscirebbe acqua da un tronco, che un solo verso dal mio cervello."

55. *Ibid.*, 2, 1182: "I lavori di poesia vogliono per natura esser corti."

56. *Ibid.*, 2, 1183: "Il poeta immagina: l'immaginazione vede il mondo come non è . . . finge, inventa, non imita . . . creatore, inventore, non imitatore." *Ibid.*, p. 1182: "Il poeta è spinto a poetare dall' intimo sentimento suo proprio . . . dal bisogno d'esprimere de' sentimenti ch'egli prova veramente."

57. *Ibid.*, p. 14: "Una maggior capacità di dolore."

58. *Ibid.*, *1*, 252–3: "Hanno questo di proprio le opere di genio, che quando anche rappresentino al vivo la nullità delle cose, quando anche dimostrino evidentemente e facciano sentire l'inevitabile infelicità della vita, quando anche esprimano le più terribili disperazioni . . . servono sempre di consolazione."

59. *Ibid.*, p. 511: "La forza creatrice dell' animo appartenente alla immaginazione, è esclusivamente propria degli antichi. Dopo che l'uomo è divenuto stabilmente infelice, e, che peggio è, l'ha conosciuto, e così ha realizzata e confermata la sua infelicità."

60. *Ibid.*, p. 163: "Così si può ben dire che in rigor di termini,

poeti non erano se non gli antichi, e non sono ora se non i fanciulli, o giovanetti, e i moderni que hanno questo nome, non sono altro che filosofi. Ed io infatti no divenni sentimentale, se non quando perduta la fantasia divenni insensibile alla natura, e tutto dedito alla ragione e al vero, in somma filosofo."

61. *Ibid.*, p. 828: "Ma la poesia, quanto è più filosofica, tanto meno è poesia."

62. *Ibid.*, p. 829: "E quivi la filosofia nuoce e distrugge la poesia, e la poesia guasta e pregiudica la filosofia. Tra questa e quella esiste una barriera insormontabile, una nemicizia giurata e mortale, che non si può nè toglier di mezzo, e riconciliare, nè dissimulare."

63. *Ibid.*, p. 87: "Tutto si è perfezionato da Omero in poi, ma non la poesia."

64. *Poesie e prose, 1,* 157; *Zibaldone, 1,* 738, 1145, 1372, 1216–7.

65. *Ibid.,* 2, 1063: "Il poema epico . . . non è che un inno in onor degli eroi o delle nazioni o eserciti; solamente un inno prolungato."

66. *Ibid.*, p. 1226: "L'epica, non solo per origine, ma totalmente, in quanto essa può esser conforme alla natura, e vera poesia, cioè consistente in brevi canti, come gli omerici, ossianici ec., ed in inni ec., rientra nella lirica."

67. On Wolf, *ibid.*, pp. 1147 ff., 115–8; on *Nibelungen, ibid.,* pp. 1261 ff., from Niebuhr, in English translation; *ibid.*, p. 1268, on Roman metrics.

68. *Ibid.*, p. 1181: "E infatti il poema epico è contro la natura della poesia: 1. domanda un piano concepito e ordinato con tutta freddezza; 2. che può aver a fare colla poesia un lavoro che domanda più e più anni d'esecuzione? la poesia sta essenzialmente in un impeto."

69. *Ibid.*, p. 1182:
Direi che la drammatica spetta alla poesia meno ancora che l'epica. . . . Il fingere di avere una passione, un carattere ch'ei non ha (cosa necessaria al drammatico) è cosa alienissima dal poeta; non meno che l'osservazione esatta e paziente de' caratteri e passioni altrui . . . Quanto più un uomo è di genio, quanto più è poeta, tanto più avrà de' sentimenti suoi proprii da esporre, tanto più sdegnerà di vestire un altro personaggio, di parlare in persona altrui, d'imitare.

70. *Ibid.*, p. 1191: "Il romanzo, la novella ec. sono all' uomo di genio assai meno alieni che il dramma, il quale gli è il più alieno di tutti i generi di letteratura, perchè è quello che esige la maggior prossimità d'imitazione, la maggior trasformazione dell' autore in altri individui, la più intera rinunzia e il più intero spoglio della propria individualita, alla quale l'uomo di genio tiene più fortemente che alcun altro."

71. *Poesie e prose, 1,* 424: "Quel miserabile mezzo dei nodi e viluppi intricatissimi in luogo della immagine continua viva ed efficace rappresentazione della natura e delle passioni umane."

72. *Zibaldone,* 2, 473–6.

73. *Ibid.,* p. 1230: "La *Divina Commedia* non è che una *lunga Lirica,* dov' è sempre in campo il poeta e i suoi propri affetti."

74. *Poesie e prose,* 2, 525, 518, etc.; *Lettere,* p. 712: "Io non trovo in lui se non pochissime, ma veramente pochissime bellezze poetiche" (1826).

75. *Zibaldone, 1,* 499, 1425.

BIBLIOGRAPHY:

THE YOUNGER GERMAN ROMANTICS

Görres is quoted from *Geistesgeschichtliche und literarische Schriften, 1* (1803–08), ed. Günther Müller (Cologne, 1926) and *Ausgewählte Werke und Briefe,* ed. Wilhelm Schellberg (Kempten, 1911). On Görres: Franz Schultz, *Josef Görres als Herausgeber, Literaturhistoriker, Kritiker,* Leipzig, 1902.

Jakob Grimm's *Kleinere Schriften* (8 vols. Berlin, 1869–90) were edited by K. Müllenhoff and E. Ippel. Wilhelm Grimm's *Kleinere Schriften* are in 4 vols., ed. G. Hinrichs, Berlin 1881–87. In addition, I quote *Achim von Arnim und Jakob und Wilhelm Grimm* (the correspondence), ed. Reinhold Steig, Stuttgart, 1904. Wilhelm Scherer's *Jakob Grimm* (Berlin, 1885) and E. Tonnelat, *Les Frères Grimm: leur œuvre de jeunesse* (Paris, 1912) are the best general books.

Arnim's *Sämtliche Werke,* ed. W. Grimm (22 vols. Berlin, 1839–56) has to be used, though far from complete. See also *Unbekannte Aufsätze und Gedichte,* ed. L. Geiger, Berlin, 1892. On Arnim: Herbert R. Liedke, *Literary Criticism and Romantic Theory in the Work of Achim von Arnim,* New York, 1937. Kleist is quoted from ed. Erich Schmidt, 5 vols. Leipzig, 1904.

Adam Müller's *Vorlesungen über die deutsche Wissenschaft und Literatur* and *Zwölf Reden über die Beredsamkeit und deren Verfall in Deutschland* are quoted from the reprints of Arthur Salz, Munich, 1920. *Über dramatische Kunst* is from *Vermischte Schriften über Staat, Philosophie und Kunst,* 2d ed. Vienna, 1817. I could see *Von der Idee des Schönen* only in the partial printing in *Phoebus,* facsimile reprint 1924. On Müller: Louis Sauzin, *Adam Heinrich Müller (1779–1829). Sa Vie et son œuvre* (Paris, 1937), 662 pp.; and Oskar Walzel, "Adam Müllers Aesthetik," in *Romantisches* (Bonn, 1934), pp. 11–250.

NOTES: THE YOUNGER GERMAN
ROMANTICS

GÖRRES

1. Josef von Görres, *Ausgewählte Werke und Briefe*, ed. Schellberg, *1*, 73 ff.

2. *Geistesgeschichtliche und literarische Schriften*, ed. Günther Müller, *1*, esp. pp. 74, 49, 93, 98, 100, 118, 120.

3. *Ibid.*, p. 178: "Naturwerke wie die Pflanzen"; p. 177: "Objekte unserer höchsten Verehrung, ehrwürdige Altertümer"; p. 281: "der neue Garten der Poesie, das Eden der Romantik"; p. 175: "der ächte, innere Geist des deutschen Volkes."

4. In Schellberg, *1*, 349:

> Wir glauben, Poesie sei eher gewesen als die Kunst, die Begei-
> sterung sei vorangegangen und die Disziplin später gefolgt. Wir
> glauben ganz unumwunden an die Existenz einer eigenen Natur-
> poesie, die denen, die sie üben, wie im Traume anfliegt, die nicht
> gelernt und nicht erworben, auch nicht in der Schule erlangt wird,
> sondern gleich der ersten Liebe ist, die der Unwissendste in einem
> Augenblicke gleich ganz weiss und ohne alle Mühseligkeit grade
> am besten dann übt, wenn er am wenigsten Studien gemacht und
> gradweise umso schlechter, je mehr er sie ergründet hat.

P. 350: "Jedes exemplarische Kunstwerk . . . wird an den Tag gelassen, wie die Natur ihre Tiere und Pflanzen von sich gelassen."

5. *Ibid.*, p. 359: "ein treuer Spiegel des Volkes"; p. 379: "lyrische Auswürfe, ein dramatisch episches Ganze . . . Denn ein unsichtbares Band geht durch alle Dinge." Cf. "Die Nation selbst hat in diesen Gesängen ihr Inneres aufgetan," etc.

6. In *Zeitschrift für Einsiedler*, reprinted in *Arnims Tröst-Einsam-keit*, ed. F. Pfaff (2d ed. Freiburg, 1890), pp. 43, 71, 117, 209: "Der gehörnte Siegfried und die Nibelungen." Also in Müller, pp. 304, 316, 323, 330.

7. Partial reprint in Schellberg, esp. p. 410. Full text in *Heidelberger Jahrbücher für Literatur*, 4 (2d half, 1811), 1201–39.

8. In *Morgenblatt für gebildete Stände* (1835), No. 78–87. Not re-printed. My account is based on Schultz, *Josef Görres als Herausgeber, Litterarhistoriker, Kritiker*, pp. 217–9.

9. *Heidelberger Jahrbücher*, 4, 1218: "lässt den Samojeden vor sich auf dem Kamele fliegend reiten, und den Araber mit Renntieren im Phaeton durch die Wüste fahren, und fliegende Fische oben im Linden-

wipfel singen, dass die Nachtigallen horchen, und Meerkatzen aufmerksam in sentimentalen Romanen blättern."

10. Müller, pp. 445–6: "Die Poesie verbirgt sich daher, wie jedes Heilige in die Dunkel der Mystik."

THE BROTHERS GRIMM

1. For details cf. Fritz Kabilinski, *Jakob Grimm als Romanist,* Gleiwitz, 1914.

2. See *Kleinere Schriften,* ed. Müllenhoff and Ippel, *4,* 100, 197, 218, 225, 416, 419, 421, 427. Grimm supported the work of Vuk Karadžić.

3. *Ibid.,* 7, 537.

4. *Ibid.,* *1,* 399–401.

5. *Ibid.,* *4,* 23, 27.

6. *Ibid.,* p. 75.

7. *Achim von Arnim und Jakob und Wilhelm Grimm,* ed. Steig, p. 116:

Die Poesie ist das was rein aus dem Gemüt ins Wort kommt . . . die Volkspoesie tritt aus dem Gemüt des Ganzen hervor; was ich unter Kunstpoesie meine, aus dem des Einzelnen. Darum nennt die neue Poesie ihre Dichter, die alte weiss keine zu nennen, sie ist durchaus nicht von einem oder zweien oder dreien gemacht worden, sondern eine Summe des Ganzen . . . Mir ist undenkbar, dass es einen Homer oder einen Verfasser der Nibelungen gegeben habe. Die Geschichte beweist den Unterschied z.B. damit, dass kein gebildetes Volk mit aller Kraft und Anstrengung ein Epos hervorzubringen vermag, und es nie vermocht hat.

8. *Ibid.,* pp. 117–8:

Die alten Menschen sind grösser, reiner und heiliger gewesen, als wir, es hat in ihnen und über sie noch der Schein des göttlichen Ausgangs geleuchtet . . . So ist mir nun die alte, epische Poesie, = Sagen- Mythengeschichte reiner und besser, ich will nicht sagen, lieber und näher, als unsere witzige, d.h. wissende, feine und zusammengesetzte . . . die alte Poesie hat eine innerlich hervorgehende Form von ewiger Giltigkeit . . . Ich sehe also in der Kunstpoesie . . . eine Zubereitung, in der Naturpoesie ein Sichvonselbstmachen.

9. *Ibid.,* p. 139: "Gar keine Werkstätten oder Überlegungen einzelner Dichter können in Betracht konnen."

10. E.g. *ibid.,* p. 139.

11. *Müllenhoff,* *4,* 13.

12. *Ibid.,* p. 84: "Die Poesie, das Epos ist nun gerade . . . diese

irdische Glückseligkeit, worin wir weben und atmen, dieses Brot des Lebens; weiter und freier als die Gegenwart, enger und eingeschränkter als die Offenbarung."

13. *Ibid.*, pp. 53–4, and *Reinhart Fuchs,* 1832.

14. Müllenhoff, *1,* 375: "Der einzelne Dichter ist es also, in dem sich die volle Natur des Volks, welchem er angehört, ausdrückt, gleichsam einfleischt."

15. *Ibid.*, pp. 74–7: "Italienische und Scandinavische Eindrücke" (1844).

16. *Achim von Arnim,* p. 140.

17. Müllenhoff, *4,* 401–2.

18. Wilhelm Grimm, *Kleinere Schriften,* ed. G. Hinrichs, *1,* 100: "Die Unschuld und Bewusstlosigkeit in welcher das Ganze sich gedichtet hat."

19. *Ibid.*, p. 108: "denn das ist der Gang des menschlichen Geistes, dass er in seiner Fortbildung immer mehr nach Abrundung und Anmut strebt, in welche die Grossheit der ersten Idee allmählich versinkt und endlich ganz verschwindet."

20. *Ibid.*, pp. 100, 112, 115: "weder direkt eingreifend in das Wesen echt deutscher Poesie . . . Manier, ganz ausser dem Geist des Volks."

21. A letter (May 17, 1809) by Jakob to Wilhelm, in *Briefwechsel zwischen Jakob und Wilhelm Grimm,* ed. H. Grimm and G. Hinrichs (Weimar, 1881) p. 98: "Sie lassen das Alte nicht als Altes stehen, sondern wollen es durchaus in unsere Zeit verpflanzen, wohin es an sich nicht mehr gehört . . . Sowenig sich fremde edele Tiere aus einem natürlichen Boden in einen andern verbreiten lassen, ohne zu leiden und zu sterben, so wenig kann die Herrlichkeit alter Poesie wieder allgemein aufleben, d.h. poetisch; allein historisch kann sie unberührt genossen werden."

22. Steig, p. 124.

23. Hinrichs, *1,* 266 ff., a review of Franz Horn's *Die schöne Literatur Deutschlands während des achtzehnten Jahrhunderts* (1812).

24. *Ibid.*, pp. 241–2: "Wir sind einmal modern, und unser Gutes ist es auch, warum soll, was unsere Zeit errungen, sich nicht äussern dürfen und ist es möglich sie zu verleugnen?"

25. See Benedetto Croce, *Poesia populare e poesia d'arte,* Bari, 1946.

26. See Theodor Frings, *Minnesinger und Troubadours,* Deutsche Akademie der Wissenschaften; Vorträge und Schriften, *34,* Berlin, 1949. Leo Spitzer, "The Mozarabic Lyric and Theodor Frings' Theories," *Comparative Literature,* 4 (1952), 1–22.

27. Cf. P. Bogatyrev and Roman Jakobson, "Die Folklore als eine

besondere Form des Schaffens," in *Donum Natalicium Schrijnen* (Nijmegen, 1929), pp. 900–13.

ARNIM AND KLEIST

1. Achim von Arnim, *Sämtliche Werke* (Charlottenburg, 1845), *13*, 444.

2. *Achim von Arnim und Clemens Brentano,* ed. R. Steig (Stuttgart, 1894), p. 38. Letter of July 9, 1802.

3. *Achim von Arnim und Jakob und Wilhelm Grimm,* ed. Steig, pp. 109–10.

4. *Ibid.,* pp. 135–6, 142. See also Steig, n. 2 above, pp. 225, 229.

5. Letter to A. W. Schlegel, September 26, 1808. Quoted by Liedke, *Literary Criticism and Romantic Theory in the Work of Achim von Arnim,* p. 91.

6. *Unbekannte Aufsätze und Gedichte,* ed. Geiger, p. 235: "doch wer keinen Sinn dafür hat, dem würde er auch mit einer weitläufigsten Auseinandersetzung nicht aufgehen. Andern aber wäre es überflüssig."

7. *Die Günderode,* ed. W. Oehlke (Berlin, 1920), p. 434: "sollte es denn nicht auch eine unmittelbare Offenbarung der Poesie geben, die vielleicht tiefer, schauerlicher ins Mark eindringt, ohne feste Grenzen der Form?—Die da schneller und natürlicher in den Geist eingreift?"

8. *Werke,* ed. Schmidt, *4*, 148: "Brief eines Dichters an einen anderen." . . . "Sprache, Rhythmus, Wohlklang, u.s.w., so reizend diese Dinge auch, insofern sie den Geist einhüllen, sein mögen, so sind sie doch an und für sich, . . . nichts als ein wahrer, obschon natürlicher und notwendiger Übelstand; und die Kunst kann, in Bezug auf sie, auf nichts gehen, als sie möglichst verschwinden zu machen."

9. *Ibid.,* p. 141: "Wir sehen, dass in dem Masse, als, in der organischen Welt, die Reflexion dunkler und schwächer wird, die Grazie darin immer strahlender und herrschender hervortritt."

10. *Ibid., 5,* 328: "Jede erste Bewegung, alles Unwillkührliche ist schön; und schief und verschroben Alles, so bald es sich selbst begreift. O der Verstand! Der unglückselige Verstand!"

ADAM MÜLLER

1. *Vorlesungen,* ed. Salz, pp. 52–3.

2. *Ibid.,* p. 54.

3. *Ibid.,* pp. 66–7.

4. *Ibid.,* p. 92.

5. *Ibid.,* pp. 197–9.

6. *Vermischte Schriften* (1817), 2, 325.

7. *Ibid.*, p. 329.

8. Delivered 1806, printed 1808, in book form 1812.

9. Delivered 1812, printed 1816.

10. *Vermischte Schriften, 2,* 218–9: "niemand kann sagen, dass er die Griechen und die romantischen Dichter begreife, der die Römer und Franzosen verächtlich bei Seite setzt und so umgekehrt; es ist nur Ein Sinn, ein ewiger Sinn der Kunst, und dieser muss ruhig und belebend durch die Kunstformen aller Zeiten hindurchzuschreiten vermögen."

11. *Ibid.*, p. 224.

12. *Zwölf Reden,* ed. Salz, p. 106.

13. *Ibid.*, pp. 110–11:

Die französische tragische Bühne ist ein auseinandergelegter Rednerstuhl, aufgeschlagen für diesen bestimmten Ort, für diese bestimmte Zeit, für diesen Hof, für diese wahre Volksversammlung von Talenten, die über dem Jahrhundert Ludwig XIV. zusammenkamen. Die französische Tragödie . . . will eine ganz bestimmte Wirkung . . . Racine hat vor seinem Schreibtisch das Porträt seines grossen Monarchen, und sein ganzes Gefolge von Heldentum und Schönheit steht vor seiner Seele . . . er will Frankreich gefallen, und denkt nicht an mehr . . . Britannikus soll in dieser französischen Hoftracht erscheinen: das römische Kostüm beobachten wäre geschmacklos, weil der Redner aus seinen Schranken treten würde; die Verwandlung der Szene wäre geschmacklos, weil eine Prätension auf Natürlichkeit darin läge, die das ganze übrige Werk und seinen Charakter zerstörte. Die französische tragische Bühne verlangt im Ton aller Schauspieler eine Art von Gesang, der allen gemein ist: man will erinnert sein, dass eigentlich nur einer spricht: der Dichter, der rhetorische Dichter. Spräche jeder Schauspieler in seinem eignen Ton und Rhythmus, so wäre es ebenso geschmacklos, als wenn ein Redner seine Stimme verwandeln, seine Partei nachmachen wollte, während er sie redend einführt. Die französische Tragödie will den Tod nicht auf der Bühne dulden, wie überhaupt die rednerische Handlung durch kein Schauspiel, kein Spektakel irgendeiner Art, durch keine unnützen Requisiten unterbrochen werden soll.

14. *Ibid.*, pp. 113–4.

15. *Vorlesungen,* p. 180.

16. *Vermischte Schriften, 2,* 108.

17. *Ibid.*, p. 167: "den Begriff der Ironie. Verlangen Sie eine deutsche Übersetzung des Worts, so weiss ich Ihnen keine bessre zu geben, als: Offenbarung der Freiheit des Künstlers oder des Menschen."

18. *Ibid.*, p. 175.
19. *Ibid.*, p. 248: "indem ein Lust-Kapital entsteht."
20. *Ibid.*, p. 184.
21. *Ibid.*, p. 246.
22. *Ibid.*, p. 185.
23. *Ibid.*, p. 151.
24. *Ibid.*, p. 154.
25. *Ibid.*, p. 99: "ich pflege sie die Spiegelscenen zu nennen."
26. *Ibid.*, p. 146, 150: "Himmelsfahrtmoment."

BIBLIOGRAPHY:

THE GERMAN PHILOSOPHERS

Solger's *Erwin* is quoted from the reprint by Rudolf Kurtz, Berlin, 1907. *Vorlesungen über Aesthetik* (Leipzig, 1829) and *Nachgelassene Schriften und Briefwechsel* (cited as *NS*), ed. L. Tieck and F. von Raumer (2 vols. Leipzig, 1826) were used. Also, *Tieck and Solger: the Complete Correspondence,* ed. Percy Matenko, New York, 1933. On Solger: Joseph E. Heller, *Solgers Philosophie der ironischen Dialektik,* Berlin, 1928; Maurice Boucher, *K. W. F. Solger, esthétique et philosophie de la présence,* Paris, 1934; and two articles by Oskar Walzel: "Methode? Ironie bei Friedrich Schlegel und bei Solger," *Helicon, 1* (1938), 33–50; and "Tragik bei Solger," *Helicon, 3* (1940), 27–49.

There are 2 eds. of Schleiermacher's aesthetics: *Vorlesungen über die Aesthetik,* ed. Carl Lommatzsch (Berlin, 1842), which reprints lecture notes from 1832–33, and *Schleiermachers Aesthetik,* ed. Rudolf Odebrecht (Berlin, 1931), which reprints the 1819 and 1825 lectures. The lectures on hermeneutics appear in *Reden und Abhandlungen,* ed. L. Jonas, Berlin, 1835. W. Dilthey, *Leben Schleiermachers* (Vol. *1*, Berlin, 1870; 2d enlarged ed. 1922) is standard, but as it reaches only to 1802 it has little immediate relevance to our topic. On aesthetics: B. Croce's chapter in *Estetica,* and "L'estetica di Federico Schleiermacher" in *Ultimi saggi* (Bari, 1948, first pub. 1933), pp. 161–79; Rudolf Odebrecht, *Schleiermachers System der Ästhetik,* Berlin, 1932. On hermeneutics: Joachim Wach, *Das Verstehen* (3 vols. Tübingen, 1926), *1*, 83–167.

Schopenhauer is quoted from *Sämtliche Werke,* ed. Arthur Hübscher, 6 vols. Leipzig, 1937 (cited as H.). Where this fails P. Deussen's ed. (Munich, 1911–42, of which only vols. 1–6, 8–11, 13–16 are published) is used. Eng. trans. R. B. Haldane and J. Kemp, *The World as Will and Idea,* 3 vols. London, 1883–86. André Fauconnet, *L'Esthétique de Schopenhauer* (Paris, 1913) is most helpful. On the theory of tragedy see Oskar Walzel, "Tragik nach Schopenhauer und von heute," in *Vom Geistesleben alter und neuer Zeit* (Leipzig, 1922), pp. 524 ff.

Hegel's *Vorlesungen über die Aesthetik* is quoted from the facsimile reprint of the original in Hermann Glockner's ed. of *Sämtliche Werke*, Stuttgart, 1928 (cited as *SW*). I quote as Vols. *1, 2,* and *3* Vols. *12, 13,* and *14,* which correspond to Vols. *10, 11,* and *12* of the original edition, 1832–44. Other references are also to Glockner's reprint. The Eng. trans., *The Philosophy of Fine Art,* by F. P. B. Osmaston (4 vols. London, 1920) was used in a few instances only.

Comment on Hegel's literary theory is surprisingly meager. See, however, Eduard von Hartmann, *Deutsche Aesthetik seit Kant* (Vol. *3* of *Ausgewählte Werke,* Leipzig, n.d.); Bosanquet; Croce; and Helmut Kuhn, *Die Vollendung der klassischen deutschen Ästhetik durch Hegel,* Berlin, 1931. In English see also Israel Knox, *The Aesthetic Theories of Kant, Hegel, and Schopenhauer,* New York, 1936; and A. C. Bradley's distinguished essay, "Hegel's Theory of Tragedy," in *Oxford Lectures on Poetry,* London, 1909.

NOTES: THE GERMAN PHILOSOPHERS

SOLGER

1. *Erwin,* ed. Kurtz, *passim.*
2. *Ibid.,* p. 394.
3. Ed. K. W. L. Heyse, 1829.
4. All this is the 2 vols. of *Nachgelassene Schriften und Briefwechsel,* ed. Tieck and von Raumer. The correspondence with Tieck was re-edited, with additions and notes, by Percy Matenko.
5. *Vorlesungen über Aesthetik,* p. 129: "Das Symbol ist die Existenz der Idee selbst; es ist das wirklich, was es bedeutet, ist die Idee in ihrer unmittelbaren Wirklichkeit. Das Symbol ist also immer selbst wahr, kein blosses Abbild von etwas Wahrem."
6. *Ibid.,* p. 187.
7. *Ibid.,* pp. 185, 115.
8. *Erwin,* p. 387.
9. *Vorlesungen,* pp. 245, 247.
10. See *NS, 2,* 555.
11. *Erwin,* p. 391.
12. *Ibid.,* p. 392.
13. *Ibid.,* p. 387: "Ich erstaune, sprach Anselm hier, über deine Kühnheit, das ganze Wesen der Kunst in die Ironie aufzulösen, welches viele für Ruchlosigkeit halten möchten."

14. *Vorlesungen,* p. 199: "denn ohne Ironie giebt es überhaupt keine Kunst."

15. *Ibid.,* p. 241: "die künstlerische Ironie. Sie macht das Wesen der Kunst, die innere Bedeutung derselben aus."

16. *Ibid.,* p. 245.

17. *Ibid.,* p. 242.

18. *NS,* 2, 513: "in beiden noch ausser der dramatischen Form ein inneres Gemeinsameres ist. Der ganze Widerstreit zwischen dem Unvollkommenen im Menschen und seiner höheren Bestimmung fängt an, uns als etwas Nichtiges zu erscheinen, worin etwas ganz anderes zu walten scheint als dieser Zwiespalt allein."

19. *Ibid.,* p. 514.

20. *Ibid.,* p. 567: "Mit der wahren Ironie ist es gerade umgekehrt: diese fängt erst recht an bei der Betrachtung des Weltgeschicks im Grossen."

21. See 1828 review of *NS* in *Sämtliche Werke,* ed. Glockner, *20,* 132–202.

22. *Der Begriff der Ironie* (Munich, 1929), p. 323.

23. *NS,* 2, 456.

24. *Ibid.,* p. 466.

25. *Ibid.,* p. 469.

26. *Erwin,* p. 258: "da er ihn doch recht als Märtyrer heiliger Gesetze geschmückt."

27. *NS, 1,* 177: "Das Drama ist die wahrste Darstellung der Gattung als des Erstgebornen und des Individuums als des Zweiten."

28. Fr. Hebbel, *Tagebuch,* entry dated July 23, 1856.

29. *NS,* 2, 536.

30. *Ibid.,* p. 541.

31. *Ibid.,* 2, 572–5, and *1,* 574.

32. *Ibid.,* 2, 586.

33. Cf. *ibid.,* p. 600.

34. *Ibid.,* p. 617.

35. *Ibid.,* p. 620.

36. Letter to Tieck, Oct. 4, 1817. Matenko, pp. 376–8. *NS, 1,* 558–60. Cf. p. 544.

37. See *ibid.,* p. 636, and letter to Tieck, Aug. 3, 1818. Matenko, pp. 469–71. *NS, 1,* 653–5.

38. *Ibid.,* p. 585.

39. *Ibid.,* pp. 175–85 (1809). Cf. *Vorlesungen,* p. 177.

SCHLEIERMACHER

1. See R. Zimmermann, *Geschichte der Ästhetik* (Vienna, 1858), pp. 608–34; Eduard von Hartmann, *Die deutsche Aesthetik seit Kant* (Berlin, 1886), pp. 156–69. There von Hartmann calls Schleiermacher's lectures "unctuous afternoon sermons delivered by a preacher in his dotage." H. Lotze, *Geschichte der Aesthetik in Deutschland* (Munich, 1868), pp. 163–7, dismisses him.

2. See the ed. and the book listed in bibliography.

3. On the early Schleiermacher see Dilthey's fine biography, and his analysis of the *Lucinde* letters, 2d ed., pp. 540 ff.

4. *Vorlesungen über die Aesthetik*, ed. Lommatzsch, pp. 67, 122: "unmittelbares Selbstbewusstsein."

5. *Ibid.*, p. 58: "Das innere Bild ist das eigentliche Kunstwerk."

6. The terms "Gefühl" and "Stimmung" prevail in the earlier lectures, "Selbstbewusstsein" in the last.

7. *Ibid.*, pp. 80–1: "es bildet nur den dunkeln Hintergrund, aus welchem das klar hervortritt, was ihn zur äusseren Production antreibt."

8. "Besinnung" or sometimes "Besonnenheit." See Odebrecht, *Schleiermachers System*, pp. 82, 97. On imagination, *ibid.*, p. 103, and *Schleiermachers Aesthetik*, ed. Odebrecht, p. 96. Schleiermacher's distinction, apparently derived from Tetens (see Odebrecht, *System*, p. 103), is identical with Coleridge's distinction between imagination and fancy. It lacks only the Schellingian superstructure.

9. Odebrecht, ed., *Aesthetik*, p. 4: "ein dunkler Ansatz zur Production."

10. *Ibid.:* "Ein Künstler würde schlecht zufrieden sein, wenn er in allen dasselbe hervorbrächte. Nur in unendlichen Modifikationen von Wirkungen kann sich das Maass eines Kunstwerkes produzieren. Nach dieser Ansicht also darf die Wirkung gar kein Gegenstand der Betrachtung sein."

11. *Ibid.*, p. 87: "Jedes Kunstwerk muss absolut für sich selbst betrachtet werden, also seinen absoluten Wert haben." Cf. Lommatzsch, pp. 217 ff.

12. Lommatzsch, pp. 118 ff., 661 ff., 690.

13. *Ibid.*, p. 686: "Das ursprüngliche Kunstwerk ist das rein Innerliche und das Herausstellen in die Erscheinung ist ein zweiter Act; es gehört aber zu der Eigenthümlichkeit der Poesie, dass sie hier beides nicht so unterscheiden kann, weil der Dichter auch nur in sich in der Form der Sprache produziren kann."

14. Odebrecht, ed., *Aesthetik,* p. 282: "Jemehr beides durchaus ineinander verwachsen ist, um desto mehr muss man es auch gleichsam auf einen Schlag entstanden denken."

15. *Ibid.,* pp. 36, 53, and *passim.* These distinctions are dropped in the later course.

16. Lommatzsch, p. 626: "Freie Productivität in der Sprache."

17. *Ibid.,* p. 633: "eine Totalität von Wohlklang"; p. 641: "Die innerliche Veränderlichkeit des Seins"; p. 642: "die reine Subjectivität der inneren Gemütsstimmung."

18. *Ibid.,* p. 642: "Die reine Objectivität des Bildes."

19. Odebrecht, p. 266: "Eine ganz strenge Verschiedenheit können wir hier so wenig als bei irgend etwas Lebendigen, wie die Kunst ist, erwarten."

20. Lommatzsch, p. 663.

21. Odebrecht, ed., *Aesthetik,* p. 88: "Nur die Volksgenossen verstehn sich mit unmittelbarer Lebendigkeit." In Lommatzsch, pp. 275 ff.

22. Odebrecht, ed., *Aesthetik,* pp. 74–5. A similar defense in *Vertraute Briefe über Lucinde,* 1800.

23. Odebrecht, ed., *Aesthetik,* p. 287: "Die Reinigung der Leidenschaften soll die Kunst bewirken."

24. *Reden und Abhandlungen,* ed. Jonas, p. 351.

25. *Ibid.,* p. 382: "Das Auslegen unterscheidet sich von dem Verstehen durchaus nur wie das laute Reden von dem innern Reden."

26. *Ibid.,* p. 354: "divinatorisch." See also pp. 360, 364, 377.

27. *Ibid.,* p. 366: "dass alles einzelne nur verstanden werden kann, vermittelst des ganzen, und also jedes Erklären des einzelnen schon das Verstehen des ganzen voraussetzt."

28. See the comments in Leo Spitzer, *Linguistics and Literary History* (Princeton, 1948), pp. 19, 33–5.

29. *Reden,* pp. 359, 375: "Morphologie der Gattung."

SCHOPENHAUER

1. Marginal note to Schelling's *Philosophische Schriften* (Landshut, 1809), p. 192, referred to above in our text, printed in *Handschriftlicher Nachlass,* ed. E. Grisebach (Leipzig, 1891–93), *3,* 129: "Eine ganz verworrene Radotage." There are favorable references to Schelling in *Gespräche und Selbstgespräche,* ed. E. Grisebach (Berlin, 1902), p. 72; and in *Briefwechsel und andere Dokumente,* ed. Max Brahm (Leipzig, 1911), p. 274.

2. *Sämtliche Werke,* ed. Hübscher, 2, 231: "Es ist der schmerzenlose Zustand, den Epikuros als das höchste Gut und als den Zustand der

Götter pries: denn wir sind, für jenen Augenblick, des schnöden Willendranges entledigt, wir feiern den Sabbath der Zuchthausarbeit des Wollens, das Rad des Ixion steht still." I quote the Eng. trans. of R. B. Haldane and J. Kemp, *1*, 254.

3. H., *2*, 293.

4. H., *3*, 494–5: "Bauchredner."

5. H., *2*, 293: "Der Darzustellende ist vom Darstellenden ganz verschieden."

6. H., *2*, 295: "Als Subjekts des reinen, willenlosen Erkennens, dessen unerschütterliche, sälige Ruhe nunmehr in Kontrast tritt mit dem Drange des immer beschränkten, immer dürftigen Wollens: die Empfindung dieses Kontrastes, dieses Wechselspieles ist eigentlich was sich im Ganzen des Liedes ausspricht und was überhaupt den lyrischen Zustand ausmacht." Eng. trans. (revised) *1*, 323.

7. Printed in Grisebach, ed., *Nachlass*, 2, 108–17.

8. *Ibid.*, p. 114.

9. H., *3*, 467–8.

10. *Nachlass*, 2, 117. This concluding paragraph was added only in 1840.

11. H., *2*, 217: "Sie wiederholt die durch reine Kontemplation aufgefassten ewigen Ideen, das Wesentliche und Bleibende aller Erscheinungen der Welt." Eng. trans., *1*, 239.

12. H., *2*, 276. Eng. trans., *1*, 302.

13. H., *2*, 286–7. Eng. trans., *1*, 313.

14. H., *2*, 284.

15. H., *3*, 488.

16. H., *2*, 287; *3*, 489.

17. H., *3*, 490.

18. H., *6*, 602.

19. *Die Genesis des Systems,* in *Sämtliche Werke,* ed. Deussen, *11*, 108–9: "Je weniger rhetorisch die Poesie ist, desto besser."

20. H., *6*, 557.

21. H., *6*, 550–1: "Das Unverständliche ist dem Unverständigen verwandt"; p. 511: "Die erste, ja, schon für sich allein beinahe ausreichende Regel des guten Stils [ist] diese, dass man etwas zu sagen habe"; p. 554: "Man gebrauche gewöhnliche Worte und sage ungewöhnliche Dinge"; p. 561: "Der leitende Grundsatz der Stilistik sollte sein, dass der Mensch nur *einen* Gedanken zur Zeit deutlich denken kann."

22. H., *6*, 528, 578, 581–3, 533.

23. H., *2*, 278; *3*, 451.

24. *Philosophische Vorlesungen,* in Deussen, *10*, 343: "Es ist übrigen₂

sehr merkwürdig, dass wir alle im Traum vollkomne Dichter sind."
Nachlass, 4, 392.

25. H., *3,* 488.

26. See *Edita und Inedita,* ed. E. Grisebach (Leipzig, 1888), p. 127.
Marginal note in Schopenhauer's own English.

27. H., *6,* 598.

28. H., *6,* 597.

29. H., *2,* 218: "So ist dagegen die Kunst überall am Ziel."

30. H., *2,* 229, 236: "Das Kunstwerk ist bloss ein Erleichterungsmittel
derjenigen Erkenntniss, in welcher jenes Wohlgefallen besteht. . . .
Das Versetzen in den Zustand des reinen Anschauens tritt am leich-
testen ein, wenn die Gegenstände demselben entgegenkommen, d.h.
durch ihre mannigfaltige und zugleich bestimmte und deutliche Gestalt leicht zu Repräsentaten ihrer Ideen werden, worin eben die
Schönheit, im objektiven Sinne, besteht." Eng. trans. (changed), *1,*
259–60.

31. H., *3,* 481. *Philosophische Vorlesungen,* in Deussen, p. 176.

32. *Ibid.,* p. 192.

33. H., *2,* 249.

34. H., *2,* 248.

35. *Philosophische Vorlesungen,* in Deussen, pp. 285, 302; on F.
Schlegel see above, p. 11.

36. H., *2,* 230: "Störende Zufälligkeiten."

37. H., *3,* 487.

38. H., *3,* 492, and Grisebach, *Gespräche,* p. 42.

39. H., *6,* 431. On Werner see *Briefe,* ed. Grisebach (1894), p. 122.
Nachlass, 4, 275: "obwohl ein *Scurra,* hat doch Genie."

40. H., *2,* 297.

41. *Philosophische Vorlesungen,* Deussen, p. 335n.

42. *Gespräche,* p. 69. *Briefwechsel,* ed. Brahm, p. 277. H., *6,* 463.

43. H., *2,* 299.

44. H., *2,* 300–1: "Sie zeigt uns das grösste Unglück nicht als eine
Ausnahme, nicht als etwas durch seltene Umstände, oder monströse
Charaktere Herbeigeführtes, sondern als etwas aus dem Tun und den
Charakteren der Menschen leicht und von selbst, fast als wesentlich
Hervorgehendes." Eng. trans., *1,* 329.

45. Quoted in H., *2,* 300, from *La vida es sueño.*

46. H., *2,* 299: "Die platte, optimistische, protestantisch-rational-
istische, oder eigentlich jüdische Weltansicht."

47. H., *3,* 495: "Der Jammer der Menschheit, die Herrschaft des
Zufalls und des Irrtums, der Fall des Gerechten, der Triumph des
Bösen. . . . Was allem Tragischen, in welcher Gestalt es auch auftrete,

den eigentümlichen Schwung zur Erhebung giebt, ist das Aufgehn der Erkenntniss, dass die Welt, das Leben, kein wahres Genügen gewähren könne, mithin unserer Anhänglichkeit nicht wert sei."

48. H., *3*, 496–7: "Ein empörendes Machwerk zu Gunsten der heidnischen Pfaffen." On Calderón's *Steadfast Prince* cf. Wilhelm Gwinner, *Schopenhauers Leben* (Leipzig, 1878), p. 77, concerning his attending a performance in 1809.

49. H., *3*, 499–500. *Philosophische Vorlesungen*, p. 348. *Genesis des Systems*, Deussen, p. 476.

50. H., *3*, 500: "Fallhöhe."

51. Especially in the early 20th century in Germany. See Oskar Walzel, "Tragik nach Schopenhauer und von heute," in *Vom Geistesleben alter und neuer Zeit* (Leipzig, 1922), pp. 524 ff.; Georg Lukács, "Zur Soziologie des modernen Dramas," *Archiv für Sozialwissenschaft und Sozialpolitik, 28* (1914), 303 ff., 662 ff.

52. Josef Körner, "Tragik und Tragödie," *Preussische Jahrbücher,* 225 (1931), 58 ff., 157 ff., 260 ff., esp. 274.

53. H., *3, 500*: "Freilich aber muss es sich beeilen, im Zeitpunkt der Freude den Vorhang fallen zu lassen, damit wir nicht sehn, was nachkommt." Eng. trans., *3*, 218.

54. *Genesis des Systems*, p. 465.

55. H., *2*, 220.

HEGEL

1. The attempt to edit the notebooks did not progress beyond a first volume, ed. Lasson, Leipzig, 1931. I have never been able to locate a copy.

2. *Sämtliche Werke, 16, 17.*

3. *Vorlesungen über die Aesthetik, SW, 1,* 68: "In dieser Weise ist das Sinnliche in der Kunst *vergeistigt,* da das Geistige in ihr versinnlicht erscheint." Cf. pp. 110, 84, 46.

4. *SW, 1,* 160: "Das sinnliche Scheinen der Idee."

5. *SW, 1,* 419.

6. *SW, 1,* 409, 2, 4.

7. *SW, 2,* 136, 234.

8. *SW, 1,* 32, 151: "Ihre Form hat aufgehört, das höchste Bedürfniss des Geistes zu sein."

9. *SW, 1,* 130.

10. *SW, 3,* 233.

11. *SW, 3,* 342; *1,* 370; *2,* 118: "Es gehören feste Grundsätze dazu, mit welchen die Gegenwart in Widerspruch steht, eine Weisheit, die

abstrakt bleibt, eine Tugend, die in starrer Energie nur an sich selber festhält."

12. *SW*, 2, 233: "Der Künstler darf nicht erst nöthig haben, mit seinem Gemüte in's Reine zu kommen, und für sein eigenes Seelenheil sorgen zu müssen: seine grosse, freie Seele muss von Hause an, ehe er an's Produciren geht, wissen und haben, woran sie ist, und ihrer sicher und in sich zuversichtlich sein."

13. *SW*, 2, 236.

14. *SW*, 2, 235.

15. *SW*, *1*, 302, 397; 2, 182, 198, 205; and esp. the review of Solger's *Nachgelassene Schriften* in *16*, esp. 139–49.

16. *SW*, 2, 235; *3*, 358.

17. *SW*, *1*, 35: "Die Kunst aber, weit entfert . . . die höchste Form des Geistes zu sein, erhält in der Wissenschaft erst ihre echte Bewährung."

18. *SW*, *3*, 226: "eine accidentellere Äusserlichkeit"; *3*, 227: "Das innere Vorstellen und Anschauen selbst."

19. *SW*, *3*, 227, 321.

20. *SW*, *3*, 274 ff.

21. *SW*, *3*, 290: "Das echte Kunsttalent bewegt sich überhaupt in seinem sinnlichen Material wie in seinem eigentlichsten heimischen Elemente, das ihn, statt hinderlich und drückend zu sein, im Gegenteil hebt und trägt."

22. *SW*, *3*, 291: "Die Versification ist eine Musik, welche, obgleich in entfernter Weise, doch schon jene dunkle aber zugleich bestimmte Richtung des Ganges und Charakters der Vorstellungen in sich widertönen lässt"; *3*, 296, 299: "der dem Ganzen ein neues eigentümliches Leben gibt."

23. *SW*, *3*, 321–5.

24. *SW*, *3*, 580.

25. *SW*, *1*, 328, 397.

26. See the whole article on Solger, n. 15 above.

27. *SW*, *1*, 557–60.

28. *SW*, *1*, 558.

29. *SW*, *1*, 534, 539: "Eine Unterbrechung des Vorstellungganges und eine stete Zerstreuung." Cf. p. 525.

30. *SW*, *1*, 540.

31. *SW*, *1*, 539: "Homer, Sophocles, bleiben, obschon auch Gleichnisse bei ihnen vorkommen, dennoch im Ganzen fast durchweg bei eigentlichen Ausdrücken stehn."

32. *SW*, 2, 4, 10, 16–7.

33. "Die Kunstreligion," sec. 7, B, in *Phänomenologie*. Hegel distinguishes between art and religion only in the 2d ed. of the *Encyclopädie* (1827), p. 563: "Die schöne Kunst hat ihre Zukunft in der wahren Religion."

34. *SW*, *1*, 443.

35. *SW*, *2*, 143.

36. *SW*, *1*, 495.

37. *SW*, *1*, 222.

38. *SW*, *1*, 40, 230.

39. *SW*, *1*, 218, 279; *2*, 15, 76.

40. *SW*, *1*, 280, 301, 346, 350.

41. *SW*, *1*, 312, 327: "Denn in ihr (der Kunst) ist nichts dunkel, sondern Alles klar und durchsichtig."

42. *SW*, *1*, 353-4.

43. *SW*, *2*, 116-8.

44. *SW*, *2*, 76: "Ein ewiger Ernst, eine unwandelbare Ruhe thront auf der Stirn der Götter, und ist ausgegossen über ihre ganze Gestalt."

45. *SW*, *2*, 77-8: "Die seligen Götter trauern gleichsam über ihre Seligkeit oder Leiblichkeit." "Der Hauch und Duft der Trauer."

46. *SW*, *2*, 218: "Ochs und Esel, die Krippe und das Stroh dürfen nicht fehlen. Und so geht es durch alles hindurch, auf dass auch in der Kunst das Wort erfüllt sei, die da niedrig sind, sollen erhöht werden."

47. *SW*, *2*, 222.

48. *SW*, *2*, 238.

49. *SW*, *2*, 240: "Ein reines Gefallen an den Gegenständen, ein unerschöpfliches Sich-ergehen der Phantasie, ein harmloses Spielen . . . Denn der Gehalt ist es, der, wie in allem Menschenwerk, so auch in der Kunst, entscheidet. Die Kunst, ihrem Begriff nach, hat nichts Anderes zu ihrem Beruf, als das in sich selbst Gehaltvolle zu adequater, sinnlicher Gegenwart herauszustellen."

50. *SW*, *1*, 27: "Die Kunst löst ihre höchste Aufgabe. . . . das Göttliche, die tiefsten Interessen des Menschen, die umfassendsten Wahrheiten des Geistes zum Bewusstsein zu bringen und auszusprechen."

51. *SW*, *1*, 30: "Die harte Rinde der Natur und gewöhnlichen Welt machen es dem Geiste saurer zur Idee durchzudringen als die Werke der Kunst."

52. *SW*, *3*, 420.

53. *SW*, *3*, 435-6, 451-2, 468.

54. *SW*, *3*, 475 ff.

55. *SW*, *3*, 338: "Wie sehr nämlich ein Epos auch die Sache der ganzen Nation ausspricht, so dichtet doch ein Volk als Gesamtheit nicht, sondern nur Einzelne."

56. *SW, 3,* 339.

57. *SW, 3,* 391: "So fügen sich allem Bisherigen die Spiele an Patroklus Grabe, die erschütternden Bitten des Priamus, die Versöhnung des Achilles, der dem Vater den Leichnam des Sohns zurückgibt, damit auch diesem die Ehre der Toten nicht fehle, zum schönsten Abschlusse befriedigend an."

58. *SW, 3,* 346–8: "Wir bekommen die Sache nicht zu sehn, sondern merken nur das Unvermögen und Abmühen des Dichters . . . Die Geschichte Christi, Jerusalem, Bethlehem, das römische Recht, selbst der trojanische Krieg haben viel mehr Gegenwart für uns als die Begebenheiten der Nibelungen."

59. *SW, 3,* 346, 405, 407.

60. *SW, 3,* 409–10: "Er senkt nun die lebendige Welt menschlichen Handelns und Leidens, und näher der individuellen Taten und Schicksale in diess wechsellose Dasein hinein . . . Denn wie die Individuen in ihrem Treiben und Leiden, ihren Absichten und ihrem Vollbringen waren, so sind sie hier, für immer, als eherne Bilder versteinert hingestellt . . . sie sind nicht in unserer Vorstellung, sondern an sich selber ewig. . . . ein Gemälde und ein Bericht des selbst Gesehenen . . . energisch bewegt, doch plastisch in Qualen starr, schreckensreich beleuchtet, doch durch Dantes eigenes Mitleid klagevoll ermässigt in der Hölle; milder, aber noch voll und rund herausgearbeitet im Fegefeuer; lichtklar endlich, und immer gestaltenlos gedankenewiger im Paradiese."

61. *SW, 3,* 370–1, 414–5.

62. *SW, 3,* 416.

63. *SW, 3,* 416–7, and cf. 373–4.

64. *SW, 3,* 342–3.

65. *SW, 3,* 395–6.

66. *SW, 2,* 217.

67. *SW, 2,* 52: "Die Götter, die sie verehrt, sind die untern Götter des Hades (*Soph. Ant.* v. 451 . . .), die inneren der Empfindung, der Liebe, des Blutes nicht die Tagesgötter des freien, selbstbewussten Volks- und Staatslebens." Cf. *3,* 551, 556.

68. *SW, 3,* 557–8: "Innerliche Aussöhnung . . . Verklärung der Seele . . . zur Einheit und Harmonie dieses sittlichen Gehaltes selber."

69. "Über *Wallenstein,*" *SW, 17,* 414: "Leben gegen Leben; aber es steht nur Tod gegen Leben auf, und unglaublich; abscheulich! der Tod siegt über das Leben. Diess ist nicht tragisch, sondern entsetzlich. Diess zerreisst das Gemüt."

70. *SW, 3,* 539.

71. *SW, 3,* 568.

72. *SW, 3,* 566: "dessen edle Seele für diese Art energischer Tätigkeit nicht geschaffen ist, und voll Ekel an der Welt und am Leben"; *3,* 574: "Doch im Hintergrunde von Hamlets Gemüt liegt von Anfang an der Tod. Die Sandbank der Endlichkeit genügt ihm nicht."

73. *SW, 3,* 574: "Eine weiche Rose im Tal dieser zufälligen Welt."

74. *SW, 2,* 197–8.

75. *SW, 3,* 542: "Individuelle Representanten . . . der in der Menschenbrust waltenden Götter." Cf. *1,* 313, where these general forces are called *Pathos.*

76. *SW, 1,* 219: "Es ist so."

77. *SW, 3,* 580.

78. *SW, 3,* 577.

79. *SW, 2,* 207: "In ihrer Gemeinheit versunken . . . Intelligenzen . . . freie Existenz . . . Bei Shakespeare finden wir keine Rechtfertigung, keine Verdamniss, sondern nur Betrachtung über das allgemeine Schicksal."

NOTES: CONCLUSION

1. There is a convenient collection of Karl Marx's and Friedrich Engels' pronouncements on literature, first prepared in Russian by Mikhail Lifschitz, *Über Kunst und Literatur: Eine Sammlung aus ihren Schriften,* Berlin, 1948. The best discussion is Georg Lukács, *Karl Marx und Friedrich Engels als Literaturhistoriker,* Berlin, 1948.

2. See H. H. Houben, *Jungdeutscher Sturm und Drang* (Leipzig, 1911), p. 186.

3. Heine calls himself "romantique défroqué" in *Geständnisse.*

4. On Carlyle see esp. C. F. Harrold, *Carlyle and German Thought,* New Haven, 1934; and my "Carlyle and the Philosophy of History," *PQ, 23* (1944), 55–76.

5. See Sigmund K. Proctor, *Thomas De Quincey's Theory of Literature,* Ann Arbor, 1943; and my argument in "De Quincey's Status in the History of Ideas," *PQ, 23* (1944), 248–72. Also, John E. Jordan, *Thomas De Quincey: Literary Critic,* Berkeley, Calif., 1952.

6. See esp. "Thoughts on Poetry and its Varieties" (1833), reprinted in *Dissertations and Discussions* (3 vols. 2d ed. London, 1867), *1,* 63–94.

7. *Keble's Lectures on Poetry* (1832–41), trans. E. K. Francis (Oxford, 1912), *1,* 22. There is excellent comment on Mill and Keble in Abrams.

8. See Bernard Weinberg, *French Realism. The Critical Reaction, 1830–1870,* Chicago, 1937.

9. There are pertinent suggestions in A. G. Lehmann, *The Symbolist Aesthetic in France 1885–1895*, Oxford, 1950.

10. See Herbert E. Bowman, *V. G. Belinski*, Cambridge, Mass., 1954.

11. On Polish criticism see P. Chmielowski, *Dzieje krytyki literarckie w Polsce*, Warsaw, 1902; and T. Grabowski, *Krytyka literarcka w Polsce w epoce romantyzmu*, Warsaw, 1931.

12. *Krásověda* (written 1820–23), partly printed in 1821, 1827, 1829. See *Dílo Františka Palackého*, (Prague, 1941), *4*, 129. Partial German translation in *Gedenkblätter. Auswahl von Denkschriften, Aufsätzen und Briefen* (Prague, 1874), pp. 3–18.

13. E. Cassirer, *Thomas Thorilds Stellung in der Geistesgeschichte des achtzehnten Jahrhunderts*, Stockholm, 1941.

14. E. Allison Peers, *A History of the Romantic Movement in Spain*, 2 vols. Cambridge, 1940; Fidelino de Figueiredo, *História da literatura romántica portuguesa (1825–1870)*, Lisbon, 1913.

15. On early American criticism see William Charvat, *The Origins of American Critical Thought: 1810–1835*, Philadelphia, 1936.

16. Vivian C. Hopkins, *Spires of Form: A Study of Emerson's Aesthetic Theory*, Cambridge, 1951. See also Wellek, "Emerson and German Philosophy," *New England Quarterly*, *16* (1943), 41–63.

17. Cf. M. Alterton, *Origins of Poe's Critical Theory*, Iowa City, Ia., 1925; Floyd Stovall, *Poe's Debt to Coleridge*, in University of Texas Studies in English, *10* (1930), 70–127.

18. Good comments in E. Rothacker, *Einleitung in die Geisteswissenschaften*, 2d ed. Tübingen, 1930. A short history of German scholarship (historical, literary, theological, etc.) in the 19th century.

CHRONOLOGICAL TABLE
OF WORKS

GERMANY

1800–01	Novalis:	*Heinrich von Ofterdingen* (published 1802)
1801	Schiller:	"Über das Erhabene"
1801	A. W. and F. Schlegel:	*Charakteristiken und Kritiken*
1801	F. Schlegel:	"Nachricht von den poetischen Werken des Boccaccio"
1801–03	Herder:	*Adrastea*
1801–04	A. W. Schlegel:	*Vorlesungen über schöne Literatur und Kunst* (published 1884)
1802	Schelling:	*Bruno*
1802	F. Schlegel:	"Über nordische Dichtkunst"
1802–03	Schelling:	*Philosophie der Kunst* (published 1859)
1803	Schelling:	*Vorlesungen über die Methode des akademischen Studiums*
1803	Schiller:	Preface to *Die Braut von Messina*
1803	F. Schlegel:	"Charakteristik des Camoëns"
1803	Tieck:	*Minnelieder des schwäbischen Zeitalters*
1804	Jean Paul:	*Vorschule der Ästhetik*
1805	Friedrich Ast:	*System der Kunstlehre*
1805	Goethe:	*Winckelmann*
1806	Adam Müller:	*Vorlesungen über deutsche Wissenschaft und Literatur*
1806–08	Arnim and Brentano:	*Des Knaben Wunderhorn*
1807	Joseph Görres:	*Die deutschen Volksbücher*
1807	Hegel:	*Phänomenologie des Geistes*
1807	F. W. Schelling:	*Über das Verhältniss der bildenden Künste zu der Natur*
1807	A. W. Schlegel:	*Comparaison des deux Phèdres*
1808	F. Schlegel:	"Anzeige von Goethes Werken"
1809–11	A. W. Schlegel:	*Vorlesungen über dramatische Kunst und Literatur* (delivered 1808–09)
1811	Heinrich von Kleist:	"Über das Marionettentheater"
1812	F. Schlegel (ed.):	*Deutsches Museum*

1812–15	Grimm:	*Kinder- und Hausmärchen*
1813–16	Goethe:	"Shakespeare und kein Ende"
1814	Goethe:	*Dichtung und Wahrheit* (3 parts; 4th part published 1832)
1815	F. Schlegel:	*Geschichte der alten und neuen Litteratur* (delivered 1812)
1815	Solger:	*Erwin*
1817	Ludwig Tieck:	*Deutsches Theater*
1818	A. W. Schlegel:	*Observations sur la langue et la littérature provençales*
1818–19	A. W. Schlegel:	*Geschichte der deutschen Sprache und Poesie* (published 1913)
1819	Schopenhauer:	*Die Welt als Wille und Vorstellung*
1820–23	F. Schlegel (ed.):	*Concordia*
1825	Tieck:	*Dramaturgische Blätter*
1825–29	Tieck:	*Dichterleben*
1826	Solger:	*Nachgelassene Schriften*
1827	Goethe:	"Nachlese zu Aristoteles' Poetik"
1829	Schiller and Goethe:	*Briefwechsel* (1794–1805)
1829	Schleiermacher:	"Über den Begriff der Hermeneutik"
1829	Solger:	*Vorlesungen über Ästhetik*
1833–34	A. W. Schlegel:	"De l'origine des romans de chevalerie"
1835	Hegel:	*Vorlesungen über die Ästhetik* (delivered 1820–29)
1836	Eckermann:	*Gespräche mit Goethe* (1823–32; 2 parts; 3rd part published 1848)
1842	Schleiermacher:	*Vorlesungen über die Ästhetik* (delivered 1832–33)
1844	Schopenhauer:	*Die Welt als Wille und Vorstellung* (Vol. 2)
1851	Schopenhauer:	*Parerga und Paralipomena*

ENGLAND AND SCOTLAND

1802	Francis Jeffrey (ed.):	*Edinburgh Review*
1802–03	Walter Scott:	*Minstrelsy of the Scottish Border*
1807	R. Southey:	*Specimens of the Later English Poets*
1808	Walter Scott:	*Life of Dryden*
1808	Coleridge:	First series of lectures on Shakespeare
1808	Charles Lamb:	*Specimens of English Dramatic Poets*
1809–10	Coleridge:	*The Friend* (collected 1812; new edition 1818)
1811	Francis Jeffrey:	"Essay on Beauty"
1811	Charles Lamb:	"On the Tragedies of Shakespeare"
1811–12	Coleridge:	Second series of lectures on Shakespeare

1812	R. Southey and Coleridge:	*Omniana*
1813–14	Coleridge:	Lectures on Shakespeare at Bristol
1814	Coleridge:	"On the Principles of Genial Criticism"
1815	Wordsworth:	*Poems . . . with a New Preface and a Supplementary Essay*
1816	Coleridge:	*The Statesman's Manual*
1817	Coleridge:	*Biographia Literaria*
1817	W. Hazlitt:	*Characters of Shakespeare's Plays*
1817	W. Hazlitt:	*The Round Table*
1818	Coleridge:	Lectures on poetry (Spenser, Milton, Dante, etc.)
1818	Coleridge:	"Of Poesy and Art"
1818	Coleridge:	"Preliminary Treatise on Method"
1818	Hazlitt:	*Lectures on the English Poets*
1818–19	Coleridge:	*Philosophical Lectures* (published 1949)
1819	Thomas Campbell:	*Specimens of the British Poets*
1819	Hazlitt:	*Lectures on the English Comic Writers*
1819	Walter Scott:	*An Essay on the Drama*
1820	W. Hazlitt:	*Lectures chiefly on the Dramatic Literature of the Age of Elizabeth*
1820	T. L. Peacock:	"Four Ages of Poetry"
1821	Byron:	*A Letter . . . on the Rev. W. L. Bowles' Strictures on . . . Pope*
1821	Walter Scott:	*Lives of the Novelists*
1821	P. B. Shelley:	*A Defence of Poetry* (published 1840)
1821–22	Hazlitt:	*Table Talk*
1822	Charles Lamb:	"On the Artificial Comedy of the Last Century"
1824	Hazlitt (ed.):	*Select British Poets*
1824	Walter Scott:	*An Essay on Romance*
1825	Thomas Carlyle:	*Life of Friedrich Schiller*
1825	Hazlitt:	*The Spirit of the Age*
1825	Macaulay:	"Milton"
1826	Hazlitt:	*The Plain Speaker*
1827	Thomas Carlyle:	"The State of German Literature"
1831	T. B. Macaulay:	"Boswell," "Byron," "Pilgrim's Progress"
1835–37	Robert Southey (ed.):	*Works of William Cowper*
1836–39	Coleridge:	*Literary Remains*
1844	Jeffrey:	*Contributions to the Edinburgh Review*

FRANCE

1801	Chateaubriand:	"Shakespeare"
1802	Chateaubriand:	*Le Génie du christianisme*

1813	Mme de Staël:	*De l' Allemagne* (printed but suppressed 1810)
1818	J. L. Geoffroy:	*Cours de littérature dramatique* (written 1800–14)
1819	Chateaubriand:	Review of Dussault
1822	Hugo:	*Odes et Ballades*
1823	Stendhal:	*Racine et Shakespeare*
1827	Hugo:	*Cromwell*
1828	Sainte-Beuve:	*Tableau de la poésie française au XVIe siècle*
1829	Sainte-Beuve:	"Boileau," "J. B. Rousseau," in *Revue de Paris*
1836	Chateaubriand:	*Essai sur la littérature anglaise*
1838	Joubert:	*Pensées* (new edition 1842; written 1782–1824)

ITALY

1816	Giovanni Berchet:	*Lettera semiseria di Grisostomo*
1818	Giacomo Leopardi:	"Discorso di un Italiano intorno alla poesia romantica" (published 1906)
1818–19		*Il Conciliatore* (Milan)
1820	A. Manzoni:	*Il Conte di Carmagnola*
		Lettre à M.C——
1823	Ugo Foscolo:	*Essays on Petrarca*
1823	A. Manzoni:	"Lettera al marchese Cesare d' Azeglio"
1845	A. Manzoni:	*Del romanzo storico*

INDEX OF NAMES

INDEX OF TOPICS AND TERMS